Office 2016 All-in-One For Dummies

A Wiley Brand

by Peter Weverka

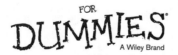

For Dummies
A Wiley Brand

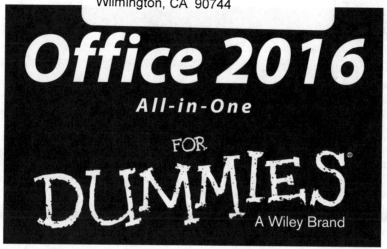

Office 2016 All-in-One For Dummies®

Published by: **John Wiley & Sons, Inc.,** 111 River Street, Hoboken, NJ 07030-5774, www.wiley.com

Published simultaneously in Canada

For general information on our other products and services, please contact our Customer Care Department within the U.S. at 877-762-2974, outside the U.S. at 317-572-3993, or fax 317-572-4002. For technical support, please visit www.wiley.com/techsupport.

Wiley publishes in a variety of print and electronic formats and by print-on-demand. Some material included with standard print versions of this book may not be included in e-books or in print-on-demand. If this book refers to media such as a CD or DVD that is not included in the version you purchased, you may download this material at http://booksupport.wiley.com. For more information about Wiley products, visit www.wiley.com.

Library of Congress Control Number: 2015951121

ISBN: 978-1-119-08312-2

ISBN 978-1-119-08313-9 (ePub); ISBN ePDF 978-1-119-08321-4 (ebk)

Manufactured in the United States of America

10 9 8 7 6 5 4 3 2

Table of Contents

Introduction

This book is for users of Microsoft Office 2016 who want to get to the heart of Office without wasting time. Don't look in this book to find out how the different applications in the Office suite work. Look in this book to find out how *you* can get *your* work done better and faster with these applications.

I show you everything you need to make the most of each of the Office applications. On the way, you have a laugh or two. No matter how much or how little skill you bring to the table, this book will make you a better, more proficient, more confident user of the Office 2016 applications.

About This Book

Besides the fact that this book is easy to read, it's different from other books about Office 2016:

- **Easy-to-find information:** I have taken great pains to make sure that the material in this book is well organized and easy to find. The descriptive headings help you find information quickly. The bulleted and numbered lists make following instructions simpler. The tables make options easier to understand and compare.
- **A task-oriented approach:** Most computer books describe what the software is, but this book explains how to complete tasks with the software. I assume that you came to this book because you want to know how to *do* something — create a table, create a chart, or give a PowerPoint presentation. You came to the right place. This book describes how to get tasks done.
- **Meaningful screen shots:** The screen shots in this book show only the part of the screen that illustrates what is being explained in the text. When instructions refer to one part of the screen, only that part of the screen is shown. I took great care to make sure that the screen shots in this book serve to help you understand the Office 2016 programs and how they work. Compare this book to the next one on the bookstore shelf. Do you see how clean the screen shots in this book are?

I want you to understand all the instructions in this book, and in that spirit, I've adopted a few conventions.

Where you see boldface letters or numbers in this book, it means to type the letters or numbers. For example, "Enter **25** in the Percentage text box" means to do exactly that: Enter the number 25.

Sometimes two tabs on the Ribbon have the same name. To distinguish tabs with the same name from one another, I sometimes include one tab's "Tools" heading in parentheses if there could be confusion about which tab I'm referring to. In PowerPoint, for example, when you see the words "(Table Tools) Design tab," I'm referring to the Design tab for creating tables, not the Design tab for changing a slide's appearance. (Book I, Chapter 1 describes the Ribbon and the tabs in detail.)

To show you how to step through command sequences, I use the ➪ symbol. For example, on the Insert tab in Word 2016, you can click the Page Number button and choose Top of Page ➪ Simple to number pages. The ➪ symbol is a shorthand method of saying "Choose Top of Page and then choose Simple."

To give most commands, you can press combinations of keys. For example, pressing Ctrl+S saves the file you're working on in the Office 2016 applications. In other words, you can hold down the Control key and press the S key to save a file. Where you see Control+, Alt+, or Shift+ and a key name or key names, press the keys simultaneously.

Foolish Assumptions

Please forgive me, but I made one or two foolish assumptions about you, the reader of this book. I assumed that:

- You own a copy of Office 2016, the latest edition of Office, and you have installed it on your computer.
- You use a Windows operating system. All people who have the Windows operating system installed on their computers are invited to read this book. It serves people who have Windows 10, Windows 8.1, Windows 8, and Windows 7.
- You are kind to foreign tourists and small animals.

Icons Used in This Book

To help you get the most out of this book, I've placed icons here and there. Here's what the icons mean:

Next to the Tip icon, you can find shortcuts and tricks of the trade to make your visit to Officeland more enjoyable.

Where you see the Warning icon, tread softly and carefully. It means that you are about to do something that you may regret later.

When I explain a juicy little fact that bears remembering, I mark it with a Remember icon. When you see this icon, prick up your ears. You will discover something that you need to remember throughout your adventures with Word, Excel, PowerPoint, or the other Office application I am demystifying.

When I am forced to describe high-tech stuff, a Technical Stuff icon appears in the margin. You don't have to read what's beside the Technical Stuff icons if you don't want to, although these technical descriptions often help you understand how a software feature works.

Beyond the Book

In addition to the information you find in the book, I have included these online bonuses:

- **Online articles covering additional topics at**

  `www.dummies.com/extras/office2016aio`

  Here you'll see how to tell Office 2016 where you prefer to store files, quickly create an index in Word 2016 by making use of a concordance file, create two data columns from one in Excel 2016, edit a video in PowerPoint 2016, copy the text from an Office 2016 file into a OneNote 2016 note, be alerted in Outlook 2016 when you get email from specific people, copy an Access 2016 report into a Word 2016 document, use images to represent data in a bar chart, put your favorite buttons on the Quick Access toolbar, and show Office 2016 files to people who don't have Office 2016 by displaying them on the Internet.

- **The Cheat Sheet for this book is at**

  (`www.dummies.com/cheatsheet/office2016aio`)

  Here you'll find descriptions of some indispensable Office 2016 commands, instructions for customizing an Office 2016 application, and tips for adding visual elements to the files you create with Office 2016.

- **Updates:** Occasionally, we have updates to our technology books. If this book does have technical updates, they will be posted at `dummies.com/go/office2016aio`.

Where to Go from Here

You are invited to read this book from start to finish or to go where you need instructions for completing a task. This book's index and table of contents will help you find the information you need.

Book I describes basic techniques that will serve you well no matter which Office 2016 application you're working in. If you came to this book to be a more capable user of Word 2016, look to Book II, which explains everything from laying out pages to taking advantage of Word's desktop publishing capabilities.

Book III delves into Excel 2016 and shows you how to construct meaningful worksheets for storing and crunching data. In Book IV, you discover how to create a PowerPoint presentation that makes the audience say, "Wow!" Book V shows you how to take and organize notes in OneNote.

Book VI explains how Outlook 2016 can help you handle your email as well as scheduling and tasks. In Book VII, you explore Access 2016, the Office application for storing and fetching data in databases.

Book VIII show how to create charts and graphs, as well as how to decorate files with shapes and pictures. In Book IX, you see how to customize Office 2016, print and otherwise distribute files, and use Publisher 2016. Book X demonstrates how you can collaborate with others using Microsoft OneDrive.

Book I

Common Office Tasks

web extras

Visit www.dummies.com for great Dummies content online.

Contents at a Glance

Chapter 1: Office Nuts and Bolts

In This Chapter

- Introducing the Office applications
- Understanding Office 365
- Exploring the Office interface
- Saving and auto-recovering your files
- Opening and closing an Office file
- Recording a file's document properties
- Clamping a password on a file

Chapter 1 is where you get your feet wet with Office 2016. Walk right to the shore and sink your toes in the water. Don't worry; I won't push you from behind.

In this chapter, you meet the Office applications and discover speed techniques for opening files. I show you around the Ribbon, Quick Access toolbar, and other Office landmarks. I also show you how to open files, save files, and clamp a password on a file.

A Survey of Office Applications

Office 2016, sometimes called the *Microsoft Office Suite,* is a collection of computer applications. Why is it called Office? I think because the people who invented it wanted to make software for completing tasks that need doing in a typical office. When you hear someone talk about "Office" or "Office software," they're talking about several different applications. Table 1-1 describes the Office applications.

Table 1-1 Office Applications

Application	*Description*
Word	A word processor for writing letters, reports, and so on. A Word file is called a *document* (see Book II).
Excel	A number cruncher for performing numerical analyses. An Excel file is called a *workbook* (see Book III).

(continued)

Table 1-1 *(continued)*

Application	*Description*
PowerPoint	A means of creating slide presentations to give in front of audiences. A PowerPoint file is called a *presentation,* or sometimes a *slide show* (see Book IV).
OneNote	A way to take notes and organize your ideas (see Book V).
Outlook	A personal information manager, scheduler, and emailer (see Book VI).
Access	A database management application (see Book VII).
Publisher	A means of creating desktop-publishing files — pamphlets, notices, newsletters, and the like (see Book IX, Chapter 3).

Microsoft offers many different versions of Office 2016, some aimed at home users and some at business users. Not all versions of Office 2016 have Outlook, Access, and Publisher. Visit this web page to compare and contrast the different versions of Office:

`https://products.office.com`

Follow these steps to find out which Office 2016 applications are installed on your computer:

1. **Open any Office 2016 application.**
2. **Click the File tab.**

   This tab is located in the upper-left corner of the screen. The Backstage window opens after you click the File tab.
3. **Select the Account category.**

   As shown in Figure 1-1, the Account window opens. Under "This Product Contains" is an icon for each Office application that is installed on your computer.
4. **Click the Back button when you finish gazing at the Account window.**

   The Back button, a left-pointing arrow, is located in the upper-left corner of the Account window.

REMEMBER

If you're new to Office, don't be daunted by the prospect of having to study so many different applications. The applications have much in common, with the same commands showing up throughout. For example, the method of choosing fonts is the same in Word, Outlook, PowerPoint, Excel, Access, and Publisher. Master one Office program and you're well on your way to mastering the next.

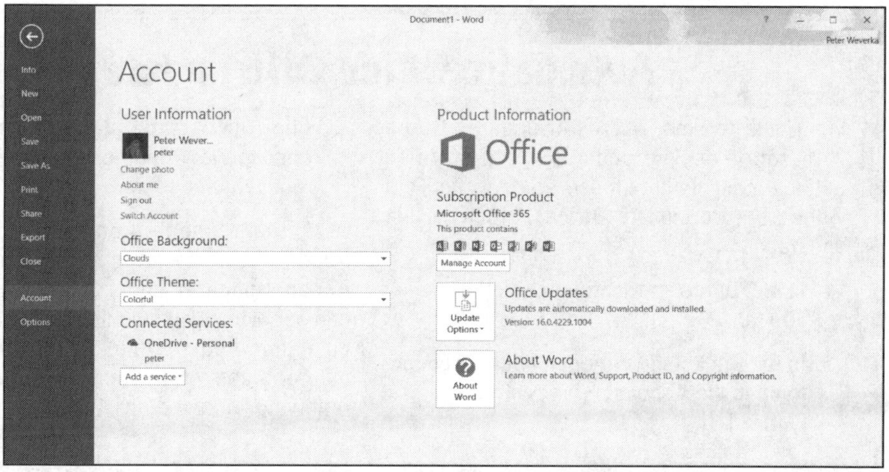

Figure 1-1: The Account window tells you which Office applications are installed.

All about Office 365

Office 365 is the name of Microsoft's online services division. To install Office 2016 software on your computer, you need an Office 365 account. In other words, you must be a paid subscriber to Office 365.

As of this writing, a subscription to the Home edition of Office 365 costs $99.99 per year or $9.99 per month (Microsoft also offers a Business edition and University edition). An Office 365 subscription entitles you to these goodies:

- ✦ The opportunity to install Office 2016 on five computers.
- ✦ The opportunity to install Word, Excel, and PowerPoint on five iPads and/or Windows tablets.
- ✦ Automatic updates to the Office software on your computer. As long as your subscription is paid up, Microsoft updates the Office software automatically.
- ✦ The opportunity to store files on OneDrive, Microsoft's cloud service. In computer jargon, *the cloud* is the name for servers on the Internet where individuals can store files. Rather than keep files on your computer, you can keep them on the Internet so that you can open them wherever your travels take you. Subscribers to Office 365 get an unlimited amount of storage space on OneDrive. (Book X explains how to store and share files with OneDrive.)

Automatic Office 2016 updates

From time to time, Microsoft updates Office 2016 software. The updates are performed automatically. Follow these steps to find out when your version of Office 2016 was last updated:

1. **In any Office application, click the File tab.**
2. **In the Backstage window, click Account to open the Account window (refer to Figure 1-1).**
3. **Click the Update Options button and choose View Updates on the drop-down menu that appears.**

Click the Manage Account button in the Account window to go online and visit your Account page at Office 365. From there, you can see when you installed Office 365 on your computer, update your credit card information, and see when your subscription needs renewing, among other things.

- The opportunity to use *Office Online,* the online versions of Word, Excel, PowerPoint, OneNote, and Outlook. To use an Office Online program, you open it in a browser and give commands through the browser window. Office Online software is useful for co-editing and sharing files.

To find out all there is to know about Office 365, visit this website:

```
http://office.microsoft.com/en-us/office365home
```

Finding Your Way Around the Office Interface

Interface, also called the *user interface,* is a computer term that describes how a software program presents itself to the people who use it (and you probably thought *interface* meant two people kissing). Figure 1-2 shows the Word interface. You will be glad to know that the interface of all the Office programs is pretty much the same.

These pages give you a quick tour of the Office interface and explain what the various parts of the interface are. Click along with me as I describe the interface and you'll know what's what by the time you finish reading these pages.

The File tab and Backstage

In the upper-left corner of the window is the *File tab* (see Figure 1-2). Clicking the File tab opens the Backstage (Microsoft's word, not mine). As shown in Figure 1-3, the *Backstage* offers commands for creating, saving, printing, and sharing files, as well as performing other file-management tasks. Notice the

Options command on the Backstage. You can choose Options to open the Options dialog box and tell the application you are working in how you want it to work.

REMEMBER

To leave the Backstage and return to the application window, click the Back button. This button is located in the upper-left corner of the Backstage.

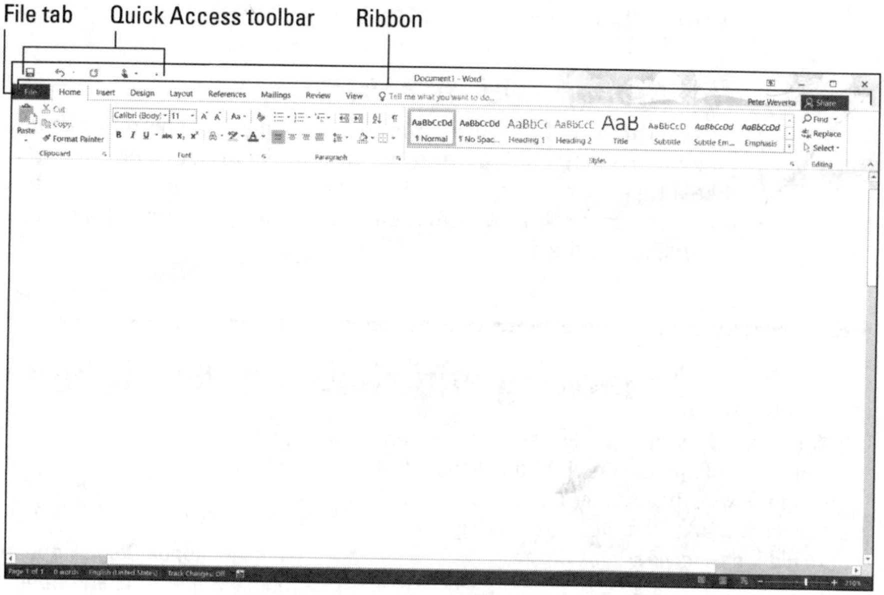

Figure 1-2: The File tab, Quick Access toolbar, and Ribbon.

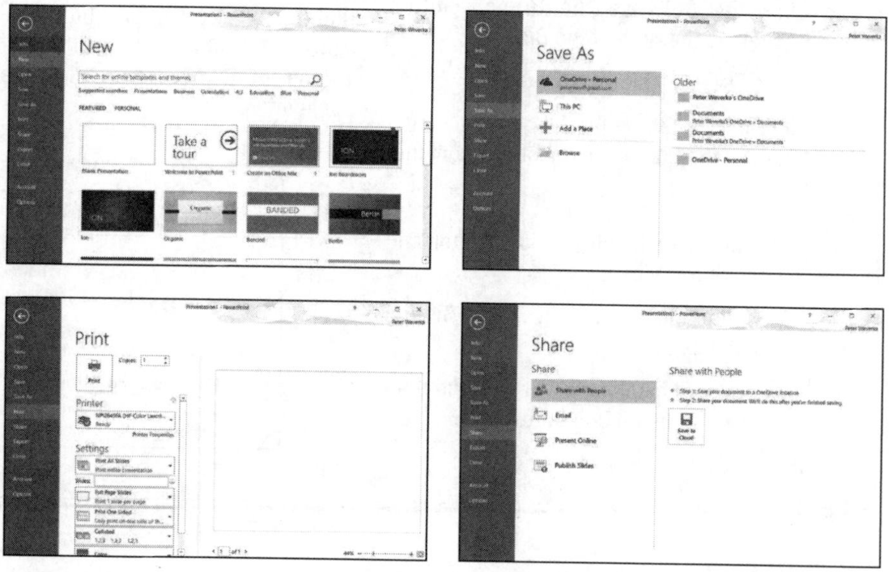

Figure 1-3: Go to the Backstage to manage, print, and share files.

The Quick Access toolbar

No matter where you travel in an Office program, you see the *Quick Access toolbar* in the upper-left corner of the screen (refer to Figure 1-2). This toolbar offers the all-important Save button, the trusty Undo button, and the convenient Repeat button (as well as the Touch/Mouse Mode button if your screen is a touchscreen). You can place more buttons on the Quick Access toolbar as well as move the toolbar lower in the window. I explain how to customize the Quick Access toolbar in Book IX, Chapter 1.

The Ribbon and its tabs

Across the top of the screen is the *Ribbon,* an assortment of different *tabs* (see Figure 1-2); click a tab to view a different set of commands and undertake a task. For example, click the Home tab to format text; click the Insert tab to insert a table or chart. Each tab offers a different set of buttons, menus, and galleries.

Collapsing and showing the Ribbon

To get more room to view items on-screen, consider collapsing the Ribbon. When the Ribbon is collapsed, only tab names on the Ribbon appear; the buttons and galleries are hidden from view.

Use these techniques to collapse the Ribbon:

- Click the Collapse the Ribbon button (located to the right of the Ribbon).
- Press Ctrl+F1.
- Right-click a tab on the Ribbon and select Collapse the Ribbon on the shortcut menu.
- Double-click a tab on the Ribbon.
- Click the Ribbon Display options button and choose Show Tabs.

Use these techniques to show the Ribbon when it is collapsed:

- Click a tab to display the Ribbon and then click the Pin the Ribbon button.
- Press Ctrl+F1.
- Right-click a tab and deselect Collapse the Ribbon.
- Double-click a tab on the Ribbon.
- Click the Ribbon Display options button and choose Show Tabs and Commands.

Want to hide the Ribbon altogether? Click the Ribbon Display Options button and choose Auto-Hide Ribbon on the drop-down list. To see the Ribbon again, click the top of the application.

Context-sensitive tabs

To keep the Ribbon from getting too crowded with tabs, Microsoft has arranged for some tabs to appear only in context — that is, they appear on the Ribbon after you insert or click something. These tabs are called *context-sensitive* tabs.

In Figure 1-4, for example, I inserted a table, and two additional tabs — the Design and the Layout tab — appear on the Ribbon under the heading "Table Tools." These context-sensitive tabs offer commands for designing and laying out tables. The idea behind context-sensitive tabs is to direct you to the commands you need and exclude all other commands.

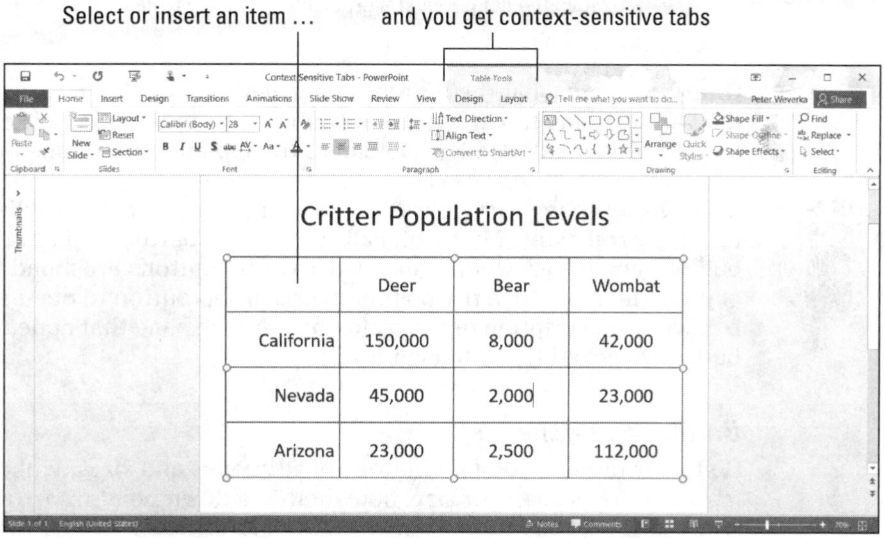

Figure 1-4: After you insert or select an item, context-sensitive tabs appear on the Ribbon.

REMEMBER

If you can't find a tab on the Ribbon, the tab is probably context-sensitive. You have to insert or select an item to make some tabs appear on the Ribbon. Context-sensitive tabs always appear on the right side of the Ribbon under a heading with the word *Tools* in its name.

The anatomy of a tab

All tabs are different in terms of the commands they offer, but all are the same insofar as how they present commands. On every tab, commands are organized in groups. On every tab, you find group buttons, buttons, and galleries. Group buttons, buttons, galleries — what's up with that?

Groups and group buttons

Commands on each tab are organized into *groups.* The names of these groups appear below the buttons and galleries on tabs. For example, the

Home tab in Excel is organized into several groups, including the Clipboard, Font, Alignment, and Number group, as shown in Figure 1-5.

Figure 1-5: Each tab is organized into groups; some groups offer group buttons.

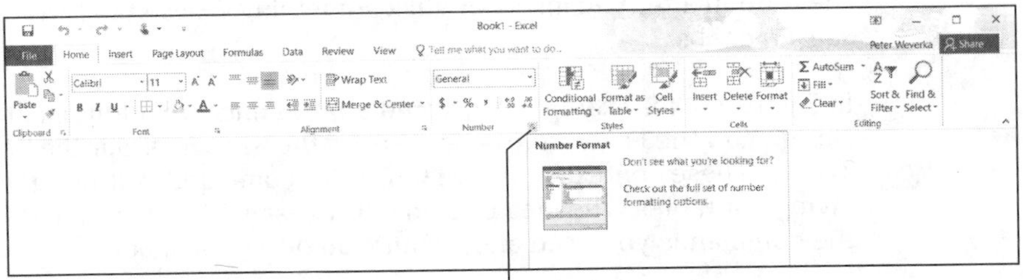

Move the pointer over a group button to see a dialog box image

Groups tell you what the buttons and galleries above their names are used for. On the Home tab in Excel, for example, the buttons in the Font group are for formatting text. Read group names to help find the command you need.

REMEMBER

Many groups have a *group button* that you can click to open a dialog box or task pane (officially, Microsoft calls these little buttons *dialog box launchers,* but let's act like grownups, shall we?). Group buttons are found to the right of group names. Move the pointer over a group button to open a pop-up help box with a description of the dialog box or task pane that appears when the button is clicked (refer to Figure 1-5).

Buttons and galleries

Go to any tab and you find buttons of all shapes and sizes. What matters isn't a button's shape or size, but whether a down-pointing arrow appears on its face. Click a button *with* an arrow and you get a drop-down list with options you can choose.

TIP

You can find out what clicking a button does by moving the pointer over it, which makes a pop-up description of the button appear.

Built in to some tabs are galleries. A *gallery* presents you with visual options for changing an item. When you move the pointer over a gallery choice, the item on your page or slide — the table, chart, or diagram, for example — changes appearance. In galleries, you can preview different choices before you click to select the choice you want.

Mini-toolbars and shortcut menus

A *mini-toolbar* is a toolbar that appears on-screen to help you do a task, as shown in Figure 1-6. You can select an option from a drop-down list or click a button on the mini-toolbar to complete a task. Mini-toolbars are very convenient. They save you the trouble of going to a different tab to complete a task.

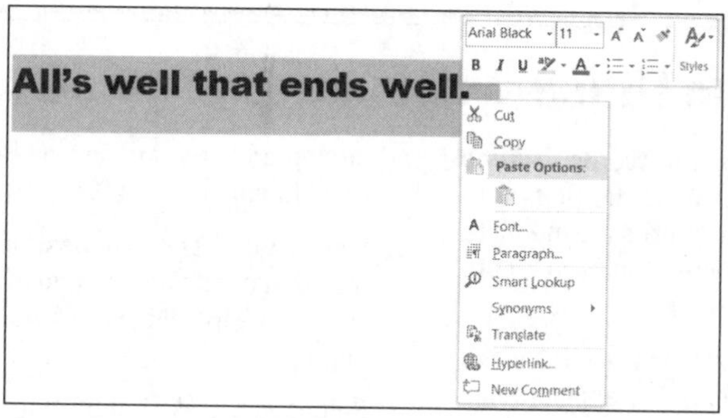

Figure 1-6: A mini-toolbar (top) and shortcut menu (bottom).

Similar to mini toolbars are the shortcut menus you get when you right-click, as shown in Figure 1-6. *Right-click* means to click the right, not the left, mouse button. Right-click just about anywhere and you get a shortcut menu of some kind.

In Word, Excel, and PowerPoint, you see a mini-toolbar *and* a shortcut menu when you right-click text.

Office 2016 for keyboard lovers

People who like to give commands by pressing keyboard shortcuts will be glad to know that Office offers Alt+key shortcuts. Press the Alt key and letters — they're called *KeyTips* — appear on tab names, as shown in Figure 1-7. After you press the Alt key, follow these instructions to make use of KeyTips:

- **Go to a tab:** Press a KeyTip on a tab to visit a tab.
- **Make KeyTips appear on menu items:** Press a KeyTip on a button or gallery to make KeyTips appear on menu items.

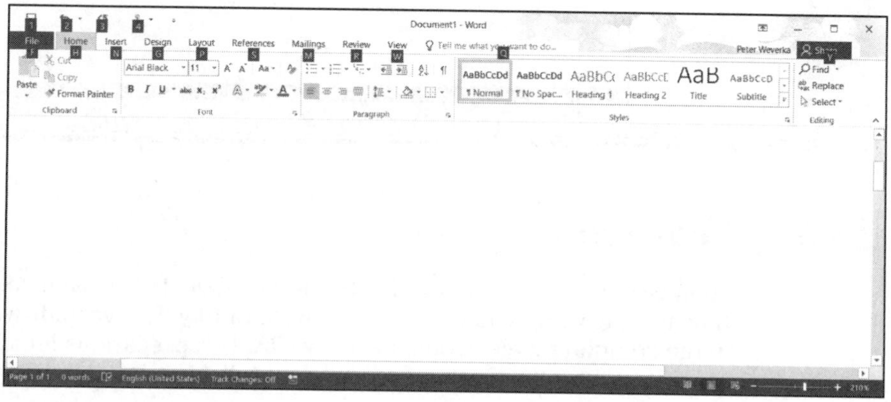

Figure 1-7: Press the Alt key to see KeyTips.

Telling Office what you want to do

In all Office applications, the words *Tell me what want me to do* appear on the Ribbon to the right of the last tab. The words are meant to help you complete tasks when you can't locate a command you're looking for.

Follow these steps the next time you can't seem to locate a command in an Office application:

1. Click the words *Tell me what want me to do* (or press Alt+Q). Your Office application presents a list of tasks in a drop-down menu called Try. Tasks you recently attempted appear under the Recently Used heading.
2. Enter a word or two to describe the task that needs completing (if the Try list doesn't list the task). A new task list appears.
3. Select your task on the list (or enter a different term to describe the task). You see a dialog box to help you complete the task.

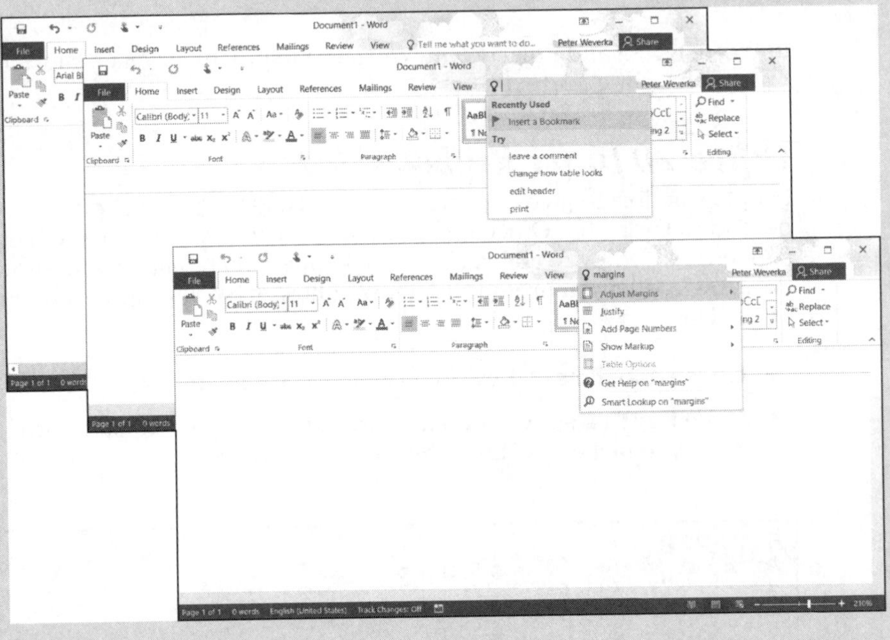

Saving Your Files

Soon after you create a new file, be sure to save it. And save your file from time to time while you work on it as well. Until you save your work, it rests in the computer's electronic memory (RAM), a precarious location. If a power outage occurs or your computer stalls, you lose all the work you did since the last time you saved your file. Make it a habit to save files every ten minutes or so, or when you complete an important task.

These pages explain how to save a file, declare where you want to save files by default, and handle files that were saved automatically after a computer failure.

Saving a file

To save a file:

- Click the Save button (you'll find it on the Quick Access toolbar).
- Press Ctrl+S.
- Go to the File tab and choose Save.

Saving a file for the first time

The first time you save a presentation, the Save As window opens. It invites you to give the file a name and choose a folder in which to store it. Enter a descriptive name in the File Name text box. To locate a folder for storing your presentation, see "Navigating the Save As and Open Windows," later in this chapter.

Converting Office 97–2003 files to 2016

When you open a file made in Office 97– 2003, the program switches to *compatibility mode.* Features that weren't part of earlier versions of the program are shut down. You can tell when a file is in compatibility mode because the words *Compatibility Mode* appear in the title bar next to the file's name.

Follow these steps to convert a 97–2003 file for use in an Office 2016 program:

1. **Go to the File tab.**
2. **Choose Info.**
3. **Click the Convert button.**

   A dialog box informs you what converting means. If you don't see the Convert option, your file has been converted already.

4. **Click OK.**

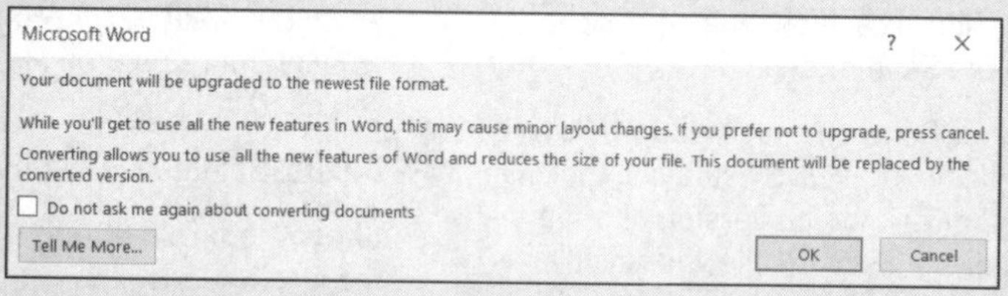

Microsoft Word
?
Your document will be upgraded to the newest file format.
While you'll get to use all the new features in Word, this may cause minor layout changes. If you prefer not to upgrade, press cancel.
Converting allows you to use all the new features of Word and reduces the size of your file. This document will be replaced by the converted version.
Do not ask me again about converting documents
Tell Me More...
OK
Cancel

Saving AutoRecovery information

To ensure against data loss owing to computer and power failures, Office saves files on its own every ten minutes. These files are saved in an AutoRecovery file. After your computer fails, you can try to recover some of the work you lost by getting it from the AutoRecovery file (see the "When disaster strikes!" sidebar).

Office saves AutoRecovery files every ten minutes, but if you want the program to save the files more or less frequently, you can change the AutoRecovery setting. Auto-recovering taxes a computer's memory. If your computer is sluggish, consider making AutoRecovery files at intervals longer than ten minutes; if your computer fails often and you're worried about losing data, make AutoRecovery files more frequently.

Follow these steps to tell Office how often to save data in an AutoRecovery file:

1. **On the File tab, choose Options.**

   The Options dialog box appears.

2. **Select the Save category.**
3. **Enter a Minutes setting in the Save AutoRecover Information Every box.**
4. **Click OK.**

When disaster strikes!

After your computer fails and you restart an Office program, you see the Document Recovery task pane with a list of files that were open when the failure occurred:

- *AutoSave* files are files that Office saves as part of its AutoRecovery procedure (see "Saving AutoRecovery information").
- *Original* files are files that you save by clicking the Save button.

The Document Recovery task pane tells you when each file was saved. By studying the time listings, you can tell which version of a file — the AutoRecovery file or the file you saved — is most up to date.

Open the drop-down list for a file and select one of these options:

- **Open/View:** Opens the file so that you can examine and work on it. If you want to keep it, click the Save button.
- **Save As:** Opens the Save As dialog box so that you can save the file under a different name. Choose this command to keep a copy of the recovered file on hand in case you need it.
- **Delete:** Deletes the AutoRecovery file.
- **Show Repairs:** Shows repairs made to the file.

Navigating the Save As and Open Windows

The Open window and Save As window offer a bunch of different ways to locate a file you want to open or locate the folder where you want to save a file. Figure 1-8 shows the Open and Save As windows. To open these windows, click the File tab and choose Open or Save As.

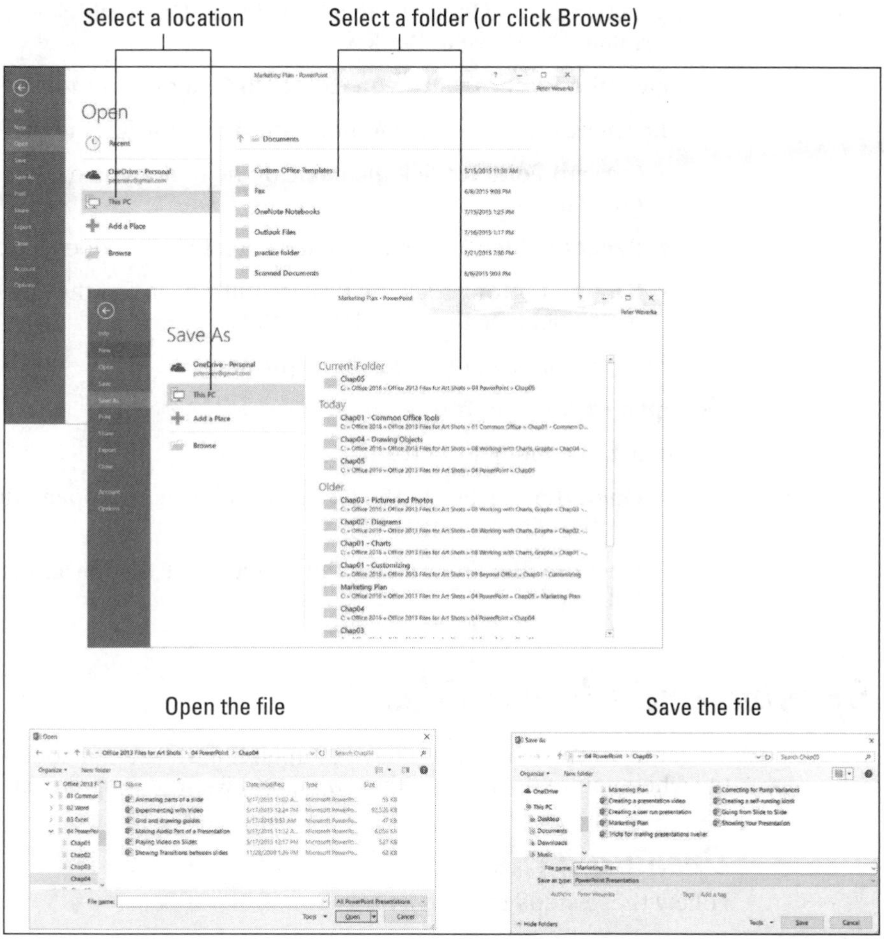

Figure 1-8: The Open window (top) and Save As window (bottom) work much the same way.

Follow these steps to open a file or save a file for the first time (or save a file under a different name or in a different location):

1. **Click the File tab.**
2. **Choose Open or Save As.**

   The Open or Save As window opens (refer to Figure 1-8).

On the Recent list, the Open window lists files you recently opened. You can open a file on this list by clicking its name. To list files you open frequently at the top of the Recent list, click the Pin This Item button. You see this button when you move the pointer over a filename on the list.

3. **Select the location where you expect to find or want to save the file (select This PC, most likely).**

   Select This PC to rummage in folders on your computer. You can also list network and OneDrive locations in the Open and Save As windows. (I explain OneDrive in Book X.)

4. **Select the folder where you expect to find or want to save the file.**

   The window provides a couple of shortcuts for finding that folder:

   - **Current Folder:** Click the name of the folder you most recently opened.
   - **Recent Folders:** Click the name of a folder you opened recently.
   - **Browse button:** Click the Browse button, and in the Open or Save As dialog box, locate and select a folder.

   The Open or Save As dialog box appears.

5. **Open or save the file.**

   At last, the moment of truth:

   - **Open the file:** Select the filename and click the Open button (or double-click the filename).
   - **Save the file:** Enter a descriptive name for the file and click the Save button.

Opening and Closing Files

To get to work on a file, you have to open it first. And, of course, you close a file when you're finished working on it and want to stop and smell the roses.

Opening a file

Follow these steps to open a file:

1. **On the File tab, choose Open (or press Ctrl+O).**

   You see the Open window. It lists files you recently opened (and files you pinned to the Recent list).

2. **If the name of the file you want to open is on the Recent list, click the name to open the file.**

   If the name isn't on the list, go to Step 3.

3. **Click the location — This PC, OneDrive, a network folder — where the file is located.**

   Click This PC if the file is located on your computer.

4. **Select the folder where the file you want to open is stored; if the folder isn't listed in the Open window, click the Browse button and select the folder in the Open dialog box.**

   The Open dialog box appears.

5. **Select the file.**

6. **Click the Open button.**

   Your file opens. You can also double-click a filename in the Open dialog box to open a file.

TIP

The fastest way to open a file is to locate it in File Explorer, the Windows file-management application, and double-click its name.

Closing a file

Closing a file is certainly easier than opening one. To close a file, save your file and use one of these techniques:

- On the File tab, choose Close. The program remains open although the file is closed.
- Click the Close button — the *X* in the upper-right corner of the window.
- Press Alt+F4.

Reading and Recording File Properties

Properties are a means of describing a file. If you manage two dozen or more files, you owe it to yourself to record properties. You can use them later to identify files.

To read property descriptions, go to the File tab, choose Info, and examine the Info window. Property descriptions are found on the right side of the window, as shown in Figure 1-9.

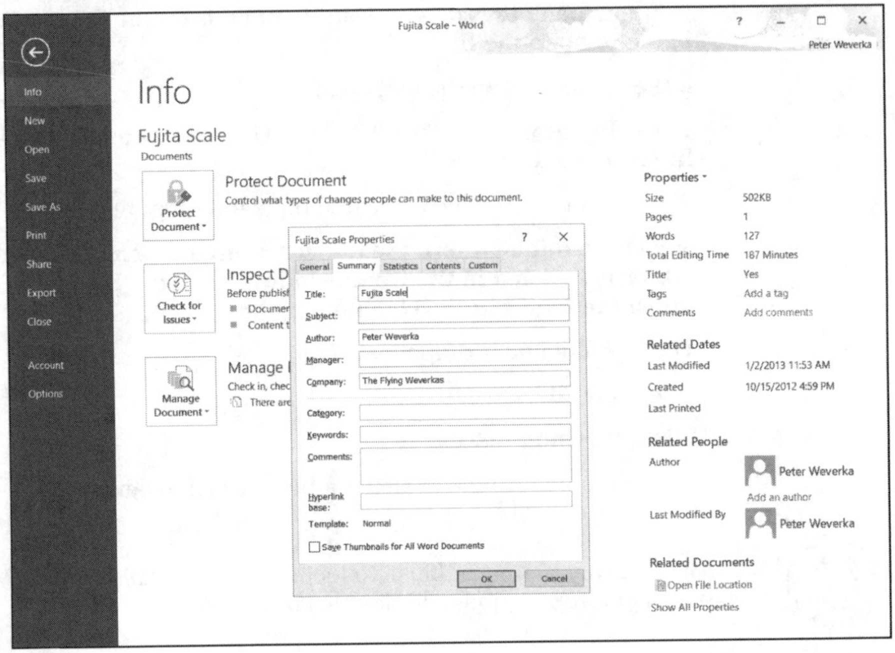

Figure 1-9: View and enter properties in the Info window.

To record even more descriptions, click the Properties button (located at the top of the file descriptions) and choose Advanced Properties on the drop-down menu. The Properties dialog box appears. Enter information about your file on the Summary and Custom tabs.

You can read a file's properties without opening a file. In Windows Explorer, File Explorer, or the Open dialog box, right-click a file's name and choose Properties. You see the Properties dialog box. Go to the Details tab to see descriptions you entered.

Locking a File with a Password

Perhaps you want to submit your file to others for critical review but you don't want any Tom, Dick, or Harry to look at your file. In that case, lock your file with a password and give out the password only to people whose opinions you trust. These pages explain how to password-protect a file, open a file that is locked with a password, and remove the password from a file.

Password-protecting a file

Follow these steps to clamp a password on a file, such that others need a password to open and perhaps also edit it:

1. **Go to the File tab and choose Info.**
2. **In the Info window, click the Protect Document (or Workbook or Presentation) button, and choose Encrypt with Password on the drop-down list.**

   The Encrypt dialog box appears, as shown in Figure 1-10.

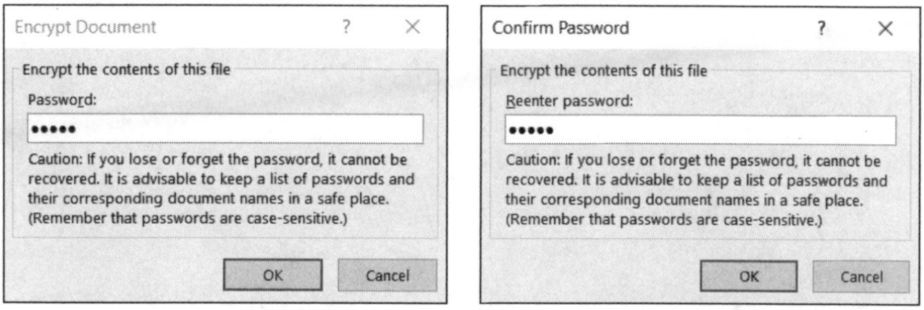

Figure 1-10: Enter passwords for the file in this dialog box.

3. **Enter a password in the Password text box and click OK.**

   Others will need the password you enter to open the file. No ifs, ands, or buts. They have to enter the password.

   Passwords are case-sensitive. In other words, you have to enter the correct combination of upper- and lowercase letters to successfully enter the password. If the password is *Valparaiso* (with an uppercase *V*), entering **valparaiso** (with a lowercase v) is deemed the wrong password and doesn't open the file.

4. **In the Confirm Password dialog box, enter the password again.**

   Figure 1-10 shows the Confirm Password dialog box.

5. **Click OK.**

   The Info window informs you that a password is required to open the file.

Removing a password from a file

Follow these steps to remove a password from a file:

1. **Open the file that needs its password removed.**
2. **Go to the File tab and choose Info to open the Info window.**
3. **Click the Protect Document button, and choose Encrypt with Password.**

   The Encrypt dialog box appears (refer to Figure 1-10).
4. **Delete the password and click OK.**

Chapter 2: Wrestling with the Text

In This Chapter

- Selecting, moving, copying, and deleting text
- Changing the appearance, size, and color of text
- Changing the case of letters
- Inserting foreign characters and symbols
- Hyperlinking to web pages and other places in a file

To enter text, all you have to do is wiggle your fingers over the keyboard. Everybody knows that. But not everyone knows all the different ways to change the look and size of text in an Office 2016 file. In this chapter, I explain how to do that as well as how to move, copy, and delete text. You find out how to quickly change a letter's case and enter a symbol or foreign character. Finally, I show you how to link your files to the Internet by fashioning a hyperlink.

Manipulating the Text

This short but important part of Chapter 2 describes the many techniques for selecting, deleting, copying, and moving text. You find an inordinate number of tips on these pages because there are so many shortcuts for manipulating text. Master the many shortcuts and you cut down considerably on the time you spend editing text.

Selecting text

Before you can do anything to text — move it, boldface it, delete it, translate it — you have to select it. Here are speed techniques for selecting text:

To Select	*Do This*
A word	Double-click the word.
A few words	Drag over the words.
A paragraph	Triple-click inside the paragraph (in Word, PowerPoint, and Outlook messages).

To Select	*Do This*
A block of text	Click the start of the text, hold down the Shift key, and click the end of the text. In Word you can also click the start of the text, press F8, and click at the end of the text.
All text	Press Ctrl+A.

TIP

Word offers a special command for selecting text with similar formats throughout a document. You can use this command to make wholesale changes to text. Select an example of the text that needs changing, and on the Home tab, click the Select button and choose Select All Text with Similar Formatting (you may have to click the Editing button first). Then choose formatting commands to change all instances of the text that you selected.

A look at the Paste options

Text adopts the formatting of neighboring text when you move or copy it to a new location. Using the Paste options, however, you can decide for yourself what happens to text formatting when you move or copy text from one place to another. To avail yourself of the Paste options:

- On the Home tab, open the drop-down list on the Paste button to see the Paste Options submenu.
- Right-click to see the Paste options on the shortcut menu.
- Click the Paste Options button to open the Paste Options submenu. This button appears after you paste text by clicking the Paste button or pressing Ctrl+V.

Choose a Paste option to determine what happens to text formatting when you move or copy text to a new location:

- **Keep Source Formatting:** The text keeps its original formatting. Choose this option to move or copy text formatting along with text to a different location.
- **Merge Formatting (Word only):** The text adopts the formatting of the text to where it is moved or copied.
- **Keep Text Only:** The text is stripped of all formatting.

In Word, you can decide for yourself what the default activity is when you paste within a document, between documents, and between programs. Go to the File tab and choose Options. In the Options dialog box, go to the Advanced category, and under Cut, Copy, and Paste, choose default options.

Moving and copying text

Office offers a number of different ways to move and copy text from place to place. Drum roll, please. . . . Select the text you want to move or copy and then use one of these techniques to move or copy it:

- **Dragging and dropping:** Move the mouse over the text and then click and drag the text to a new location. *Drag* means to hold down the mouse button while you move the pointer on-screen. If you want to copy rather than move the text, hold down the Ctrl key while you drag.
- **Using the Clipboard:** Move or copy the text to the Clipboard by clicking the Cut or Copy button, pressing Ctrl+X or Ctrl+C, or right-clicking and choosing Cut or Copy on the shortcut menu. The text is moved or copied to an electronic holding tank called the *Clipboard.* Paste the text by clicking the Paste button, pressing Ctrl+V, or right-clicking and choosing Paste. You can find the Paste, Cut, and Copy buttons on the Home tab.

Taking advantage of the Clipboard task pane

The Windows Clipboard is a piece of work. After you copy or cut text with the Cut or Copy command, the text is placed on the Clipboard. The Clipboard holds the last 24 items that you cut or copied. You can open the Clipboard task pane and view the last 24 items you cut or copied to the Clipboard and cut or copy them anew, as shown in Figure 2-1.

To open the Clipboard task pane, go to the Home tab and click the Clipboard group button (it's to the right of the word *Clipboard* in the upper-left corner of the screen). Icons next to the items tell you where they came from. To copy an item, click it or open its drop-down list and choose Paste. The Clipboard is available to all Office applications; it's especially useful for copying text and graphics from one Office application to another.

Deleting text

To delete text, select it and press the Delete key. By the way, you can kill two birds with one stone by selecting text and then starting to type. The letters you type immediately take the place of and delete the text you selected.

REMEMBER

You can always click the Undo button (or press Ctrl+Z) if you regret deleting text. This button is located on the Quick Access toolbar.

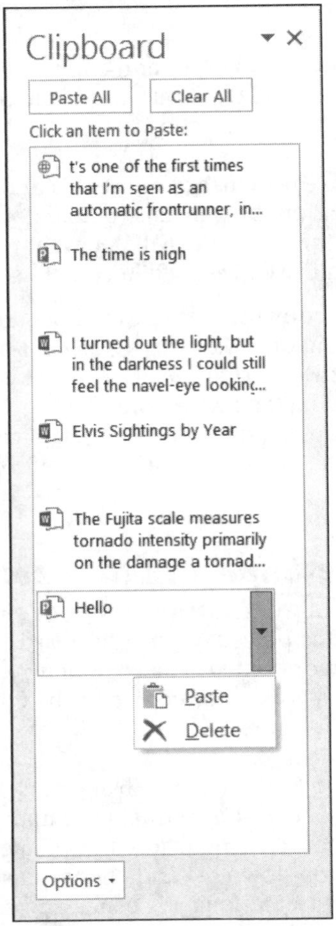

Figure 2-1: The Clipboard task pane in action.

Changing the Look of Text

What text looks like is determined by its font, the size of the letters, the color of the letters, and whether text effects or font styles such as italic or boldface are in the text. What text looks like really matters in Word and PowerPoint because files you create in those applications are meant to be read by all and sundry. Even in Excel, Access, and Outlook messages, however, font choices matter because the choices you make determine whether your work is easy to read and understand.

A *font* is a collection of letters, numbers, and symbols in a particular typeface, including all italic and boldface variations of the letters, numbers, and symbols. Fonts have beautiful names, and some of them are many centuries old. Most computers come with these fonts: Arial, Tahoma, Times New Roman, and Verdana. By default, Office often applies the Calibri font to text.

Font styles include boldface, italic, and underline. By convention, headings are boldface. Italic is used for emphasis and to mark foreign words in text. Office provides a number of text effects. *Text effects,* also known as *text attributes*, include strikethrough and superscript. Use text effects sparingly.

The following pages look at the different ways to change the font, font size, and color of text, as well as how to assign font styles and text effects to text.

Choosing fonts for text

If you aren't happy with the fonts you choose, select the text that needs a font change and change fonts with one of these techniques:

- ✦ **Mini-toolbar:** Move the pointer over the selected text. You see the mini-toolbar. Move the pointer over this toolbar and choose a font in the Font drop-down list, as shown in Figure 2-2.
- ✦ **Shortcut menu:** Right-click the selected text and choose a new font on the shortcut menu.

The Format Painter: A fast way to change the look of text

When you're in a hurry to change the look of text and reformat paragraphs, consider using the Format Painter. This nifty tool works something like a paintbrush. You drag it over text to copy formats from place to place. Follow these instructions to use the Format Painter:

1. **Click a place with text and paragraph formats that you want to copy elsewhere (or select the text).**
2. **On the Home tab (or the Format Text tab in an Outlook message), click or double-click the Format Painter button (or press Ctrl+Shift+C).**

   You can find the Format Painter button in the Clipboard group. Click the button to copy formats once; double-click to copy formats to more than one location. The pointer changes into a paintbrush.
3. **Drag the pointer across text to which you want to copy the formats.**

   You can go from place to place with the Format Painter.
4. **Click the Format Painter button a second time or press Esc when you finish using the Format Painter.**

   Press Esc or click the Format Painter button again to cease using the Format Painter if you used it to copy formats to more than one location.

At the opposite end of the spectrum from the Format Painter button is the Clear All Formatting button on the Home tab. You can select text and click this button to strip text of all its formats, whatever they may be.

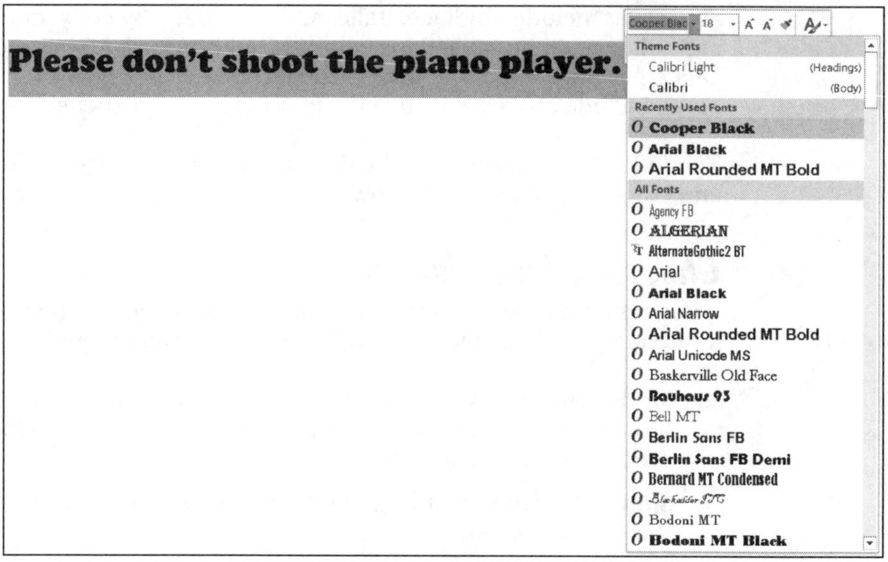

Figure 2-2: Changing fonts by way of the mini-toolbar.

- **Font drop-down list:** On the Home tab, open the Font drop-down list (or press Ctrl+Shift+F) and choose a font.
- **Font dialog box:** On the Home tab, click the Font group button. You see the Font dialog box. Select a font and click OK.

TIP

Avoid using too many different fonts, because a file with too many fonts looks like alphabet soup. The object is to choose a font that helps set the tone. An aggressive sales pitch calls for a strong, bold font; a technical presentation calls for a font that is clean and unobtrusive. Make sure that the fonts you select help communicate your message.

Changing the font size of text

Font size is measured in *points;* a point is $1/72$ of an inch. The golden rule of font sizes goes something like this: the larger the font size, the more important the text. This is why headings are larger than footnotes. Select your text and use one of these techniques to change the font size of the letters:

- **Mini-toolbar:** Move the pointer over the text, and when you see the mini-toolbar, move the pointer over the toolbar and choose a font size on the Font Size drop-down list (refer to Figure 2-2).
- **Font Size drop-down list:** On the Home tab, open the Font Size drop-down list and choose a font size. You can live-preview font sizes this way.
- **Font dialog box:** On the Home tab, click the Font group button (or press Ctrl+Shift+P), and in the Font dialog box, choose a font size and click OK.

Installing and removing fonts on your computer

If Windows is installed on your computer, so are many different fonts. The names of these fonts appear on the Font drop-down list, Font dialog box, and mini-toolbar. Do you have enough fonts on your computer? Do you want to remove fonts to keep the Font drop-down list from being overcrowded?

Font files are kept in the `C:\Windows\Fonts` folder on your computer. Here are instructions for handling fonts:

- **Installing new fonts:** Place the font file in the `C:\Windows\Fonts` folder.
- **Removing a font:** Move the font file out of the `C:\Windows\Fonts` folder. Store font files you don't want in another folder where you can resuscitate them if need be.
- **Examining fonts:** Double-click a font file to examine a font more closely. A window opens, and you see precisely what the font looks like. Do you know why "The quick brown fox jumps over the lazy dog" appears in this window? Because that sentence includes every letter in the alphabet.

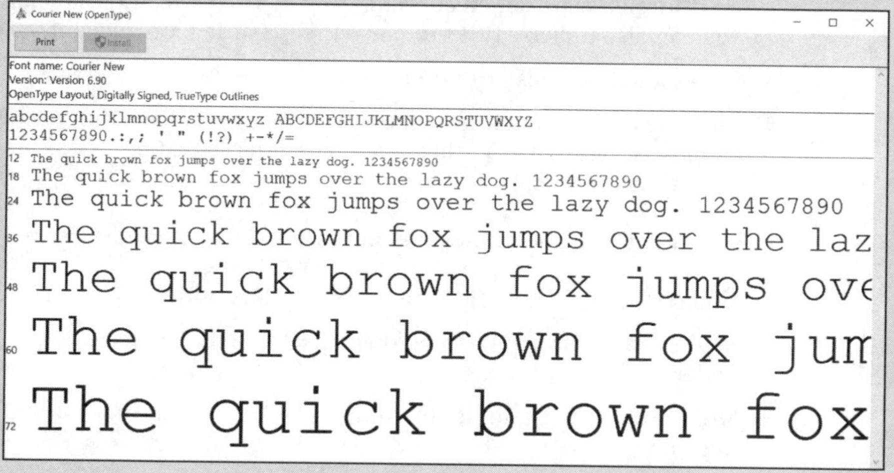

- **Increase Font Size and Decrease Font Size buttons:** Click these buttons (or press Ctrl+] or Ctrl+[) to increase or decrease the point size by the next interval on the Font Size drop-down list. You can find the Increase Font Size and Decrease Font Size buttons on the Home tab and the mini-toolbar. Watch the Font Size list or your text and note how the text changes size. This is an excellent technique when you want to "eyeball it" and you don't care to fool with the Font Size drop-down list or Font dialog box.

TIP

Click the Increase Font Size and Decrease Font Size buttons when you're dealing with fonts of different sizes and you want to proportionally change the size of all the letters. Drag the pointer over the text to select it before clicking one of the buttons.

TIP

If the font size you want isn't on the Font Size drop-down list, enter the size. For example, to change the font size to 13.5 points, type **13.5** in the Font Size box and press Enter.

Applying font styles to text

There are four — count 'em, four — font styles: regular, bold, italic, and underline:

- **Regular**: This style is just Office's way of denoting an absence of any font style.
- **Italic**: Italic is used for emphasis, when introducing a new term, and to mark foreign words such as *violà, gung hay fat choy,* and *Qué magnifico!* You can also italicize titles to make them a little more elegant.
- **Bold:** Bold text calls attention to itself.
- **Underline:** Underlined text also calls attention to itself, but use underlining sparingly. Later in this chapter, "Underlining text" looks at all the ways to underline text.

Select text and use one of these techniques to apply a font style to it:

- **Home tab:** Click the Bold, Italic, or Underline button.
- **Keyboard:** Press Ctrl+B to boldface text, Ctrl+I to italicize it, or Ctrl+U to underline it.
- **Mini-toolbar:** The mini-toolbar offers the Bold, Italic, and Underline buttons.
- **Font dialog box:** Select a Font Style option in the Font dialog box. To open this dialog box, visit the Home tab and click the Font group button (or press Ctrl+D).

To remove a font style, click the Bold, Italic, or Underline button a second time. You can also select text and then click the Clear Formatting button on the Home tab (in Word, PowerPoint, and Publisher).

Applying text effects to text

Text effects have various uses, some utilitarian and some strictly for yucks. Be careful with text effects. Use them sparingly and to good purpose. To apply a text effect, start on the Home tab (or the Format Text tab in Outlook messages) and do one of the following:

+ Click a text effect button on the Home tab.
+ Click the Font group button (or press Ctrl+D) and choose a text effect in the bottom half of the Font dialog box, as shown in Figure 2-3.

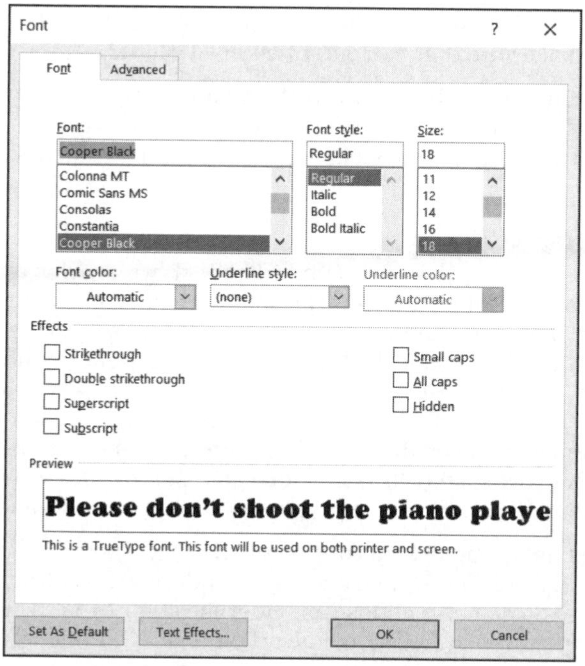

Figure 2-3: Text effects in the Font dialog box (Word).

Here's a rundown of the different text effects (not all these effects are available in PowerPoint, Excel, Publisher, and Outlook):

+ **Strikethrough and double strikethrough:** By convention, *strikethrough* is used to show where passages are struck from a contract or other important document. Double strikethrough, for all I know, is used to shows where passages are struck out forcefully. Use these text effects to demonstrate ideas that you reject.
+ **Subscript:** A *subscripted* letter is lowered in the text. In this chemical formula, the 2 is lowered to show that two atoms of hydrogen are needed along with one atom of oxygen to form a molecule of water: H_2O. (Press Ctrl+=.)
+ **Superscript:** A *superscripted* letter or number is one that is raised in the text. Superscript is used in mathematical and scientific formulas, in ordinal numbers (1st, 2nd, 3rd), and to mark footnotes. In the theory of relativity, the 2 is superscripted: $E = mc^2$. (Press Ctrl+Shift+plus sign.)

- **Small Caps:** A *small cap* is a small capital letter. You can find many creative uses for small caps. An all-small-cap title looks elegant. Be sure to type lowercase letters in order to create small caps. Type an uppercase letter, and Office refuses to turn it into a small cap. Not all fonts can produce small capital letters.
- **All Caps:** The All Caps text effect merely capitalizes all letters. Use it in styles to make sure that you enter text in all capital letters.
- **Equalize Character Height (PowerPoint only):** This effect makes all characters the same height and stretches the characters in text. You can use it to produce interesting effects in text box announcements.

Underlining text

You can choose among 17 ways to underline text, with styles ranging from Words Only to Wavy Line, and you can select a color for the underline in Word, PowerPoint, and Outlook. If you decide to underline titles, do it consistently. To underline text, select the text that you want to underline, go to the Home tab, and pick your poison:

- On the Home tab, click the Underline button. A single line runs under all the words you selected. In Word, you can open the drop-down list on the Underline button and choose from several ways to underline text.
- Click the Font group button (or press Ctrl+D) to open the Font dialog box (refer to Figure 2-3) and then choose an underline style from the drop-down list. You can also choose an underline color from the Underline Color drop-down list (in Word, PowerPoint, and Outlook). The color you select applies to the underline, not to the words being underlined.

To remove an underline from text, select the text and then click the Underline button on the Home tab.

Changing the color of text

Before you change the color of text, peer at your computer screen and examine the background theme or color you chose. Unless the color of the text is different from the theme or color, you can't read the text. Besides choosing a color that contributes to the overall tone, choose a color that is easy to read.

Select the text that needs touching up and use one of these techniques to change its color:

- On the mini-toolbar, open the drop-down list on the Font Color button and choose a color, as shown in Figure 2-4.
- On the Home tab, open the drop-down list on the Font Color button and choose a color.

- On the Home tab, click the Font group button (or press Ctrl+D) to open the Font dialog box, open the Font Color drop-down list, and choose a color.

Figure 2-4: Choosing a font color on the mini-toolbar.

TIP

The Font Color drop-down list offers theme colors and standard colors. You are well advised to choose a theme color. These colors are deemed *theme colors* because they jibe with the theme you choose for your file.

Quick Ways to Handle Case, or Capitalization

Case refers to how letters are capitalized in words and sentences. Table 2-1 explains the different cases, and Figure 2-5 demonstrates why paying attention to case matters. In the figure, the PowerPoint slide titles are presented using different cases, and the titles are inconsistent with one another. In one slide, only the first letter in the title is capitalized (sentence case); in another slide, the first letter in each word is capitalized (capitalize each word); in another, none of the letters is capitalized (lowercase); and in another, all the letters are capitalized (uppercase). In your titles and headings, decide on a capitalization scheme and stick with it for consistency's sake.

To change case in Word and PowerPoint, all you have to do is select the text, go to the Home tab, click the Change Case button, and choose an option on the drop-down list:

- **Sentence case:** Renders the letters in sentence case.
- **lowercase:** Makes all the letters lowercase.
- **UPPERCASE**: Renders all the letters as capital letters.
- **Capitalize Each Word:** Capitalizes the first letter in each word. If you choose this option for a title or heading, go into the title and lowercase the first letter of articles *(the, a, an),* coordinate conjunctions *(and, or, for, nor),* and prepositions unless they're the first or last word in the title.
- **tOGGLE cASE:** Choose this option if you accidentally enter letters with the Caps Lock key pressed.

Table 2-1 Cases for Headings and Titles

Case	*Description*	*Example Title*
Sentence case	The first letter in the first word is capitalized; all other words are lowercase unless they are proper names.	Man bites dog in January
Lowercase	All letters are lowercase unless they are proper names.	man bites dog in January
Uppercase	All letters are uppercase no matter what.	MAN BITES DOG IN JANUARY
Capitalize each word	The first letter in each word is capitalized.	Man Bites Dog In January

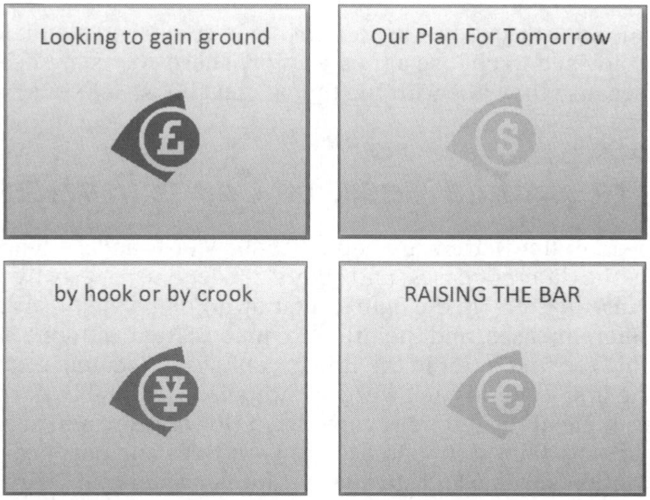

Figure 2-5: Capitalization schemes (clockwise from upper-left): sentence case; capitalize each word; uppercase; lowercase.

TIP

You can also change case by pressing Shift+F3. Pressing this key combination in Word and PowerPoint changes characters to uppercase, lowercase, each word capitalized, and back to uppercase again.

Entering Symbols and Foreign Characters

Don't panic if you need to enter an umlaut, grave accent, or cedilla because you can do it by way of the Symbol dialog box, as shown in Figure 2-6. You can enter just about any symbol and foreign character by way of this dialog box. Click where you want to enter a symbol or foreign character and follow these steps to enter it:

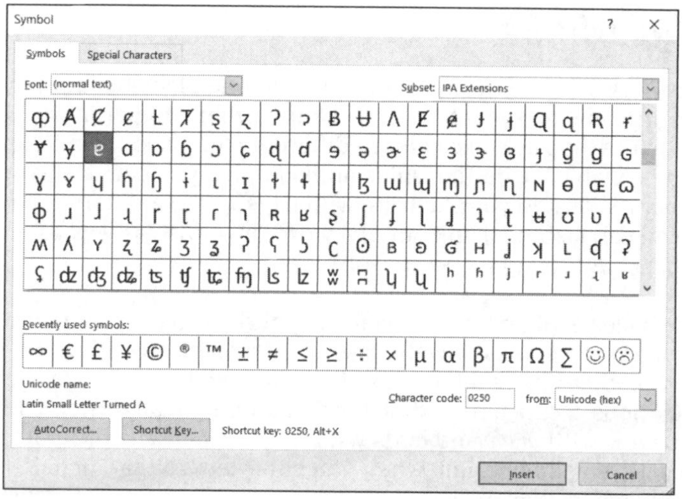

Figure 2-6: To enter a symbol or foreign character, select it and click the Insert button.

1. **On the Insert tab, click the Symbol button. (You may have to click the Symbols button first, depending on the size of your screen.)**

   In Word, Outlook, and Publisher, click More Symbols after you click the Symbol button if no symbol on the drop-down list does the job for you. You see the Symbol dialog box (refer to Figure 2-6).

2. **If you're looking to insert a symbol, not a foreign character, choose Webdings or Wingdings 1, 2, or 3 in the Font drop-down list.**

   Webdings and the Wingdings fonts offer all kinds of weird and wacky symbols.

3. **Select a symbol or foreign character.**

   You may have to scroll to find the one you want.

4. **Click the Insert button to enter the symbol and then click Close to close the dialog box.**

TIP

The Symbol dialog box lists the last several symbols or foreign characters you entered under Recently Used Symbols. See whether the symbol you need is listed there. It spares you the trouble of rummaging in the Symbol dialog box. In Word, Outlook, and Publisher, you see the last several symbols or foreign characters you entered on a drop-down list after you click the Symbol button.

Creating Hyperlinks

A *hyperlink* is an electronic shortcut from one place to another. If you've spent any time on the Internet, you know what a hyperlink is. Clicking hyperlinks on the Internet takes you to different web pages or different places on the same web page. In the Office applications, you can use hyperlinks to connect readers to your favorite web pages or to a different page, slide, or file. You can fashion a link out of a word or phrase as well as any object — a graphic image, text box, shape, or picture.

These pages explain how to insert a hyperlink to another place in your file as well as create links to web pages. You also discover how to enter an email hyperlink that makes it easy for others to email you. By the way, the Office applications create a hyperlink for you automatically when you type a word that begins with *www* and ends with *.com* or *.net*. The programs create an automatic email hyperlink when you enter letters that include the at symbol (@) and end in *.com* or *.net*.

Linking a hyperlink to a web page

It could well be that a web page on the Internet has all the information your readers need. In that case, you can link to the web page so that viewers can visit it in the course of viewing your file. When a viewer clicks the link, a web browser opens and the web page appears.

Follow these steps to hyperlink your file to a web page on the Internet:

1. **Select the text or object that will form the hyperlink.**

   For example, select a line of text or phrase if you want viewers to be able to click it to go to a web page.

2. **On the Insert tab, click the Hyperlink button (or press Ctrl+K).**

   Depending on the size of your screen, you may have to click the Links button before you can get to the Hyperlink button. You see the Insert Hyperlink dialog box, as shown in Figure 2-7. You can also open this dialog box by right-clicking an object or text and choosing Hyperlink on the shortcut menu.

3. **Under Link To, select Existing File or Web Page.**

4. **In the Address text box, enter the address of the web page to which you want to link, as shown in Figure 2-7.**

   From easiest to hardest, here are techniques for entering web page addresses:

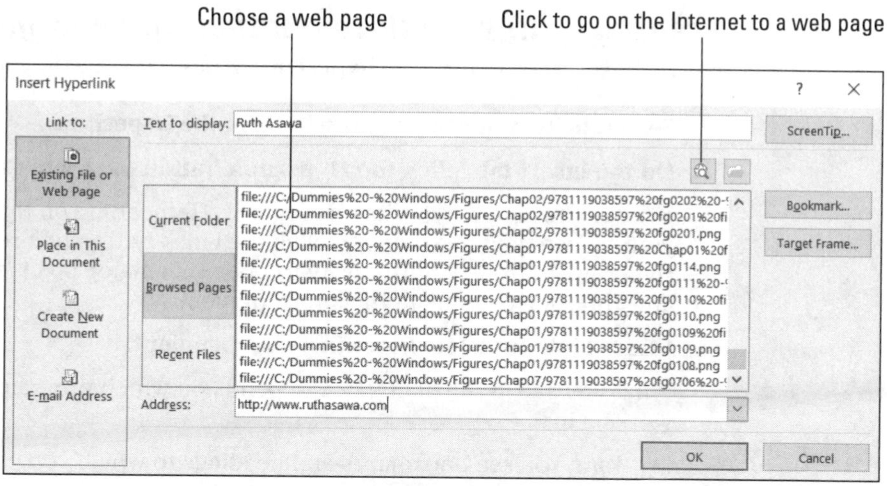

Figure 2-7: Enter the web page target in the Address text box to create a hyperlink to a web page.

- *Click the Browse the Web button:* Your web browser opens after you click this button. Go to the web page you want to link to, copy the page's address in your web browser, and paste the address in the Address text box. (Figure 2-7 shows where the Browse the Web button is.)
- *Click Browsed Pages:* The dialog box lists web pages you recently visited after you click this button, as shown in Figure 2-7. Choose a web page.
- *Type (or copy) a web page address into the Address text box:* Enter the address of the web page. You can right-click the text box and choose Paste to copy a web page address into the text box.

5. **Click the ScreenTip button, enter a ScreenTip in the Set Hyperlink ScreenTip dialog box, and click OK.**

   Viewers can read the ScreenTip you enter when they move their pointers over the hyperlink.

6. **Click OK in the Insert Hyperlink dialog box.**

   I would test the hyperlink if I were you to make sure it takes viewers to the right web page. To test a hyperlink, Ctrl+click it or right-click it and choose Open Hyperlink on the shortcut menu.

Creating a hyperlink to another place in your file

Follow these steps to create a hyperlink to another place in your file:

1. **Select the text or object that will form the hyperlink.**
2. **On the Insert tab, click the Hyperlink button (or press Ctrl+K).**

   You see the Insert Hyperlink dialog box. (Depending on the size of your screen, you may have to click the Links button before you see the Hyperlink button.) Another way to open this dialog box is to right-click and choose Hyperlink in the shortcut menu.
3. **Under Link To, select Place in This Document.**

   What you see in the dialog box depends on which program you're working in:

   - *Word:* You see bookmarks and headings to which you've assigned a heading style.
   - *PowerPoint:* You see a list of slides in your presentation, as well as links to the first, last, next, and previous slide, as shown in Figure 2-8.
   - *Excel:* You see boxes for entering cell references and defined cell names.

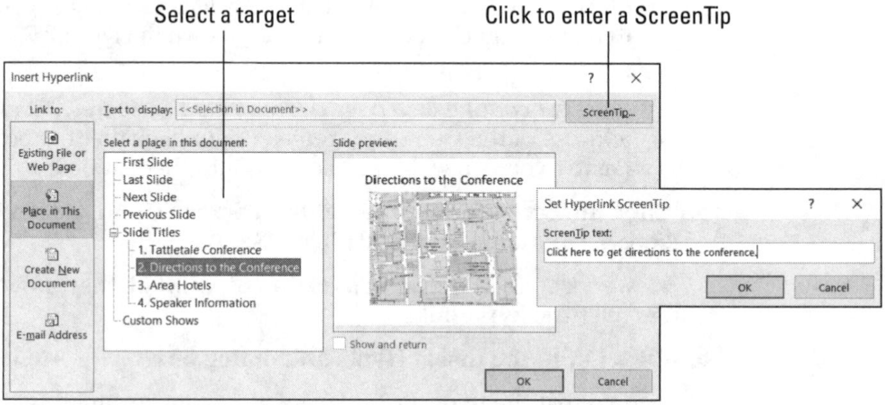

Figure 2-8: You can also create a hyperlink to a different place in a file.

4. **Select the target of the hyperlink.**
5. **Click the ScreenTip button.**

   You see the Set Hyperlink ScreenTip dialog box, as shown in Figure 2-8.

6. **Enter a ScreenTip and click OK.**

   When viewers move their pointers over the link, they see the words you enter. Enter a description of where the hyperlink takes you.

7. **Click OK in the Insert Hyperlink dialog box.**

   To test your hyperlink, move the pointer over it. You should see the ScreenTip description you wrote. Ctrl+click the link to see if it takes you to the right place.

Creating an email hyperlink

An *email hyperlink* is one that opens an email program. These links are sometimes found on web pages so that anyone visiting a web page can conveniently send an email message to the person who manages the web page. When you click an email hyperlink, your default email program opens. And if the person who set up the link was thorough about it, the email message is already addressed and given a subject line.

TIP

Include an email hyperlink in a file if you're distributing the file to others and you would like them to be able to comment on your work and send the comments to you.

Follow these steps to put an email hyperlink in a file:

1. **Select the words or object that will constitute the link.**
2. **On the Insert tab, click the Hyperlink button (or press Ctrl+K).**

   The Insert Hyperlink dialog box appears.

3. **Under Link To, click E-Mail Address.**

   Text boxes appear for entering an email address and a subject message.

4. **Enter your email address and a subject for the messages that others will send you.**

   Office inserts the word *mailto:* before your email address as you enter it.

5. **Click OK.**

   Test the link by Ctrl+clicking it. Your default email program opens. The email message is already addressed and given a subject.

Repairing and removing hyperlinks

From time to time, check the hyperlinks in your file to make sure they still work. Clicking a hyperlink and having nothing happen is disappointing. Hyperlinks get broken when web pages and parts of files are deleted.

To repair or remove a hyperlink, right-click the link and choose Edit Hyperlink on the shortcut menu (or click in the link and then click the Hyperlink button on the Insert tab). You see the Edit Hyperlink dialog box. This dialog box looks and works just like the Insert Hyperlink dialog box. Sometimes you can repair a link simply by editing it in this dialog box.

- **Repairing a link**: Select a target in your file or a web page and click OK.
- **Removing a link:** Click the Remove Link button. You can also remove a hyperlink by right-clicking the link and choosing Remove Hyperlink on the shortcut menu.

Chapter 3: Speed Techniques Worth Knowing About

In This Chapter

- Undoing mistakes and repeating actions
- Zooming to get a better view of your work
- Working with two different files at the same time
- Instructing Office to correct typos automatically
- Entering hard-to-type text with the AutoCorrect command

This brief chapter takes you on a whirlwind tour of shortcut commands that can save you time and effort no matter which Office application you're working in. This chapter is devoted to people who want to get it done quickly and get away from their computers. It explains the Undo and Repeat commands, zooming in and out, and opening more than one window on the same file. You also discover how to display windows in different ways, correct your typos automatically, and enter hard-to-type terminology with a simple flick of the wrist.

Undoing and Repeating Commands

If I were to choose two commands for the Hall of Fame, they would be the Undo command and the Repeat command. One allows you to reverse actions you regret doing, and the other repeats a previous action without you having to choose the same commands all over again. Undo and Repeat are explained forthwith.

Undoing a mistake

Fortunately for you, all is not lost if you make a big blunder because Office has a marvelous little tool called the Undo command. This command "remembers" your previous editorial and formatting changes. As long as you catch your error in time, you can undo your mistake.

Click the Undo button on the Quick Access toolbar (or press Ctrl+Z) to undo your most recent change. If you made your error and went on to do something else before you caught it, open the drop-down list on the Undo button.

It lists your previous actions, as shown in Figure 3-1. Click the action you want to undo, or if it isn't on the list, scroll until you find the error and then click it.

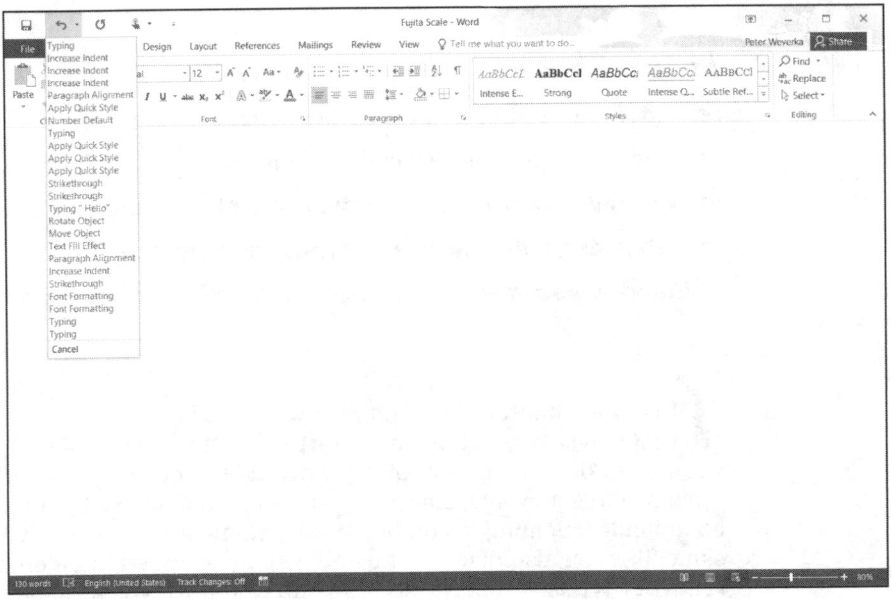

Figure 3-1: Fixing a mistake with the Undo drop-down list.

Remember, however, that choosing an action far down the Undo list also reverses the actions before it on the list. For example, if you undo the 19th action on the list, you also undo the 18 more recent actions above it.

Repeating an action — and quicker this time

The Quick Access toolbar offers a button called Repeat that you can click to repeat your last action. This button can be a mighty, mighty timesaver. For example, if you just changed fonts in one heading and you want to change another heading in the same way, select the heading and click the Repeat button (or press F4 or Ctrl+Y). Move the pointer over the Repeat button to see, in a pop-up box, what clicking it does.

You can find many creative uses for the Repeat command if you use your imagination. For example, if you had to type "I will not talk in class" a hundred times as a punishment for talking in class, you could make excellent use of the Repeat command to fulfill your punishment. All you would have to do is write the sentence once and then click the Repeat button 99 times.

After you click the Undo button, the Repeat button changes names and becomes the Redo button. Click the Redo button to "redo" the command you "undid." In other words, if you regret clicking the Undo button, you can turn back the clock by clicking Redo.

Zooming In, Zooming Out

Eyes weren't meant to stare at the computer screen all day, which makes the Zoom controls all the more valuable. You can find these controls on the View tab and in the lower-right corner of the window, as shown in Figure 3-2. Use them freely and often to enlarge or shrink what is on the screen and preserve your eyes for important things, such as gazing at the sunset.

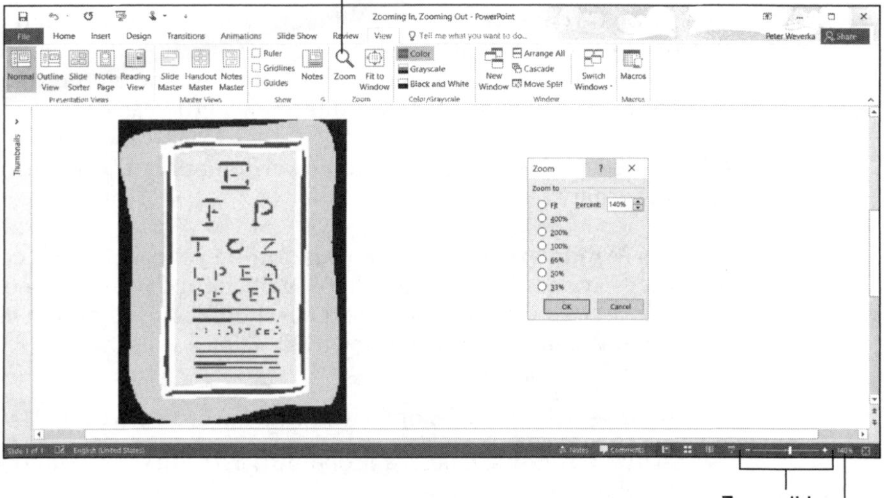

Figure 3-2: The Zoom controls.

Meet the Zoom controls:

- **Zoom dialog box:** Click the Zoom button on the View tab or the Zoom box (the % listing) to display the Zoom dialog box, as shown in Figure 3-2. From there, you can select an option button or enter a Percent measurement.

- **Zoom button:** Click the Zoom In or Zoom Out button on the Zoom slider to zoom in or out in 10-percent increments.
- **Zoom slider:** Drag the *Zoom slider* left to shrink or right to enlarge what is on your screen.
- **Mouse wheel:** If your mouse has a wheel, you can hold down the Ctrl key and spin the wheel to quickly zoom in or out.

Each Office program offers its own special Zoom commands in the Zoom group on the View tab. In Word, for example, you can display one page or two pages; in Excel, you can click the Zoom to Selection button and enlarge a handful of cells. Make friends with the Zoom commands. They never let you down.

Viewing a File Through More Than One Window

By way of the commands in the Window group in the View tab, you can be two places simultaneously, at least where Office is concerned. You can work on two files at once. You can place files side by side on the screen and do a number of other things to make your work a little easier.

On the View tab, Word, Excel, and PowerPoint offer these buttons in the Window group:

- **New Window:** Opens another window on your file so you can be two places at once in the same file. To go back and forth between windows, click a taskbar button or click the Switch Windows button and choose a window name on the drop-down list. Click a window's Close button when you finish looking at it.
- **Arrange All:** Arranges open windows onscreen so that all are visible.
- **Switch Windows:** Opens a drop-down list with open windows so you can travel between windows.

You can also take advantage of these Window buttons in Word and Excel to compare files:

- **View Side by Side:** Displays files side by side so you can compare and contrast them.
- **Synchronous Scrolling:** Permits you to scroll two files at the same rate so you can proofread one against the other. To use this command, start by clicking the View Side by Side button. After you click the Synchronous Scrolling button, click the Reset Window Position button so both files are displayed at the same size onscreen.
- **Reset Window Position:** Makes files being shown side by side the same size onscreen to make them easier to compare.

Correcting Typos on the Fly

The unseen hand of Office 2016 corrects some typos and misspellings automatically. For example, try typing **accomodate** with one *m* — Office corrects the misspelling and inserts the second *m* for you. Try typing **perminent** with an *i* instead of an *a* — the invisible hand of Office corrects the misspelling, and you get *permanent.* While you're at it, type a colon and a close parenthesis **:)** — you get a smiley face.

As good as the AutoCorrect feature is, you can make it even better. You can also add the typos and misspellings you often make to the list of words that are corrected automatically.

Office corrects common spelling errors and turns punctuation mark combinations into symbols as part of its AutoCorrect feature. To see which typos are corrected and which punctuation marks are turned into symbols, open the AutoCorrect dialog box by following these steps:

1. **On the File tab, choose Options.**

   You see the Options dialog box.
2. **Go to the Proofing category.**
3. **Click the AutoCorrect Options button.**

   The AutoCorrect dialog box opens.
4. **Go to the AutoCorrect tab.**

   As shown in Figure 3-3, the AutoCorrect tab lists words that are corrected automatically. Scroll down the Replace list and have a look around. Go ahead. Make yourself at home.

No doubt you make the same typing errors and spelling errors time and time again. To keep from making these errors, you can tell Office to correct them for you automatically. You do that by entering the misspelling and its corrected spelling in the AutoCorrect dialog box (see Figure 3-3):

TIP

You can also remove misspellings and typos from the list of words that are corrected automatically. To remove a word from the list of corrected words, select it in the AutoCorrect dialog box and click the Delete button.

Enter a typo and its replacement

AutoCorrect: English (United States) ? ✕

AutoCorrect Math AutoCorrect AutoFormat As You Type AutoFormat Actions

☑ Show AutoCorrect Options buttons

☑ Correct TWo INitial CApitals Exceptions...

☑ Capitalize first letter of sentences

☑ Capitalize first letter of table cells

☑ Capitalize names of days

☑ Correct accidental usage of cAPS LOCK key

☑ Replace text as you type

Replace: With: ⦿ Plain text ○ Formatted text

Wazerka	Weverka

wa snot	was not
waht	what
warrent	warrant
wasnt	wasn't
watn	want
we;d	we'd
we;ll	we'll

Add Delete

☑ Automatically use suggestions from the spelling checker

OK Cancel

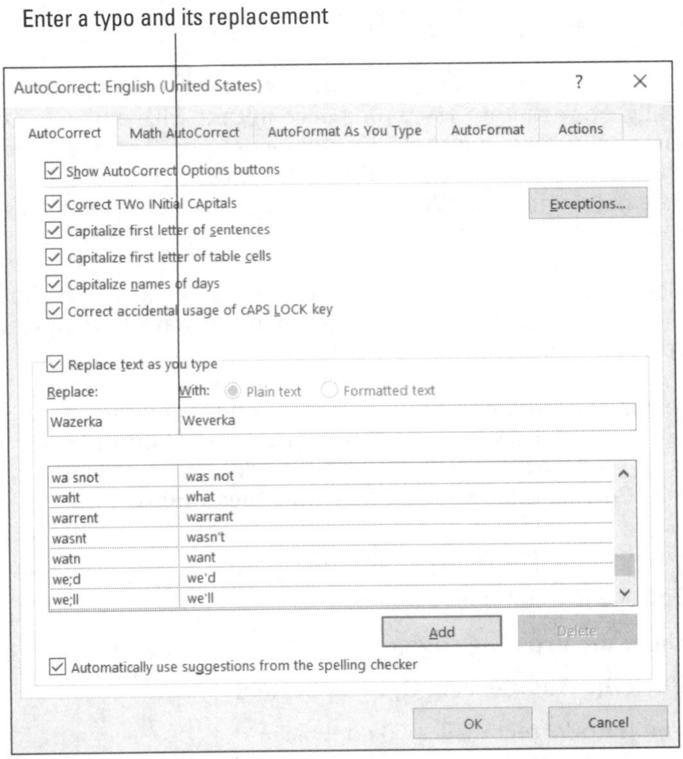

Figure 3-3: As you type, words in the Replace column are replaced automatically with words in the With column.

Entering Text Quickly with the AutoCorrect Command

The preceding part of this chapter explains how you can use the AutoCorrect command to help correct typing errors, but with a little cunning, you can also use it to quickly enter hard-to-type jargon, scientific names, and the like. To open the AutoCorrect dialog box, click the File tab, choose Options, go to the Proofing category in the Options dialog box, and then click the AutoCorrect Options button. Select the AutoCorrect tab in the AutoCorrect dialog box, as shown in Figure 3-4.

In the Replace column in the AutoCorrect tab are hundreds of common typing errors and codes that Office corrects automatically. The program corrects the errors by entering text in the With column whenever you mistakenly type the letters in the Replace column. However, you can also use this dialog box for the secondary purpose of quickly entering text.

Enter text to trigger AutoCorrect

What's entered when you type the text

AutoCorrect: English (United States) ? ✕

| AutoCorrect | Math AutoCorrect | AutoFormat As You Type | AutoFormat | Actions |

☑ Show AutoCorrect Options buttons

☑ Correct TWo INitial CApitals Exceptions...

☑ Capitalize first letter of sentences

☑ Capitalize first letter of table cells

☑ Capitalize names of days

☑ Correct accidental usage of cAPS LOCK key

☑ Replace text as you type

Replace: With: ◉ Plain text ○ Formatted text

/cs cordyceps sinensis

(c)	©
(e)	€
(r)	®
(tm)	™
...	...
:(☹
:-(☹

 Add Delete

☑ Automatically use suggestions from the spelling checker

 OK Cancel

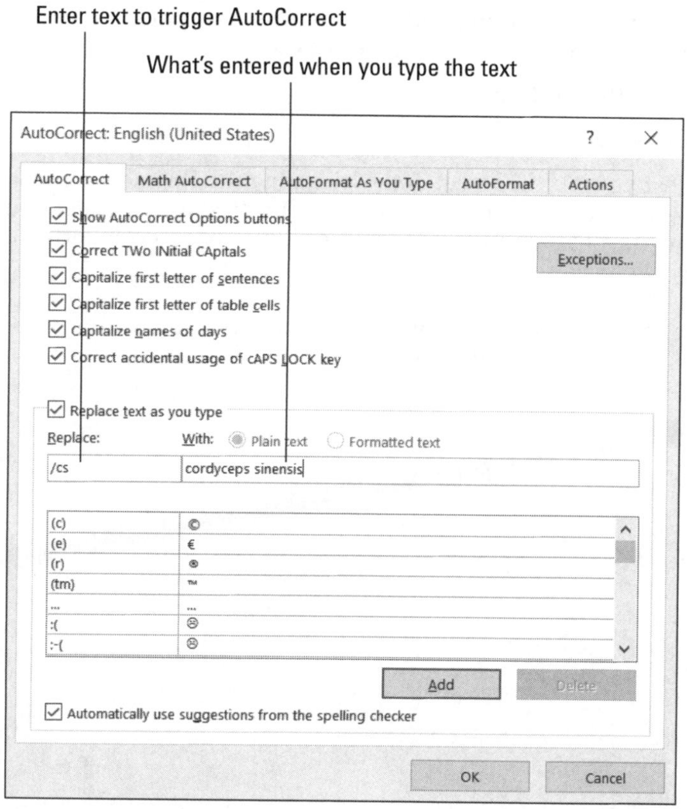

Figure 3-4:
With a little
cunning,
you can use
AutoCorrect
to enter
hard-to-type
text.

To make AutoCorrect work as a means of entering text, you tell Office
to enter the text whenever you type three or four specific characters. In
Figure 3-4, for example, Office is instructed to insert the words *cordyceps
sinensis* (a mushroom genus) whenever I enter the characters **/cs** (and press
the spacebar). Follow these steps to use AutoCorrect to enter text:

1. **Open the AutoCorrect tab of the AutoCorrect dialog box (see
 Figure 3-4).**

2. **In the Replace text box, enter the three or four characters that will
 trigger the AutoCorrect mechanism and make it enter your text.**

 Don't enter a word, or characters that you might really type someday,
 in the Replace box. If you do, the AutoCorrect mechanism might kick
 in when you least expect it. Enter three or four characters that never
 appear together. And start all AutoCorrect entries with a slash (/). You
 might forget which characters trigger the AutoText entry or decide
 to delete your AutoCorrect entry someday. By starting it with a slash,
 you can find it easily in the AutoCorrect dialog box at the top of the
 Replace list.

3. **In the With text box, enter the hard-to-type name or word(s) that will appear when you enter the Replace text.**
4. **Click the Add button.**
5. **Click OK.**

   Test your AutoCorrect entry by typing the Replace text you entered in Step 2 (which, of course, includes the slash I recommended) and pressing the spacebar. (AutoCorrect doesn't do its work until you press the spacebar.)

To delete an AutoCorrect entry, open the AutoCorrect dialog box, select the entry, and click the Delete button.

Book II

Word 2016

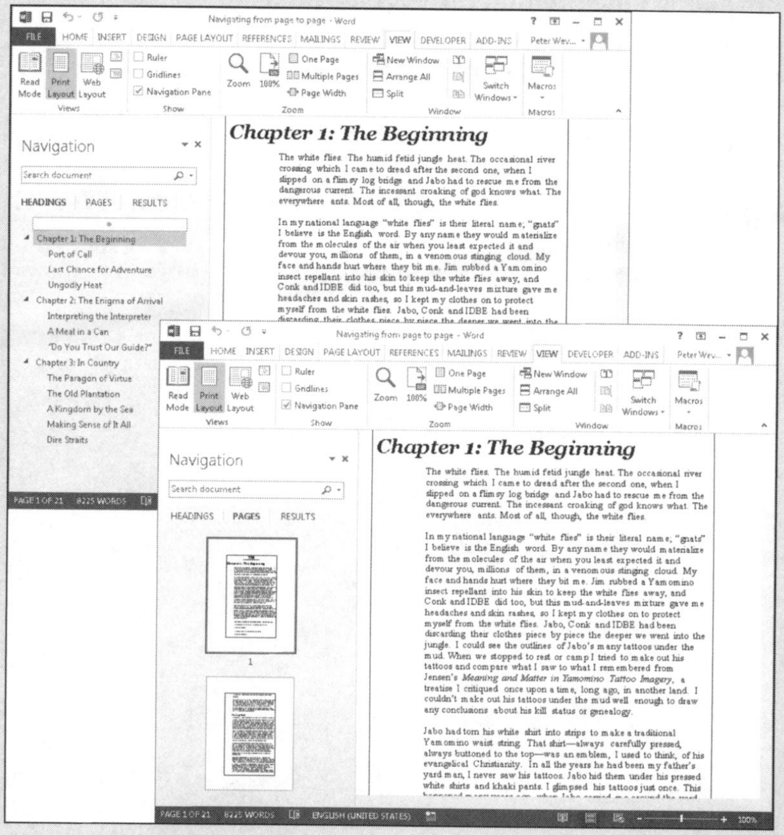

Go to www.dummies.com/extras/office2016aio to discover a simple trick for quickly marking entries for an index.

Contents at a Glance

Chapter 1: Speed Techniques for Using Word

In This Chapter

- Getting acquainted with the Word screen
- Creating a Word document
- Changing your view of a document
- Selecting text so that you can copy, move, or delete it
- Getting from place to place in long documents
- Pasting one Word document into another
- Creating data-entry forms

This chapter explains shortcuts and commands that can help you become a speedy user of Word 2016. Everything in this chapter was put here so that you can get off work earlier and take the slow, scenic route home. Starting here, you discover how to create and change your view of documents. You find out how to select text, get from place to place, and mark your place in long documents. You also explore how to insert one document into another and create data-entry forms to make entering information a little easier.

Book I, Chapter 2 explains the basics of entering and formatting text in Word 2016 and the other Office 2016 applications.

Introducing the Word Screen

Seeing the Word screen for the first time is like trying to find your way through Tokyo's busy Ikebukuro subway station. It's intimidating. But when you start using Word, you quickly learn what everything is. To help you get going, Figure 1-1 shows you the different parts of the screen. Here are shorthand descriptions of these screen parts:

- **Word button:** In the upper-left corner of the screen, the Word button offers a menu for restoring, moving, sizing, minimizing, maximizing, and closing the Word window.

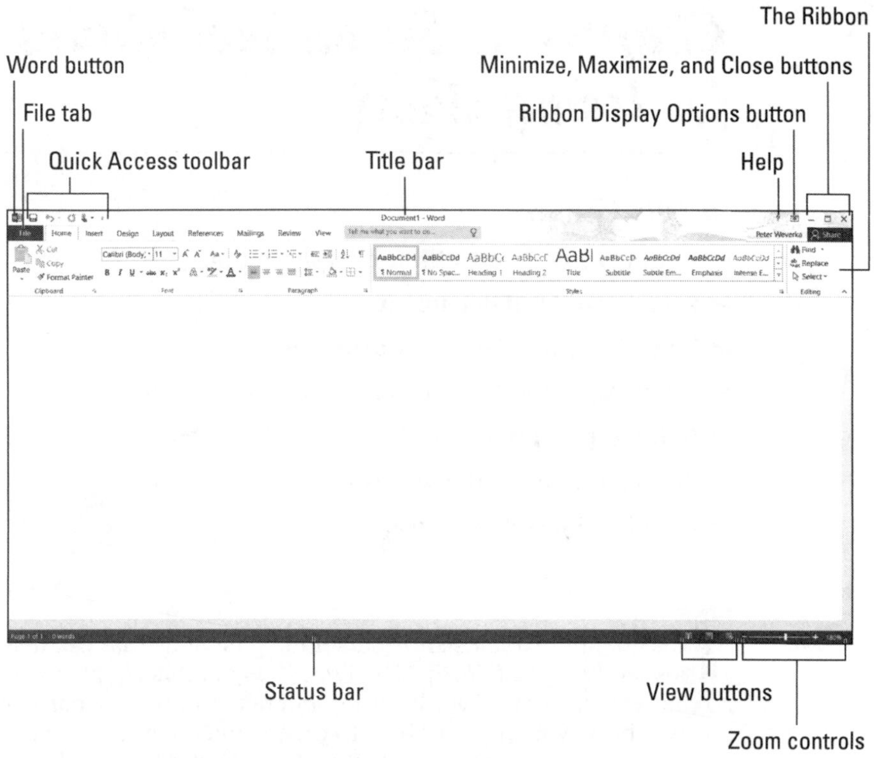

Figure 1-1: The Word screen.

- **Quick Access toolbar:** This toolbar offers the Save, Undo, Repeat, and Customize buttons (and on touchscreens, the Touch/Mouse mode button). Wherever you go in Word, you see the Quick Access toolbar. Book I, Chapter 1 explains the toolbar in detail; Book IX, Chapter 1 explains how to customize and move the Quick Access toolbar.
- **Title bar:** At the top of the screen, the title bar tells you the name of the document you're working on.
- **Ribbon Display Options button:** Clicking this button opens a menu for handling the Ribbon.
- **Minimize, Restore, Close buttons:** These three magic buttons make it very easy to shrink, enlarge, and close the window you are working in.
- **File tab:** Go to the File tab to do file-management tasks.
- **The Ribbon:** Select a tab on the Ribbon to undertake a new task. (Book I, Chapter 1 explains the Ribbon in detail, and Book IX, Chapter 1 explains how to customize the Ribbon.)

- **Status bar:** The status bar gives you basic information about where you are and what you're doing in a document. It tells you what page and what section you're in, and the total number of pages and words in your document. Book IX, Chapter 1 explains how to customize the status bar.
- **View buttons:** Click one of these buttons — Read Mode, Print Layout, or Web Layout — to change your view of a document. (Later in this chapter, "Getting a Better Look at Your Documents" describes the different ways to view a document.)
- **Zoom controls:** Use these controls to zoom in and out on your work.

Creating a New Document

Document is just a fancy word for a letter, report, announcement, or proclamation that you create with Word. All documents are created using a special kind of file called a *template*. The template provides the formats — the fonts, styles, margin specifications, layouts and other stuff — that give a document its appearance.

When you create a document, you are asked to choose a template to establish what your document will look like. If your aim is to create an academic report, flyer, newsletter, calendar, résumé, or other sophisticated document, see if you can spare yourself the formatting work by choosing the appropriate template when you create your document. (Chapter 3 of this mini-book explains templates in detail and how to create your own templates.)

Follow these basic steps to create a document:

1. **On the File tab, choose New.**

   The New window shown in Figure 1-2 appears.
2. **Click to select a template.**

   A preview window appears with a description of the template you chose, as shown in Figure 1-2.
3. **Click the Create button in the preview window.**

   Your new Word document opens.

Use these techniques in the New window to choose a template and create a document:

- **Choose the blank document template:** Choose Blank Document to create a bare-bones document with few styles. Blank Document is the default template for creating documents. (By pressing Ctrl+N, you can create a new document without opening the New window.)

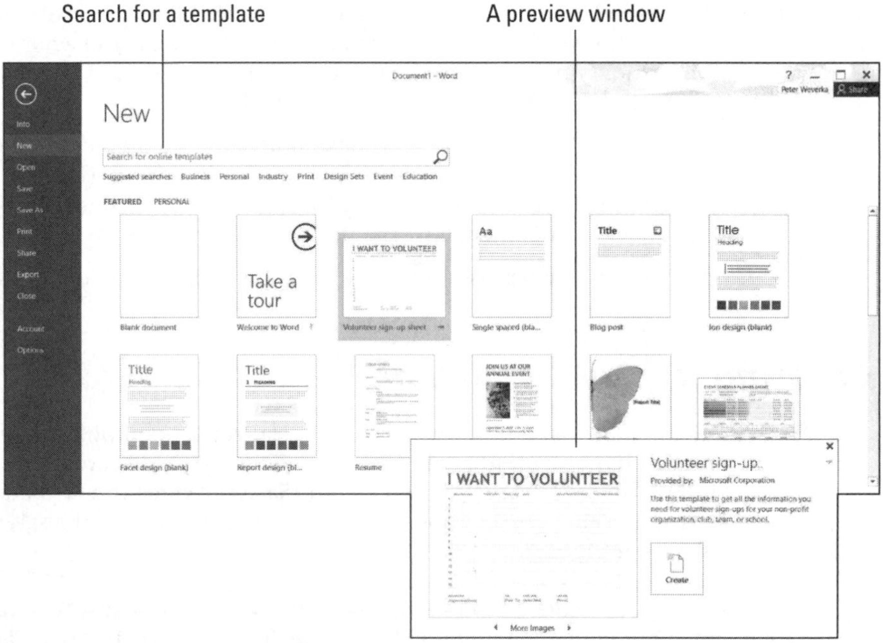

Figure 1-2: To create a document, choose a template in the New window.

- **Search online for a template:** Enter a search term in the Search box and click the Start Searching button (or click a suggested search term). Templates appear in the New window. You can click a template to examine it closely in a preview window (refer to Figure 1-2). Click the Create button to create a document from the template.
- **Choose a template:** Select a template to examine it in a preview window (refer to Figure 1-2). Click the Create button in the preview window to create a document from the template.
- **Choose a personal template:** On the Personal tab, click to select a template and create a document. A personal template is one that you created or copied to your computer or network. Chapter 3 of this minibook explains how to create templates. The Personal tab appears in the New window only if you've created templates or copied them to your computer.

TIP

If your search for the perfect template takes you too far afield, you can click the Home button to return to the New window.

TIP

To find out which template was used to create a document, go to the File tab, choose Info, and in the Info window, click the Show All Properties link (it's located in the lower-right corner of the window). The Properties list appears. Among other things, it tells you the template with which the document was created.

Welcome back!

To help you pick up where you left off, the Welcome back! notice appears when you reopen a Word document. It tells you which page you read most recently, the heading on that page, and when you last viewed the page.

Click the Welcome back! notice (or the Welcome back! icon) to go to directly to the page you last read.

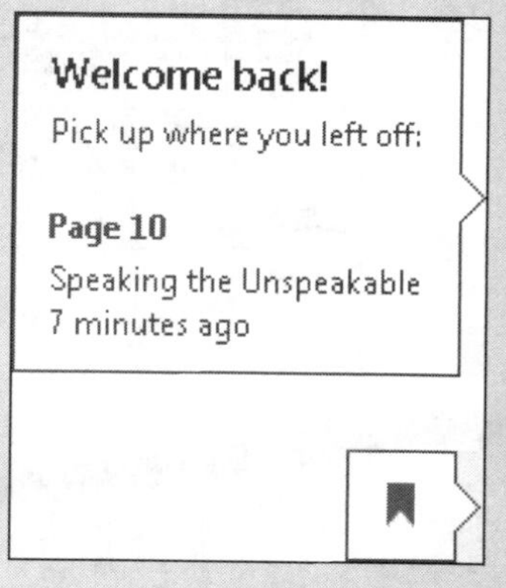

Book I, Chapter 1 explains how to save documents after you create them, as well as how to open a document you want to work on.

Getting a Better Look at Your Documents

A computer screen can be kind of confining. There you are, staring at the darn thing for hours at a stretch. Do you wish the view were better? The Word screen can't be made to look like the Riviera, but you can examine documents in different ways and work in two places at one time in the same document. Better read on.

Viewing documents in different ways

In word processing, you want to focus sometimes on the writing, sometimes on the layout, and sometimes on the organization of your work. To help you stay in focus, Word offers different ways of viewing a document. Figure 1-3 shows these views. These pages explain how to change views, the five different views, and why to select one over the other. (Be sure to visit Book I, Chapter 3 as well; it describes how to view a document through more than one window and how to open a second window in a document.)

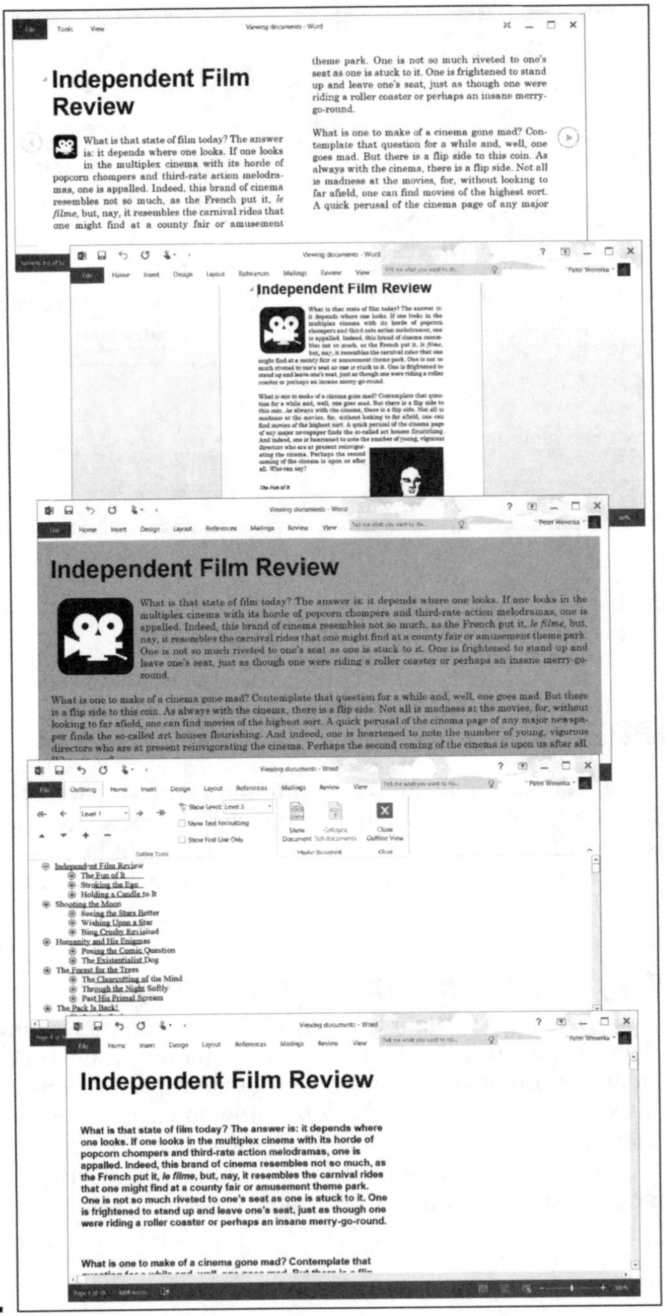

Figure 1-3: The different document views (top to bottom): Read Mode, Print Layout, Web Layout, Outline, and Draft.

Changing views

Use these techniques to change views:

- ✦ Click one of the three View buttons on the right side of the status bar.
- ✦ On the View tab, click one of the five buttons in the Views group.

Read mode

Switch to Read mode to focus on the text itself and proofread your documents. You can't enter or edit text in Read mode. Everything is stripped away — the Ribbon, scroll bars, status bar, and all. All you see are the text and artwork in your documents. Read mode is designed for reading documents on tablet computers.

Print Layout view

Switch to Print Layout view to see the big picture. In this view, you can see what your document will look like when you print it. You can see graphics, headers, footers, and even page borders in Print Layout view. You can also see clearly where page breaks occur (where one page ends and the next begins). In Print Layout view, you can click the One Page, Multiple Pages, or Page Width button on the View tab to display more or fewer pages on your screen.

Web Layout view

Switch to Web Layout view to see what your document would look like as a web page. Background colors appear (if you chose a theme or background color for your document). Text is wrapped to the window rather than around the artwork in the document. Book IX, Chapter 2 explains how to save an Office file, a Word document included, as a web page.

Outline view

Switch to Outline view to see how your work is organized. In this view, you can see only the headings in a document. You can get a sense of how your document unfolds and easily move sections of text backward and forward in a document. In other words, you can reorganize a document in Outline view. Chapter 8 of this mini-book explains outlines in torturous detail.

Draft view

Switch to Draft view when you're writing a document and you want to focus on the words. Pictures, shapes, and other distractions don't appear in this view, nor do page breaks (although you can clearly see section breaks). Draft view is best for writing first drafts.

Read mode zooming

While you're in Read mode, you can double-click a table, image, or chart to enlarge it onscreen and get a better look at it. Moreover, after the item gets enlarged, you can click the Zoom button (the magnifying glass) to enlarge it several times more.

To shrink an item back to size, press Esc or click onscreen (don't click the item itself).

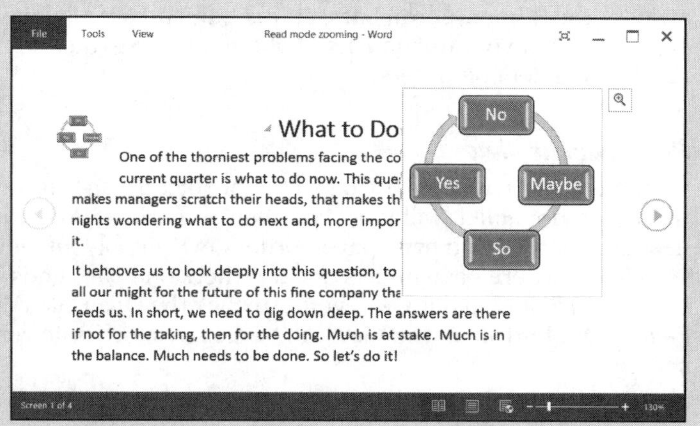

Splitting the screen

Besides opening a second window on a document (a subject of Book I, Chapter 3), you can be two places at one time in a Word document by splitting the screen. One reason you might do this: You're writing a long report and want the introduction to support the conclusion, and you also want the conclusion to fulfill all promises made by the introduction. That's difficult to do sometimes, but you can make it easier by splitting the screen so that you can be two places at one time as you write your introduction and conclusion.

Splitting a window means to divide it into north and south halves, as shown in Figure 1-4. In a split screen, two sets of scroll bars appear so that you can travel in one half of the screen without disturbing the other half. Follow these steps to split the screen:

1. **On the View tab, click the Split button.**

   A gray line appears onscreen.

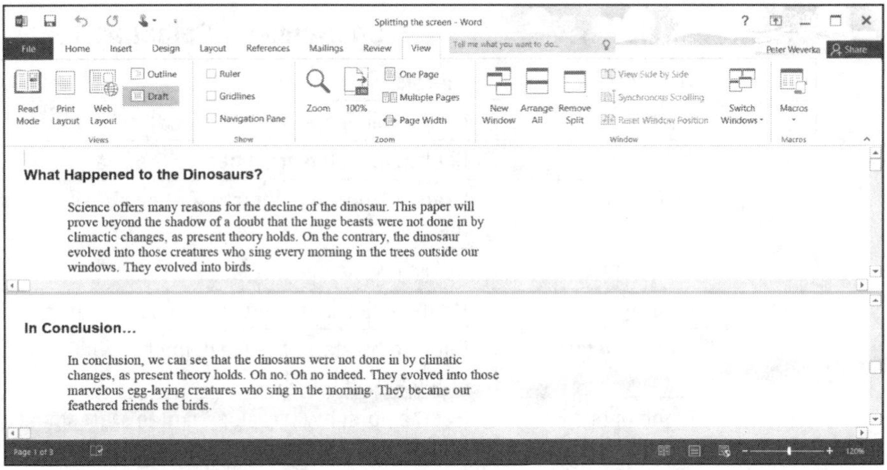

Figure 1-4: A split screen.

2. **Drag the gray line until the gray line is where you want the split to be.**

   You get two screens split down the middle. You can also split the screen by pressing Alt+Ctrl+S.

When you tire of this split-screen arrangement, click the Remove Split button on the View tab or drag the line to the top or bottom of the screen. You can also double-click the line that splits the screen in two.

TIP

In a split screen, you can choose a different view for the different halves. For example, click in the top half of the screen and choose Outline view to see your document in outline form, and click on the bottom half and choose Draft view to see the other half in Draft view. This way, for example, you can see the headings in a document while you write the introduction.

Selecting Text in Speedy Ways

Book I, Chapter 2 explains how to enter text and change its appearance and size. After you enter text, you inevitably have to copy, move, or delete it, but you can't do those tasks until you select it first. Table 1-1 describes short-cuts for selecting text.

If a bunch of highlighted text is onscreen and you want it to go away but it won't (because you pressed F8), press the Esc key.

Table 1-1 Shortcuts for Selecting Text

To Select This	*Do This*
A word	Double-click the word.
A line	Click in the left margin next to the line.
Some lines	Drag the mouse pointer over the lines or drag it down the left margin.
A sentence	Ctrl+click the sentence.
A paragraph	Double-click in the left margin next to the paragraph.
A mess of text	Click at the start of the text, hold down the Shift key, and click at the end of the text.
A gob of text	Put the cursor where you want to start selecting, press F8, and press an arrow key, drag the mouse, or click at the end of the selection.
Text with the same formats	On the Home tab, click the Select button and choose Select Text with Similar Formatting (you may have to click the Editing button first).
A document	Hold down the Ctrl key and click in the left margin; triple-click in the left margin; press Ctrl+A; or go to the Home tab, click the Select button, and choose Select All (you may have to click the Editing button first).

TIP

After you press F8, all the keyboard shortcuts for moving the cursor also work for selecting text. For example, press F8 and then press Ctrl+Home to select everything from the cursor to the top of the document. Later in this chapter, "Keys for getting around" describes keyboard shortcuts for getting from place to place.

Viewing the hidden format symbols

Sometimes it pays to see the hidden format symbols when you're editing and laying out a document. The symbols show line breaks, tab spaces, paragraph breaks, and the space or spaces between words. To see the hidden format symbols, go to the Home tab and click the Show/Hide ¶ button (or press Ctrl+Shift+8). Click the button again to hide the symbols.

Here's what the hidden symbols look like onscreen.

Symbol	**How to Enter**
Line break (↵)	Press Shift+Enter
Optional hyphen -(-)	Press Ctrl+hyphen
Paragraph (¶)	Press Enter
Space (·)	Press the spacebar
Tab (→)	Press Tab

Moving Around Quickly in Documents

Besides sliding the scroll bar, Word offers a handful of very speedy techniques for jumping around in documents: pressing shortcut keys, using the Go To command, and navigating with the Navigation pane. Read on to discover how to get there faster, faster, faster.

Keys for getting around quickly

One of the fastest ways to go from place to place is to press the keys and key combinations listed in Table 1-2.

Table 1-2 Keys for Moving Around Documents

Key to Press	*Where It Takes You*
PgUp	Up the length of one screen
PgDn	Down the length of one screen
Home	To the start of the line
End	To the end of the line
Ctrl+PgUp	To the previous page in the document
Ctrl+PgDn	To the next page in the document
Ctrl+Home	To the top of the document
Ctrl+End	To the bottom of the document

TIP

Here's a useful keystroke for getting from place to place: Shift+F5. Press it once to go to the location of your most recent edit. Press it two or three times to go back one or two edits before that. Pressing Shift+F5 is useful when you want to return to the place where you made an edit but can't quite remember where that place is.

Navigating from page to page or heading to heading

In lengthy documents such as the one in Figure 1-5, the best way to get from place to place is to make use of the Navigation pane. Click a heading or a page in the Navigation pane and Word takes you there in the twinkling of an eye.

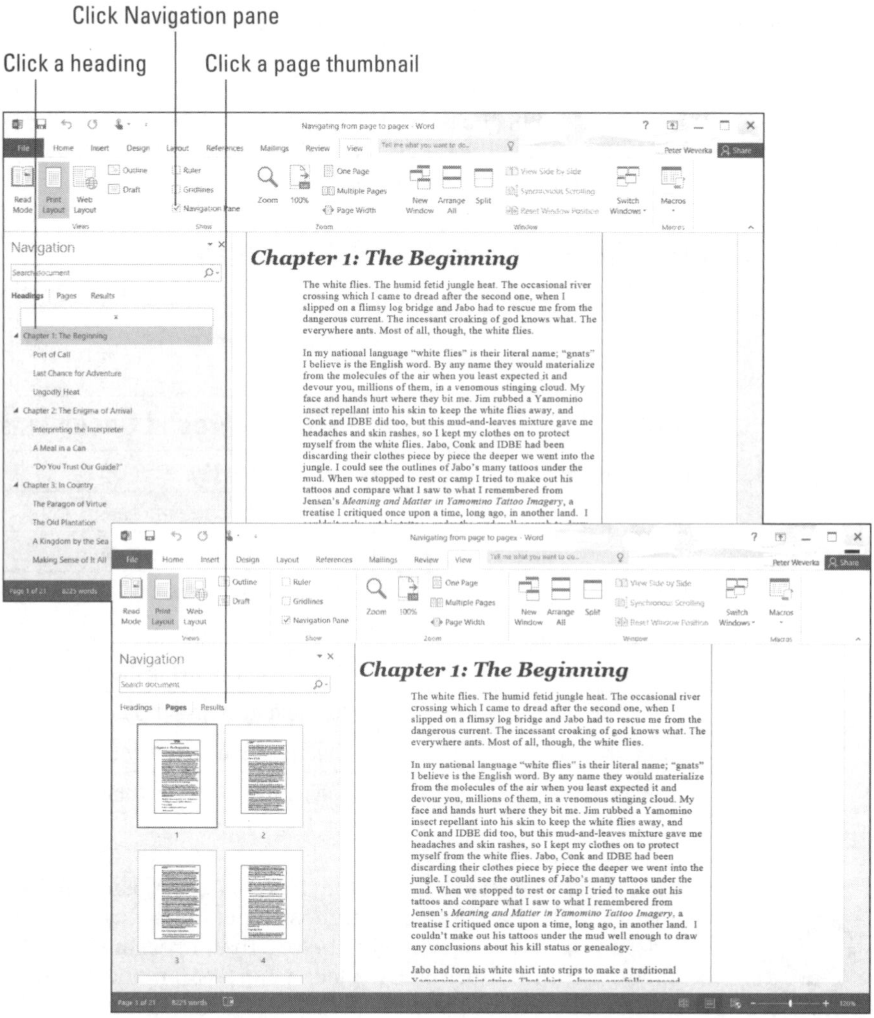

Figure 1-5: In the Navigation pane, click a heading or page thumbnail to go from place to place.

To display the Navigation pane, go to the View tab and click the Navigation Pane check box (you may have to click the Show button first). Then select a tab in the Navigation pane and go to it:

✦ **Going from heading to heading:** Select the Headings tab. Headings in your document appear (provided you assigned heading styles to headings). You can use the Navigation pane like a table of contents and click headings to get from place to place. Right-click a heading and choose a heading-level option on the shortcut menu to tell Word which headings to display. You can also right-click a heading and choose Expand All or Collapse All to see or hide lower-level headings.

✦ **Going from page to page:** Select the Pages tab. A thumbnail image of each page in the document appears. To quickly move from page to page, use the scroll bar in the Navigation pane or click a page thumbnail. Each thumbnail is numbered so that you always know which page you're viewing.

Going there fast with the Go To command

Another fast way to go from place to place in a document is to use the Go To command. On the Home tab, open the drop-down list on the Find button and choose Go To (you may have to click the Editing button first). You see the Go To tab of the Find and Replace dialog box, shown in Figure 1-6. You can also open this dialog box by pressing Ctrl+G or F5.

The Go to What menu in this dialog box lists everything that can conceivably be numbered in a Word document, and other things, too. Click a menu item, enter a number, choose an item from the drop-down list, or click the Previous, Next, or Go To buttons to go elsewhere.

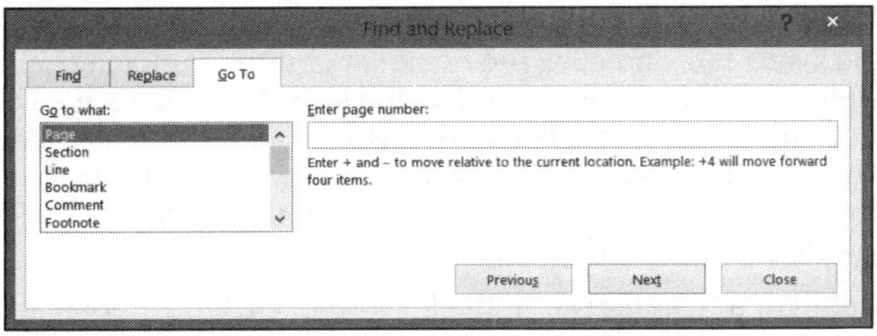

Figure 1-6: Using the Go To command.

Bookmarks for hopping around

Rather than press PgUp or PgDn or click the scroll bar to thrash around in a long document, you can use *bookmarks*. All you do is put a bookmark in an important spot in your document that you'll return to many times. To return to that spot, open the Bookmark dialog box and select a bookmark name, as shown in Figure 1-7. True to the craft, the mystery writer whose bookmarks are shown in Figure 1-7 wrote the end of the story first and used bookmarks to jump back and forth between the beginning and end to make all the clues fit together.

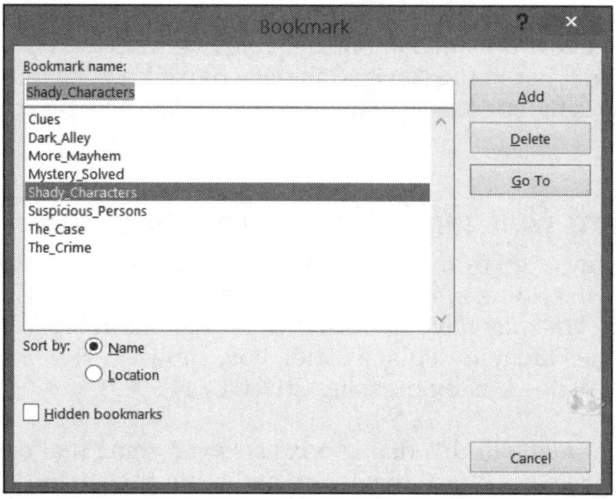

Figure 1-7: The Bookmark dialog box.

Follow these instructions to handle bookmarks:

- **Inserting a bookmark:** Click where you want the bookmark to go, visit the Insert tab, and click the Bookmark button (you may have to click the Links button first, depending on the size of your screen). Then, in the Bookmark dialog box, type a descriptive name in the Bookmark Name box, and click the Add button. Bookmarks can't start with numbers or include blank spaces. You can also open the Bookmark dialog box by pressing Ctrl+Shift+F5.
- **Going to a bookmark:** On the Insert tab, click the Bookmark button (you may have to click the Links button first), double-click the bookmark in the Bookmark dialog box, and click the Close button.
- **Deleting a bookmark:** Select the bookmark in the Bookmark dialog box and click the Delete button.

Word uses bookmarks for many purposes. For example, bookmarks indicate where cross-references are located in a document.

Inserting a Whole File into a Document

One of the beautiful things about word processing is being able to recycle documents. Say that you wrote an essay on the Scissor-Tailed Flycatcher that would fit very nicely in a broader report on North American birds. You can insert the Scissor-Tailed Flycatcher document into your report document:

1. **Place the cursor where you want to insert the document.**
2. **On the Insert tab, open the drop-down list on the Object button and choose Text from File.**

   You see the Insert File dialog box. (The Object button is located in the Text group on the right side of the Ribbon.)
3. **Find and select the file you want to insert.**
4. **Click the Insert button.**

Entering Information Quickly in a Computerized Form

A *form* is a means of soliciting and recording information. You can use forms like the one shown in Figure 1-8 to enter data faster and to reduce data-entry errors. Instead of entering all the information by hand, you or a data-entry clerk can choose entries from combo boxes, drop-down lists, and date pickers. You save time because you don't have to enter all the information by hand, and the information you enter is more likely to be accurate because you choose it from prescribed lists instead of entering it yourself.

To create a form like the one shown in Figure 1-8, start by creating a template for your form and putting *data-entry controls* — the combo boxes, drop-down lists, and date pickers — in the form. To fill out a form, you create a document from the form template and go to it. These pages explain how to create a form and use forms to record information.

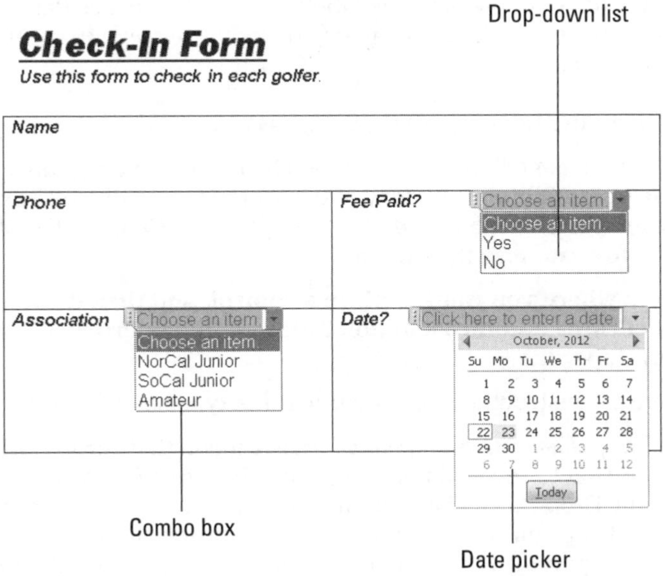

Figure 1-8: A data-entry form.

Creating a computerized form

The first step in creating a data-entry form is to create a template for holding the form. After that, you design the form itself by labeling the data fields and creating the data-entry controls. Better keep reading.

Creating a template to hold the form

Follow these steps to create a new template:

1. **Press Ctrl+N to create a new document.**
2. **On the File tab, choose Save As.**

   You see the Save As window.
3. **Click the Browse button.**

   The Save As dialog box opens.
4. **Open the Save As Type menu and choose Word Template.**
5. **Enter a descriptive name for your template and click the Save button.**

   Word stores your template in the Default Personal Templates Location folder. Chapter 3 of this mini-book explains templates in detail and explains where this folder is located.

Creating the form and data-entry controls

Your next task is to create the form and data-entry controls for your template. Enter labels on the form where you will enter information. The form in Figure 1-8, for example, has five labels: Name, Phone, Fee Paid?, Association, and Date. After you enter the labels, follow these steps to create the data-entry controls:

1. **Display the Developer tab, if necessary.**

   If this tab isn't showing, go to the File tab, choose Options, and on the Customize Ribbon category of the Word Options dialog box, select the Developer check box and click OK. (Book IX, Chapter 1 explains in detail how to customize the Ribbon.)
2. **Click where you want to place a control, and then create the control by clicking a Controls button followed by the Properties button on the Developer tab.**

   Here are instructions for creating three types of controls:

   - *Drop-down list:* A *drop-down list* is a menu that "drops" when you open it to reveal different option choices (refer to Figure 1-8). Click the Drop-Down List Content Control button and then the Properties button. You see the Content Control Properties dialog box, as shown in Figure 1-9. For each option you want to place on the drop-down list, click the Add button, and in the Add Choice dialog box, enter the option's name in the Display Name text box and click OK, as shown in Figure 1-9.

- *Combo box:* Like a drop-down list, a *combo box* "drops" to reveal choices. However, as well as choosing an option on the drop-down list, data-entry clerks can enter information in the box (refer to Figure 1-8). Click the Combo Box Content Control button and then the Properties button. In the Content Control Properties dialog box, enter option names the same way you enter them in a drop-down list, as shown in Figure 1-9.
- *Date picker:* A *date picker* is a mini-calendar from which data-entry clerks can enter a date (refer to Figure 1-8). Click the Date Picker Content Control button and then the Properties button. In the Content Control Properties dialog box, choose a display format for dates and click OK.

3. **Click the Save button to save your template.**

   Now you're ready to use your newly made form to enter data.

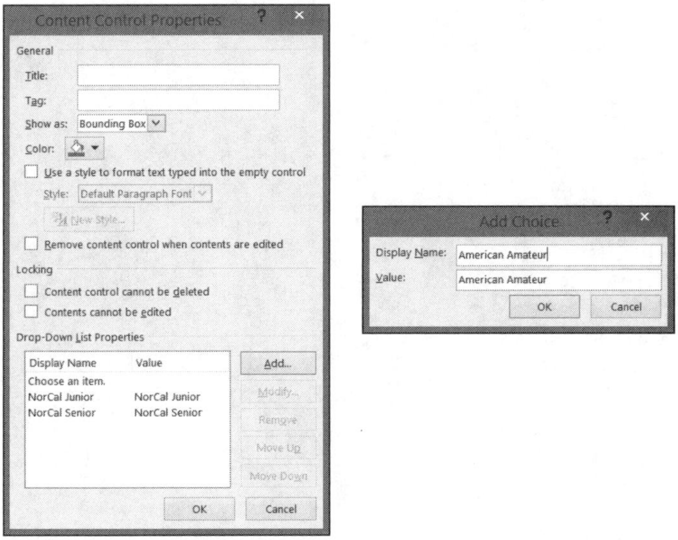

Figure 1-9: Click the Add button to create options for a drop-down menu or combo box.

Entering data in the form

Now that you have the template, you or someone else can enter data cleanly in easy-to-read forms:

1. **On the File tab, choose New.**

   You see the New window.

2. **Click the Personal tab.**

   This tab lists templates stored on your computer.

3. **Double-click the name of the template you created for entering data in your form.**

   The form appears.

4. **Enter information in the input fields.**

   Press the up or down arrow, or press Tab and Shift+Tab to move from field to field. You can also click input fields to move the cursor there.

5. **When you're done, print the document or save it.**

Chapter 2: Laying Out Text and Pages

In This Chapter

- Entering a section break
- Starting a new line and page
- Changing the margins
- Indenting text
- Numbering pages and handling headers and footers
- Adjusting the space between lines and paragraphs
- Handling bulleted and numbered lists
- Hyphenating the text

This chapter explains how to format text and pages. A well-laid-out document says a lot about how much time and thought was put into it. This chapter presents tips, tricks, and techniques for making pages look just right.

In this chapter, you learn what section breaks are and why they are so important to formatting. You discover how to establish the size of margins, indent text, number pages, construct headers and footers, determine how much space appears between lines of text, handle lists, and hyphenate text.

Paragraphs and Formatting

Back in English class, your teacher taught you that a paragraph is a part of a longer composition that presents one idea or, in the case of dialogue, presents the words of one speaker. Your teacher was right, too, but for word-processing purposes, a paragraph is a lot less than that. In word processing, a paragraph is simply what you put on-screen before you press the Enter key.

For instance, a heading is a paragraph. If you press Enter on a blank line to go to the next line, the blank line is considered a paragraph. If you type **Dear John** at the top of a letter and press Enter, "Dear John" is a paragraph.

REMEMBER

It's important to know this because paragraphs have a lot to do with formatting. If you click the Paragraph group button on the Home tab and monkey around with the paragraph formatting in the Paragraph dialog box, your changes affect everything in the paragraph where the cursor is located. To make format changes to a whole paragraph, all you have to do is place the cursor there. You don't have to select the paragraph. And if you want to make format changes to several paragraphs, all you have to do is select those paragraphs first.

Inserting a Section Break for Formatting Purposes

When you want to change page numbering schemes, headers and footers, margin sizes, and page orientations in a document, you have to create a *section break* to start a new section. Word creates a new section for you when you create newspaper-style columns or change the size of margins.

Follow these steps to create a new section:

1. **Click where you want to insert a section break.**
2. **On the Layout tab, click the Breaks button.**

   You open a drop-down list.
3. **Under Section Breaks on the drop-down list, select a section break.**

Figure 2-1 shows what the different section breaks look like in Draft view. All four section break options create a new section, but they do so in different ways:

- **Next Page:** Inserts a page break as well as a section break so that the new section can start at the top of a new page (the next one). Select this option to start a new chapter, for example.
- **Continuous:** Inserts a section break in the middle of a page. Select this option if, for example, you want to introduce newspaper-style columns in the middle of a page.
- **Even Page:** Starts the new section on the next even page. This option is good for two-sided documents in which the headers on the left- and right-side pages are different.
- **Odd Page:** Starts the new section on the next odd page. You might choose this option if you have a book in which chapters start on odd pages. (By convention, that's where they start.)

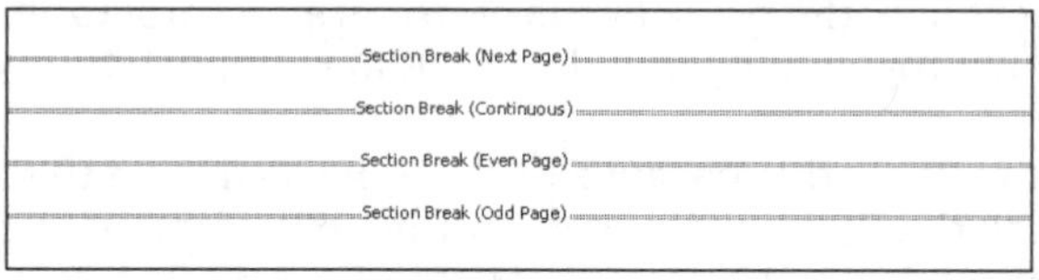

Figure 2-1: Section breaks in Draft view.

To delete a section break, make sure that you are in Draft view so that you can see section breaks, click the dotted line, and press the Delete key.

In the same way that paragraph marks store formats for a paragraph, section breaks store formats for an entire section. When you delete a section break, you apply new formats, because the section is folded into the section that formerly followed it and the section you deleted adopts that next section's formats. Because it's easy to accidentally delete a section break and create havoc, I recommend working in Draft view when your document has many section breaks. In Draft view, you can tell where a section ends because `Section Break` and a double dotted line appear on-screen. The only way to tell where a section ends in Print Layout view is to click the Show/Hide¶ button on the Home tab. (You can make section information appear on the status bar. Right-click the status bar and choose Section on the pop-up menu.)

Seeing what the formats are

Sometimes seeing how text was formatted merely by looking is difficult. However, by pressing Shift+F1, you can see precisely how text and paragraphs were formatted in the Reveal Formatting task pane. It describes how the text, paragraph, and section where the cursor is located are formatted.

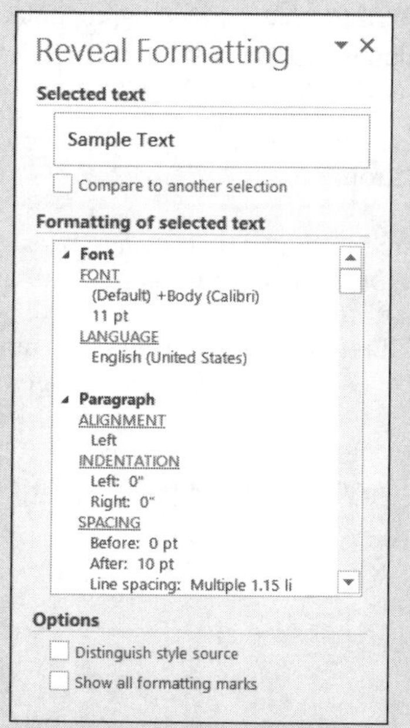

While the Reveal Formatting task pane is open, you can take advantage of these amenities:

- **Compare one part of a document to another:** Click the Compare to Another Section check box and then click another part of your document. The Reveal Formatting task pane describes how the two parts differ. Knowing how parts of a document differ can be invaluable when you're creating and modifying styles.
- **Find out which style was assigned:** Click the Distinguish Style Source check box. The task pane lists the style you assigned to the part of your document where the cursor is located.
- **See the formatting marks:** Click the Show All Formatting Marks check box. You can see where paragraphs end, where line breaks are, and where tab spaces were entered. Clicking this check box is the equivalent to clicking the Show/Hide¶ button on the Home tab.

Breaking a Line

To break a line of text before it reaches the right margin without starting a new paragraph, press Shift+Enter. Figure 2-2 shows how you can press Shift+Enter to make lines break better. The paragraphs are identical, but I broke lines in the right-side paragraph to make the text easier to read. Line breaks are marked with the ↵ symbol. To erase line breaks, click the Show/Hide¶ button to see these symbols and then backspace over them.

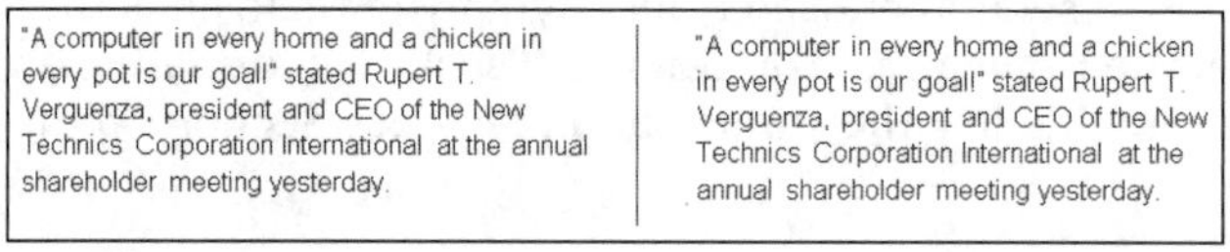

"A computer in every home and a chicken in
every pot is our goal!" stated Rupert T.
Verguenza, president and CEO of the New
Technics Corporation International at the annual
shareholder meeting yesterday.
"A computer in every home and a chicken
in every pot is our goal!" stated Rupert T.
Verguenza, president and CEO of the New
Technics Corporation International at the
annual shareholder meeting yesterday.

Figure 2-2: Break lines to make reading easier.

Starting a New Page

Word gives you another page so that you can keep going when you fill up one page. But what if you're impatient and want to start a new page right away? Whatever you do, *don't* press Enter again and again until you fill up the page. Instead, create a *hard page break* by doing one the following on the Insert tab:

- ✦ Click the Page Break button (or press Ctrl+Enter). Word starts a new page at the cursor position. (You can also go to the Layout tab, click the Breaks button, and choose Page on the drop-down list.)
- ✦ Click the Blank Page button. Word enters two hard page breaks to create an empty, blank page at the cursor position.

REMEMBER

Figure 2-3 shows, in Draft view, the difference between a soft page break and a hard page break. Word inserts a *soft page break* when the page is full and another page is needed; only you can create a hard page break. In Draft view, soft page breaks are marked with a dotted line; hard page breaks are marked with the words `Page Break` and a line. You can't tell where hard page breaks are in Print Layout view.

To delete a hard page break, switch to Draft view, double-click the words `Page Break`, and press the Delete key.

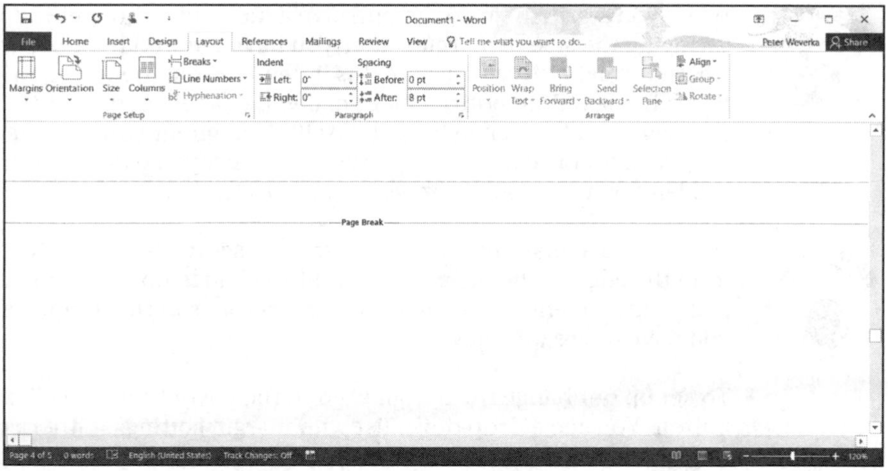

Figure 2-3: In Draft view, a soft page break (top) and hard page break (bottom).

Setting Up and Changing the Margins

Margins are the empty spaces along the left, right, top, and bottom of a page, as shown in Figure 2-4. Headers and footers fall, respectively, in the top and bottom margins. And you can put graphics, text boxes, and page numbers in the margins as well. Margins serve to frame the text and make it easier to read.

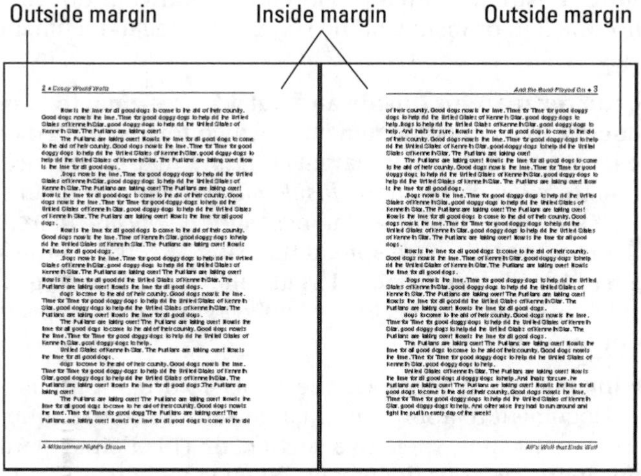

Figure 2-4: Margins in a two-sided document.

When you start a new document, give a moment's thought to the margins. Changing the size of margins after you have entered the text, graphics, and whatnot can be disastrous. Text is indented from the left and right margins. Pages break on the bottom margin. If you change margin settings, indents and page breaks change for good or ill throughout your document. By setting the margins carefully from the beginning, you can rest assured that text will land on the page where you want it to land.

Don't confuse margins with indents. Text is indented from the margin, not from the edge of the page. If you want to change how far text falls from the page edge, indent it. To change margin settings in the middle of a document, you have to create a new section.

To set up or change the margins, go to the Layout tab and click the Margins button. You see a drop-down list with margin settings. Either choose a setting or select Custom Margins to open the Margins tab of the Page Setup dialog box and choose among these commands for handling margins:

- **Changing the size of the margins:** Enter measurements in the Top, Bottom, Left, and Right boxes to tell Word how much blank space to put along the sides of the page.
- **Making room for the gutter:** The *gutter* is the part of the paper that the binding eats into when you bind a document. Enter a measurement in the Gutter box to increase the left or inside margin and make room for the binding. Notice on the pages of this book, for example, that the margin closest to the binding is wider than the outside margin. Choose Top on the Gutter Position menu if you intend to bind your document from the top, not the left, or inside, of the page. Some legal documents are bound this way.
- **Using mirror margins (inside and outside margins) in two-sided documents:** In a bound document in which text is printed on both sides of the pages, the terms left margin and right margin are meaningless. What matters instead is in the *inside margin*, the margin in the middle of the page spread next to the bindings, and the *outside margin*, the margin on the outside of the page spread that isn't affected by the bindings (refer to Figure 2-4). Choose Mirror Margins on the Multiple Pages drop-down list and adjust the margins accordingly if you intend to print on both sides of the paper.
- **Applying margin changes:** On the Apply To drop-down list, choose Whole Document to apply your margin settings to the entire document; This Section to apply them to a section; or This Point Forward to change margins in the rest of a document. When you choose This Point Forward, Word creates a new section.

If you're in a hurry to change margins, you can change them on the ruler. Display the ruler and drag the Left Margin, Right Margin, or Top Margin marker. You can find these markers by moving the pointer onto a ruler and looking for the two-headed arrow near a margin boundary. It appears, along with a pop-up label, when the pointer is over a margin marker.

To get a good look at where margins are, go to the File tab and choose Options. In the Word Options dialog box, select the Advanced category, and click the Show Text Boundaries check box (you'll find it under "Show Document Content").

Indenting Paragraphs and First Lines

An *indent* is the distance between a margin and the text, not the edge of the page and the text. Word offers a handful of ways to change the indentation of paragraphs. You can change the indentation of first lines as well as entire paragraphs. To start, select all or part of the paragraphs you want to re-indent (just click in a paragraph if you want to re-indent only one paragraph). Then click an Indent button, fiddle with the indentation marks on the ruler, or go to the Paragraph dialog box. All three techniques are described here.

Clicking an Indent button (for left-indents)

On the Home tab, click the Increase Indent or Decrease Indent button (or press Ctrl+M or Ctrl+Shift+M) to move a paragraph a half-inch farther away from or closer to the left margin. If you created tab stops, text is indented to the next or previous tab stop as well as to the next or previous half-inch. This is the fastest way to indent text, although you can't indent first lines or indent from the right margin this way.

"Eye-balling it" with the ruler

You can also change indentations by using the ruler to "eyeball it." This technique requires some dexterity with the mouse or your finger, but it allows you to see precisely where paragraphs and the first lines of paragraphs are indented. If necessary, display the ruler by going to the View tab and clicking the Ruler check box. Then click in or select the paragraph or paragraphs that need indenting and use these techniques to re-indent them:

- **Indenting an entire paragraph from the left margin:** Drag the *left-indent marker* on the ruler to the right. Figure 2-5 shows where this marker is located. Dragging the left-indent marker moves the first-line indent marker as well.

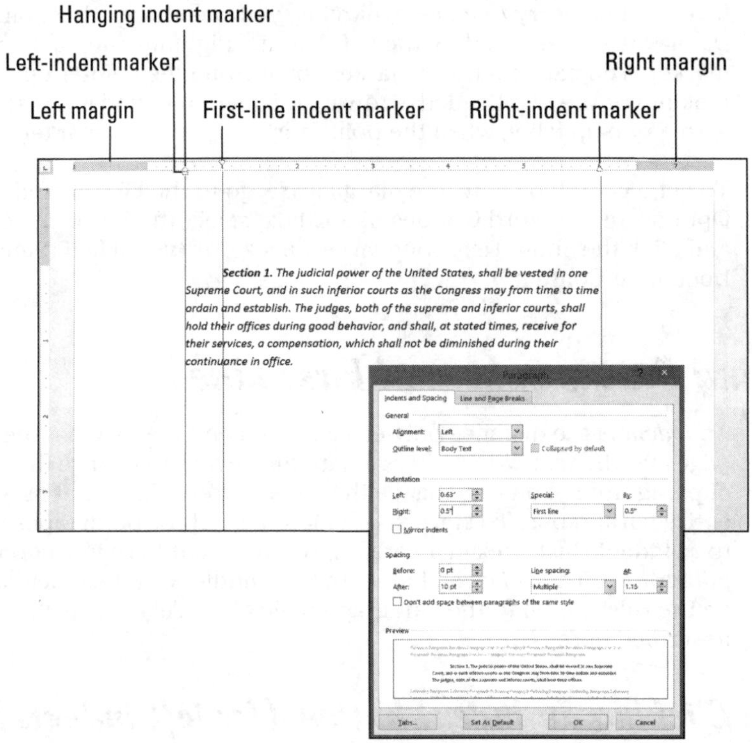

Figure 2-5: Indenting with the ruler (top) and Paragraph dialog box (bottom).

- **Indenting the first line of a paragraph:** Drag the *first-line indent marker* to the right (refer to Figure 2-5). This marker determines how far the first line of the paragraph is indented.
- **Making a hanging indent:** Drag the *hanging indent marker* to the right of the first-line indent marker (refer to Figure 2-5). A *hanging indent* is one in which the first line of a paragraph appears to "hang" into the left margin because the second and subsequent lines are indented to the right of the start of the first line. Bulleted and numbered lists employ hanging indents.
- **Indenting an entire paragraph from the right margin:** Drag the *right-indent marker* to the left (refer to Figure 2-5).

Notice the shaded areas on the left and right side of the ruler. These areas represent the page margins.

Indenting in the Paragraph dialog box

Yet another way to indent a paragraph or first line is to visit the Paragraph dialog box, as shown in Figure 2-5. Click in or select the paragraph or paragraphs in question, go to the Home or Layout tab, and click the Paragraph group button (the small button to the right of the word “Paragraph” in the Paragraph group). You see the Indents and Spacing tab of the Paragraph dialog box. Change the indentation settings. If you want to indent the first line or create a hanging indent, choose First Line or Hanging on the Special drop-down list and enter a measurement in the By box.

Numbering the Pages

How do you want to number the pages in your document? You can number them in sequence starting with the number 1, start numbering pages with a number other than 1, use Roman numerals or other number formats, and include chapter numbers in page numbers. What’s more, you can number the pages differently in each section of your document as long as you divided your document into sections.

When it comes to numbering pages, you can proceed in two ways, as shown in Figure 2-6:

- ✦ Put a page number by itself on the pages of your document.
- ✦ Include the page number in the header or footer.

After you enter a page number, you can format it in different ways in the Page Number Format dialog box (refer to Figure 2-6) and (Header & Footer Tools) Design tab.

REMEMBER

To handle page numbers (as well as headers and footers), you must be in Print Layout view. Click the Print Layout view button on the status bar or go to the View tab and click the Print Layout button.

Numbering with page numbers only

Follow these steps to insert a page number by itself in the header, footer, or margin of the pages:

1. **On the Insert tab, click the Page Number button.**
2. **On the drop-down list, choose where on the page you want to put the page number (Top of Page, Bottom of Page, or Page Margins).**
3. **On the submenu that appears, choose a page number option.**

   The farther you scroll on the submenu, the fancier the page number formats are.

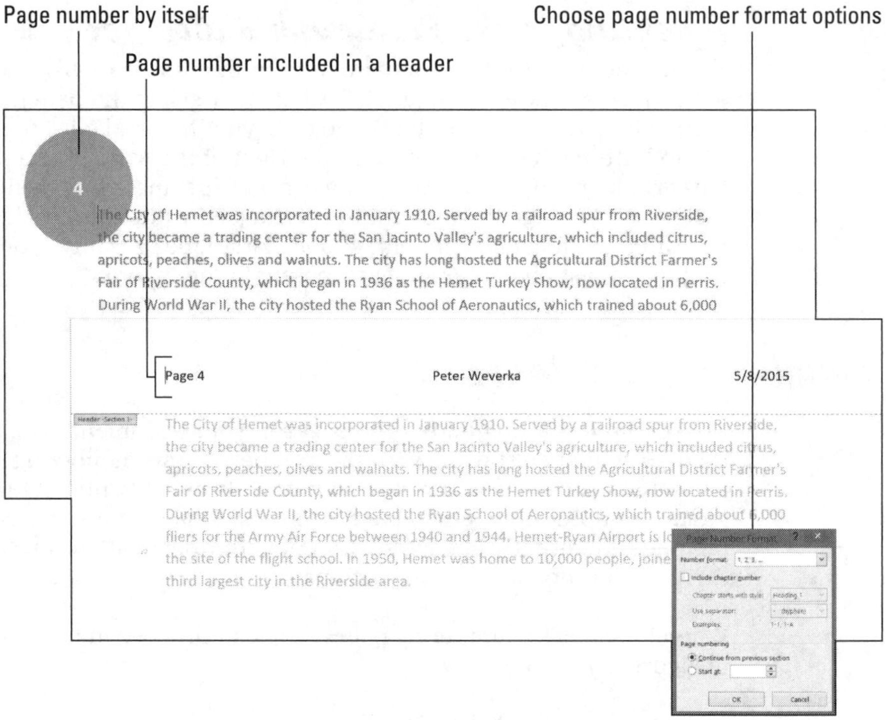

Figure 2-6: Ways to display page numbers on document pages.

If you change your mind about the page number format you choose, switch to Print Layout view and double-click in the header or footer where the page number is displayed. The (Header & Footer Tools) Design tab opens. Click the Page Number button and make a different choice, or choose Remove Page Numbers.

Including a page number in a header or footer

To put the page number part in a header or footer, double-click in the header or footer where you want the page number to appear (later in this chapter, "Putting Headers and Footers on Pages" explains headers and footers). Then follow these steps to insert the page number:

1. **On the (Header & Footer Tools) Design tab, click the Page Number button.**
2. **Choose Current Position.**

   You see a submenu with page number choices.

3. **Scroll through the submenu and choose a page number format.**

   The "Page X of Y" option is for listing the total number of pages in a document as well as the page number. For example, page 2 of a 10-page document is numbered "Page 2 of 10."

Changing page number formats

Change page number formats in the Page Number Format dialog box (refer to Figure 2-6). To display this dialog box, make sure you're in Print Layout view and double-click your header or footer. Then use one of the following methods to change page number formats:

- On the Insert tab, click the Page Number button and choose Format Page Numbers.
- On the (Header & Footer Tools) Design tab, click the Page Number button and choose Format Page Numbers.

In the Page Number Format dialog box, make your page numbers just so:

- **Choosing a different number format:** Open the Number Format drop-down list and choose a page-numbering format. You can use numbers, letters, or roman numerals.
- **Including chapter numbers in page numbers:** If your document generates chapter numbers automatically from headings assigned the same style (a subject not covered in this book), you can include the chapter number in the page number. Click the Include Chapter Number check box, choose a style, and choose a separator to go between the chapter number and page number.
- **Numbering each section separately:** Click the Start At option button (not the Continue from Previous Section button) to begin counting pages anew at each section in your document. Earlier in this chapter, "Inserting a Section Break for Formatting Purposes" explains sections.
- **Start numbering pages at a number other than 1:** Click the Start At option button and enter a number other than 1.

TIP

To keep some pages in a document from being numbered, create a section for those pages, and then remove page numbers from the section. To paginate your document, Word skips the section you created and resumes numbering pages in the following section.

Editing PDF files

PDF stands for *portable document file.* PDFs are designed to be read with the Adobe Reader program. Almost anywhere you go on the Internet, you stumble upon PDFs. The PDF format is a popular means of sharing and distributing files.

You can edit a PDF file in Word. Open the PDF as you would any text file and start editing. In my experiments, most of the PDF formats carry over to Word. I had some trouble with tables and images, but I didn't have any serious trouble.

Book IX, Chapter 2 explains how to save a Word file as a PDF file.

Putting Headers and Footers on Pages

A *header* is a little description that appears along the top of a page so that the reader knows what's what. Usually, headers include the page number and a title, and often the author's name appears in the header as well. A *footer* is the same thing as a header except that it appears along the bottom of the page, as befits its name.

These pages explain everything a mere mortal needs to know about headers and footers. Meanwhile, here are the ground rules for managing them:

✦ **Switching to Print Layout view:** To enter, read, edit or delete headers and footers, you must be in Print Layout view. You can't see headers and footers in the other views.

✦ **Displaying the (Header & Footer Tools) Design tab:** As shown in Figure 2-7, you manage headers and footers by way of buttons on the (Header & Footer Tools) Design tab. To display this tab after you create a header or footer, switch to Print Layout view and double-click a header or footer.

✦ **Closing the (Header & Footer Tools) Design tab:** Click the Close Header and Footer button or double-click outside the header or footer.

✦ **Placing different headers and footers in the same document:** To change headers or footers in the middle of a document, you have to create a new section. See "Inserting a Section Break for Formatting Purposes" earlier in this chapter.

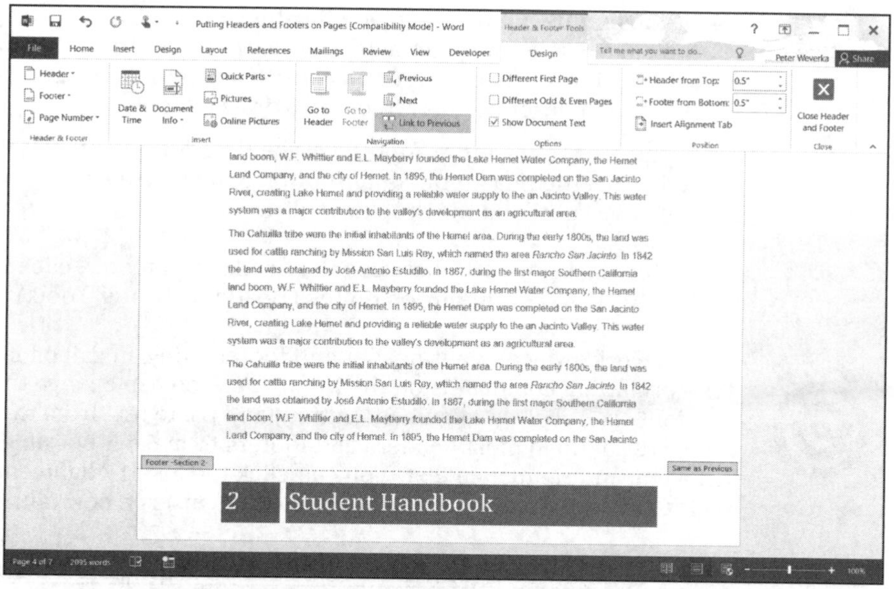

Figure 2-7: Manage headers and footers on the (Header & Footer Tools) Design tab.

Creating, editing, and removing headers and footers

Follow these instructions to create, edit, and delete headers and footers:

- **Creating a header or footer:** On the Insert tab, click the Header or the Footer button, and choose a header or footer on the gallery. The gallery presents headers or footers with preformatted page numbers, dates, and places to enter a document title and author's name. Click More Headers (or Footers) from Office.com to download headers or footers from Microsoft. (Later in this chapter, "Fine-tuning a header or footer" explains how to insert the date and time and change headers and footers from section to section.)
- **Choosing a different header or footer:** Don't like the header or footer you chose? If necessary, double-click your header or footer to display. Then click the Header or Footer button and choose a new header or footer from the gallery.
- **Editing a header or footer:** Double-click the header or footer. The cursor moves into the header or footer so that you can enter or format text. You can also click the Header or the Footer button and choose Edit Header or Edit Footer on the drop-down list.

- **Changing the appearance of a header or footer:** Click a shape or text box in a header or footer and visit the (Drawing Tools) Format tab to change the shape or text box's color, background, or size. (Book VIII, Chapter 4 describes the Office 2016 drawing tools.)
- **Removing a header or footer:** On the (Header & Footer Tools) Design tab, click the Header or Footer button and choose Remove Header or Remove Footer on the drop-down list.

To switch back and forth between the header and footer, click the Go to Header or Go to Footer button on the (Header & Footer Tools) Design tab.

TIP

As you work away on your header and footer, you can call on most of the text-formatting commands on the Home tab. You can change the text's font and font size, click an alignment button, and paste text from the Clipboard. Tabs are set up in most headers and footers to make it possible to center, left-align, and right-align text. You can click the Insert Alignment Tab button on the (Header & Footer Tools) Design tab to insert a new tab.

Creating your own header or footer for the gallery

When you click the Header or the Footer button on the Insert tab, a gallery appears with headers or footers. You can create your own header or footer and place it on this gallery. For example, create a header or footer with your company logo. After you design and create your header or footer, follow these instructions to wrangle with it:

- **Placing a header or footer in the gallery:** Select your header or footer by dragging over it or by clicking in the margin to its left. On the (Header & Footer Tools) Design tab, click the Quick Parts button and choose Save Selection to Quick Part Gallery. You see the Create New Building Block dialog box. Enter a descriptive name for the header or footer, choose Footers or Headers on the Gallery drop-down list, and click OK.
- **Inserting a header or footer you created:** On the Insert tab, click the Header or Footer button and choose your header or footer in the gallery. It is located in the Built-In or General category, depending on where you chose to put it.
- **Removing and editing headers or footers:** On the Insert tab, click the Quick Parts button and choose Building Blocks Organizer. The Building Blocks Organizer dialog box appears. Select your header or footer and click the Delete button to remove it from the gallery or the Edit Properties button to change its name, gallery assignment, or category assignment.

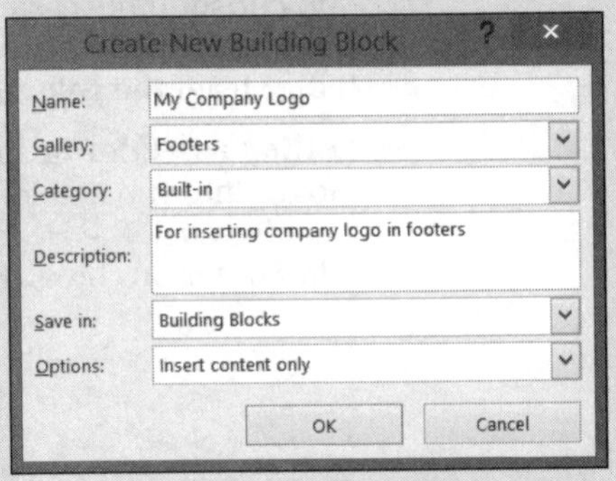

Fine-tuning a header or footer

Here is advice for making a perfect header on the (Header & Footer Tools) Design tab:

- **Inserting a page number:** See "Including a page number in a header or footer" and "Changing page number formats" earlier in this chapter.
- **Inserting the date and time:** Click the Date & Time button, choose a date format in the Date and Time dialog box, and click OK. Click the Update Automatically check box if you want the date to record when you print the document, not when you created your header or footer.
- **Changing headers and footers from section to section:** Use the Link to Previous button to determine whether headers and footers are different from section to section (you must divide a document into sections to have different headers and footers). Deselecting this button tells Word that you want your header or footer to be different from the header or footer in the previous section of the document; selecting this button (clicking it so it looks selected) tells Word that you want your header or footer to be the same as the header or footer in the previous section of your document. To make a different header or footer, deselect the Link to Previous button and enter a different header or footer.

  REMEMBER: When the header or footer is the same as that of the previous section, the Header or Footer box reads `Same as Previous` (refer to Figure 2-7); when the header or footer is different from that of the previous section, the words `Same as Previous` don't appear. You can click the Previous or Next button to examine the header or footer in the previous or next section.
- **Different headers and footers for odd and even pages:** Click the Different Odd & Even Pages check box to create different headers and footers for odd and even pages. As "Setting Up and Changing the Margins" explains earlier in this chapter, documents in which text is printed on both sides of the page can have different headers and footers for the left and right side of the page spread. The Header or Footer box reads Odd or Even to tell you which side of the page spread you're dealing with as you enter your header or footer.
- **Removing headers and footers from the first page:** Click the Different First Page check box to remove a header or footer from the first page of a document or section. Typically, the first page of letters and reports are not numbered.

Adjusting the Space between Lines

To change the spacing between lines, select the lines whose spacing you want to change, or simply put the cursor in a paragraph if you're changing the line spacing throughout a paragraph (if you're just starting a document, you're ready to go). Then, on the Home tab, click the Line and Paragraph Spacing button and choose an option on the drop-down list.

To take advantage of more line-spacing options, open the Paragraph dialog box, as shown in Figure 2-8. Use either of these techniques to open the Paragraph dialog box:

- ✦ Go to the Home tab or Layout tab and click the Paragraph group button.
- ✦ On the Home tab, click the Line and Paragraph Spacing button and choose Line Spacing Options on the drop-down list.

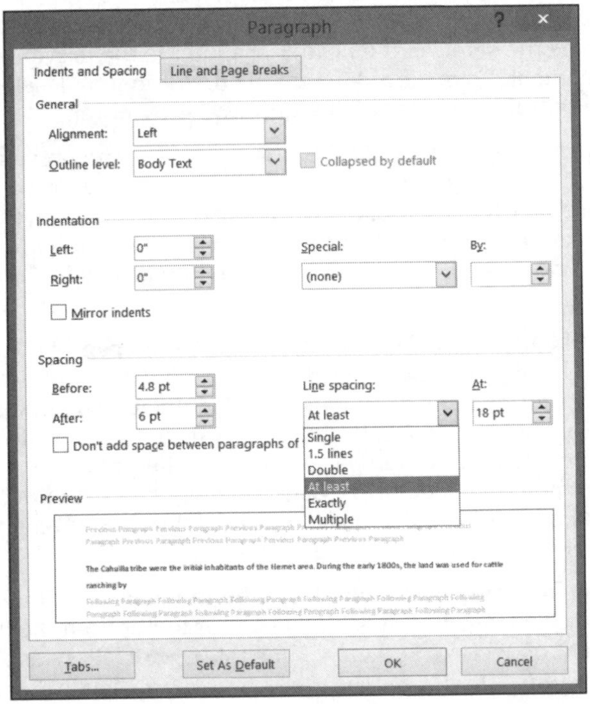

Figure 2-8: In the Paragraph dialog box, choose Spacing options to decide the amount of space between paragraphs and lines.

Besides single-, 1.5-, and double-spacing, the Paragraph dialog box offers these Line Spacing options:

- ✦ **At Least:** Choose this one if you want Word to adjust for tall symbols or other unusual text. Word adjusts the lines but makes sure there is, at minimum, the number of points you enter in the At box between each line.
- ✦ **Exactly:** Choose this one and enter a number in the At box if you want a specific amount of space between lines.
- ✦ **Multiple:** Choose this one and put a number in the At box to get triple-spaced, quadruple-, quintuple-, or any other number of spaced lines.

TIP

To quickly single-space text, click the text or select it if you want to change more than one paragraph, and press Ctrl+1. To quickly double-space text, select the text and press Ctrl+2. Press Ctrl+5 to put one and a half lines between lines of text.

The Design tab offers a command called Paragraph Spacing for changing the overall look of paragraphs. Click the Paragraph Spacing button and choose an option on the drop-down list to make paragraphs and lines of text more compact, tight, open, or relaxed.

Adjusting the Space Between Paragraphs

Rather than press Enter to put a blank line between paragraphs, you can open the Paragraph dialog box and enter a point-size measurement in the Before or After text box (see Figure 2-8). The Before and After measurements place a specific amount of space before and after paragraphs.

WARNING!

Truth be told, the Before and After options are for use with styles (a subject of the next chapter). When you create a style, you can tell Word to always follow a paragraph in a certain style with a paragraph in another style. For example, a paragraph in the Chapter Title style might always be followed by a paragraph in the Chapter Intro style. In cases like these, when you know that paragraphs assigned to one type of style will always follow paragraphs assigned to another style, you can confidently put space before and after paragraphs. But if you use the Before and After styles indiscriminately, you can end up with large blank spaces between paragraphs.

Go to the Home tab and use one of these techniques to adjust the amount of space between paragraphs:

- ✦ Click the Line and Paragraph Spacing button and choose Add Space Before Paragraph or Add Space after Paragraph on the drop-down list. These commands place 10 points of blank space before or after the paragraph that the cursor is in.

- Click the Paragraph group button to open the Paragraph dialog box (see Figure 2-8), and enter point-size measurements in the Before and After boxes (or choose Auto in these boxes to enter one blank line between paragraphs in whatever your Line-Spacing choice is). The Don't Add Space between Paragraphs of the Same Style check box tells Word to ignore Before and After measurements if the previous or next paragraph is assigned the same style as the paragraph that the cursor is in.

Creating Numbered and Bulleted Lists

What is a word-processed document without a list or two? It's like an emperor with no clothes. Numbered lists are invaluable in manuals and books like this one that present a lot of step-by-step procedures. Use bulleted lists when you want to present alternatives to the reader. A *bullet* is a black, filled-in circle or other character. These pages explain numbered lists, bulleted lists, and multilevel lists.

Simple numbered and bulleted lists

The fastest, cleanest, and most honest way to create a numbered or bulleted list is to enter the text without any concern for numbers or bullets. Just press Enter at the end of each step or bulleted entry. When you're done, select the list, go to the Home tab, and click the Numbering or Bullets button. You can also click the Numbering or Bullets button and start typing the list. Each time you press Enter, Word enters the next number or another bullet.

Meanwhile, here are some tricks for handling lists:

- **Ending a list:** Press the Enter key twice after typing the last entry in the list.
- **Removing the numbers or bullets:** Select the list and click the Numbering or Bullets button.
- **Adjusting how far a list is indented:** Right-click anywhere in the list, choose Adjust List Indents, and enter a new measurement in the Text Indent box.
- **Resuming a numbered list:** Suppose that you want a numbered list to resume where a list you entered earlier ended. In other words, suppose that you left off writing a four-step list, put in a graphic or some paragraphs, and now you want to resume the list at Step 5. Click the Numbering button to start numbering again. The AutoCorrect Options button appears. Click it and choose Continue Numbering, or right-click and choose Continue Numbering on the shortcut menu.
- **Starting a new list:** Suppose that you want to start a brand-new list right away. Right-click the number Word entered and choose Restart at 1 on the shortcut menu.

Automatic lists and what to do about them

Word creates automatic lists for you whether you like it or not. To see what I mean, type the number 1, type a period, and press the spacebar. Word immediately creates a numbered list. In the same manner, Word creates a bulleted list when you type an asterisk (*) and press the spacebar.

Some people find this kind of behind-the-scenes skullduggery annoying. If you are one such person, do one of the following to keep Word from making lists automatically:

- Click the AutoCorrect Options button — it appears automatically — and choose Stop Automatically Creating Lists.
- On the File tab, choose Options, select the Proofing category in the Word Options dialog box, and click the AutoCorrect Options button. On the AutoFormat As You Type tab in the AutoCorrect dialog box, deselect the Automatic Numbered Lists and Automatic Bulleted Lists check boxes.

Constructing lists of your own

If you're an individualist and you want numbered and bulleted lists to work your way, follow these instructions for choosing unusual bullet characters and number formats:

- **Choosing a different numbering scheme:** On the Home tab, open the drop-down list on the Numbering button and choose a numbering scheme. You can also choose Define New Number Format. As shown in Figure 2-9, you see the Define New Number Format dialog box, where you can choose a number format, choose a font for numbers, and toy with number alignments.
- **Choosing a different bullet character:** On the Home tab, open the drop-down list on the Bullets button and choose a different bullet character on the drop-down list. You can also choose Define New Bullet to open the Define New Bullet dialog box, shown in Figure 2-9, and click the Symbol button to choose a bullet character in the Symbol dialog box (Book I, Chapter 2 describes symbols). The dialog box also offers opportunities for indenting bullets and the text that follows them in unusual ways.

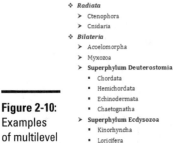

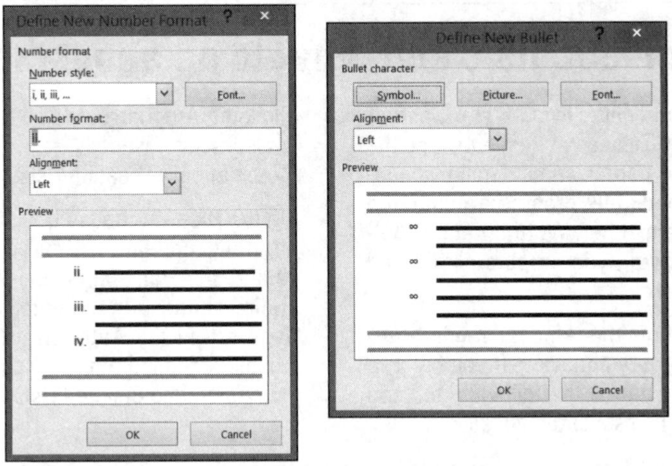

Figure 2-9: Customizing a numbered or bulleted list.

Managing a multilevel list

A *multilevel list,* also called a *nested list*, is a list with subordinate entries, as shown in Figure 2-10. To create a multilevel list, you declare what kind of list you want, and then, as you enter items for the list, you indent the items that you want to be subordinate. Follow these steps to create a multilevel list:

1. **On the Home tab, click the Multilevel List button and choose what kind of list you want.**

   If none of the lists suit you, you can choose Define New Multilevel List and create a new kind of list in the Define New Multilevel List dialog box.

2. **Enter the items for the list, pressing Enter as you complete each one.**
3. **Select a list item (or items) and click the Increase Indent button (or press Ctrl+M) to make the items subordinate in the list; click the Decrease Indent button (or press Ctrl+Shift+M) to raise their rank in the list.**

   Repeat Step 3 until the list is just so.

- ❖ ***Radiata***
  - ➤ Ctenophora
  - ➤ Cnidaria
- ❖ ***Bilateria***
  - ➤ Acoelomorpha
  - ➤ Myxozoa
  - ➤ **Superphylum Deuterostomia**
    - ▪ Chordata
    - ▪ Hemichordata
    - ▪ Echinodermata
    - ▪ Chaetognatha
  - ➤ **Superphylum Ecdysozoa**
    - ▪ Kinorhyncha
    - ▪ Loricifera
    - ▪ Priapulida

1) ***Radiata***
   a) Ctenophora
   b) Cnidaria
2) ***Bilateria***
   a) Acoelomorpha
   b) Myxozoa
   c) **Superphylum Deuterostomia**
      i) Chordata
      ii) Hemichordata
      iii) Echinodermata
      iv) Chaetognatha
   d) **Superphylum Ecdysozoa**
      i) Kinorhyncha
      ii) Loricifera
      iii) Priapulida

1. ***Radiata***
   1.1. Ctenophora
   1.2. Cnidaria
2. ***Bilateria***
   2.1. Acoelomorpha
   2.2. Myxozoa
   2.3. **Superphylum Deuterostomia**
      2.3.1. Chordata
      2.3.2. Hemichordata
      2.3.3. Echinodermata
      2.3.4. Chaetognatha
   2.4. **Superphylum Ecdysozoa**
      2.4.1. Kinorhyncha
      2.4.2. Loricifera
      2.4.3. Priapulida

Figure 2-10: Examples of multilevel lists.

Working with Tabs

Tabs are a throwback to the days of the typewriter, when it was necessary to make tab stops in order to align text. Except for making leaders and aligning text in headers and footers, everything you can do with tabs can also be done by creating a table — and it can be done far faster. All you have to do is align the text inside the table and then remove the table borders. (Chapter 4 of this mini-book explains tables.)

A *tab stop* is a point around which or against which text is formatted. As shown in Figure 2-11, Word offers five tab types for aligning text: Left, Center, Right, Decimal, and Bar (a bar tab stop merely draws a vertical line on the page). When you press the Tab key, you advance the text cursor by one tab stop. Tab stops are shown on the ruler; symbols on the ruler tell you what type of tab you're dealing with.

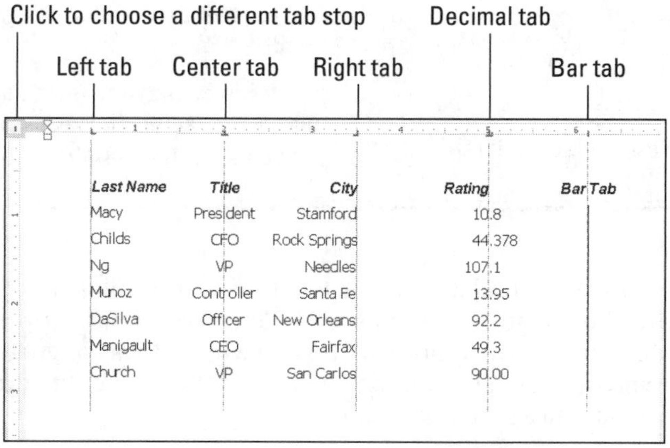

Figure 2-11: Different kinds of tab stops.

By default, tabs are left-aligned and are set at half-inch intervals. Display the ruler (click the Ruler check box on the View tab) and follow these steps to change tabs or change where tabs appear on the ruler:

1. **Select the paragraphs that need different tab settings.**
2. **Click the Tab box on the left side of the ruler as many times as necessary to choose the kind of tab you want.**

   Symbols on the tab box indicate which type of tab you're choosing.
3. **Click on the ruler where you want the tab to go.**

   You can click as many times as you want and enter more than one kind of tab.

All about tab leaders

In my opinion, the only reason to fool with tabs and tab stops is to create tab leaders like the ones shown here. A *leader* is a series of punctuation marks — periods in the illustration — that connect text across a page. Leaders are very elegant. For the figure, I used left-aligned tab stops for the characters' names and right-aligned tab stops for the players' names. I included leaders so that you can tell precisely who played whom.

THE PLAYERS

Romeo..	McGeorge Wright
Juliet...	Gabriela Hernandez
Mercutio...	Chris Suzuki
Lady Capulet................................	Mimi Hornstein

Follow these steps to create tab leaders:

1. **Enter the text and, in each line, enter a tab space between the text on the left side and the text on the right side.**
2. **Select the text you entered.**
3. **On the Home tab, click the Paragraph group button, and in the Paragraph dialog box, click the Tabs button.**

   You see the Tabs dialog box.
4. **Enter a position for the first new tab in the Tab Stop Position box.**
5. **Under Leader in the dialog box, select the punctuation symbol you want for the leader.**
6. **Click OK, display the ruler, and drag tab markers to adjust the space between the text on the left and right.**

To move a tab stop, drag it to a new location on the ruler. Text that is aligned with the tab stop moves as well. To remove a tab stop, drag it off the ruler. When you remove a tab stop, text to which it was aligned is aligned to the next remaining tab stop on the ruler or to the next default tab stop if you didn't create any tab stops of your own.

Sometimes it's hard to tell where tabs were put in the text. To find out, click the Show/Hide ¶ button on the Home tab to see the formatting characters, including the arrows that show where the Tab key was pressed.

Hyphenating Text

The first thing you should know about hyphenating words is that you may not need to do it. Text that hasn't been hyphenated is much easier to read, which is why the majority of text in this book, for example, isn't hyphenated. It has a *ragged right margin,* to borrow typesetter lingo. Hyphenate only when text is trapped in columns or in other narrow places, or when you want a very formal-looking document.

Do not insert a hyphen simply by pressing the hyphen key, because the hyphen will stay there even if the word moves to the middle of a line and doesn't need to be broken in half. Instead, when a big gap appears in the right margin and a word is crying out to be hyphenated, put the cursor where the hyphen needs to go and press Ctrl+hyphen. This way, you enter what is called a *discretionary hyphen,* and the hyphen appears only if the word breaks at the end of a line. (To remove a discretionary hyphen, press the Show/Hide ¶ button so that you can see it, and then backspace over it.)

Automatically and manually hyphenating a document

Select text if you want to hyphenate part of a document, not all of it, and use one of these techniques to hyphenate words that break on the end of a line of text:

- **Automatic hyphenation:** On the Layout tab, click the Hyphenation button and choose Automatic on the drop-down list. Word hyphenates your document (or a portion of your document, if you selected it first).

  You can tell Word how to hyphenate automatically by clicking the Hyphenation button and choosing Hyphenation Options. You see the Hyphenation dialog box shown in Figure 2-12. Deselect the Hyphenate Words in CAPS check box if you don't care to hyphenate words in uppercase. Words that fall in the hyphenation zone are hyphenated, so enlarging the hyphenation zone means a less ragged right margin but more ugly hyphens, and a small zone means fewer ugly hyphens but a more ragged right margin. You can limit how many hyphens appear consecutively by entering a number in the Limit Consecutive Hyphens To box.

- **Manual hyphenation:** On the Layout tab, click the Hyphenation button and choose Manual on the drop-down list. Word displays a box with some hyphenation choices in it, as shown in Figure 2-12. The cursor blinks on the spot where Word suggests putting a hyphen. Click Yes or No to accept or reject Word's suggestion. Keep accepting or rejecting Word's suggestions until the text is hyphenated.

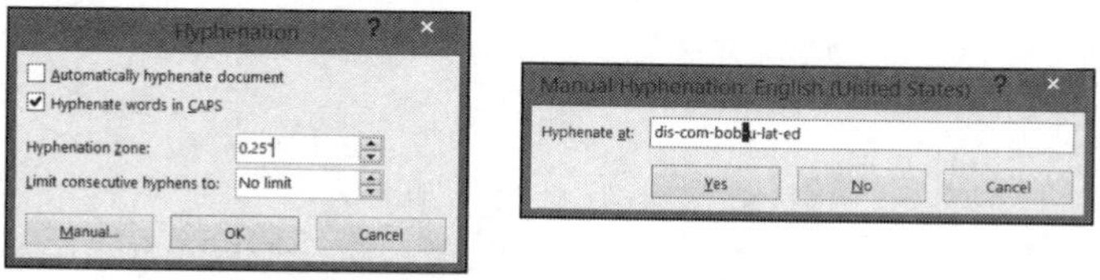

Figure 2-12: Telling Word how to hyphenate (left) and deciding where a hyphen goes (right).

Unhyphenating and other hyphenation tasks

More hyphenation esoterica:

- **Unhyphenating:** To "unhyphenate" a document or text you hyphenated automatically, go to the Layout tab, click the Hyphenation button, and choose None on the drop-down menu.
- **Preventing text from being hyphenated:** Select the text and, on the Home tab, click the Paragraph group button. In the Paragraph dialog box, select the Line and Page Breaks tab, and select the Don't Hyphenate check box. (If you can't hyphenate a paragraph, it's probably because this box was selected unintentionally.)

Em and en dashes

Here is something about hyphens that editors and typesetters know, but the general public does not know: There is a difference between hyphens and dashes. Most people insert a hyphen where they ought to use an em dash or an en dash:

- An *em dash* looks like a hyphen but is wider — it's as wide as the letter *m*. The previous sentence has an em dash in it. Did you notice?
- An *en dash* is the width of the letter *n*. Use en dashes to show inclusive numbers or time periods, like so: pp. 45–50; Aug.–Sept. 1998; Exodus 16:11–16:18. An en dash is a little bit longer than a hyphen.

To place an em or en dash in a document and impress your local typesetter or editor, not to mention your readers, use these techniques:

- **Em dash:** Press Ctrl+Alt+– (the minus sign key on the Numeric keypad).
- **En dash:** Press Ctrl+– (on the numeric keypad).

You can also enter an em or en dash by following these steps:

1. **Go to the Insert tab.**
2. **Click the Symbol button and choose More Symbols on the drop-down list.**

   The Symbol dialog box opens.
3. **Go to the Special Characters tab.**
4. **Choose Em Dash or En Dash.**

Chapter 3: Word Styles

In This Chapter

- Discovering how styles and templates work
- Applying a new style
- Creating your own styles
- Altering a style
- Creating a new template

Welcome to what may be the most important chapter of this book — the most important in Book II, anyway. Styles can save a ridiculous amount of time that you would otherwise spend formatting and wrestling with text. And many Word features rely on styles. You can't create a table of contents or use the Navigation pane unless each heading in your document has been assigned a heading style. Nor can you take advantage of Outline view and the commands for moving text around in that view. You can't cross-reference headings or number the headings in a document.

If you want to be stylish, at least where Word is concerned, you have to know about styles.

All About Styles

A *style* is a collection of formatting commands assembled under one name. When you apply a style, you give many formatting commands simultaneously, and you spare yourself the trouble of visiting numerous tabs and dialog boxes to format text. Styles save time and make documents look more professional. Headings assigned the same style — Heading1, for example — all look the same. When readers see that headings and paragraphs are consistent with one another across all the pages of a document, they get a warm, fuzzy feeling. They think the person who created the document really knew what he or she was doing.

Styles and templates

REMEMBER

Every document comes with built-in styles that it inherits from the template with which it was created. You can create your own styles to supplement styles from the template. For that matter, you can create a template, populate it with styles you design, and use your new template to create distinctive letters or reports for your company.

A simple document created with the Blank Document template — a document that you create by pressing Ctrl+N — has only a few styles, but a document that was created with a sophisticated template comes with many styles. The Oriel Report template, for example, comes with styles for formatting titles, subtitles, headings, and quotations. Figure 3-1 illustrates how choosing styles from a template changes text formatting. Notice how choosing style options in the Styles pane reformats the text.

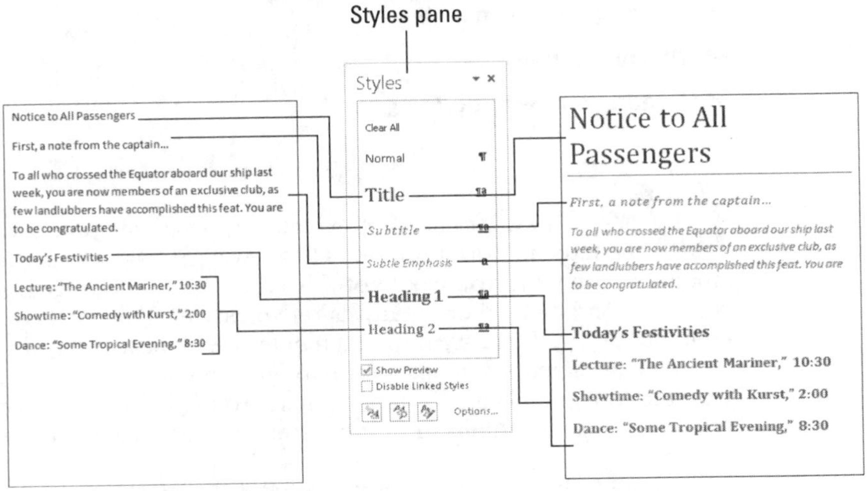

Figure 3-1: Apply styles to reformat text.

Types of styles

In the Styles pane (refer to Figure 3-1), the symbol next to each style name tells you what type of style you're dealing with. Word offers three style types:

- **Paragraph styles:** Determine the formatting of entire paragraphs. A paragraph style can include these settings: font, paragraph, tab, border, language, bullets, numbering and text effects. Paragraph styles are marked with the paragraph symbol (¶).
- **Character styles:** Apply to text, not to paragraphs. You select text before you apply a character style. Create a character style for text that is hard to lay out and for foreign-language text. A character style can include these settings: font, border, language, and text effects. When you apply a character style to text, the character-style settings override the paragraph-style settings. For example, if the paragraph style calls for 14-point Arial font but the character style calls for 12-point Times Roman font, the character style wins. Character styles are marked with the letter *a*.

- **Linked (paragraph and character):** Apply paragraph formats as well as text formats throughout a paragraph. These styles are marked with the paragraph symbol (¶) as well as the letter *a*.

Applying Styles to Text and Paragraphs

Word offers several ways to apply a style, and you are invited to choose the one that works best for you. These pages explain how to apply a style and tell Word how to present style names in the various places where style names are presented for your enjoyment and pleasure.

Applying a style

REMEMBER

The first step in applying a style is to select the part of your document that needs a style change:

- **A paragraph or paragraphs:** Because paragraph styles apply to all the text in a paragraph, you need only click in a paragraph before applying a style to make a style apply throughout the paragraph. To apply a style to several paragraphs, select all or part of them.
- **Text:** To apply a character style, select the letters whose formatting you want to change.

Next, apply the style with one of these techniques:

- **Styles gallery:** On the Home tab, choose a style in the Styles gallery (depending on the size of your screen, you may have to click the Styles button first). Figure 3-2 shows where the Styles gallery is located. The formatted letters above each style name in the gallery show you what your style choice will do to paragraphs or text. You can "live-preview" styles on the Styles gallery by moving the pointer over style names.
- **Styles pane:** On the Home tab, click the Styles group button to open the Styles pane, and select a style, as shown in Figure 3-2. Click the Show Preview check box at the bottom of the Styles pane to see formatted style names in the pane and get an idea of what the different styles are. You can drag the Styles pane to different locations on your screen. It remains on-screen after you leave the Home tab.
- **Apply Styles task pane:** Choose a style on the Apply Styles task pane, as shown in Figure 3-2. To display this task pane, go to the Home tab, open the Styles gallery, and choose Apply Styles (look for this option at the bottom of the gallery). You can drag the Apply Styles task pane to a corner of the screen. As does the Styles pane, the Apply Styles task pane remains on-screen after you leave the Home tab.

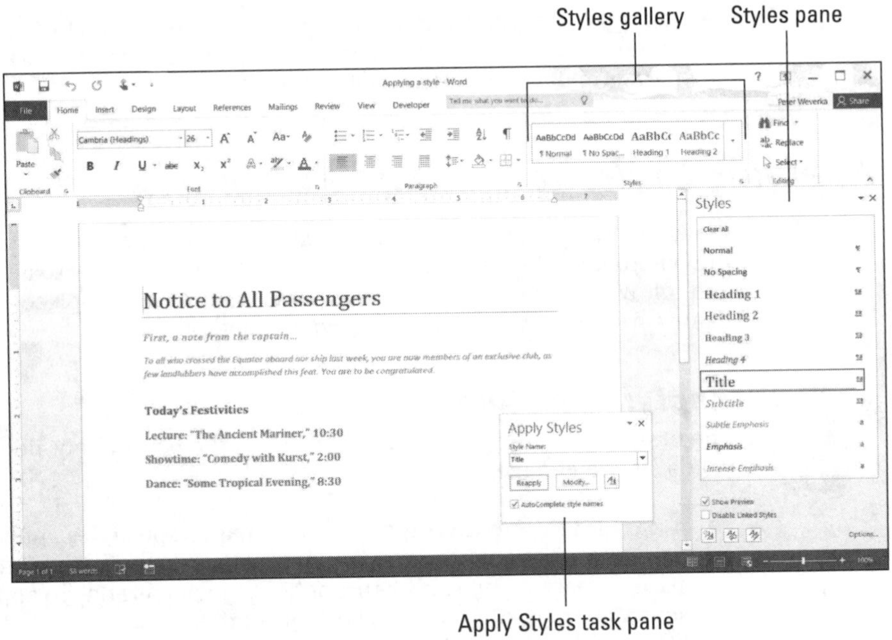

Figure 3-2: The three ways to apply a style.

To strip a paragraph or text of its style and give it the generic Normal style, select it and choose Clear Formatting in the Styles gallery or Clear All at the top of the Styles pane.

Experimenting with style sets

A *style set* is a slight variation on the styles in the template you chose when you created your document. Figure 3-3 shows examples of style sets. Style sets include Classic, Elegant, Fancy, and Modern. Choosing a style set imposes a slightly different look on your document — you make it classier, more elegant, fancier, or more modern. All templates, even those you create yourself, offer style sets. Style sets are a convenient way to experiment with the overall look of a document.

Keyboard shortcuts for applying styles

A handful of keyboard shortcuts can be very handy when applying paragraph styles:

- Normal: Ctrl+Shift+N
- Heading 1: Ctrl+Alt+1
- Heading 2: Ctrl+Alt+2
- Heading 3: Ctrl+Alt+3
- Next higher heading: Alt+Shift+←
- Next lower heading: Alt+Shift+→

You can assign keyboard shortcuts to styles. Book IX, Chapter 1 explains how.

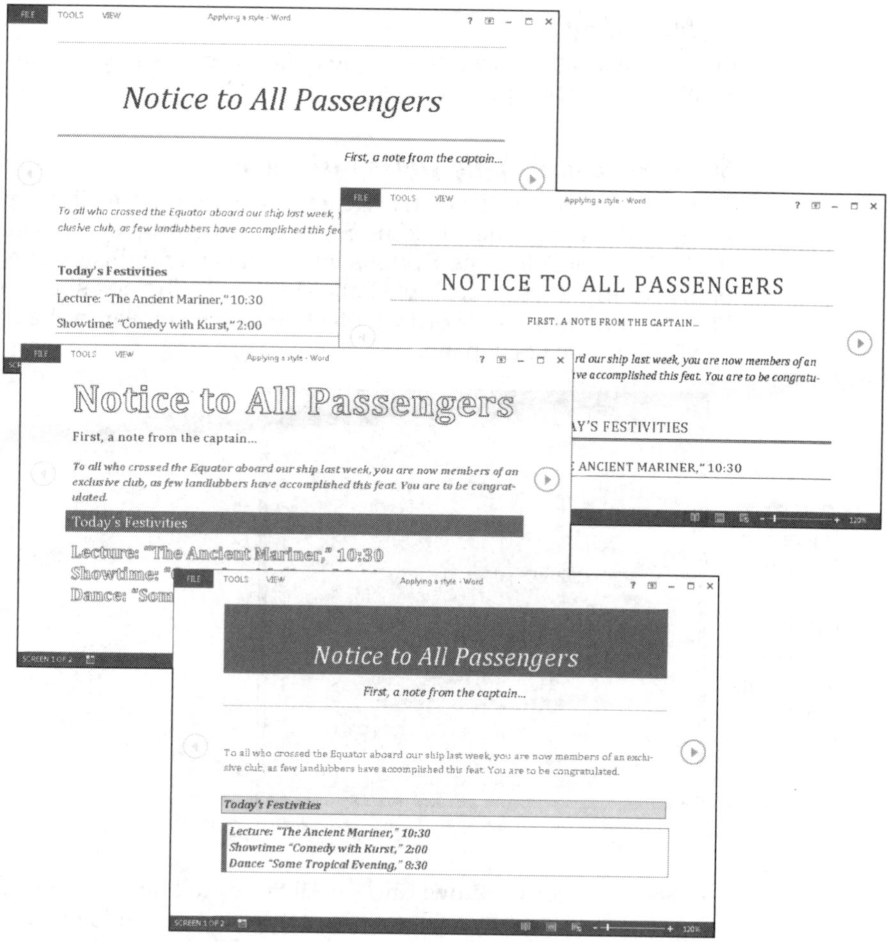

Figure 3-3: Examples of style sets.

To experiment with style sets, go to the Design tab and choose an option in the Style Set gallery.

To return to the original styles in a template, open the Style Set gallery and choose Reset to the Default Style Set.

Choosing which style names appear on the Style menus

One of the challenges of applying styles is finding the right style to apply in the Styles gallery, Styles pane, or Apply Styles task pane (refer to Figure 3-2). All three can become crowded with style names. To make finding and choosing styles names easier, you can decide for yourself which names appear on the three style menus.

Styles gallery

In the Styles gallery, remove a style name by right-clicking it and choosing Remove from Style gallery.

Styles pane and Apply styles task pane

To decide for yourself which style names appear in the Styles pane and Apply Styles task pane, click the Styles group button on the Home tab, and in the Styles pane, click the Options link (you can find this link near the bottom of the pane). You see the Style Pane Options dialog box shown in Figure 3-4. Choose options to tell Word which style names appear in the Styles pane and Apply Styles task pane:

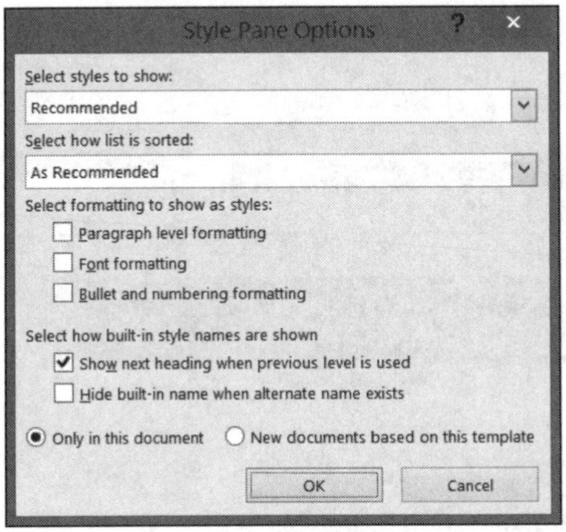

Figure 3-4: Deciding which names to put in the Styles pane and Apply Styles task pane.

- **Select Styles to Show:** Choose All Styles to show all style names. The other options place a subset of names in the window and task pane. Recommended style names are those Microsoft thinks you need most often.
- **Select How List Is Sorted:** Choose an option to describe how to list styles. Except for Based On, these options, I think, are self-explanatory. The Based On option lists styles in alphabetical order according to which style each style is based on (later in this chapter, “Creating a style from the ground up” explains how the based on setting is used in constructing styles).
- **Select Formatting to Show As Styles:** Choose options to declare which styles to list — those that pertain to paragraph level formatting, fonts, and bulleted and numbered lists.
- **Select How Built-In Style Names Are Shown:** Choose options to tell how to handle built-in styles, the obscure styles that Word applies on its own when you create tables of contents and other self-generating lists.

Determining which style is in use

How can you tell which style has been applied to a paragraph or text? Sometimes you need to know which style is in play before you decide whether applying a different style is necessary.

Click the paragraph or text and use these techniques to find out which style was applied to it:

- **Glance at the Styles gallery and Styles pane to see which style is selected.** The selected style is the one that was applied to your paragraph or text.
- **Click the Style Inspector button at the bottom of the Style pane.** The Style Inspector pane opens and lists the current style.
- **Press Shift+F1.** The Reveal Formatting task pane opens. It lists the style that was applied to the paragraph or text.

If you're especially keen to know about styles in your document, you can make style names appear to the left of the text in Outline and Draft view. On the File tab, choose Options. In the Word Options dialog box, go to the Advanced tab and enter .5 or another measurement in the Style Area Pane Width in Draft and Outline Views box (look for this box under "Display"). You can drag the border of the Style Area pane to enlarge or shrink it.

- **Apply to this document or to the template as well:** Click the Only in This Document option button to apply your choices only to the document you're working on; click the New Documents Based on This Template option button to apply your choices to your document and to all future documents you create with the template you're using.

Creating a New Style

You can create a new style by creating it from a paragraph or building it from the ground up. To do a thorough job, build it from the ground up because styles you create this way can be made part of the template you are currently working in and can be copied to other templates (later in this chapter, "Creating and Managing Templates" explains templates).

Creating a style from a paragraph

Follow these steps to create a new style from a paragraph:

1. **Click in a paragraph whose formatting you want to turn into a style.**
2. **On the Home tab, open the Styles gallery and choose Create a Style.**

   You see the Create New Style from Formatting dialog box.

3. **Enter a name for your new style.**
4. **Click OK.**

   A style you create this way becomes a part of the document you're working on; it isn't made part of the template from which you created your document.

Creating a style from the ground up

To make a style available in documents you will create in the future, make it part of a template and build it from the ground up. In the Styles pane, click the New Style button (you can find it at the bottom of the pane). You see the Create New Style from Formatting dialog box shown in Figure 3-5. Fill in the dialog box and click OK.

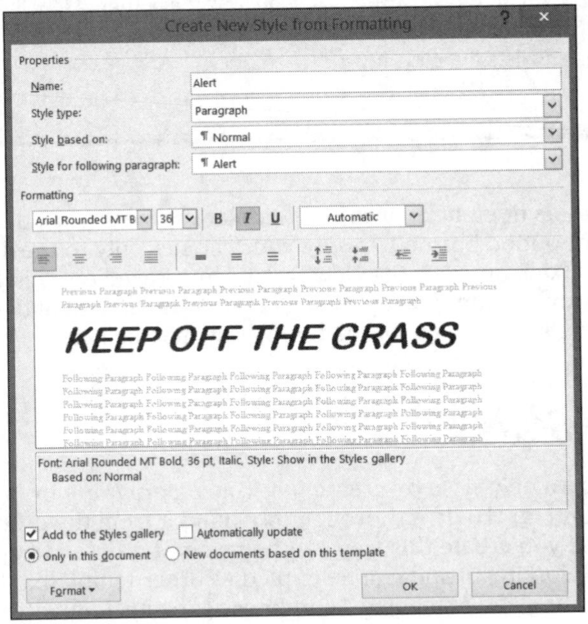

Figure 3-5: Creating a brand-spanking-new style.

Here's a rundown of the options in the Create New Style from Formatting dialog box:

- **Name:** Enter a descriptive name for the style.
- **Style Type:** On the drop-down list, choose a style type ("Types of Styles," earlier in this chapter, describes the style types).

- **Style Based On:** If your new style is similar to a style that is already part of the template with which you created your document, choose the style to get a head start on creating the new one. Be warned, however, that if you or someone else changes the Based On style, your new style will inherit those changes and be altered as well.
- **Style for Following Paragraph:** Choose a style from the drop-down list if the style you're creating is always followed by an existing style. For example, a new style called Chapter Title might always be followed by a style called Chapter Intro Paragraph. For convenience, someone who applies the style you're creating and presses Enter automatically applies the style you choose here on the next line of the document. Applying a style automatically to the following paragraph saves you the trouble of having to apply the style yourself.
- **Formatting:** Choose options from the menus or click buttons to fashion or refine your style (you can also click the Format button to do this).
- **Add to Styles Gallery:** Select this check box to make the style's name appear in the Styles gallery, Styles pane, and Apply Styles task pane.
- **Automatically Update:** Normally, when you make a formatting change to a paragraph, the style assigned to the paragraph does not change at all, but the style does change if you check this box. Checking this box tells Word to alter the style itself each time you alter a paragraph to which you've assigned the style. With this box checked, all paragraphs in the document that were assigned the style are altered each time you change a single paragraph that was assigned the style.
- **Only in This Document/New Documents Based on This Template:** To make your style a part of the template from which you created your document as well as the document itself, click the New Documents Based on This Template option button. This way, new documents you create that are based on the template you are using can also make use of the new style.
- **Format:** This is the important one. Click the button and make a formatting choice. Word takes you to dialog boxes so that you can create or refine the style.

Modifying a Style

What if you decide at the end of an 80-page document that all 35 introductory paragraphs to which you assigned the Intro Para style look funny? If you clicked the Automatically Update check box in the Create New Style from Formatting dialog box when you created the style, all you have to do is alter a paragraph to which you assigned the Intro Para style to alter all 35 introductory paragraphs. However, if you decided against updating styles automatically, you can still change the introductory paragraphs throughout your document.

Follow these steps to modify a style that isn't updated automatically:

1. **Click in any paragraph, table, or list to which you've assigned the style; if you want to modify a character style, select the characters to which you've assigned the style.**
2. **In the Styles pane or Apply Styles task pane, make sure the name of the style you want to modify is selected.**

   If the right name isn't selected, select it now in the Styles pane or Apply Styles task pane.
3. **In the Styles pane, open the style's drop-down list and choose Modify, as shown in Figure 3-6; in the Apply Styles task pane, click the Modify button.**

   You see the Modify Style dialog box. Does the dialog box look familiar? It is identical to the Create New Style from Formatting dialog box you used to create the style in the first place (refer to Figure 3-5).
4. **Change the settings in the Modify Styles dialog box and click OK.**

   The previous section in this chapter explains the settings.

Figure 3-6: Choosing to modify a style.

After you modify a style, all paragraphs or text to which the style was assigned are instantly changed. You don't have to go back and reformat text and paragraphs throughout your document.

Creating and Managing Templates

As I explain at the start of this chapter, every document you create is fashioned from a *template*. The purpose of a template is to store styles for documents. In the act of creating a document, you choose a template, and the styles on the template become available to you when you work on your document (Chapter 1 of this mini-book explains how to choose a template when you create a new document).

For example, when you select Blank Template in the New window or press Ctrl+N, you create a document with the Blank Document template, a relatively simple template with few styles. When you create a document with a template from Office.com or a template from the New window, more styles are available to you because these templates are more sophisticated.

To save time formatting your documents, you are invited to create templates with styles that you know and love. You can create a new template on your own or create a template by assembling styles from other templates and documents. Styles in templates, like styles in documents, can be modified, deleted, and renamed.

To create a document from a template you created yourself, open the New window (on the File tab, choose New), click the Personal tab, and select your template (see Chapter 1 of this mini-book for details).

To find out which template was used to create a document, go to the File tab and choose Info. Then click the Show All Properties link in the Info window. You see a list of document properties, including the name of the template used to create the document.

Creating a new template

How do you want to create a new template? You can do it on your own or assemble styles from other templates. Read on.

Creating a template on your own

One way to create a template is to start by opening a document with many or all the styles you know and love. When you save this document as a template, you pass along the styles in the document to the template, and you save yourself the trouble of creating styles for the template after you create it.

Follow these steps to create a template on your own:

1. **Create a new document or open a document with styles that you can recycle.**
2. **On the File tab, choose Save As.**

   The Save As window opens.
3. **Click This PC.**
4. **Click the Browse button.**

   The Save As dialog box appears.
5. **Open the Save As Type menu and choose Word Template.**

   The Save As dialog box opens to the folder where templates are stored on your computer.
6. **Enter a name for your template.**
7. **Click the Save button.**

Create, modify, and delete styles as necessary (see "Creating a New Style" and "Modifying a Style" earlier in this chapter).

Telling Word where templates are stored

The first time you create a template, Word stores it in this folder:

- `C:\Users\`*Username*`\Documents\Custom Office Templates`

However, in previous versions of Word, templates were stored in one of these folders:

- `C:\Users\Owner\Documents\Custom Office Templates`
- `C:\Users\`*Username*`\AppData\Roaming\Microsoft\Templates`

To keep all you templates in one place, either move them to the `C:\Users\`*Username*`\Documents\Custom Office Templates` folder or tell Word where you prefer to store templates.

Follow these steps to tell Word where you keep templates on your computer:

1. **On the File tab, choose Options.**

   The Word Options dialog box opens.
2. **Go to the Save category.**
3. **In the Default Personal Templates Location text box, enter the path to the folder where you prefer to store templates.**
4. **Click OK.**

If you're having trouble finding the Templates folder, go to the File tab and choose Options. In the Word Options dialog box, go to the Advanced Category and scroll to the File Locations button. Clicking this button opens the File Locations dialog box, where, under User Templates, you can see the name of the folder in which your templates are stored.

Assembling styles from different documents and templates

Suppose that you like a style in one document and you want to copy it to another so that you can use it there. Or you want to copy it to a template to make it available to documents created with the template. Read on to find out how to copy styles between documents and between templates.

Copying a style from one document to another

Copy a style from one document to another when you need the style on a one-time basis. Follow these steps:

1. **Select a paragraph that was assigned the style you want to copy.**

   Be sure to select the entire paragraph. If you want to copy a character style, select text to which you have assigned the character style.

2. **Press Ctrl+C or right-click and choose Copy to copy the paragraph to the Clipboard.**
3. **Switch to the document you want to copy the style to and press Ctrl+V or click the Paste button on the Home tab.**
4. **Delete the text you just copied to your document.**

   The style remains in the Styles pane and Styles gallery even though the text is deleted. You can call upon the style whenever you need it.

Copying styles to a template

Use the Organizer to copy styles from a document to a template or from one template to another. After making a style a part of a template, you can call upon the style in other documents. You can call upon it in each document you create or created with the template. Follow these steps to copy a style into a template:

1. **Open the document or template with the styles you want to copy.**

   Later in this chapter, "Opening a template so that you can modify it" explains how to open a template.

2. **In the Styles pane, click the Manage Styles button.**

   This button is located at the bottom of the window. The Manage Styles dialog box appears.

3. **Click the Import/Export button.**

   You see the Organizer dialog box shown in Figure 3-7. Styles in the document or template that you opened in Step 1 appear in the In list box on the left side.

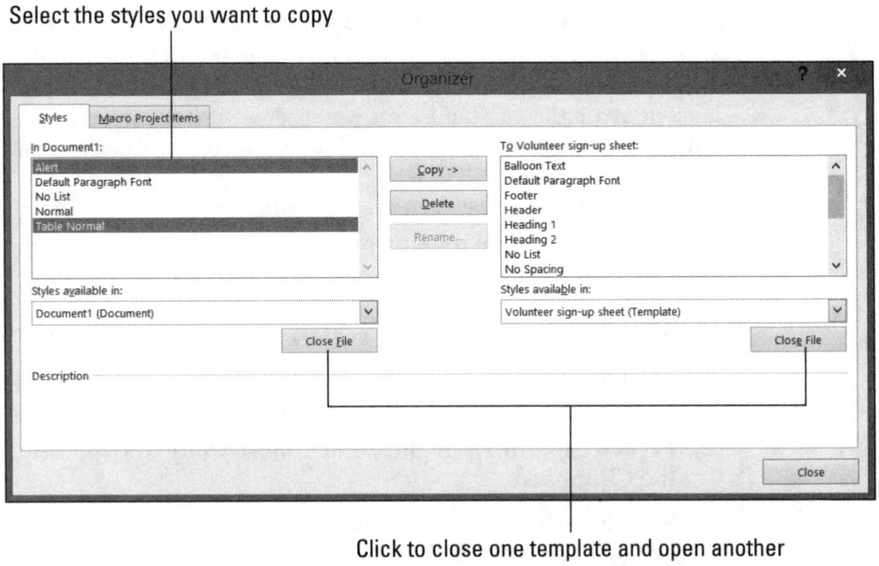

Figure 3-7: Copying styles to a template.

4. **Click the Close File button on the right side of the dialog box.**

   The button changes names and becomes the Open File button.

5. **Click the Open File button and, in the Open dialog box, find and select the template to which you want to copy styles; then, click the Open button.**

   See the sidebar "Telling Word where templates are stored," earlier in this chapter, if you have trouble finding the Templates folder.

   The names of styles in the template you chose appear on the right side of the Organizer dialog box.

6. **In the Organizer dialog box, Ctrl+click to select the names of styles on the left side of the dialog box that you want to copy to the template listed on the right side of the dialog box.**

   As you click the names, they become highlighted.

7. **Click the Copy button.**

   The names of styles that you copied appear on the right side of the Organizer dialog box.

8. **Click the Close button and click Save when Word asks whether you want to save the new styles in the template.**

Attaching a different template to a document

It happens in the best of families. You create or are given a document only to discover that the wrong template is attached to it. For times like those, Word gives you the opportunity to switch templates. Follow these steps:

1. **On the Developer tab, click the Document Template button.**

   You see the Templates and Add-Ins dialog box. If the Developer tab isn't displayed on your screen, go to the File tab, choose Options, visit the Customize Ribbon category in the Word Options dialog box, select the Developer check box, and click OK.

2. **Click the Attach button to open the Attach Template dialog box.**

3. **Find and select the template you want and click the Open button.**

   You return to the Templates and Add-ins dialog box, where the name of the template you chose appears in the Document Template box.

4. **Click the Automatically Update Document Styles check box.**

   Doing so tells Word to apply the styles from the new template to your document.

5. **Click OK.**

Opening a template so that you can modify it

Follow these steps to open a template in Word and be able to modify it:

1. **On the File tab, choose Open.**

   You see the Open window.

2. **Click This PC.**
3. **Click the Browse button.**
4. **In the Open dialog box, go to the Templates folder where you store templates.**

   See the sidebar "Telling Word where templates are stored," earlier in this chapter, if you have trouble finding the Templates folder.

5. **Select the template.**
6. **Click the Open button.**

The template opens in the Word window. Style modifications you make in the template become available to all documents that were fashioned from the template.

Modifying, deleting, and renaming styles in templates

Modify, delete, and rename styles in a template the same way you do those tasks to styles in a document (see "Modifying a Style" earlier in this chapter). However, in the Modify Style dialog box, select the New Documents Based on This Template option button before clicking OK.

Your style modifications will apply to all documents you create in the future with your template. For the style modifications to take effect in documents you already created with your template, tell Word to automatically update document styles in those documents. Follow these steps:

1. **Save and close your template if it is still open.**

   If any documents you fashioned from the template are open, close them as well.

2. **Open a document that you want to update with the style modifications you made to the template.**
3. **Go to the Developer tab.**

   To display this tab if necessary, open the File tab, choose Options, go to the Customize Ribbon category in the Word Options dialog box, select the Developer check box, and click OK.

4. **Click the Document Template button.**

   The Templates and Add-ins dialog box opens. It should list the path to the Templates folder and the template you modified. If the wrong template is listed, click the Attach button and select the correct template in the Attach Template dialog box.

5. **Select the Automatically Update Document Styles check box.**
6. **Click OK.**

Chapter 4: Constructing the Perfect Table

In This Chapter

- Understanding table jargon
- Creating a table and entering the text and numbers
- Changing the size of rows and columns
- Aligning table text in various ways
- Merging and splitting cells to make interesting layouts
- Decorating a table with table styles, colors, and borders
- Doing math calculations in a Word table
- Discovering an assortment of table tricks

The best way to present a bunch of data at one time in Word is to do it in a table. Viewers can compare and contrast the data. They can compare Elvis sightings in different cities or income from different businesses. They can contrast the number of socks lost in different washing machine brands. A table is a great way to plead your case or defend your position. Readers can see right away whether the numbers back you up. They can refer to your table to get the information they need.

As everyone who has worked on tables knows, however, tables are a chore. Getting all the columns to fit, making columns and rows the right width and height, and editing the text in a table isn't easy. This chapter explains how to create tables, enter text in tables, change the number and size of columns and rows, lay out tables, format tables, and do the math in tables. You'll also discover a few tricks — including using a picture for the background — that only magicians know. And to start you on the right foot, I begin by explaining table jargon.

Talking Table Jargon

As with much else in Computerland, tables have their own jargon. Figure 4-1 describes this jargon. Sorry, but you need to catch up on these terms to construct the perfect table:

- **Cell:** The box that is formed where a row and column intersect. Each cell holds one data item.
- **Header row:** The name of the labels along the top row that explain what is in the columns below.
- **Row labels:** The labels in the first column that describe what is in each row.
- **Borders:** The lines in the table that define where the rows and columns are.
- **Gridlines:** The gray lines that show where the columns and rows are. Unless you've drawn borders around all the cells in a table, you can't tell where rows and columns begin and end without gridlines. To display or hide the gridlines, go to the (Table Tools) Layout tab and click the View Gridlines button.

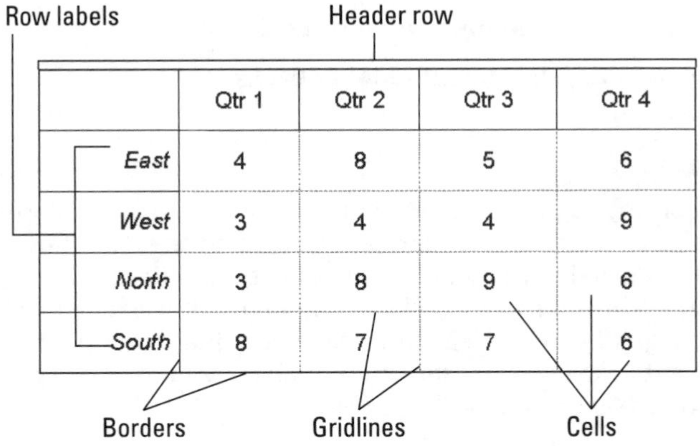

Figure 4-1: The parts of a table.

Creating a Table

Word offers several ways to create a table:

- **Drag on the Table menu.** On the Insert tab, click the Table button, point in the drop-down list to the number of columns and rows you want, click, and let go of the mouse button, as shown in Figure 4-2.
- **Use the Insert Table dialog box.** On the Insert tab, click the Table button and choose Insert Table on the drop-down list. The Insert Table dialog box appears (see Figure 4-2). Enter the number of columns and rows you want and click OK.

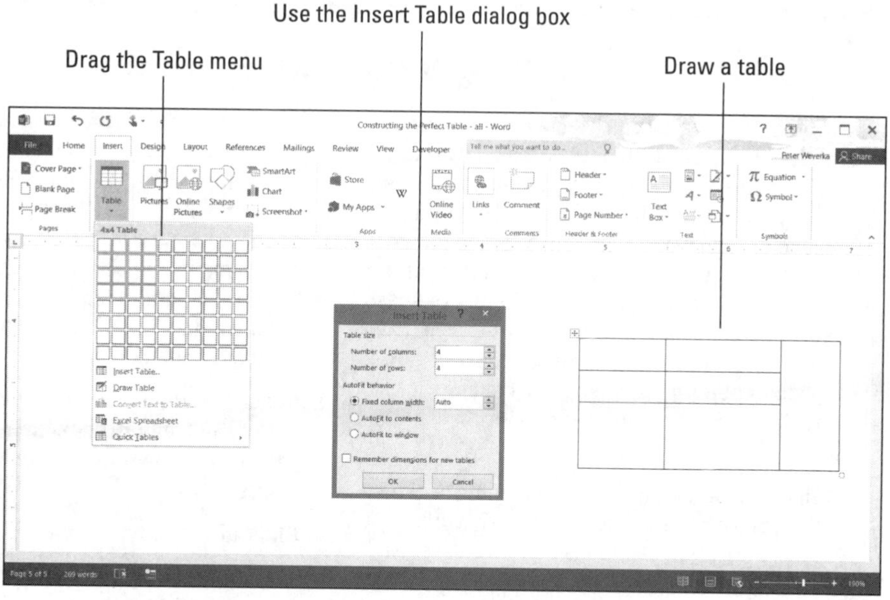

Figure 4-2: Some techniques for creating a table.

- **Draw a table.** On the Insert tab, click the Table button and then choose Draw Table on the drop-down list. The pointer changes into a pencil. Use the pencil to draw table borders, rows, and columns. If you make a mistake, click the Eraser button on the (Table Tools) Layout tab and drag it over the parts of the table you regret drawing (you may have to click the Draw Borders button first). When you finish drawing the table, press Esc.
- **Create a quick table.** On the Insert tab, click the Table button and choose Quick Tables on the drop-down list. Then select a ready-made table on the submenu. You have to replace the sample data in the quick table with your own data.
- **Construct a table from an Excel worksheet.** On the Insert tab, click the Table button, and choose Excel Spreadsheet. An Excel worksheet appears and — *gadzooks!* — you see Excel tabs and commands where Word tabs and commands used to be. The worksheet you just created is embedded in your file. Whenever you click the worksheet, Excel menus and commands instead of Word menus and commands appear on-screen. Click outside the worksheet to return to Word.

REMEMBER

After you create a table, you get two new tabs on the Ribbon. The (Table Tools) Design tab offers commands for changing the look of the table; the (Table Tools) Layout tab is for changing around the rows and columns.

To delete a table, go to the (Table Tools) Layout tab, click the Delete button, and choose Delete Table on the drop-down list.

Turning a list into a table

In order to turn a list into a table, all components of the list — each name, address, city name, state, and zip code listing, for example — must be separated from the next component by a tab space or a comma. Word looks for tab spaces or commas when it turns a list into a table, and the program separates data into columns according to where the tab spaces or commas are located. You have to prepare your list carefully by entering tab spaces or commas in all the right places before you can turn a list into a table.

Follow these steps to turn a list into a table after you've done all the preliminary work:

1. **Select the list.**
2. **On the Insert tab, click the Table button and choose Convert Text To Table on the drop-down list.**

   You see the Convert Text to Table dialog box. Note the number in the Number of Columns box. It should list the number of components into which you separated your list. If the number doesn't match the number of components, you misplaced a tab entry or comma in your list. Click Cancel, return to your list, and examine it to make sure each line has been divided into the same number of components.
3. **Under Separate Text At, choose the Tabs or Commas option, depending on which you used to separate the components on the list.**
4. **Click OK.**

You can turn a table into a list by clicking the Convert to Text button on the (Table Tools) Layout tab (you may have to click the Data button first, depending on the size of your screen).

Entering the Text and Numbers

After you've created the table, you can start entering text and numbers. All you have to do is click in a cell and start typing. Select your table and take advantage of these techniques to make the onerous task of entering table data a little easier:

- **Quickly changing a table's size**: Drag the bottom or side of a table to change its overall size. To make the table stretch from page margin to page margin, go to the (Table Tools) Layout tab, click the AutoFit button, and choose AutoFit Window.
- **Moving a table**: Switch to Print Layout view and drag the table selector (the square in the upper-left corner of the table).
- **Choosing your preferred font and font size**: Entering table data is easier when you're working in a font and font size you like. Select the table, visit the Home tab, and choose a font and font size there. To select a table, go to the (Table Tools) Layout tab, click the Select button, and choose Select Table on the drop-down list.

✦ **Quickly inserting a new row:** Click in the last column of the last row in your table and press the Tab key to quickly insert a new row at the bottom of the table.

TIP

Here are some shortcuts for moving the cursor in a table:

Press	*Moves the Cursor to*
Tab	Next column in row
Shift+Tab	Previous column in row
↓	Row below
↑	Row above
Alt+Home	Start of row
Alt+End	End of row
Alt+Page Up	Top of column
Alt+Page Down	Bottom of column

Selecting Different Parts of a Table

It almost goes without saying, but before you can reformat, alter, or diddle with table cells, rows, or columns, you have to select them:

✦ **Selecting cells:** To select a cell, click in it. You can select several adjacent cells by dragging the pointer over them.

✦ **Selecting rows:** Move the pointer to the left of the row and click when you see the right-pointing arrow; click and drag to select several rows. You can also go to the (Table Tools) Layout tab, click inside the row you want to select, click the Select button, and choose Select Row on the drop-down list. To select more than one row at a time, select cells in the rows before choosing the Select Row command.

✦ **Selecting columns:** Move the pointer above the column and click when you see the down-pointing arrow; click and drag to select several columns. You can also start from the (Table Tools) Layout tab, click in the column you want to select, click the Select button, and choose Select Column in the drop-down list. To select several columns, select cells in the columns before choosing the Select Column command.

✦ **Selecting a table:** On the (Table Tools) Layout tab, click the Select button, and choose Select Table on the drop-down list (or press Alt+5 on the numeric keypad).

Laying Out Your Table

Very likely, you created too many or too few columns or rows for your table. Some columns are probably too wide and others too narrow. If that's the case, you have to change the table layout by deleting, inserting, and changing the size of columns and rows, not to mention changing the size of the table itself. In other words, you have to modify the table layout. (Later in this chapter, "Decorating your table with borders and colors" shows how to put borders around tables and embellish them in other ways.)

Changing the size of a table, columns, and rows

The fastest way to adjust the width of columns, the height of rows, and the size of a table itself is to "eyeball it" and drag the mouse:

✦ **Column or row:** Move the pointer onto a gridline or border, and when the pointer changes into a double-headed arrow, start dragging. Tug and pull, tug and pull until the column or row is the right size.

  You can also go to the (Table Tools) Layout tab and enter measurements in the Height and Width text boxes to change the width of a column or the height of a row. The measurements affect entire columns or rows, not individual cells.

✦ **A table:** Select your table and use one of these techniques to change its size:

  • *Dragging:* Drag the top, bottom, or side of the table. You can also drag the lower-right corner to change the size vertically and horizontally.

  • *Height and Width text boxes:* On the (Table Tools) Layout tab, enter measurements in the Height and Width text boxes.

  • *Table Properties dialog box:* On the (Table Tools) Layout tab, click the Cell Size group button, and on the Table tab of the Table Properties dialog box, enter a measurement in the Preferred Width text box.

Adjusting column and row size

Resizing columns and rows can be problematic in Word. For that reason, Word offers special commands on the (Table Tools) Layout tab for adjusting the width and height of rows and columns:

✦ **Making all columns the same width:** Click the Distribute Columns button to make all columns the same width. Select columns before giving this command to make only the columns you select the same width.

✦ **Making all rows the same height:** Click the Distribute Rows button to make all rows in the table the same height. Select rows before clicking the button to make only the rows you select the same height.

You can also click the AutoFit button on the (Table Tools) Layout tab, and take advantage of these commands on the drop-down list for handling columns and rows:

- **AutoFit Contents:** Make each column wide enough to accommodate its widest entry.
- **AutoFit Window:** Stretch the table so that it fits across the page between the left and right margin.
- **Fixed Column Width:** Fix the column widths at their current settings.

Inserting columns and rows

The trick to inserting (and deleting) columns and rows is to correctly select part of the table first. You can insert more than one column or row at a time by selecting more than one column or row before giving the Insert command. To insert two columns, for example, select two columns and choose an Insert command; to insert three rows, select three rows and choose an Insert command. Earlier in this chapter, "Selecting Different Parts of a Table" explains how to make table selections.

Word offers many, many ways to insert columns and rows. Too many ways, if you ask me.

On the (Table Tools) Layout tab

Go to the (Table Tools) Layout tab and follow these instructions to insert and delete columns and rows:

- **Inserting columns:** Select a column or columns and click the Insert Left or Insert Right button.
- **Inserting rows:** Select a row or rows and click the Insert Above or Insert Below button.

To insert a row at the end of a table, move the pointer into the last cell in the last row and press the Tab key.

Right-clicking

Follow these steps to insert columns or rows by right-clicking:

1. **Select column or rows.**
2. **Right-click to display the mini-toolbar.**

   Figure 4-3 shows the mini-toolbar you see when you right-click a table.
3. **Click the Insert button on the mini-toolbar.**
4. **Click an Insert button (Above, Below, Left, or Right).**

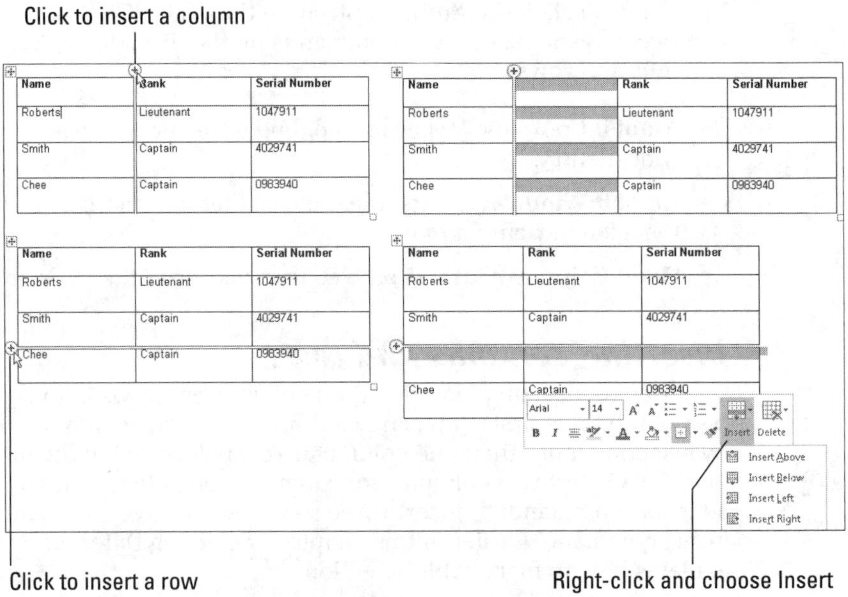

Figure 4-3: The one-click and right-click techniques for inserting columns and rows.

One-Click Row and One-Click Column buttons

To insert one row or one column, click a One-Click button, as shown in Figure 4-3. The One-Click Column button appears when you move the pointer between columns at the top of a table; the One-Click Row button appears when you move the pointer between rows on the left side of a table. Click a One-Click button to insert one column or one row.

Deleting columns and rows

Go to the (Table Tools) Layout tab and use these techniques to delete columns and rows:

- **Deleting columns:** Click in the column you want to delete, click the Delete button, and choose Delete Columns on the drop-down list. Select more than one column to delete more than one. (You can also right-click and choose Delete Columns.)
- **Deleting rows:** Click in the row you want to delete, click the Delete button, and choose Delete Rows. Select more than one row to delete more than one. (You can also right-click and choose Delete Rows.)

REMEMBER

Pressing the Delete key after you select a column or row deletes the data in the column or row, not the column or row itself.

Moving columns and rows

Because there is no elegant way to move a column or row, you should move only one at a time. If you try to move several simultaneously, you open a can of worms that is best left unopened. To move a column or row:

1. **Select the column or row you want to move.**

   Earlier in this chapter, "Selecting Different Parts of a Table" explains how to select columns and rows.

Sorting, or reordering a table

On the subject of moving columns and rows, the fastest way to rearrange the rows in a table is to sort the table. *Sorting* means to rearrange all the rows in a table on the basis of data in one or more columns. For example, a table that shows candidates and the number of votes they received could be sorted in alphabetical order by the candidates' names or in numerical order by the number of votes they received. Both tables present the same information, but the information is sorted in different ways.

The difference between ascending and descending sorts is as follows:

- Ascending arranges text from A to Z, numbers from smallest to largest, and dates from earliest to latest.
- Descending arranges text from Z to A, numbers from largest to smallest, and dates from latest to earliest.

When you rearrange a table by sorting it, Word rearranges the formatting as well as the data. Do your sorting before you format the table.

Follow these steps to sort a table:

1. **On the (Table Tools) Layout tab, click the Sort button.**

   You see the Sort dialog box. Depending on the size of your screen, you may have to click the Data button before you see the Sort button.
2. **In the first Sort By drop-down list, choose the column you want to sort with.**
3. **If necessary, open the first Type drop-down list and choose Text, Number, or Date to describe what kind of data you're dealing with.**
4. **Select the Ascending or Descending option button to declare whether you want an ascending or descending sort.**
5. **If necessary, on the first Then By drop-down list, choose the tiebreaker column.**

   If two items in the Sort By columns are alike, Word looks to your Then By column choice to break the tie and place one row before another in the table.
6. **Click OK.**

When you sort a table, Word ignores the *header row* — the first row in the table — and doesn't move it. However, if you want to include the header row in the sort, click the No Header Row option button in the Sort dialog box.

2. **Right-click in the selection and choose Cut on the shortcut menu.**

   The column or row is moved to the Clipboard.

3. **Insert a new column or row where you want the column or row to be.**

   Earlier in this chapter, "Inserting columns and rows" explains how.

4. **Move the column or row:**
   - **Column:** Click in the topmost cell in your new column and then click the Paste button (on the Home tab) or press Ctrl+V.
   - **Row:** Click in the first column of the row you inserted and then click the Paste button (on the Home tab) or press Ctrl+V.

Aligning Text in Columns and Rows

Aligning text in columns and rows is a matter of choosing how you want the text to line up vertically and how you want it to line up horizontally. Follow these steps to align text in a table:

1. **Select the cells, columns, or rows, with text that you want to align (or select your entire table).**
2. **Go to the (Table Tools) Layout tab.**
3. **Click an Align button (you may have to click the Alignment button first, depending on the size of your screen).**

Figure 4-4 shows where the Align buttons are on the (Table Tools) Layout tab and how these options align text in a table.

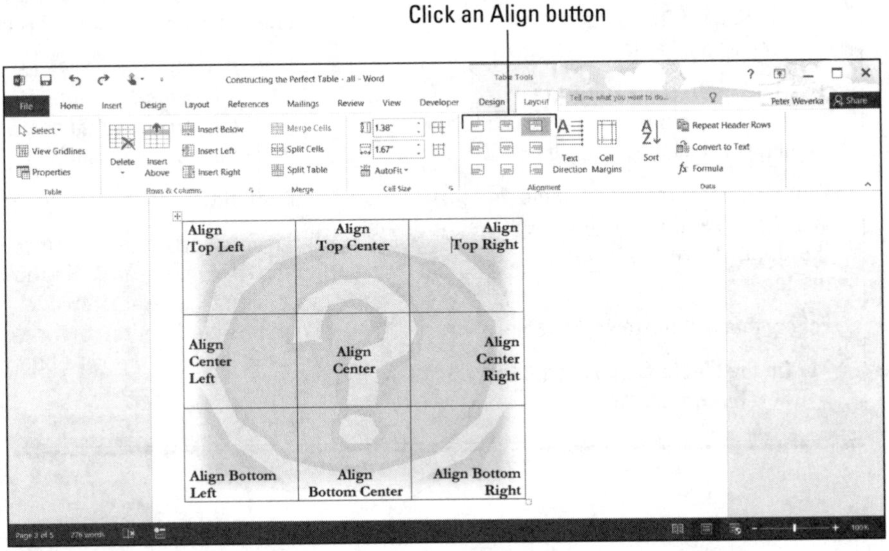

Figure 4-4: Word offers nine ways to align text.

Merging and Splitting Cells

Merge and split cells to make your tables a little more elegant than run-of-the-mill tables. *Merge* cells to break down the barriers between cells and join them into one cell; *split* cells to divide a single cell into several cells (or several cells into several more cells). In the table shown in Figure 4-5, cells in rows and columns have been split or merged to create a curious-looking little table.

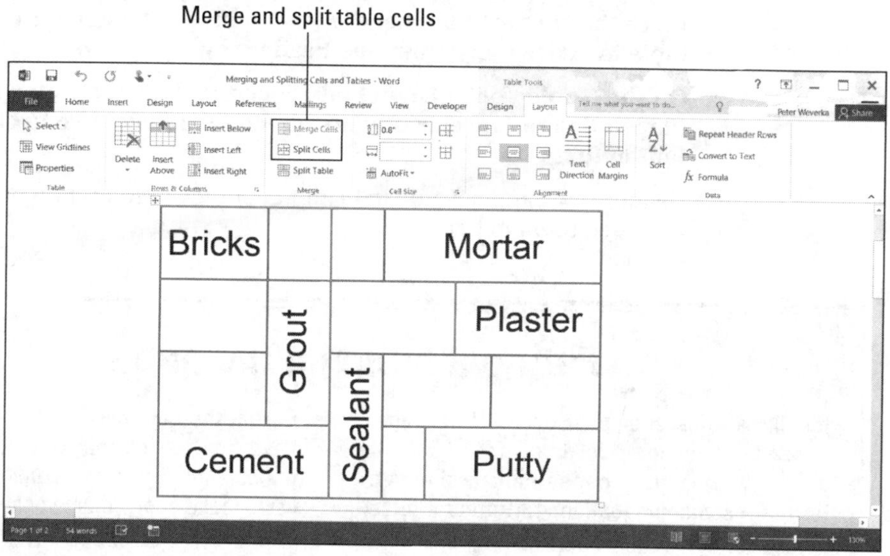

Figure 4-5: Merge and split cells to create unusual tables.

Select the cells you want to merge or split, go to the (Table Tools) Layout tab, and follow these instructions to merge or split cells:

- ✦ **Merging cells:** Click the Merge Cells button (you can also right-click and choose Merge Cells).
- ✦ **Splitting cells:** Click the Split Cells button (you can also right-click and choose Split Cells). In the Split Cells dialog box, declare how many columns and rows you want to split the cell into and then click OK.

Another way to merge and split cells is to click the Draw Table or Eraser button on the (Table Tools) Layout tab. Click the Draw Table button and then draw lines through cells to split them. Click the Eraser button and drag over or click the boundary between cells to merge cells. Press Esc when you finish drawing or erasing table cell boundaries.

Need to split a table? Place the cursor in what you want to be the first row of the new table, go to the (Table Tools) Layout tab, and click the Split Table button.

Repeating Header Rows on Subsequent Pages

TIP

Making sure that the *header row,* sometimes called the *heading row,* appears on a new page if the table breaks across pages is essential. The header row is the first row in the table, the one that usually describes what is in the columns below. Without a header row, readers can't tell what the information in a table means. Follow these steps to make the header row (or rows) repeat on the top of each new page that a table appears on:

1. **Place the cursor in the header row or select the header rows if your table includes more than one header row.**
2. **On the (Table Tools) Layout tab, click the Repeat Header Rows button (depending on the size of your screen, you may have to click the Data button first).**

   Header rows appear only in Print Layout view, so don't worry if you can't see them in Draft view.

Fitting a table on the page

Ideally, a table should fit on a single page, because studying table data that is spread across two or more pages can be difficult. Here are some suggestions for fitting a table on a single page:

- **Present the table in landscape mode:** In Landscape mode, a page is turned on its ear so that it is wider than it is tall and you have room for more table columns. To print in Landscape mode, however, you must create a new section for the pages in question. To change the page orientation, go to the Layout tab, click the Orientation button, and choose Landscape.
- **Shrink the font size:** Sometimes shrinking the font size throughout a table shrinks the table just enough to fit it on a page. To shrink fonts throughout a table, go to the Home tab and click the Decrease Font Size button (or press Ctrl+[). Keep decreasing the font size until the table fits on one page.
- **Shrink the columns:** On the (Table Tools) Layout tab, click the AutoFit button, and choose AutoFit Contents on the drop-down list to make each column only wide enough to accommodate its widest entry.
- **Change the orientation of header row text:** In a top-heavy table in which the header row cells contain text and the cells below contain numbers, you can make the entire table narrower by changing the orientation of the text in the header row. To turn text on its ear, select the cells whose text needs a turn, go to the (Table Tools) Layout tab, and click the Text Direction button. Keep clicking until the text turns the direction you want.

Chances are, if your table can't fit on one page, presenting the information in a table isn't the best option. Try presenting it in bulleted or numbered lists. Or present the information in short paragraphs under small fourth- or fifth-level headings.

Formatting Your Table

After you enter text in the table, lay out the columns and rows, and make them the right size, the fun begins. Now you can dress up your table and make it look snazzy. You can choose colors for columns and rows. You can play with the borders that divide the columns and rows and shade columns, rows, and cells by filling them with gray shades or a black background. Read on to find out how to do these tricks.

Designing a table with a table style

TIP

The fastest way to get a good-looking table is to select a table style in the Table Styles gallery, as shown in Figure 4-6. A *table style* is a ready-made assortment of colors and border choices. You can save yourself a lot of formatting trouble by selecting a table style. After you select a table style, you can modify it by selecting or deselecting check boxes in the Table Style Options group on the (Table Tools) Design tab.

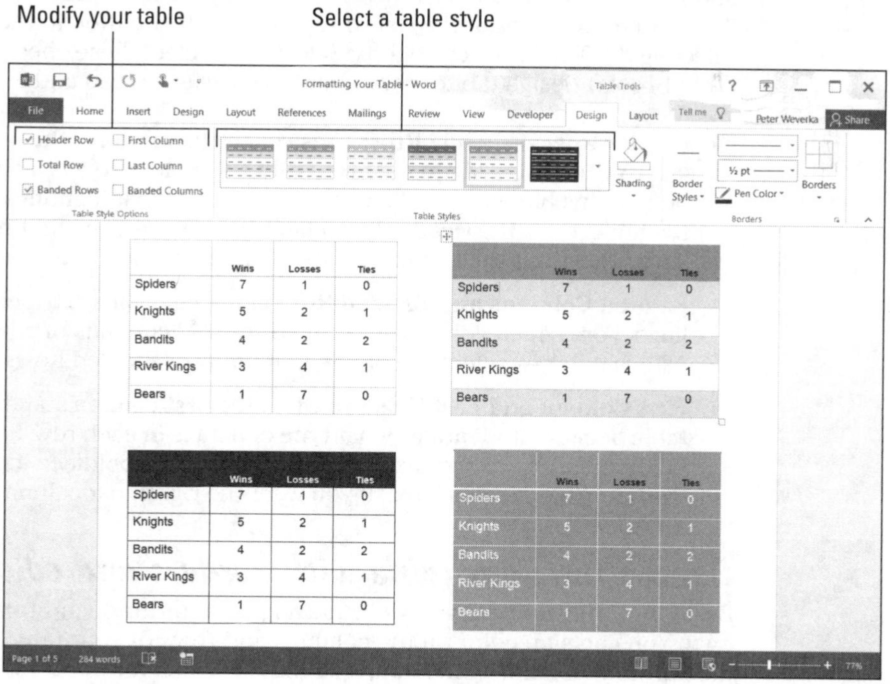

Figure 4-6: You have many opportunities for designing tables.

Click anywhere in your table and follow these steps to choose a table style:

1. **Go to the (Table Tools) Design tab.**
2. **Open the Table Styles gallery and move the pointer over table style choices to live-preview the table.**
3. **Select a table style.**

   To remove a table style, open the Table Styles gallery and choose Clear.

TIP

For consistency's sake, choose a similar table style — or better yet the same table style — for all the tables in your document. This way, your work doesn't become a showcase for table styles.

Calling attention to different rows and columns

On the (Table Tools) Design tab, Word offers Table Style Options check boxes for calling attention to different rows or columns (refer to Figure 4-6). For example, you can make the first row in the table, called the header row, stand out by selecting the Header Row check box. If your table presents numerical data with total figures in the last row, you can call attention to the last row by selecting the Total Row check box. Select or deselect these check boxes on the (Table Tools) Design tab to make your table easier to read and understand:

- **Header Row and Total Row:** These check boxes make the first row and last row in a table stand out. Typically, the header row is a different color or contains boldface text because it is the row that identifies the data in the table. Click the Header Row check box to make the first row stand out; if you also want the last row to stand out, click the Total Row check box.
- **Banded Columns and Banded Rows:** *Banded* means "striped" in Office lingo. For striped columns or striped rows — columns or rows that alternate in color — select the Banded Columns or Banded Rows check box.
- **First Column and Last Column:** Often the first column stands out in a table because it identifies what type of data is in each row. Select the First Column check box to make it a different color or boldface its text. Check the Last Column check box if you want the rightmost column to stand out.

Decorating your table with borders and colors

Besides relying on a table style, you can play interior decorator on your own. You can slap color on the columns and rows of your table, draw borders around columns and rows, and choose a look for borders. Figure 4-7 shows the drop-down lists on the (Table Tools) Design tab that pertain to table decoration. Use these drop-down lists to shade table columns and rows and draw table borders.

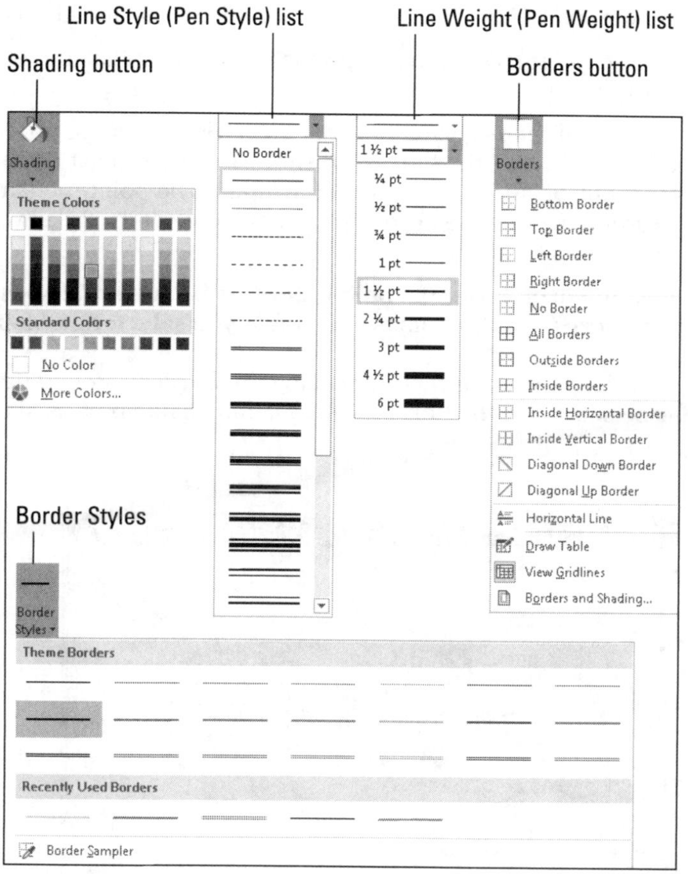

Figure 4-7: Tools on the (Table Tools) Design tab for decorating tables.

Designing borders for your table

Follow these steps to fashion a border for your table or a part of your table:

1. **Go to the (Table Tools) Design tab.**
2. **Select the part of your table that needs a new border.**

   To select the entire table, go to the (Table Tools) Layout tab, click the Select button, and choose Select Table.
3. **Create a look for the table borders you will apply or draw.**

   As shown in Figure 4-7, use all or some of these techniques to devise a border:

   - **Border style:** Open the drop-down list on the Border Styles button and choose the border style that most resembles the one you want.

- **Line style:** Open the Line Style drop-down list and choose a style.
- **Line weight:** Open the Line Weight drop-down list and choose a line thickness.

TIP

If a table on the page you're looking at already has the border you like, you can "sample" the border. Open the drop-down list on the Border Styles button and choose Border Sampler. The pointer changes to an eyedropper. Click the border you want to select its style, weight, and color settings.

4. **Open the drop-down list on the Borders button and choose where to place borders on the part of the table you selected in Step 2.**

You can also change borders by clicking the Borders group button and making selections in the Borders and Shading dialog box, as shown in Figure 4-8.

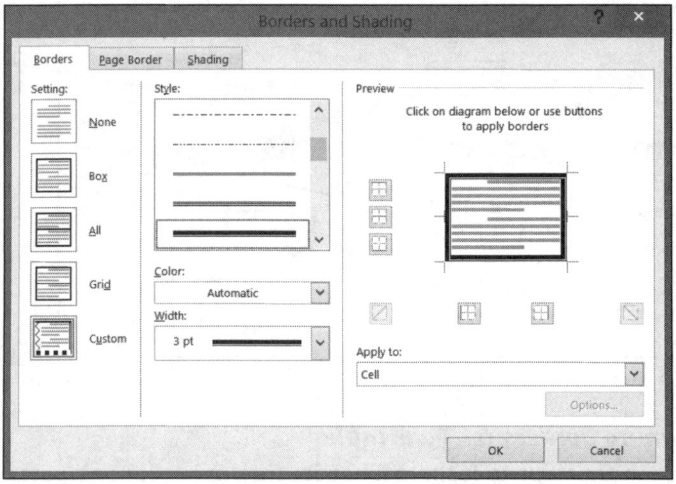

Figure 4-8: You can draw borders with the Borders and Shading dialog box.

Selecting colors for columns, rows, or your table

Follow these steps to paint columns, rows, or your table a new color:

1. **Select the part of the table that needs a paint job.**
2. **In the (Table Tools) Design tab, open the drop-down list on the Shading button and choose a color (refer to Figure 4-7).**

Later in this chapter, "Using a picture as the table background" explains how to use a picture as the background in a table.

Using Math Formulas in Tables

No, you don't have to add the figures in columns and rows yourself; Word gladly does that for you. Word can perform other mathematical calculations as well. Follow these steps to perform mathematical calculations and tell Word how to format sums and products:

1. **Put the cursor in the cell that will hold the sum or product of the cells above, below, to the right, or to the left.**
2. **On the (Table Tools) Layout tab, click the Formula button.**

   Depending on the size of your screen, you may have to click the Data button first. The Formula dialog box appears, as shown in Figure 4-9. In its wisdom, Word makes an educated guess about what you want the formula to do and places a formula in the Formula box.

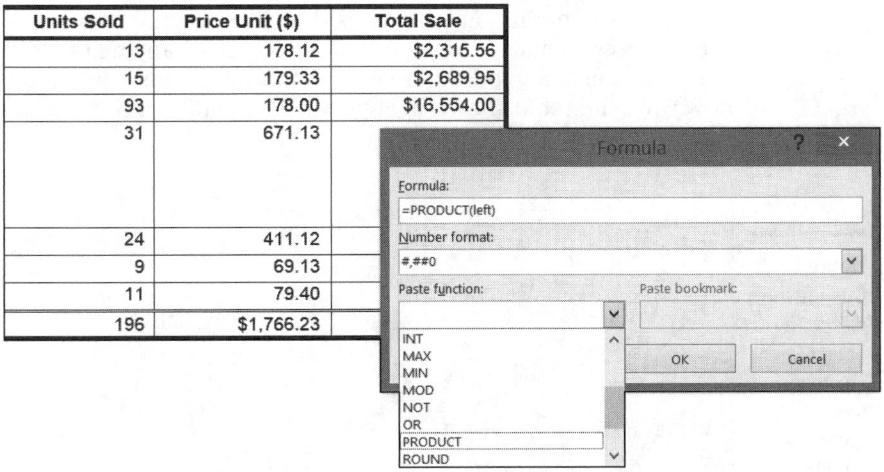

Figure 4-9: A math formula in a table.

3. **If this isn't the formula you want, delete everything except the equal sign in the Formula box, open the Paste Function drop-down list, and choose another function for the formula.**

   For example, choose PRODUCT to multiply figures. You may have to type **left**, **right**, **above**, or **below** in the parentheses within the formula to tell Word where it can find the figures you want to compute.

4. **In the Number Format drop-down list, choose a format for your number.**
5. **Click OK.**

TIP

Word doesn't calculate blank cells in formulas. Enter 0 in blank cells if you want them to be included in calculations. You can copy functions from one cell to another to save yourself the trouble of opening the Formula dialog box.

Neat Table Tricks

The rest of this chapter details a handful of neat table tricks to make your tables stand out in a crowd. Why should all tables look alike? Read on to discover how to make text in the header row stand on its ear, wrap text around a table, put a picture behind a table, draw diagonal border lines, draw on top of a table, and wrap slide text around a table.

Changing the direction of header row text

In a top-heavy table in which the cells in the first row contain text and the cells below contain numbers, consider changing the direction of the text in the first row to make the table easier to read. Changing text direction in the first row is also a good way to squeeze more columns into a table. Consider how wide the table shown in Figure 4-10 would be if the words in the first row were displayed horizontally.

	Yes	No	Maybe	Often	Never
Prof. Plum in the Library	✓				
Miss Scarlet in the Drawing Room		✓			
Col. Mustard in the Dining Room					✓

Figure 4-10: Change the direction of text to squeeze more columns on a table.

Follow these steps to change the direction of text on a table.

1. **Select the row that needs a change of text direction.**

   Usually, that's the first row in a table.

2. **Go to the (Table Tools) Layout tab.**
3. **Keep clicking the Text Direction button until text lands where you want it to land.**

You may have to click the Alignment button before you can see the Text Direction button.

4. **Change the height of the row to make the vertical text fit.**

   As "Changing the size of a table, columns, and rows" explains earlier in this chapter, you can change the height of a row by going to the (Table Tools) Layout tab and entering a measurement in the Height box.

Wrapping text around a table

Nothing is sadder than a forlorn little table all alone on a page. To keep tables from being lonely, you can wrap text around them, as shown in Figure 4-11.

Fujita Scale

Scale	Wind Speed (mph)
F0	40–72
F1	73–112
F2	113–157
F3	158–206
F4	207–260
F5	261–318

The Fujita scale measures tornado intensity primarily on the damage a tornado does to buildings and vegetation. Meteorologists determine official Fujita scale measurements by surveying damage on the ground and by air. They take into account eyewitness testimony, media reports, ground-swirl patterns, radar tracking imagery, and, if video is available, videogrammetry.

Figure 4-11: Wrap text to keep tables from being lonely.

To wrap text around a table, drag it into the text (drag the selection handle in the upper-left corner of the table). Nine times out of ten, that's all there is to it, but if the text doesn't wrap correctly, follow these steps to wrap your table:

1. **On the (Table Tools) Layout tab, click the Cell Size group button.**

   The Table Properties dialog box opens.

2. **On the Table tab, under Text Wrapping, select the Around option.**
3. **Click the Positioning button.**

   The Table Positioning dialog box appears.

4. **Select the Move with Text check box and click OK.**

   By selecting Move with Text, you make sure that the table stays with the surrounding text when you insert or delete text.

5. **Click OK in the Table Properties dialog box.**

Using a picture as the table background

As Figure 4-12 demonstrates, a picture used as the background in a table looks mighty nice. To make it work, however, you need a graphic that serves well as the background. For Figure 4-12, I got around this problem by recoloring my graphic (Book VIII, Chapter 3 explains how to recolor a graphic.) You also need to think about font colors. Readers must be able to read the table text, and that usually means choosing a white or light font color for text so that the text can be read over the graphic. For Figure 4-12, I selected a white font color.

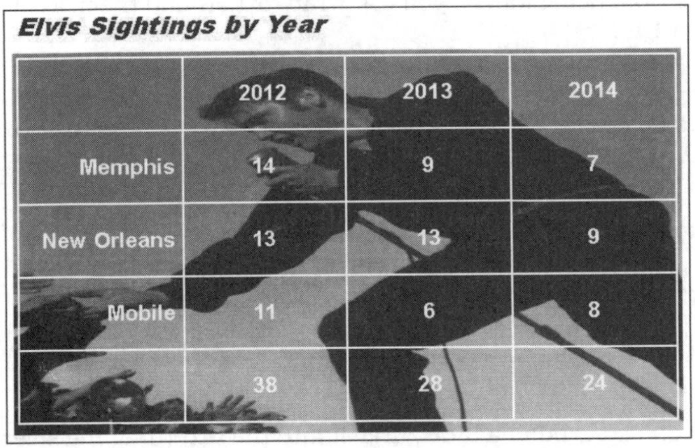

	2012	2013	2014
Memphis	14	9	7
New Orleans	13	13	9
Mobile	11	6	8
	38	28	24

Figure 4-12: A well-chosen graphic in a table background helps indicate what the table is all about.

Placing a graphic behind a table requires a fair bit of work, but the results are well worth the effort. First you insert the graphic and perhaps recolor it. Then you create the table. Lastly, you make the table fit squarely on top of the graphic and perhaps group the objects together.

Follow these steps to place a graphic behind a table:

1. **Insert the graphic, resize it, and format the graphic.**

   Book VIII, Chapter 3 explains how to insert and resize graphics. To insert a graphic, go to the Insert tab and click the Pictures or Online Pictures button. To resize it, drag a selection handle; make the graphic as big as you want your table to be. To recolor a graphic similar to the job done to the graphic in Figure 4-12, select the (Picture Tools) Format tab, click the Color button, and choose an option.

2. **Click the Layout Options button (it's located to the right of the picture) and choose Behind Text on the drop-down list.**

   Choosing Behind Text tells Word to put the graphic behind the text. You can also go to the (Picture Tools) Format tab, click the Wrap Text button, and choose Behind Text.

3. **Insert the table and make it roughly the same size as the graphic.**

   These tasks are explained earlier in this chapter. To change the size of a table, drag a selection handle on its corner or side. Place the table nearby the graphic, but not right on top of it.

4. **On the (Table Tools) Design tab, open the Table Styles gallery, and choose Clear.**

   With the table styles out of the way, you can see the graphic clearly through your table.

5. **Enter the data in the table, select a font and font color, select a border and border color, and align the text.**

   These tasks (except for selecting fonts) are described throughout this chapter. The easiest way to choose a font and font color for a table is to select the table, go to the Home tab, and select a font and font size.

6. **Move the table squarely on top of the graphic and then make the table and graphic roughly the same size.**

Here are a few tricks that are worth knowing when you're handling a graphic and table:

✦ If the graphic is in front of the table, select the graphic, go to the (Picture Tools) Format tab, open the drop-down list on the Send Backward button, and choose Send Behind Text.

✦ To make the text in the table legible, use a light-colored font. As well, use white or light-colored table borders so that the borders can be clearly seen.

Drawing diagonal lines on tables

Draw diagonal lines across table cells to cancel out those cells or otherwise make cells look different. In Figure 4-13, diagonal lines are drawn on cells to show that information that would otherwise be in the cells is either not available or is not relevant.

Figure 4-13: Diagonal lines mark off cells as different.

	Mon.	Tues.	Wed.	Thurs.	Fri.	Sat.	Sun.
McKeef	8:00			3:00		8:00	2:15
Arnez	9:00	6:00	2:30	12:00	8:15		4:00
Danes	9:30		2:00	7:30		3:30	7:30
Minor		12:00	4:15	5:15	2:00		
Krupf	3:30	6:00		12:00	2:30	9:00	9:00
Gough	3:00			7:00	3:30	4:530	3:30
Gonzalez	12:00	7:15	8:30				10:15

To draw diagonal lines across cells, select the cells that need diagonal lines, and on the (Table Tools) Design tab, open the drop-down list on the Borders button, and choose Diagonal Down Border or Diagonal Up Border.

To remove diagonal lines, open the drop-down list on the Borders button and choose Diagonal Down Border or Diagonal Up Border again.

Drawing on a table

When you want to call attention to data in one part of a table, draw a circle around the data. By "draw" I mean make an Oval shape and place it over the data you want to highlight, as shown in Figure 4-14. Book VIII, Chapter 4 explains the drawing tools in detail. To spare you the trouble of turning to that chapter, here are shorthand instructions for drawing on a table:

1. **On the Insert tab, click the Shapes button and select the Oval shape on the drop-down list.**

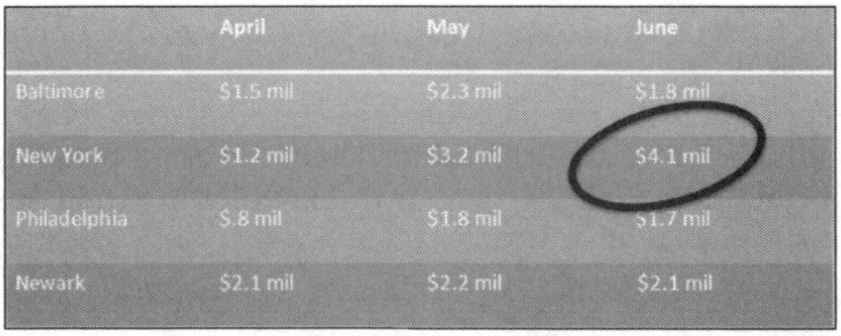

Figure 4-14: You can circle data to highlight it.

2. **On a corner of your page, away from the table, drag to draw the oval.**
3. **On the (Drawing Tools) Format tab, open the drop-down list on the Shape Fill button and choose No Fill.**
4. **Open the drop-down list on the Shape Outline button and choose a very dark color.**
5. **Open the drop-down list on the Shape Outline button, choose Weight, and choose a thick line.**
6. **Drag the oval over the data on your table that you want to highlight.**

   If the oval is obscured by the table, go to the (Drawing Tools) Format tab, and click the Bring Forward button (click the Arrange button, if necessary, to see this button). While you're at it, consider rotating the oval a little way to make it appear as though it was drawn by hand on the table.

Chapter 5: Taking Advantage of the Proofing Tools

In This Chapter

- **Fixing spelling errors and customizing the spelling dictionary**
- **Repairing grammatical errors in documents**
- **Looking up a word definition**
- **Finding text — and replacing it if you want**
- **Conducting outside research while you work in Word**
- **Looking for a better word in the thesaurus**
- **Working with and translating foreign language text**

I was going to call this chapter "Foolproofing Your Work," but that seemed kind of presumptuous because keeping every error from slipping into your work is well-nigh impossible. Still, you can do a good job of proofing your work and eliminating errors by using the tools that Word provides for that purpose. This chapter describes how to proof your work for spelling and grammatical errors. It shows how to find text, find and replace text, and how to conduct research in reference books and on the Internet without leaving Word. You also find out how to translate text and proof foreign language text. The proofing tools are not foolproof, but they're close to it.

The F7 key is the key to the kingdom when it comes to proofing Word documents. Here is the magic of pressing F7 and various key combinations:

- **F7:** Run a spell-check
- **Alt+F7:** Scroll to the next misspelling
- **Ctrl+F7:** Get a word definition
- **Shift+F7:** Open the Thesaurus

Correcting Your Spelling Errors

Word keeps a dictionary in its hip pocket, which is a good thing for you. Who wants to be embarrassed by a spelling error? Word consults its dictionary when you enter text in a document. To correct misspellings, you can either address them one at a time or start the spell checker and proof many pages simultaneously.

Don't trust the smell checker to be accurate all the time. It doesn't really locate misspelled words — it locates words that aren't in its dictionary. For example, if you write "Nero diddled while Rome burned," the spell checker doesn't catch the error. Nero *fiddled* while Rome burned, but because *diddle* is a legitimate word in the spelling dictionary, the spell checker overlooks the error. The moral: Proofread your documents carefully and don't rely on the spell checker to catch all your smelling errors.

Correcting misspellings one at a time

One way to handle misspelled words is to use the one-at-a-time method of spell-checking. As shown in Figure 5-1, you can right-click each word that is underlined in red and choose a correct spelling from the shortcut menu. After you choose a word from the shortcut menu, it replaces the misspelling that you right-clicked.

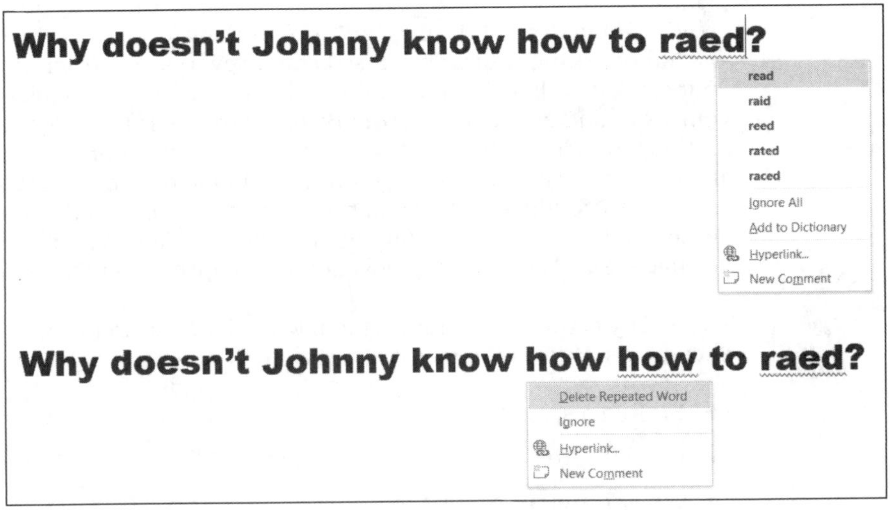

Figure 5-1: Right-click a word underlined in red to correct a typo or repeated word.

Words entered twice are also flagged in red, in which case the shortcut menu offers the Delete Repeated Word option so that you can delete the second word (see Figure 5-1). You can also click Ignore All to tell Word when a word is correctly spelled and shouldn't be flagged, or click Add to Dictionary, which adds the word to the Office spelling dictionary and declares it a correctly spelled word.

> **Getting rid of the squiggly red lines**
>
> More than a few people think that the squiggly red lines that appear under misspelled words are annoying. To keep those lines from appearing, go to the File tab, choose Options, and go to the Proofing category in the Options dialog box. Then deselect the Check Spelling As You Type check box.
>
> Even with the red lines gone, you can do a quick one-at-a time spell-check. Press Alt+F7 to scroll to the next misspelling and display a shortcut menu for fixing it.

Running a spell-check

Instead of correcting misspellings one at a time, you can run a spell-check on your work. Start your spell-check with one of these methods:

- ✦ Press F7.
- ✦ Go to the Review tab and click the Spelling & Grammar button.
- ✦ On the status bar, click the Proofing Errors button. (Move the pointer over this button to see a pop-up message that tells you whether Word has found proofing errors in your document.)

You see the Spelling task pane, as shown in Figure 5-2. As I explain shortly, Word offers all sorts of amenities for handling misspelled words, but here are options for correcting known misspellings in the Spelling task pane:

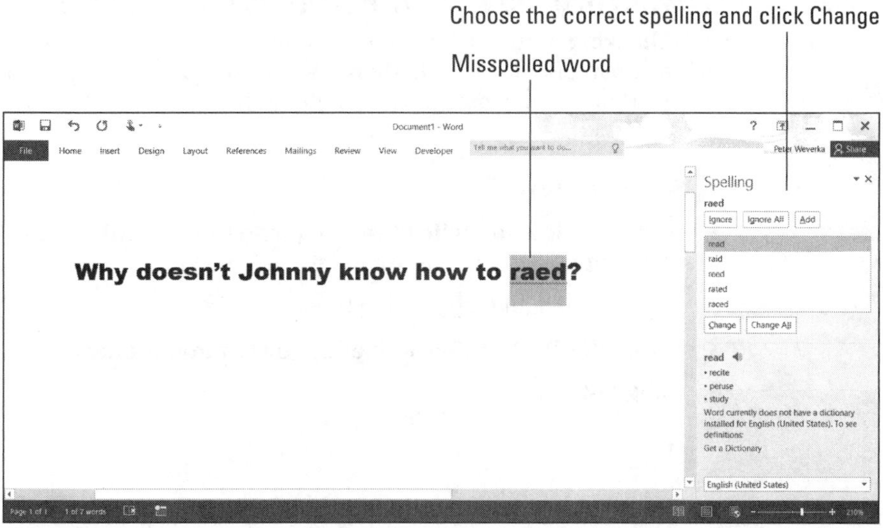

Figure 5-2: Correcting a misspelling in the Spelling task pane.

- Select the correct spelling and click the Change button.
- Click in the page you're working on and correct the misspelling there; then click the Resume button.

If the word in question isn't a misspelling, tell Word how to handle the word by clicking one of these buttons:

- **Ignore:** Ignores this instance of the misspelling but stops on it again if the same misspelling appears later.
- **Ignore All:** Ignores the misspelling throughout the document you're working on and in all other open documents as well.
- **Change/Delete:** Enters the selected word in the document where the misspelling used to be. When the same word appears twice in a row, the Delete button appears. Click the Delete button to delete the second word in the pair.
- **Change All:** Replaces all instances of the misspelled word with the word that you select. Click the Change All button to correct a misspelling that occurs throughout a document.
- **Add:** Adds the misspelling to the Office spelling dictionary. By clicking the Add button, you tell Word that the misspelling is a legitimate word or name.

REMEMBER

Office programs share the same spelling dictionary. For example, words you add to the spelling dictionary in Word are deemed correct spellings in PowerPoint presentations, Excel spreadsheets, Publisher publications, Access databases, and Outlook e-mails.

Preventing text from being spell checked

Spell-checking address lists, lines of computer code, and foreign languages such as Spanglish for which Microsoft doesn't offer foreign language dictionaries is a thorough waste of time. Follow these steps to tell the spell checker to ignore text:

1. **Select the text.**
2. **In the Review tab, click the Language button and choose Set Proofing Language on the drop-down list.**

   You see the Language dialog box.
3. **Select the Do Not Check Spelling or Grammar check box.**
4. **Click OK.**

Checking for Grammatical Errors in Word

Much of what constitutes good grammar is, like beauty, in the eye of the beholder. Still, you can do your best to repair grammatical errors in Word documents by getting the assistance of the grammar checker. The grammar checker identifies grammatical errors, explains what the errors are, and gives you the opportunity to correct the errors.

Figure 5-3 shows the grammar checker in action. To correct grammatical errors:

- **Correct errors one at a time:** Right-click and choose an option on the shortcut menu, as shown in Figure 5-3. Grammatical errors are underlined in blue.
- **Open the Grammar task pane:** Press F7, click the Spelling & Grammar button on the Review tab, or click the Proofing Errors button on the status bar. The Grammar task pane opens. Select a correction and click Change or click the Ignore button to disregard the grammar error.

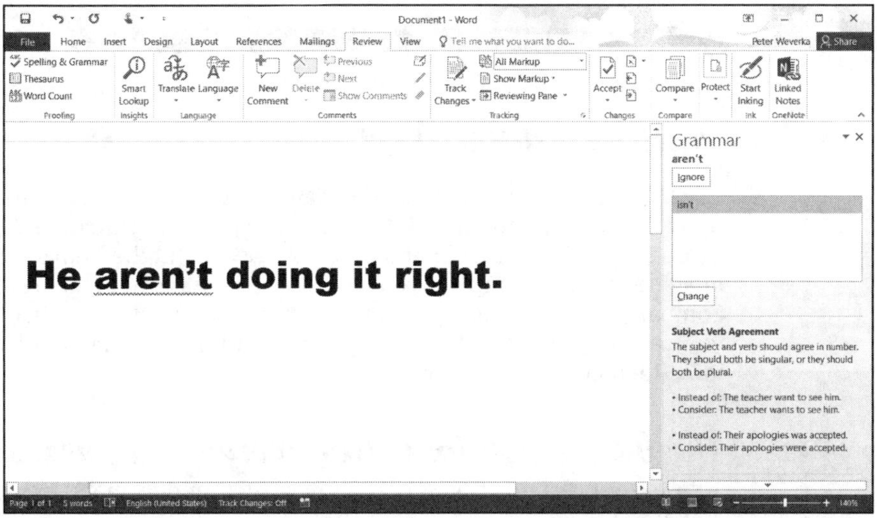

Figure 5-3: Fix grammatical errors with the grammar checker.

If you want to fine-tune how Word runs its grammar checker, go to the File tab and choose Options, and in the Word Options dialog box, go to the Proofing category. Under When Correcting Spelling and Grammar in Word, choose whether to mark grammatical errors with blue lines, check for grammatical as well as spelling errors, and in the Writing Style drop-down list, how stringent you want the rules of grammar to be.

Getting a Word Definition

Rather than reach for a large, unwieldy dictionary, you can get a word definition in the Dictionary task pane, as shown in Figure 5-4. Click the word that needs defining and press Ctrl+F7 to get its definition.

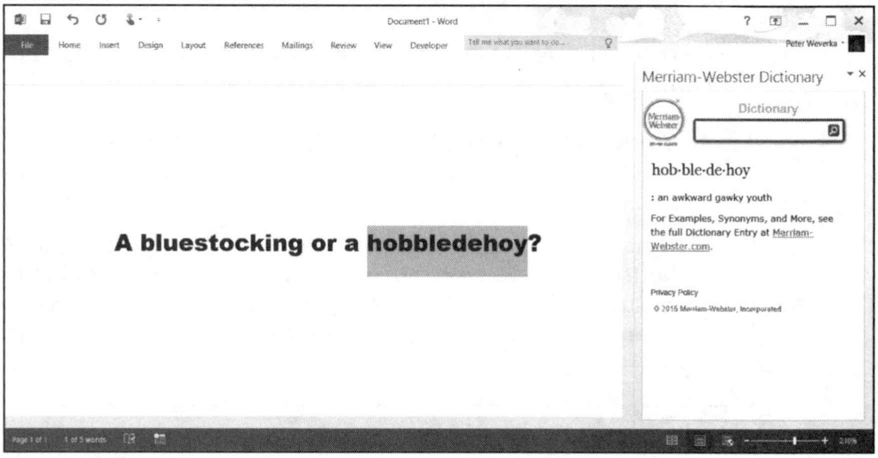

Figure 5-4: The Dictionary task pane in action.

Finding and Replacing Text

Use the Find command to locate a name or text passage. Use its twin, the powerful Replace command, to find and replace a name or text passage throughout a document. For an idea of how useful the Replace command is, imagine that the company you work for just changed its name and the old company name is in many different places. By using the Replace command, you can replace the old company name with the new name throughout a long document in a matter of seconds.

The basics: Finding stray words and phrases

To locate stray words, names, text passages, and formats, follow these basic steps:

1. **Press Ctrl+F or go to the Home tab and click the Find button.**

   The Navigation pane appears so that you can enter search criteria in the Results tab, as shown in Figure 5-5.

2. **Enter the word or phrase in the search text box.**

   After you enter the word or phrase, the Navigation pane lists each instance of the term you're looking for and the term is highlighted in your document wherever it is found (see Figure 5-5).

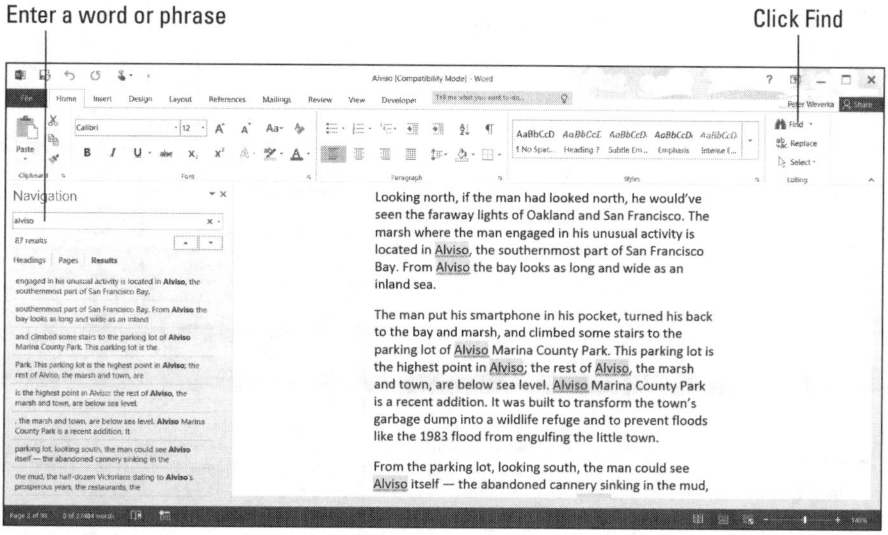

Figure 5-5: Conducting a Find operation in Word.

3. **If you want to conduct a narrow search, click the Find Options button — located to the right of the Search text box in the Navigation pane — and make a choice on the drop-down list.**

   Later in this chapter, "Narrowing your search" explains how to make searches more efficient by choosing options on this drop-down list.

4. **Click an instance of the search term in the Navigation pane to scroll to a location in your document where the search term is located.**

   To go from search term to search term, you can also scroll in the Navigation pane, click the Previous button or Next button (located below the Search text box), or press Ctrl+Page Up or Ctrl+Page Down.

Narrowing your search

To narrow your search, click the Find Options button in the Navigation pane, as shown in Figure 5-6. Then choose an option on the drop-down list:

- **Options:** Opens the Find Options dialog box so that you can select options to narrow your search. Table 5-1 explains these options.
- **Advanced Find:** Opens the Find tab of the Find and Replace dialog box so that you can select options to narrow the search. Table 5-1 explains these options. (You can also open this dialog box on the Home tab by opening the drop-down menu on the Find button and choosing Advanced Find.) Choose Advanced Find if you want to search using font, paragraph, and other formats as well as advanced search criteria. By clicking the Format button and Special button, you can search for text that was formatted a certain way, as well as for special characters such as paragraph marks and page breaks.

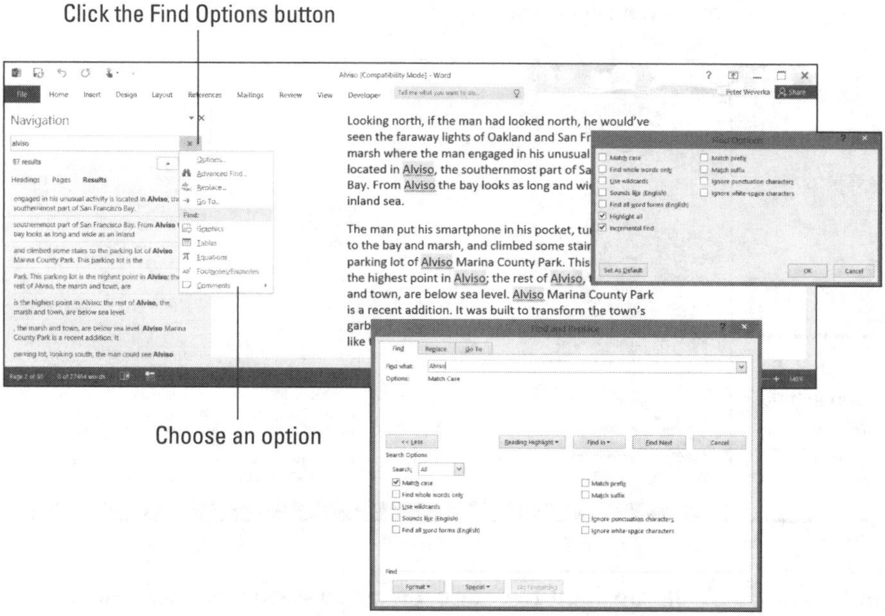

Figure 5-6: Conducting a narrow search.

- **Find (Graphics, Tables, Equations, Footnotes/Endnotes, Comments):** Search for a particular object type. For example, choose Tables to search for tables.

REMEMBER

Click the More button in the Find and Replace dialog box to see all the search options.

WARNING!

After you finish conducting a search for formatted text, don't forget to click the No Formatting button in the Find and Replace dialog box. (You can't conduct a normal search again unless you turn format searching off.)

Using wildcard operators to refine searches

Word permits you to use wildcard operators in searches. A *wildcard operator* is a character that represents characters in a search expression. Wildcards aren't for everybody. Using them requires a certain amount of expertise, but after you know how to use them, wildcards can be invaluable in searches and macros. Table 5-2 explains the wildcard operators that you can use in searches. Click the Use Wildcards check box if you want to search using wildcards.

Table 5-1 Search Options in the Find Options and Find and Replace Dialog Box

Option	*Description*
Match Case	Searches for words with upper- and lowercase letters that exactly match those in the search text box. When the Match Case option is selected, a search for *bow* finds *bow,* but not *Bow* or *BOW.*
Find Whole Words Only	Normally, a search for *bow* yields *elbow, bowler, bow-wow,* and all other words with the letters *b-o-w* (in that order). Choose this option and you get only *bow.*
Use Wildcards	Choose this option to use wildcards in searches. (See "Using wildcard operators to refine searches," later in this chapter.)
Sounds Like	Search for words that sound like the one in the Search text box. A search for *bow* with this option selected finds *beau,* for example. However, it doesn't find *bough.* This command isn't very reliable.
Find All Word Forms	Takes into account verb conjugations and plurals in searches. With this option, you get *bows, bowing,* and *bowed* as well as *bow.*
Highlight All[1]	Highlights search results on the page. (Click the Reading Highlight button in the Find and Replace dialog box.)
Incremental Find[1]	Searches for and highlights text as you type it in the Search text box.
Match Prefix	A *prefix* is a syllable appearing before the root or stem of a word to alter its meaning. For example, *co, mid, non,* and *un* are prefixes in the words *coauthor, midtown, nonviolent,* and *unselfish.* Choose this option and enter a prefix in the Find What text box to locate words that begin with the prefix you enter.
Match Suffix	A *suffix* is a syllable or two appearing at the end of a word that alters its meaning. For example, *age, ish,* and *ness* are suffixes in the words *spillage, smallish,* and *darkness.* Choose this option and enter a suffix in the Find What text box to find words that end with the same suffix.
Ignore Punctuation Characters	Search in text for word phrases without regard for commas, periods, and other punctuation marks. For example, a search for *Yuma Arizona* finds *Yuma, Arizona* (with a comma) in the text.

(continued)

Table 5-1 *(continued)*

Option	*Description*
Ignore White Space Characters	Search in text for word phrases without regard for white space caused by multiple blank spaces or tab entries.
Format (button)[2]	Search for text formatted a certain way. For example, search for boldface text. After you click the Format button in the Find and Replace dialog box, you can choose a format type on the drop-down list — Font, Paragraph, Tabs, Language, Frame, Style, or Highlight. A Find dialog box opens so that you can describe the format you're looking for. Select options in the dialog box to describe the format and click OK.
Special (button)[2]	Search for special characters such as paragraph marks and em dashes. (See "Searching for special characters," later in this chapter.)

[1] Find Options dialog box only
[2] Find and Replace dialog box only

WARNING!

You can't conduct a whole-word-only search with a wildcard. For example, a search for **f*s** not only finds *fads* and *fits* but also all text strings that begin with *f* and end with *s,* such as *for the birds.* Wildcard searches can yield many, many results and are sometimes useless.

TIP

To search for an asterisk (*), question mark (?), or other character that serves as a wildcard search operator, place a backslash (\) before it in the text box.

Searching for special characters

Table 5-3 describes the *special characters* you can look for in Word documents. To look for the special characters listed in the table, enter the character directly in the text box or click the Special button in the Find and Replace dialog box, and then choose a special character from the pop-up list. Be sure to enter lowercase letters. For example, you must enter **^n**, not **^N**, to look for a column break. ***Note:*** A caret (^) precedes special characters.

Before searching for special characters, go to the Home tab and click the Show/Hide¶ button. That way, you see special characters — also known as *hidden format symbols* — on-screen when Word finds them.

Table 5-2 Wildcards for Searches

Operator	*What It Finds*	*Example*
?	Any single character	**b?t** finds *bat, bet, bit,* and *but.*
*	Zero or more characters	**t*o** finds *to, two,* and *tattoo.*
[*xyz*]	A specific character, *x, y,* or *z*	**t[aeiou]pper** finds *tapper, tipper,* and *topper.*
[*x-z*]	A range of characters, *x* through *z*	**[1-4]000** finds *1000, 2000, 3000,* and *4000,* but not *5000.*
[!*xy*]	Not the specific character or characters, *xy*	**p[!io]t** finds *pat* and *pet,* but not *pit* or *pot.*
<	Characters at the beginning of words	**<info** finds *information, infomaniac,* and *infomercial.*
>	Characters at the end of words	**ese>** finds *these, journalese,* and *legalese.*
@@	One or more instances of the previous character	**sho@@t** finds *shot* and *shoot.*
{*n*}	Exactly *n* instances of the previous character	**sho{2}t** finds *shoot* but not *shot.*
{*n*,}	At least *n* instances of the previous character	**^p{3,}** finds three or more paragraph breaks in a row, but not a single paragraph break or two paragraph breaks in a row.
{*n*,*m*}	From *n* to *m* instances of the previous character	**10{2,4}** finds *100, 1000,* and *10000,* but not *10* or *100000.*

TIP

Creative people find many uses for special characters in searches. The easiest way to find section breaks, column breaks, and manual line breaks in a document is to enter **^b**, **^n**, or **^l**, respectively, and start searching. By combining special characters with text, you can make find-and-replace operations more productive. For example, to replace all double hyphens (–) in a document with em dashes (—), enter **–** in the Find What text box and **^m** in the Replace With text box. This kind of find-and-replace operation is especially useful for cleaning documents that were created in another program and then imported into Word.

Table 5-3	**Special Characters for Searches**
To Find/Replace	*Enter*
Manual Formats That Users Insert	
Column break	^n
Field[1]	^d
Manual line break (↵)	^l
Manual page break	^m
No-width non break	^z
No-width optional break	^x
Paragraph break (¶)	^p
Section break[1]	^b
Section character	^%
Tab space (→)	^t
Punctuation Marks	
1/4 em space	^q
Caret (^)	^^
Ellipsis	^i
Em dash (—)	^+
En dash (–)	^=
Full-width ellipses	^j
Nonbreaking hyphen	^~
Optional hyphen	^-
White space (one or more blank spaces)[1]	^w
Characters and Symbols	
Foreign character	You can type foreign characters in the Find What and Replace With text boxes
ANSI and ASCII characters and symbols	^*nnnn*, where *nnnn* is the four-digit code
Any character[1]	^?
Any digit[1]	^#
Any letter[1]	^$
Clipboard contents[2]	^c
Contents of the Find What box[2]	^&

To Find/Replace	*Enter*
Elements of Reports and Scholarly Papers	
Endnote mark[1]	^e
Footnote mark[1]	^f
Graphic[1]	^g

[1] *For use in find operations only*
[2] *For use in replace operations only*

Conducting a find-and-replace operation

Conducting a find-and-replace operation is the spitting image of conducting a find operation. Figure 5-7 shows the Replace dialog box, the place where you declare what you want to find and what to replace it with. Do the options and buttons in the dialog box look familiar? They do if you read the previous handful of pages about searching because the Replace options are the same as the Find options.

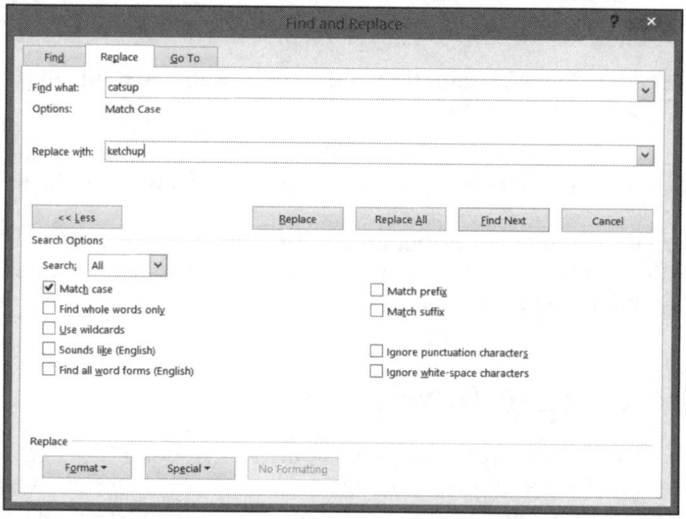

Figure 5-7: Using the powerful Replace command.

The key to a successful find-and-replace operation is making sure you *find* exactly what you want to find and replace. One way to make sure that you find the right text is to start by running a Find operation. If the program finds precisely the text you want, you're in business. Click the Replace tab in the Find and Replace dialog box and then enter the replacement text.

To locate and replace words, names, or text passages with the Find command, follow these steps:

1. **Press Ctrl+H or go to the Home tab and click the Replace button.**

   The Find and Replace dialog box appears (see Figure 5-7).

2. **Describe the text that needs replacing.**

   Earlier in this chapter, "The basics: Finding stray words and phrases" explains how to construct a search. Try to narrow your search so you find only the text you're looking for.

3. **Click the Find Next button.**

   Did your program find what you're looking for? If it didn't, describe the search again.

4. **Enter the replacement text in the Replace With text box.**

   You can select replacement text from the drop-down list.

5. **Either replace everything simultaneously or do it one at a time.**

   Click one of these buttons:

   - Click Replace All to make all replacements in an instant.
   - Click Find Next and then either click Replace to make the replacement or Find Next to bypass it.

   Click the Replace All button only if you are very, very confident that the thing your program found is the thing you want to replace.

Be sure to examine your document after you conduct a find-and-replace operation. You never know what the powerful Replace command will do. If the command makes a hash of your document, click the Undo button.

Researching a Topic Inside Word

Thanks to the Research task pane, your desk needn't be as crowded as before. The Research task pane offers dictionaries, foreign language dictionaries, a thesaurus, language translators, and encyclopedias, as well as Internet searching, all available from inside Word (and the other Office programs too). As shown in Figure 5-8, the Research task pane can save you a trip to the library.

The task pane offers menus and buttons for steering a search in different directions, but no matter what you want to research in the Research task pane, start your search the same way:

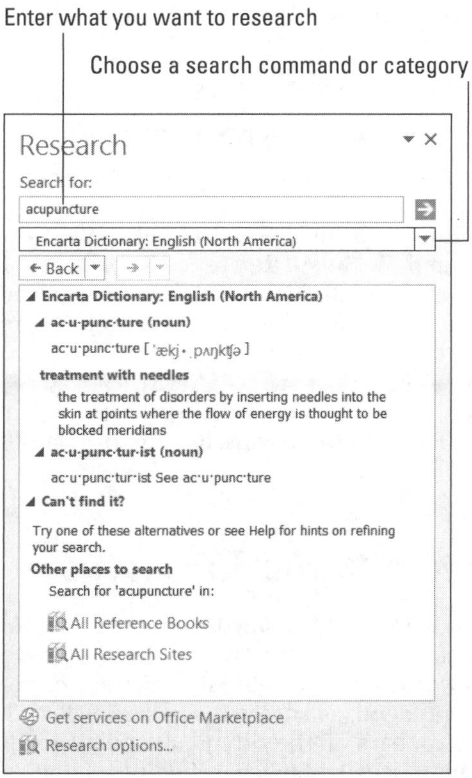

Figure 5-8: The Research task pane is like a mini reference library.

1. **Either click in a word or select the words that you want to research.**

   For example, if you want to translate a word, click it. Clicking a word or selecting words saves you the trouble of entering words in the Search For text box, but if no word in your document describes what you want to research, don't worry about it. You can enter the subject of your search later.

2. **Alt+click the word or words you want to research. (In Excel and PowerPoint, you can also click the Research button on the Review tab.)**

   The Research task pane appears (refer to Figure 5-8). If you've researched since you started running Word, the options you chose for your last research project appear in the task pane.

3. **Enter a research term in the Search For text box (if one isn't there already).**

4. **Open the Search For drop-down list and tell Word where to steer your search.**

   Choose a reference book or research website.

5. **Click the Start Searching button (or press Enter).**

   The results of your search appear in the Research task pane.

If your search yields nothing worthwhile or nothing at all, scroll to the bottom of the task pane and try the All Reference Books or All Research Sites link. The first link searches all reference books — the dictionaries, thesauruses, and translation service. The second searches research sites — Bing, Factiva iWorks, and HighBeam Research.

TIP

You can retrace a search by clicking the Back button or Forward button in the Research task pane. These buttons work like the Back and Forward buttons in a web browser.

Finding the Right Word with the Thesaurus

If you can't find the right word or if the word is on the tip of your tongue but you can't quite remember it, you can always give the Thesaurus a shot. To find synonyms for a word, start by right-clicking the word and choosing Synonyms on the shortcut menu, as shown in Figure 5-9. With luck, the synonym you're looking for appears on the submenu, and all you have to do is click to enter the synonym. Usually, however, finding a good synonym is a journey, not a Sunday stroll.

To search for a good synonym, click the word in question and open the Thesaurus task pane with one of these techniques:

- Press Shift+F7.
- Right-click the word and choose Synonyms ⇨ Thesaurus.
- Go to the Review tab and click the Thesaurus button.

The Thesaurus task pane opens. It offers a list of synonyms and sometimes includes an antonym or two at the bottom. Now you're getting somewhere:

- **Choosing a synonym:** Move the pointer over the synonym you want, open its drop-down list, and choose Insert.
- **Finding a synonym for a synonym:** If a synonym intrigues you, click it. The task pane displays a new list of synonyms.
- **Searching for antonyms:** If you can't think of the right word, type its antonym in the text box and then look for an "antonym of an antonym" in the task pane.

Figure 5-9: Searching for a synonym.

Proofing Text Written in a Foreign Language

In the interest of cosmopolitanism, Word gives you the opportunity to make foreign languages a part of documents. To enter and edit text in a foreign language, start by installing proofing tools for the language. With the tools installed, you tell Word where in your document a foreign language is used. After that, you can spell check text written in the language.

To spell check text written in Uzbek, Estonian, Afrikaans, and other languages apart from English, French, and Spanish, you have to obtain additional proofing tools from Microsoft. These can be obtained at the Microsoft Download Center at `www.microsoft.com/en-us/download` (enter **proofing tools** in the Search box). Proofing tools include a spell checker, grammar checker, thesaurus, hyphenator, AutoCorrect list, and translation dictionary, but not all these tools are available for every language.

REMEMBER

The status bar along the bottom of the screen lists the current language. Glance at the status bar if you aren't sure which language Word is whispering in your ear.

Telling Office which languages you will use

Follow these steps to inform Word that you will use a language or languages besides English in your documents:

1. **On the Review tab, click the Language button and choose Language Preferences.**

   The Word Options dialog box opens to the Language category.

2. **Open the Add Additional Editing Languages drop-down list, select a language, and click the Add button to make that language a part of your documents.**
3. **Click OK.**

Marking text as foreign language text

The next step is to tell Office where in your document you're using a foreign language. After you mark the text as foreign language text, Office can spell check it with the proper dictionaries. Follow these steps to mark text so that Office knows in which language it was written:

1. **Select the text that you wrote in a foreign language.**
2. **Go to the Review tab.**
3. **Click the Language button and choose Set Proofing Language on the drop-down list.**

   You see the Language dialog box, as shown in Figure 5-10.

4. **Select a language and click OK.**

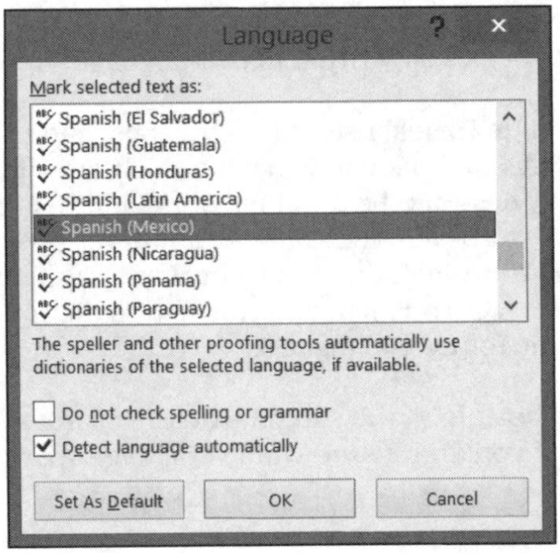

Figure 5-10: Identifying foreign language words for spell-checking.

Translating Foreign Language Text

Office offers a gizmo for translating words and phrases from one language to another. The translation gizmo gives you the opportunity to translate single words and phrases as well as entire documents, although, in my experience, it is only good for translating words and phrases. To translate an entire document, you have to seek the help of a real, native speaker.

Follow these steps to translate foreign language text:

1. **Select the word or phrase that needs translating.**
2. **On the Review tab, click the Translate button and choose a Translate option on the drop-down list.**

   Office offers these ways to translate words:

   - *Translate Document:* Word sends the text to Microsoft Translator, a translation service, and the translated text appears on a web page. Copy the text and do what you will with it. (If the wrong translation languages are listed, choose correct languages from the drop-down lists on the top of the web page.)
   - *Translate Selected Text:* The Research task pane opens, as shown in Figure 5-11. Choose a From and To option to translate the word from one language to another.

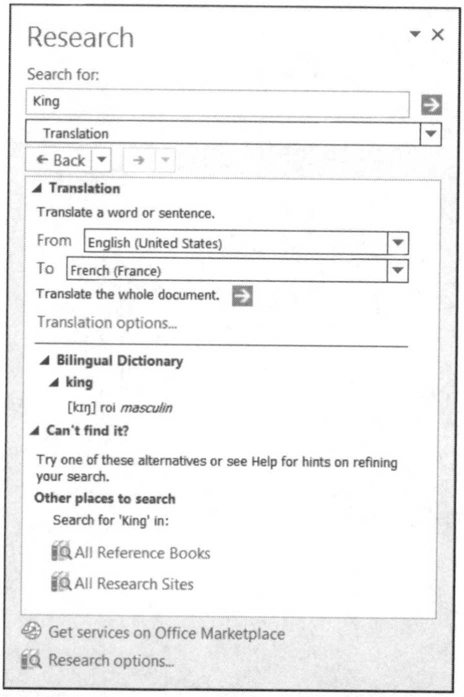

Figure 5-11: Use the Research task pane to translate a word or phrase.

Chapter 6: Desktop Publishing with Word

In This Chapter

- **Choosing a new theme**
- **Putting borders on pages**
- **Considering ways to desktop-publish in Word**
- **Wrapping text around graphics and other objects**
- **Putting text boxes in documents**
- **Decorating pages with drop caps and watermarks**
- **Running text in newspaper-style columns**
- **Printing landscape documents on various sizes of paper**
- **Showing video in a document**

Once upon a time, word processors were nothing more than glorified typewriters. They were good for typing and basic formatting, and not much else. But over the years, Microsoft Word has become a desktop publishing program in its own right. This chapter explains a few desktop publishing features that can make your documents stand out in the crowd — themes, columns, text boxes, page borders, watermarks, video, and drop caps, to name a few.

Experimenting with Themes

A *theme* is a colorful, ready-made design for headings and text. Each theme imposes a slightly different look on a document. If you want to experiment with themes, theme style sets, theme colors, and theme fonts, more power to you, but be prepared to click the Undo button and backtrack as you rummage around for the right look for your document. Figure 6-1 shows some theme experiments.

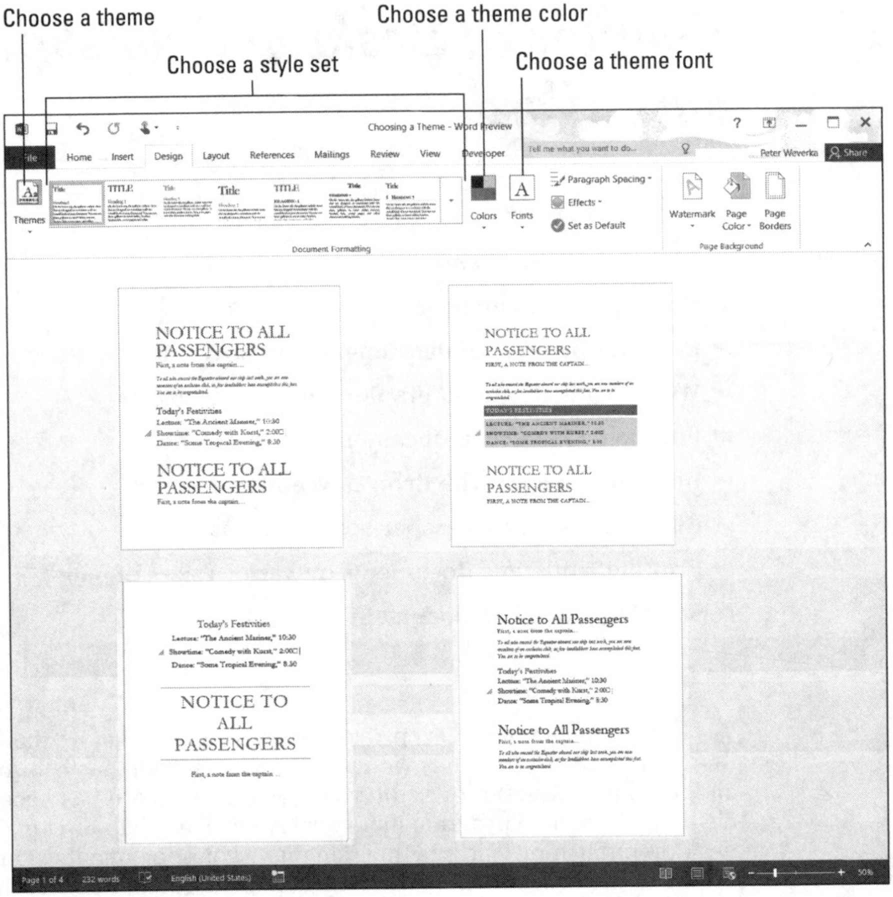

Figure 6-1: On the Design tab, experiment with themes, style sets, theme colors, and theme fonts.

Starting on the Design tab, follow these instructions to experiment with themes:

- **Choosing a new theme:** Click the Themes button and choose a theme on the drop-down list.
- **Choosing a new style set:** On the Theme Styles gallery, choose a style set.
- **Choosing a new set of colors for your theme:** Click the Theme Colors button, slide the pointer over the different color sets on the drop-down list, and see what effect they have on your document.
- **Changing the fonts:** Click the Theme Fonts button and choose a combination of fonts on the drop-down list for the headings and text in your document.

Sprucing Up Your Pages

You can play interior decorator with the pages of a document by putting a border around pages, splashing color on pages, and taking advantage of the predesigned cover pages that Word provides for you. Keep reading if making the pages of your document a little prettier interests you.

Decorating a page with a border

Word offers a means of decorating title pages, certificates, menus, and similar documents with a page border. Besides lines, you can decorate the sides of a page with stars, pieces of cake, and other artwork. If you want to place a border around a page in the middle of a document, you must create a section break where the page is.

Before you create your border, place the cursor on the page where the border is to appear. Place the cursor on the first page of a document if you want to put a border around only the first page. If your document is divided into sections and you want to put borders around certain pages in a section, place the cursor in the section — either in the first page if you want the borders to go around it, or in a subsequent page.

With the cursor in the right place, follow these steps to decorate your page or pages with a border:

1. **Go to the Design tab and click the Page Borders button.**

   You see the Borders and Shading dialog box, as shown in Figure 6-2.

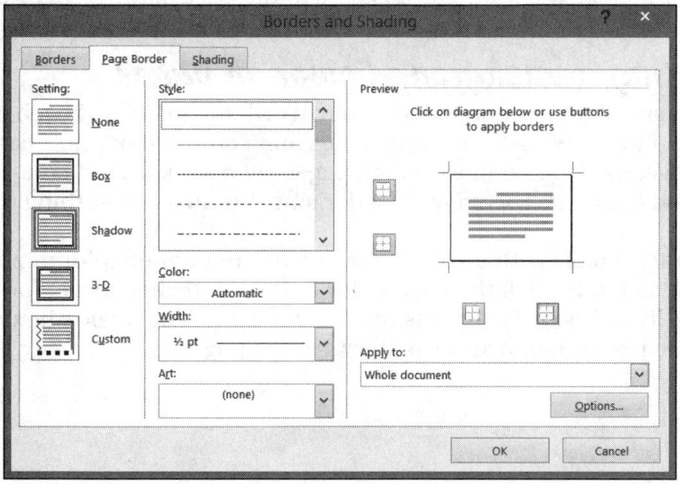

Figure 6-2: Putting borders on pages.

2. **Under Setting, choose which kind of border you want.**

   Use the None setting to remove borders.

3. **On the Apply To drop-down menu, tell Word which page or pages in the document get borders.**
4. **Select options to construct the border you want and then click OK.**

The Page Border tab offers a bunch of tools for fashioning a border:

- **Line for borders:** Under Style, scroll down the list and choose a line for the borders. You will find interesting choices at the bottom of the menu. Be sure to look in the Preview window to see what your choices in this dialog box add up to.
- **Color for borders:** Open the Color drop-down list and choose a color for the border lines if you want a color border.
- **Width of borders:** If you chose artwork for the borders, use the Width drop-down list to tell Word how wide the lines or artwork should be.
- **Artwork for borders**: Open the Art drop-down list and choose a symbol, illustration, star, piece of cake, or other artwork, if that is what you want for the borders. You will find some amusing choices on this long list, including ice cream cones, bats, and umbrellas.
- **Borders on different sides of the page:** Use the four buttons in the Preview window to tell Word on which sides of the page to draw borders. Click these buttons to remove or add borders, as you wish.
- **Distance from edge of page:** Click the Options button and fill in the Border and Shading Options dialog box if you want to get specific about how close the borders can come to the edge of the page or pages.

Putting a background color on pages

Especially if you intend to save your Word document as a web page, you will be glad to know that putting a background color on pages is easy. You can't, however, pick and choose which pages get a background color. Putting background colors on the pages of a document is an all-or-nothing proposition.

To grace a page with a background color or gradient color mixture, go to the Design tab, click the Page Color button, and choose a color on the drop-down list. Choose Fill Effects to open the Fill Effects dialog box and apply gradient color mixtures or patterns to the pages.

Getting Word's help with cover letters

Writing and designing a cover page for a letter, resume, or report is a chore. Word can't dictate a cover page for you, but it can provide a handsome preformatted cover page that looks nice at the front of a report or article. Figure 6-3 shows example of cover pages.

To place a cover page at the start of a document, go to the Insert tab, click the Cover Page button, and choose a cover page on the gallery.

Figure 6-3: Examples of ready-made cover pages.

Making Use of Charts, Diagrams, Shapes, and Photos

Figure 6-4 shows a newsletter that includes a chart, diagram, shape, and photo. You are invited to include these items in your Word documents, and you'll be glad to know that including them isn't very much trouble.

- **Charts:** A chart is an excellent way to present data for comparison purposes. The pie slices, bars, columns, or lines tell readers right away which business is more productive, for example, or who received the most votes. Book VIII, Chapter 1 explains how to create charts.
- **Diagrams:** A diagram allows readers to quickly grasp an idea, relationship, or concept. Instead of explaining an abstract idea, you can portray it in a diagram. Book VIII, Chapter 2 explains diagrams.
- **Shapes and lines:** Shapes and lines can also illustrate ideas and concepts. You can also use them for decorative purposes in Word documents. Book VIII, Chapter 4 explains how to draw lines, arrows, and shapes.
- **Photos:** Photos make a document livelier. They add a little color to documents. Book VIII, Chapter 3 explains how to place photos in documents.

Figure 6-4: This newsletter includes a photo, chart, diagram, and shape, image.

Working with the Drawing Canvas

As Book VIII, Chapter 4 explains, shapes and lines are a great way to illustrate ideas. You can in effect doodle on the page and give readers another insight into what you want to explain. In Word, however, drawing lines and shapes is problematic unless you draw them on the drawing canvas.

The *drawing canvas* works like a corral to hold lines and shapes. After you create a drawing canvas, you can draw inside it as though you were drawing on a little page, as shown in Figure 6-5. You can treat the drawing canvas as an object in its own right. You can move it, along with the things inside it, to new locations. You can also, by way of the (Drawing Tools) Format tab, give the drawing canvas an outline shape and fill color. The drawing canvas makes working with objects on a page, especially lines and shapes, that much easier.

Follow these steps to create a drawing canvas for holding lines and shapes:

1. **Place the cursor roughly where you want the drawing canvas to be.**
2. **Go to the Insert tab.**
3. **Click the Shapes button and choose New Drawing Canvas.**

   You can find the New Drawing Canvas command at the bottom of the Shapes drop-down list. A drawing canvas appears on your screen.

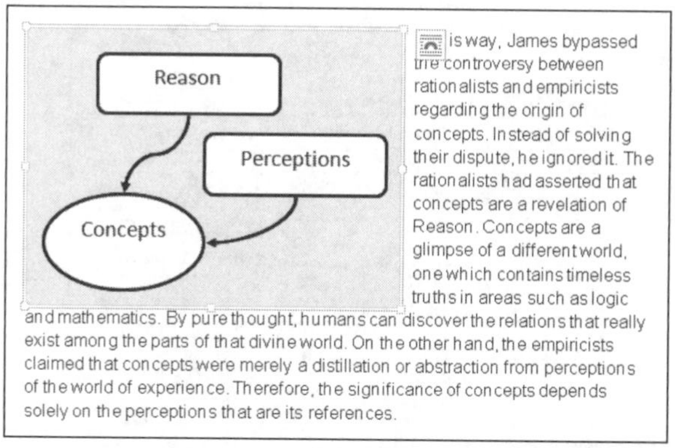

Reason
Perceptions
Concepts
is way, James bypassed the controversy between rationalists and empiricists regarding the origin of concepts. Instead of solving their dispute, he ignored it. The rationalists had asserted that concepts are a revelation of Reason. Concepts are a glimpse of a different world, one which contains timeless truths in areas such as logic and mathematics. By pure thought, humans can discover the relations that really exist among the parts of that divine world. On the other hand, the empiricists claimed that concepts were merely a distillation or abstraction from perceptions of the world of experience. Therefore, the significance of concepts depends solely on the perceptions that are its references.

Figure 6-5: The drawing canvas — a corral for shapes and lines.

The drawing canvas is an object in its own right. You can wrap text around it, give it an outline, and give it a color fill. You can drag it to a new location. To change its size, drag a handle on the side or corner.

Positioning and Wrapping Objects Relative to the Page and Text

"Object" is just Office's generic term for a shape, line, text box, image, photo, diagram, WordArt image, or chart that you insert in a document. Book VIII, Chapter 4 explains how to manipulate an object — how to change its size, shape, and other qualities. When you place an object in a Word document, you have to consider more than its size and shape. You also have to consider where to position it on the page and how to wrap text around it. In Word lingo, *wrap* refers to what text does when it butts heads with a shape, text box, photo, diagram, or other object. You must be in Print Layout view to wrap and position objects on a page.

When you insert an object, it lands *inline with text.* That means it lands against the left margin and text doesn't wrap around its side. Before you can change the position of an object, you must select it and choose a text-wrapping option apart from Inline with Text.

Wrapping text around an object

Figure 6-6 illustrates the 15 different ways you can wrap text around an object. Select the object you want to wrap text around and use one of these techniques to wrap text around the object:

- ✦ Click the Layout Options button (it's located to the right of the object) and choose an option on the drop-down list, as shown in Figure 6-7.

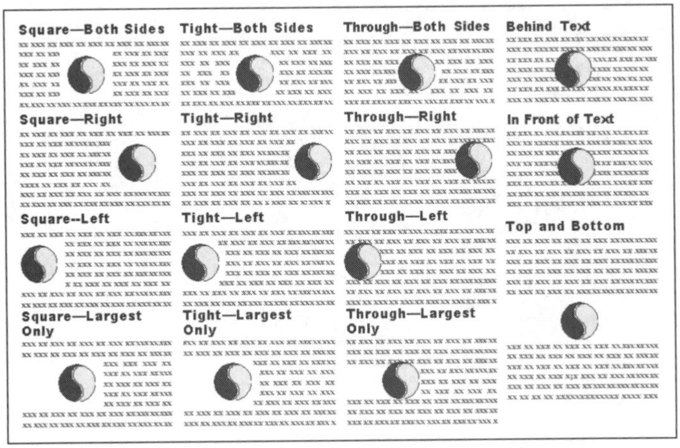

Figure 6-6: All the ways to wrap text in a Word document.

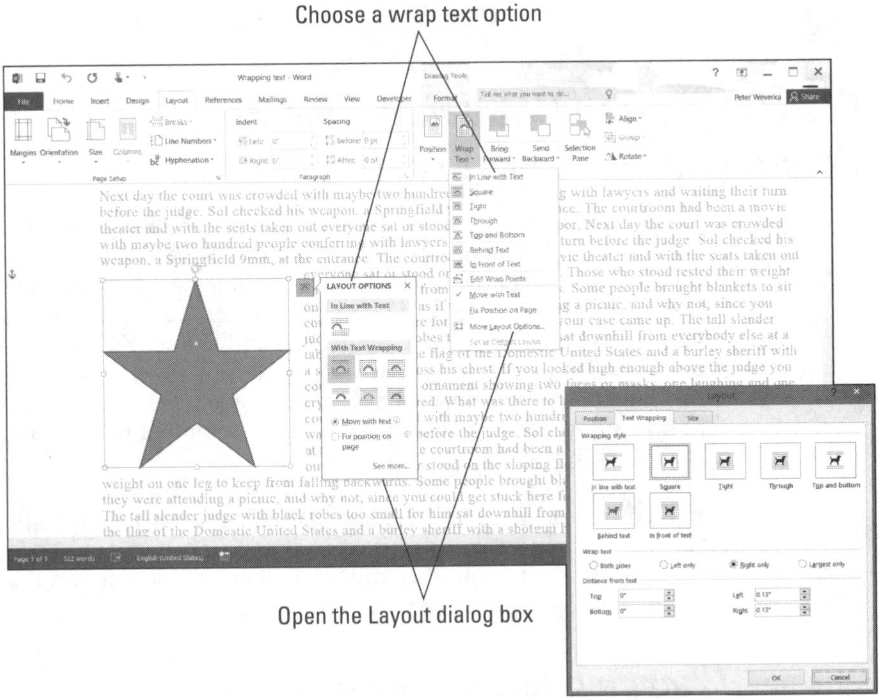

Figure 6-7: Choosing how to wrap text.

- ✦ On the Layout or Format tab, click the Wrap Text button and choose an option on the drop-down list, as shown in Figure 6-7. (You may have to click the Arrange button first, depending on the size of your screen.)
- ✦ Open the Layout dialog box, go to the Text Wrapping tab, and choose a wrapping style and side around which to wrap text. Figure 6-6 shows

what the different combinations of Wrapping Style and Wrap Text options do. To open the Layout dialog box:

- Click the Layout Options button (to the right of the object) and click the See More link on the drop-down list.
- Click the Wrap Text button and choose More Layout Options on the drop-down list.

TIP

Wrapped text looks best when it is justified and hyphenated. That way, text can get closer to the object that is being wrapped.

Positioning an object on a page

To position an object in a Word page, you can drag it to a new location. As Book VIII, Chapter 4 explains in torturous detail, dragging means to select the object, move the pointer over its perimeter, click when you see the four-headed arrow, and slide the object to a new location.

To make positioning objects on a page a little easier, Word also offers Position commands for moving objects to specific places on the page. For example, you can place an object squarely in a corner or middle of the page.

Wrapping text with precision

You can decide for yourself how close or far text is from an object when you wrap text. Select the object, and on the Format tab, click the Wrap Text button and choose Edit Wrap Points on the drop-down list. Small black squares called *wrap points* appear around the object, as shown in this illustration. Click and drag the wrap points to push text away from or bring text closer to the object in question.

Statue of Liberty
The Statue of Liberty, officially titled Liberty Enlightening the World (la Liberté éclairant le monde), dedicated on October 28, 1886, is a monument that commemorates the centennial of the signing of the United States Declaration of Independence. It was given to the United States by the people of France to acknowledge the friendship between the two countries established during the American Revolution. The statue represents a woman wearing a stola, a radiant crown and sandals, trampling a broken chain, carrying a torch in her raised right hand and a tabula ansata tablet, where the date of the Declaration of Independence is inscribed, in her left arm.

Select your object, go to the Layout or Format tab, and use one of these techniques to move your object precisely into place:

- ✦ Click the Position button and select a With Text Wrapping option on the drop-down list, as shown in Figure 6-8. (You may have to click the Arrange button first, depending on the size of your screen.) These options position an object squarely in a corner, a side, or the middle of the page.
- ✦ Click the Position button and choose More Layout Options on the drop-down list, or click the Size group button on the Format tab and select the Position tab in the Layout dialog box. Then choose position options. Go to the Layout dialog box when you want to place objects in the very same position on different pages.

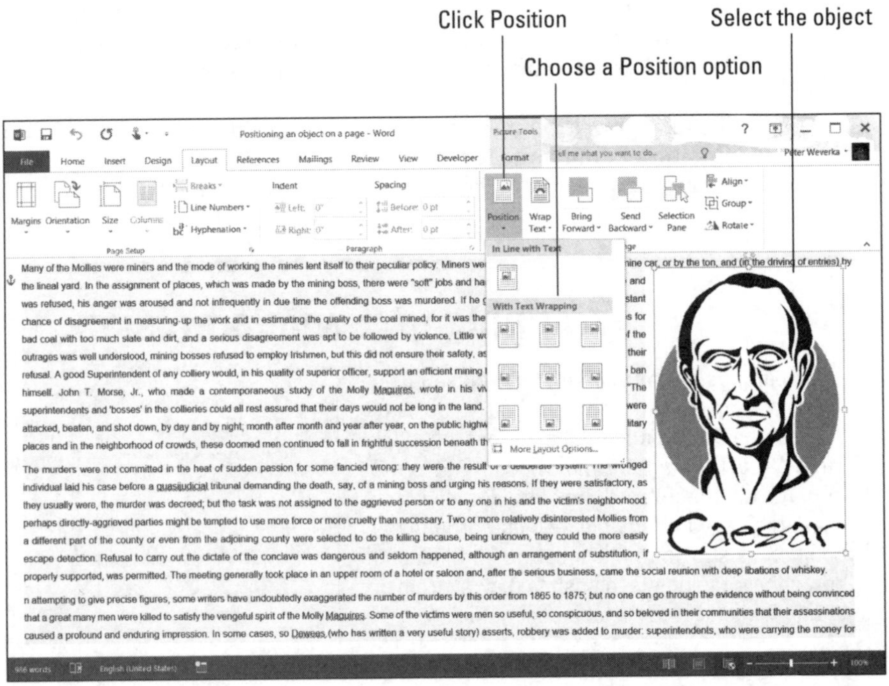

Figure 6-8: The Position options place an object on one part of the page.

REMEMBER

When you insert an object, Word attaches it to the paragraph where the cursor is located when you make the insertion. For that reason, if you move that paragraph to another page or the paragraph gets moved as you edit text, the object moves right along with the paragraph. You can locate the paragraph to which an object is connected by clicking the object. The anchor symbol appears beside the paragraph to which the object is connected.

Working with Text Boxes

Put text in a text box when you want a notice or announcement to stand out on the page. Like other objects, text boxes can be shaded, filled with color, and given borders, as the examples in Figure 6-9 demonstrate. You can also lay them over graphics to make for interesting effects. I removed the borders and the fill color from the text box on the right side of Figure 6-9, but rest assured, the text in this figure lies squarely in a text box. (Book VIII, Chapter 4 explains how to give borders, shading, and color to objects such as text boxes.)

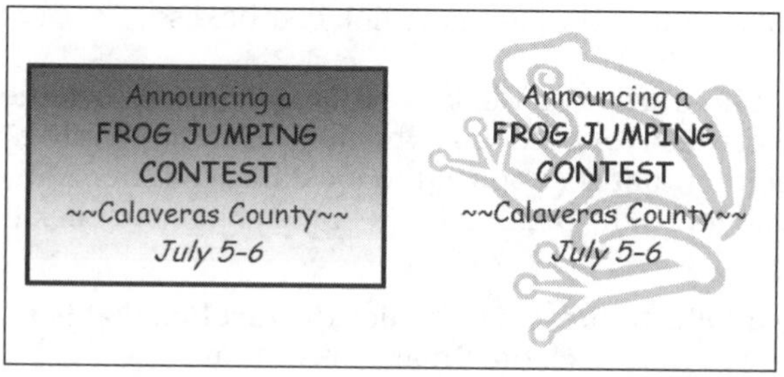

Figure 6-9: Examples of text boxes.

You can move a text box around at will on the page until it lands in the right place. You can even use text boxes as columns and make text jump from one text box to the next in a document — a nice feature, for example, when you want a newsletter article on page 1 to be continued on page 2. Instead of cutting and pasting text from page 1 to page 2, Word moves the text for you as the column on page 1 fills up.

Inserting a text box

To create a text box, go to the Insert tab, click the Text Box button, and use one of these techniques:

- **Choose a ready-made text box:** Scroll in the drop-down list and choose a preformatted text box.
- **Draw a conventional text box:** Choose Draw Text Box on the drop-down list, and then click and drag to draw the text box. Lines show you how big it will be when you release the mouse button.

After you insert the text box, you can type text in it and call on all the formatting commands on the (Drawing) Format tab. These commands are explained in Book VIII, Chapter 4. It also describes how to turn a shape such as a circle or triangle into a text box (create the shape, right-click it and choose Add Text, and start typing).

TIP

Here's a neat trick: You can turn the text in a text box on its side so that it reads from top to bottom or bottom to top, not from left to right. Create a text box, enter the text, go to the (Drawing Tools) Format tab, click the Text Direction button, and choose a Rotate option on the drop-down list.

Making text flow from text box to text box

As I mention earlier, you can link text boxes so that the text in the first box is pushed into the next one when it fills up. To link text boxes, start by creating all the text boxes that you need. You cannot link one text box to another if the second text box already has text in it. Starting on the (Drawing Tools) Format tab, follow these directions to link text boxes:

- **Creating a forward link:** Click a text box and then click the Create Link button to create a forward link. The pointer changes into a very odd-looking pointer that is supposed to look like a pitcher. Move the odd-looking pointer to the next text box in the chain and click there to create a link.
- **Breaking a link:** To break a link, click the text box that is to be the last in the chain, and then click the Break Link button.

Dropping In a Drop Cap

A *drop cap* is a large capital letter that "drops" into the text, as shown in Figure 6-10. Drop caps appear at the start of chapters in many books, this book included, and you can find other uses for them, too. In Figure 6-10, one drop cap marks the A side of a list of songs on a homemade music CD.

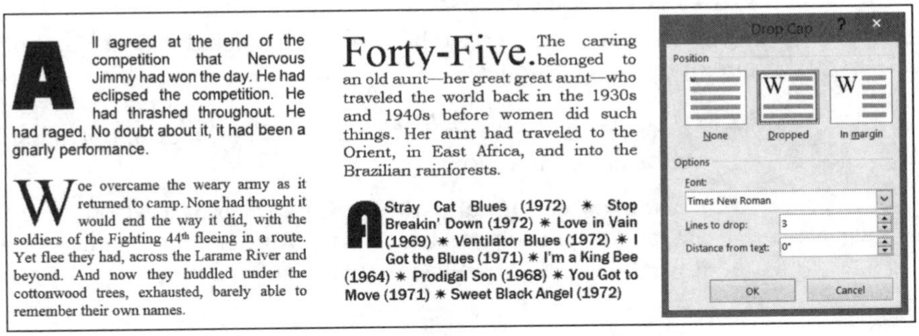

Figure 6-10: Creating a drop cap.

To create a drop cap, start by clicking anywhere in the paragraph whose first letter you want to "drop." If you want to "drop" more than one character at the start of the paragraph, select the characters. Then go to the Insert tab, click the Drop Cap button, and choose Dropped or Drop Cap Options. Choosing Drop Cap Options opens the Drop Cap dialog box shown in Figure 6-10, where you can experiment with these options:

- **Position:** Choose which kind of drop cap you want. In Margin places the drop cap to the left of the paragraph, in the margin, not in the paragraph itself.
- **Font:** Choose a font from the Font drop-down list. Choose a different font from the text in the paragraph.
- **Lines to Drop:** Enter the number of text lines to drop the letter.
- **Distance from Text:** Keep the 0 setting unless you're dropping an *I*, *1*, or other skinny letter or number.

Click the Drop Cap button and choose None to remove a drop cap.

Watermarking for the Elegant Effect

A *watermark* is a pale image or set of words that appears behind text on each page in a document. True watermarks are made in the paper mold and can be seen only when the sheet of paper is held up to a light. You can't make true watermarks with Word, but you can make the closest thing to them that can be attained in the debased digital world in which we live. Figure 6-11 shows two pages of a letter in which the paper has been "watermarked." Watermarks are one of the easiest formatting tricks to accomplish in Word.

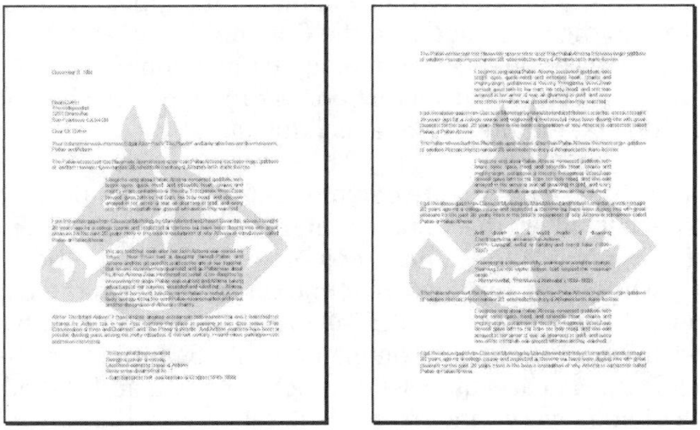

Figure 6-11: Watermarks showing faintly on the page.

To create a watermark for every page of a document, go to the Design tab and click the Watermark button. From the drop-down list, create your watermark:

- **Prefabricated text watermark:** Scroll down the list and choose an option. You will find "Confidential," "Urgent," and other text watermarks.
- **Picture watermark:** Choose Custom Watermark, and in the Printed Watermark dialog box, click the Picture Watermark option button. Then click the Select Picture button. In the Insert Pictures dialog box, select a graphics file to use for the watermark and click the Insert button. Back in the Printed Watermark dialog box, choose or enter a size for the graphic on the Scale drop-down menu. I don't recommend unchecking the Washout check box — do so and your image may be so dark it obscures the text.
- **Text watermark:** Choose Custom Watermark and, in the Printed Watermark dialog box, click the Text Watermark option button. Type a word or two in the Text box (or choose an entry from the drop-down menu). Choose a font, size, color, and layout for the words. If you uncheck the Semitransparent check box, you do so at your peril because the watermark words may be too dark on the page.

To tinker with a watermark, reopen the Printed Watermark dialog box. To remove a watermark, click the Watermark button and choose Remove Watermark on the drop-down list.

Putting Newspaper-Style Columns in a Document

Columns look great in newsletters and similar documents. And you can pack a lot of words in columns. I should warn you, however, that the Columns command is only good for creating columns that appear on the same page. Running text to the next page with the Columns command can be problematic. If you're serious about running text in columns, I suggest either constructing the columns from text boxes or using Publisher, another Office program. Book IX, Chapter 3 explains Publisher.

TIP

Sometimes it is easier to create columns by creating a table or by using text boxes, especially when the columns refer to one another. In a two-column résumé, for example, the left-hand column often lists job titles ("Facsimile Engineer") whose descriptions are found directly across the page in the right-hand column ("I Xeroxed stuff all day long"). Creating a two-column résumé with Word's Columns command would be futile because making the columns line up is nearly impossible. Each time you add something to the left-hand column, everything *snakes* — it gets bumped down in the left-hand column and the right-hand column as well.

Doing the preliminary work

TIP

Before you put text in newspaper-style columns, write it. Take care of the spelling, grammar, and everything else first because making text changes to words after they've been arranged in columns is difficult. Columns appear only in Print Layout view.

Running text into columns

To "columnize" text, select it, go to the Layout tab, and click the Columns button. Then either choose how many columns you want on the drop-down list or choose More Columns to create columns of different widths.

You see the Columns dialog box shown in Figure 6-12 if you choose More Columns. Here are the options in the Columns dialog box:

- **Preset columns:** Select a Presets box to choose a preset number of columns. Notice that, in some of the boxes, the columns aren't of equal width.

Figure 6-12: Running text in columns.

- **Number of columns:** If a preset column doesn't do the trick, enter the number of columns you want in the Number of Columns box.
- **Line between columns:** A line between columns is mighty elegant and is difficult to draw on your own. Choose the Line Between check box to run lines between columns.
- **Columns width:** If you uncheck the Equal Column Width check box, you can make columns of unequal width. Change the width of each column by using the Width boxes.
- **Space between columns:** Enter a measurement in the Spacing boxes to determine how much space appears between columns.
- **Start new column:** This check box is for putting empty space in a column, perhaps to insert a text box or picture. Place the cursor where you want the empty space to begin, choose This Point Forward on the Apply To drop-down list, and click the Start New Column check box.

Word creates a new section if you selected text before you columnized it, and you see your columns in Print Layout view. Chapter 2 of this mini-book explains sections.

To "break" a column in the middle and move text to the next column, click where you want the column to break and press Ctrl+Shift+Enter or go to the Layout tab, click the Breaks button, and choose Column on the drop-down list.

Landscape Documents

A *landscape* document is one in which the page is wider than it is long, like a painting of a landscape, as shown on the right side of Figure 6-13. Most documents, like the pages of this book, are printed in *portrait* style, with the short sides of the page on the top and bottom. However, creating a landscape document is sometimes a good idea because a landscape document stands out from the usual crowd of portrait documents and sometimes printing in landscape mode is necessary to fit text, tables, and graphics on a single page.

You're ready to go if you want to turn all the pages in your document into landscape pages. To turn some of the pages into landscape pages, create a section for the pages that need to appear in Landscape mode and click in the section (Chapter 2 of this mini-book explains sections). Starting on the Layout tab, use these techniques to change the page orientation:

- **Landscape pages:** Click the Orientation button and choose Landscape on the drop-down list.
- **Portrait pages:** Click the Orientation button and choose Portrait on the drop-down list.

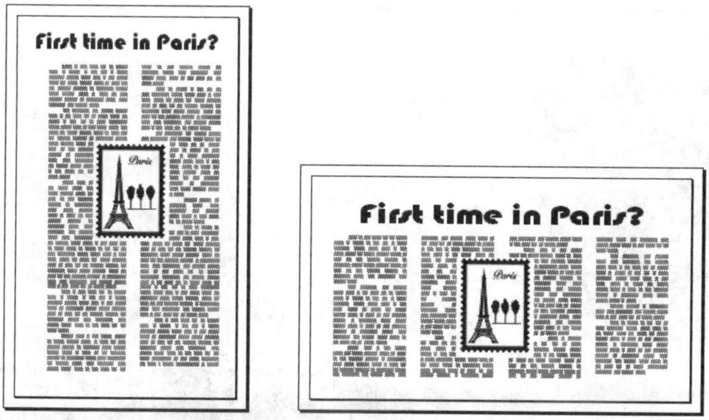

Figure 6-13: A portrait document (left) and landscape document (right).

Printing on Different Size Paper

You don't have to print exclusively on standard 8.5 x 11 paper; you can print on legal-size paper and other sizes of paper as well. A newsletter with an unusual shape really stands out in a crowd and gets people's attention. Go to the Layout tab and use one of these techniques to change the size of the paper on which you intend to print a document:

- Click the Size button and choose an option on the drop-down list.
- Click the Size button and choose More Paper Sizes. You see the Paper tab in the Page Setup dialog box. Choose a setting on the Paper Size drop-down list. If none of the settings suits you, enter your own settings in the Width and Height text boxes.

Showing Online Video in a Document

When words and pictures don't do the job, consider making video a part of your document with the Online Video command. This command establishes a link between your document and a video on the Internet. You see the first frame of the video in the Word document, as shown in Figure 6-14. Clicking the Play button in this frame opens a video viewer so you can play the video.

To insert an online video in a document, go to the Insert tab and click the Online Video button. The Insert Video dialog box appears. Use it to search for an online video with the Bing search engine, search for an online video at YouTube, or enter the video's online address. As shown in Figure 6-14, the search results window gives you the opportunity to preview a video by clicking the View Larger button.

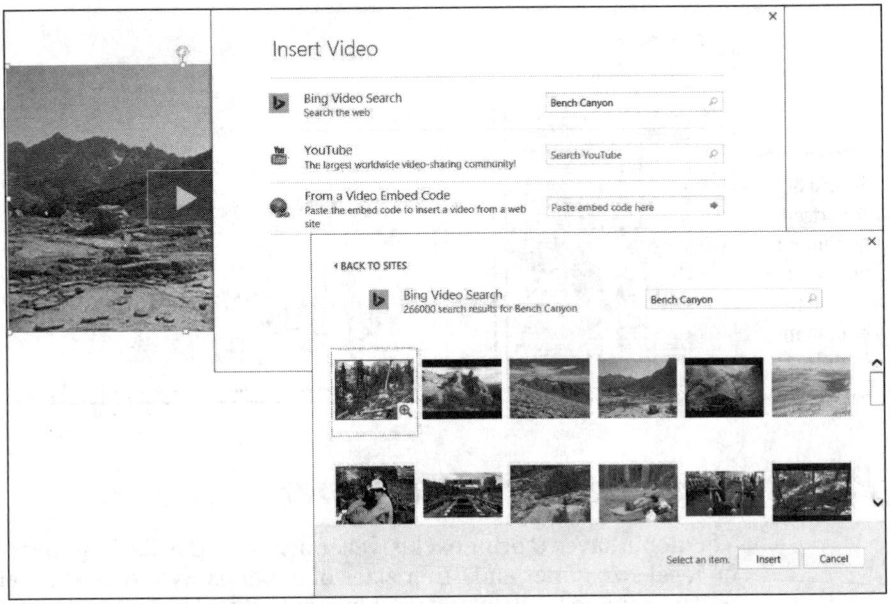

Figure 6-14: Making video part of a Word document.

Chapter 7: Getting Word's Help with Office Chores

In This Chapter

- **Commenting on others' work**
- **Tracking revisions to documents**
- **Printing envelopes and labels**
- **Mail merging for form letters and bulk mailing**

This chapter is dedicated to the proposition that everyone should get their work done sooner. It explains how Word can be a help in the office, especially when it comes to working on team projects. This chapter explains comments, using revision marks to record edits, and mail merging, Microsoft's term for generating form letters, labels, and envelopes for mass mailings.

Book X explains another way to collaborate on team projects — by collaborating online with OneDrive.

Highlighting Parts of a Document

In my work, I often use the Highlight command to mark paragraphs and text that need reviewing later. And on rainy days, I use it to splash color on my documents and keep myself amused. Whatever your reasons for highlighting text in a document, go to the Home tab and use one of these techniques to do it:

- **Select text and then choose a highlighter:** Select the text you want to highlight, and then either click the Text Highlight Color button (if it's displaying your color choice) or open the drop-down list on the button and choose a color.
- **Choose a highlighter and then select text:** Either click the Text Highlight Color button (if it's already displaying your color choice) or open the drop-down list on the button and choose a color. The pointer changes into a crayon. Drag across the text you want to highlight. When you finish highlighting, click the Text Highlight Color button again or press Esc.

To remove highlights, select the highlighted text, open the drop-down list on the Text Highlight Color button, and choose No Color. Select the entire document (press Ctrl+A) and choose No Color to remove all highlights from a document.

Highlight marks are printed along with the text. To keep highlights from being printed, go to the File tab, choose Options, visit the Display category in the Word Options dialog box, and deselect the Show Highlighter Marks check box.

Commenting on a Document

People collaborating on a document can write comments and in so doing prove that two heads are better than one. Comments give you the opportunity to suggest improvements, plead with your collaborators, debate your editor, and praise others, all in the interest of turning out a better document.

To enter and read comments, go to the Review tab, as shown in Figure 7-1. These pages explain how to enter comments, examine comments, hide and display comments, and do all else that pertains to commenting on a document.

Entering a comment

In my experience, Print Layout view is the best view for entering and reading comments. Use these techniques to write comments:

- **Entering a comment:** Select the word or sentence that you want to comment on. Then, on the Review tab, click the New Comment button and enter your comment in a balloon on the right side of the screen or the Revision pane on the left side.
- **Commenting on a comment:** Display the comment that needs commentary in a balloon and click the button in the upper-right corner of the balloon (see Figure 7-1). Space (and your name) appears in the balloon so that you can write a comment about the comment. Collaborators can discuss topics in this way.

REMEMBER

Whether you enter and read comments in the Revisions pane on the left side of the screen or balloons on the right side depends on your Show Markup choice. Click the Show Markup button on the Review tab, choose Balloons, and choose an option on the submenu to display comments in different ways. See "Viewing and displaying comments," the next topic in this chapter, for details.

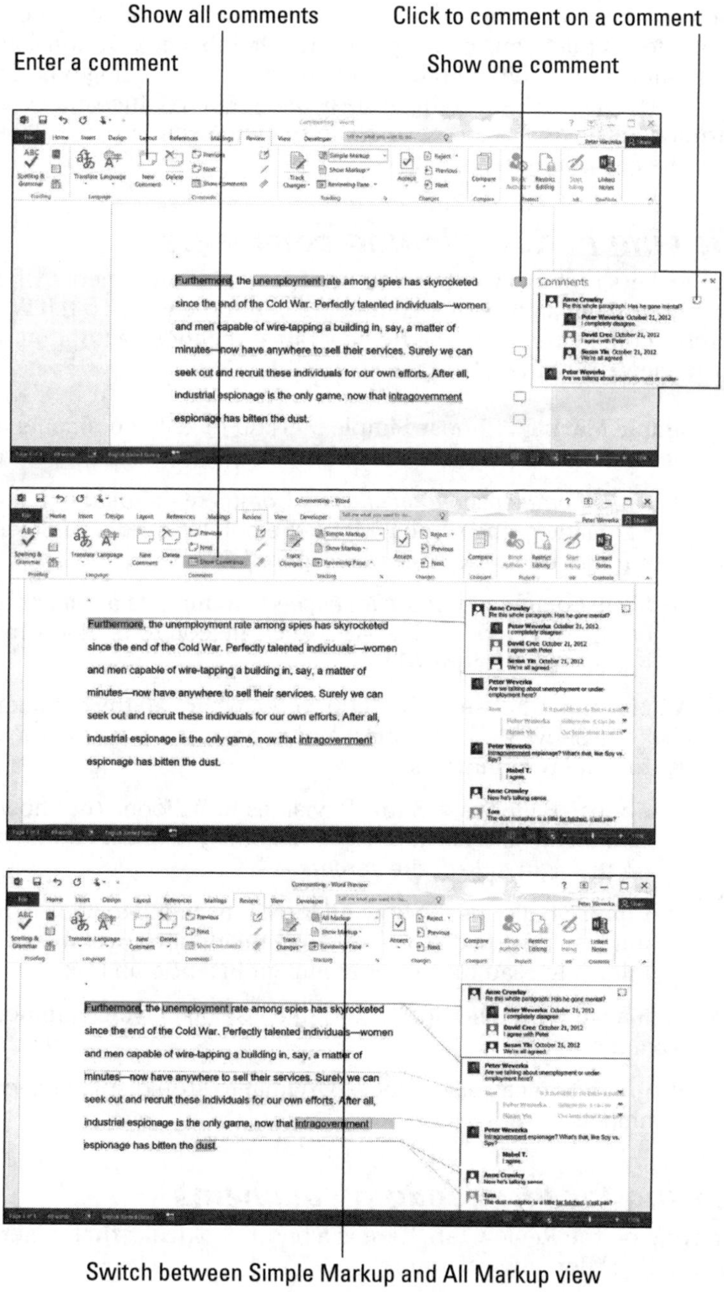

Figure 7-1: Comments as icons in Simple Markup view (top); comments shown in Simple Markup view (middle); comments in All Markup view (bottom).

Each comment lists the name of the person who wrote it. If a comment you wrote doesn't list your name, go to the File tab, click Options, and enter your user name in the General tab of the Word Options dialog box. Select the Always Use These Values Regardless of Sign In to Office check box if you are enrolled in Office 365 and you sign in to Office.com under a different name than the one you entered.

Viewing and displaying comments

The makers of Word want you to be able to view comments when necessary but shunt them aside when comments get in the way. To tell Word how to display comments, go to the Review tab and choose an option on the Display for Review drop-down list (see Figure 7-1):

- **Simple Markup:** Choose Simple Markup to keep comments from crowding the screen. Then click the Show Comments button if necessary:
  - *Show Comments button clicked.* Comments appear in balloons on the right side of the screen. Move the pointer over a comment to see what it refers to on the page (see Figure 7-1).
  - *Show Comments button not clicked.* Comments are marked by icons on the right side of the page. Click an icon to read a comment in a balloon (see Figure 7-1).
- **All Markup:** Choose All Markup to see where all the comments are. Then click the Show Markup button and choose an option on the drop-down list to display comments:
  - Choose Balloons ⇨ Show Revisions in Balloons (or Show Only Comments and Formatting in Balloons) to show comments in balloons on the right side of the screen.
  - Choose Balloons ⇨ Show All Revisions Inline to show commenters' initials in the text. You can move the pointer over a commenter's initials to read his or her comment in a pop-up box.
- **No Markup:** Choose No Markup to cease displaying comment icons or comments.
- **Original:** You can also choose Original to stop displaying icons and comments.

Caring for and feeding comments

Starting on the Review tab, here is a handful of tasks that deserve comment (if you'll pardon my little pun):

- **Editing a comment:** Display the comment and edit its text.
- **Going from comment to comment:** Click the Previous or Next button.

- **Displaying comments by a specific reviewer:** Click the Show Markup button, choose Specific People, and deselect All Reviewers on the submenu. Then click the button again, choose Specific People, and choose the name of a reviewer. To see all comments again, click the Show Markup button and choose Specific People ➪ All Reviewers.
- **Deleting comments:** Delete one, all, or some comments:
  - **Deleting a comment:** Select a comment and click the Delete button. You can also right-click and choose Delete Comment.
  - **Deleting all the comments in the document:** Open the drop-down list on the Delete button and choose Delete All Comments in Document.
  - **Deleting comments made by one or two people:** First, isolate comments made by people whose comments you want to delete (see "Displaying comments by a particular reviewer" earlier in this list). Then open the drop-down list on the Delete button and choose Delete All Comments Shown.
- **Marking a comment as done:** Rather than delete a comment, you can mark it as done to keep a record of it. Comments marked this way are shown in gray text. To mark a comment as done, right-click it and choose Mark Comment Done on the shortcut menu.
- **Drawing to make a comment:** Click the Ink Comment button. Then draw on the comment in the place that Word provides. You can click the Eraser button to erase your doodlings.

Tracking Changes to Documents

When many hands go into revising a document, figuring out who made changes to what is impossible. What's more, it's impossible to tell what the first draft looked like. Sometimes it's hard to tell whether the changes were for good or ill. To help you keep track of changes to documents, Word offers the Track Changes command. When this command is in effect:

- Changes to a document are recorded in a different color, with one color for each reviewer.
- New text is underlined; deleted text is crossed out.

By moving the pointer over a change, you can read the name of the person who made it as well as the words that were inserted or deleted. You can see changes as well in the Reviewing pane. As you review changes, you can accept or reject each change. You can also see the original document, a copy with revisions, or the final copy simply by making a choice from the Display for Review drop-down list on the Review tab.

To give you an idea of what tracking marks look like, Figure 7-2 shows the first two sentences of Vladimir Nabokov's autobiography *Speak, Memory* with marks showing where the author made additions and deletions to the original draft.

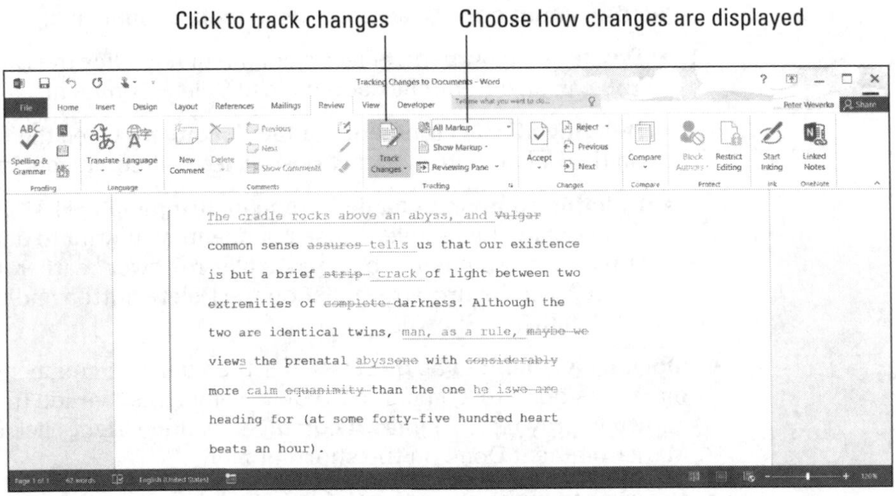

Figure 7-2: A document with change marks and changes showing.

Telling Word to start marking changes

To start tracking where editorial changes are made to a document, turn Track Changes on. You can do that with one of these techniques:

- On the Review tab, click the Track Changes button (or open its drop-down list and choose Track Changes).
- Press Ctrl+Shift+E.
- On the status bar, click the words *Track Changes* so that the status bar reads "Track Changes: On." If you don't see the words *Track Changes* on the status bar and you want to see them there, right-click the status bar and select Track Changes on the pop-up menu.

To stop tracking changes to a document, click the Track Changes button again, press Ctrl+Shift+E again, or click the words *Track Changes* on the status bar so that the words read "Track Changes: Off."

Reading and reviewing a document with change marks

Reading and reviewing a document with change marks isn't easy. The marks can get in the way. Fortunately, Word offers the Display for Review menu on the Review tab for dealing with documents that have been scarred by change marks. Choose options on the Display for Review drop-down list to get a better idea of how your changes are taking shape:

- **Get an idea where changes were made:** Choose Simple Markup. A vertical line appears on the left side of the page to show where changes were made. (This line doesn't appear in Draft and Outline view.)
- **See where additions and deletions were made:** Choose All Markup (refer to Figure 7-2). Additions are underlined and deleted text is crossed through.
- **See what the document would look like if you accepted all changes:** Choose No Markup. All change marks are stripped away and you see what your document would look like if you accepted all changes made to it.
- **See what the document would look like if you rejected all changes:** Choose Original. You get the original, pristine document back.

Requiring your collaborators to track changes

As well as insist that your collaborators track the changes they make to a document, you can compel them to do so. You can lock your document so that all editorial changes made to it are tracked with revision marks.

To lock a document against anyone's making changes without the changes being tracked, go to the Review tab, open the drop-down list on the Track Changes button, and choose Lock Tracking. Then enter and reenter a password in the Lock Tracking dialog box.

All changes are tracked automatically in a document that has been locked against anyone's turning off the track changes mechanism.

To unlock a document so that you and your collaborators can once again turn the track changes feature on or off, open the drop-down list on the Track Changes button and deselect Lock Tracking. Then enter the password in the Unlock Tracking dialog box.

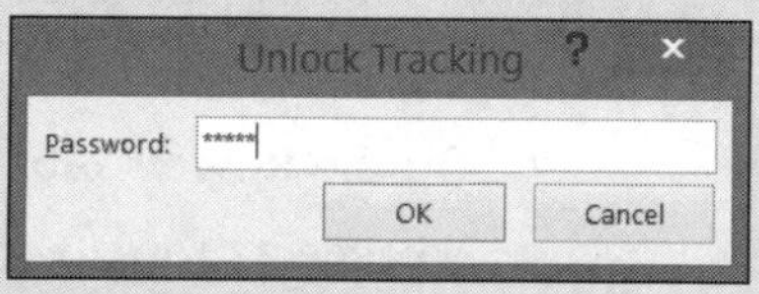

Marking changes when you forgot to turn on change marks

Suppose that you write the first draft of a document and someone revises it but that someone doesn't track changes. How can you tell where changes were made? For that matter, suppose that you get hold of a document, you change it around without tracking changes, and now you want to see what your editorial changes did to the original copy. I have good news: You can compare documents to see the editorial changes that were made to them. Word offers a command for comparing the original document to a revised edition and another for comparing two different revised editions of the same document.

After you make the comparison, Word creates a third document similar to the one shown in Figure 7-3. In the Source Document pane on the right side of the window, you can see the documents you're comparing. The Compared Document pane, meanwhile, shows who made changes and what those changes are.

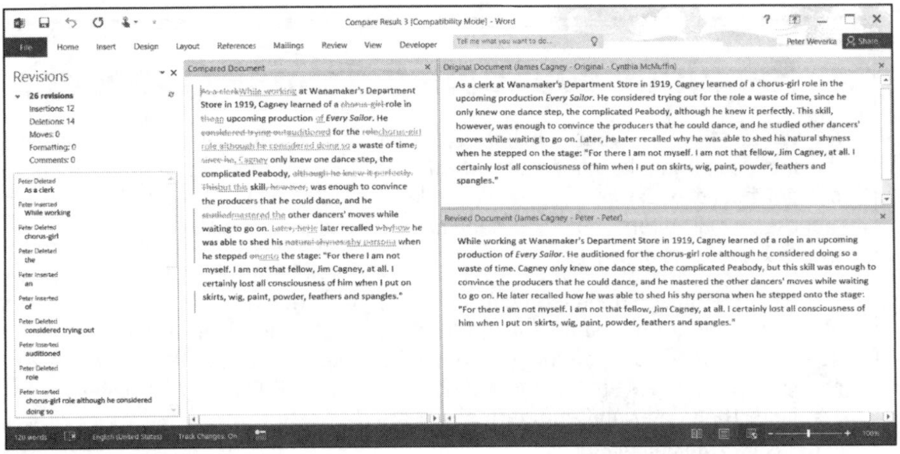

Figure 7-3: Comparing documents to see where editorial changes were made.

Follow these steps to compare an original document to its revised copy or two revised copies:

1. **On the Review tab, click the Compare button.**

   You see a drop-down list (depending on the size of your screen, you may have to choose Compare more than once to get to the drop-down list).

2. **On the drop-down list, choose Compare to compare the original document to its revised edition; choose Combine to compare two editions of the same document that were revised separately.**

   You see the Compare Documents dialog box or the Combine Documents dialog box, as shown in Figure 7-4. These dialog boxes work the same way.

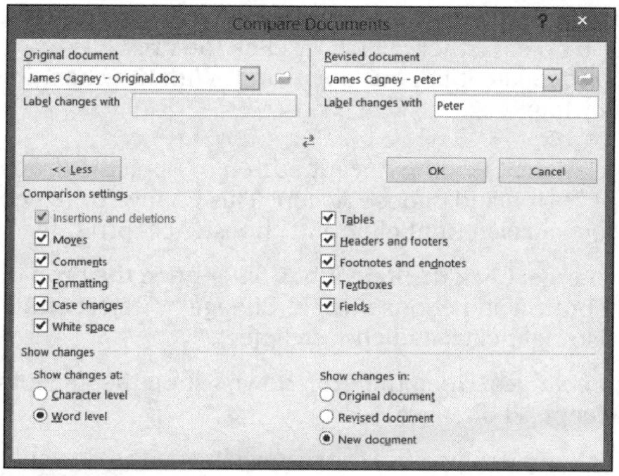

Figure 7-4: Choosing which documents to compare.

3. **On the Original Document drop-down list, choose the original or a revised edition of the document; if its name isn't there, click the Browse button and select it in the Open dialog box.**
4. **On the Revised Document drop-down list, choose a revised copy, or else click the Browse button and select it in the Open dialog box.**
5. **Click the More button.**

   You see more options for comparing or combining documents.
6. **If you so desire, deselect Comparison Settings check boxes to tell Word what you want to compare.**
7. **Click OK.**

   Word creates a new document that shows where changes were made to the original copy or where the revised copies differ (refer to Figure 7-3). You can save this document if you want to.

TIP

To help with document comparisons, you can tell Word what to display in the Source Documents pane on the right side of the screen. On the Review tab, click the Compare button, choose Show Source Documents, and choose an option on the submenu. You can hide the source documents, show the original document, show the revised edition, or show both editions.

Accepting and rejecting changes to a document

TIP

Word gives you the chance to accept or reject changes one at a time, but in my considerable experience with changes (I am a sometime editor), I find that the best way to handle changes is to go through the document, reject the changes you don't care for, and when you have finished reviewing, accept all the remaining changes. That way, reviewing changes is only half as tedious.

Whatever your preference for accepting or rejecting changes, start by selecting a change. To do so, either click it or click the Previous or Next button on the Review tab to locate it in your document. With the change selected, do one of the following:

- **Accept a change:** Click the Accept button or open the drop-down list on the Accept button and choose Accept This Change or Accept and Move to Next. You can also right-click and choose Accept.
- **Reject a change:** Click the Reject button or open the drop-down list on the Reject button and choose Reject Change or Reject and Move to Next. You can also right-click and choose Reject.
- **Accept all changes:** Open the drop-down list on the Accept button and choose Accept All Changes.
- **Reject all changes:** Open the drop-down list on the Reject button and choose Reject All Changes.

TIP

By way of the Accept and Reject buttons, you can also accept or reject all changes made by a single reviewer. First, isolate the reviewer's changes by clicking the Show Markup button, choosing Specific People, and selecting a reviewer's name. Then open the drop-down list on the Accept or Reject button, and choose Accept All Changes Shown or Reject All Changes Shown.

Printing an Address on an Envelope

Printing addresses gives correspondence a formal, official look. It makes you look like a big shot. (Later in this chapter, "Churning Out Letters, Labels, and Envelopes for Mass Mailings" explains how to print more than one envelope at a time). Here's how to print an address and a return address on an envelope:

1. **To save a bit of time, open the document that holds the letter you want to send; then select the name and address of the person you want to send the letter to.**

   By doing so, you save yourself from having to type the address. However, you don't have to open a document to start with.

2. **On the Mailings tab, click the Envelopes button (you may have to click the Create button first, depending on the size of your screen).**

   The Envelopes tab of the Envelopes and Labels dialog box appears, as shown in Figure 7-5.

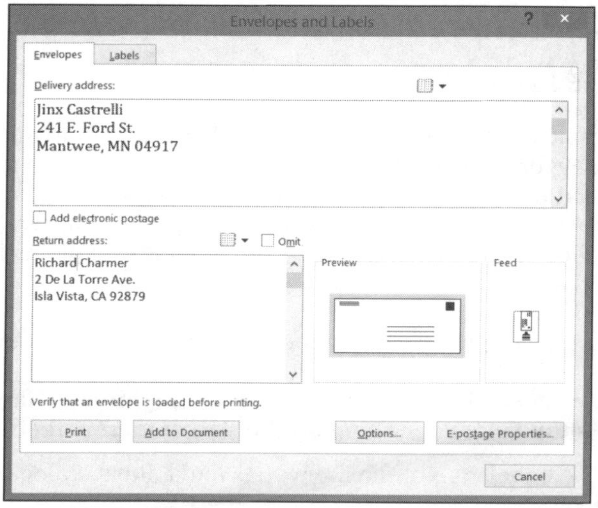

Figure 7-5: Printing on an envelope.

3. **Enter a name and address in the Delivery Address box (the address is already there if you selected it in Step 1).**
4. **Enter your return address in the Return Address box, if you want.**
5. **Click the Omit check box if you don't want your return address to appear on the envelope.**
6. **Click the Options button, and in the Envelope Options dialog box, tell Word what size your envelopes are and how your printer handles envelopes.**

   Tell Word about your envelopes on the Envelope Options and Printing Options tabs, and click OK:

   - *Envelope Options tab:* Choose an envelope size, a font for printing the delivery and return address, and a position for the addresses. The sample envelope in the Preview shows you what your position settings do when the envelope is printed.
   - *Printing Options tab:* Choose a technique for feeding envelopes to your printer. Consult the manual that came with your printer, select one of the Feed Method boxes, click the Face Up or Face Down option button, and open the Feed From drop-down list to tell Word which printer tray the envelope is in or how you intend to stick the envelope in your printer.
7. **Click the Print button.**

   All that trouble just to print an address on an envelope!

Printing a Single Address Label (Or a Page of the Same Label)

If you need to print a single label or a sheet of labels that are all the same, you can do it. Before you start printing, however, take note of the label's brand name and product number. You are asked about brand names and product numbers when you print labels. (Later in this chapter, "Churning Out Letters, Labels, and Envelopes for Mass Mailings" explains how to print multiple labels as part of a mass mailing.)

Follow these steps to print a single label or a sheet full of identical labels:

1. **On the Mailings tab, click the Labels button (you may have to click the Create button first, depending on the size of your screen).**

   You see the Labels tab of the Envelopes and Labels dialog box, as shown in Figure 7-6.

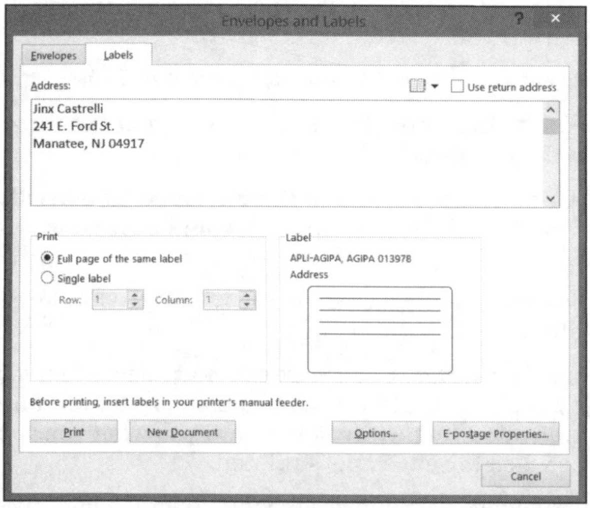

Figure 7-6: Printing labels.

2. **Enter the label — the name and address — in the Address box.**
3. **Either click the Options button or click the label icon in the Label box to open the Label Options dialog box.**
4. **In the Printer Information area, select either Continuous-Feed Printers or Page Printers to declare which kind of printer you have; on the Tray drop-down list, choose the option that describes how you will feed labels to your printer.**

5. **Open the Label Vendors drop-down list and choose the brand or type of labels that you have.**

   If your brand is not on the list, click the Details button, and describe your labels in the extremely confusing Information dialog box. A better way, however, is to measure your labels and see whether you can find a label of the same size by experimenting with Product Number and Label Information combinations.

6. **In the Product Number menu, select the product number listed on the box that your labels came in.**

   Look in the Label Information box on the right to make sure that the Height, Width, and Page Size measurements match those of the labels you have.

7. **Click OK to return to the Envelopes and Labels dialog box.**
8. **Choose a Print option.**

   Tell Word to print a single label or a sheet full of labels:

   - *Full Page of the Same Label:* Select this option button if you want to print a pageful of the same label. Likely, you'd choose this option to print a pageful of your own return addresses. Click the New Document button after you make this choice. Word creates a new document with a pageful of labels. Save and print this document on a sheet of labels.
   - *Single Label:* Select this option button to print one label. Then enter the row and column where the label is located and click the Print button.

Churning Out Letters, Envelopes, and Labels for Mass Mailings

Thanks to the miracle of computing, you can churn out form letters, labels, and envelopes for a mass mailing in the privacy of your home or office, just as the big companies do. Churning out form letters, envelopes, and labels is easy, as long as you take the time to prepare the source file. The *source file* is the file that the names and addresses come from. A Word table, an Excel worksheet, a Microsoft Access database table or query, or an Outlook Contacts list or Address Book can serve as the source file. (Book VI explains Outlook; Book III explains Excel; Book VII explains Access.)

To generate form letters, envelopes, or labels, you merge the form letter, envelope, or label document with a source file. Word calls this process *merging.* During the merge, names and addresses from the source file are plugged into the appropriate places in the form letter, envelope, or label document. When the merge is complete, you can either save the form letters, envelopes, or labels in a new file or start printing right away.

The following pages explain how to prepare the source file and merge addresses from the source file with a document to create form letters, labels, or envelopes. Then you discover how to print the form letters, labels, or envelopes after you have generated them.

TIP

Word offers a mail-merge wizard (*wizard* is Microsoft's name for a step-by-step procedure you can follow to accomplish a task). If you want to try your hand at using the wizard to complete a mail merge, go to the Mailings tab, click the Start Mail Merge button, and choose Step by Step Mail Merge Wizard on the drop-down list. Good luck to you!

Preparing the source file

If you intend to get addresses for your form letters, labels, or envelopes from an Outlook Contact List or Address Book on your computer, you're ready to go. However, if you haven't entered the addresses yet or you are keeping them in a Word table, Excel worksheet, Access database table, or Access query, make sure that the data is in good working order:

- **Word table:** Save the table in its own file and enter a descriptive heading at the top of each column. In the merge, when you tell Word where to plug in address and other data, you will do so by choosing a heading name from the top of a column. In Figure 7-7, for example, the column headings are Last Name, First Name, Street, and so on. (Chapter 4 of this mini-book explains how to construct a Word table.)

Last Name	First Name	Street	City	State	ZIP	Birthday
Creed	Hank	443 Oak St.	Atherton	CA	93874	July 31
Daws	Leon	13 Spruce St.	Colma	CA	94044	April 1
Maves	Carlos	11 Guy St.	Reek	NV	89201	February 28
Ng	Winston	1444 Unger Ave.	Colma	CA	94404	November 12
Smith	Jane	121 First St.	Colma	CA	94044	January 10
Weiss	Shirley	441 Second St.	Poltroon	ID	49301	May 4

Figure 7-7: A Word source table for a mail merge.

- **Excel worksheet:** Arrange the worksheet in table format with a descriptive heading atop each column and no blank cells in any columns. Word will plug in addresses and other data by choosing heading names.
- **Access database table or query:** Make sure that you know the field names in the database table or query where you keep the addresses. During the merge, you will be asked for field names. By the way, if you're comfortable in Access, query a database table for the records you will need. As you find out shortly, Word offers a technique for choosing only the records you want for your form letters, labels, or envelopes. However, by querying first in Access, you can start off with the records you need and spare yourself from having to choose records in Word.

A Word table, Excel worksheet, or Access table or query can include more than address information. Don't worry about deleting information that isn't required for your form letters, labels, and envelopes. As you find out soon, you get to decide which information to take from the Word table, Excel worksheet, or Access table or query.

Merging the document with the source file

After you prepare the source file, the next step in generating form letters, labels, or envelopes for a mass mailing is to merge the document with the source file. Follow these general steps to do so:

1. **Create or open a document.**
   - *Form letters:* Either create a new document and write your form letter, being careful to leave out the parts of the letter that differ from recipient to recipient, or open a letter you have already written and delete the addressee's name, the address, and other parts of the letter that are particular to each recipient.
   - *Envelopes:* Create a new document.
   - *Labels:* Create a new document.
2. **On the Mailings tab, click the Start Mail Merge button.**
3. **Choose Letters, Envelopes, or Labels on the drop-down list.**
4. **Prepare the groundwork for creating form letters, envelopes, or labels for a mass mailing.**

   What you do next depends on what kind of mass mailing you want to attempt:

   - *Form letters:* You're ready to go. The text of your form letter already appears onscreen if you followed the directions for creating and writing it in Step 1.
   - *Envelopes:* You see the Envelope Options dialog box, where, on the Envelope Options and Printing Options tabs, you tell Word what size envelope you will print on. See "Printing an Address on an Envelope," earlier in this chapter, for instructions about filling out these tabs (see Step 6). A sample envelope appears onscreen.
   - *Labels:* You see the Label Options dialog box, where you tell Word what size labels to print on. See "Printing a Single Address Label (Or a Page of the Same Label)" earlier in this chapter, if you need advice for filling out this dialog box (refer to Steps 4 through 7).

5. **Click the Select Recipients button and choose an option on the drop-down list to direct Word to your source file or the source of your address and data information.**

   Earlier in this chapter, "Preparing the source file" explains what a source file is. Your options are as follows:

   - *Addresses from a Word table, Excel worksheet, Access database table, or Access query:* Choose Use an Existing List. You see the Select Data Source dialog box. Locate the Word file, the Excel worksheet, or the Access database, select it, and click Open.

     If you select an Excel worksheet or Access database, you see the Select Table dialog box. Select the worksheet, table, or query you want and click the OK button.

   - **Addresses from Microsoft Outlook:** Choose Choose from Outlook Contacts (Outlook must be your default e-mail program to get addresses from Outlook). Then, in the Select Contacts dialog box, choose Contacts and click OK. The Mail Merge Recipients dialog box appears (skip to Step 7).

6. **Click the Edit Recipient List button.**

   The Mail Merge Recipients dialog box appears, as shown in Figure 7-8.

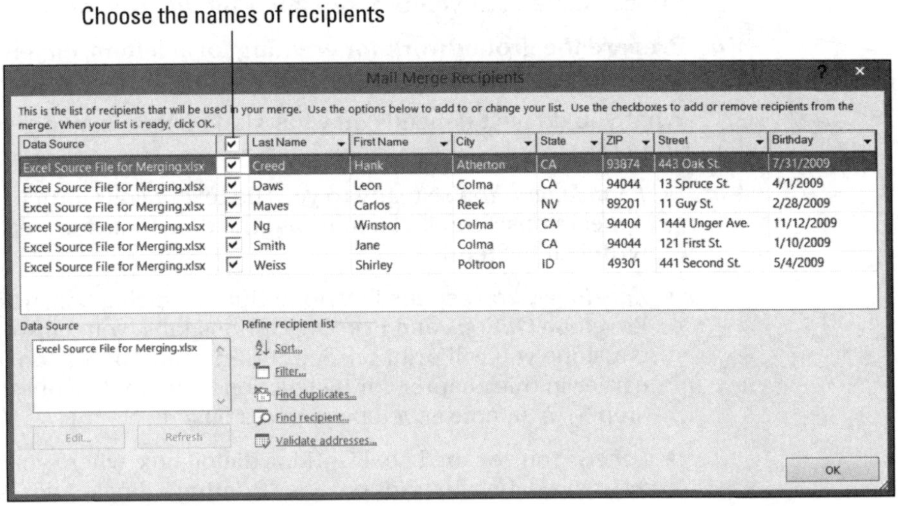

Figure 7-8: Choosing who gets mail.

7. **In the Mail Merge Recipients dialog box, select the names of people to whom you will send mail; then click OK.**

   To select recipients' names, check or uncheck the boxes on the left side of the dialog box.

8. **Enter the address block on your form letters, envelopes, or labels.**

   The *address block* is the address, including the recipient's name, company, title, street address, city, and ZIP Code. If you're creating form letters, click in the sample letter where the address block will go. If you're printing on envelopes, click in the middle of the envelope where the delivery address will go. Then follow these steps to enter the address block:

   a. Click the Address Block button. The Insert Address Block dialog box appears, as shown in Figure 7-9.

   b. Choose a format for entering the recipient's name in the address block. As you do so, watch the Preview window; it shows the actual names and addresses that you selected in Step 7.

   c. Click the Match Fields button. You see the Match Fields dialog box, shown in Figure 7-9.

   d. Using the drop-down lists on the right side of the dialog box, match the fields in your source file with the address block fields on the left side of the dialog box. In Figure 7-9, for example, the Street field is the equivalent of the Address 1 field on the left side of the dialog box, so Street is chosen from the drop-down list to match Address 1.

   e. Click OK in the Match Fields dialog box and the Insert Address Block dialog box. The `<<AddressBlock>>` field appears in the document where the address will go. Later, when you merge your document with the data source, real data will appear where the field is now. Think of a field as a kind of placeholder for data.

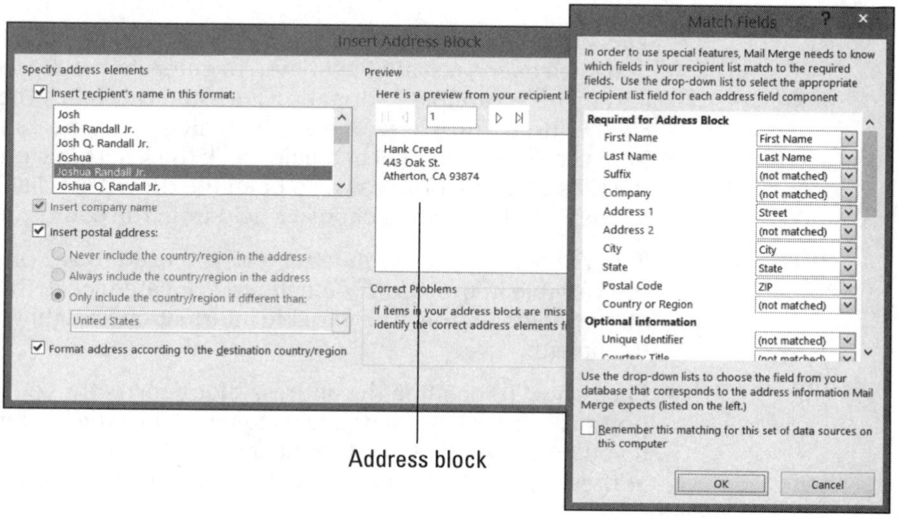

Figure 7-9: Creating the address block (left) and linking it with address fields (right).

9. **Click the Preview Results button on the Mailings tab to see real data rather than fields.**

   Now you can see clearly whether you entered the address block correctly. If you didn't enter it correctly, click the Match Fields button (it's in the Write & Insert Fields group) to open the Match Fields dialog box and make new choices.

10. **Put the finishing touches on your form letters, labels, or envelopes:**

    • *Form letters:* Click where the salutation ("Dear John") will go and then click the Greeting Line button. You see the Insert Greeting Line dialog box, shown in Figure 7-10. Make choices in this dialog box to determine how the letters' salutations will read.

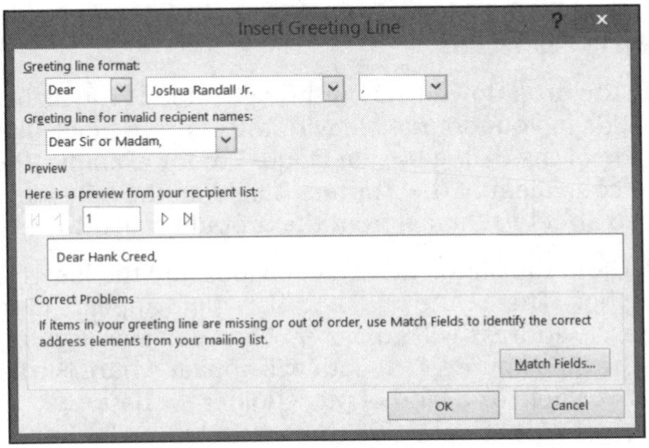

Figure 7-10: Entering the greeting.

The body of your form letter may well include other variable information such as names and birthdays. To enter that stuff, click in your letter where variable information goes and then click the Insert Merge Field button. The Insert Merge Field dialog box appears and lists fields from the source file. Select a field, click the Insert button, and click the Close button. (You can also open the drop-down list on the Insert Merge Field button and choose a field from the source file.)

If you're editing your form letter and you need to see precisely where the variable information you entered is located, click the Highlight Merge Fields button. The variable information is highlighted in your document.

    • *Envelopes:* To position the address block correctly, you may have to press the Enter key and tab keys to move it to the center of envelope. If you don't like the fonts or font sizes on the envelope, select an address, go to the Home tab, and change fonts and font sizes there.

To enter a return address, click in the upper-left corner of the envelope and enter it there.

- *Labels:* Click the Update Labels button to enter all recipients' labels in the sample document.

11. **Click the Next Record and Previous Record buttons on the Mailings tab to skip from recipient to recipient and make sure that you have entered information correctly.**

    These buttons are located in the Preview Results group. The items you see onscreen are the same form letters, envelopes, or labels you will see when you have finished printing. (Click the Preview Results button if you see field names rather than people's names and addresses.)

If an item is incorrect, open the source file and correct it there. When you save the source file, the correction is made in the sample document.

At last — you're ready to print the form letters, envelopes, or labels. Take a deep breath and keep reading.

Printing form letters, envelopes, and labels

After you have gone to the trouble to prepare the data file and merge it with the document, you're ready to print your form letters, envelopes, or labels. Start by loading paper, envelopes, or sheets of labels in your printer:

- **Form letters:** Form letters are easiest to print. Just put the paper in the printer.
- **Envelopes:** Not all printers are capable of printing envelopes one after the other. Sorry, but you probably have to consult the dreary manual that came with your printer to find out the correct way to load envelopes.
- **Labels:** Load the label sheets in your printer.

Now, to print the form letters, envelopes, or labels, save the material in a new document or send it straight to the printer:

- **Saving in a new document:** Click the Finish & Merge button and choose Edit Individual Documents (or press Alt+Shift+N). You see the Merge to New Document dialog box. Click OK. After Word creates the document, save it and print it. You can go into the document and make changes here and there before printing. In form letters, for example, you can write a sentence or two in different letters to personalize them.

- **Printing right away:** Click the Finish & Merge button and choose Print Documents (or press Alt+Shift+M) to print the form letters, envelopes, or labels without saving them in a document. Click OK in the Merge to Printer dialog box and then negotiate the Print dialog box.

TIP

Save the form letters, labels, or envelopes in a new document if you intend to print them at a future date or ink is running low on your printer and you may have to print in two or more batches. Saving in a new document permits you to generate the mass mailing without having to start all over again with the merge process and all its tedium.

Chapter 8: Tools for Reports and Scholarly Papers

In This Chapter

- **Putting a list in alphabetical order**
- **Working in Outline view**
- **Collapsing and expanding headings**
- **Creating a table of contents**
- **Indexing and cross-referencing your work**
- **Managing footnotes and endnotes**
- **Putting together a bibliography**

This chapter is hereby dedicated to everyone who has had to delve into the unknown and write a report about it. Writing reports, manuals, and scholarly papers is not easy. You have to explore uncharted territory. You have to contemplate the ineffable. And you have to write bibliographies and footnotes and maybe an index, too. Word cannot take you directly to uncharted territory, but it can take some of the sting out of it.

This chapter explains how to construct an outline, handle footnotes and endnotes, generate a table of contents, index a document, include cross-references in documents, and stitch together a bibliography.

Alphabetizing a List

Which comes first in an alphabetical list, "San Jose, California" or "San José, Costa Rica"? You could research the matter on your own, delving into various dictionaries and online references, or you could rely on the Sort button for the answer. Follow these steps to quickly alphabetize a list:

1. **Select the list.**
2. **On the Home tab, click the Sort button.**

   You see the Sort Text dialog box. The Then By options are for sorting tables; they don't concern you, because you're sorting a list.

3. **Click OK.**

   That was easy.

Outlines for Organizing Your Work

Outline view is a great way to see at a glance how your document is organized and whether you need to organize it differently. To take advantage of this feature, you must have assigned heading styles to the headings in your document (Chapter 3 of this mini-book explains styles). In Outline view, you can see all the headings in your document. If a section is in the wrong place, you can move it simply by dragging an icon or by clicking one of the buttons on the Outlining tab. To change the rank of a heading, simply click a button to promote or demote it.

To switch to Outline view, go to the View tab and click the Outline button (or press Alt+Ctrl+O). You see the Outlining tab, as shown in Figure 8-1. Rather than see text, you see the headings in your document, as well as the first line underneath each heading. Now you get a sense of what is in your document and whether it is organized well. By choosing an option from the Show Level drop-down list, you can decide which headings to see onscreen.

To leave Outline view when you're done reorganizing your document, click the Close Outline View button or a view button apart from Outline.

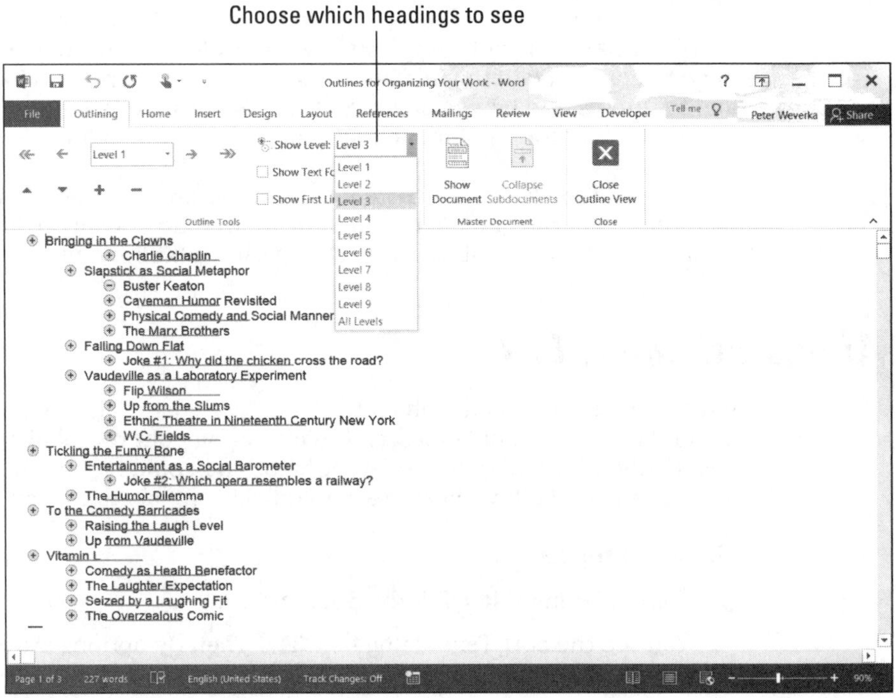

Figure 8-1: A document in Outline view.

Viewing the outline in different ways

Before you start rearranging your document in Outline view, get a good look at it:

- **View some or all headings:** Choose an option from the Show Level drop-down list (refer to Figure 8-1). To see only first-level headings, for example, choose Level 1. To see first-, second-, and third-level headings, choose Level 3. Choose All Levels to see all the headings.
- **View heading formats:** Click the Show Text Formatting check box. When this check box is selected, you can see how headings were formatted and get a better idea of their ranking in your document.
- **View or hide the subheadings in one section:** To see or hide the subheadings and text in one section of a document, select that section by clicking the plus sign beside its heading; then, click the Expand button (or press Alt+Shift+plus sign) to see the subheadings, or click the Collapse button (or press Alt+Shift+minus sign) to hide the subheadings. You can also double-click the plus sign beside a heading to view or hide its subheadings. (Later in this chapter, "Collapsing and Expanding Parts of a Document" explains how to view or hide subheadings in Print Layout view.)
- **View or hide paragraph text:** Click the Show First Line Only check box (or press Alt+Shift+L). When this check box is selected, you see only the first line in each paragraph. First lines are followed by an ellipsis (. . .) so you know that more text follows.

REMEMBER

Notice the plus and minus icons next to the headings and the text. A plus icon means that the item has subheadings and text under it. For example, headings almost always have plus icons because text comes after them. A minus icon means that nothing is found below the item in question. For example, body text usually has a minus icon because body text is lowest on the Outline totem pole.

Rearranging document sections in Outline view

Outline view is mighty convenient for moving sections in a document and for promoting and demoting sections. Use these techniques to rearrange and reorganize your document:

- **Move a section:** To move a section up or down in the document, select it and click the Move Up or Move Down button (or press Alt+Shift+↑ or Alt+Shift+↓). You can also drag the plus sign to a new location. If you want to move the subheadings and subordinate text along with the section, be sure to click the Collapse button to tuck all the subheadings and subtext into the heading before you move it.

- **Promote and demote headings:** Click the heading and then click the Promote button or Demote button (or press Alt+Shift+← or Alt+Shift+→). For example, you can promote a Level 3 heading to Level 2 by clicking the Promote button. Click the Promote To Heading 1 button to promote any heading to a first-level heading; click the Demote To Body text button to turn a heading into prose.
- **Choose a new level for a heading:** Click the heading and choose a new heading level from the Outline Level drop-down list.

Collapsing and Expanding Parts of a Document

As long as you apply heading styles (Heading 1, Heading 2, and so on) to headings, you can collapse and expand parts of a document. Click the Collapse button next to a heading to conceal its subheadings and subtext. Collapsing clears the screen of material that doesn't require your attention. Click the Expand button next to a heading to display its subheadings and subtext.

Figure 8-2 demonstrates expanding and collapsing. Use these techniques to collapse or expand the subheadings and subtext under a heading:

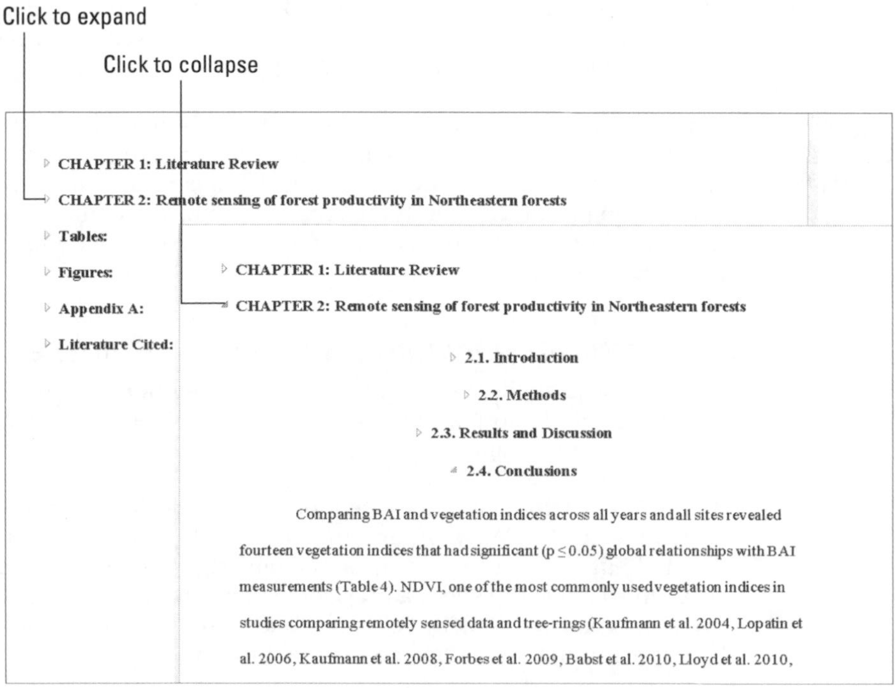

Figure 8-2: Collapse subheadings and subtext under a heading to keep the screen from getting crowded.

- **Collapsing:** Click the Collapse button to the left of a heading.
- **Expanding:** Move the pointer over a heading to display its Expand button; then click the Expand button.

You can collapse headings by default. On the Home tab, click the Paragraph group button to open the Paragraph dialog box. On the Indents and Spacing tab, choose an outline level and select the Collapsed by Default check box.

Generating a Table of Contents

A book-size document or long report isn't worth very much without a table of contents (TOC). How else can readers find what they're looking for? Generating a table of contents with Word is easy, as long as you give the headings in the document different styles — Heading 1, Heading 2, and so on (Chapter 3 of this mini-book explains styles). The beautiful thing about Word TOCs is the way they can be updated nearly instantly. If you add a new heading or erase a heading, you can update the TOC with a snap of your fingers. Moreover, you can quickly go from a TOC entry to its corresponding heading in a document by Ctrl+clicking the entry.

Before you create your TOC, create a new section in which to put it and number the pages in the new section with Roman numerals (Chapter 2 of this mini-book explains sections and how to number pages). TOCs, including the TOC in this book, are usually numbered in this way. The first entry in the TOC should cite page number 1. If you don't heed my advice and create a new section, the TOC will occupy the first few numbered pages of your document, and the numbering scheme will be thrown off.

Creating a TOC

To create a table of contents, place the cursor where you want the TOC to go, visit the References tab, and click the Table of Contents button. On the drop-down list, choose one of Word's automatic TOC options or choose Custom Table of Contents to fashion a TOC on your own in the Table of Contents dialog box. (See "Customizing a TOC," later in this chapter, for information about fashioning a TOC in the Table of Contents dialog box.)

Suppose that you want to copy a TOC to another document? To copy a TOC, drag the pointer down its left margin to select it, and then press Ctrl+Shift+F9. Next, use the Copy and Paste commands to copy the TOC to the other document. Because Word gives the text of TOCs the Hyperlink character style, you have to change the color of the text in the TOC (it's blue) and remove the underlines. As for the original TOC, you "disconnected" it from the headings in your document when you pressed Ctrl+Shift+F9. Press the Undo button to undo the effects of pressing Ctrl+Shift+F9 and "disconnecting" your TOC from the headers to which it refers.

Updating and removing a TOC

Follow these instructions to update and remove a TOC:

- **Updating a TOC:** If you add, remove, or edit a heading in your document, your TOC needs updating. To update it, go to the References tab and click the Update Table button, or click in the TOC and press F9. A dialog box asks how to update the TOC. Either update the page numbers only or update the entire table, including all TOC entries and page numbers.
- **Removing a TOC:** On the References tab, click the Table of Contents button and choose Remove Table of Contents on the drop-down list.

Customizing a TOC

Want to tinker with your TOC? You can number the headings in different ways and tell Word to include or exclude certain headings.

To change around a TOC, click inside it, go to the References tab, click the Table of Contents button, and choose Custom Table of Contents on the drop-down list. You see the Table of Contents dialog box shown in Figure 8-3. Choose options to declare which headings you want for your TOC and how you want to format it:

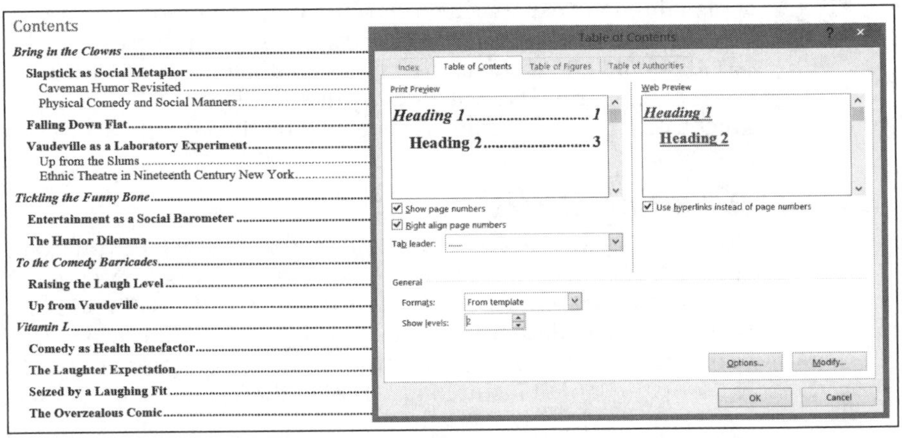

Figure 8-3: You can decide for yourself which headings go in a TOC and how it's numbered.

- **Showing page numbers:** Deselect the Show Page Numbers box if you want your TOC to be a simple list that doesn't refer to headings by page.
- **Aligning the page numbers:** Select the Right Align Page Numbers check box if you want page numbers to line up along the right side of the TOC so that the ones and tens line up under each other.

- **Choosing a tab leader:** A *leader* is the punctuation mark that appears between the heading and the page number the heading is on. If you don't want periods as the leader, choose another leader or choose (None).
- **Choosing a format:** Choose a format from the Formats drop-down list if you don't care to use the one from the template. Just be sure to watch the Print Preview and Web Preview boxes to see the results of your choice.
- **Choosing a TOC depth:** The Show Levels box determines how many heading levels are included in the TOC. Unless your document is a legal contract or other formal paper, enter a **2** or **3** here. A TOC is supposed to help readers find information quickly. Including lots of headings that take a long time to read through defeats the purpose of having a TOC.

Changing the structure of a TOC

Sometimes the conventional TOC that Word generates doesn't do the trick. Just because a heading has been given the Heading 1 style doesn't mean that it should receive first priority in the TOC. Suppose that you created another style called Chapter Title that should stand taller in the hierarchy than Heading 1. In that case, you need to rearrange the TOC so that Heading 1 headings rank second, not first, in the TOC hierarchy.

Use the Table of Contents Options and Style dialog boxes to tinker with a TOC. These dialog boxes are shown in Figure 8-4. To open them, click, respectively, the Options button or Modify button in the Table of Contents dialog box (refer to Figure 8-3).

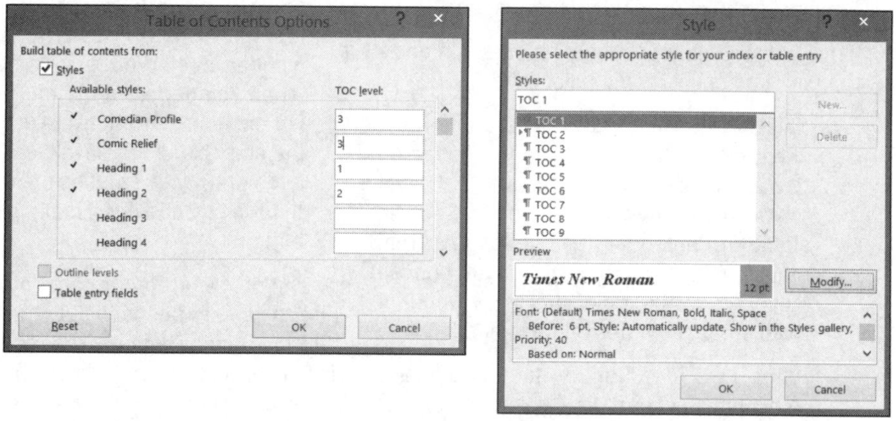

Figure 8-4: Changing a TOC's structure and formatting.

- **Assigning TOC levels to paragraph styles:** The Table of Contents Options dialog box lists each paragraph style in the document you're working in. For headings you want to appear in the TOC, enter a number in the TOC Level text box to determine the headings' rank. If headings assigned the Heading 1 style are to rank second in the TOC, for example, enter a 2 in Heading 1's TOC Level text box. You can exclude headings from a TOC by deleting a number in a TOC Level box.
- **Including table entry fields:** To include text you marked for entry in the TOC, select the Table Entry Fields check box in the Table of Contents Options dialog box (later in this chapter, the sidebar "Marking oddball text for inclusion in the TOC" explains how TOC fields work).
- **Changing the look of TOC entries:** The Style dialog box you see when you click the Modify button gives you the chance to choose new fonts, character styles, and font sizes for TOC entries if you generated your TOC from a template. Click the Modify button. Then, in the Style dialog box, choose options to format the TOC style. For example, click the Bold button to boldface TOC entries. (Chapter 3 of this mini-book explains modifying styles.)

Marking oddball text for inclusion in the TOC

Table of contents entries can refer to a particular place in a document, not just to headings that have been assigned heading styles. For example, you can include figure captions.

Use one of these techniques to mark an entry in your document for inclusion in the TOC:

- Click in the heading, figure caption, or whatnot. Next, click the Add Text button on the References tab and choose a TOC level on the drop-down list (the Do Not Show in Table of Contents option keeps text from being included in the TOC). If you choose Level 2, for example, the entry appears with other second-level headings.
- Click in a heading or text and press Alt+Shift+O. Then, in the Mark Table of Contents Entry dialog box, make sure that the words you want to appear in the TOC appear in the Entry text box (edit or enter the words if need be), and make sure that C (for Contents) appears in the Table Identifier box. In the Level box, enter a number to tell Word how to treat the entry when you generate the table of contents. For example, entering **1** tells Word to treat the entry like a first-level heading and give it top priority. A **3** places the entry with the third-level headings. Finally, click the Mark button.

When you generate the table of contents, be sure to include the oddball entries. To do that, click the Options button in the Table of Contents dialog box and, in the Table of Contents Options dialog box (refer to Figure 8-4), select the Table Entry Fields check box.

Indexing a Document

A good index is a thing of beauty. User manuals, reference works of any length, and reports that readers will refer to all require indexes. Except for the table of contents, the only way to find information in a long document is to look in the index. An index at the end of a company report reflects well on the person who wrote the report. It gives the appearance that the author put in a fair amount of time to complete the work, even if he or she didn't really do that.

An index entry can be formatted in many ways. You can cross-reference index entries, list a page range in an index entry, and break out an index entry into subentries and sub-subentries. To help you with your index, Figure 8-5 explains indexing terminology.

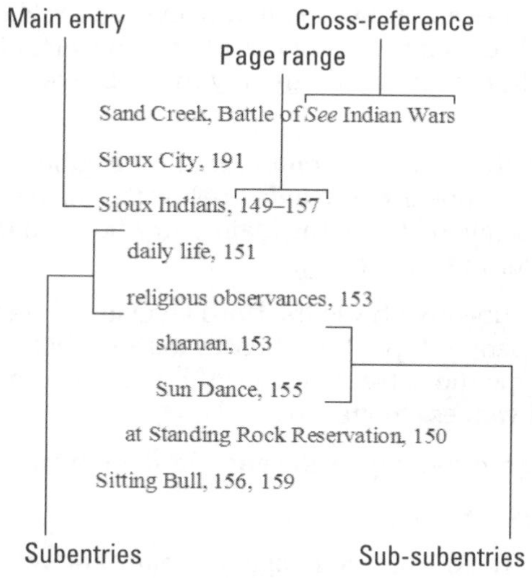

Figure 8-5: Different ways of handling index entries.

REMEMBER

Writing a good index entry is as hard as writing a good, descriptive heading. As you enter index entries in your document, ask yourself how you would look up information in the index, and enter your index entries accordingly.

Marking index items in the document

The first step in constructing an index is to mark index entries in your document. Marking index items yourself is easier than it seems. After you open the Mark Index Entry dialog box, it stays open so that you can scroll through your document and make entries.

1. **If you see a word or phrase in your document that you can use as a main, top-level entry, select it; otherwise, place the cursor in the paragraph or heading whose topic you want to include in the index.**

   You can save a little time by selecting a word, as I describe shortly.

2. **On the References tab, click the Mark Entry button (or press Alt+Shift+X).**

   The Mark Index Entry dialog box appears. If you selected a word or phrase, it appears in the Main Entry box.

3. **Choose how you want to handle this index entry (refer to Figure 8-5 to see the various ways to make index entries).**

   When you enter the text, don't put a comma or period after it. Word does that when it generates the index. The text that you enter appears in your index.

   - *Main Entry:* If you're entering a main, top-level entry, leave the text in the Main Entry box (if it's already there), type new text to describe this entry, or edit the text that's already there. Leave the Subentry box blank.
   - *Subentry:* To create a subentry, enter text in the Subentry box. The subentry text will appear in the index below the main entry text, so make sure that some text is in the Main Entry box and that the subentry text fits under the main entry.
   - *Sub-subentry:* A sub-subentry is the third level in the hierarchy. To create a sub-subentry, type the subentry in the Subentry box, enter a colon (:), and type the sub-subentry without entering a space, like so: **religious observances:shaman**.

4. **Decide how to handle the page reference in the entry.**

   Again, your choices are many:

   - *Cross-reference:* To go without a page reference and refer the reader to another index entry, click the Cross-Reference option button and type the other entry in the text box after the word *See.* What you type here appears in your index, so be sure that the topic you refer the reader to is really named in your index.
   - *Current Page:* Click this option to enter a single page number after the entry.
   - *Page Range:* Click this option if you're indexing a subject that covers several pages in your document. A page range index entry looks something like this: "Sioux Indians, 149–157." To make a page range entry, you must create a bookmark first. Leave the Mark Index Entry dialog box, select the text in the page range, and press Ctrl+Shift+F5 or click the Bookmark button on the Insert tab. In the Bookmark dialog box, enter a name in the Bookmark Name box, and click the Add button. (Chapter 1 of this mini-book explains bookmarks.)

5. **You can boldface or italicize a page number or page range by clicking a Page Number Format check box.**

   In some indexes, the page or page range where the topic is explained in the most depth is italicized or boldfaced so that readers can get to the juiciest parts first.

6. **If you selected a single word or phrase in Step 1, you can click the Mark All button to have Word go through the document and mark all words that are identical to the one in the Main Entry box; click Mark to put this single entry in the index.**

   Click outside the Mark Index Entry dialog box and find the next topic or word that you want to mark for the index. Then click the Mark Entry button on the References tab and make another entry.

REMEMBER

A bunch of ugly field codes appear in your document after you mark an index entry. You can render them invisible by clicking the Show/Hide¶ button on the Home tab (or pressing Ctrl+Shift+8).

Generating the index

After you mark all the index entries, it's time to generate the index:

1. **Place the cursor where you want the index to go, most likely at the end of the document.**

   You might type the word **Index** at the top of the page and format the word in a decorative way.

2. **On the References tab, click the Insert Index button.**

   You see the Index dialog box shown in Figure 8-6.

3. **Choose options in the dialog box and click OK.**

   As you make your choices, watch the Print Preview box to see what happens.

Here are the options in the Index dialog box:

✦ **Type:** Choose Run-in if you want subentries and sub-subentries to run together; choose Indented to indent subentries and sub-subentries below main entries (refer to Figure 8-6).

✦ **Columns:** Stick with 2, unless you don't have subentries or sub-subentries and you can squeeze three columns on the page or you are working on a landscape document.

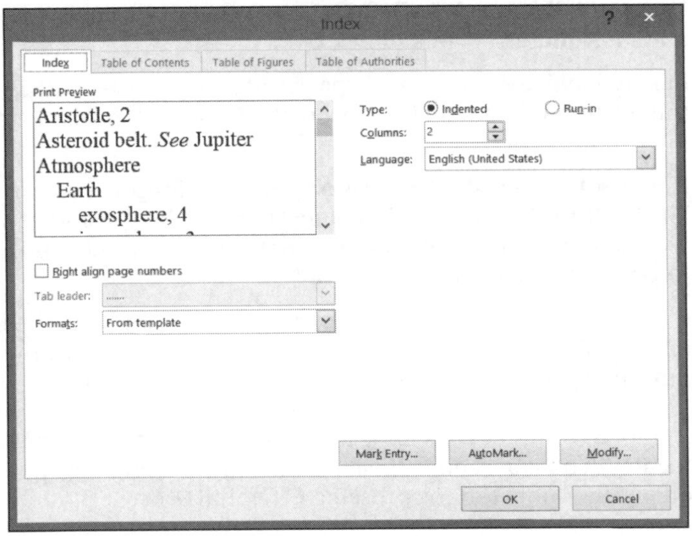

Figure 8-6: Generating an index.

- **Language:** Choose a language for the table, if necessary and if you have installed a foreign language dictionary. If you have installed the dictionary, you can run the spell-checker over your index and make sure that the entries are spelled correctly. (Chapter 5 of this mini-book explains foreign language dictionaries.)
- **Right Align Page Numbers:** Normally, page numbers appear right after entries and are separated from entries by a comma, but you can right-align the entries so that they line up under one another with this option.
- **Tab Leader:** Some index formats place a *leader* between the entry and the page number. A leader is a series of dots or dashes. If you're working with a format that has a leader, you can choose a leader from the drop-down list.
- **Formats:** Word offers a number of attractive index layouts. You can choose one from the list.
- **Modify:** Click this button if you're adventurous and want to create an index style of your own (Chapter 3 explains styles).

To update an index after you create or delete entries, click it and then click the Update Index button on the References tab or right-click the index and then choose Update Field on the shortcut menu.

Editing an index

After you generate an index, read it carefully to make sure that all entries are useful to readers. Inevitably, something doesn't come out right, but you can edit index entries as you would the text in a document. Index field markers are enclosed in curly brackets with the letters *XE* and the text of the index entry in quotation marks, like so: `{ XE: "Wovoka: Ghost Dance" }`. To edit an index marker, click the Show/Hide¶ button on the Home tab (or press Ctrl+Shift+8) to see the field markers and find the one you need to edit. Then delete letters or type letters as you would do normal text.

TIP

Here's a quick way to find index field markers: After clicking the Show/Hide¶ button, with the index fields showing, press Ctrl+G to open the Go To tab of the Find and Replace dialog box. In the Go To menu, choose Field; type **XE** in the Enter Field Name box, and click the Next button until you find the marker you want to edit. You can also use the Find command on the Home tab to look for index entries. Word finds index entries as well as text as long as you click the Show/Hide¶ button to display index fields in your document.

Putting Cross-References in a Document

Cross-references are very handy indeed. They tell readers where to go to find more information about a topic. The problem with cross-references, however, is that the thing being cross-referenced really has to be there. If you tell readers to go to a heading called "The Cat's Pajamas" on page 93, and neither the heading nor the page is really there, readers curse and tell you where to go, instead of the other way around.

Fortunately for you, Word lets you know when you make errant cross-references. You can refer readers to headings, page numbers, footnotes, endnotes, and plain-old paragraphs. And as long you create captions for your cross-references with the Insert Caption button on the References tab, you can also make cross-references to equations, figures, graphs, listings, programs, and tables. If you delete the thing that a cross-reference refers to and render the cross-reference invalid, Word tells you about it the next time you update your cross-references. Best of all, if the page number, numbered item, or text that a cross-reference refers to changes, so does the cross-reference.

Follow these steps to create a cross-reference:

1. **Write the first part of the cross-reference text.**

   For example, you could write **To learn more about these cowboys of the pampas, see page** and then type a blank space. The blank space separates the word *page* from the page number in the cross-reference. If you are referring to a heading, write something like **For more information, see** ". Don't type a blank space this time because the cross-reference heading text will appear right after the double quotation mark.

2. **On the References tab, click the Cross-Reference button.**

   The Cross-Reference dialog box appears, as shown in Figure 8-7.

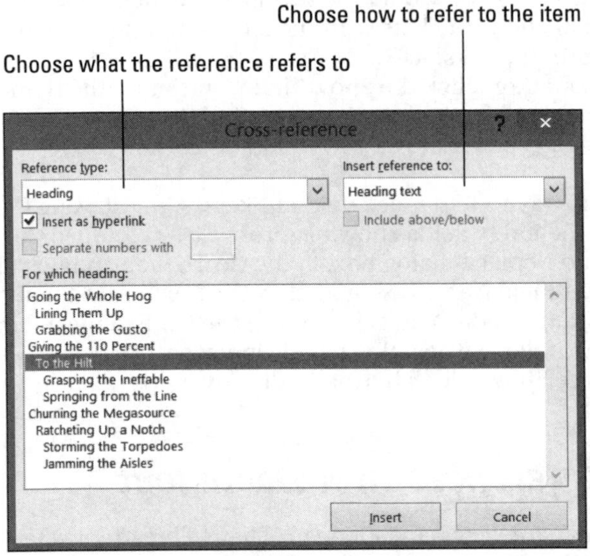

Figure 8-7: Entering a cross-reference.

3. **Choose what type of item you're referring to in the Reference Type drop-down list.**

   If you're referring to a plain old paragraph, choose Bookmark. Then click outside the dialog box, scroll to the paragraph you're referring to, and place a bookmark there. (Chapter 1 of this mini-book explains bookmarks.)

4. **Make a choice in the Insert Reference To box to refer to text, a page number, or a numbered item.**

   The options in this box are different, depending on what you chose in Step 3.

   - *Text:* Choose this option (Heading Text, Entire Caption, and so on) to include text in the cross-reference. For example, choose Heading Text if your cross-reference is to a heading.
   - *Number:* Choose this option to insert a page number or other kind of number, such as a table number, in the cross-reference.
   - *Include Above/Below:* Check this box to include the word *above* or *below* to tell readers where, in relation to the cross-reference, the thing being referred to is located in your document.

5. **If you wish, leave the check mark in the Insert as Hyperlink check box to create a hyperlink as well as a cross-reference.**

   With a hyperlink, someone reading the document onscreen can Ctrl+click the cross-reference and go directly to what it refers to.

6. **In the For Which box, tell Word where the thing you're referring to is located.**

   To do so, select a heading, bookmark, footnote, endnote, equation, figure, graph, or whatnot. In long documents, you almost certainly have to click the scroll bar to find the one you want.

7. **Click the Insert button and then click the Close button.**
8. **Back in your document, enter the rest of the cross-reference text, if necessary.**

When you finish creating your document, update all the cross-references. To do that, press Ctrl+A to select the entire document. Then press F9 or right-click in the document and choose Update Field on the shortcut menu.

TIP

If the thing referred to in a cross-reference is no longer in your document, you see `Error! Reference source not found` where the cross-reference should be. To find cross-reference errors in long documents, look for the word *Error!* with the Find command (press Ctrl+F). Investigate what went wrong, and repair or delete errant cross-references.

Putting Footnotes and Endnotes in Documents

A *footnote* is a bit of explanation, a comment, or a reference that appears at the bottom of the page and is referred to by a number or symbol in the text. An *endnote* is the same thing, except that it appears at the end of the section, chapter, or document. If you've written a scholarly paper of any kind, you know what a drag footnotes and endnotes are.

You will be glad to know that Word takes some of the drudgery out of footnotes and endnotes. For example, if you delete or add a note, all notes after the one you added or deleted are renumbered. And you don't have to worry about long footnotes because Word adjusts the page layout to make room for them. You can change the numbering scheme of footnotes and endnotes at will. When you are reviewing a document, all you have to do is move the pointer over a footnote or endnote citation. The note icon appears, as does a pop-up box with the text of the note.

Entering a footnote or endnote

To enter a footnote or endnote in a document:

1. **Place the cursor in the text where you want the note's number or symbol to appear.**
2. **On the References tab, click the Insert Footnote button (or press Ctrl+Alt+F) or the Insert Endnote button (or press Ctrl+Alt+D).**

   In Print Layout view, Word scrolls to the bottom of the page or the end of the document or section so that you can enter the note, as shown in Figure 8-8. If you are in Draft view, the Notes pane opens at the bottom of the screen with the cursor beside the number of the note you're about to enter.

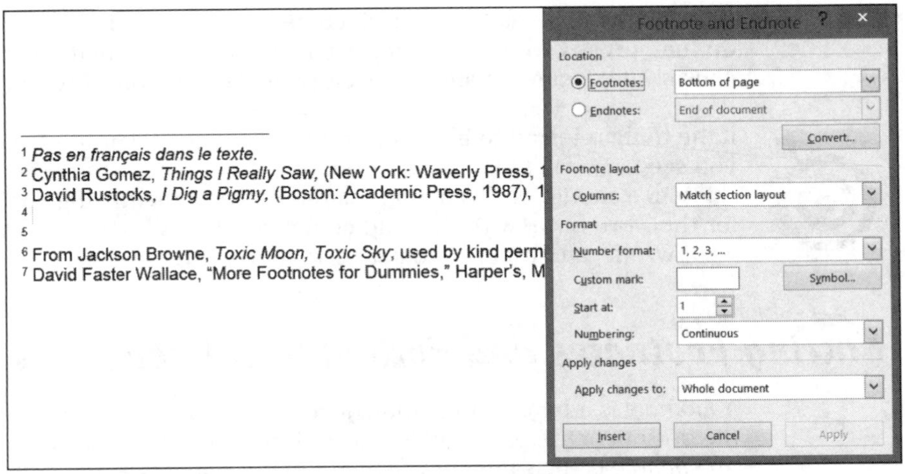

Figure 8-8: Entering a footnote in Print Layout view (left); the Footnote and Endnote dialog box (right).

3. **Enter your footnote or endnote.**
4. **In Print Layout view, scroll upward to return to the main text; click the Close button in the Notes pane if you're in Draft view.**

Click the Show Notes button at any time to see your notes in the Notes pane, at the bottom of the page, or at the end of the section or document.

TIP

To quickly return from writing a note to the place in your document where the footnote or endnote number citation is located, double-click the number citation at the bottom of the page (in Print Layout view) or the Notes pane (in Draft view). For example, if you just finished entering footnote 3, double-click the number *3*.

Choosing the numbering scheme and position of notes

Choosing the numbering scheme and positioning of endnotes and footnotes is quite easy. On the References tab, click the Footnotes group button. The Footnote and Endnote dialog box appears (refer to Figure 8-8). Tell Word where to place your notes:

- **Footnotes:** Choose Bottom of Page to put footnotes at the bottom of the page no matter where the text ends; choose Below Text to put footnotes directly below the last line of text on the page.
- **Endnotes:** Choose End of Section if your document is divided into sections (such as chapters) and you want endnotes to appear at the back of sections; choose End of Document to put all endnotes at the very back of the document.
- **Columns:** If you want to run footnotes or endnotes into columns, choose the number of columns you want.

In the Format area, tell Word how to number the notes:

- **Number Format:** Choose A B C, i ii iii, or another numbering scheme, if you want. You can also enter symbols by choosing the last option on this drop-down list.
- **Custom Mark:** You can mark the note with a symbol by clicking the Symbol button and choosing a symbol in the Symbol dialog box. If you go this route, you have to enter a symbol each time you insert a note. Not only that, you may have to enter two or three symbols for the second and third notes on each page or document because Word can't renumber symbols.
- **Start At:** To start numbering the notes at a place other than 1, A, or i, enter **2**, **B**, **ii**, or whatever in this box.
- **Numbering:** To number the notes continuously from the start of your document to the end, choose Continuous. Choose Restart Each Section to begin anew at each section of your document. For footnotes, you can begin anew on each page by choosing Restart Each Page.

By the way, the Convert button in the Footnote and Endnote dialog box is for fickle scholars who suddenly decide that their endnotes should be footnotes or vice versa. Click it and choose an option in the Convert Notes dialog box to turn footnotes into endnotes, turn endnotes into footnotes, or — in documents with both endnotes and footnotes — make the endnotes footnotes and the footnotes endnotes.

Deleting, moving, and editing notes

If a devious editor tells you that a footnote or endnote is in the wrong place, that you don't need a note, or that you need to change the text in a note, all is not lost:

- **Editing:** To edit a note, double-click its number or symbol in the text. You see the note onscreen. Edit the note at this point.
- **Moving:** To move a note, select its number or symbol in the text and drag it to a new location, or cut and paste it to a new location.
- **Deleting:** To delete a note, select its number or symbol and press the Delete key.

Footnotes and endnotes are renumbered when you move or delete one of them.

Compiling a Bibliography

A *bibliography* is a list, usually in alphabetical order by author name, of all the books, journal articles, websites, interviews, and other sources used in the writing of an article, report, or book. Writing a good bibliography is a chore. Besides keeping careful track of sources, you have to list them correctly. Does the author's name or work's name come first in the citation? How do you list a website or magazine article without an author's name?

Word's Bibliography feature is very nice in this regard: It solves the problem of how to enter citations for a bibliography. All you have to do is enter the bare facts about the citation — the author's name, title, publication date, publisher, and so on — and Word presents this information correctly in the bibliography. You can choose among several popular bibliographical styles (APA, Chicago, and others) from the Style drop-down list, as shown in Figure 8-9. After you make your choice, Word reformats all bibliography citations. You don't have to worry about whether titles should be underlined or italicized, or how authors' names should be listed in the bibliography.

Inserting a citation for your bibliography

An abbreviated citation appears in the text of your document in between parentheses where you enter a citation; the complete citation appears in the bibliography. After you enter the information about a citation, entering it a second time is easy because Word keeps a master list of all citations you have used in your work, both in the document you're working on and your other documents. To enter a citation, click in your document at the place that refers to the source, go to the References tab, and use one of these techniques to enter the citation:

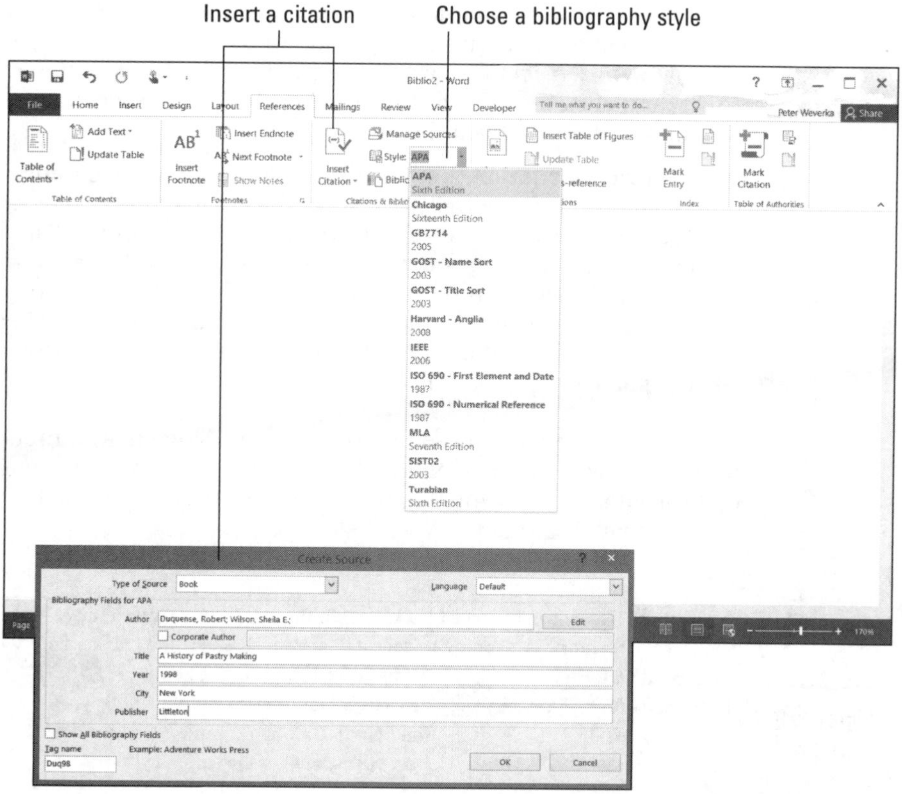

Figure 8-9: Adding a citation (left) and formatting citations (right) for a bibliography.

- **Entering a citation you've already entered in your document:** Click the Insert Citation button and choose the citation on the drop-down list. The top of the drop-down list presents citations you've already entered.
- **Creating a new citation:** Click the Insert Citation button and choose Add New Source. You see the Create Source dialog box shown in Figure 8-9. Choose an option on the Type of Source drop-down list and enter particulars about the source. You can click the Show All Bibliography Fields check box to enlarge the dialog box and enter all kinds of information about the source. Whether clicking the check box is necessary depends on how detailed you want your bibliography to be.
- **Inserting a citation placeholder:** Click the Insert Citation button and choose Add New Placeholder if you're in a hurry and you don't currently have all the information you need to describe the source. The Placeholder Name dialog box appears. Enter a placeholder name for the source and click OK. Later, when you have the information for the source,

either click the citation in the text and choose Edit Source on its drop-down list or click the Manage Sources button, and in the Source Manager dialog box, select the placeholder name (it has a question mark next to it) and click the Edit button. You see the Edit Source dialog box. Enter the information and click OK.

- **Inserting a citation you've entered in another document:** Click the Manage Sources button. You see the Source Manager dialog box. In the Master List, select the source you need if the source is listed; otherwise, click the Browse button, select the document with the source in the Open Source List dialog box, and click Open). Next, click the Copy button to copy sources from the Master List into your document. Then click Close and enter the citation by clicking the Insert Citation button and choosing the name of the citation you copied.

Your citation appears in text in parentheses. Move the pointer over the citation and click it to see an inline drop-down menu. From this menu, you can edit the citation as it appears in-text as well as edit it in the bibliography, as shown in Figure 8-10.

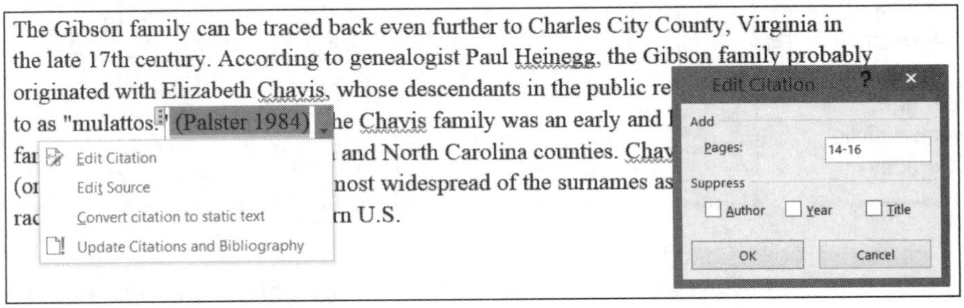

Figure 8-10: In-text citations have inline drop-down lists.

Editing a citation

Use one of these techniques to edit a citation:

- Open the citation's inline drop-down menu (refer to Figure 8-10) and choose Edit Source. You see the Edit Source dialog box, where you can edit the citation.
- Click the Manage Sources button on the References tab. The Source Manager dialog box appears. Select the citation, click the Edit button, and change around the citation in the Edit Source dialog box.

Changing how citations appear in text

Citations appear in text enclosed in parentheses. Use one of these techniques to change how a citation appears in the text of your document:

✦ **Changing what's in parentheses:** Open the citation's drop-down menu and choose Edit Citation. You see the Edit Citation dialog box (refer to Figure 8-10). To suppress the author's name, year, or title from appearing inside parentheses, select the Author, Year, or Title check box (whether the citation in parentheses lists the author, year, or title depends on which citation style you choose). To make page numbers appear with the citation, enter page numbers in the Pages box.

✦ **Removing the in-text citation:** Swipe over the citation to select it and press Delete. Removing an in-text citation this way does not prevent the citation from appearing in the bibliography.

Generating the bibliography

Go to the References tab and follow these steps to generate your bibliography:

1. **Click in your document where you want the bibliography to appear.**

   Probably that place is toward the end of the document.

2. **On the References tab, open the Style drop-down list and choose a style.**

   If you're generating your bibliography for a paper you will submit to a journal or institution, ask the editors which style they prefer for bibliographies and choose that style from the list.

3. **Click the Manage Sources button.**

   You see the Source Manager dialog box. Citations in the Current List box will appear in your bibliography.

4. **If necessary, address citations in the Current List box.**

   If you entered any citation placeholders, their names appear in the list next to question marks. Select these placeholders, click the Edit button, and enter information in the Edit Source dialog box.

   To keep a citation from appearing in the bibliography, select it and click the Delete button.

5. **Click the Close button in the Source Manager dialog box.**

6. **Click the Bibliography button and choose a built-in bibliography or the Insert Bibliography command on the drop-down list.**

There it is — your bibliography.

Book III

Excel 2016

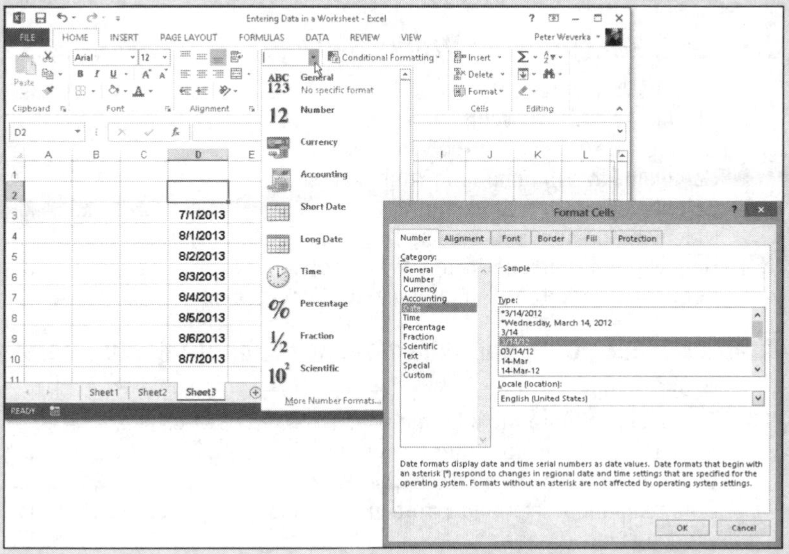

Visit www.dummies.com/extras/office2016aio to see how to turn one column of data (for example, a Name column) into two columns of data (for example, a First Name and Last Name column).

Contents at a Glance

Chapter 1: Up and Running with Excel

In This Chapter

- Creating an Excel workbook
- Understanding what a worksheet is
- Entering text as well as numeric, date, and time data
- Using the AutoFill command to enter lists and serial data
- Setting up data-validation rules

This chapter introduces *Microsoft Excel,* the official number cruncher of Office 2016. The purpose of Excel is to track, analyze, and tabulate numbers. Use the program to project profits and losses, formulate a budget, or analyze Elvis sightings in North America. Doing the setup work takes time, but after you enter the numbers and tell Excel how to tabulate them, you're on Easy Street. Excel does the math for you. All you have to do is kick off your shoes, sit back, and see how the numbers stack up.

This chapter explains what a workbook and a worksheet is, and how rows and columns on a worksheet determine where cell addresses are. You also discover tips and tricks for entering data quickly in a worksheet and how to construct data-validation rules to make sure that data is entered accurately.

Creating a New Excel Workbook

Workbook is the Excel term for the files you create with the Excel. When you create a workbook, you are given the choice of creating a blank workbook or creating a workbook from a template.

A *template* is a preformatted workbook designed for a specific purpose, such as budgeting, tracking inventories, or tracking purchase orders. Creating a workbook from a template is mighty convenient if you happen to find a template that suits your purposes, but in my experience, you almost always have to start from a generic, blank workbook because your data is your own. You need a workbook you create yourself, not one created from a template by someone else.

To create a workbook, begin by going to the File tab and choosing New. You see the New window shown in Figure 1-1. This window offers templates for creating workbooks and the means to search for templates online.

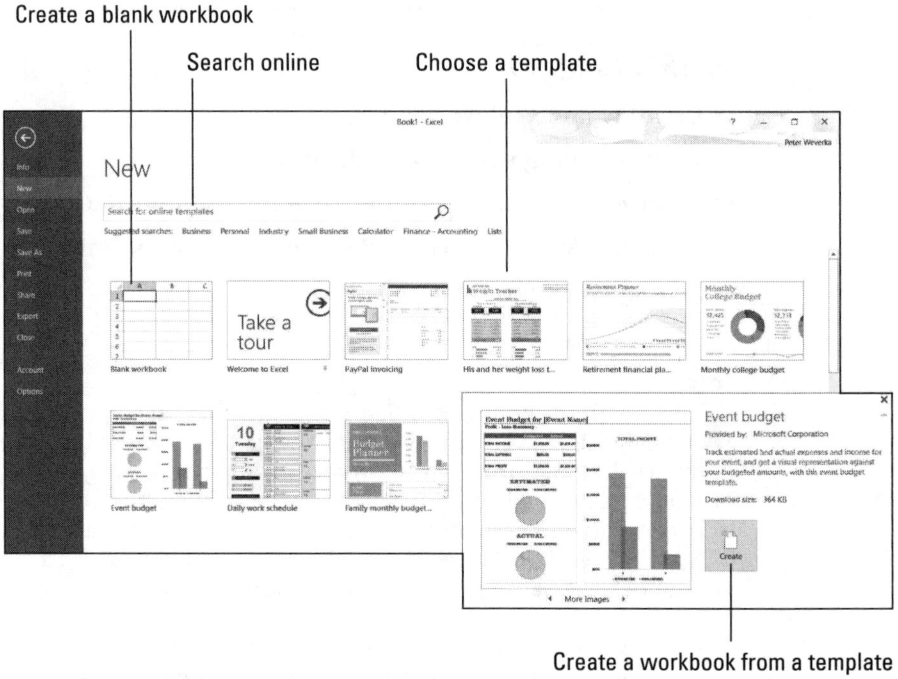

Figure 1-1: Create a workbook by starting in the New window.

Use these techniques in the New window to choose a template and create a workbook:

- ✦ **Choose the blank workbook template:** Choose Blank Workbook to create a plain template.

  Press Ctrl+N to create a new, blank workbook without opening the New window.

- ✦ **Choose a template:** Select a template to examine it in a preview window (refer to Figure 1-1). If you like what you see, click the Create button in the preview window to create a document from the template.

- **Search online for a template:** Enter a search term in the Search box and click the Start Searching button (or click a suggested search term). New templates appear in the New window. Click a template to preview it (see Figure 1-1). Click the Create button in the preview window to create a document from the template.

Book I, Chapter 1 explains how to save Office application files after you create them, as well as how to open them.

Getting Acquainted with Excel

If you've spent any time in an Office application, much of the Excel screen may look familiar to you. The buttons on the Home tab — the Bold and the Align buttons, for example — work the same in Excel as they do in Word. The Font and Font Size drop-down lists work the same as well. Any command in Excel that has to do with formatting text and numbers works the same in Excel and Word.

As mentioned earlier, an Excel file is a *workbook.* Each workbook comprises one or more worksheets. A *worksheet,* also known as a *spreadsheet,* is a table into which you enter data and data labels. Figure 1-2 shows a worksheet with data about rainfall in different counties.

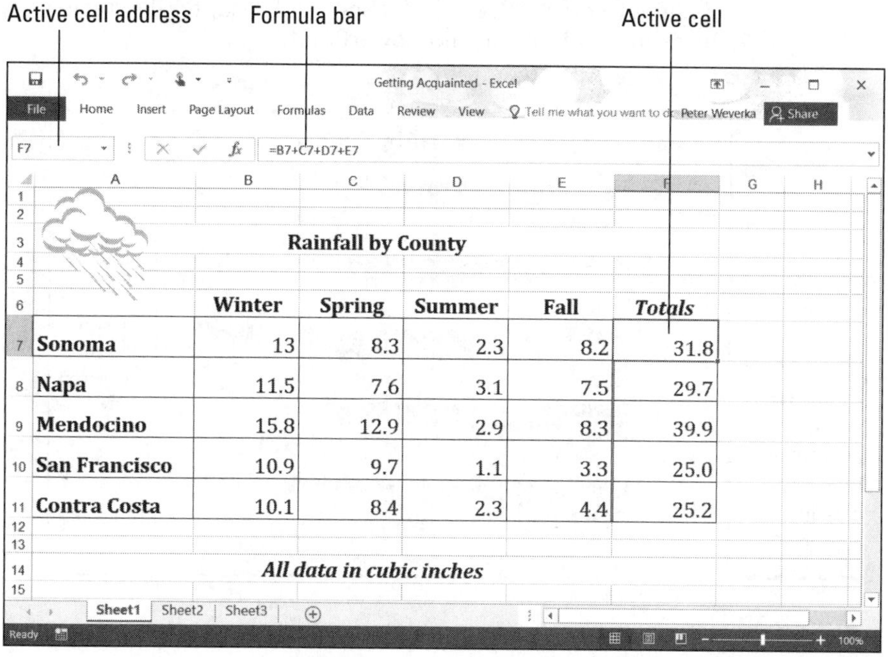

Figure 1-2: The Excel screen.

A worksheet works like an accountant's ledger — only it's much easier to use. Notice how the worksheet is divided by gridlines into columns (A, B, C, and so on) and rows (1, 2, 3, and so on). The rectangles where columns and rows intersect are *cells,* and each cell can hold one data item, a formula for calculating data, or nothing at all.

Each cell has a different cell address. In Figure 1-2, cell B7 holds 13, the amount of rain that fell in Sonoma County in the winter. Meanwhile, as the Formula bar at the top of the screen shows, cell F7, the *active cell,* holds the formula `=B7+C7+D7+E7`, the sum of the numbers in cells — you guessed it — B7, C7, D7, and E7.

REMEMBER

The beauty of Excel is that the program does all the calculations and recalculations for you after you enter the data. If I were to change the number in cell B7, Excel would instantly recalculate the total amount of rainfall in Sonoma County in cell F7. People like myself who struggled in math class will be glad to know that you don't have to worry about the math because Excel does it for you. All you have to do is make sure that the data and the formulas are entered correctly.

After you enter and label the data, enter the formulas, and turn your worksheet into a little masterpiece, you can start analyzing the data. For example, you can also generate charts like the one in Figure 1-3. Do you notice any similarities between the worksheet in Figure 1-2 and the chart in Figure 1-3? The chart is fashioned from data in the worksheet, and it took me about half a minute to create that chart. (Book VIII, Chapter 4 explains how to create charts in Excel, Word, and PowerPoint.)

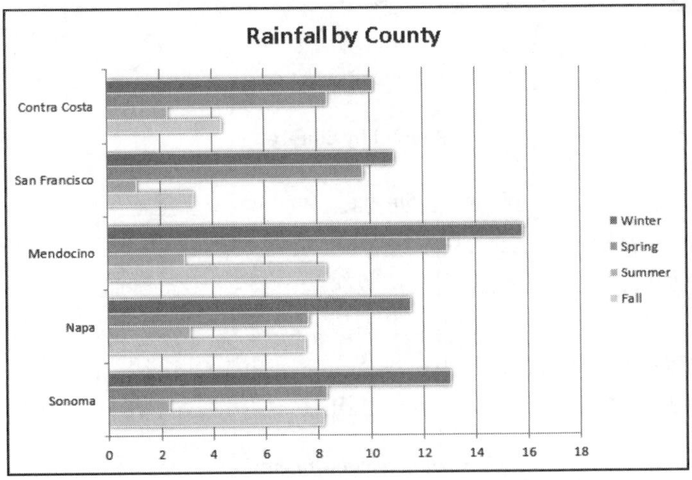

Figure 1-3: A chart generated from the data in Figure 1-2.

Rows, columns, and cell addresses

Not that anyone needs them all, but an Excel worksheet has numerous columns and more than 1 million rows. The rows are numbered, and columns are labeled A to Z, then AA to AZ, then BA to BZ, and so on. The important thing to remember is that each cell has an address whose name comes from a column letter and a row number. The first cell in row 1 is A1, the second is B1, and so on. You need to enter cell addresses in formulas to tell Excel which numbers to compute.

To find a cell's address, either make note of which column and row it lies in or click the cell and glance at the Formula bar (refer to Figure 1-2). The left side of the Formula bar lists the address of the *active cell,* the cell that is selected in the worksheet. In Figure 1-2, cell F7 is the active cell.

Workbooks and worksheets

By default, each workbook includes one worksheet, called Sheet1, but you can add more worksheets. Think of a workbook as a stack of worksheets. Besides calculating the numbers in cells across the rows or down the columns of a worksheet, you can make calculations throughout a workbook by using numbers from different worksheets in a calculation. Chapter 2 of this mini-book explains how to add worksheets, rename worksheets, and do all else that pertains to them.

Entering Data in a Worksheet

Entering data in a worksheet is an irksome activity. Fortunately, Excel offers a few shortcuts to take the sting out of it. These pages explain how to enter data in a worksheet, what the different types of data are, and how to enter text labels, numbers, dates, and times.

The basics of entering data

What you can enter in a worksheet cell falls into four categories:

- Text
- A value (numeric, date, or time)
- A logical value (True or False)
- A formula that returns a value, logical value, or text

Still, no matter what type of data you're entering, the basic steps are the same:

1. **Click the cell where you want to enter the data or text label.**

   As shown in Figure 1-4, a square appears around the cell to tell you that the cell you clicked is now the active cell. Glance at the left side of the Formula bar if you're not sure of the address of the cell you're about to enter data in. The Formula bar lists the cell address.

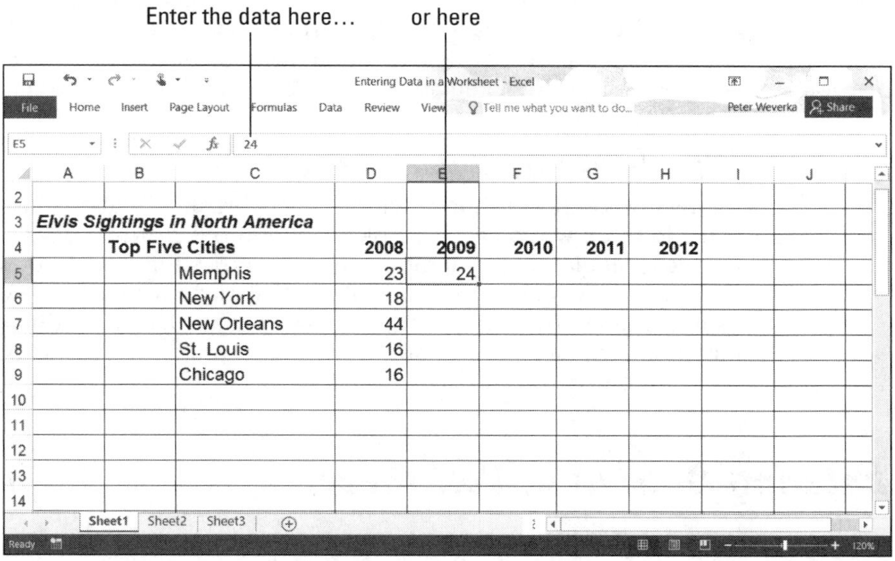

Figure 1-4: Entering data.

2. **Type the data in the cell.**

   If you find typing in the Formula bar easier, click and start typing there. As soon as you type the first character, the Cancel button (an *X*) and Enter button (a check mark) appear beside the Insert Function button (labeled *fx*) on the Formula bar.

3. **Press the Enter key to enter the number or label.**

   Besides pressing the Enter key, you can also press an arrow key (←, ↑, →, ↓), press Tab, or click the Enter button (the check mark) on the Formula bar.

   If you change your mind about entering data, click the Cancel button or press Esc to delete what you entered and start over.

Chapter 3 of this mini-book explains how to enter logical values and formulas. The next several pages describe how to enter text labels, numeric values, date values, and time values.

Entering text labels

Sometimes a text entry is too long to fit in a cell. How Excel accommodates text entries that are too wide depends on whether data is in the cell to the right of the one you entered the text in:

- If the cell to the right is empty, Excel lets the text spill into the next cell.
- If the cell to the right contains data, the entry gets cut off. Nevertheless, the text you entered is in the cell. Nothing gets lost when it can't be displayed onscreen. You just can't see the text or numbers except by glancing at the Formula bar, where the contents of the active cell can be seen in its entirety.

Use these techniques to solve the problem of text that doesn't fit in a cell:

- Widen the column to allow room for more text.
- Shorten the text entry.
- Reorient the text (Chapter 4 of this mini-book explains how to do it).
- Wrap the contents of the cell. *Wrapping* means to run the text down to the next line, much the way the text in a paragraph runs to the next line when it reaches the right margin. Excel makes rows taller to accommodate wrapped text in a cell. To wrap text in cells, select the cells, go to the Home tab, and click the Wrap Text button (you can find it in the Alignment group).

Entering numeric values

When a number is too large to fit in a cell, Excel displays pounds signs (###) instead of a number or displays the number in scientific notation (8.78979E+15). You can always glance at the Formula bar, however, to find out the number in the active cell. As well, you can always widen the column to display the entire number.

To enter a fraction in a cell, enter a 0 or a whole number, a blank space, and the fraction. For example, to enter ⅜, type a **0**, press the spacebar, and type **3/8**. To enter 5⅜, type the **5**, press the spacebar, and type **3/8**. For its purposes, Excel converts fractions to decimal numbers, as you can see by looking in the Formula bar after you enter a fraction. For example, 5⅜ displays as 5.375 in the Formula bar.

Here's a little trick for entering numbers with decimals quickly in all the Excel files you work on. To spare yourself the trouble of pressing the period key (.), you can tell Excel to enter the period automatically. Instead of entering **12.45**, for example, you can simply enter **1245**. Excel enters the period for you: 12.45. To perform this trick, go to the File tab, choose Options, visit the Advanced category in the Excel Options dialog box, click the

Automatically Insert a Decimal Point check box, and in the Places text box, enter the number of decimal places you want for numbers. Deselect this option when you want to go back to entering numbers the normal way.

Entering date and time values

Dates and times can be used in calculations, but entering a date or time value in a cell can be problematic because these values must be entered in such a way that Excel can recognize them as dates or times, not text.

Not that you necessarily need to know it, but Excel converts dates and times to serial values for the purpose of being able to use dates and times in calculations. For example, July 31, 2004, is the number 38199. July 31, 2004, at Noon is 38199.5. These serial values represent the number of whole days since January 1, 1900. The portion of the serial value to the right of the decimal point is the time, represented as a portion of a full day.

Entering date values

You can enter a date value in a cell in just about any format you choose, and Excel understands that you're entering a date. For example, enter a date in any of the following formats and you'll be all right:

m/d/yy	7/31/16
m-d-yyyy	7-31-2016
d-mmm-yy	31-Jul-16

Here are some basic things to remember about entering dates:

- **Date formats:** You can quickly apply a format to dates by selecting cells and using one of these techniques:
  - On the Home tab, open the Number Format drop-down list and choose Short Date (*m/d/yyyy;* 7/31/2016) or Long Date (*day of the week, month, day, year;* Wednesday, July 31, 2016), as shown in Figure 1-5.
  - On the Home tab, click the Number group button to open the Number tab of the Format Cells dialog box. As shown in Figure 1-5, choose the Date category and then choose a date format.
- **Current date:** Press Ctrl+; (semicolon) to enter the current date.
- **Current year's date:** If you don't enter the year as part of the date, Excel assumes that the date you entered is in the current year. For example, if you enter a date in the *m/d* (7/31) format during the year 2016, Excel enters the date as 7/31/16. As long as the date you want to enter is the current year, you can save a little time when entering dates by not entering the year because Excel enters it for you.

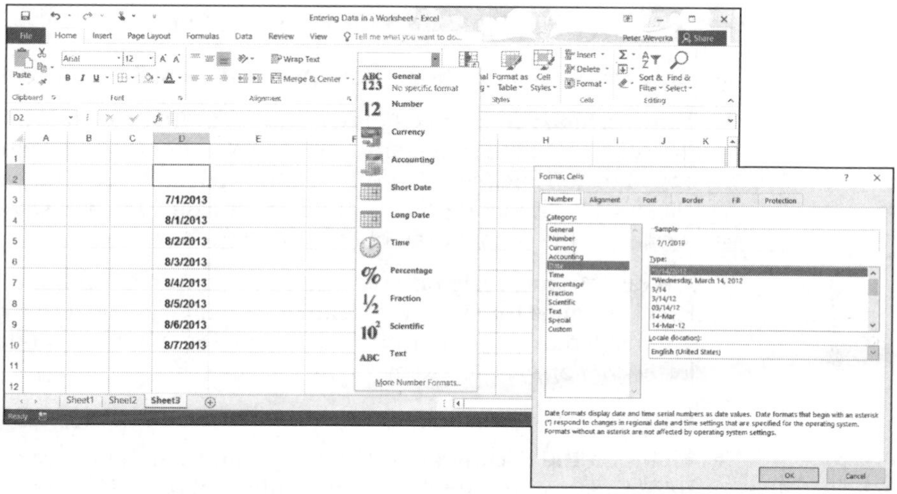

Figure 1-5: Format dates and numbers on the Number Format drop-down list or Format Cells dialog box.

- **Dates on the Formula bar:** No matter which format you use for dates, dates are displayed in the Formula bar in the format that Excel prefers for dates: *m/d/yyyy* (7/31/2016). How dates are displayed in the worksheet is up to you.

REMEMBER

- **20th and 21st century two-digit years:** When it comes to entering two-digit years in dates, the digits 30 through 99 belong to the 20th century (1930–1999), but the digits 00 through 29 belong to the 21st century (2000–2029). For example, 7/31/13 refers to July 31, 2013, not July 31, 1910. To enter a date in 1929 or earlier, enter four digits instead of two to describe the year: **7-31-1929**. To enter a date in 2030 or later, enter four digits instead of two: **7-31-2030**.

REMEMBER

- **Dates in formulas:** To enter a date directly in a formula, enclose the date in quotation marks. (Make sure that the cell where the formula is entered has been given the Number format, not the Date format.) For example, the formula `=TODAY()-"1/1/2016"` calculates the number of days that have elapsed since January 1, 2016. Formulas are the subject of Chapter 3 of this mini-book.

Entering time values

Excel recognizes time values that you enter in the following ways:

h:mm AM/PM	3:31 AM
h:mm:ss AM/PM	3:31:45 PM

Here are some things to remember when entering time values:

- **Use colons:** Separate hours, minutes, and seconds with a colon (:).
- **Time formats:** To change to the *h:mm:ss* AM/PM time format, select the cells, go to the Home tab, open the Number Format drop-down list, and choose Time (see Figure 1-5). You can also change time formats by clicking the Number group button on the Home tab and selecting a time format on the Number tab of the Format Cells dialog box.
- **AM or PM time designations:** Unless you enter AM or PM with the time, Excel assumes that you're operating on military time. For example, 3:30 is considered 3:30 a.m.; 15:30 is 3:30 p.m. Don't enter periods after the letters *am* or *pm* (don't enter a.m. or p.m.).
- **Current time:** Press Ctrl+Shift+; (semicolon) to enter the current time.
- **Times on the Formula bar:** On the Formula bar, times are displayed in this format: *hours:minutes:seconds,* followed by the letters AM or PM. However, the time format used in cells is up to you.

Entering data with Flash Fill

Don't look now, but Excel is peering over your shoulder to see whether it can enter data for you with Flash Fill, a mechanism whereby Excel recognizes the data you want to enter and offers to enter it on your behalf. When Excel recognizes a pattern in the data and thinks it can fill in a column for you, a ghostly image of the data Excel wants to enter appears in the column. Press Enter if you want to enter this data.

After you press Enter, the Flash Fill Options button appears. Click it to open a menu with options for Undoing Flash Fill and selecting cells.

Flash Fill is useful for cleaning up worksheets with data that you imported from a comma- or tab-delimited file. Often this data arrives in a mishmash with data from different categories in the same column.

Date	Transaction	Score	Name
2/2/2013	Weverka-4971	48	Weverka
2/2/2013	Johnson-891	42	Johnson
2/3/2013	McKeil- 497	78	McKeil
2/4/2013	Munoz-9071	23	Munoz
2/4/2013	Hong-9781	12	Hong
2/5/2013	Chester-9714	34	Chester

Combining date and time values

You can combine dates and time values by entering the date, a blank space, and the time:

- 7/31/13 3:31 am
- 7-31-13 3:31:45 pm

Quickly Entering Lists and Serial Data with the AutoFill Command

Data that falls into the "serial" category — month names, days of the week, and consecutive numbers and dates, for example — can be entered quickly with the AutoFill command. Believe it or not, Excel recognizes certain kinds of serial data and enters it for you as part of the AutoFill feature. Instead of laboriously entering this data one piece at a time, you can enter it all at one time by dragging the mouse. Follow these steps to "autofill" cells:

1. **Click the cell that is to be first in the series.**

   For example, if you intend to list the days of the week in consecutive cells, click where the first day is to go.

2. **Enter the first number, date, or list item in the series.**

3. **Move to the adjacent cell and enter the second number, date, or list item in the series.**

   If you want to enter the same number or piece of text in adjacent cells, it isn't necessary to take this step, but Excel needs the first and second items in the case of serial dates and numbers so that it can tell how much to increase or decrease the given amount or time period in each cell. For example, entering **5** and **10** tells Excel to increase the number by 5 each time so that the next serial entry is 15.

4. **Select the cell or cells you just entered data in.**

   To select a single cell, click it; to select two, drag over the cells. Chapter 2 of this mini-book describes all the ways to select cells in a worksheet.

5. **Click the AutoFill handle and start dragging in the direction in which you want the data series to appear on your worksheet.**

   The *AutoFill handle* is the little green square in the lower-right corner of the cell or block of cells you selected. As you drag, the serial data appears in a pop-up box, as shown in Figure 1-6.

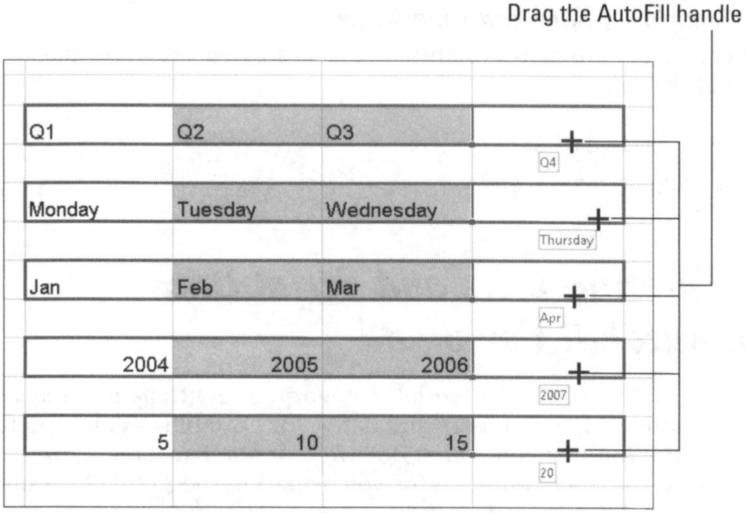

Figure 1-6: Entering serial data and text.

The AutoFill Options button appears after you enter the serial data. Click it and choose an option if you want to copy cells or fill the cells without carrying along their formats.

To enter the same number or text in several empty cells, drag over the cells to select them or select each cell by holding down the Ctrl key as you click. Then type a number or some text and press Ctrl+Enter.

Creating your own AutoFill list

As you probably know, Excel is capable of completing lists on its own with the AutoFill feature. You can enter the days of the week or month names simply by entering one day or month and dragging the AutoFill handle to enter the others. Here's some good news: The AutoFill command can also reproduce the names of your coworkers, the roster of a softball team, street names, or any other list that you care to enter quickly and repeatedly in a worksheet.

Follow these steps to enter items for a list so that you can enter them in the future by dragging the AutoFill handle:

1. **If you've already entered items for the list on your worksheet, select the items.**

   If you haven't entered the items yet, skip to Step 2.

2. **On the File tab, and choose Options to open the Excel Options dialog box.**
3. **Go to the Advanced category.**
4. **Click the Edit Custom Lists button (you have to scroll down to find it).**

   You see the Custom Lists dialog box.

5. **In the List Entries box, do one of the following:**

   If you selected the items in Step 1, click the Import button. The items you selected appear in the List Entries box.

   If you need to enter items for the list, enter them in the List Entries box, with one item on each line.

6. **Click the Add button.**

7. **Click OK.**

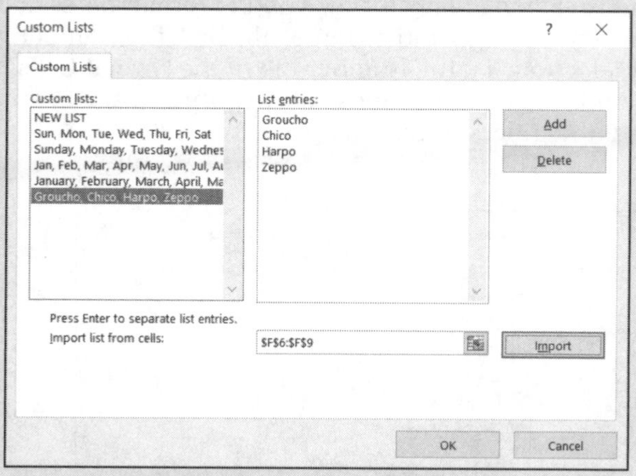

Formatting Numbers, Dates, and Time Values

When you enter a number that Excel recognizes as belonging to one of its formats, Excel assigns the number format automatically. Enter **45%**, for example, and Excel assigns the Percentage number format. Enter **$4.25**, and Excel assigns the Currency number format. Besides assigning formats by hand, however, you can assign them to cells from the get-go and spare yourself the trouble of entering dollar signs, commas, percent signs, and other extraneous punctuation. All you have to do is enter the raw numbers. Excel does the window dressing for you.

Excel offers five number-formatting buttons on the Home tab — Accounting Number Format, Percent Style, Comma Style, Increase Decimal, and Decrease Decimal. Select cells with numbers in them and click one of these buttons to change how numbers are formatted:

✦ **Accounting Number Format:** Places a dollar sign before the number and gives it two decimal places. You can open the drop-down list on this button and choose a currency symbol apart from the dollar sign.

- **Percent Style:** Places a percent sign after the number and converts the number to a percentage.
- **Comma Style:** Places commas in the number.
- **Increase Decimal:** Increases the number of decimal places by one.
- **Decrease Decimal:** Decreases the number of decimal places by one.

To choose among many formats and to format dates and time values as well as numbers, go to the Home tab, click the Number group button, and make selections on the Number tab of the Format Cells dialog box. Figure 1-7 shows this dialog box. Choose a category and select options to describe how you want numbers or text to appear.

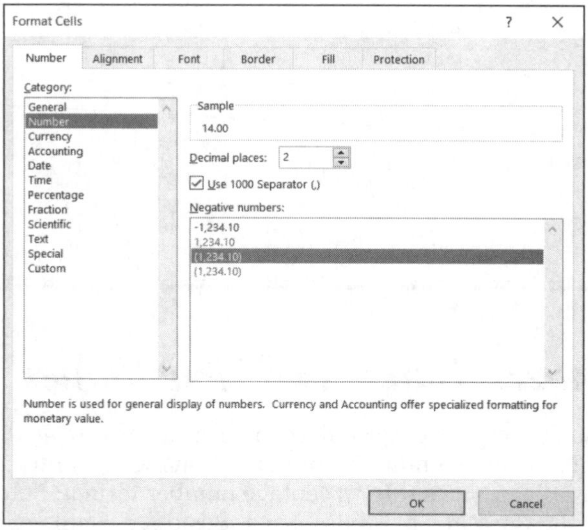

Figure 1-7: The Number category of the Format Cells dialog box.

To strip formats from the data in cells, select the cells, go to the Home tab, click the Clear button, and choose Clear Formats.

TIP: Entering ZIP Codes can be problematic because Excel strips the initial zero from the number if it begins with a zero. To get around this problem, visit the Number tab of the Format Cells dialog box (see Figure 1-7), choose Special in the Category list, and select a ZIP Code option.

Establishing Data-Validation Rules

By nature, people are prone to enter data incorrectly because the task of entering data is so dull. This is why data-validation rules are invaluable. A *data-validation rule* is a rule concerning what kind of data can be entered in a cell. When you select a cell that has been given a rule, an input message tells you what to enter, as shown in Figure 1-8. And if you enter the data incorrectly, an error alert tells you as much, also shown in Figure 1-8.

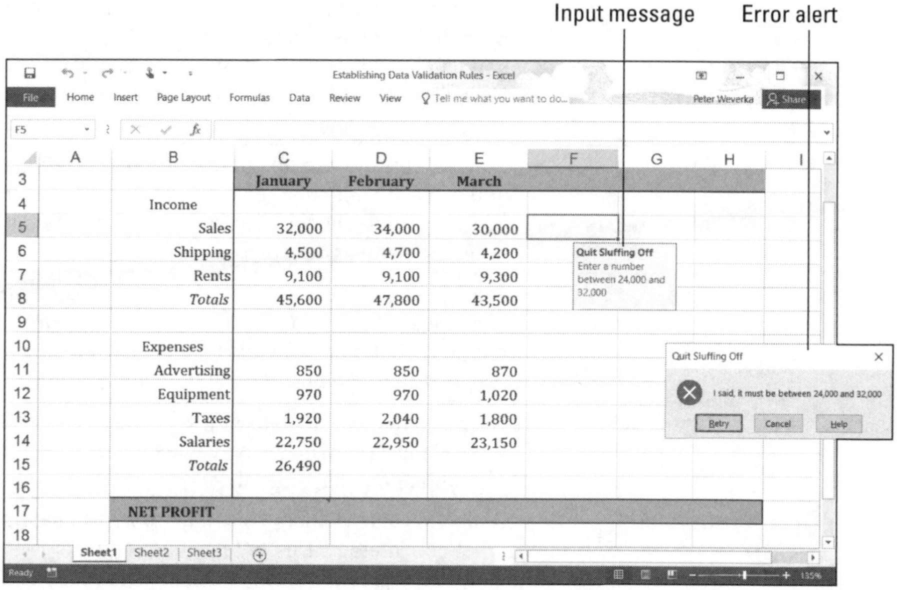

Figure 1-8: A data-validation rule in action.

Data-validation rules are an excellent defense against sloppy data entry and that itchy feeling you get when you're in the middle of an irksome task. In a cell that records date entries, you can require dates to fall in a certain time frame. In a cell that records text entries, you can choose an item from a list instead of typing it yourself. In a cell that records numeric entries, you can require the number to fall within a certain range. Table 1-1 describes the different categories of data-validation rules.

Table 1-1 Data-Validation Rule Categories

Rule	*What Can Be Entered*
Any Value	Anything whatsoever. This is the default setting.
Whole Number	Whole numbers (no decimal points allowed). Choose an operator from the Data drop-down list and values to describe the range of numbers that can be entered.
Decimal	Same as the Whole Number rule except numbers with decimal points are permitted.

(continued)

Table 1-1 ***(continued)***

Rule	*What Can Be Entered*
List	Items from a list. Enter the list items in cells on a worksheet, either the one you're working in or another. Then reopen the Data Validation dialog box, click the Range Selector button (you can find it on the right side of the Source text box), and select the cells that hold the list. The list items appear in a drop-down list on the worksheet.
Date	Date values. Choose an operator from the Data drop-down list and values to describe the date range. Earlier in this chapter, "Entering date and time values" describes the correct way to enter date values.
Time	Time values. Choose an operator from the Data drop-down list and values to describe the date and time range. Earlier in this chapter, "Entering date and time values" describes the correct way to enter a combination of date and time values.
Text Length	A certain number of characters. Choose an operator from the Data drop-down list and values to describe how many characters can be entered.
Custom	A logical value (True or False). Enter a formula that describes what constitutes a true or false data entry.

Follow these steps to establish a data-validation rule:

1. **Select the cell or cells that need a rule.**
2. **On the Data tab, click the Data Validation button.**

   As shown in Figure 1-9, you see the Settings tab of the Data Validation dialog box.
3. **On the Allow drop-down list, choose the category of rule you want.**

   Table 1-1, earlier in this chapter, describes these categories.
4. **Enter the criteria for the rule.**

   What the criteria is depends on what rule category you're working in. Table 1-1 describes how to enter the criteria for rules in each category. You can refer to cells in the worksheet by selecting them. To do that, either select them directly or click the Range Selector button and then select them.

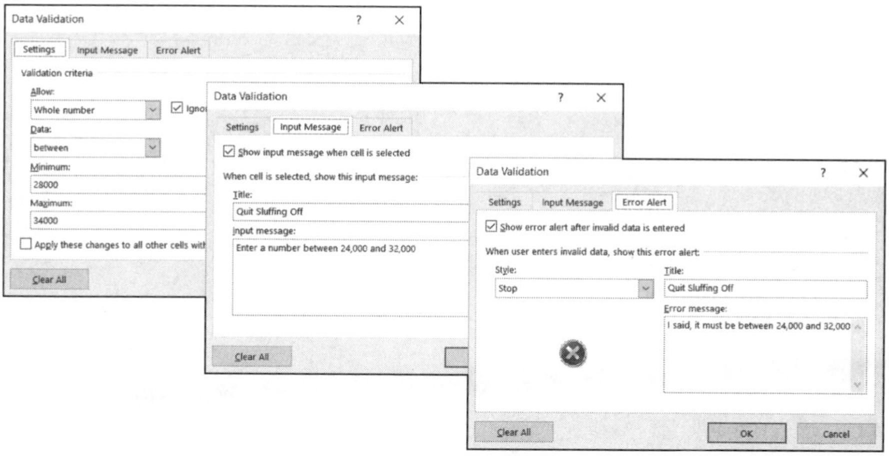

Figure 1-9: Creating a data-validation rule.

5. **On the Input Message tab, enter a title and input message.**

   You can see a title ("Quit Sluffing Off") and input message ("Enter a number between 24,000 and 32,000") in Figure 1-8. The title appears in boldface. Briefly describe what kind of data belongs in the cell or cells you selected.

6. **On the Error Alert tab, choose a style for the symbol in the Message Alert dialog box, enter a title for the dialog box, and enter a warning message.**

   In the error message in Figure 1-8, shown previously, the Stop symbol was chosen. The title you enter appears across the top of the dialog box, and the message appears beside the symbol.

7. **Click OK.**

   To remove data-validation rules from cells, select the cells, go to the Data tab, click the Data Validation button, and on the Settings tab of the Data Validation dialog box, click the Clear All button, and click OK.

Chapter 2: Refining Your Worksheet

In This Chapter

- Changing worksheet data
- Going here and there in a worksheet
- Freezing and splitting columns and rows to make data entry easier
- Documenting a worksheet with comments
- Selecting cells
- Copying and moving data
- Inserting, deleting, and renaming worksheets
- Hiding and protecting worksheets so that they can't be altered

This chapter delves into the workaday world of worksheets (say that three times fast). It explains how to edit worksheet data and move quickly here and there in a worksheet. You also discover techniques for entering data quickly, selecting cells, and copying and moving data in cells. This chapter describes how to move, delete, and rename worksheets as well as protect them from being edited or altered.

Editing Worksheet Data

Not everyone enters data correctly the first time. To edit data you entered in a cell, do one of the following:

- **Double-click the cell.** Doing so places the cursor squarely in the cell, where you can start deleting or entering numbers and text.
- **Click the cell and press F2.** This technique also lands the cursor in the cell.
- **Click the cell you want to edit.** With this technique, you edit the data on the Formula bar.

If nothing happens when you double-click, or if pressing F2 lands the cursor in the Formula bar, not a cell, somebody has been fooling with the Options settings. On the File tab, choose Options, select the Advanced category in the Excel Options dialog box, and click the Allow Editing Directly in Cells check box.

Moving Around in a Worksheet

Going from place to place gets progressively more difficult as a worksheet gets larger. Luckily for you, Excel offers keyboard shortcuts for jumping around. Table 2-1 describes these keyboard shortcuts.

Table 2-1 Keyboard Shortcuts for Getting Around in Worksheets

Press. . .	*To Move the Selection. . .*
Home	To column A
Ctrl+Home	To cell A1, the first cell in the worksheet
Ctrl+End	To the last cell in the last row with data in it
←, →, ↑, ↓	To the next cell
Ctrl+←, →, ↑, ↓	In one direction toward the nearest cell with data in it or to the first or last cell in the column or row
PgUp or PgDn	Up or down one screen's worth of rows
Ctrl+PgUp or Ctrl+PgDn	Backward or forward through the workbook, from worksheet to worksheet

As well as pressing keys, you can use these techniques to get from place to place in a worksheet:

- **Scroll bars:** Use the vertical and horizontal scroll bars to move to different areas. Drag the scroll box to cover long distances. To cover long distances very quickly, hold down the Shift key as you drag the scroll box on the vertical scroll bar.
- **Scroll wheel on the mouse:** If your mouse is equipped with a scroll wheel, turn the wheel to quickly scroll up and down.
- **Name box:** Enter a cell address in the Name box and press Enter to go to the cell. The Name box is found to the left of the Formula bar.

- **The Go To command:** On the Home tab, click the Find & Select button and choose Go To on the drop-down list (or press Ctrl+G or F5). You see the Go To dialog box. Enter a cell address in the Reference box and click OK. Cell addresses you've already visited with the Go To command are already listed in the dialog box. Click the Special button to open the Go To Special dialog box and visit a formula, comment, or other esoteric item.
- **The Find command:** On the Home tab, click the Find & Select button and choose Find on the drop-down list (or press Ctrl+F). Enter the data you seek in the Find What box and click the Find Next button. Click the Find All button to find all instances of the item you're looking for. A list of the items appears at the bottom of the dialog box; click an item to go to it.

To scroll to the active cell if you no longer see it onscreen, press Ctrl+Backspace.

Getting a Better Look at the Worksheet

Especially when you're entering data, it pays to get a good look at the worksheet. You need to know which column and row you're entering data in. These pages explain techniques for changing your view of a worksheet so that you always know where you are. Read on to discover how to freeze, split, and hide columns and rows. (On the subject of changing views, Book I, Chapter 3 explains an essential technique for changing views: zooming in and zooming out.)

Freezing and splitting columns and rows

Sometimes your adventures in a worksheet take you to a faraway cell address, such as X31 or C39. Out there in the wilderness, it's hard to tell where to enter data because you can't see the data labels in the first column or first row that tell you where to enter data on the worksheet.

To see one part of a worksheet no matter how far you stray from it, you can *split* the worksheet or *freeze* columns and rows onscreen. In Figure 2-1, I split the worksheet so that column A (Property) always appears onscreen, no matter how far I scroll to the right; similarly, row 1 (Property, Rent, Management Fees, and so on) also appears at the top of the worksheet no matter how far I scroll down. Notice how the row numbers and column letters are interrupted in Figure 2-1. Because I split the screen, I always know what data to enter in a cell because I can clearly see property names in the first column and the column headings along the top of the worksheet.

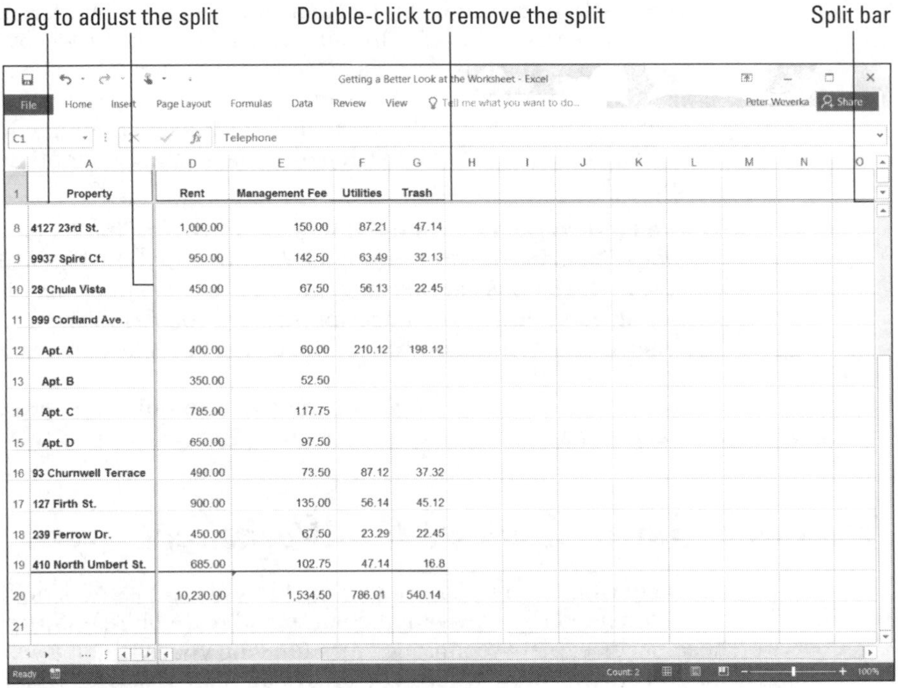

Figure 2-1: Splitting a worksheet.

Freezing columns or rows on a worksheet works much like splitting except that lines instead of gray bars appear onscreen to show which columns and rows are frozen, and you can't adjust where the split occurs by dragging the boundary where the worksheet is split.

Giving the Split or Freeze Panes command

Follow these steps to split or freeze columns and rows onscreen:

1. **Click the cell that is directly below the row you want to freeze or split and is in the column to the right of the column that you want to freeze or split.**

   In other words, click where you want the split to occur.

2. **On the View tab, split or freeze the columns and rows.**

   Go to the View tab and use one of these techniques:

   - **Splitting:** Click the Split button and then click and drag the split bars to split the screen horizontally or vertically (refer to Figure 2-1). The other way to split a worksheet is to grab hold of a *split bar,* the little division markers directly above the vertical scroll bar and directly to the right of the horizontal scroll bar (in the lower-right corner of your screen). You can tell where split bars are because the pointer turns into a double arrow when it's over a split bar.

- **Freezing:** Click the Freeze Panes button and choose one of three Freeze options on the drop-down list. The second and third options, respectively, freeze the top row or first column. The first option, Freeze Panes, freezes the column(s) to the left and the row(s) above the cell you selected in Step 1.

Bars or lines appear onscreen to show which row(s) and column(s) have been frozen or split. Move where you will in the worksheet. The column(s) and row(s) you froze or split stay onscreen.

Unsplitting and unfreezing

Use one of these techniques to keep your worksheet from splitting or freezing to death:

✦ **Unsplitting:** Click the Split button again; double-click one of the split bars to remove it; or drag a split bar into the top or left side of the worksheet window.

✦ **Unfreezing:** On the View tab, click the Freeze Panes button and choose Unfreeze Panes on the drop-down list.

Hiding columns and rows

Another way to take the clutter out of a worksheet is to temporarily hide columns and rows:

✦ **Hiding columns or rows:** Drag over the column letters or row numbers of the columns or rows that you want to hide. Dragging this way selects entire columns or rows. Then go to the Home tab, click the Format button, choose Hide & Unhide, and choose Hide Columns or Hide Rows.

✦ **Unhiding columns and rows:** Select columns to the right and left of the hidden columns, or select rows above and below the hidden rows. To select columns or rows, drag over their letters or numbers. Then go to the Home tab, click the Format button, choose Hide & Unhide, and choose Unhide Columns or Unhide Rows.

TIP

It's easy to forget where you hid columns or rows. To make sure all columns and rows in your worksheet are displayed, click the Select All button (or press Ctrl+A) to select your entire worksheet. Then go to the Home tab, click the Format button and choose Hide & Unhide ➪ Unhide Columns; click the Format button again and choose Hide & Unhide ➪ Unhide Rows.

Your own customized views

After you go to the trouble of freezing the screen or zooming in to a position you're comfortable with, you may as well save your view of the screen as a customized view. That way, you can call upon the customized view whenever you need it. View settings, the window size, the position of the grid onscreen, and cells that are selected can all be saved in a customized view.

Follow these steps to create a customized view:

1. **On the View tab, click the Custom Views button.**

   You see the Custom Views dialog box. It lists views you've already created, if you've created any.

2. **Click the Add button.**

   The Add View dialog box appears.

3. **Enter a name for the view and click OK.**

To switch to a customized view, click the Custom Views button, select a view in the Custom Views dialog box, and click the Show button.

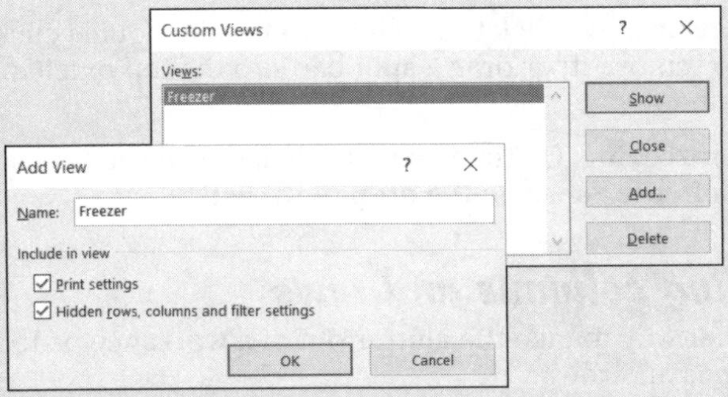

Comments for Documenting Your Worksheet

It may happen that you return to your worksheet days or months from now and discover to your dismay that you don't know why certain numbers or formulas are there. For that matter, someone else may inherit your worksheet and be mystified as to what the heck is going on. To take the mystery out of a worksheet, document it by entering comments here and there.

A *comment* is a note that describes part of a worksheet. Each comment is connected to a cell. You can tell where a comment is because a small red triangle appears in the upper-right corner of cells that have been commented on. Move the pointer over one of these triangles and you see the pop-up box, a comment, and the name of the person who entered the comment, as shown in Figure 2-2. Click the Show All Comments button on the Review tab to see every comment in a worksheet.

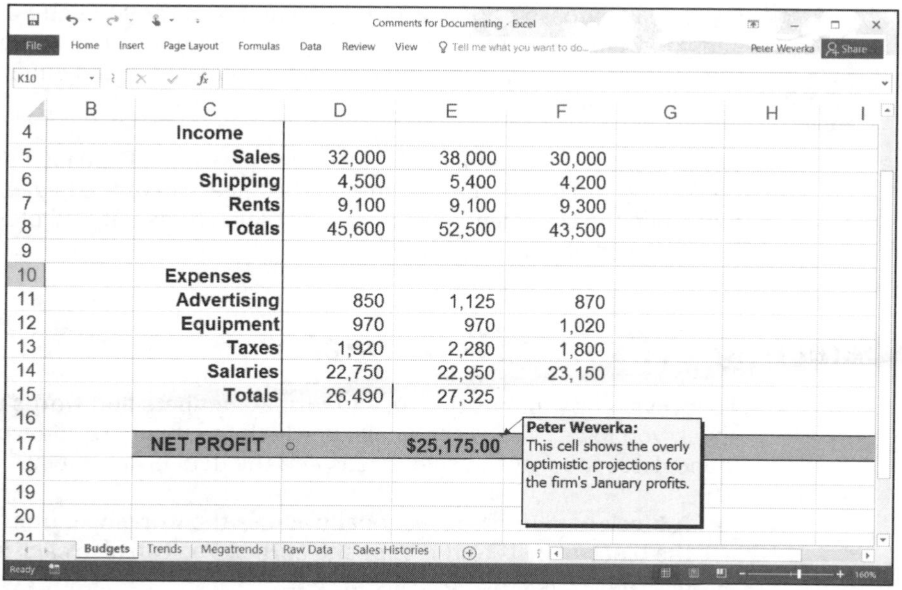

Figure 2-2: Comments explain what's what in a worksheet.

Here's everything a mere mortal needs to know about comments:

- **Entering a comment:** Click the cell that deserves the comment, go to the Review tab, and click the New Comment button. Enter your comment in the pop-up box. Click in a different cell when you finish entering your comment.
- **Reading a comment:** Move the pointer over the small red triangle and read the comment in the pop-up box (refer to Figure 2-2). You can also right-click a cell and choose Show/Hide Comment.
- **Finding comments:** On the Review tab, click the Previous or Next button to go from comment to comment.
- **Editing a comment:** Select the cell with the comment, and on the Review tab, click the Edit Comment button, and edit the comment in the pop-up box. You can also right-click the cell and choose Edit Comment.
- **Deleting comments:** On the Review tab, click a cell with a comment, and then click the Delete button, or right-click the cell and choose Delete Comment. To delete several comments, select them by Ctrl+clicking and then click the Delete button.
- **Deleting all comments in a worksheet:** Select all comments and then, on the Review tab, click the Delete button. You can select all comments by clicking the Find & Select button on the Home tab and choosing Comments on the drop-down list.

If your name doesn't appear in the pop-up box after you enter a comment and you want it to appear there, go to the File tab, choose Options, select the General category in the Excel Options dialog box, and enter your name in the User Name text box.

You can print the comments in a worksheet. On the Page Layout tab, click the Page Setup group button, and on the Sheet tab of the Page Setup dialog box, open the Comments drop-down list and choose At End of Sheet or As Displayed on Sheet.

Selecting Cells in a Worksheet

To format, copy, move, delete, and format numbers and words in a worksheet, you have to select the cells in which the numbers and words are found. Here are ways to select cells and the data inside them:

- **A block of cells:** Drag diagonally across the worksheet from one corner of the block of cells to the opposite corner. You can also click in one corner and Shift+click the opposite corner.
- **Adjacent cells in a row or column:** Drag across the cells.
- **Cells in various places:** While holding down the Ctrl key, click different cells.
- **A row or rows:** Click a row number to select an entire row. Click and drag down the row numbers to select several adjacent rows.
- **A column or columns:** Click a column letter to select an entire column. Click and drag across letters to select adjacent columns.
- **Entire worksheet:** Click the Select All button, the square to the left of the column letters and above the row numbers; press Ctrl+A; or press Ctrl+Shift+Spacebar.

Press Ctrl+Spacebar to select the column that the active cell is in; press Shift+Spacebar to select the row where the active cell is.

You can enter the same data item in several different cells by selecting cells and then entering the data in one cell and pressing Ctrl+Enter. This technique comes in very handy, for example, when you want to enter a placeholder zero (0) in several different cells.

Deleting, Copying, and Moving Data

In the course of putting together a worksheet, it is sometimes necessary to delete, copy, and move cell contents. Here are instructions for doing these chores:

- **Deleting cell contents:** Select the cells and then press the Delete key; on the Home tab, click the Clear button and choose Clear Contents; or right-click and choose Clear Contents. (Avoid the Delete button on the Home tab for deleting cell contents. Clicking that button deletes cells as well as their contents.)
- **Copying and moving cell contents:** Select the cells and use one of these techniques:
  - *Cut or Copy and Paste commands:* When you paste the data, click where you want the first cell of the block of cells you're copying or moving to go. (Book I, Chapter 2 explains copying and moving data in detail.) Be careful not to overwrite cells with data in them when you copy or move data. After you paste data, you see the Paste Options button. Click this button and choose an option from the drop-down list to format the data in different ways.
  - *Drag and drop:* Move the pointer to the edge of the cell block, click when you see the four-headed arrow, and start dragging. Hold down the Ctrl key to copy the data.

Handling the Worksheets in a Workbook

A workbook can hold more than one worksheet. Keeping more than one worksheet in the same workbook has advantages. For example, in a workbook that tracks monthly income from rental properties, you can record monthly income on 12 worksheets, 1 for each month. By constructing formulas that calculate income data across the 12 worksheets, you can track annual income from the properties.

As Figure 2-3 shows, Excel places a tab at the bottom of the screen for each worksheet in a workbook. Worksheets are named Sheet1, Sheet2, and so on, but you can change their names. Click a tab to go from worksheet to worksheet. Right-click a tab open a shortcut menu with commands for handling worksheets.

Follow these instructions to move among, add, delete, rename, and change the order of worksheets:

- **Inserting a new worksheet:** Click the New Sheet button (you can find it in the lower-left corner of the screen to the right of the worksheet tab); press Shift+F11; or on the Home tab, open the drop-down list on the Insert button and choose Insert Sheet.
- **Moving among worksheets:** To go from one worksheet to another, click a worksheet tab along the bottom of the screen. If you can't see a tab, click one of the scroll arrows to the left of the worksheet tabs.

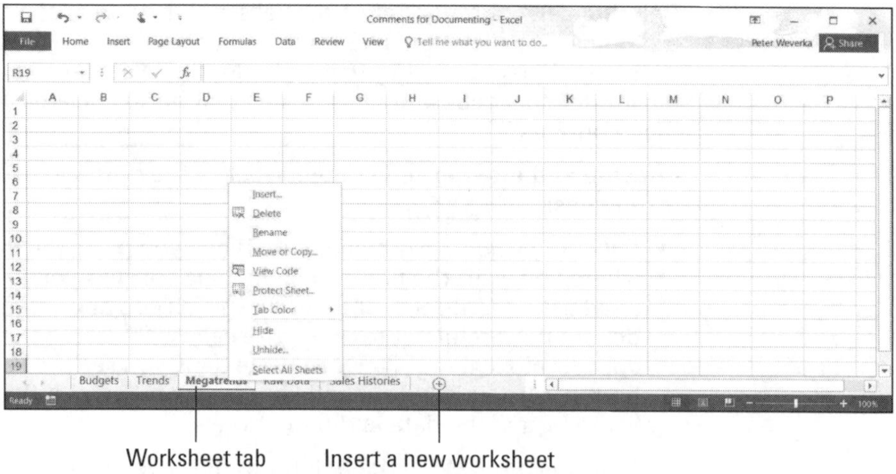

Figure 2-3: You can have multiple worksheets in a workbook.

- **Renaming a worksheet:** Right-click the worksheet tab, choose Rename on the shortcut menu, type a new name, and press Enter. You can also go to the Home tab, click the Format button, choose Rename Sheet on the drop-down list, and enter a new name. Spaces are allowed in names, and names can be 31 characters long. Brackets ([ ]) are allowed in names, but you can't use these symbols: / \ : ? and * .
- **Selecting worksheets:** Click the worksheet's tab to select it. To select several worksheets, Ctrl+click their tabs or click the first tab and then Shift+click the last tab in the set. To select all the worksheets, right-click a tab and choose Select All Sheets on the shortcut menu.
- **Rearranging worksheets:** Drag the worksheet tab to a new location. As you drag, a tiny black arrow and a page icon appear to show you where the worksheet will land after you release the mouse button. You can also select a sheet, go to the Home tab, click the Format button, and choose Move or Copy Sheet on the drop-down list. The Move or Copy dialog box appears, as shown in Figure 2-4. Select the sheet in the Before Sheet list where you want the worksheet to go and click OK.
- **Deleting a worksheet:** Select the sheet, and on the Home tab, open the drop-down list on the Delete button and choose Delete Sheet. You can also right-click a worksheet tab and choose Delete. Be careful, because you can't restore your deleted worksheet by pressing the Undo button.
- **Copying a worksheet:** Select the sheet, hold down the Ctrl key, and drag the worksheet tab to a new location.

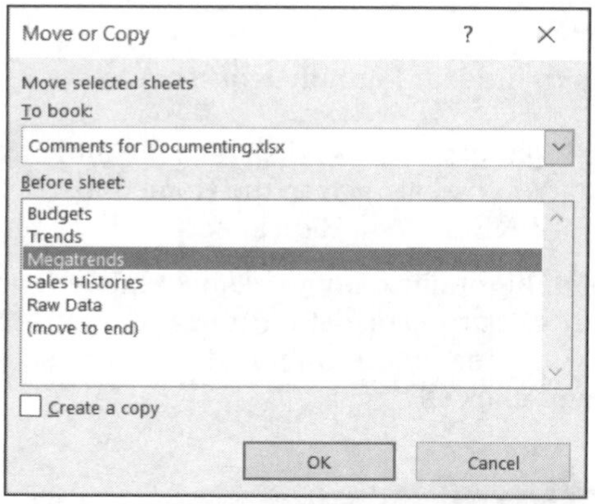

Figure 2-4: Besides dragging it, you can move a worksheet by using this dialog box.

- **Moving a worksheet to another notebook:** Make sure that the other workbook is open, open the drop-down list on the Format button, and choose Move or Copy Sheet. Then select the other workbook's name in the Move or Copy dialog box and click OK.
- **Color-coding a worksheet:** Right-click a worksheet tab and choose Tab Color. Then select a color in the submenu, or choose More Colors and select a color in the Colors dialog box.

TIP

You can change the size of columns or apply numeric formats to the same addresses in different worksheets by selecting all the sheets first and then formatting one worksheet. The formats apply to all the worksheets that you select. Being able to format several different worksheets simultaneously comes in handy, for example, when your workbook tracks monthly data and each worksheet pertains to one month. Another way to handle worksheets with similar data is to create the first worksheet and copy it to the second, third, and fourth worksheets with the Copy and Paste commands.

Keeping Others from Tampering with Worksheets

People with savvy and foresight sometimes set up workbooks so that one worksheet holds raw data and the other worksheets hold formulas that calculate the raw data. This technique prevents others from tampering with the raw data. Furthermore, if the worksheet with raw data is hidden, the chance that it will be tampered with is lower; and if the worksheet is protected, people can't tamper with it unless they have a password. These pages explain how to hide a worksheet so that others are less likely to find it. I also tell you how to protect a worksheet from being edited.

Hiding a worksheet

Follow these instructions to hide and unhide worksheets:

- **Hiding a worksheet:** Right-click the worksheet's tab and choose Hide on the shortcut menu. You can also go to the Home tab, click the Format button, and choose Hide &Unhide ➪ Hide Sheet.
- **Unhiding a worksheet:** Right-click any worksheet tab and choose Unhide; or go to the Home tab, click the Format button, and choose Hide & Unhide ➪ Unhide Sheet. Then, in the Unhide dialog box, select the sheet you want to unhide and click OK.

Protecting a worksheet

Protecting a worksheet means to restrict others from changing it — from formatting it, inserting new rows and columns, or deleting rows and columns, among other tasks. You can also prevent any editorial changes whatsoever from being made to a worksheet. Follow these steps to protect a worksheet from tampering by others:

1. **Select the worksheet that needs protection.**
2. **On the Review tab, click the Protect Sheet button.**

   You see the Protect Sheet dialog box shown in Figure 2-5. You can also open this dialog box by going to the Home tab, clicking the Format button, and choosing Protect Sheet.

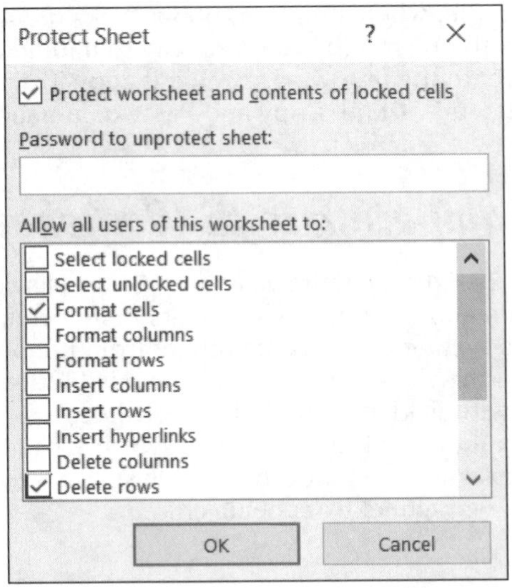

Figure 2-5: Select what you want others to be able to do.

3. **Enter a password in the Password to Unprotect Sheet box if you want only people with the password to be able to unprotect the worksheet after you protect it.**
4. **On the Allow All Users of This Worksheet To list, select the check box next to the name of each task that you want to permit others to do.**

   For example, click the Format Cells check box if you want others to be able to format cells.

   TIP: Deselect the Select Locked Cells check box to prevent any changes from being made to the worksheet. By default, all worksheet cells are locked, and by preventing others from selecting locked cells, you effectively prevent them from editing any cells.
5. **Click OK.**

   If you entered a password in Step 3, you must enter it again in the Confirm Password dialog box and click OK.

To unprotect a worksheet that you protected, go to the Review tab and click the Unprotect Sheet button. You must enter a password if you elected to require others to have a password before they can unprotect a worksheet.

Chapter 3: Formulas and Functions for Crunching Numbers

In This Chapter

- Constructing a formula
- Using cell ranges in formulas
- Naming cell ranges
- Referring to cells in other worksheets
- Copying formulas to other columns and rows
- Preventing errors in formulas
- Using functions in formulas

Formulas are where it's at as far as Excel is concerned. After you know how to construct formulas, and constructing them is pretty easy, you can put Excel to work. You can make the numbers speak to you. You can turn a bunch of unruly numbers into meaningful figures and statistics.

This chapter explains what a formula is, how to enter a formula, and how to enter a formula quickly. You also discover how to copy formulas from cell to cell and how to keep formula errors from creeping into your workbooks. Finally, this chapter explains how to make use of the hundred or so functions that Excel offers.

How Formulas Work

A *formula,* you may recall from the sleepy hours you spent in math class, is a way to calculate numbers. For example, 2+3=5 is a formula. When you enter a formula in a cell, Excel computes the formula and displays its results in the cell. Click in cell A3 and enter **=2+3**, for example, and Excel displays the number 5 in cell A3.

Referring to cells in formulas

As well as numbers, Excel formulas can refer to the contents of different cells. When a formula refers to a cell, the number in the cell is used to compute the formula. In Figure 3-1, for example, cell A1 contains the number 2; cell A2 contains the number 3; and cell A3 contains the formula `=A1+A2`. As shown in cell A3, the result of the formula is 5. If I change the number in cell A1 from 2 to 3, the result of the formula in cell A3 (`=A1+A2`) becomes 6, not 5. When a formula refers to a cell and the number in the cell changes, the result of the formula changes as well.

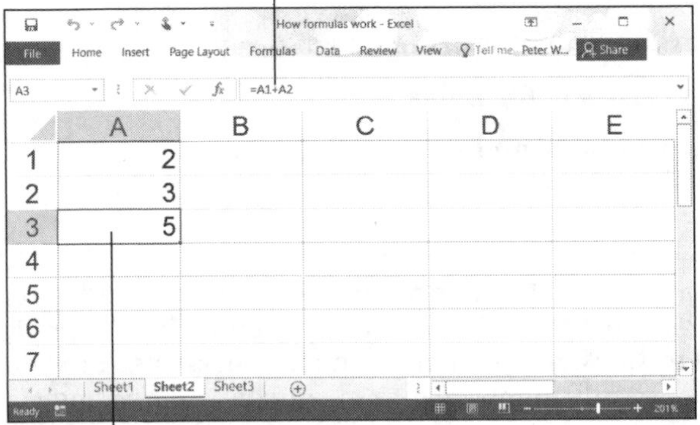

Figure 3-1: A simple formula.

To see the value of using cell references in formulas, consider the worksheet shown in Figure 3-2. The purpose of this worksheet is to track the budget of a school's Parent Teacher Association (PTA):

- Column C, Actual Income, lists income from different sources.
- Column D, Projected Income, shows what the PTA members thought income from these sources would be.
- Column E, Over/Under Budget, shows how actual income compares to projected income from the different sources.

As the figures in the Actual Income column (column C) are updated, figures in the Over/Under Budget column (column E) and the Total Income row (row 8) change instantaneously. These figures change instantaneously because the formulas refer to the numbers in cells, not to unchanging numbers (known as *constants*).

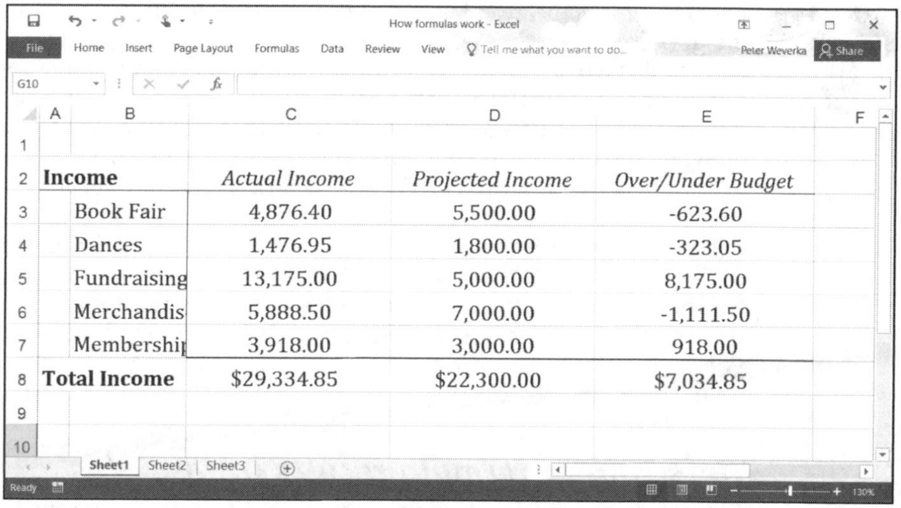

Figure 3-2: Using formulas in a worksheet.

Figure 3-3 shows the formulas used to calculate the data in the worksheet in Figure 3-2. In column E, formulas deduct the numbers in column D from the numbers in column C to show where the PTA over- or under-budgeted for the different sources of income. In row 8, you can see how the `SUM` function is used to total cells in rows 3 through 7. The end of this chapter explains how to use functions in formulas.

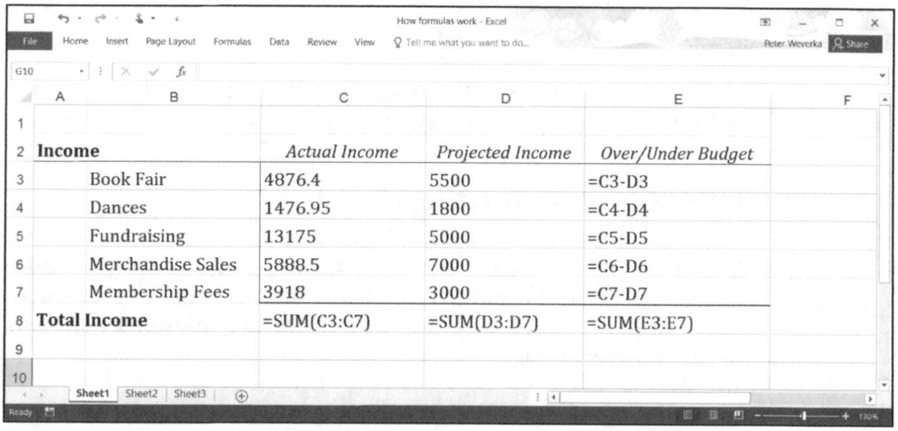

Figure 3-3: The formulas used to generate the numbers in Figure 3-2.

REMEMBER

Excel is remarkably good about updating cell references in formulas when you move cells. To see how good Excel is, consider what happens to cell addresses in formulas when you delete a row in a worksheet. If a formula refers to cell C1 but you delete row B, row C becomes row B and the value in cell C1 changes addresses from C1 to B1. You would think that references in formulas to cell C1 would be out of date, but you would be wrong. Excel automatically adjusts all formulas that refer to cell C1. Those formulas now refer to cell B1 instead.

In case you're curious, you can display formulas in worksheet cells instead of the results of formulas, as was done in Figure 3-3, by pressing Ctrl+' (apostrophe) or clicking the Show Formulas button on the Formulas tab (you may have to click the Formula Auditing button first, depending on the size of your screen). Click the Show Formulas button a second time to see formula results again.

Referring to formula results in formulas

Besides referring to cells with numbers in them, you can refer to formula results in a cell. Consider the worksheet shown in Figure 3-4. The purpose of this worksheet is to track scoring by the players on a basketball team over three games:

- ✦ The Totals column (column E) shows the total points each player scored in the three games.
- ✦ The Average column (column F), using the formula results in the Totals column, determines how much each player has scored on average. The Average column does that by dividing the results in column E by 3, the number of games played.

In this case, Excel uses the results of the total-calculation formulas in column E to compute average points per game in column F.

Operators in formulas

Addition, subtraction, and division aren't the only operators you can use in formulas. Table 3-1 explains the arithmetic operators you can use and the key you press to enter each operator. In the table, operators are listed in the order of precedence (see the "The order of preference" sidebar for an explanation of precedence).

Another way to compute a formula is to make use of a function. As "Working with Functions" explains later in this chapter, a function is a built-in formula that comes with Excel. `SUM`, for example, adds the numbers in cells. `AVG` finds the average of different numbers.

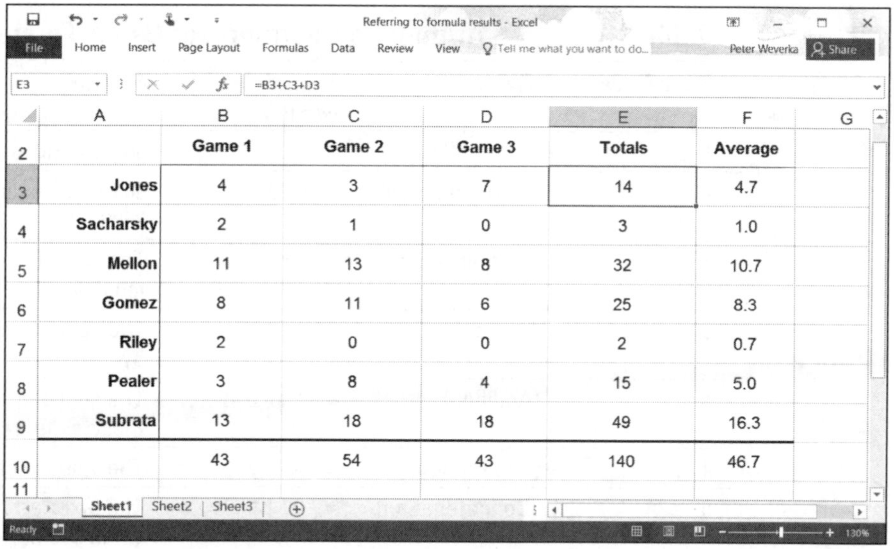
Referring to formula results - Excel

E3 =B3+C3+D3

	Game 1	Game 2	Game 3	Totals	Average
Jones	4	3	7	14	4.7
Sacharsky	2	1	0	3	1.0
Mellon	11	13	8	32	10.7
Gomez	8	11	6	25	8.3
Riley	2	0	0	2	0.7
Pealer	3	8	4	15	5.0
Subrata	13	18	18	49	16.3
	43	54	43	140	46.7

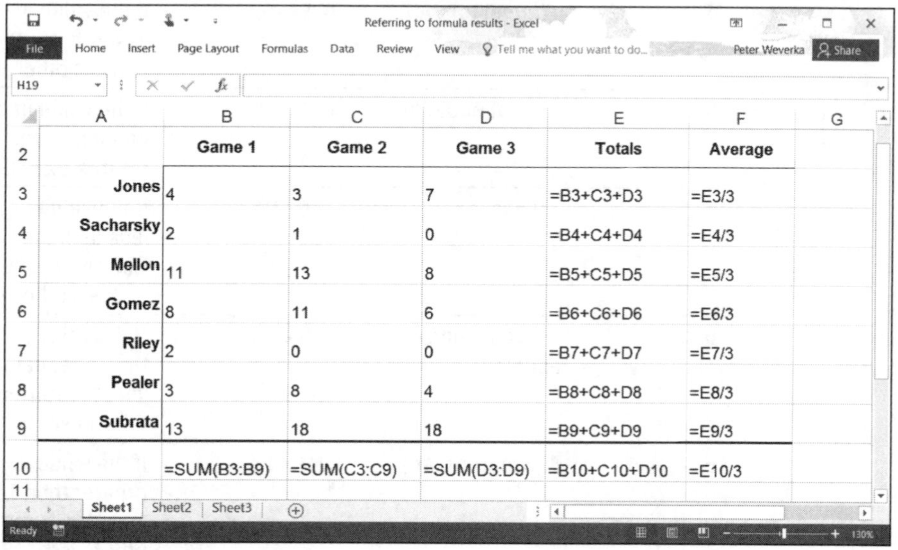
Referring to formula results - Excel

	Game 1	Game 2	Game 3	Totals	Average
Jones	4	3	7	=B3+C3+D3	=E3/3
Sacharsky	2	1	0	=B4+C4+D4	=E4/3
Mellon	11	13	8	=B5+C5+D5	=E5/3
Gomez	8	11	6	=B6+C6+D6	=E6/3
Riley	2	0	0	=B7+C7+D7	=E7/3
Pealer	3	8	4	=B8+C8+D8	=E8/3
Subrata	13	18	18	=B9+C9+D9	=E9/3
	=SUM(B3:B9)	=SUM(C3:C9)	=SUM(D3:D9)	=B10+C10+D10	=E10/3

Figure 3-4: Using formula results as other formulas.

Table 3-1 Arithmetic Operators for Use in Formulas

Precedence	*Operator*	*Example Formula*	*Returns*
1	% (Percent)	=50%	50 percent, or 0.5
2	^ (Exponentiation)	=50^2,	50 to the second power, or 2500
3	* (Multiplication)	=E2*4	The value in cell E2 multiplied by 4
3	/ (Division)	=E2/3	The value in cell E2 divided by 3
4	+ (Addition)	=F1+F2+F3,	The sum of the values in those cells
4	– (Subtraction)	=G5-8,	The value in cell G5 minus 8
5	& (Concatenation)	="Part No. "&D4	The text *Part No.* and the value in cell D4
6	= (Equal to)	=C5=4,	If the value in cell C5 is equal to 4, returns TRUE; returns FALSE otherwise
6	<> (Not equal to)	=F3<>9	If the value in cell F3 is *not* equal to 9, returns TRUE; returns FALSE otherwise
6	< (Less than)	=B9<E11	If the value in cell B9 is less than the value in cell E11; returns TRUE; returns FALSE otherwise
6	<= (Less than or equal to)	=A4<=9	If the value in cell A4 is less than or equal to 9, returns TRUE; returns FALSE otherwise
6	> (Greater than)	=E8>14	If the value in cell E8 is greater than 14, returns TRUE; returns FALSE otherwise
6	>= (Greater than or equal to)	=C3>=D3	If the value in cell C3 is greater than or equal to the value in cell D3; returns TRUE; returns FALSE otherwise

The order of precedence

When a formula includes more than one operator, the order in which the operators appear in the formula matters a lot. Consider this formula:

```
=2+3*4
```

Does this formula result in 14 (2+[3*4]) or 20 ([2+3]*4)? The answer is 14 because Excel performs multiplication before addition in formulas. In other words, multiplication takes precedence over addition.

The order in which calculations are made in a formula that includes different operators is called the *order of precedence.* Be sure to remember the order of precedence when you construct complex formulas with more than one operator:

1. Percent (%)
2. Exponentiation (^)
3. Multiplication (*) and division (/); leftmost operations are calculated first
4. Addition (+) and subtraction (-); leftmost operations are calculated first
5. Concatenation (&)
6. Comparison (<, <=, >,>=, and <>)

To get around the order of precedence problem, enclose parts of formulas in parentheses. Operations in parentheses are calculated before all other parts of a formula. For example, the formula `=2+3*4` equals 20 when it is written this way: `=(2+3)*4`.

The Basics of Entering a Formula

No matter what kind of formula you enter, no matter how complex the formula is, follow these basic steps to enter it:

1. **Click the cell where you want to enter the formula.**
2. **Click in the Formula bar if you want to enter the data there rather than the cell.**
3. **Enter the equal sign (=).**

   REMEMBER

   You must be sure to enter the equal sign before you enter a formula. Without it, Excel thinks you're entering text or a number, not a formula.
4. **Enter the formula.**

   For example, enter **=B1*.06**. Make sure that you enter all cell addresses correctly. By the way, you can enter lowercase letters in cell references.

Excel changes them to uppercase after you finish entering the formula. The next section in this chapter explains how to enter cell addresses quickly in formulas.

5. **Press Enter or click the Enter button (the check mark on the Formulabar).**

   The result of the formula appears in the cell.

Speed Techniques for Entering Formulas

Entering formulas and making sure that all cell references are correct is a tedious activity, but fortunately for you, Excel offers a few techniques to make entering formulas easier. Read on to find out how ranges make entering cell references easier and how you can enter cell references in formulas by pointing and clicking. You also find instructions here for copying formulas.

Clicking cells to enter cell references

The hardest part about entering a formula is entering the cell references correctly. You have to squint to see which row and column the cell you want to refer to is in. You have to carefully type the right column letter and row number. However, instead of typing a cell reference, you can click the cell you want to refer to in a formula.

In the course of entering a formula, simply click the cell on your worksheet that you want to reference. As shown in Figure 3-5, shimmering marquee lights appear around the cell that you clicked so that you can clearly see which cell you're referring to. The cell's reference address, meanwhile, appears in the Formula bar. In Figure 3-5, I clicked cell F3 instead of entering its reference address on the Formula bar. The reference F3 appears on the Formula bar, and the marquee lights appear around cell F3.

Get in the habit of pointing and clicking cells to enter cell references in formulas. Clicking cells is easier than typing cell addresses, and the cell references are entered more accurately.

Entering a cell range

A *cell range* is a line or block of cells in a worksheet. Instead of typing cell reference addresses one at a time, you can simply select cells on your worksheet. In Figure 3-6, I selected cells C3, D3, E3, and F3 to form cell range C3:F3. This spares me the trouble of entering one at a time the cell addresses that I want in the range. The formula in Figure 3-6 uses the `SUM` function to total the numeric values in cell range C3:F3. Notice the marquee lights around the range C3:F3. The lights show precisely which range you're selecting. Cell ranges come in especially handy where functions are concerned (see "Working with Functions," later in this chapter).

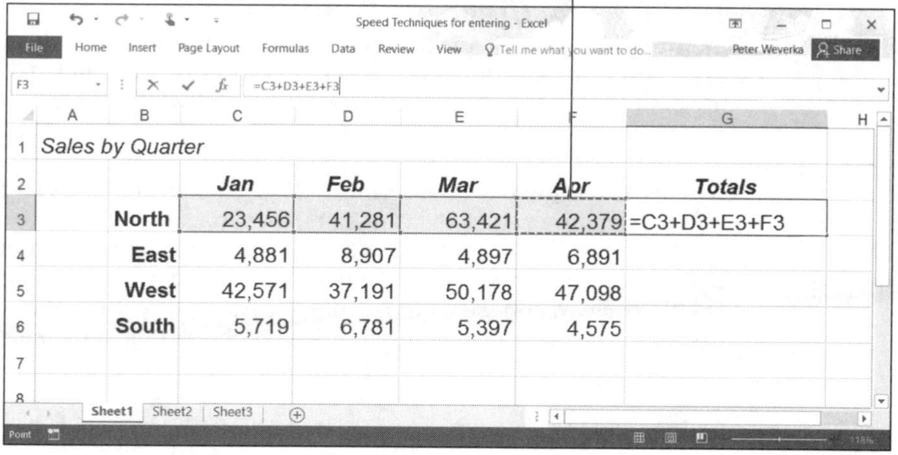

Figure 3-5: Clicking to enter a cell reference.

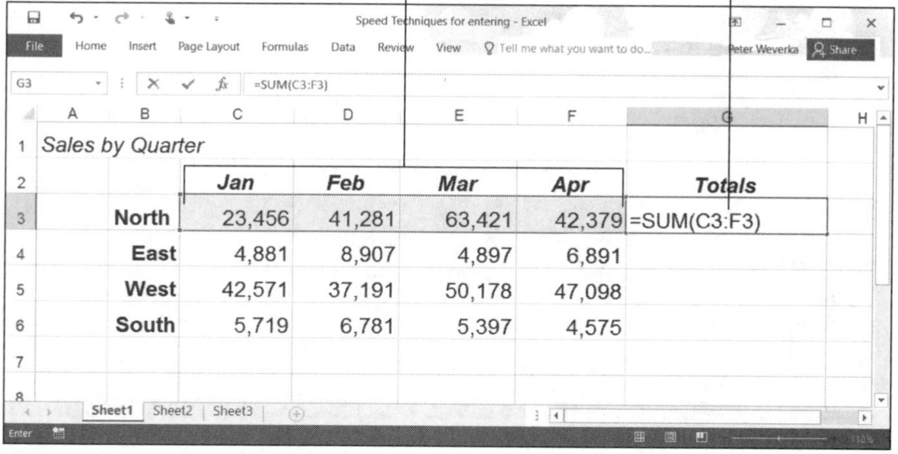

Figure 3-6: Using a cell range in a formula.

Book III Chapter 3

Formulas and Functions for Crunching Numbers

To identify a cell range, Excel lists the outermost cells in the range and places a colon (:) between cell addresses:

- ✦ A cell range comprising cells A1, A2, A3, and A4 is listed this way: A1:A4.
- ✦ A cell range comprising a block of cells from A1 to D4 is listed this way: A1:D4.

You can enter cell ranges on your own without selecting cells. To do so, type the first cell in the range, enter a colon (:), and type the last cell.

Naming cell ranges so that you can use them in formulas

Whether you type cell addresses yourself or drag across cells to enter a cell range, entering cell address references is a chore. Entering **=C1+C2+C3+C4**, for example, can cause a finger cramp; entering **=SUM(C1:C4)** is no piece of cake, either.

To take the tedium out of entering cell ranges in formulas, you can name cell ranges. Then, to enter a cell range in a formula, all you have to do is select a name in the Paste Name dialog box or click the Use in Formula button on the Formulas tab, as shown in Figure 3-7. Naming cell ranges has an added benefit: You can choose a name from the Name Box drop-down list and go directly to the cell range whose name you choose, as shown in Figure 3-7.

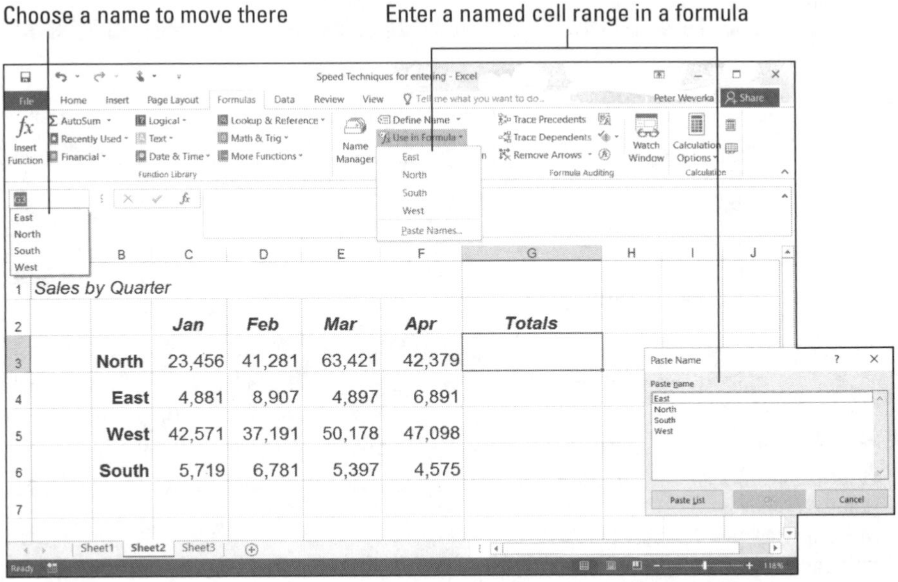

Figure 3-7: Choosing a named cell range.

WARNING!

Naming cell ranges has one disadvantage, and it's a big one. Excel doesn't adjust cell references when you copy a formula with a range name from one cell to another. A range name always refers to the same set of cells. Later in this chapter, "Copying Formulas from Cell to Cell" explains how to copy formulas.

Creating a cell range name

Follow these steps to create a cell range name:

1. **Select the cells that you want to name.**
2. **On the Formulas tab, click the Define Name button.**

   You see the New Name dialog box.
3. **Enter a descriptive name in the Name box.**

   Names can't begin with a number or include blank spaces.
4. **On the Scope drop-down list, choose Workbook or a worksheet name.**

   Choose a worksheet name if you intend to use the range name you're creating only in formulas that you construct in a single worksheet. If your formulas will refer to cell range addresses in different worksheets, choose Workbook so that you can use the range name wherever you go in your workbook.
5. **Enter a comment to describe the range name, if you want.**

   Enter a comment if doing so will help you remember where the cells you're naming are located or what type of information they hold. As I explain shortly, you can read comments in the Name Manager dialog box, the place where you go to edit and delete range names.
6. **Click OK.**

TIP

In case you're in a hurry, here's a fast way to enter a cell range name: Select the cells for the range, click in the Name Box (you can find it on the left side of the Formula bar, as shown in Figure 3-7), enter a name for the range, and press the Enter key.

Entering a range name as part of a formula

To include a cell range name in a formula, click in the Formula bar where you want to enter the range name and then use one of these techniques to enter the name:

- ✦ On the Formulas tab, click the Use in Formula button and choose a cell range name on the drop-down list (refer to Figure 3-7).
- ✦ Press F3 or click the Use in Formula button and choose Paste Names on the drop-down list. You see the Paste Name dialog box (refer to Figure 3-7). Select a cell range name and click OK.

Quickly traveling to a cell range that you named

To go quickly to a cell range you named, open the drop-down list on the Name Box and choose a name (refer to Figure 3-7). The Name Box drop-down list is located on the left side of the Formula bar.

To make this trick work, the cursor can't be in the Formula bar. The Name Box drop-down list isn't available when you're constructing a formula.

Managing cell range names

To rename, edit, or delete cell range names, go to the Formulas tab and click the Name Manager button. You see the Name Manager dialog box, as shown in Figure 3-8. This dialog box lists names, cell values in names, the worksheet on which the range name is found, and whether the range name can be applied throughout a workbook or only in one worksheet. To rename, edit, or delete a cell range name, select it in the dialog box and use these techniques:

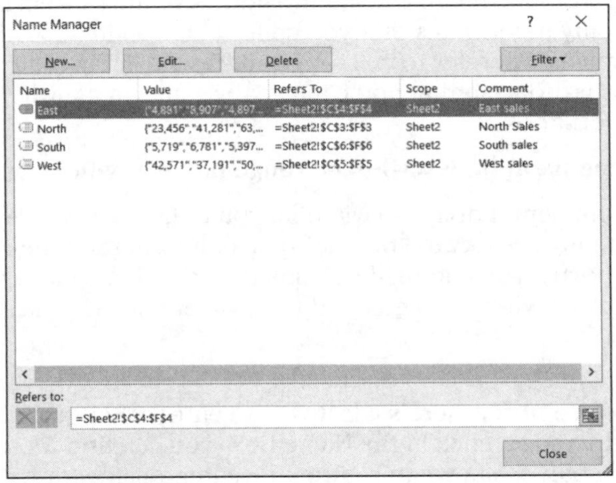

Figure 3-8: The Name Manager dialog box.

- **Renaming:** Click the Edit button and enter a new name in the Edit Name dialog box.
- **Reassigning cells:** To assign different cells to a range name, click the Edit button. You see the Edit Name dialog box. To enter a new range of cells, either enter the cells' addresses in the Refers To text box or click the Range Selector button (it's to the right of the text box), drag across the cells on your worksheet that you want for the cell range, and click the Cell Selector button again to return to the Edit Name dialog box.
- **Deleting:** Click the Delete button and click OK in the confirmation box.

Referring to cells in different worksheets

Excel gives you the opportunity to use data from different worksheets in a formula. If one worksheet lists sales figures from January and the next lists sales figures from February, you can construct a "grand total" formula in either worksheet to tabulate sales in the two-month period. A reference to a cell on a different worksheet is called a *3D reference.*

Construct the formula as you normally would, but when you want to refer to a cell or cell range in a different worksheet, click a worksheet tab to move to the other worksheet and select the cell or range of cells there. Without returning to the original worksheet, complete your formula in the Formula bar and press Enter. Excel returns you to the original worksheet, where you can see the results of your formula.

The only odd thing about constructing formulas across worksheets is the cell references. As a glance at the Formula bar tells you, cell addresses in cross-worksheet formulas list the sheet name and an exclamation point (!) as well as the cell address itself. For example, this formula in Sheet 1 adds the number in cell A4 to the numbers in cells D5 and E5 in Sheet 2:

```
=A4+Sheet2!D5+Sheet2!E5
```

This formula in Sheet 2 multiplies the number in cell E18 by the number in cell C15 in Worksheet 1:

```
=E18*Sheet1!C15
```

This formula in Sheet 2 finds the average of the numbers in the cell range C7:F7 in Sheet 1:

```
=AVERAGE(Sheet1!C7:F7)
```


Copying Formulas from Cell to Cell

Often in worksheets, you use the same formula across a row or down a column, but different cell references are used. For example, in the worksheet shown in Figure 3-9, column F totals the rainfall figures in rows 7 through 11. To enter formulas for totaling the rainfall figures in column F, you could laboriously enter formulas in cells F7, F8, F9, F10, and F11. But a faster way is to enter the formula once in cell F7 and then copy the formula in F7 down the column to cells F8, F9, F10, and F11.

When you copy a formula to a new cell, Excel adjusts the cell references in the formula so that the formula works in the cells to which it has been copied. Astounding! Opportunities to copy formulas abound on most worksheets. And copying formulas is the fastest and safest way to enter formulas in a worksheet.

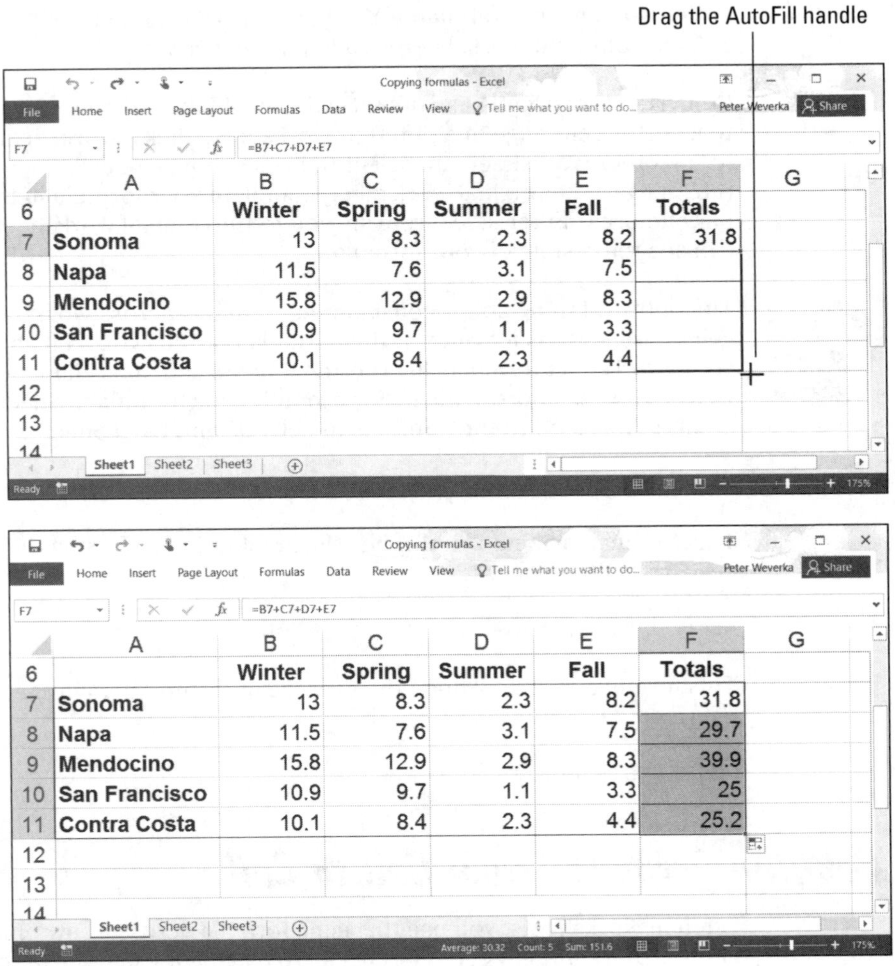

Figure 3-9: Copying a formula.

Follow these steps to copy a formula:

1. **Select the cell with the formula you want to copy down a column or across a row.**
2. **Drag the AutoFill handle across the cells to which you want to copy the formula.**

   This is the same AutoFill handle you drag to enter serial data (see Chapter 1 of this mini-book about entering lists and serial data with the AutoFill command). The AutoFill handle is the small green square in the lower-right corner of the cell. When you move the mouse pointer over it, it changes to a black cross. Figure 3-9 shows a formula being copied.

3. **Release the mouse button.**

   If I were you, I would click in the cells to which you copied the formula and glance at the Formula bar to make sure that the formula was copied correctly. I'd bet you it was.

You can also copy formulas with the Copy and Paste commands. Just make sure that cell references refer correctly to the surrounding cells.

Detecting and Correcting Errors in Formulas

It happens. Everyone makes an error from time to time when entering formulas in cells. Especially in a worksheet in which formula results are calculated into other formulas, a single error in one formula can spread like a virus and cause miscalculations throughout a worksheet. To prevent that calamity, Excel offers several ways to correct errors in formulas. You can correct them one at a time, run the error checker, and trace cell references, as the following pages explain.

TIP

By the way, if you want to see formulas in cells instead of formula results, go to the Formulas tab and click the Show Formulas button or press Ctrl+' (apostrophe). Sometimes seeing formulas this way helps to detect formula errors.

Correcting errors one at a time

When Excel detects what it thinks is a formula that has been entered incorrectly, a small green triangle appears in the upper-left corner of the cell where you entered the formula. And if the error is especially egregious, an *error message,* a cryptic three- or four-letter display preceded by a pound sign (#), appears in the cell. Table 3-2 explains common error messages.

To find out more about a formula error and perhaps correct it, select the cell with the green triangle and click the Error button. This small button appears beside a cell with a formula error after you click the cell, as shown in Figure 3-10. The drop-down list on the Error button offers opportunities for correcting formula errors and finding out more about them.

Running the error checker

Another way to tackle formula errors is to run the error checker. When the checker encounters what it thinks is an error, the Error Checking dialog box tells you what the error is, as shown in Figure 3-10.

Table 3-2 Common Formula Error Messages

Message	*What Went Wrong*
`#DIV/0!`	You tried to divide a number by a zero (0) or an empty cell.
`#NAME`	You used a cell range name in the formula, but the name isn't defined. Sometimes this error occurs because you type the name incorrectly. (Earlier in this chapter, "Naming cell ranges so that you can use them in formulas" explains how to name cell ranges.)
`#N/A`	The formula refers to an empty cell, so no data is available for computing the formula. Sometimes people enter N/A in a cell as a placeholder to signal the fact that data isn't entered yet. Revise the formula or enter a number or formula in the empty cells.
`#NULL`	The formula refers to a cell range that Excel can't understand. Make sure that the range is entered correctly.
`#NUM`	An argument you use in your formula is invalid.
`#REF`	The cell or range of cells that the formula refers to aren't there.
`#VALUE`	The formula includes a function that was used incorrectly, takes an invalid argument, or is misspelled. Make sure that the function uses the right argument and is spelled correctly.

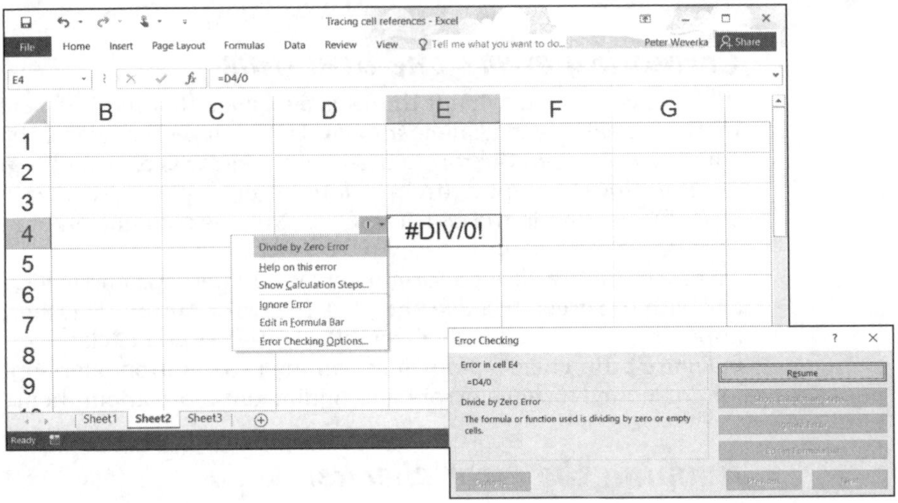

Figure 3-10: Ways to detect and correct errors.

To run the error checker, go to the Formulas tab and click the Error Checking button (you may have to click the Formula Auditing button first, depending on the size of your screen).

If you see clearly what the error is, click the Edit in Formula Bar button, repair the error in the Formula bar, and click the Resume button in the dialog box (you find this button at the top of the dialog box). If the error isn't one that really needs correcting, either click the Ignore Error button or click the Next button to send the error checker in search of the next error in your worksheet.

Tracing cell references

In a complex worksheet in which formulas are piled on top of one another and the results of some formulas are computed into other formulas, it helps to be able to trace cell references. By tracing cell references, you can see how the data in a cell figures into a formula in another cell; or, if the cell contains a formula, you can see which cells the formula gathers data from to make its computation. You can get a better idea of how your worksheet is constructed, and in so doing, find structural errors more easily.

Figure 3-11 shows how cell tracers describe the relationships between cells. A *cell tracer* is a blue arrow that shows the relationships between cells used in formulas. You can trace two types of relationships:

- ✦ **Tracing precedents:** Select a cell with a formula in it and trace the formula's *precedents* to find out which cells are computed to produce the results of the formula. Trace precedents when you want to find out where a formula gets its computation data. Cell tracer arrows point from the referenced cells to the cell with the formula results in it.

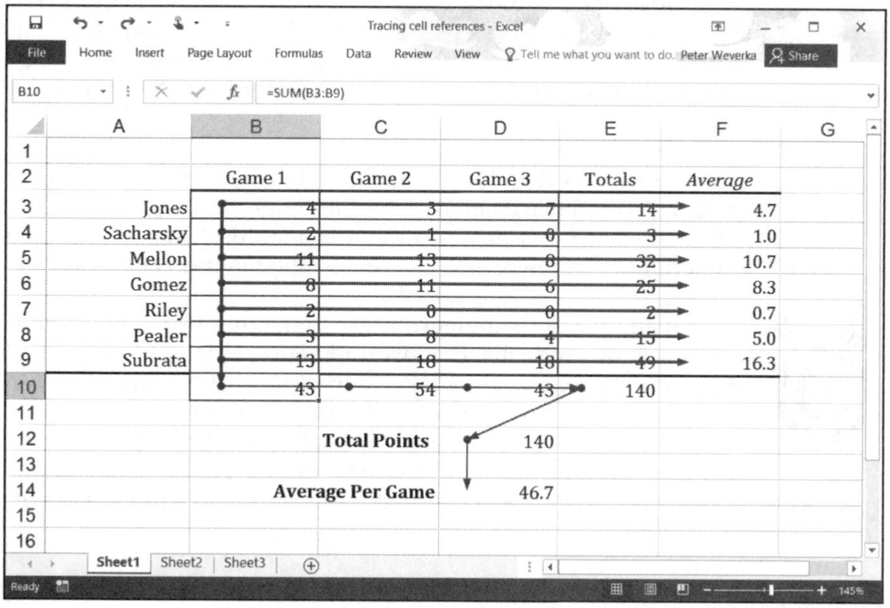

Figure 3-11: Tracing the relationships between cells.

To trace precedents, go to the Formulas tab and click the Trace Precedents button (you may have to click the Formula Auditing button first, depending on the size of your screen).

- **Tracing dependents:** Select a cell and trace its *dependents* to find out which cells contain formulas that use data from the cell you selected. Cell tracer arrows point from the cell you selected to cells with formula results in them. Trace dependents when you want to find out how the data in a cell contributes to formulas elsewhere in the worksheet. The cell you select can contain a constant value or a formula in its own right (and contribute its results to another formula).

  To trace dependents, go to the Formulas tab and click the Trace Dependents button (you may have to click the Formula Auditing button first, depending on the size of your screen).

To remove the cell tracer arrows from a worksheet, go to the Formulas tab and click the Remove Arrows button. You can open the drop-down list on this button and choose Remove Precedent Arrows or Remove Dependent Arrows to remove only cell-precedent or cell-dependent tracer arrows.

Working with Functions

A *function* is a canned formula that comes with Excel. Excel offers hundreds of functions, some of which are very obscure and fit only for use by rocket scientists or securities analysts. Other functions are very practical. For example, you can use the `SUM` function to quickly total the numbers in a range of cells. Rather than enter `=C2+C3+C4+C5` on the Formula bar, you can enter `=SUM(C2:C5)`, which tells Excel to total the numbers in cell C2, C3, C4, and C5. To obtain the product of the number in cell G4 and .06, you can use the `PRODUCT` function and enter `=PRODUCT(G4,.06)` on the Formula bar.

These pages explain how to use functions in formulas. You discover how to construct the arguments, enter function names, and get Excel's help with entering functions. Later in this chapter, "A Look at Some Very Useful Functions" examines how to use specific functions in formulas.

TIP

To get an idea of the numerous functions that Excel offers, go to the Formulas tab and click the Insert Function button. You see the Insert Function dialog box shown in Figure 3-12. (Later in this chapter, I show you how this dialog box can help with using functions in formulas.) Choose a function category in the dialog box, choose a function name, and read the description. You can click the Help on This Function link to open the Excel Help window and get a thorough description of a function and how it's used.

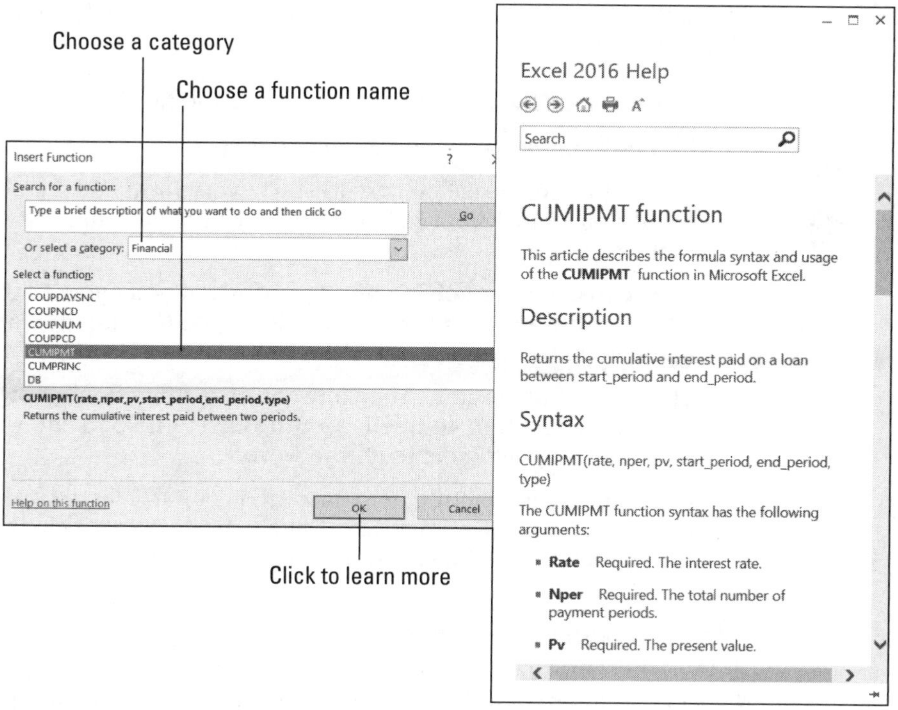

Figure 3-12: The Insert Function dialog box.

Using arguments in functions

Every function takes one or more *arguments.* Arguments are the cell references or numbers, enclosed in parentheses, which the function acts upon. For example, `=AVERAGE(B1:B4)` returns the average of the numbers in the cell range B1 through B4; `=PRODUCT(6.5,C4)` returns the product of multiplying the number 6.5 by the number in cell C4. When a function requires more than one argument, enter a comma between the arguments (enter a comma without a space).

Entering a function in a formula

To enter a function in a formula, you can enter the function name by typing it in the Formula bar, or you can rely on Excel to enter it for you. Enter function names yourself if you're well acquainted with a function and comfortable using it.

No matter how you want to enter a function as part of a formula, start this way:

1. **Select the cell where you want to enter the formula.**
2. **In the Formula bar, type an equal sign (=).**

   Please, please, please be sure to start every formula by entering an equal sign (=). Without it, Excel thinks you're entering text or a number in the cell.
3. **Start constructing your formula, and when you come to the place where you want to enter the function, type the function's name or call upon Excel to help you enter the function and its arguments.**

   The upcoming section, "Manually entering a function" shows how to type in the function yourself; "Getting Excel's help to enter a function" shows how to get Excel to do the work.

   If you enter the function on your own, it's up to you to type the arguments correctly; if you get Excel's help, you also get help with entering the cell references for the arguments.

Manually entering a function

Be sure to enclose the function's argument or arguments in parentheses. Don't enter a space between the function's name and the first parenthesis. Likewise, don't enter a comma and a space between arguments; enter a comma, nothing more:

```
=SUM(F11,F14,23)
```

You can enter function names in lowercase. Excel converts function names to uppercase after you click the Enter button or press Enter to complete the formula. Entering function names in lowercase is recommended because doing so gives you a chance to find out whether you entered a function name correctly. If Excel doesn't convert your function name to uppercase, you made a typing error when you entered the function name.

Getting Excel's help to enter a function

Besides entering a function by typing it, you can do it by way of the Function Arguments dialog box, as shown in Figure 3-13. The beauty of using this dialog box is that it warns you if you enter arguments incorrectly. What's more, the Function Arguments dialog box shows you the results of the formula as you construct it so that you can tell whether you're using the function correctly.

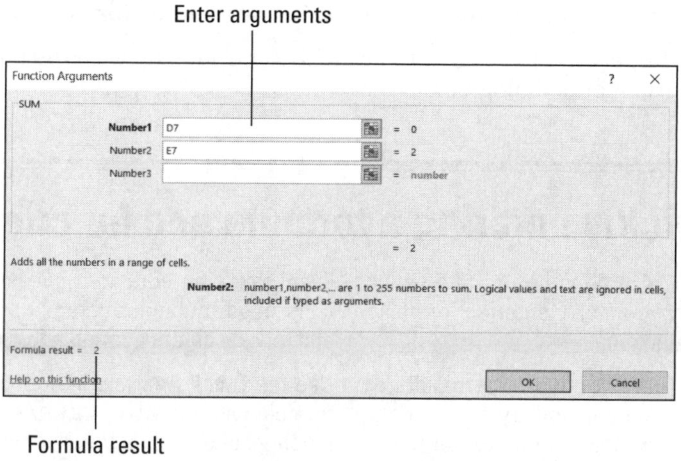

Figure 3-13: The Function Arguments dialog box.

Follow these steps to get Excel's help with entering a function as part of a formula:

1. **On the Formulas tab, tell Excel which function you want to use.**

   You can do that with one of these techniques:

   - **Click a Function Library button:** Click the button whose name describes what kind of function you want and choose the function's name on the drop-down list. You can click the Financial, Logical, Text, Date & Time, Lookup & Reference, Math & Trig, or More Functions buttons.
   - **Click the Recently Used button:** Click this button and choose the name of a function you used recently.
   - **Click the Insert Function button:** Clicking this button opens the Insert Function dialog box (refer to Figure 3-12). Find and choose the name of a function. You can search for functions or choose a category and then scroll the names until you find the function you want.

   You see the Function Arguments dialog box (refer to Figure 3-13). It offers boxes for entering arguments for the function to compute.

2. **Enter arguments in the spaces provided by the Function Arguments dialog box.**

   To enter cell references or ranges, you can click or select cells in your worksheet. If necessary, click the Range Selector button (you can find it to the right of an argument text box) to shrink the Function Arguments dialog box and get a better look at your worksheet.

3. **Click OK when you finish entering arguments for your function.**

   I hope you didn't have to argue too strenuously with the Function Arguments dialog box.

Quickly entering a formula and function

Excel offers the AutoSum button and Quick Analysis button for quickly entering formulas that include a function.

Click the cell where you want the results of your formula to appear and try these techniques for constructing formulas with the AutoSum button:

- On the Home or Formulas tab, click the AutoSum button to total nearby cells.
- On the Home or Formulas tab, open the drop-down list on the AutoSum button and choose Sum, Average, Count Numbers, Max, or Min. Respectively, these functions total, average, obtain the number of, obtain the highest value in, or obtain the lowest value in nearby cells.

Excel takes an educated guess as to which cells need totaling, averaging, or whatever, and quickly enters a formula for you.

Use the Quick Analysis button to construct a formula with the `SUM`, `AVERAGE`, or `COUNT` function, or one of their variations:

1. **Select the cells that will be used as arguments by the function.**

   The Quick Analysis button appears.

2. **Click the Quick Analysis button.**
3. **Choose Totals in the pop-up window.**
4. **Move the pointer over the various functions and glance at your worksheet to see the results of your formulas.**
5. **Select a function.**

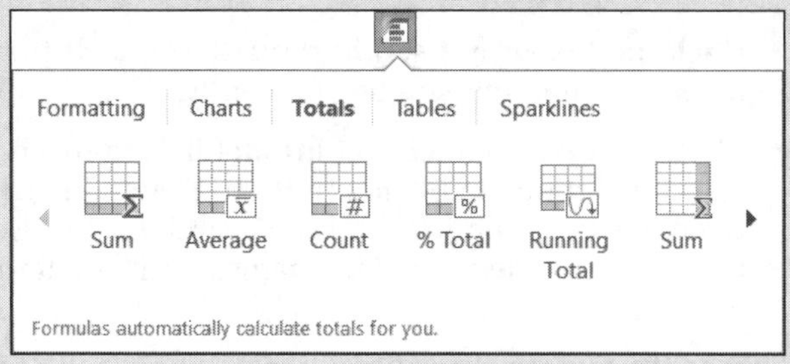

A Look at Some Very Useful Functions

Starting with Table 3-3, the remainder of this chapter looks into functions that I consider especially useful or interesting. After you spend some time constructing formulas, you'll come up with your own list of useful or interesting functions.

Table 3-3 Common Functions and Their Use

Function	*Returns*
AVERAGE(*number1,number2,...*)	The average of the numbers in the cells listed in the arguments.
COUNT(*value1,value2,...*)	The number of cells that contain the numbers listed in the arguments.
MAX(*number1,number2,...*)	The largest value in the cells listed in the arguments.
MIN(*number1,number2,...*)	The smallest value in the cells listed in the arguments.
PRODUCT(*number1,number2,...*)	The product of multiplying the cells listed in the arguments.
STDEV(*number1,number2,...*)	An estimate of standard deviation based on the sample cells listed in the argument.
STDEVP(*number1,number2,...*)	An estimate of standard deviation based on the entire sample cells listed in the arguments.
SUM(*number1,number2,...*)	The total of the numbers in the arguments.
VAR(*number1,number2,...*)	An estimate of the variance based on the sample cells listed in the arguments.
VARP(*number1,number2,...*)	A variance calculation based on all cells listed in the arguments.

AVERAGE for Averaging Data

Might as well start with an easy one. The AVERAGE function averages the values in a cell range. In Figure 3-14, for example, AVERAGE is used to compute the average rainfall in a three-month period in three different counties.

Use AVERAGE as follows:

```
AVERAGE(cell range)
```

Excel ignores empty cells and logical values in the cell range; cells with 0 are computed.

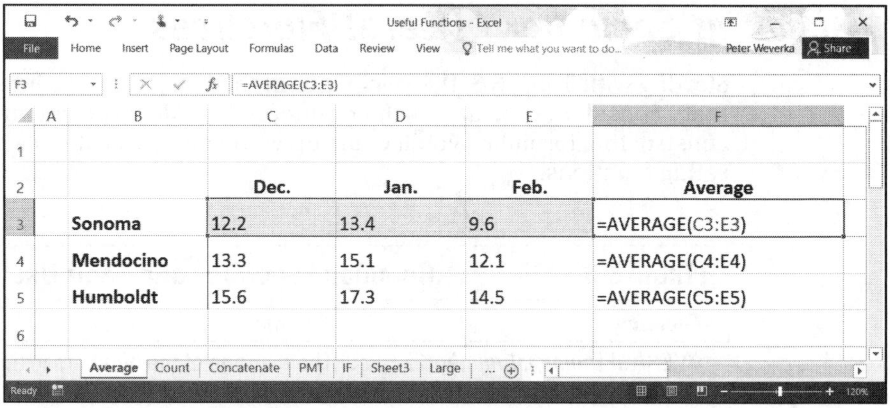

Figure 3-14: Using AVERAGE to find average rainfall data.

COUNT and COUNTIF for Tabulating Data Items

Use COUNT, a statistical function, to count how many cells have data in them. Numbers and dates, not text entries, are counted. The COUNT function is useful for tabulating how many data items are in a range. In the spreadsheet at the top of Figure 3-15, for example, COUNT is used to compute the number of mountains listed in the data:

```
COUNT(C5:C9)
```

Use COUNT as follows:

```
COUNT(cell range)
```

Similar to COUNT is the COUNTIF function. It counts how many cells in a cell range have a specific value. To use COUNTIF, enter the cell range and a criterion in the argument, as follows. If the criterion is a text value, enclose it in quotation marks.

```
COUNTIF(cell range, criterion)
```

At the bottom of Figure 3-15, the formula determines how many of the mountains in the data are in Nepal:

```
=COUNTIF(D5:D9,"Nepal")
```

CONCATENATE for Combining Values

CONCATENATE, a text function, is useful for combining values from different cells into a single cell. In the spreadsheet at the top of Figure 3-16, for example, values from three columns are combined in a fourth column to list peoples' names in their entirety.

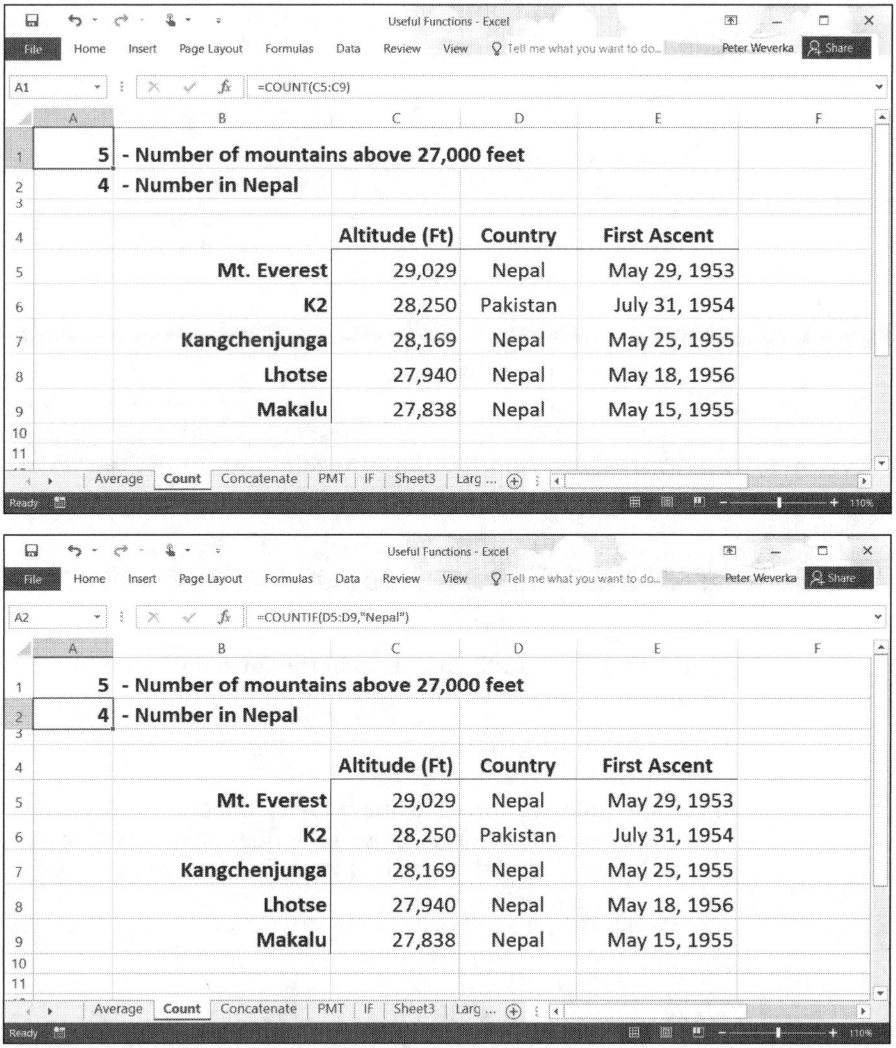

Figure 3-15: The COUNT (above) and COUNTIF (below) function at work.

Use CONCATENATE as follows:

```
CONCATENATE(text1,text2,text3...)
```

To include blank spaces in the text you're combining, enclose a blank space between quotation marks as an argument. Moreover, you can include original text in the concatenation formula as long as you enclose it in quotation marks and enter it as a separate argument. In Figure 3-16, I had to include a

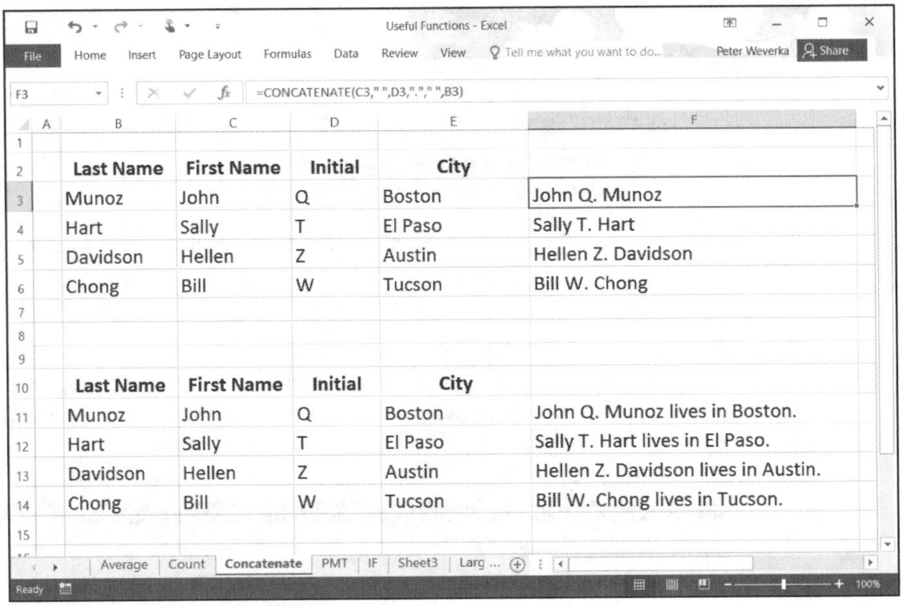

Figure 3-16: Use the CONCATENATE function to combine values from cells.

period after the middle initial, so in the formula, I entered a period in quotation marks as an argument:

```
=CONCATENATE(C3," ",D3,"."," ",B3)
```

In the spreadsheet shown at the bottom of Figure 3-16, I used the CONCATENATE function to write sentences ("John Q. Munoz lives in Boston."). I included the words "lives in" in the formula, as follows:

```
=CONCATENATE(C11," ",D11,"."," ",B11," ","lives in","
    ",E11,".")
```

PMT for Calculating How Much You Can Borrow

If you're looking to buy a house, a car, or another expensive item for which you have to borrow money, the question to ask yourself is: How much can I borrow and make the monthly payment on the loan without stressing my budget unnecessarily? Can you safely make a monthly payment of $1,000, $1,500, $2,000? How much you can afford to pay each month to service a loan determines how much you can realistically borrow.

Use the PMT (payment) function to explore how much you can borrow given different interest rates and different amounts. PMT determines how much you have to pay annually on different loans. After you determine how much you have to pay annually, you can divide this amount by 12 to see how much you have to pay monthly.

Use the PMT function as follows to determine how much you pay annually for a loan:

```
PMT(interest rate, number of payments, amount of loan)
```

As shown in Figure 3-17, set up a worksheet with five columns to explore loan scenarios:

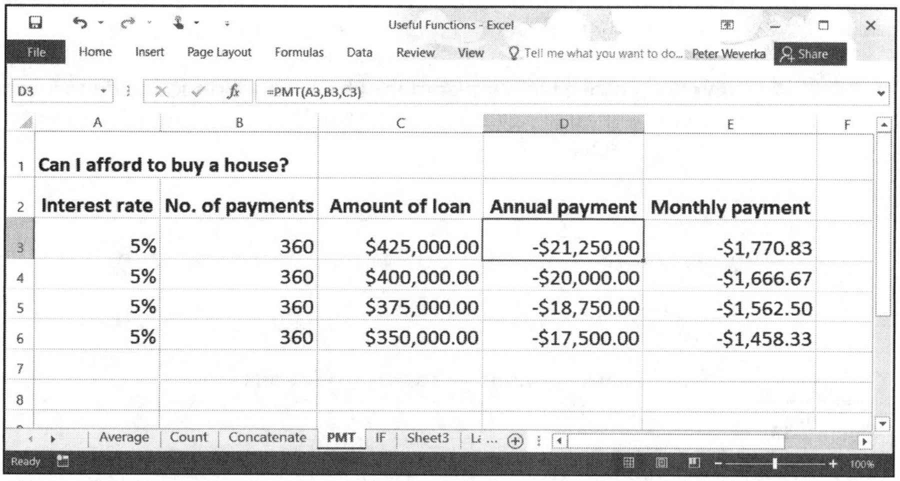

	A	B	C	D	E
1	Can I afford to buy a house?				
2	Interest rate	No. of payments	Amount of loan	Annual payment	Monthly payment
3	5%	360	$425,000.00	-$21,250.00	-$1,770.83
4	5%	360	$400,000.00	-$20,000.00	-$1,666.67
5	5%	360	$375,000.00	-$18,750.00	-$1,562.50
6	5%	360	$350,000.00	-$17,500.00	-$1,458.33
7					
8					

Figure 3-17: Exploring loan scenarios with the PMT function.

- **Interest rate (column A):** Because the interest rate on loans is expressed as a percentage, format this column to accept numbers as percentages (click the Percent Style button on the Home tab).
- **No. of payments (column B):** Typically, loan payments are made monthly. For a thirty-year home loan mortgage, enter 360 in this column (12 months × 30 years); for a 15-year mortgage, enter 180 (12 months × 15 years). Enter the total number of loan payments you will make during the life of the loan.
- **Amount of loan (column C):** Enter the amount of the loan.
- **Annual payment (column D):** Enter a formula with the PMT function in this column to determine how much you have to pay annually for the loan. In Figure 3-17, the formula is

  ```
  =PMT(A3,B3,C3)
  ```

- **Monthly payment (column E):** Divide the annual payment in column D by 12 to determine the monthly payment:

  ```
  =D3/12
  ```

After you set up the worksheet, you can start playing with different loan scenarios — different interest rates and amounts — to find out how much you can comfortably borrow and comfortably pay each month to pay back the loan.

IF for Identifying Data

The IF function examines data and returns a value based on criteria you enter. Use the IF function to locate data that meets a certain threshold. In the worksheet shown in Figure 3-18, for example, the IF function is used to identify teams that are eligible for the playoffs. To be eligible, a team must have won more than six games. The IF function identifies whether a team has won more than six games and, in the Playoffs column, enters the word *Yes* or *No* accordingly.

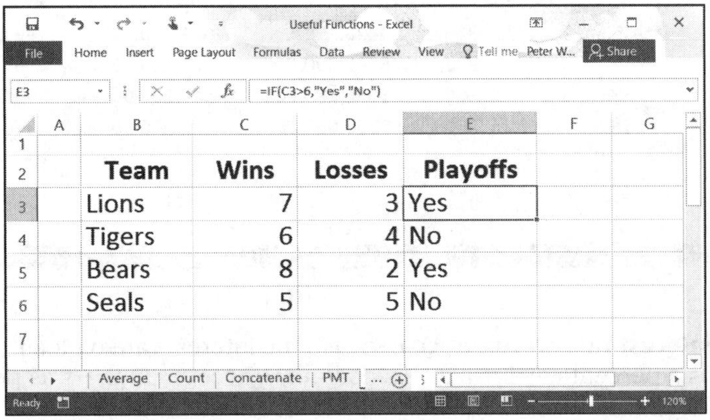

Figure 3-18: Exploring loan scenarios with the PMT function.

Use the IF function as follows:

```
IF(logical true-false test, value if true, value if false)
```

Instructing Excel to enter a value if the logical true-false test comes up false is optional; you must supply a value to enter if the test is true. Enclose the value in quotation marks if it is a text value such as the word *Yes* or *No*.

In Figure 3-18, the formula for determining whether a team made the playoffs is as follows:

```
=IF(C3>6,"Yes","No")
```

If the false "No" value was absent from the formula, teams that didn't make the playoffs would not show a value in the Playoffs column; these teams' Playoffs column would be empty.

LEFT, MID, and RIGHT for Cleaning Up Data

Sometimes when you import data from another software application, especially if it's a database application, the data arrives with unneeded characters. You can use the LEFT, MID, RIGHT, and TRIM functions to remove these characters:

- LEFT returns the leftmost characters in a cell to the number of characters you specify. For example, in a cell with CA_State, this formula returns CA, the two leftmost characters in the text:

  ```
  =LEFT(A1,2)
  ```

- MID returns the middle characters in a cell starting at a position you specify to the number of characters you specify. For example, in a cell with http://www.dummies.com, this formula uses MID to remove the extraneous seven characters at the beginning of the URL and get www.dummies.com:

  ```
  =MID(A1,7,50)
  ```

- RIGHT returns the rightmost characters in a cell to the number of characters you specify. For example, in a cell containing the words *Vitamin B1*, this formula returns B1, the two rightmost characters in the name of the vitamin:

  ```
  =RIGHT(A1,2)
  ```

- TRIM, except for single spaces between words, removes all blank spaces from inside a cell. Use TRIM to remove leading and trailing spaces. This formula removes unwanted spaces from the data in cell A1:

  ```
  =TRIM(A1)
  ```


PROPER for Capitalizing Words

The PROPER function makes the first letter of each word in a cell uppercase. As are LEFT and RIGHT, it is useful for cleaning up data you imported from elsewhere. Use PROPER as follows:

```
PROPER(cell address)
```

LARGE and SMALL for Comparing Values

Use the LARGE and SMALL functions, as well as their cousins MIN, MAX, and RANK, to find out where a value stands in a list of values. For example, use LARGE to locate the ninth oldest man in a list, or MAX to find the oldest man. Use MIN to find the smallest city by population in a list, or SMALL to find the fourth smallest. The RANK function finds the rank of a value in a list of values.

Use these functions as follows:

✦ MIN returns the smallest value in a list of values. For the argument, enter a cell range or cell array. In the worksheet shown in Figure 3-19, the following formula finds the fewest number of fish caught at any lake on any day:

```
=MIN(C3:G7)
```

✦ SMALL returns the *n*th smallest value in a list of values. This function takes two arguments, first the cell range or cell array, and next the position, expressed as a number, from the smallest of all values in the range or array. In the worksheet shown in Figure 3-19, this formula finds the second smallest number of fish caught in any lake:

```
=SMALL(C3:G7,2)
```

✦ MAX returns the largest value in a list of values. Enter a cell range or cell array as the argument. In the worksheet shown in Figure 3-19, this formula finds the most number of fish caught in any lake:

```
=MAX(C3:G7)
```

✦ LARGE returns the *n*th largest value in a list of values. This function takes two arguments, first the cell range or cell array, and next the position, expressed as a number, from the largest of all values in the range or array. In the worksheet shown in Figure 3-19, this formula finds the second largest number of fish caught in any lake:

```
=LARGE(C3:G7,2)
```

✦ RANK returns the rank of a value in a list of values. This function takes three arguments:

- The cell with the value used for ranking
- The cell range or cell array with the comparison values for determining rank
- Whether to rank in order from top to bottom (enter 0 for descending) or bottom to top (enter 1 for ascending)

In the worksheet shown in Figure 3-19, this formula ranks the total number of fish caught in Lake Temescal against the total number of fish caught in all five lakes:

```
=RANK(H3,H3:H7,0)
```

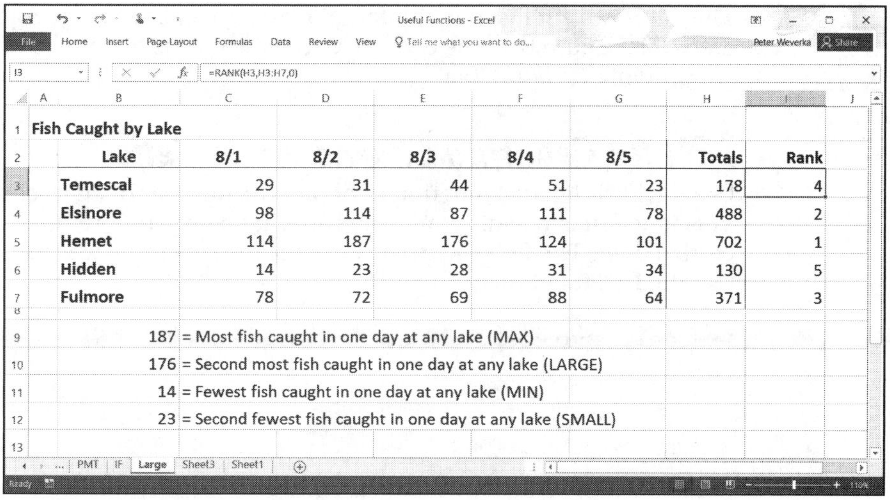

	Lake	8/1	8/2	8/3	8/4	8/5	Totals	Rank
1	Fish Caught by Lake							
3	Temescal	29	31	44	51	23	178	4
4	Elsinore	98	114	87	111	78	488	2
5	Hemet	114	187	176	124	101	702	1
6	Hidden	14	23	28	31	34	130	5
7	Fulmore	78	72	69	88	64	371	3

Figure 3-19: Using functions to compare values.

NETWORKDAY and TODAY for Measuring Time in Days

Excel offers a couple of date functions for scheduling, project planning, and measuring time periods in days.

NETWORKDAYS measures the number of workdays between two dates (the function excludes Saturdays and Sundays from its calculations). Use this function for scheduling purposes to determine the number of workdays needed to complete a project. Use NETWORKDAYS as follows:

```
NETWORKDAYS(start date, end date)
```

TODAY gives you today's date, whatever it happens to be. Use this function to compute today's date in a formula. The TODAY function takes no arguments and is entered like so, parentheses included:

```
TODAY()
```

To measure the number of days between two dates, use the minus operator and subtract the latest date from the earlier one. For example, this formula measures the number of days between 1/1/2016 and 6/1/20165:

```
="6/1/2016"-"1/1/20165"
```

The dates are enclosed in quotation marks to make Excel recognize them as dates. Make sure that the cell where the formula is located is formatted to show numbers, not dates.

LEN for Counting Characters in Cells

Use the LEN (length) function to obtain the number of characters in a cell. This function is useful for making sure that characters remain under a certain limit. The LEN function counts blank spaces as well as characters. Use the LEN function as follows:

```
LEN(cell address)
```

Chapter 4: Making a Worksheet Easier to Read and Understand

In This Chapter

- **Aligning numbers and text**
- **Changing column and row sizes**
- **Applying cell styles to data in cells**
- **Splashing color on a worksheet**
- **Drawing borders between cells and titles**
- **Making worksheets fit well on the page**
- **Preparing a worksheet before you print it**

This short and pithy chapter explains how to dress a worksheet in its Sunday best in case you want to print and present it to others. It explains how to align numbers and text, insert rows and columns, and change the size of rows and columns. You find out how to decorate a worksheet with colors and borders as well as create and apply styles to make formatting tasks go more quickly. Finally, this chapter describes everything you need to know before you print a worksheet, including how to make it fit on one page and repeat row labels and column names on all pages.

Laying Out a Worksheet

Especially if you intend to print your worksheet, you may as well dress it in its Sunday best. And you can do a number of things to make worksheets easier to read and understand. You can change character fonts. You can draw borders around or shade important cells. You can also format the numbers so that readers know, for example, whether they're staring at dollar figures or percentages. This part of Chapter 4 is dedicated to the proposition that a worksheet doesn't have to look drab and solemn.

Aligning numbers and text in columns and rows

To start with, numbers in worksheets are right-aligned in cells, and text is left-aligned. Numbers and text sit squarely on the bottom of cells. You can, however, change the way that data is aligned. For example, you can make data float at the top of cells rather than rest at the bottom, and you can center or justify data in cells. Figure 4-1 illustrates different ways to align text and numbers. How text is aligned helps people make sense of your worksheets. In Figure 4-1, for example, Income and Expenses are left-aligned so that they stand out and make it clearer what the right-aligned column labels below are all about.

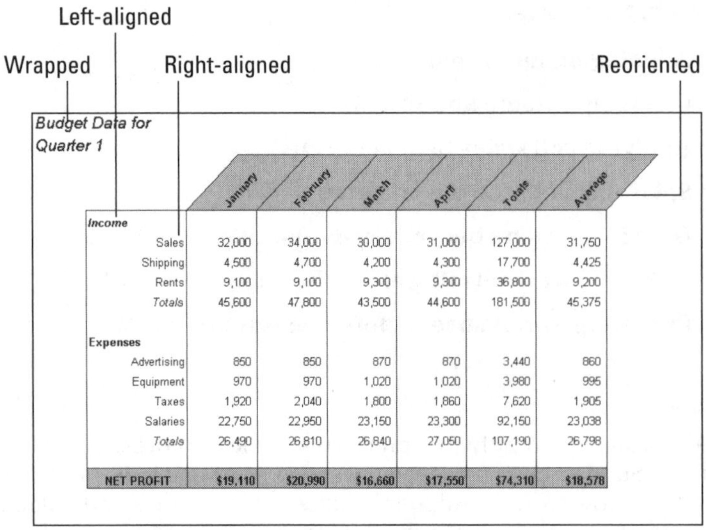

Figure 4-1: Ways to align data.

Select the cells whose alignment needs changing and follow these instructions to realign data in the cells:

- **Changing the horizontal (side-to-side) alignment:** On the Home tab, click the Align Left, Center, or Align Right button. You can also click the Alignment group button, and on the Alignment tab of the Format Cells dialog box, choose an option on the Horizontal drop-down list. Figure 4-2 shows the Format Cells dialog box.
- **Changing the vertical (top-to-bottom) alignment:** On the Home tab, click the Top Align, Middle Align, or Bottom Align button. You can also click the Alignment group button to open the Format Cells dialog box (refer to Figure 4-2) and choose an option on the Vertical drop-down list. The Justify option makes all the letters or numbers fit in a cell, even if it means wrapping text to two or more lines.
- **Reorienting the cells:** On the Home tab, click the Orientation button and choose an option on the drop-down list. (For Figure 4-2, I chose the Angle Counterclockwise option.) You can also click the Alignment group button, and on the Alignment tab of the Format Cells dialog box (refer to Figure 4-2), drag the diamond in the Orientation box or enter a number in the Degrees text box.

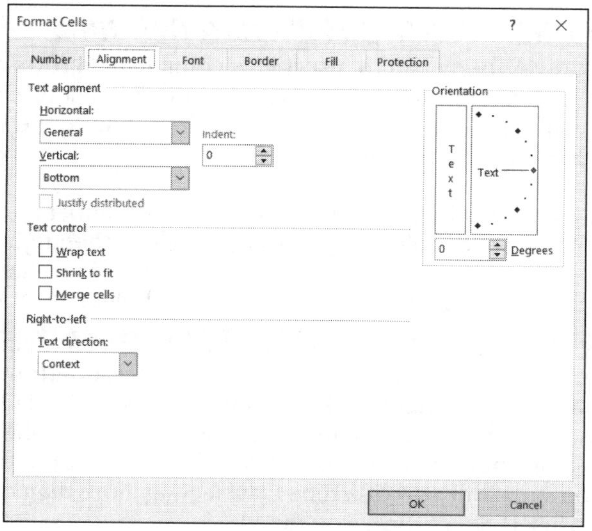

Figure 4-2: The Alignment tab of the Format Cells dialog box.

TIP

Changing the orientation of text in cells is an elegant solution to the problem of keeping a worksheet from getting too wide. Numbers are usually a few characters wide, but heading labels can be much wider than that. By changing the orientation of a heading label, you make columns narrower and keep worksheets from growing too wide to fit on the screen or page.

Merging and centering text across several cells

In the illustration shown here, "Sales Totals by Regional Office" is centered across four different cells. Normally, text is left aligned, but if you want to center it across several cells, drag across the cells to select them, go to the Home tab, and click the Merge & Center button. Merging and centering allows you to display text across several columns.

To "unmerge and uncenter" cells, select the text that you merged and centered, open the drop-down list on the Merge & Center button, and choose Unmerge Cells. You can also deselect the Merge Cells check box in the Format Cells dialog box (refer to Figure 4-2).

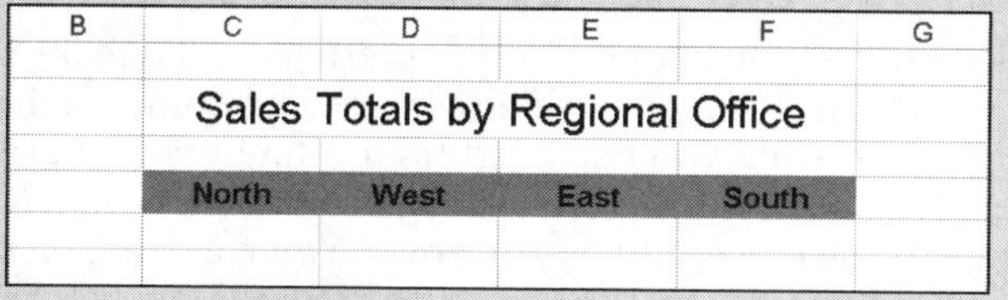

Inserting and deleting rows and columns

At some point, everybody has to insert new columns and rows and delete ones that are no longer needed. Make sure before you delete a row or column that you don't delete data that you really need. Do the following to insert and delete rows and columns:

- **Deleting rows or columns:** Drag across the row numbers or column letters of the rows or columns you want to delete; then right-click and choose Delete, or, on the Home tab, open the drop-down list on the Delete button and select Delete Sheet Rows or Delete Sheet Columns.
- **Inserting rows:** Select the row below the row you want to insert; then, on the Home tab, open the drop-down list on the Insert button and choose Insert Sheet Rows, or right-click the row you selected and choose Insert on the shortcut menu. For example, to insert a new row above row 11, select the current row 11 before choosing Insert Sheet Rows. You can insert more than one row at a time by selecting more than one row before giving the Insert Sheet Rows command.
- **Inserting columns:** Select the column to the right of where you want the new column to be; then, on the Home tab, open the drop-down list on the Insert button and choose Insert Sheet Columns, or right-click the column you selected and choose Insert on the shortcut menu. You can insert more than one column this way by selecting more than one column before giving the Insert command.

TIP

A fast way to insert several rows or columns is to insert one and keep pressing F4 (the Repeat command) until you insert all the rows or columns you need.

After you insert rows or columns, the Insert Options button appears. Click it and choose an option from the drop-down list if you want your new row or column to have the same or different formats as the row or column you selected to start the Insert operation.

REMEMBER

To insert more than one row or column at a time, select more than one row number or column letter before giving the Insert command.

Changing the size of columns and rows

By default, columns are 8.11 characters wide. To make columns wider, you have to widen them yourself. Rows are 14.4 points high, but Excel makes them higher when you enter letters or numbers that are taller than 14.4 points (72 points equals one inch). Excel offers a bunch of different ways to change the size of columns and rows. You can start on the Home tab and choose options on the Format button drop-down list, as shown in Figure 4-3,

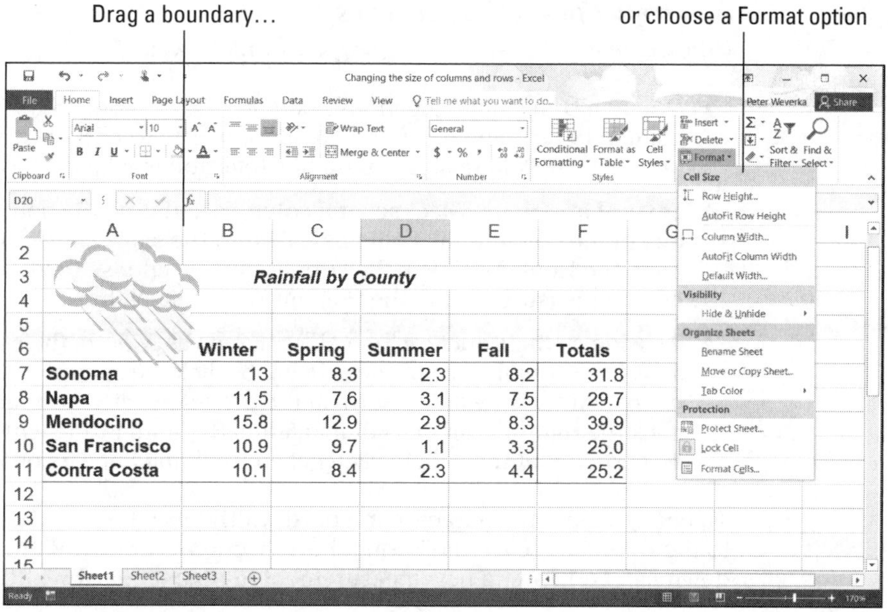

Figure 4-3: Ways to change the size of columns and rows.

or you can rely on your wits and change sizes manually by dragging or double-clicking the boundaries between row numbers or column letters.

Before you change the size of columns or rows, select them (Chapter 2 of this mini-book explains how). Click or drag across row numbers to select rows; click or drag across column letters to select columns.

Adjusting the height of rows

Here are ways to change the height of rows:

✦ **One at a time:** Move the mouse pointer onto the boundary between row numbers and, when the pointer changes to a cross, drag the boundary between rows up or down. A pop-up box tells you how tall the row will be after you release the mouse button.

✦ **Several at a time:** Select several rows and drag the boundary between one of the rows. When you do so, all rows change height. You can also go to the Home tab, click the Format button, choose Row Height, and enter a measurement in the Row Height dialog box.

✦ **Tall as the tallest entry:** To make a row as tall as its tallest cell entry, double-click the border below a row number (after you've selected a row) or go to the Home tab, click the Format button, and choose AutoFit Row Height.

Adjusting the width of columns

Here are ways to make columns wider or narrower:

- **One at a time:** Move the mouse pointer onto the boundary between column letters, and when the pointer changes to a cross, drag the border between the columns. A pop-up box tells you what size the column is.
- **Several at a time:** Select several columns and drag the boundary between one of the columns; all columns adjust to the same width. You can also go to the Home tab, click the Format button, choose Column Width, and enter a measurement in the Column Width dialog box.
- **As wide as their entries:** To make columns as wide as their widest entries, select the columns, go to the Home tab, click the Format button, and choose AutoFit Column Width on the drop-down list. You can also double-click the right border of a column letter. By "auto-fitting" columns, you can be certain that the data in each cell in a column appears onscreen.

To change the 8.11-character standard width for columns in a worksheet, go to the Home tab, click the Format button, choose Default Width on the drop-down list, and enter a new measurement in the Standard Width dialog box.

Decorating a Worksheet with Borders and Colors

The job of gridlines is simply to help you line up numbers and letters in cells. By default, gridlines aren't printed, and because gridlines aren't printed, drawing borders on worksheets is absolutely necessary if you intend to print your worksheet. Use borders to steer the reader's eye to the most important parts of your worksheet — the totals, column labels, and heading labels. You can also decorate worksheets with colors. This part of the chapter explains how to put borders and colors on worksheets.

Cell styles for quickly formatting a worksheet

A *style* is a collection of formats — boldface text, a background color, or a border around cells — that can be applied all at once to cells without having to visit a bunch of different dialog boxes or give a bunch of different commands. Styles save time. If you find yourself choosing the same formatting commands time and time again, consider creating a style. That way, you can apply all the formats simultaneously and go to lunch earlier. Excel comes with many built-in styles, and you can create styles of your own, as the following pages explain.

Applying a built-in cell style

By way of the Cell Styles gallery on the Home tab, you can choose from any number of attractive styles for cells in a worksheet. Excel offers styles for titles and headings, styles for calling attention to what kind of data is in cells, and styles to accent cells. Follow these steps to reformat cells by choosing a cell style:

1. **Select the cells that need a new look.**
2. **On the Home tab, click the Cell Styles button.**

   As shown in Figure 4-4, the Cell Styles gallery opens.

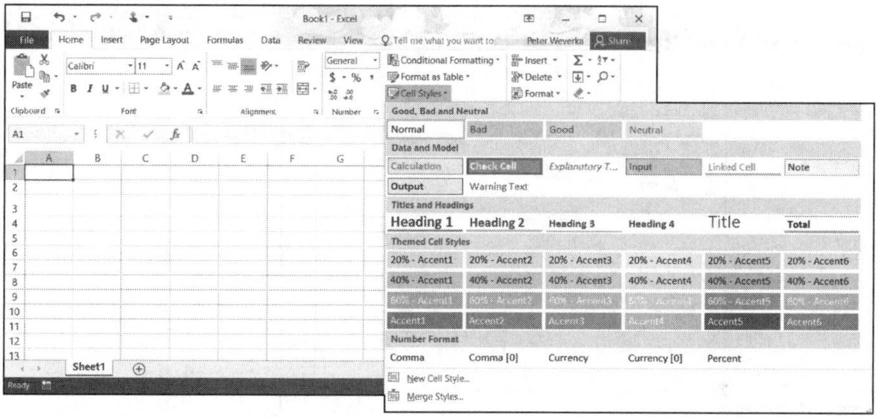

Figure 4-4: Choosing a new style from the Cell Styles gallery.

3. **Select a cell style.**

   The Cell Styles gallery is divided into categories. Find a style that suits your purposes.

TIP

To remove a style from cells, select the cells, open the Cell Styles gallery, and choose Normal. (You find Normal in the "Good, Bad and Neutral" category.)

Creating your own cell style

The names of cell styles you create on your own are placed at the top of the Cell Styles gallery under the Custom heading. Create a cell style if you're the creative type or if no built-in style meets your high standards. Follow these steps to create a cell style:

1. **Apply the formatting commands you want for your style to a single cell.**

   For example, left-align cell data. Or apply a fill color to the cells (see "Decorating worksheets with colors," later in this chapter). Or change fonts and font sizes. Knock yourself out. Choose all the formatting commands you want for your new style.

2. **On the Home tab, click the Cell Styles button to open the Cell Styles gallery.**

   Depending on the size of your screen, you may have to click the Styles button and then click the More button first.

3. **Choose New Cell Style at the bottom of the gallery.**

   You see the Style dialog box shown in Figure 4-5. It lists formatting specifications that you chose for the cell you selected in Step 1. If these specifications aren't what you're after, or if you want to change a specification, you can click the Format button and construct your new style in the Format Cells dialog box.

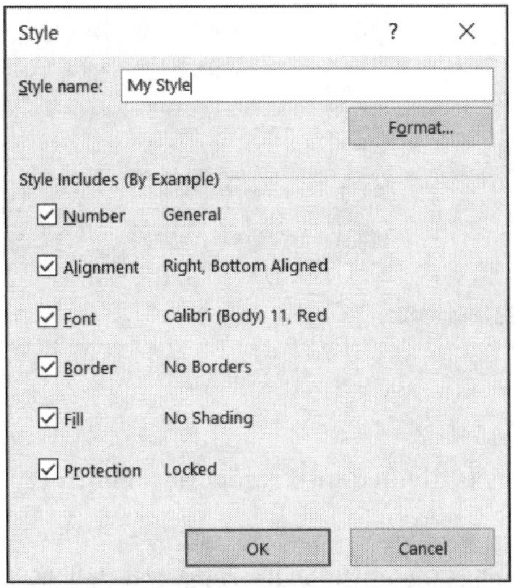

Figure 4-5: Creating a new style for the Cell Styles gallery.

4. **Enter a descriptive name for your style in the Style Name text box.**
5. **Click OK.**

   Next time you open the Cell Styles gallery, you see the name of your style at the top under Custom.

To remove a style you created from the Cell Styles gallery, right-click its name in the gallery and choose Delete on the shortcut menu.

Formatting cells with table styles

Especially if your worksheet data is arranged neatly into columns and rows so that it looks like a conventional table, one of the easiest ways to decorate cells is to take advantage of table styles. Excel offers many preformatted table styles that you can apply to columns and rows on a worksheet.

Follow these steps to experiment with table styles:

1. **Select the cells you want to format as a table.**
2. **On the Home tab, click the Format As Table button and select a table style in the gallery.**

   The Format As Table dialog box appears.
3. **If the cells you want to format include headers, the labels at the top of column rows that describe the data in the columns below, select the My Table Has Headers check box.**
4. **Click OK in the Format As Table dialog box.**

   You can go to the (Table Tools) Design tab to refine your table. Choose a different table style in the gallery if you don't care for the style you chose.

To remove a table style from cells, select the cells, go to the (Table Tools) Design tab, and choose Clear in the Table Styles gallery.

As Chapter 5 of this mini-book explains, choosing the Format As Table command can be a way to filter and sort table data. This is why the Format As Table command places filter buttons in the first row of tables. To remove these filter buttons, deselect the Filter Button check box on the (Table Tools) Design tab.

Slapping borders on worksheet cells

Put borders on worksheet cells to box in cells, draw lines beneath cells, or draw lines along the side of cells. Borders can direct people who review your worksheet to its important parts. Typically, for example, a line appears above the Totals row of a worksheet to separate the Totals row from the rows above and help readers locate cumulative totals.

To draw borders on a worksheet, start by selecting the cells around which or through which you want to place borders. Then do one of the following to draw the borders:

- **Borders button:** On the Home tab, open the drop-down list on the Borders button (it's in the Font group) and choose a border, as shown in Figure 4-6.
- **Drawing:** On the Home tab, open the drop-down list on the Borders button and choose Draw Border or Draw Border Grid. Then drag on the screen to draw the borders. Press Esc when you finish drawing.

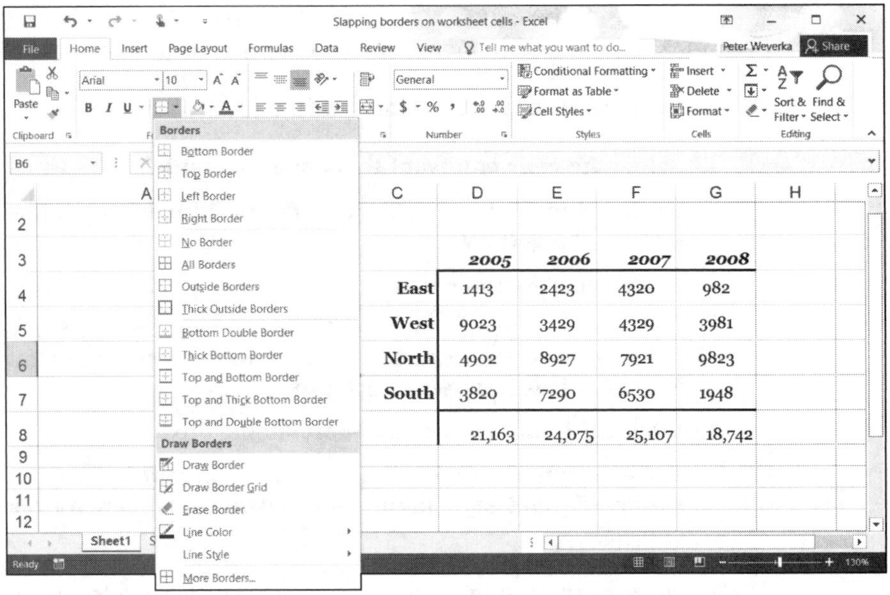

Figure 4-6: Drawing a border with the Borders button.

- **Format Cells dialog box:** On the Home tab, click the Format button and choose Format Cells, or choose More Borders on the Borders button drop-down list. The Format Cells dialog box opens, as shown in Figure 4-7. On the Border tab, select a border style and either click in the Border box to tell Excel where to draw the border or click a Presets button. The Border tab offers different lines for borders and colors for borderlines as well.

To remove the border from cells, select the cells, open the drop-down list on the Borders button, and choose No Border.

Decorating worksheets with colors

Apply background colors to cells to make them stand out or help the people who review your worksheets understand how they are laid out. Select the cells that need a background color and use these techniques to splash color on your worksheet:

- On the Home tab, click the Format button and choose Format Cells on the drop-down list. You see the Format Cells dialog box. On the Fill tab, select a color and click OK. Figure 4-7 shows what the Fill tab looks like.
- On the Home tab, open the drop-down list on the Fill Color button and select a color.

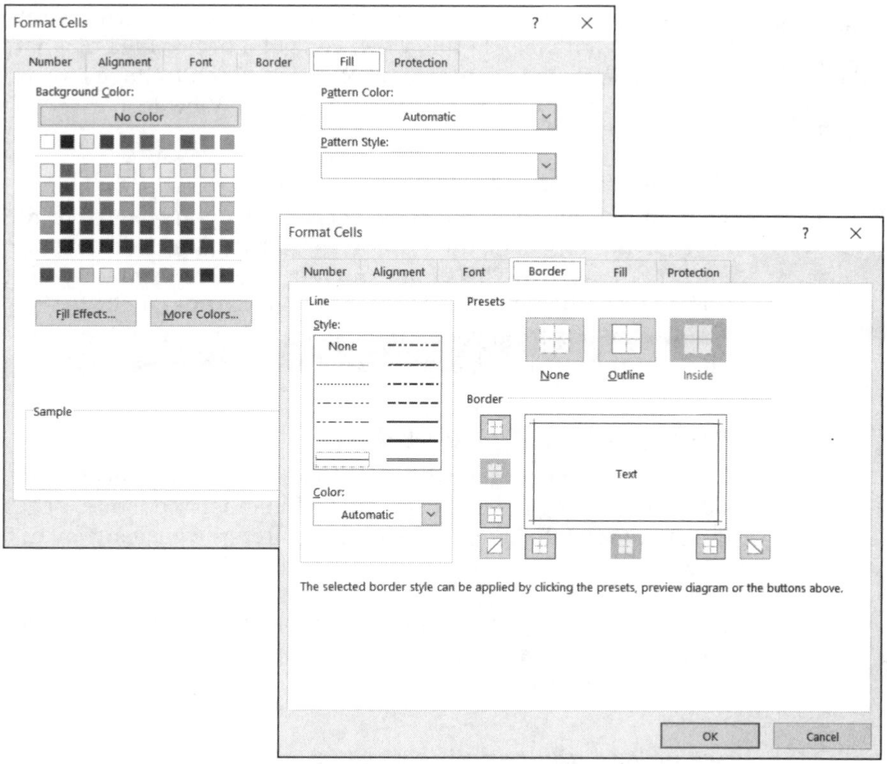

Figure 4-7: Go to the Format Cells dialog box to apply color (left) or draw borders (right).

Getting Ready to Print a Worksheet

Printing a worksheet isn't simply a matter of giving the Print command. A worksheet is a vast piece of computerized sprawl. Most worksheets don't fit neatly on a single page. If you simply click the Print button to print your worksheet, you wind up with page breaks in unexpected places, both on the right side of the page and the bottom. Read on to discover how to set up a worksheet so that the people you hand it to can read and understand it.

Making a worksheet fit on a page

Unless you tell it otherwise, Excel prints everything from cell A1 to the last cell with data in it in the southeast corner of the worksheet. Usually, it isn't necessary to print all those cells because some of them are blank. And printing an entire worksheet often means breaking the page up in all kinds of awkward places. To keep that from happening, following are some techniques for making a worksheet fit tidily on one or two pages.

As you experiment with the techniques described here, switch occasionally to Page Layout view. In this view, you get a better idea of what your worksheet will look like when you print it. To switch to Page Layout view, click the Page Layout button on the status bar or View tab.

Printing part of a worksheet

To print part of a worksheet, select the cells you want to print, go to the Page Layout tab, click the Print Area button, and choose Set Print Area on the drop-down list. This command tells Excel to print only the cells you selected. On the worksheet, a box appears around cells in the print area. To remove the box from your worksheet, click the Print Area button and choose Clear Print Area on the drop-down list.

Printing a landscape worksheet

If your worksheet is too wide to fit on one page, try turning the page on its side and printing in landscape mode. In landscape mode, pages are wider than they are tall. Landscape mode is often the easiest way to fit a worksheet on a page.

To make yours a landscape worksheet instead of a portrait worksheet, go to the Page Layout tab, click the Orientation button, and choose Landscape on the drop-down list.

Seeing and adjusting the page breaks

Reading a worksheet is extremely difficult when it's broken awkwardly across pages. Where one page ends and the next begins is a *page break.* Use these techniques to see where page breaks occur, adjust the position of page breaks, and insert and remove page breaks:

- **Viewing where page breaks occur:** Click the Page Break Preview button on the status bar or View tab. As shown in Figure 4-8, you switch to Page Break Preview view. In this view, page numbers appear clearly on the worksheet and dashed lines show you where Excel wants to break the pages.
- **Adjusting page break positions:** In Page Break Preview view, drag a dashed line to adjust the position of a page break. After you drag a dashed line, it ceases being a default page break and becomes a manual page break. Manual page breaks are marked by solid lines, not dashed lines (see Figure 4-8). You can drag them, too. Excel shrinks the numbers and letters on your worksheet if you try to squeeze too much data on a worksheet by dragging a page break.

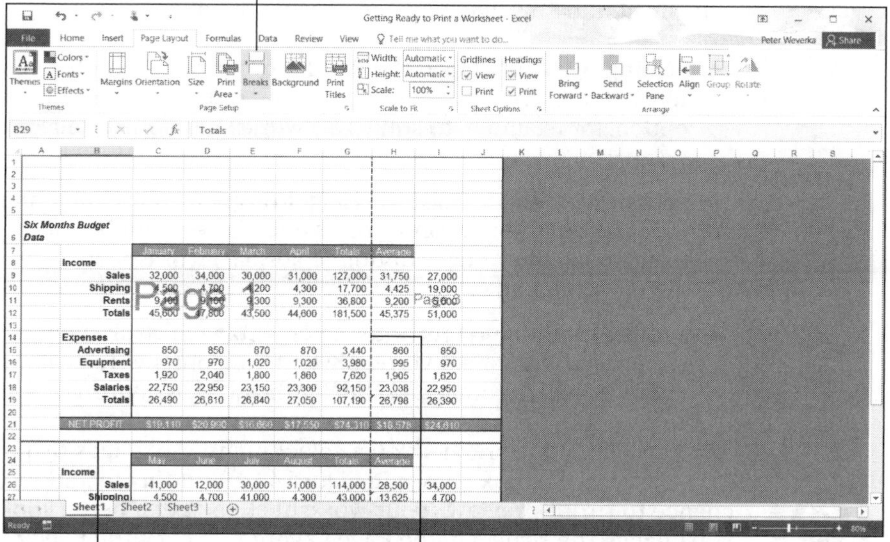

Figure 4-8: Deciding where pages break.

- **Inserting a page break:** Select the cell directly below where you want the horizontal break to occur and directly to the right of where you want the vertical break to be, go to the Page Layout tab, click the Breaks button, and choose Insert Page Break. Drag a page break to adjust its position.
- **Removing a page break:** Select a cell directly below or directly to the right of the page break, go to the Page Layout tab, click the Breaks button, and choose Remove Page Break.
- **Removing all manual page breaks:** To remove all manual page breaks you inserted, go to the Page Layout tab, click the Breaks button, and choose Reset All Page Breaks.

Switch to Page Layout or Normal view after you're done fooling with page breaks. You can clearly see page breaks in Page Layout view. In Normal view, page breaks are marked by a dotted line.

"Scaling to fit" a worksheet

To scale the numbers and letters in a worksheet and make them a bit smaller so that they fit on a page, you can experiment with the Scale to Fit options.

These options are located on the Page Layout tab. Starting in Page Layout view, go to the Page Layout tab and test-drive these options to make your worksheet fit on a single page or a certain number of pages:

- **Scaling by width:** Open the Width drop-down list and choose an option to make your worksheet fit across one or more pages. Choose the 1 Page option, for example, to squeeze a worksheet horizontally so that it fits on one page.
- **Scaling by height:** Open the Height drop-down list and choose an option to make your worksheet fit across on a select number of pages. For example, choose the 2 Pages option to shrink a worksheet vertically so that it fits on two pages.
- **Scaling by percentage:** Enter a percentage measurement in the Scale box to shrink a worksheet vertically and horizontally. To scale this way, you must choose Automatic in the Width and Height drop-down lists.

TIP

You can also fit a worksheet on a select number of pages by going to the Page Setup dialog box shown in Figure 4-9. With this technique, you get a chance to "print-preview" your worksheet and get a better look at it after you change the scale. On the Page Layout tab, click the Page Setup group button to open the Page Setup dialog box. On the Page tab of the dialog box, select the Fit To option button and enter the ideal number of pages you want for your worksheet in the Page(s) Wide By and Tall text boxes. Excel shrinks the data as much as is necessary to make it fit on the number of pages you asked for. Click the Print Preview button to preview your worksheet in the Print window and find out whether shrinking your worksheet this way helps.

Adjusting the margins

Another way to stuff all the data onto one page is to narrow the margins a bit. Go to the Page Layout tab and use either of these techniques to adjust the size of the margins:

- Click the Margins button and choose Narrow on the drop-down list.
- Click the Page Setup group button, and on the Margins tab of the Page Setup dialog box, change the size of the margins, as shown in Figure 4-9. By clicking the Print Preview button, you can preview your worksheet in the Print window and adjust margins there by dragging them. Select the Show Margins button to display the margins. (This little button is in the lower-right corner of the Print window.)

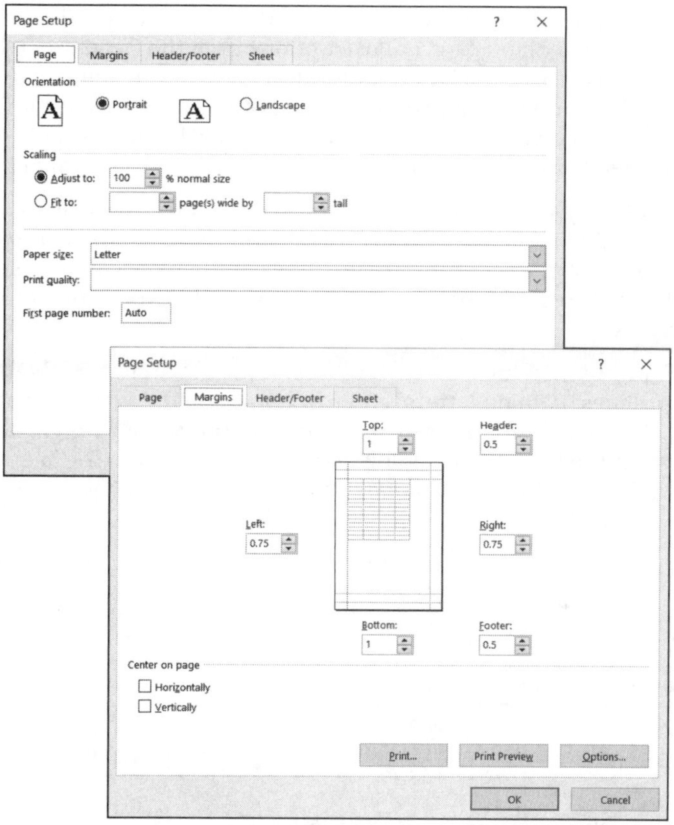

Figure 4-9: The Page (left) and Margins tab (right) of the Page Setup dialog box.

Making a worksheet more presentable

Before you print a worksheet, visit the Page Setup dialog box and see what you can do to make your worksheet easier for others to read and understand. To open the Page Setup dialog box, go to the Page Layout tab and click the Page Setup group button. Here are your options:

✦ **Including page numbers on worksheets:** On the Page tab of the Page Setup dialog box (refer to Figure 4-9), enter **1** in the First Page Number text box. Then, on the Header/Footer tab, open the Header or Footer drop-down list and choose an option that includes a page number. Choosing the Page 1 of ? option, for example, enters the page number and the total number of pages in the worksheet in your header or footer.

- **Putting headers and footers on pages:** On the Header/Footer tab of the Page Setup dialog box, choose options from the Header and Footer drop-down lists. You can find options for listing the file name, page numbers, the date, and your name. By clicking the Custom Header or Custom Footer button, you can open the Header or Footer dialog box and construct a header or footer there. Figure 4-10 shows the Footer dialog box.
- **Centering worksheet data on the page:** On the Margins tab of the page Setup dialog box, select Horizontally or Vertically to center the worksheet relative to the top or bottom or sides of the page. You can select both check boxes. The preview screen shows what your choices mean in real terms.
- **Printing gridlines, column letters, and row numbers:** By default, the gridlines, column letters, and row numbers that you know and love in a worksheet aren't printed, but you can print them by going to the Sheet tab of the Page Setup dialog box and selecting the Gridlines check box as well as the Row and Column Headings check box.

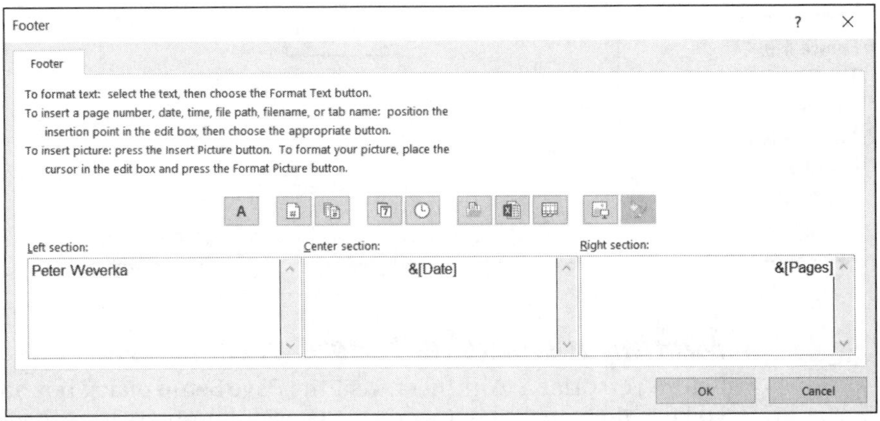

Figure 4-10: Constructing a fancy footer.

Repeating row and column headings on each page

If your worksheet is a big one that stretches beyond one page, you owe it to the people who view your worksheet to repeat row and column headings from page to page. Without these headings, no one can tell what the data in the worksheet means. Follow these steps to repeat row and column headings from page to page:

1. **On the Page Layout tab, click the Print Titles button.**

   You see the Sheet tab of the Page Setup dialog box.

2. **Select the Row and Column Headings check box.**

   You can find this check box under Print.

3. **To repeat rows, click the Range Selector button next to the Rows to Repeat at Top text box; to repeat columns, click the Range Selector button next to the Columns to Repeat at Left text box.**

   These buttons are located on the right side of the dialog box. The dialog box shrinks so that you can get a better look at your worksheet.

4. **Select the row or column with the labels or names you need.**

   As long as they're next to each other, you can select more than one row or column by dragging over the row numbers or column letters.

5. **Click the Range Selector button to enlarge the dialog box and see it again.**

   The text box now lists a cell range address.

6. **Repeat Steps 3 through 5 to select column or row headings.**

7. **Click OK to close the Page Setup dialog box.**

   If I were you, I would click the Print Preview button in the Page Setup dialog box first to make sure that row and column headings are indeed repeating from page to page.

To remove row and column headings, return to the Sheet tab of the Page Setup dialog box and delete the cell references in the Rows to Repeat at Top text box and the Columns to Repeat at Left text box. You can also press Ctrl+F3 and delete Print_Titles in the Name Manager dialog box.

Chapter 5: Advanced Techniques for Analyzing Data

In This Chapter

- **Generating a sparkline chart**
- **Using conditional formats to call attention to data**
- **Sorting information in a worksheet list**
- **Filtering a list to find the information you need**
- **Using the Goal Seek command to produce formula results**
- **Performing what-if analyses with data tables**
- **Examining data with a PivotTable**

This chapter offers a handful of tricks for analyzing the data that you so carefully and lovingly enter in a worksheet. Delve into this chapter to find out what sparklines are and how to manage, sort, and filter data in lists. You also discover how conditional formats can help data stand out, how the Goal Seek command can help you target values in different kinds of analyses, and how you can map out different scenarios with data by using one- and two-input data tables. Finally, this chapter explains how a PivotTable can help turn an indiscriminate list into a meaningful source of information.

Seeing What the Sparklines Say

Maybe the easiest way to analyze information in a worksheet is to see what the sparklines say. Figure 5-1 shows examples of sparklines. In the form of a tiny line or bar chart, sparklines tell you about the data in a row or column.

Follow these steps to create a sparkline chart:

1. **Select the cell where you want the chart to appear.**
2. **On the Insert tab, click the Line, Column, or Win/Loss button.**

   The Create Sparklines dialog box appears.
3. **Drag in a row or column of your worksheet to select the cells with the data you want to analyze.**
4. **Click OK in the Create Sparklines dialog box.**

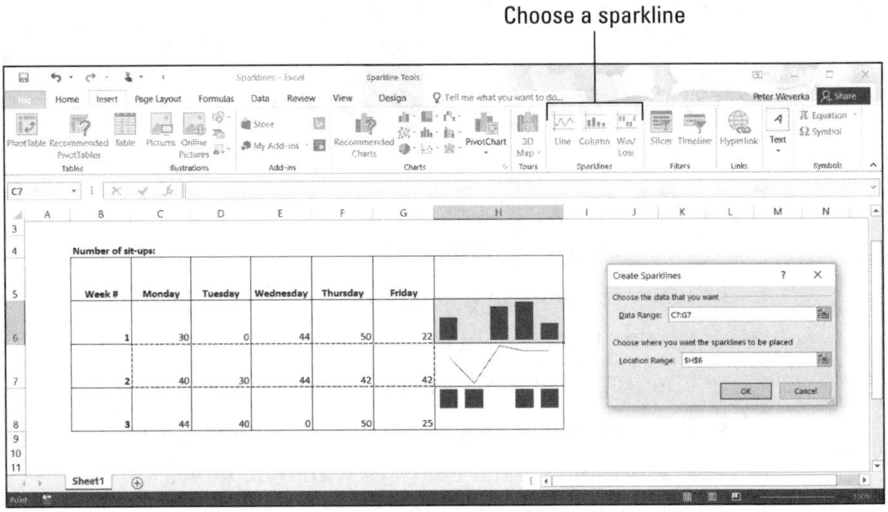

Figure 5-1: Sparklines in action (top to bottom): Column, Line, and Win/Loss.

To change the look of a sparkline chart, go to the (Sparkline Tools) Design tab. There you will find commands for changing the color of the line or bars, choosing a different sparkline type, and doing one or two other things to pass the time on a rainy day. Click the Clear button to remove a sparkline chart.

TIP

You can also create a sparkline chart with the Quick Analysis button. Drag over the cells with the data you want to analyze. When the Quick Analysis button appears, click it, choose Sparklines in the pop-up window, and then choose Line, Column, or Win/Loss.

Conditional Formats for Calling Attention to Data

A *conditional format* is one that applies when data meets certain conditions. To call attention to numbers greater than 10,000, for example, you can tell Excel to highlight those numbers automatically. To highlight negative numbers, you can tell Excel to display them in bright red. Conditional formats help you analyze and understand data better.

Select the cells that are candidates for conditional formatting and follow these steps to tell Excel when and how to format the cells:

1. **On the Home tab, click the Conditional Formatting button (you may have to click the Styles button first, depending on the size of your screen).**

2. **Choose Highlight Cells Rules or Top/Bottom Rules on the drop-down list.**

   You see a submenu with choices about establishing the rule for whether values in the cells are highlighted or otherwise made more prominent:

   - *Highlight Cells Rules:* These rules are for calling attention to data if it falls in a numerical or date range, or it's greater or lesser than a specific value. For example, you can highlight cells that are greater than 400.
   - *Top/Bottom Rules:* These rules are for calling attention to data if it falls within a percentage range relative to all the cells you selected. For example, you can highlight cells with data that falls in the bottom 10-percent range.

3. **Choose an option on the submenu.**

   You see a dialog box similar to the ones in Figure 5-2.

4. **On the left side of the dialog box, establish the rule for flagging data.**
5. **On the With drop-down list, choose how you want to call attention to the data.**

   For example, you can display the data in red or yellow. You can choose Custom Format on the drop-down list to open the Format Cells dialog box and choose a font style or color for the text.

6. **Click OK.**

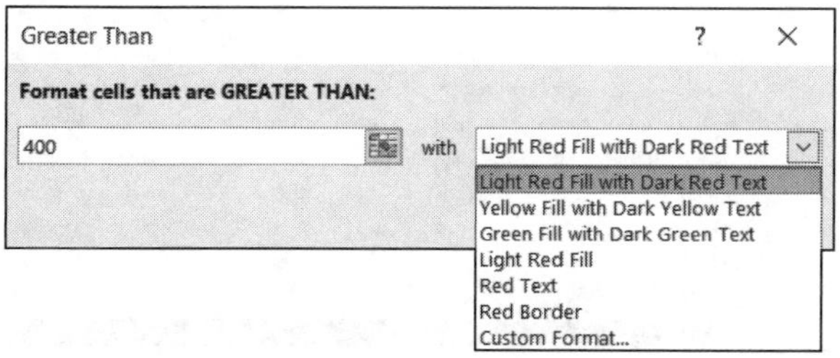

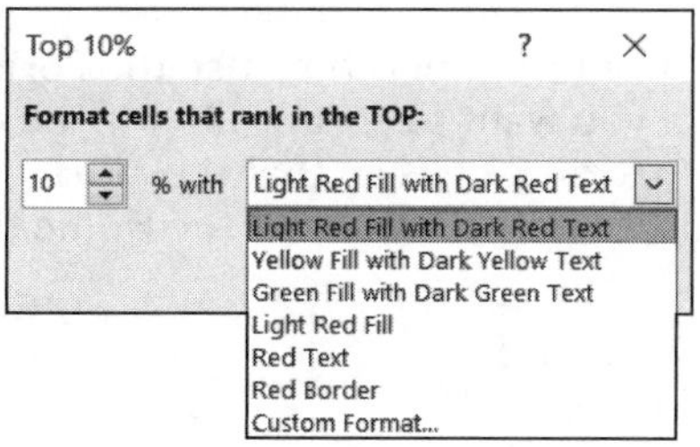

Figure 5-2: Establishing a condition format for data.

To remove conditional formats, select the cells with the formats, go to the Home tab, click the Conditional Formatting button, and choose Clear Rules ⇨ Clear Rules from Selected Cells.

You can also establish conditional formats by selecting cells and clicking the Quick Analysis button (or pressing Ctrl+Q). In the pop-up window, choose Formatting and then click Greater Than or Top 10% to create a highlight-cell or top/bottom rule.

Managing Information in Lists

Although Excel is a spreadsheet program, many people use it to keep and maintain lists, such as the list shown in Figure 5-3. Addresses, inventories, and employee data are examples of information that typically is kept in lists. These pages explain how to sort and filter a list to make it yield more information. Sort a list to put it in alphabetical or numeric order; filter a list to isolate the information you need.

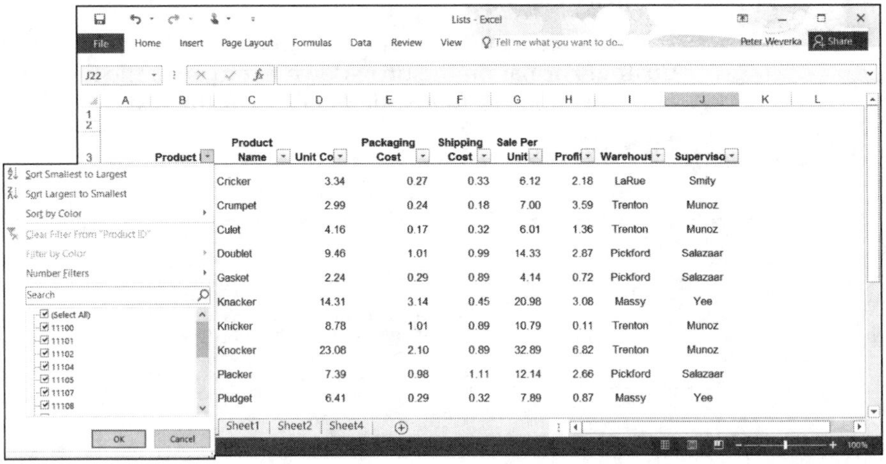

Figure 5-3: A list in a worksheet.

REMEMBER

Before you attempt a sort or filter operation, use the Format As Table command to capture the data you want to sort or filter in a list. Chapter 4 of this minibook explains how to format cells so that they form a table. (Hint: Select the cells, click the Format As Table button on the Home tab, and select a table style in the gallery.)

Sorting a list

Sorting means to rearrange the rows in a list on the basis of data in one or more columns. Sort a list on the Last Name column, for example, to arrange the list in alphabetical order by last name. Sort a list on the ZIP Code column to arrange the rows in numerical order by ZIP Code. Sort a list on the Birthday column to arrange it chronologically from earliest born to latest born.

Here are all the ways to sort a list:

✦ **Sorting on a single column:** Click any cell in the column you want to use as the basis for the sort. For example, to sort item numbers from smallest to largest, click in the Item Number column. Then use one of these techniques to conduct the sort operation:

- On the Data tab, click the Sort Smallest to Largest or Sort Largest to Smallest button. These buttons are located in the Sort & Filter group.
- Open the drop-down menu on the column heading and choose Sort Smallest to Largest or Sort Largest to Smallest on the drop-down menu (see Figure 5-3). Click the Filter button if you don't see the drop-down menus.

✦ **Sorting on more than one column:** Click the Sort button on the Data tab. You see the Sort dialog box, as shown in Figure 5-4. Choose which columns you want to sort with and the order in which you want to sort. To add a second or third column for sorting, click the Add Level button.

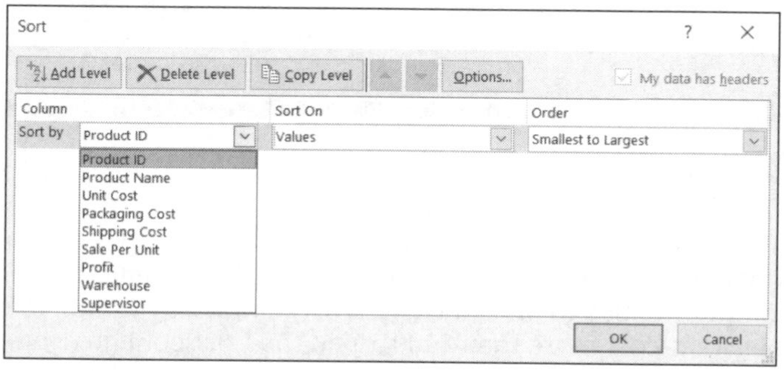

Figure 5-4: Sort to arrange the list data in different ways.

Filtering a list

Filtering means to scour a worksheet list for certain kinds of data. To filter, you tell Excel what kind of data you're looking for, and the program assembles rows with that data to the exclusion of rows that don't have the data. You end up with a shorter list with only the rows that match your filter criteria. Filtering is similar to using the Find command except that you get more than one row in the results of the filtering operation. For example, in a list of addresses, you can filter for addresses in California. In a price list, you can filter for items that fall within a certain price range.

To filter data, your list needs column headers, the descriptive labels in the first row that describe what is in the columns below. Excel needs column headers to identify and be able to filter the data in the rows. Each column header must have a different name.

To filter a list, start by going to the Data tab and clicking the Filter button. As shown in Figure 5-5, a drop-down list appears beside each column header.

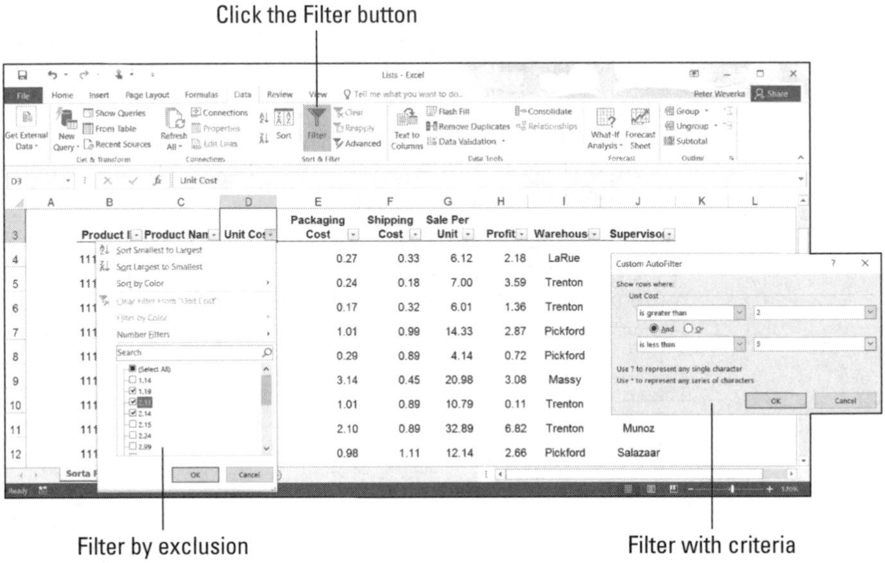

Figure 5-5: Filter a worksheet to isolate data.

Your next task is to open a drop-down list in the column that holds the criteria you want to use to filter the list. For example, if you want to filter the list to items that cost more than $100, open the Cost column drop-down list; if you want to filter the list so that only the names of employees who make less than $30,000 annually appears, open the Salary drop-down list.

After you open the correct column drop-down list, tell Excel how you want to filter the list:

- **Filter by exclusion:** On the drop-down list, deselect the Select All check box and then select the check box next to each item you *don't* want to filter out. For example, to filter an Address list for addresses in Boston, Chicago, and Miami, deselect the Select All check box and then select the check boxes next to Boston, Chicago, and Miami on the drop-down list. Your filter operation turns up only addresses in those three cities.
- **Filter with criteria:** On the drop-down list, choose Number Filters, and then choose a filter operation on the submenu (or simply choose Custom Filter). You see the Custom AutoFilter dialog box.

Choose an operator (equals, is greater than, or another) from the drop-down list, and either enter or choose a target criterion from the list on the right side of the dialog box. You can search by more than one criterion. Select the And option button if a row must meet both criteria to be selected, or select the Or option button if a row can meet either criterion to be selected.

Click the OK button on the column's drop-down list or the Custom AutoFilter dialog box to filter your list.

To see all the data in the list again — to *unfilter* the list — click the Clear button on the Data tab.

Forecasting with the Goal Seek Command

In a conventional formula, you provide the raw data and Excel produces the results. With the Goal Seek command, you declare what you want the results to be and Excel tells you the raw data you need to produce those results. The Goal Seek command is useful in analyses when you want the outcome to be a certain way and you need to know which raw numbers will produce the outcome that you want.

Figure 5-6 shows a worksheet designed to find out the monthly payment on a mortgage. With the PMT function, the worksheet determines that the monthly payment on a $250,000 loan with an interest rate of 6.5 percent and to be paid over a 30-year period is $1,580.17. Suppose, however, that the person who calculated this monthly payment determined that he or she could pay more than $1,580.17 per month? Suppose the person could pay $1,750 or $2,000 per month. Instead of an outcome of $1,580.17, the person wants to know how much he or she could borrow if monthly payments — the outcome of the formula — were increased to $1,750 or $2,000.

To make determinations such as these, you can use the Goal Seek command. This command lets you experiment with the arguments in a formula to achieve the results you want. In the case of the worksheet in Figure 5-6, you can use the Goal Seek command to change the argument in cell C3, the total amount you can borrow, given the outcome you want in cell C6, $1,750 or $2,000, the monthly payment on the total amount.

Follow these steps to use the Goal Seek command to change the inputs in a formula to achieve the results you want:

1. **Select the cell with the formula whose arguments you want to experiment with.**

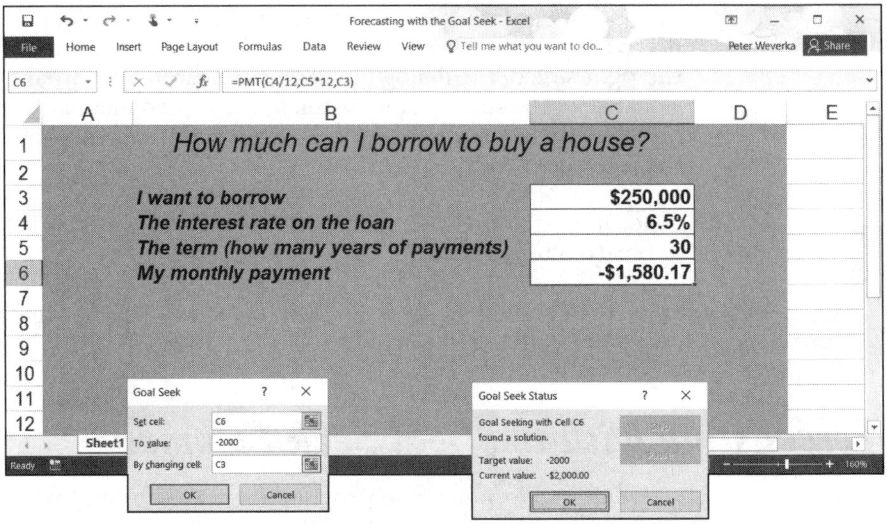

Figure 5-6: Experimenting with the Goal Seek command.

2. **On the Data tab, click the What-If Analysis button and choose Goal Seek on the drop-down list.**

   You see the Goal Seek dialog box shown in Figure 5-6. The address of the cell you selected in Step 1 appears in the Set Cell box.

3. **In the To Value text box, enter the target results you want from the formula.**

   In the example in Figure 5-6, you enter -1750 or -2000, the monthly payment you can afford for the 30-year mortgage.

4. **In the By Changing Cell text box, enter the address of the cell whose value is unknown.**

   To enter a cell address, go outside the Goal Seek dialog box and click a cell on your worksheet. In Figure 5-6, you select the address of the cell that shows the total amount you want to borrow.

5. **Click OK.**

   The Goal Seek Status dialog box appears, as shown in Figure 5-6. It lists the target value that you entered in Step 3.

6. **Click OK.**

   On your worksheet, the cell with the argument you wanted to alter now shows the target you're seeking. In the case of the example worksheet in Figure 5-6, you can borrow $316,422 at 6.5 percent, not $250,000, by raising your monthly mortgage payments from $1,580.17 to $2,000.

Performing What-If Analyses with Data Tables

For something a little more sophisticated than the Goal Seek command (which I describe in the preceding section), try performing what-if analyses with data tables. With this technique, you change the data in input cells and observe what effect changing the data has on the results of a formula. The difference between the Goal Seek command and a data table is that with a data table, you can experiment simultaneously with many different input cells and in so doing experiment with many different scenarios.

Using a one-input table for analysis

In a *one-input table,* you find out what the different results of a formula would be if you changed one *input cell* in the formula. In Figure 5-7, that input cell is the interest rate on a loan. The purpose of this data table is to find out how monthly payments on a $250,000, 30-year mortgage are different, given different interest rates. The interest rate in cell B4 is the input cell.

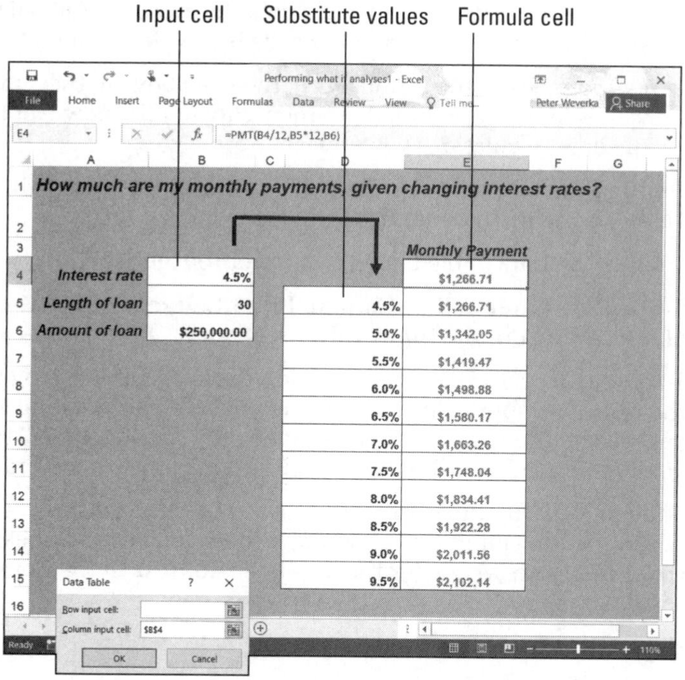

Figure 5-7: A one-input data table.

Follow these steps to create a one-input table:

1. **On your worksheet, enter values that you want to substitute for the value in the input cell.**

   To make the input table work, you have to enter the substitute values in the right location:

   - *In a column:* Enter the values in the column starting one cell below and one cell to the left of the cell where the formula is located. In Figure 5-7, for example, the formula is in cell E4 and the values are in the cell range D5:D15.
   - *In a row:* Enter the values in the row starting one cell above and one cell to the right of the cell where the formula is.

2. **Select the block of cells with the formula and substitute values.**

   Select a rectangle of cells that encompasses the formula cell, the cell beside it, all the substitute values, and the empty cells where the new calculations will soon appear.

   - *In a column:* Select the formula cell, the cell to its left, all the substitute-value cells, and the cells below the formula cell.
   - *In a row:* Select the formula cell, the cell above it, the substitute values in the cells directly to the right, and the now-empty cells where the new calculations will appear.

3. **On the Data tab, click the What-If Analysis button and choose Data Table on the drop-down list.**

   You see the Data Table dialog box (refer to Figure 5-7).

4. **In the Row Input Cell or Column Input Cell text box, enter the address of the cell where the input value is located.**

   To enter this cell address, go outside the Data Table dialog box and click the cell. The input value is the value you're experimenting with in your analysis. In the case of the worksheet shown in Figure 5-7, the input value is located in cell B4, the cell that holds the interest rate.

   If the new calculations appear in rows, enter the address of the input cell in the Row Input Cell text box; if the calculations appear in columns (refer to Figure 5-7), enter the input cell address in the Column Input Cell text box.

5. **Click OK.**

   Excel performs the calculations and fills in the table.

To generate the one-input table, Excel constructs an array formula with the `TABLE` function. If you change the cell references in the first row or plug in different values in the first column, Excel updates the one-input table automatically.

Using a two-input table for analysis

In a two-input table, you can experiment with two input cells rather than one. Getting back to the example of the loan payment in Figure 5-7, you can calculate not only how loan payments change as interest rates change but also how payments change if the life of the loan changes. Figure 5-8 shows a two-input table for examining monthly loan payments given different interest rates and two different terms for the loan, 15 years (180 months) and 30 years (360 months).

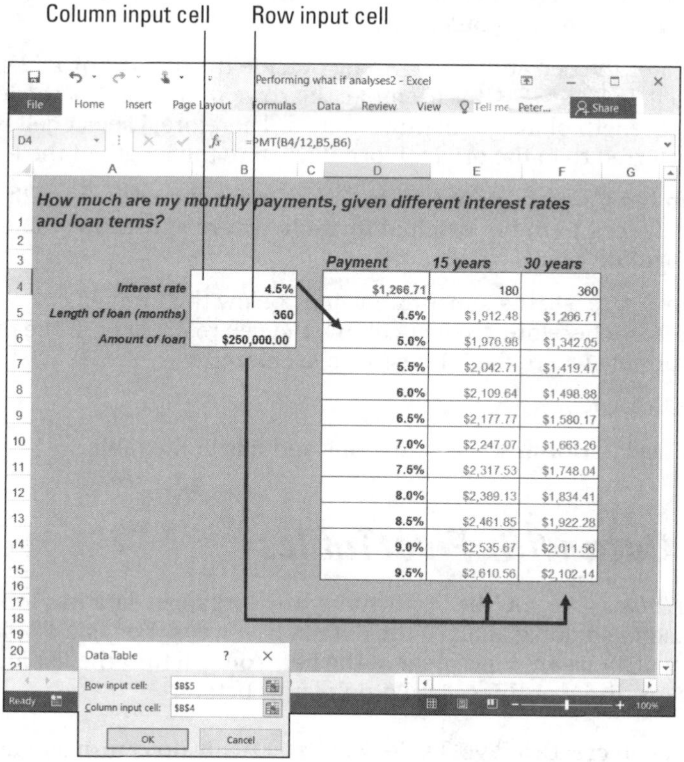

Figure 5-8: A two-input data table.

Follow these steps to create a two-input data table:

1. **Enter one set of substitute values below the formula in the same column as the formula.**

   In Figure 5-8, different interest rates are entered in the cell range D5:D15.

2. **Enter the second set of substitute values in the row to the right of the formula.**

   In Figure 5-8, 180 and 360 are entered. These numbers represent the number of months of the life of the loan.

3. **Select the formula and all substitute values.**

   Do this correctly and you select three columns, including the formula, the substitute values below it, and the two columns to the right of the formula. You select a big block of cells (the range D4:F15, in this example).

4. **On the Data tab, click the What-If Analysis button and choose Data Table on the drop-down list.**

   The Data Table dialog box appears (refer to Figure 5-8).

5. **In the Row Input Cell text box, enter the address of the cell referred to in the original formula where substitute values to the right of the formula can be plugged in.**

   Enter the cell address by going outside the dialog box and selecting a cell. In Figure 5-8, for example, the rows to the right of the formula are for length of loan substitute values. Therefore, I select cell B5, the cell referred to in the original formula where the length of the loan is listed.

6. **In the Column Input Cell text box, enter the address of the cell referred to in the original formula where substitute values below the formula are.**

   In Figure 5-8, the substitute values below the formula cell are interest rates. Therefore, I select cell B4, the cell referred to in the original formula where the interest rate is entered.

7. **Click OK.**

   Excel performs the calculations and fills in the table.

Analyzing Data with PivotTables

PivotTables give you the opportunity to reorganize data in a long worksheet list and in so doing analyze the data in new ways. You can display data such that you focus on one aspect of the list. You can turn the list inside out and perhaps discover things you didn't know before.

When you create a PivotTable, what you really do is turn a multicolumn list into a table for the purpose of analysis. For example, the four-column list in Figure 5-9 records items purchased in two grocery stores over a four-week period. The four columns are

- *Item:* The items purchased.
- *Store:* The grocery store (Safepath or Wholewallet) where the items were purchased.
- *Cost:* The cost of the items.
- *Week:* When the items were purchased (Week 1, 2, 3, or 4).

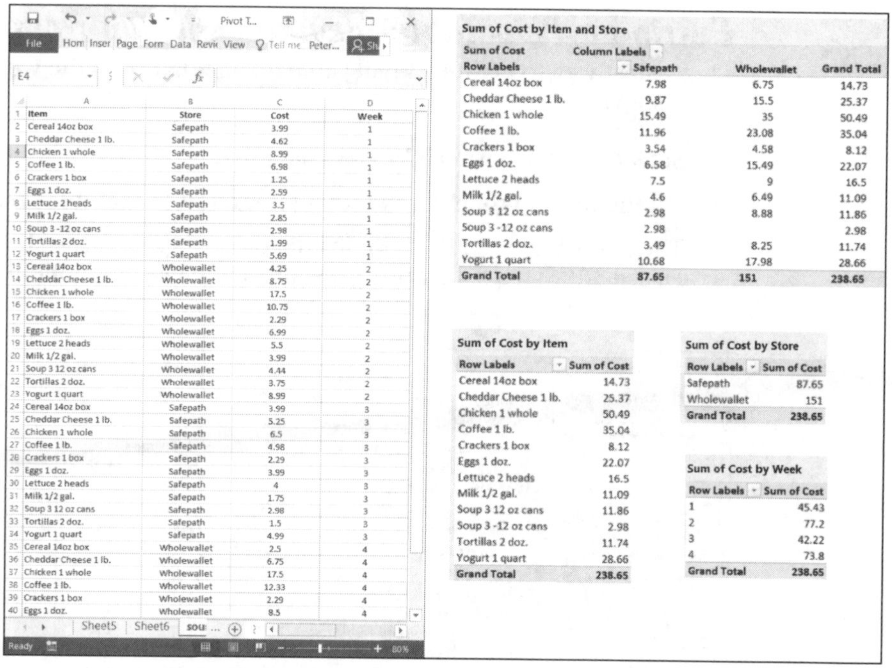

Figure 5-9: A raw multicolumn list (left) turned into meaningful PivotTables (right).

This raw list doesn't reveal anything; it's hardly more than a data dump. However, as Figure 5-9 shows, by turning the list into PivotTables, you can tease the list to find out, among other things:

- ✦ How much was spent item-by-item in each grocery store, with the total spent for each item (Sum of Cost by Item and Store)
- ✦ How much was spent on each item (Sum of Cost by Item)
- ✦ How much was spent at each grocery store (Sum of Cost by Store)
- ✦ How much was spent each week (Sum of Cost by Week)

REMEMBER

Make sure that the list you want to analyze with a PivotTable has column headers. Column headers are the descriptive labels that appear across the top of columns in a list. Excel needs column headers to construct PivotTables.

Getting a PivotTable recommendation from Excel

The easiest way to create a PivotTable is to let Excel do the work. Follow these steps:

1. **Select a cell anywhere in your data list.**
2. **On the Insert tab, click the Recommended PivotTables button.**

   The Recommended PivotTables dialog box appears, as shown in Figure 5-10. This dialog box presents a number of PivotTables.

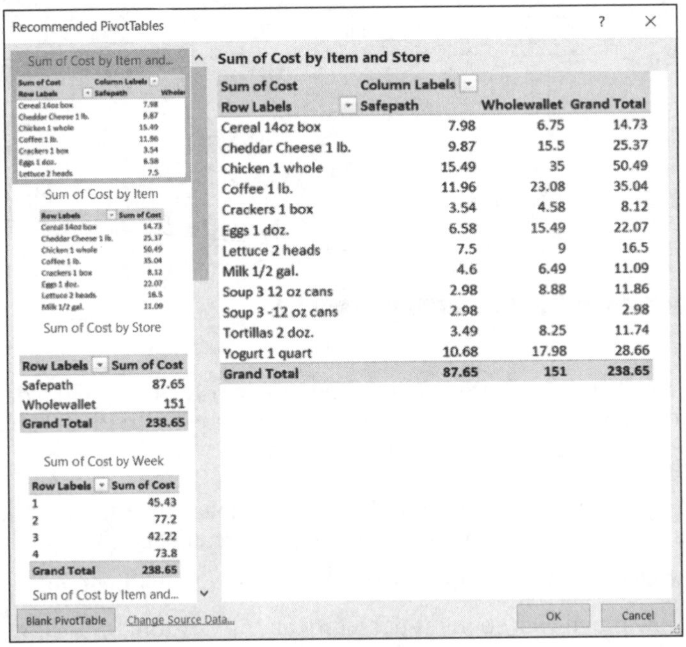

Figure 5-10: These PivotTables come highly recommended.

3. **Scroll the list of PivotTables on the left side of the dialog box, selecting each one and examining it on the right side of the dialog box.**
4. **Select a PivotTable and click OK.**

   The PivotTable appears on a new worksheet.

Creating a PivotTable from scratch

Follow these steps to create a PivotTable on your own:

1. **Select a cell anywhere in your data list.**

2. **On the Insert tab, click the PivotTable button.**

   Excel selects what it believes is your entire list, and you see the Create PivotTable dialog box. If the list isn't correctly selected, click outside the dialog box and select the data you want to analyze.

3. **Choose the New Worksheet option.**

   You can choose the Existing Worksheet option and select cells on your worksheet to show Excel where you want to place the PivotTable, but in my experience, creating it on a new worksheet and moving it later is the easier way to go.

   The (PivotTable Tools) Analyze tab and PivotTable Fields task pane appear, as shown in Figure 5-11. The task pane lists the names of fields, or column headings, from your table.

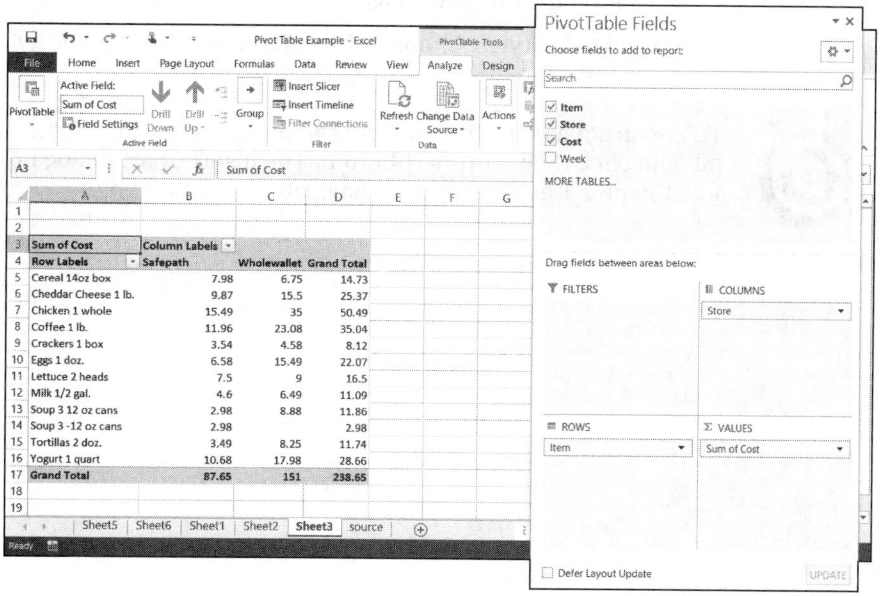

Figure 5-11: Constructing a PivotTable on the (PivotTable Tools) Analyze tab.

4. **In the PivotTable Fields task pane, drag field names into the four areas (Filters, Columns, Rows, and Values) to construct your PivotTable.**

   As you construct your table, you see it take shape onscreen. You can drag fields in and out of areas as you please. Drag one field name into each of these areas:

   - **Rows:** The field whose data you want to analyze.
   - **Columns:** The field by which you want to measure and compare data.

- **Values:** The field with the values used for comparison.
- **Filters (optional):** A field you want to use to sort table data. (This field's name appears in the upper-left corner of the PivotTable. You can open its drop-down list to sort the table; see "Sorting a list," earlier in this chapter.)

Putting the finishing touches on a PivotTable

Go to the (PivotTable Tools) Design tab to put the finishing touches on a PivotTable:

- **Grand Totals:** Excel totals columns and rows in PivotTables. If you prefer not to see these "grand totals," click the Grand Totals button and choose an option to remove them from rows, columns, or both.
- **Report Layout:** Click the Report Layout button and choose a PivotTable layout on the drop-down list.
- **PivotTable Styles:** Choose a PivotTable style to breathe a little color into your PivotTable.

TIP

To construct a chart from a PivotTable, go to the (PivotTable Tools) Analyze tab and click the PivotChart button. The Insert Chart dialog box opens. Book VIII, Chapter 1 explains how to navigate this dialog box.

Book IV

PowerPoint 2016

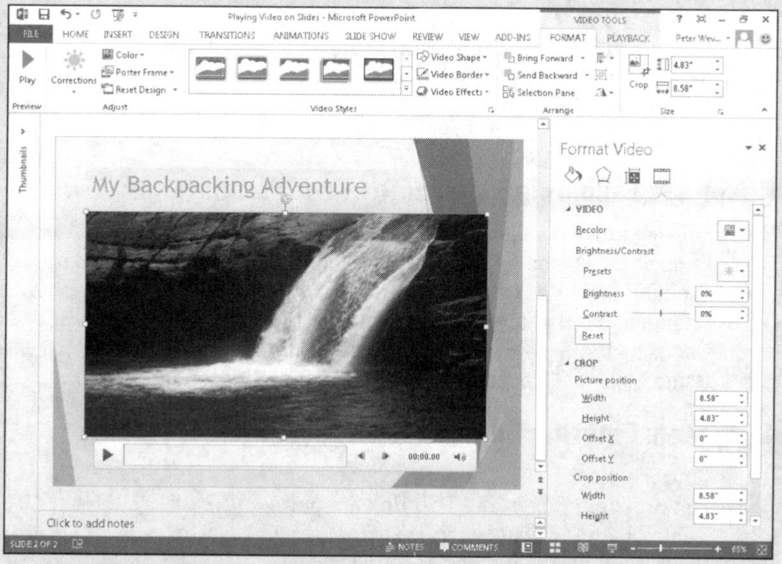

Check out www.dummies.com/extras/office2016aio to see how you can edit a video on a PowerPoint slide.

Contents at a Glance

Chapter 1: Getting Started in PowerPoint

In This Chapter

- Introducing PowerPoint
- Finding your way around the screen
- Understanding what creating a presentation is all about
- Creating a presentation
- Inserting the slides
- Changing views of the screen
- Rearranging the Slides and Notes panes
- Manipulating slides
- Creating a photo album
- Hiding slides for use in a presentation

It's impossible to sit through a conference, seminar, or trade show without seeing at least one PowerPoint presentation. PowerPoint has found its way into nearly every office and boardroom. I've heard of a man (a very unromantic man) who proposed to his wife by way of a PowerPoint presentation.

As nice as PowerPoint can be, it has its detractors. If the software isn't used properly, it can come between the speaker and the audience. In a *New Yorker* article titled "Absolute PowerPoint: Can a Software Package Edit Our Thoughts?," Ian Parker argued that PowerPoint may actually be more of a hindrance than a help in communicating. PowerPoint, Parker wrote, is "a social instrument, turning middle managers into bullet-point dandies." The software, he added, "has a private, interior influence. It edits ideas. . . . It helps you make a case, but also makes its own case about how to organize information, how to look at the world."

To make sure that you use PowerPoint wisely, this chapter shows what creating a PowerPoint presentation entails. After a brief tour of PowerPoint, you find out how to create presentations, get a better view of your work, insert slides, put together a photo album, and hide slides.

Getting Acquainted with PowerPoint

Figure 1-1 (top) shows the PowerPoint window. That thing in the middle of the window is a *slide,* the PowerPoint word for an image that you show your audience. Surrounding the slide are many tools for entering text and decorating slides. When the time comes to show your slides to an audience, you dispense with the tools and make the slide fill the screen, as shown in Figure 1-1 (bottom).

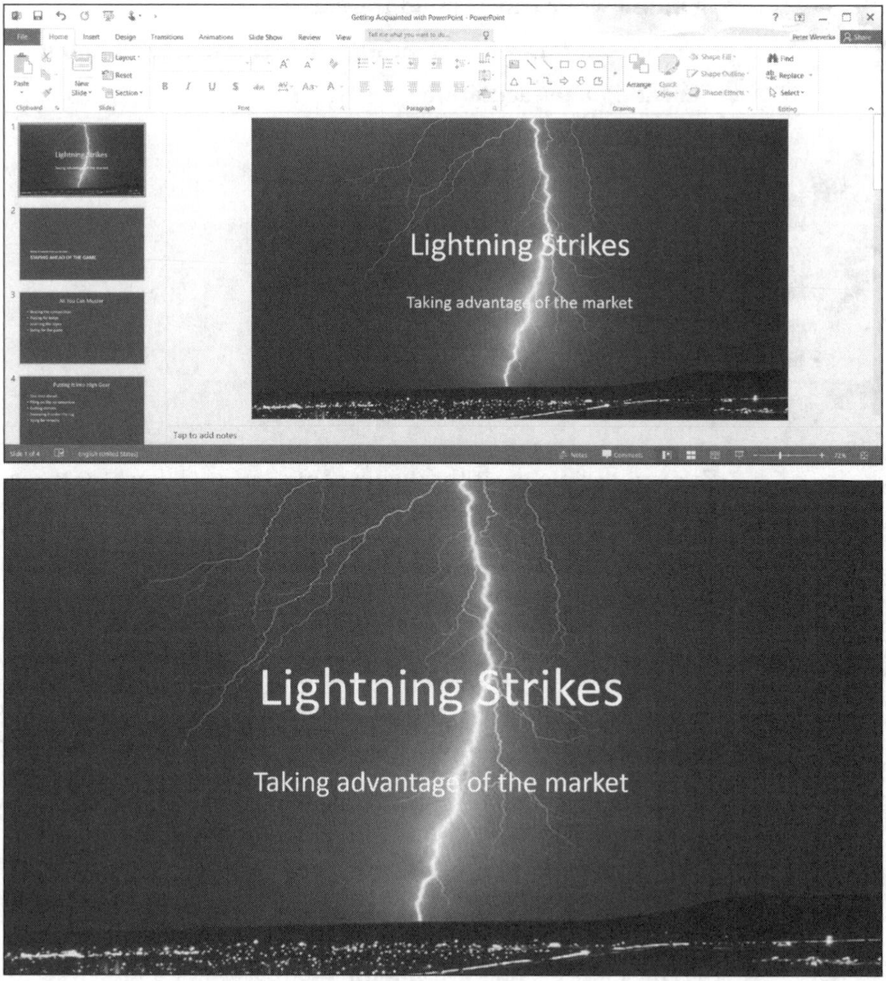

Figure 1-1: The PowerPoint window (top) and a slide as it looks in a presentation (bottom).

To make PowerPoint do your bidding, you need to know a little jargon:

- **Presentation:** All the slides, from start to finish, that you show your audience. Sometimes presentations are called "slide shows."
- **Slides:** The images you create with PowerPoint. During a presentation, slides appear onscreen one after the other.
- **Notes:** Printed pages that you, the speaker, write and print so that you know what to say during a presentation. Only the speaker sees notes. Chapter 5 in this mini-book explains notes.
- **Handout:** Printed pages that you may give to the audience along with a presentation. A handout shows the slides in the presentation. Handouts are also known by the somewhat derogatory term *leave-behinds.* Chapter 5 of this mini-book explains handouts.

A Brief Geography Lesson

Figure 1-2 shows the different parts of the PowerPoint screen. I'd hate for you to get lost in PowerPoint Land. Fold down the corner of this page so that you can return here if screen terminology confuses you:

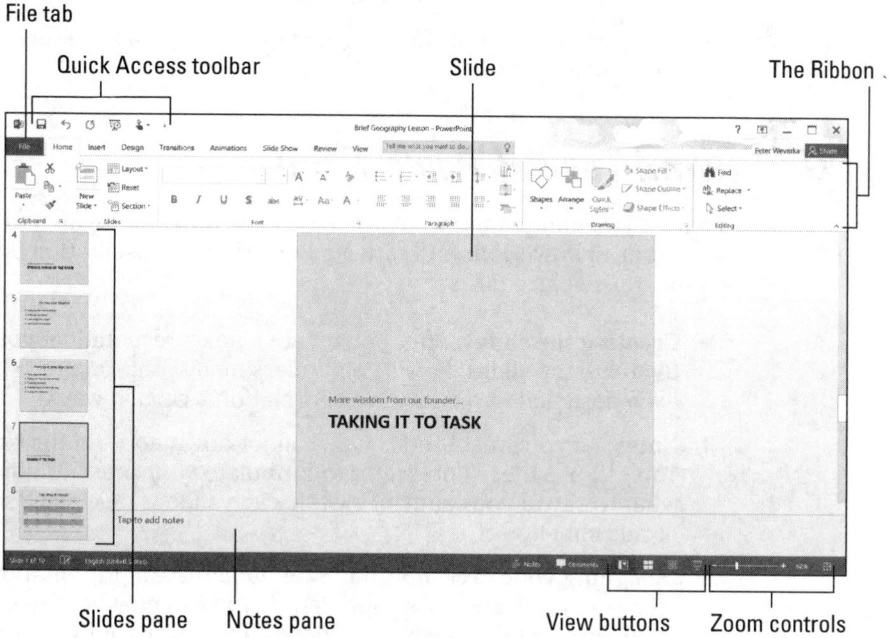

Figure 1-2: The different parts of the PowerPoint screen.

- **File tab:** The tab you visit to create, open, and save PowerPoint presentations, as well as do other file-management tasks.
- **Quick Access toolbar:** A toolbar with four buttons — Save, Undo, Repeat, and Start From Beginning (as well as Touch/Mouse Mode if your computer has a touchscreen). You see this toolbar wherever you go in PowerPoint.
- **Ribbon:** The place where the tabs are located. Click a tab — Home, Insert, Design, Transitions, Animations, Slide Show, Review, or View — to start a task.
- **Slides pane:** In Normal view, the place on the left side of the screen where you can see the slides or the text on the slides in your presentation. Scroll in the Slides pane to move backward and forward in a presentation.
- **Slide window:** Where a slide (in Normal view) or slides (in Slide Sorter view) are displayed. Scroll to move backward or forward in your presentation.
- **Notes pane:** Where you type notes (in Normal view) that you can refer to when giving your presentation. The audience can't see these notes — they're for you and you alone. See Chapter 5 of this mini-book for details.
- **View buttons:** Buttons you can click to switch to (from left to right) Normal, Slide Sorter, Reading View, and Slide Show. See "Getting a Better View of Your Work," later in this chapter.
- **Zoom controls:** Tools for enlarging or shrinking a slide (in Normal and Slide Sorter view).

A Whirlwind Tour of PowerPoint

To help you understand what you're getting into, you're invited on a whirlwind tour of PowerPoint. Creating a PowerPoint presentation entails completing these basic tasks:

- **Creating the slides:** After you create a new presentation, your next task is to create the slides. PowerPoint offers many preformatted slide layouts, each designed for presenting information a certain way.
- **Notes:** As you create slides, you can jot down notes in the Notes pane. You can use these notes later to formulate your presentation and decide what to say to your audience while each slide is onscreen (see Chapter 5 of this mini-book).
- **Designing your presentation**: After you create a presentation, the next step is to think about its appearance. You can change slides' colors and backgrounds, as well as choose a *theme* for your presentation, an all-encompassing design that applies to all (or most of) the slides (see Chapter 2 of this mini-book).

- **Inserting tables, charts, diagrams, and shapes:** A PowerPoint presentation should be more than a loose collection of bulleted lists. Starting on the Insert tab, you can place tables, charts, and diagrams on slides, as well as adorn your slides with text boxes, WordArt images, and shapes (see Chapter 4 of this mini-book).
- **"Animating" your slides:** PowerPoint slides can play video and sound, as well as be "animated" (see Chapter 4 of this mini-book). You can make the items on a slide move on the screen. As a slide arrives, you can make it spin or flash.
- **Delivering your presentation:** During a presentation, you can draw on the slides. You can also blank the screen and show slides out of order. In case you can't be there in person, PowerPoint gives you the opportunity to create self-running presentations and presentations that others can run on their own. You can also distribute presentations on CDs and as videos (see Chapter 5 of this mini-book).

Creating a New Presentation

All PowerPoint presentations are created using a template, A *template* is a blueprint for creating slides. Each template comes with its own particular slide layouts, colors, and fonts. When you create a presentation, you are invited to choose the template best suited for your audience. Figure 1-3 shows examples of templates.

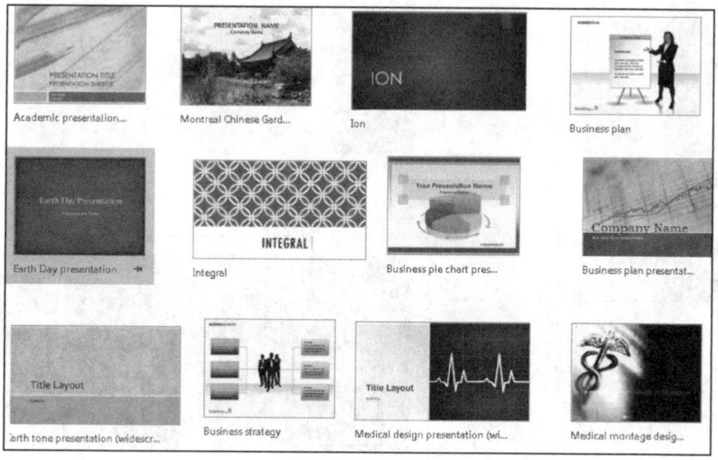

Figure 1-3: Examples of PowerPoint templates.

PowerPoint offers these templates for creating presentations:

- **The Blank Presentation template:** A bare-bones template that you can use as the starting point for designing a presentation on your own.
- **Built-In templates:** Sophisticated templates designed by Microsoft artists. Figure 1-4 shows some of these templates in the New window, the window where you create presentations.
- **Online templates:** Sophisticated templates from Microsoft that you can download to your computer.
- **Personal templates:** Templates that you or someone apart from Microsoft designed and created. Many companies provide templates with their company colors and fonts for employees to use when creating PowerPoint presentations.

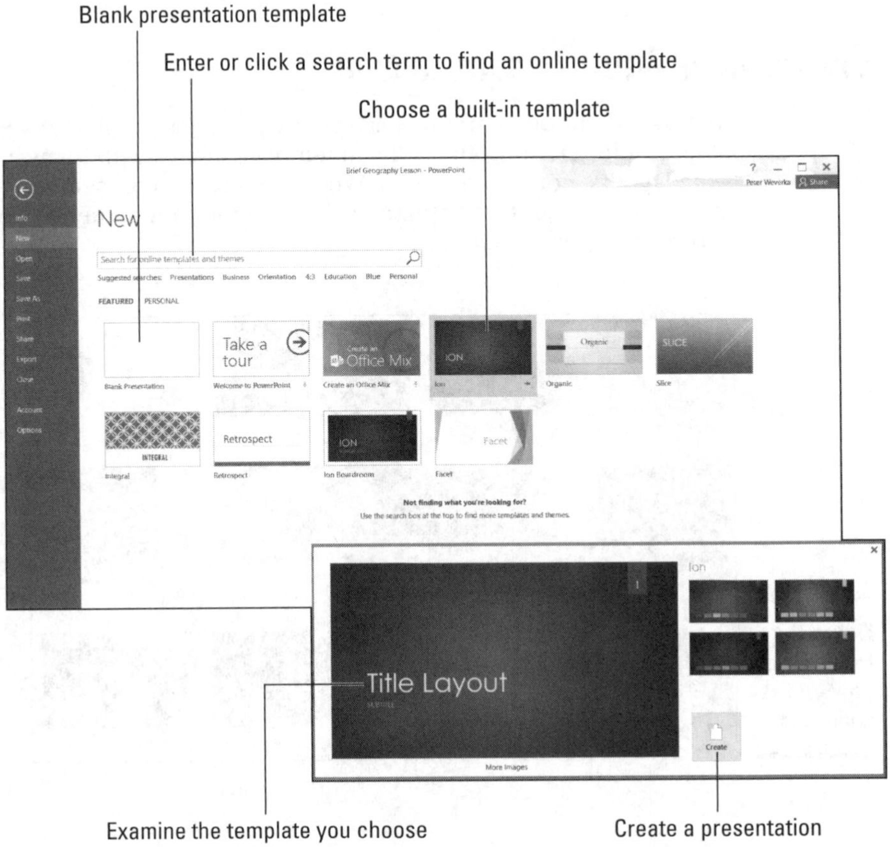

Figure 1-4: In the New window, choose a template for creating a presentation.

Built-in and online templates are a mixed blessing. They're designed by artists and they look very good. Some templates come with *boilerplate text* — already written material that you can recycle into your presentation. However, presentations made from templates are harder to modify. Sometimes the design gets in the way. As well, a loud or intricate background may overwhelm a diagram or chart you want to put on a slide.

Follow these steps to create a PowerPoint presentation:

1. **Click the File tab.**
2. **Choose New.**

   The New window opens (refer to Figure 1-4).
3. **Choose a template.**

   Choose the template that is best suited for the audience who will see your presentation.

   - **Blank Presentation:** Click the Blank Presentation icon. A new presentation is created. (By pressing Ctrl+N, you can create a new, blank presentation without even opening the New window.)
   - **Built-in template:** Select a featured template in the New window. A preview window opens so that you can examine the slide layouts and themes that the template offers (refer to Figure 1-4). Click the Close button to return to the New window; click the Create button to create a presentation with the template you selected.
   - **Online template:** Search for a template online by entering a search term or clicking a suggested search term (refer to Figure 1-4). When you select a template, a preview window opens so that you can examine it more thoroughly. Click the Create button to create a presentation; click the Home button to return to the New window.
   - **Personal template:** Click the Personal tab to go to the folder where your personal templates are stored. Then select a template and click the Create button. The Personal tab appears in the New window only if you've created templates or copied them to your computer.

Where personal templates are stored on your computer depends on which Windows operating system you have and whether you upgraded from an earlier version of Office. To tell PowerPoint where your personal templates are stored, click the File tab and choose Options. In the PowerPoint Options dialog box, go to the Save category, and in the Default Personal Templates Location text box, enter the path to the folder where you keep personal templates. Your personal templates are likely stored in one of these folders:

```
C:\Users\Name\AppData\Roaming\Microsoft\PowerPoint
```

```
C:\Users\Name\Documents\Custom Office Templates
```

Advice for Building Persuasive Presentations

Before you create any slides, think about what you want to communicate to your audience. Your goal isn't to dazzle the audience with your PowerPoint skills, but communicate something — a company policy, the merits of a product, the virtues of a strategic plan. Your goal is to bring the audience around to your side. To that end, here is some practical advice for building persuasive presentations:

- **Start by writing the text in Word.** Start in Microsoft Word, not PowerPoint, so you can focus on the words. In Word, you can clearly see how a presentation develops. You can make sure that your presentation builds to its rightful conclusion. PowerPoint has a special command for getting headings from a Word file. (See "Conjuring slides from Word document headings," later in this chapter.)
- **When choosing a design, consider the audience.** A presentation to the American Casketmakers Association calls for a mute, quiet design; a presentation to the Cheerleaders of Tomorrow calls for something bright and splashy. Select a slide design that sets the tone for your presentation and wins the sympathy of the audience.
- **Keep it simple.** To make sure that PowerPoint doesn't upstage you, keep it simple. Make use of the PowerPoint features, but do so judiciously. An animation in the right place at the right time can serve a valuable purpose. It can highlight an important part of a presentation and grab the audience's attention. But stuffing a presentation with too many gizmos turns a presentation into a carnival sideshow and distracts from your message.
- **Follow the one-slide-per-minute rule.** At the very minimum, a slide should stay onscreen for at least one minute. If you have 15 minutes to speak, you're allotted no more than 15 slides for your presentation, according to the rule.
- **Beware the bullet point.** Terse bullet points have their place in a presentation, but if you put them there strictly to remind yourself what to say next, you're doing your audience a disfavor. Bullet points can cause drowsiness. They can be a distraction. The audience skims the bullets when it should be attending to your voice and the argument you're making. When you're tempted to use a bulleted list, consider using a table, chart, or diagram instead. Figure 1-5 demonstrates how a bulleted list can be presented instead in a table, chart, or diagram.
- **Take control from the start.** Spend the first minute introducing yourself to the audience without running PowerPoint (or, if you do run PowerPoint, put a simple slide with your company name or logo onscreen). Make eye contact with the audience. This way, you establish your credibility. You give the audience a chance to get to know you.

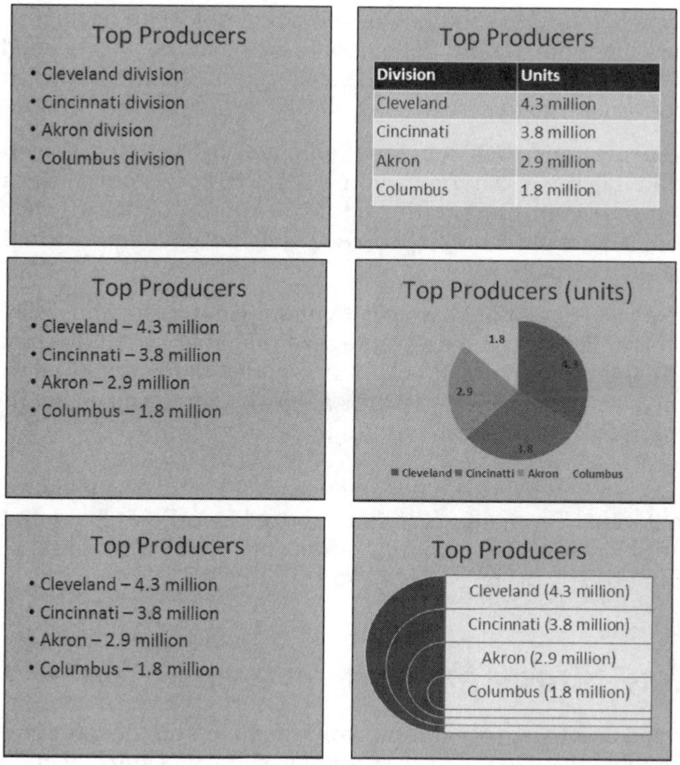

Figure 1-5: List information presented in a table (top), chart (middle), and diagram (bottom).

- **Make clear what you're about.** In the early going, state very clearly what your presentation is about and what you intend to prove with your presentation. In other words, state the conclusion at the beginning as well as the end. This way, your audience knows exactly what you're driving at and can judge your presentation according to how well you build your case.
- **Personalize the presentation.** Make the presentation a personal one. Tell the audience what *your* personal reason for being there is or why *you* work for the company you work for. Knowing that you have a personal stake in the presentation, the audience is more likely to trust you. The audience understands that you're not a spokesperson, but a *speaker* — someone who has come before them to make a case for something that you believe in.
- **Tell a story.** Include an anecdote in the presentation. Everybody loves a pertinent and well-delivered story. This piece of advice is akin to the previous one about personalizing your presentation. Typically, a story illustrates a problem for *people* and how *people* solve the problem.

Even if your presentation concerns technology or an abstract subject, make it about people. "The people in Shaker Heights needed faster Internet access," not "the data switches in Shaker Heights just weren't performing fast enough."

- **Rehearse and then rehearse some more.** The better you know your material, the less nervous you will be. To keep from getting nervous, rehearse your presentation until you know it backward and forward. Rehearse it out loud. Rehearse it while imagining you're in the presence of an audience.
- **Use visuals, not only words, to make your point.** You really owe it to your audience to take advantage of the table, chart, diagram, and picture capabilities of PowerPoint. People understand more from words and pictures than they do from words alone. It's up to you — not the slides — as the speaker to describe topics in detail with words.

Want to see how PowerPoint can suck the life and drama out of a dramatic presentation? Try visiting the Gettysburg PowerPoint Presentation, a rendering of Lincoln's Gettysburg Address in PowerPoint. Yikes! You can find it here: `http://vimeo.com/7849863`.

Creating New Slides for Your Presentation

After you create a presentation, your next step on the path to glory is to start adding the slides. To create a new slide, you start by choosing a slide layout. *Slide layouts* are the preformatted slide designs that help you enter text, graphics, and other things. Some slide layouts have *text placeholder frames* for entering titles and text; some come with *content placeholder frames* designed especially for inserting a table, chart, diagram, picture, clip-art image, or media clip.

When you add a slide, select the slide layout that best approximates the slide you have in mind for your presentation. Figure 1-6 shows the slide layouts that are available when you create a presentation with the Blank Presentation template. These pages explain how to insert slides and harvest them from Word document headings.

Inserting a new slide

Follow these steps to insert a new slide in your presentation:

1. **Select the slide that you want the new slide to go after.**

   In Normal view, select the slide on the Slides pane. In Slide Sorter view, select the slide in the main window.

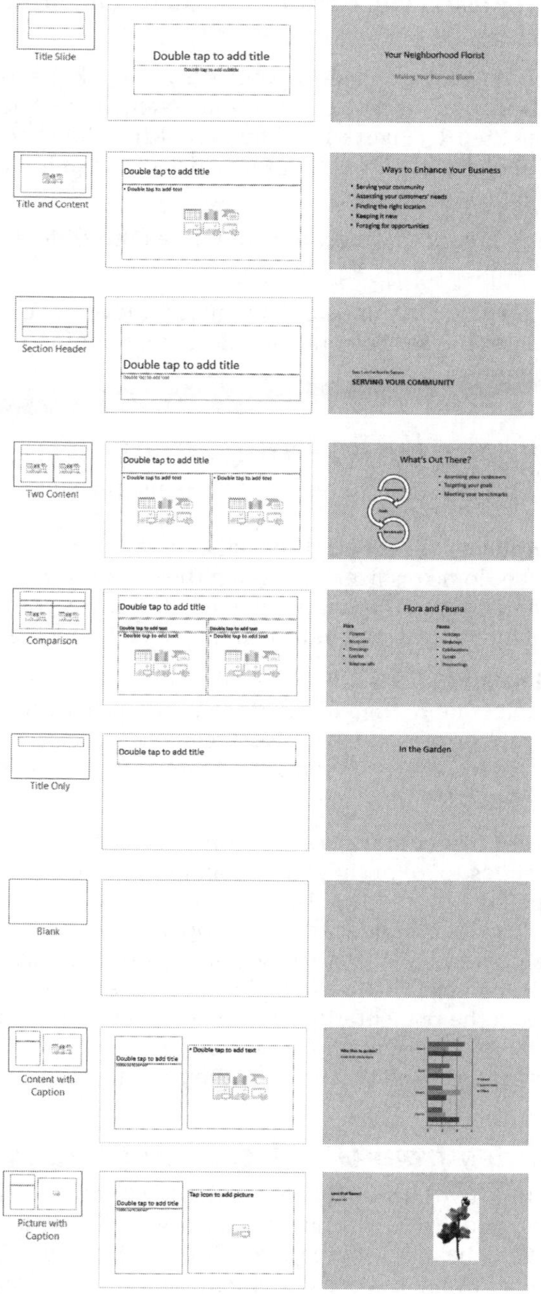

Figure 1-6: The first step in creating a slide is to choose a slide layout. The left side of this figure shows the slide layouts on the New Slide drop-down list.

2. **On the Home or Insert tab, click the bottom half of the New Slide button.**

   You see a drop-down list of slide layouts. (If you click the top half of the New Slide button, you insert a slide with the same layout as the one you selected in Step 1.) Figure 1-6 shows what the slide layouts look like (left), what a slide looks like right after you insert it (middle), and finished slides (right).

3. **Select the slide layout that best approximates the slide you want to create.**

   Don't worry too much about selecting the right layout. You can change slide layouts later on, as "Selecting a different layout for a slide" explains later in this chapter.

TIP

Speed techniques for inserting slides

When you're in a hurry, use these techniques to insert a slide:

✦ **Creating a duplicate slide:** Select the slide or slides you want to duplicate, and on the Home or Insert tab, open the drop-down list on the New Slide button and choose Duplicate Selected Slides. You can also open the drop-down menu on the Copy button and choose Duplicate.

✦ **Copying and pasting slides:** Click the slide you want to copy (or Ctrl+click to select more than one slide) and then click the Copy button on the Home tab (or press Ctrl+C). Next, click to select the slide that you want the copied slide (or slides) to appear after and click the Paste button (or press Ctrl+V).

✦ **Recycling slides from other presentations:** Select the slide that you want the recycled slides to follow in your presentation, and on the Home or Insert tab, open the drop-down list on the New Slide button and choose Reuse Slides. The Reuse Slides task pane opens. Open the drop-down list on the Browse button, choose Browse File, and select a presentation in the Browse dialog box. The Reuse Slides task pane shows thumbnail versions of slides in the presentation you selected. One at a time, click slides to add them to your presentation. You can right-click a slide and choose Insert All Slides to grab all the slides in the presentation.

Conjuring slides from Word document headings

If you think about it, Word headings are similar to slide titles. Headings, like slide titles, introduce a new topic. If you know your way around Word and you want to get a head start creating a PowerPoint presentation, you can borrow the headings in a Word document for your PowerPoint slides. After you import the headings from Word, you get one slide for each Level 1 heading (headings given the Heading 1 style). Level 1 headings form the title of the slides, Level 2 headings form first-level bullets, Level 3 headings form second-level bullets, and so on. Paragraph text isn't imported. Figure 1-7 shows what headings from a Word document look like after they land in a PowerPoint presentation.

Each level-1 heading in the Word document becomes a slide title in PowerPoint

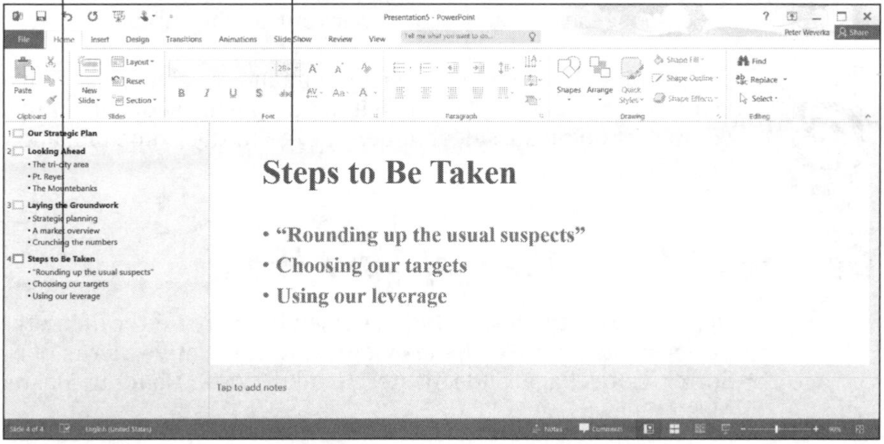

Figure 1-7: Headings from a Word document imported into a PowerPoint presentation.

Follow these steps to use headings in a Word document to create slides in a PowerPoint presentation:

1. **On the View tab, click the Outline View button.**

   The Outline tab displays slide text (see Figure 1-7). You get a better sense of how headings from the Word document land in your presentation by viewing your presentation from the Outline tab.

2. **Select the slide that the new slides from the Word document will follow.**

3. **On the Home or Insert tab, open the drop-down list on the New Slide button and choose Slides from Outline.**

   You see the Insert Outline dialog box.

4. **Select the Word document with the headings you want for your presentation and click the Insert button.**

   Depending on how many first-level headings are in the Word document, you get a certain number of new slides. These slides probably need work. The Word text may need tweaking to make it suitable for a PowerPoint presentation.

Selecting a different layout for a slide

If you mistakenly choose the wrong layout for a slide, all is not lost. You can start all over. You can graft a new layout onto your slide with one of these techniques:

- ✦ On the Home tab, click the Layout button and choose a layout on the drop-down list.
- ✦ Right-click the slide (being careful not to right-click a frame or object), choose Layout, and choose a layout on the submenu.

PowerPoint also offers the Reset command for giving a slide its original layout after you've fiddled with it. If you push a slide all out of shape and you regret doing so, select your slide, go to the Home tab, and click the Reset button.

Getting a Better View of Your Work

Depending on the task at hand, some views are better than others. These pages explain how to change views and the relative merits of Normal, Slide Sorter, Notes Page, Slide Master, Reading View, Handout Master, and Notes Master view.

Changing views

PowerPoint offers two places to change views:

- ✦ **View buttons on the status bar:** Click a View button — Normal, Slide Sorter, Reading View, or Slide Show — on the status bar to change views, as shown in Figure 1-8.
- ✦ **View tab:** On the View tab, click a button on the Presentation Views or Master Views group, as shown in Figure 1-8.

Looking at the different views

Here is a survey of the different views with suggestions about using each one:

- ✦ **Normal view for examining slides:** Switch to Normal view and select a slide in the Slides pane when you want to examine a slide. In this view, thumbnail slides appear in the Slides pane, and you can see your slide in all its glory in the middle of the screen.

Click a View button on the View tab...

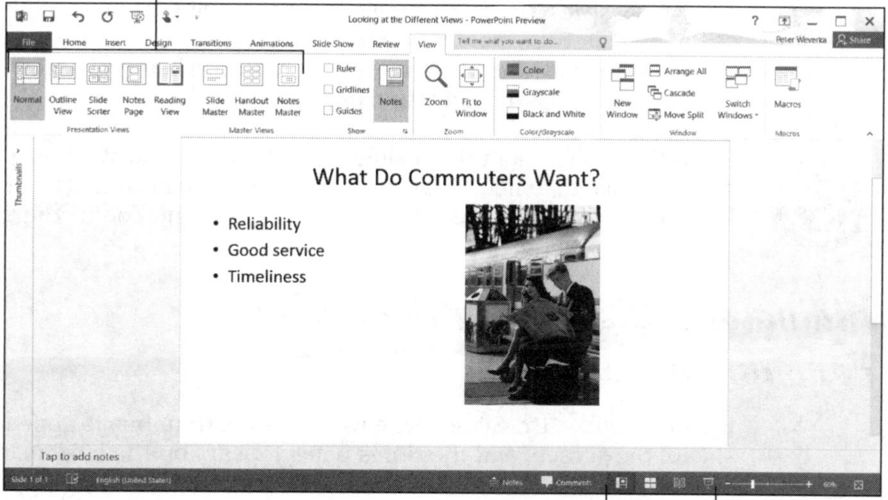

or click a View button on the status bar

Figure 1-8: Techniques for changing views.

- **Outline view for fiddling with text:** Switch to Outline view to enter or read text (refer to Figure 1-7). The words appear in outline form on the left side of the screen. Outline view is ideal for focusing on the words in a presentation.
- **Slide Sorter view for moving and deleting slides:** In Slide Sorter view, you see thumbnails of all the slides in the presentation (use the Zoom slider to change the size of thumbnails). From here, moving slides around is easy, and seeing many slides simultaneously gives you a sense of whether the different slides are consistent with one another and how the whole presentation is shaping up. The slides are numbered so that you can see where they appear in a presentation.
- **Notes Page view for reading your speaker notes:** In Notes Page view, you see notes you've written to aid you in your presentation, if you've written any. You can write notes in this view as well as in the Notes pane in Normal view. Chapter 5 of this mini-book explains notes pages.
- **Reading View view for focusing on slides' appearance:** In Reading View view, you also see a single slide, but it appears onscreen with the View buttons and with buttons for moving quickly from slide to slide. Switch to Reading View view to proofread slides and put the final touches on a presentation.

- **The Master views for a consistent presentation:** The Master views — Slide Master, Handout Master, and Notes Master — are for handling *master styles,* the formatting commands that pertain to all the slides in a presentation, handouts, and notes. To switch to these views, go to the View tab and click the appropriate button. Chapter 2 of this mini-book looks into master slides and master styles.

TIP

PowerPoint offers a button called Fit Slide to Current Window that you can click to make the slide fill the window. This little button is located in the lower-right corner of the screen, to the right of the Zoom controls.

Hiding and Displaying the Slides Pane and Notes Pane

In Normal view, the Slides pane with its slide thumbnails appears on the left side of the screen, and the Notes pane appears on the bottom of the screen so that you can scribble notes about slides. Sometimes these panes just take up valuable space. They clutter the screen and occupy real estate that could be better used for formatting slides. Follow these instructions to temporarily close the Slides and Notes panes:

- **Hiding and displaying the Notes pane:** Click the Notes button on the status bar or View tab. To change the size of the Notes pane, move the pointer over the border between the pane and the rest of the screen, and after the pointer changes to a two-headed arrow, drag the border.
- **Hiding and displaying the Slides pane:** To hide the Slides pane, move the pointer over the border between the pane and the middle of the screen, and when the pointer changes to a two-headed arrow, drag the border to the left. To display the Slides pane, click the Thumbnails button.

REMEMBER

You can change the size of either pane by moving the pointer over its border and then clicking and dragging.

Selecting, Moving, and Deleting Slides

As a presentation takes shape, you have to move slides forward and backward. Sometimes you have to delete a slide. And you can't move or delete slides until you select them first. Herewith are instructions for selecting, moving, and deleting slides.

Selecting slides

The best place to select slides is Slide Sorter view (if you want to select several at a time). Use one of these techniques to select slides:

- **Select one slide:** Click the slide.
- **Select several different slides**: Hold down the Ctrl key and click each slide in the Slides pane or in Slide Sorter view.
- **Select several slides in succession:** Hold down the Shift key and click the first slide and then the last one.
- **Select a block of slides:** In Slide Sorter view, drag across the slides you want to select. Be sure when you click and start dragging that you don't click a slide.
- **Selecting all the slides:** On the Home tab, click the Select button and choose Select All on the drop-down list.

Moving slides

To move or rearrange slides, you're advised to go to Slide Sorter view. Select the slide or slides that you want to move and use one of these techniques to move slides:

- **Dragging and dropping:** Click the slides you selected and drag them to a new location.
- **Cutting and pasting:** On the Home tab, cut the slide or slides to the Windows Clipboard (click the Cut button, press Ctrl+X, or right-click and choose Cut). Then select the slide that you want the slide or slides to appear after and give the Paste command (click the Paste button, press Ctrl+V, or right-click and choose Paste). You can right-click between slides to paste with precision.

Deleting slides

Before you delete a slide, think twice about deleting. Short of using the Undo command, you can't resuscitate a deleted slide. Select the slide or slides you want to delete and use one of these techniques to delete slides:

- Press the Delete key.
- Right-click and choose Delete Slide on the shortcut menu.

Putting Together a Photo Album

Photo album is just PowerPoint's term for inserting many photographs into a presentation all at once. You don't necessarily have to stuff the photo album with travel or baby pictures for it to be a proper photo album. The Photo Album is a wonderful feature because you can use it to dump a bunch of photos in a PowerPoint presentation without having to create slides one at a time, insert the photos, and endure the rest of the rigmarole. Create a photo album to quickly place a bunch of photos on PowerPoint slides.

Creating your photo album

PowerPoint creates a new presentation for you when you create a photo album. To start, take note of where on your computer the photos you want for the album are. Then go to the Insert tab and click the Photo Album button. You see the Photo Album dialog box, as shown in Figure 1-9. For such a little thing, the Photo Album dialog box offers many opportunities for constructing a PowerPoint presentation. Your first task is to decide which pictures you want for your album. Then you choose a slide layout for the pictures.

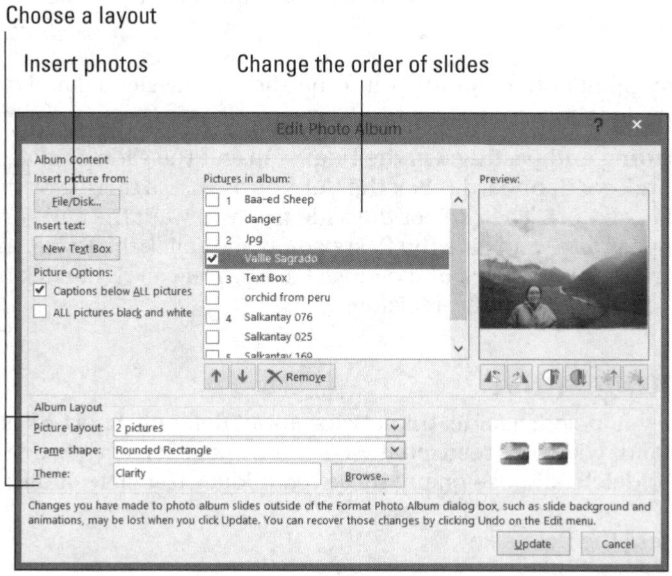

Figure 1-9: Create a photo album in this dialog box.

Inserting pictures and creating slides

Here is the lowdown on choosing pictures for a photo album:

- **Inserting photos:** Click the File/Disk button and choose photos in the Insert New Pictures dialog box. You can select more than one photo at a time by Ctrl+clicking. The filenames of photos you selected appear in the Pictures in Album box. Slide numbers appear as well so that you know which photos are on which slides.
- **Deciding how photos are framed:** Open the Frame Shape drop-down list and choose an option for placing borders or rounded corners on your photos. (This option isn't available if you choose Fit to Slide on the Picture Layout drop-down list.)
- **Inserting a text box:** Insert a text box if you want to enter commentary in your photo album. In the Pictures in Album box, select the picture or text box that you want your new text box to go after and then click the New Text Box button. Later, you can go into your presentation and edit the placeholder text, which PowerPoint aptly enters as *Text Box.*
- **Providing captions for all pictures:** To place a caption below all the pictures in your photo album, select the Captions Below ALL Pictures check box. PowerPoint initially places the picture file name in the caption, but you can delete this caption and enter one of your own. (To select this option, you must choose a picture layout option besides Fit to Slide.)
- **Changing the order of pictures:** Select a picture in the Pictures in Album box and then click an arrow button to move it forward or backward in the presentation.
- **Changing the order of slides**: Ctrl+click to select each picture on a slide. Then click an arrow as many times as necessary to move the slide forward or backward in the presentation.
- **Removing a picture:** Select a picture in the Pictures in Album box and click the Remove button to remove it from your photo album. You can Ctrl+click pictures to select more than one.

Choosing a layout for slides

Your next task is to go to the bottom of the Photo Album dialog box (refer to Figure 1-9) and choose a layout for the slides in the presentation. Open the Picture Layout drop-down list to choose one of the seven picture layouts:

- Choose Fit to Slide for a presentation in which each picture occupies an entire slide.
- Choose a "pictures" option to fit 1, 2, or 4 pictures on each slide.
- Choose a "pictures with" option to fit 1, 2, or 4 pictures as well as a text title frame on each slide.

Changing the look of pictures

The Photo Album dialog box (refer to Figure 1-9) offers a handful of tools for changing the look of the pictures. When you use these tools, keep your eye on the Preview box — it shows you what you're doing to your picture.

- **Making all photos black and white:** Select the ALL Pictures Black and White check box.
- **Rotating pictures:** Click a Rotate button to rotate a picture clockwise or counterclockwise.
- **Changing the contrast:** Click a Contrast button to sharpen or mute the light and dark colors or shades in the picture.
- **Changing the brightness**: Click a Brightness button to make a picture brighter or more somber.
- **Choosing a frame shape for pictures:** If you opted for a "picture" or "picture with" slide layout, you can choose a shape — Soft Edge Rectangle, Compound Frame, or others — for your pictures on the Frame Shape drop-down list.
- **Choosing a theme for your photo album:** If you selected a "picture" or "picture with" slide layout, you can choose a theme for your slide presentation. Click the Browse button and choose a theme in the Choose Theme dialog box.

At last, click the Create button when you're ready to create the photo album. PowerPoint attaches a title slide to the start of the album that says, *Photo Album* with your name below.

Putting on the final touches

Depending on the options you chose for your photo album, it needs all or some of these final touches:

- **Fix the title slide:** Your title slide should probably say more than the words *Photo Album* and your name.
- **Fill in the text boxes:** If you asked text boxes with your photo album, by all means, replace PowerPoint's generic text with meaningful words of your own.
- **Write the captions:** If you asked for photo captions, PowerPoint entered photo file names below photos. Replace these file names with something more descriptive.

Editing a photo album

To go back into the Photo Album dialog box and rearrange the photos in your album, go to the Insert tab, open the drop-down list on the Photo Album button, and choose Edit Photo Album on the drop-down list. You see the Edit Photo Album dialog box. It looks and works exactly like the Photo Album dialog box (refer to Figure 1-9). Of course, you can also edit your photo album by treating it like any other PowerPoint presentation. Change the theme, fiddle with the slides, and do what you will to torture your photo album into shape.

Hidden Slides for All Contingencies

Hide a slide when you want to keep it on hand "just in case" during a presentation. Hidden slides don't appear in slide shows unless you shout *Ollie ollie oxen free!* and bring them out of hiding. Although you, the presenter, can see hidden slides in Normal view and Slide Sorter view, where their slide numbers are crossed through, the audience doesn't see them in the course of a presentation unless you decide to show them. Create hidden slides if you anticipate having to steer your presentation in a different direction — to answer a question from the audience, prove your point more thoroughly, or revisit a topic in more depth. Merely by right-clicking and choosing a couple of commands, you can display a hidden slide in the course of a slide show.

Hiding a slide

TIP

The best place to put hidden slides is the end of a presentation where you know you can find them. Follow these steps to hide slides:

1. **Select the slide or slides that you want to hide.**
2. **On the Slide Show tab, click the Hide Slide button.**

   You can also right-click a slide in the Slides pane or Slide Sorter view and choose Hide Slide. Hidden slides' numbers are crossed through in the Slides pane and the Slide Sorter window.

To unhide a slide, click the Hide Slide button again or right-click the slide and choose Hide Slide.

Showing a hidden slide during a presentation

Hidden slides don't appear during the course of a presentation, but suppose that the need arises to show one. Before showing a hidden slide, take careful note of which slide you're viewing now. You have to return to this slide after viewing the hidden slide. Follow these steps to view a hidden slide during a presentation:

1. **Click the Slides button (located in the lower-left corner of the screen).**

   You see a screen with thumbnail versions of the slides in your presentation. You can also open this screen by right-clicking and choosing See All Slides.

2. **Select a hidden slide so that the audience can view it.**

   You can tell which slides are hidden because their slide numbers are enclosed in parentheses.

How do you resume your presentation after viewing a hidden slide? If you look at only one hidden slide, you can right-click and choose Last Viewed on the shortcut menu to return to the slide you saw before the hidden slide. If you've viewed several hidden slides, right-click the screen, choose See All Slides, and select a slide to pick up where you left off.

Chapter 2: Fashioning a Look for Your Presentation

In This Chapter

- Introducing themes and slide backgrounds
- Choosing themes and theme variants
- Creating a solid color, gradient, picture, and texture slide background
- Selecting a theme or background for specific slides
- Changing the size of slides
- Redesigning your presentation with master slides

From the audience's point of view, this chapter is the most important in this mini-book. What your presentation looks like — which theme and background style you select for the slides in your presentation — sets the tone. From the very first slide, the audience judges your presentation on its appearance. When you create a look for your presentation, what you're really doing is declaring what you want to communicate to your audience.

This chapter explains how to handle slide backgrounds. It examines what you need to consider when you select colors and designs for backgrounds. You also discover how to select and customize a theme, and how to create your own slide backgrounds. This chapter looks into how to change the background of some but not all of the slides in a presentation. It also explains how to use master slides and master styles to make sure that slides throughout your presentation are consistent with one another.

Looking at Themes and Slide Backgrounds

What a presentation looks like is mostly a matter of the theme you choose and the slide backgrounds you make for the slides in your presentation. A *theme* is a "canned" slide design. Themes are designed by graphic artists. Most themes include sophisticated background patterns and colors. As well, you can create a background of your own from a single color, a gradient mixture of two colors, or a picture.

Figure 2-1 shows examples of themes. When you installed PowerPoint on your computer, you also installed a dozen or more themes, and you can acquire more themes online from Office.com and other places. After you select a theme, you can select a theme variant — a slight variation on the theme you selected.

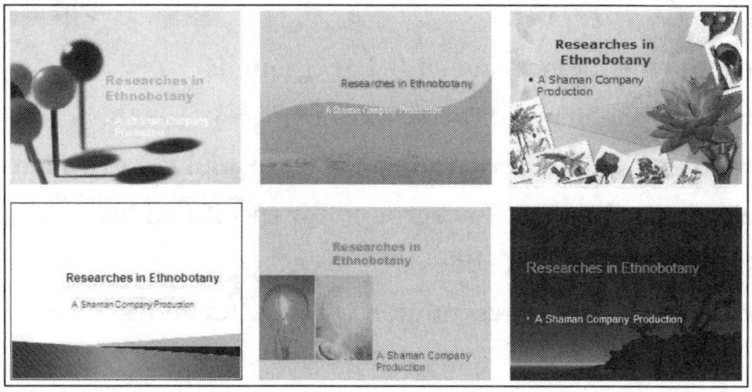

Figure 2-1: Examples of themes.

Figure 2-2 shows examples of backgrounds you can create yourself. Self-made backgrounds are not as intrusive as themes. The risk of the background overwhelming the lists, tables, charts, and other items in the forefront of slides is less when you fashion a background style yourself. You can apply a background that you create to a single slide or all the slides in your presentation.

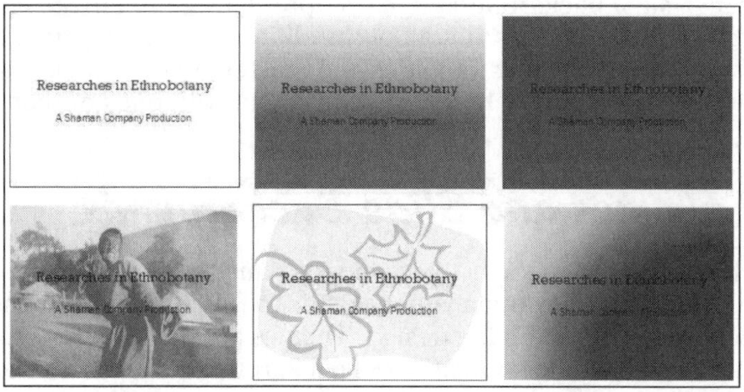

Figure 2-2: Examples of background styles (clockwise from upper left): plain style, gradient, solid color, customized radial gradient, picture, and photo.

To choose a theme or create slide backgrounds, start on the Design tab, as shown in Figure 2-3. The Design tab offers themes, theme variants, and the Format Background pane, the place to go when you want to fashion a fashionable background for slides.

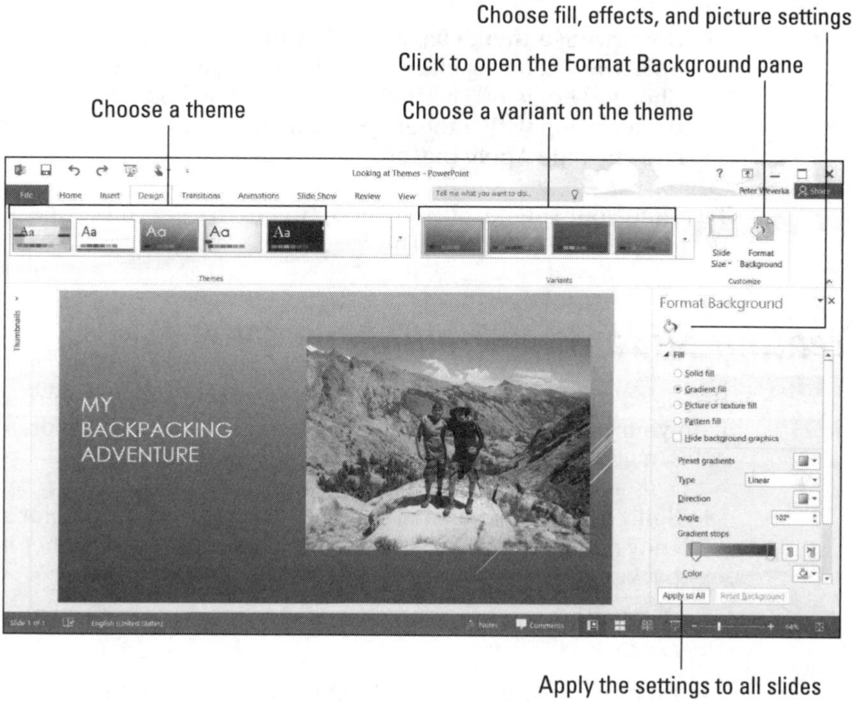

Figure 2-3: Decide what your presentation looks like on the Design tab.

More than any other design decision, what sets the tone for a presentation are the colors you select for slide backgrounds. If the purpose of your presentation is to show photographs you took on a vacation to Arizona's Painted Desert, select light-tone, hot colors for the slide backgrounds. If your presentation is an aggressive sales pitch, consider a black background. There is no universal color theory for selecting the right colors in a design because everyone is different. Follow your intuition. It will guide you to the right background color choices.

Choosing a Theme for Your Presentation

PowerPoint offers many different themes in the Themes gallery, and if you happen to have PowerPoint presentations at hand, you can borrow a theme from another presentation. Experimenting with themes is easy. You are hereby encouraged to test different themes until you find the right one.

Starting on the Design tab, use one of these techniques to select a new theme for your presentation:

- **Selecting a theme in the Themes gallery:** Open the Themes gallery and move the pointer over different themes to "live-preview" them. Click a theme to select it.
- **Borrowing a theme from another presentation:** On the Design tab, open the Themes gallery, and click Browse for Themes. You see the Choose Theme or Themed Document dialog box. Locate and select a presentation with a theme you can commandeer for your presentation and click the Apply button.

To refine your theme, choose an option in the Variants gallery on the Design tab.

Creating Slide Backgrounds on Your Own

Besides a theme, your other option for creating slide backgrounds is to do it on your own. For a background, you can have a solid color, a transparent color, a gradient blend of colors, a picture, or an image.

- **Solid color:** A single, uniform color. You can adjust a color's transparency and in effect "bleach out" the color to push it farther into the background.
- **Gradient:** A mixture of different colors with the colors blending into one another.
- **Picture:** A picture you get from the Internet or store on your computer.
- **Pattern:** A pattern such as stripes or diamonds.
- **Texture:** A uniform pattern that gives the impression that the slide is displayed on a material such as cloth or stone.

How to create these kinds of slide backgrounds on your own is the subject of the next several pages.

Using a solid (or transparent) color for the slide background

Using a solid or transparent color for the background gives your slides a straightforward, honest look. Because all the slides are the same color or transparent color, the audience can focus better on the presentation itself rather than the razzle-dazzle. Follow these steps to use a solid or transparent color as the background for slides:

1. **On the Design tab, click the Format Background button.**

   The Format Background pane opens.

2. **Click the Solid Fill option button.**
3. **Click the Color button and choose a color on the drop-down list.**

   The muted theme colors are recommended because they look better in the background, but you can select a standard color or click the More Colors button and select a color in the Colors dialog box.

4. **Drag the Transparency slider if you want a "bleached out" color rather than a slide color.**

   At 0% transparency, you get a solid color; at 100%, you get no color at all.

5. **Click the Apply to All button and then the Close button (the *X*) to close the Format Background pane.**

   I sincerely hope you like your choice of colors, but if you don't, try, try, try again.

Creating a gradient color blend for slide backgrounds

Gradient refers to how and where two or more colors grade, or blend, into one another on a slide. As well as the standard linear gradient direction, you can opt for a radial, rectangular, or path gradient direction. Figure 2-4 shows examples of gradient fill backgrounds. These backgrounds look terribly elegant. Using a gradient is an excellent way to create an original background that looks different from all the other presenter's slide backgrounds.

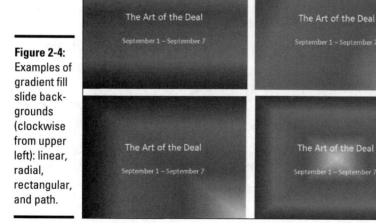

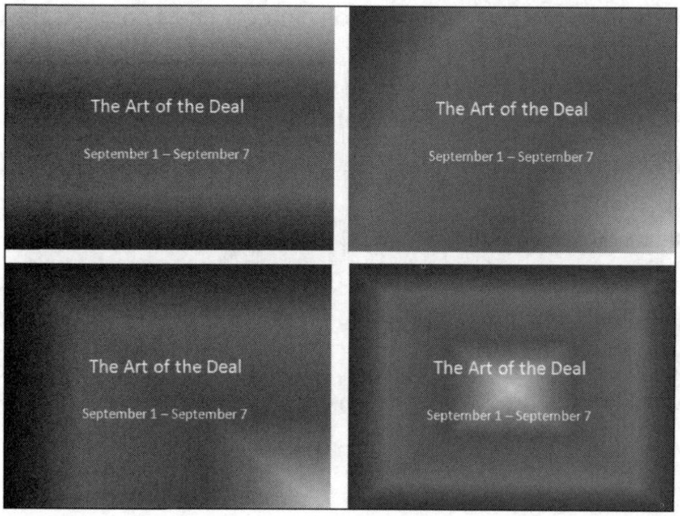

Figure 2-4: Examples of gradient fill slide backgrounds (clockwise from upper left): linear, radial, rectangular, and path.

Follow these steps to create a gradient background for slides:

1. **On the Design tab, click the Format Background button to open the Format Background pane.**
2. **Click the Gradient Fill option button.**

   Before you experiment with gradients, try opening the Preset Gradients drop-down list to see whether one of the ready-made gradient options does the job for you.
3. **On the Type drop-down list, choose what type of gradient you want — Linear, Radial, Rectangular, Path, or Shade from Title (see Figure 2-4).**

   If you choose Linear, you can enter a degree measurement in the Angle box to change the angle at which the colors blend. At 90 degrees, for example, colors blend horizontally across the slide; at 180 degrees, they blend vertically.
4. **Create a gradient stop for each color transition you want on your slides.**

   Gradient stops determine where colors are, how colors transition from one to the next, and which colors are used. You can create as many gradient stops as you want. Here are techniques for handling gradient stops:

   - *Adding a gradient stop:* Click the Add Gradient Stop button. A new gradient stop appears on the slider. Drag it to where you want the color blend to occur.
   - *Removing a gradient stop:* Select a gradient stop on the slider and click the Remove Gradient Stop button.
   - *Choosing a color for a gradient stop:* Select a gradient stop on the slider, click the Color button, and choose a color on the drop-down list.
   - *Positioning a gradient stop:* Drag a gradient stop on the slider or use the Position box to move it to a different location.
5. **Drag the Brightness slider to make the colors dimmer or brighter.**
6. **Drag the Transparency slider to make the colors on the slides more or less transparent.**

   At 0% transparency, you get solid colors; at 100%, you get no color at all.
7. **Click the Apply to All button.**

   Very likely, you have to experiment with stop colors and stop positions until you blend the colors to your satisfaction. Good luck.

Placing a picture in the slide background

As long as they're on the pale side or you've made them semitransparent, pictures from Office.com or the Internet do fine for slide backgrounds. They look especially good in title slides. Figure 2-5 shows examples of pictures as backgrounds. As Book VIII, Chapter 3 explains, Office.com offers numerous photos and pictures. You're invited to place one in the background of your slides by following these steps:

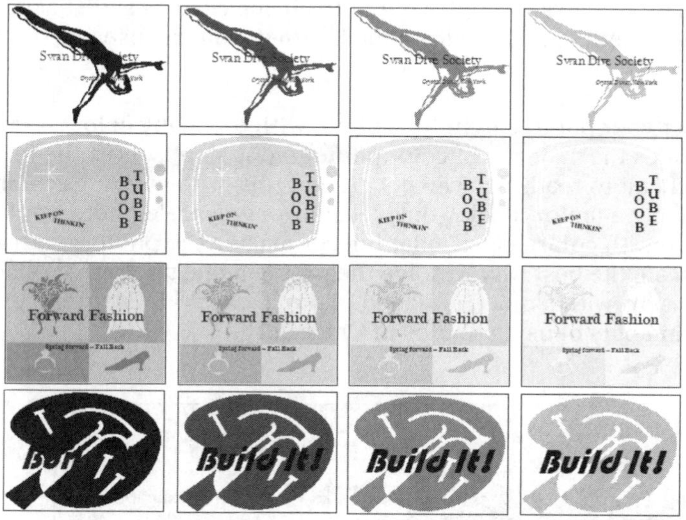

Figure 2-5: For backgrounds, a picture usually has to be at least somewhat transparent. These slides are (from left to right) 0%, 40%, 65%, and 85% transparent.

1. **On the Design tab, click the Format Background button to open the Format Background pane.**
2. **Click the Picture or Texture Fill option button.**
3. **Click the Online button.**

   You see the Insert Pictures dialog box.
4. **Search for and select a picture that you can use in the background of your slides.**

   Book VIII, Chapter 3 explains the ins and outs of trolling for pictures.
5. **In the Format Background pane, enter a Transparency measurement.**

   Drag the Transparency slider or enter a measurement in the box. The higher the measurement, the more transparent the image is (see Figure 2-5).

6. **Enter measurements in the Offsets boxes to make your picture fill the slide.**
7. **Click the Apply to All button and then click Close.**

   There you have it. The picture you selected lands in the slides' backgrounds.

Using a photo of your own for a slide background

Figure 2-6 shows examples of photos being used as slide backgrounds. Besides getting a photo from the Internet, you can use one of your own photos.

Select your photo carefully. A photo with too many colors — and that includes the majority of color photographs — obscures the text and makes it difficult to read. You can get around this problem by "recoloring" a photo to give it a uniform color tint, selecting a grayscale photograph, selecting a photo with colors of a similar hue, or making the photo semitransparent, but all in all, the best way to solve the problem of a photo that obscures the text is to start with a quiet, subdued photo. (Book VIII, Chapter 3 explains all the ins and outs of using photos in Office 2016.)

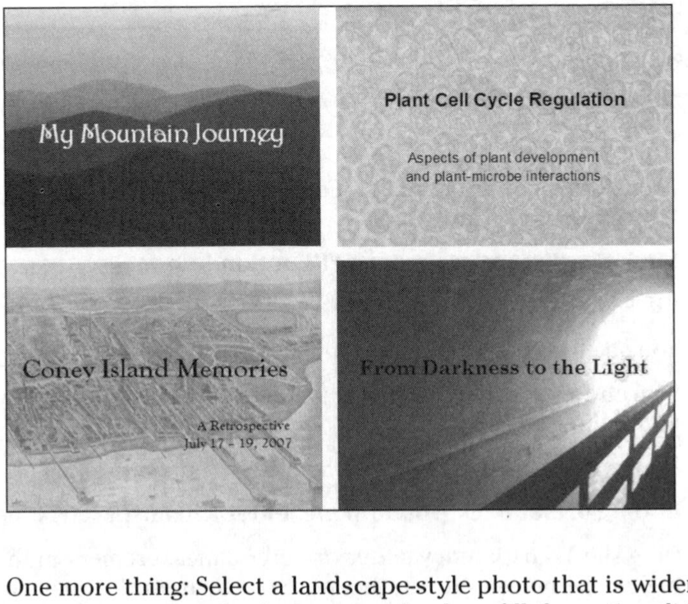

Figure 2-6: Examples of pictures used as slide backgrounds.

One more thing: Select a landscape-style photo that is wider than it is tall. PowerPoint expands photos to make them fill the entire slide background. If you select a skinny, portrait-style photo, PowerPoint has to do a lot of expanding to make it fit on the slide, and you end up with a distorted background image.

Follow these steps to use a picture as a slide background:

1. **On the Design tab, click the Format Background button to open the Format Background tab.**
2. **Click the Picture or Texture Fill option button.**
3. **Click the File button.**

   The Insert Picture dialog box appears.
4. **Locate the photo you want, select it, and click the Insert button.**

   The picture lands on your slide.
5. **Enter a Transparency measurement to make the photo fade a bit into the background.**

   Drag the slider or enter a measurement in the Transparency box. The higher percentage measurement you enter, the more "bleached out" the picture is.
6. **Using the Offsets text boxes, enter measurements to make your picture fit on the slides.**
7. **Click the Picture icon in the Format Background pane.**
8. **Experiment with the Picture Corrections and Picture Color options to make your picture more suitable for a background.**
9. **Click the Apply to All button.**

   How do you like your slide background? You may have to open the Format Background pane again and play with the transparency setting. Only the very lucky and the permanently blessed get it right the first time.

Using a texture for a slide background

Yet another option for slide backgrounds is to use a texture. As shown in Figure 2-7, a *texture* gives the impression that the slide is displayed on a material such as marble or parchment. A texture can make for a very elegant slide background. Follow these steps to use a texture as a slide background:

1. **On the Design tab, click the Format Background button to open the Format Background pane.**
2. **Click the Picture or Texture Fill option button.**
3. **Click the Texture button and choose a texture on the drop-down list.**
4. **Enter a Transparency measurement to make the texture less imposing.**

   Drag the slider or enter a measurement in the Transparency box.
5. **Click the Apply to All button and then click Close.**

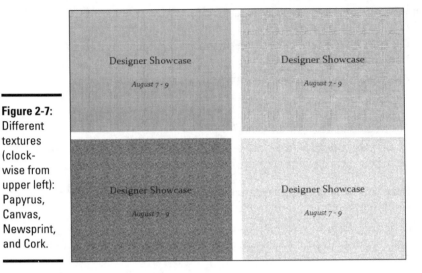

Figure 2-7: Different textures (clockwise from upper left): Papyrus, Canvas, Newsprint, and Cork.

Changing the Background of a Single or Handful of Slides

To make a single slide (or a handful of slides) stand out in a presentation, change their background or theme. A different background tells your audience that the slide being presented is a little different from the one before it. Maybe it imparts important information. Maybe it introduces another segment of the presentation. Use a different background or theme to mark a transition, indicate that your presentation has shifted gears, or mark a milestone in your presentation.

Follow these steps to change the background of one or several slides in your presentation:

1. **In Slide Sorter view, select the slide or slides that need a different look.**

   You can select more than one slide by Ctrl+clicking slides.

2. **On the Design tab, choose a different theme or background for the slides you selected.**

   How you do this depends on whether you're working with a theme or a slide background:

   - *Theme:* In the Themes gallery, right-click a theme and choose Apply To Selected Slides.
   - *Slide background:* Make like you're creating a background style for all the slides (see "Creating Slide Backgrounds on Your Own" earlier in this chapter) but don't click the Apply to All button.

WARNING!

When you assign a different theme to some of the slides in a presentation, PowerPoint creates another Slide Master. You may be surprised to discover that when you add a new slide to your presentation, a second, third, or fourth set of slide layouts appears on the New Slide drop-down list. These extra layouts appear because your presentation has more than one Slide Master. Later in this chapter, "Using Master Slides and Master Styles for a Consistent Design," explains what Slide Masters are.

Choosing the Slide Size

By default, slides in PowerPoint 2016 presentations are 16:9 ratio widescreen slides. In versions of PowerPoint prior to 2013, slides were 4:3 ratio standard size. The widescreen slide size is meant to accommodate modern letterbox computer screens, which are wider than they were in the past.

To change the size of the slides in a presentation, go to the Design tab and click the Slide Size button. Then, on the drop-down list, choose Standard (4:3), choose Widescreen (16:9), or choose Custom Slide Size and choose a different size in the Slide Size dialog box.

All slides in a presentation must be the same size. Sorry, you can't mix and match slides of different sizes.

Using Master Slides and Master Styles for a Consistent Design

Consistency is everything in a PowerPoint design. Consistency of design is a sign of professionalism and care. In a consistent design, the fonts and font sizes on slides are consistent from one slide to the next, the placeholder text frames are in the same positions, and the text is aligned the same way across different slides. In the bulleted lists, each entry is marked with the same bullet character. If the corner of each slide shows a company logo, the logo appears in the same position.

It would be torture to have to examine every slide to make sure it is consistent with the others. In the interest of consistency, PowerPoint offers master styles and master slides. A *master slide* is a model slide from which the slides in a presentation inherit their formats. A *master style* is a format that applies to many different slides. Starting from a master slide, you can change a master style and in so doing, reformat many slides the same way. These pages explain how master slides can help you quickly redesign a presentation.

Switching to Slide Master view

To work with master slides, switch to *Slide Master view,* as shown in Figure 2-8. From this view, you can start working with master slides:

1. **Go to the View tab.**
2. **Click the Slide Master button.**

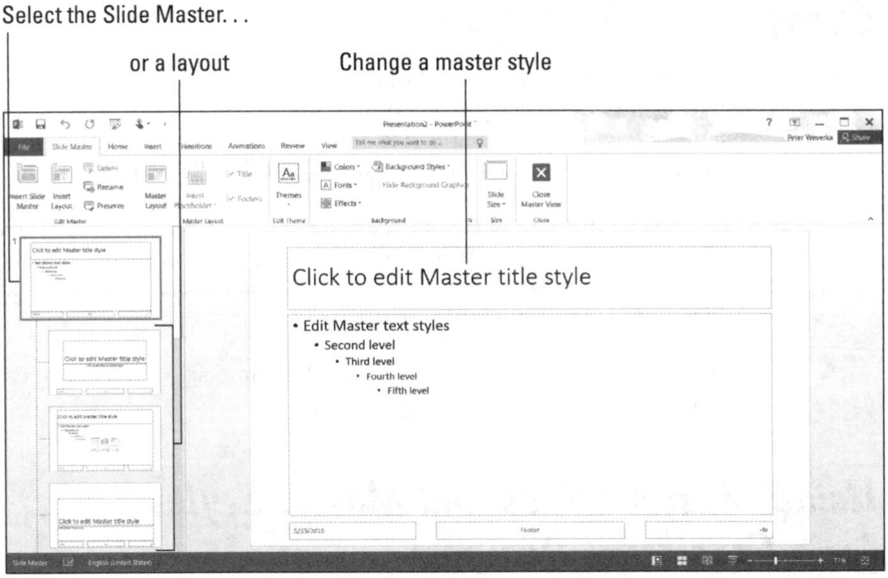

Figure 2-8: In Slide Master view, you can reformat many different slides simultaneously.

In Slide Master view, you can select a master slide in the Slides pane, format styles on a master slide, and in this way reformat many different slides. (Click the Close Master View button or a view button such as Normal or Slide Sorter to leave Slide Master view.)

Understanding master slides and master styles

Master slides are special, high-powered slides. Use master slides to deliver the same formatting commands to many different slides. Whether the commands affect all the slides in your presentation or merely a handful of slides depends on whether you format the Slide Master (the topmost slide in Slide Master view) or a layout (one of the other slides):

- **The Slide Master:** The *Slide Master* is the first slide in the Slides pane in Slide Master view (refer to Figure 2-8). It's a little bigger than the master slides, as befits its status as Emperor of All Slides. Formatting changes you make to the Slide Master affect all the slides in your presentation. When you select a theme for your presentation, what you're really doing is assigning a theme to the Slide Master. Because formatting commands given to the Slide Master apply throughout a presentation, the theme design and colors are applied to all slides. If you want a company logo to appear on all your slides, place the logo on the Slide Master.
- **Layouts:** As you know, you choose a slide layout — Title and Content, for example — on the New Slide drop-down list to create a new slide. In Slide Master view, PowerPoint provides one *layout* for each type of slide layout in your presentation. By selecting and reformatting a layout in Slide Master view, you can reformat all slides in your presentation that were created with the same slide layout. For example, to change fonts, alignments, and other formats on all slides that you created with the Title layout, select the Title layout in Slide Master view and change master styles on the Title layout. Each layout controls its own little fiefdom in a PowerPoint presentation — a fiefdom comprised of slides created with the same slide layout.
- **Master styles:** Each master slide — the Slide Master and each layout — offers you the opportunity to click to edit master styles (refer to Figure 2-8). The master style governs how text is formatted on slides. By changing a master style on a master slide, you can change the look of slides throughout a presentation. For example, by changing the Master Title Style font, you can change fonts in all the slide titles in your presentation.

PowerPoint's Slide Master–layouts–slides system is designed on the "trickle down" theory. When you format a master style on the Slide Master, formats trickle down to layouts and then to slides. When you format a master style on a layout, the formats trickle down to slides you created using the same slide layout. This chain-of-command relationship is designed to work from the top down, with the master slide and layouts barking orders to the slides below. In the interest of design consistency, slides take orders from layouts, and layouts take orders from the Slide Master.

TIP

In Slide Master view, you can move the pointer over a layout thumbnail in the Slides pane to see a pop-up box that tells you the layout's name and which slides in your presentation "use" the layout. For example, a pop-up box that reads "Title and Content Layout: used by slide(s) 2-3, 8" tells you that slides 2 through 3 and 8 in your presentation are governed by the Title and Content layout.

Editing a master slide

Now that you know the relationship among the Slide Master, layouts, and slides, you're ready to start editing master slides. To edit a master slide, switch to Slide Master view, select a master slide, and change a master style. To insert a picture on a master slide, visit the Insert tab.

Changing a master slide layout

Changing the layout of a master slide entails changing the position and size of text frames and content frames as well as removing these frames:

- **Changing size of frames:** Select the frame you want to change, and then move the pointer over a frame handle on the corner, side, top or bottom of the frame and drag when you see the double-headed arrow.
- **Moving frames:** Move the pointer over the perimeter of a frame, click when you see the four-headed arrow, and drag.
- **Removing a frame from the Slide Master:** Click the perimeter of the frame to select it and then press Delete.
- **Adding a frame to the Slide Master:** Select the slide master, and on the Slide Master tab, click the Master Layout button. You see the Master Layout dialog box. Select the check box beside the name of each frame you want to add and click OK.

Chapter 3: Entering the Text

In This Chapter

- **Entering and changing the font, size, and color of text**
- **Creating text boxes and text box shapes**
- **Handling overflow text in text boxes and frames**
- **Aligning the text in text boxes and text frames**
- **Creating bulleted and numbered lists**
- **Placing footers and headers on slides**

This chapter explains how to change the appearance of text, create text boxes, and create text box shapes. I solve the riddle of what to do when text doesn't fit in a text box or text placeholder frame. You also discover how to align text, handle bulleted and numbered lists, and put footers and headers on all or some of the slides in your presentation.

By the time you finish reading this chapter, if you read it all the way through, you will be one of those people others turn to when they have a PowerPoint question about entering text on slides. You'll become a little guru in your own right.

Entering Text

No presentation is complete without a word or two, which is why the first thing you see when you add a new slide to a presentation are the words "Click to add text." As soon as you "click," the words of instruction disappear, and you're free to enter a title or text of your own. Most slides include a text placeholder frame at the top for entering a slide title; many slides also have another, larger text placeholder frame for entering a bulleted list.

As shown in Figure 3-1, the easiest way to enter text on slides is to click in a text placeholder frame and start typing. The other way is to switch to Outline view and enter text in the Slides pane (see Figure 3-1).

Enter text on slides the same way you enter text in a Word document — by wiggling your fingers over the keyboard. While you're at it, you can change fonts, the font size of text, and the color of text, as the following pages explain. (Chapter 1 of this mini-book describes how to get the text for slides from the headings in a Word document; Book I, Chapter 2 explains everything a sane person needs to know about handling fonts.)

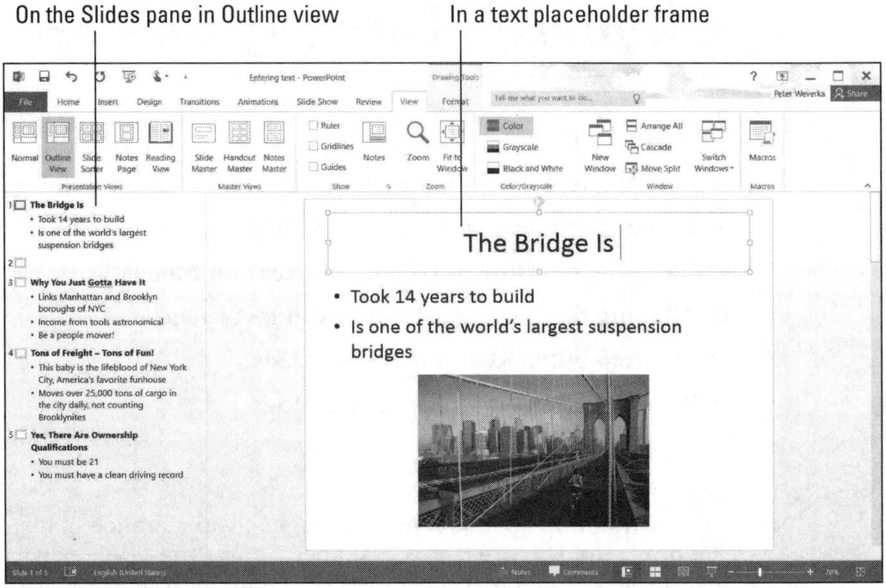

Figure 3-1: Ways of entering text.

Choosing fonts for text

If you aren't happy with the fonts in your presentation, you have two ways to remedy the problem:

- **Dig in and choose new fonts on a slide-by-slide basis.** Select the text, go to the Home tab, and choose a font from the Font drop-down list or the Font dialog box.
- **Choose a new font on a master slide to change fonts throughout your presentation.** Chapter 2 of this mini-book explains master slides and how you can use them to change formats simultaneously on many slides. In Slide Master view, select a master slide and change its fonts on the Home tab.

Changing the font size of text

For someone in the back row of an audience to be able to read text in a PowerPoint presentation, the text should be no smaller than 28 points. Try this simple test to see whether text in your presentation is large enough to read: Stand five or so feet from your computer and see whether you can read the text. If you can't read it, make it larger.

Go to the Home tab and select the text whose size you want to change. Then use one of these techniques to change font sizes:

- **Font Size drop-down list:** Open this list and choose a point size. To choose a point size that isn't on the list, click in the Font Size text box, enter a point size, and press Enter.
- **Font dialog box:** Click the Font group button to open the Font dialog box. Then either choose a point size from the Size drop-down list or enter a point size in the Size text box and click OK.
- **Increase Font Size and Decrease Font Size buttons:** Click these buttons (or press Ctrl+Shift+> or Ctrl+Shift+<) to increase or decrease the point size by the next interval on the Font Size drop-down list. Watch the Font Size list or your text and note how the text changes size. This is an excellent technique when you want to "eyeball it" and you don't care to fool with the Font Size list or Font dialog box.

Changing the look of text

For the daring and experimental, PowerPoint offers about a hundred different ways to change the look of text. You can change colors, make the text glow, and make the text cast a shadow, among other things.

Select the text that needs a makeover and then use one of these techniques to change its appearance:

- **Changing color:** On the Home tab, open the drop-down list on the Font Color button and choose a color. You can also click the Font group button to open the Font dialog box and choose a color there.
- **Choosing text fills, outlines, and effects:** On the Design tab, click the Format Background button and then select Text Options in the Format Shape pane. As shown in Figure 3-2, the Format Shape pane offers many ways to change the appearance of text:

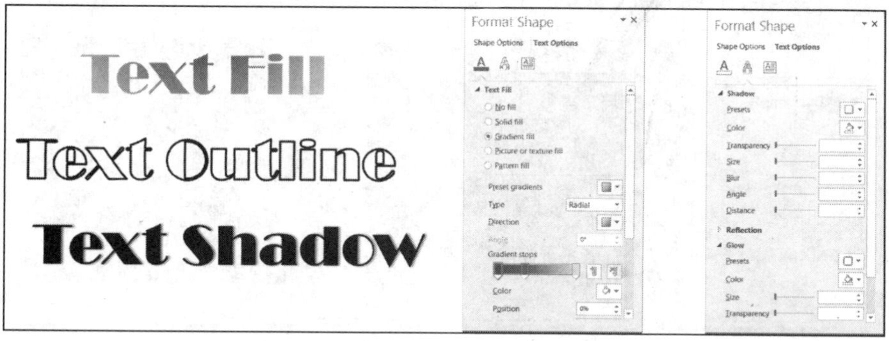

Figure 3-2: The Format Shape pane offers many commands for changing the look of text.

- **Text Fill:** Show the text in gradients, textures, or patterns. You can assign a transparent color to text by choosing a color and dragging the Transparency slider.
- **Text Outline:** Change the text outline — the outermost lines that form the letters and numbers. Try this: Under Text Fill, choose the No Fill option, and then choose a solid line as the text outline (refer to Figure 3-2).
- **Text Effects:** Give the letters and numbers a shadow, a glow, a softer edge, or another dimension. Before you experiment with these commands, try choosing an option on the Presets menu. Preset options demonstrate what these text effects can do and give you a head start in fashioning a text effect.

TIP

Before you change the look of text, peer into your computer screen and examine the background theme or color you selected for your slides. Unless the text is a different color from the background, the audience can't read the text. As you experiment with changing the look of text, make sure that your audience can still read the text.

Fixing a top-heavy title

In typesetting terminology, a *top-heavy title* is a title in which the first line is much longer than the second. Whenever a title extends to two lines, it runs the risk of being top-heavy. Unsightly top-heavy titles look especially bad on PowerPoint slides, where text is blown up to 40 points or more.

To fix a top-heavy title, click where you prefer the lines to break and then press Shift+Enter. Pressing Shift+Enter creates a *hard line break*, a forced break at the end of one line. (To remove a hard line break, click where the break occurs and then press the Delete key.)

The only drawback of hard line breaks is remembering where you made them. In effect, the line breaks are invisible. When you edit a title with a line break, the line break remains, and unless you know it's there, you discover the line breaking in an odd place. The moral is: If you're editing a title and the text keeps moving to the next line, you may have entered a hard line break and forgotten about it.

The Last Days of the California
Grizzly

The Last Days of
the California Grizzly

Fun with Text Boxes and Text Box Shapes

Text boxes give you an opportunity to exercise your creativity. They add another element to slides. Use them to position text wherever you want, annotate a chart or equation, or place an announcement on a slide. You can even create a vertical text box in which the text reads from top to bottom instead of left to right, or turn a text box into a circle, arrow, or other shape. Figure 3-3 shows examples of text boxes and text box shapes.

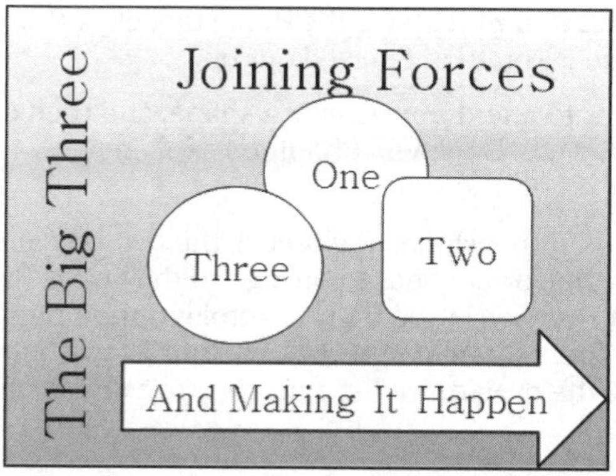

Figure 3-3: Examples of text boxes and text box shapes.

In Office terminology, a PowerPoint text box is an object. Book VIII, Chapter 4 explains all the different techniques for handling objects, including how to make them overlap and change their sizes. Here are the basics of handling text boxes in PowerPoint:

- **Creating a text box:** On the Insert tab, click the Text Box button and move the pointer to a part of the slide where you can see the *text box pointer,* a downward-pointing arrow. Then click and start dragging to create your text box, and enter the text.
- **Filling a text box with color:** On the (Drawing Tools) Format tab, choose a style on the Shape Styles gallery or click the Shape Fill button and select a color. You can also go to the Design tab, click the Format Background button, and select a color, picture, pattern, or gradient in the Format Shape pane.

- **Rotating a text box (text included):** Use one of these techniques to rotate a text box along with the text inside it:
  - Drag the rotation handle, the circle above the text box.
  - On the (Drawing Tools) Format tab, click the Rotate button and choose a Rotate or Flip command on the drop-down list.
  - On the (Drawing Tools) Format tab, click the Size group button (you may have to click the Size button first) and, in the Format Shape pane, enter a measurement in the Rotation box.
- **Changing the direction of text:** On the Home tab, click the Text Direction button and choose a Rotate or Stacked option.
- **Turning a shape into a text box:** Create a shape, and then click in the shape and start typing. (Book VIII, Chapter 4 explains how to create a shape.)
- **Turning a text box into a shape:** Right-click the text box and choose Format Shape. In the Format Shape pane, go to the Size & Properties tab. Then, under Text Box, select the Do Not AutoFit option button. Next, on the (Drawing Tools) Format tab, click the Edit Shape button, choose Change Shape on the drop-down list, and choose a shape on the Change Shape submenu.

TIP

Many people object to the small text boxes that appear initially when you create a text box. If you prefer to establish the size of text boxes when you create them, not when you enter text, change the AutoFit setting and then create a default text box with the new setting. The next section in this chapter explains how to change the AutoFit settings.

Controlling How Text Fits in Text Frames and Text Boxes

When text doesn't fit in a text placeholder frame or text box, PowerPoint takes measures to make it fit. In a text placeholder frame, PowerPoint shrinks the amount of space between lines and then it shrinks the text itself. When text doesn't fit in a text box, PowerPoint enlarges the text box to fit more text. PowerPoint handles overflow text as part of its AutoFit mechanism.

How AutoFit works is up to you. If, like me, you don't care for how PowerPoint enlarges text boxes when you enter the text, you can tell PowerPoint not to "AutoFit" text, but instead to make text boxes large from the get-go. And if you don't care for how PowerPoint shrinks text in text placeholder frames, you can tell PowerPoint not to shrink text. These pages explain how to choose AutoFit options for overflow text in your text frames and text boxes.

Choosing how AutoFit works in text frames

When text doesn't fit in a text placeholder frame and PowerPoint has to "AutoFit" the text, the AutoFit Options button appears beside the text box. Click this button to open a drop-down list with options for handling overflow text, as shown in Figure 3-4. The AutoFit options — along with a couple of other techniques, as I explain shortly — represent the "one at a time" way of handling overflow text. You can also change the default AutoFit options for handling overflow text, as I also explain if you'll bear with me a while longer and quit your yawning.

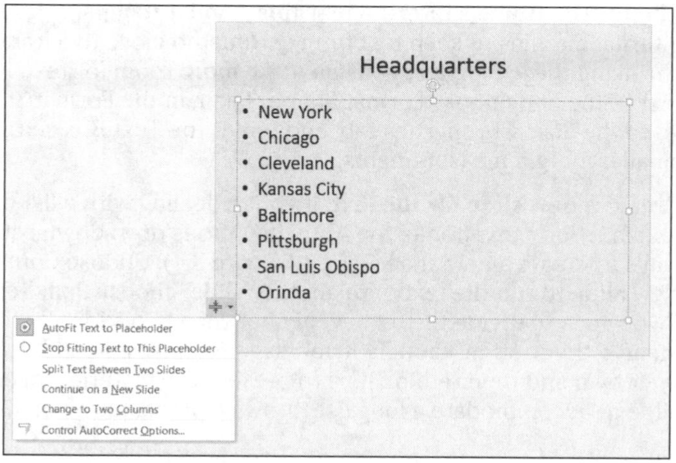

Figure 3-4: The laundry list of AutoFit options.

"AutoFitting" the text one frame at a time

WARNING!

When text doesn't fit in a text placeholder frame, especially a title frame, the first question to ask is, "Do I want to fool with the integrity of the slide design?" Making the text fit usually means shrinking the text, enlarging the text frame, or compromising the slide design in some way, but audiences notice design inconsistencies. Slides are shown on large screens where design flaws are easy to see.

Making text fit in a text frame usually means making a compromise. Here are different ways to handle the problem of text not fitting in a text frame. Be prepared to click the Undo button when you experiment with these techniques:

✦ **Edit the text:** Usually when text doesn't fit in a frame, the text needs editing. It needs to be made shorter. A slide is not a place for a treatise. Editing the text is the only way to make it fit in the frame without compromising the design.

- **Enlarge the frame:** Click the AutoFit Options button and choose Stop Fitting Text to This Placeholder on the shortcut menu (see Figure 3-4). Then select the frame and drag the bottom or top selection handle to enlarge it.
- **Decrease the font size:** Select the text, go to the Home tab, and choose a smaller Font Size measurement. You can also click the Decrease Font Size button (or press Ctrl+<) to decrease the font size.
- **Decrease the amount of spacing between lines:** On the Home tab, click the Paragraph group button to open the Paragraph dialog box and decrease the After measurement under Spacing.
- **Change the frame's internal margins:** Similar to a page, text frames have internal margins to keep text from getting too close to a frame border. By shrinking these margins, you can make more room for text. Right-click the text frame and choose Format Shape. Then, in the Format Shape pane, go to the Size & Properties tab, and under the Text Box settings, enter smaller margin measurements.
- **Create a new slide for the text:** If you're dealing with a list or paragraph text in a body text frame, the AutoFit Options drop-down list offers two ways to create a new slide (refer to Figure 3-4). Choose Continue on a New Slide to run the text onto another slide; choose Split Text Between Two Slides to divide the text evenly between two slides. I don't recommend either option, though. If you need to make a new slide, do it on your own and then rethink how to present the material. Inserting a new slide to accommodate a long list throws a presentation off-track.

Choosing default AutoFit options for text frames

Unless you change the default AutoFit options, PowerPoint shrinks the amount of space between lines and then shrinks the text itself to make text fit in text placeholder frames. Follow these steps if you want to decide for yourself whether PowerPoint "auto-fits" text in text frames:

1. **Open the AutoFormat As You Type tab in the AutoCorrect dialog box.**

   Here are the two ways to get there:

   - Click the AutoFit Options button (refer to Figure 3-4) and choose Control AutoCorrect Options on the drop-down list.
   - On the File tab, choose Options to open the PowerPoint Options dialog box. In the Proofing category, click the AutoCorrect Options button.

2. **Deselect the AutoFit Title Text to Placeholder check box to prevent auto-fitting in title text placeholder frames.**
3. **Deselect the AutoFit Body Text to Placeholder check box to prevent auto-fitting in text placeholder frames apart from title frames.**
4. **Click OK.**

Choosing how AutoFits works in text boxes

PowerPoint offers three options for handling overflow text in text boxes:

- **Do Not AutoFit:** Doesn't fit text in the text box but lets text spill out
- **Shrink Text on Overflow:** Shrinks the text to make it fit in the text box
- **Resize Shape to Fit Text:** Enlarges the text box to make the text fit inside it

Follow these steps to tell PowerPoint how or whether to fit text in text boxes:

1. **Select the text box.**
2. **Right-click the text box and choose Format Shape.**

   The Format Shape dialog box pane opens.
3. **Go to the Size & Properties tab.**
4. **Display the Text Box options.**
5. **Choose an AutoFit option: Do Not AutoFit, Shrink Text on Overflow, or Resize Shape to Fit Text.**

Positioning Text in Frames and Text Boxes

How text is positioned in text frames and text boxes is governed by two sets of commands: the Align Text commands and the Align commands. These commands are located on the Home tab. By choosing combinations of Align and Align Text commands, you can land text where you want it in a text frame or text box. Just wrestle with these two commands until you land your text where you want it to be in a text frame or box:

- Align commands control horizontal (left-to-right) alignments. On the Home tab, click the Align Left (press Ctrl+L), Center (press Ctrl+E), Align Right (press Ctrl+R), or Justify button.
- Align Text commands control vertical (up-and-down) alignments. On the Home tab, click the Align Text button and choose Top, Middle, or Bottom on the drop-down list, as shown in Figure 3-5.

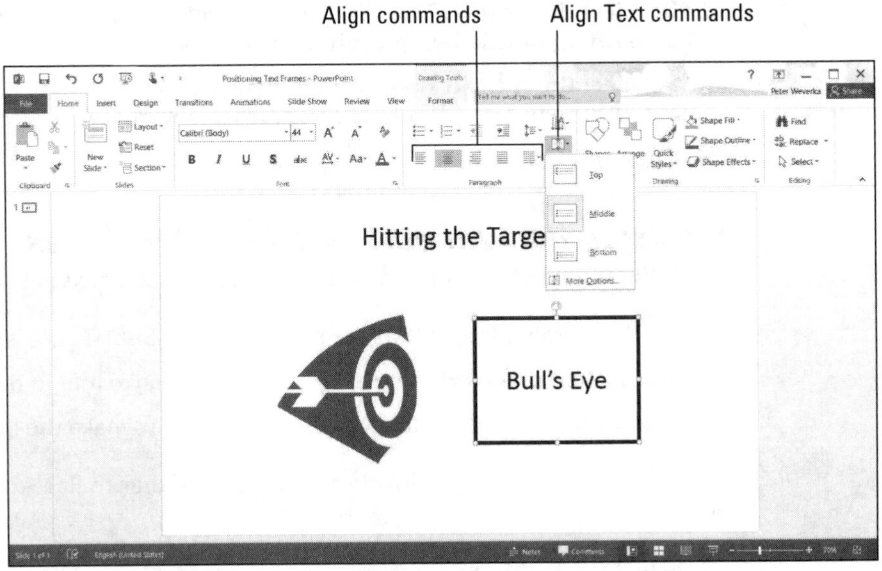

Figure 3-5: Choose an Align Text and an Align command to position text in text frames and boxes.

Handling Bulleted and Numbered Lists

What is a PowerPoint presentation without a list or two? It's like an emperor without any clothes on. This part of the chapter explains everything there is to know about bulleted and numbered lists.

Lists can be as simple or complex as you want them to be. PowerPoint offers a bunch of different ways to format lists, but if you're in a hurry or you don't care whether your lists look like everyone else's, you can take advantage of the Numbering and Bullets buttons and go with standard lists. Nonconformists and people with nothing else to do, however, can try their hand at making fancy lists. The following pages cover that topic, too.

Creating a standard bulleted or numbered list

In typesetting terms, a *bullet* is a black, filled-in circle or other character that marks an item on a list. Many slide layouts include text frames that are formatted already for bulleted lists. All you have to do in these text frames is "Click to add text" and keep pressing the Enter key while you enter items for your bulleted list. Each time you press Enter, PowerPoint adds another bullet to the list. Bulleted lists are useful when you want to present the audience with alternatives or present a list in which the items aren't ranked in any order. Use a numbered list to rank items in a list or present step-by-step instructions.

Follow these instructions to create a standard bulleted or numbered list:

✦ **Creating a bulleted list:** Select the list if you've already entered the list items, go to the Home tab, and click the Bullets button. You can also right-click, choose Bullets on the shortcut menu, and choose a bullet character on the submenu if you don't care for the standard, black, filled-in circle.

✦ **Creating a numbered list:** Select the list if you've already entered the list items, go to the Home tab, and click the Numbering button. You can also right-click, choose Numbering on the shortcut menu, and select a numbering style on the submenu.

✦ **Converting a numbered to a bulleted list (or vice versa):** Drag over the list to select it, go to the Home tab, and then click the Bullets or Numbering button.

To remove the bullets or numbers from a list, select the list, open the drop-down list on the Bullets or Numbering button, and choose None.

Choosing a different bullet character, size, and color

As Figure 3-6 demonstrates, the black filled-in circle isn't the only character you can use to mark items in a bulleted list. You can also opt for what PowerPoint calls *pictures* (colorful bullets of many sizes and shapes) or symbols from the Symbol dialog box. While you're at it, you can change the bullets' color and size.

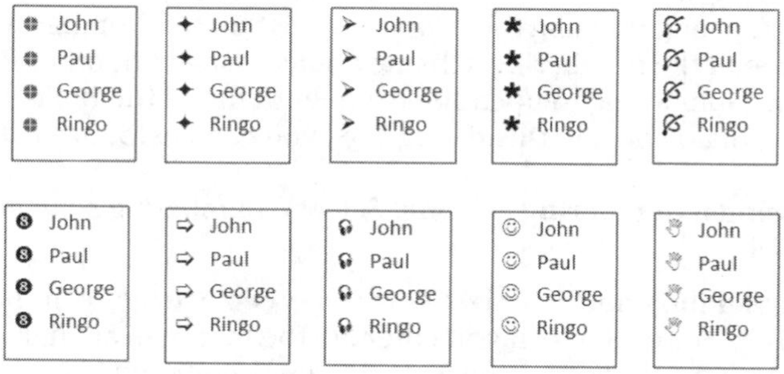

Figure 3-6: Examples of characters you can use for bulleted lists.

If you decide to change the bullet character in your lists, be consistent from slide to slide. Unless you want to be goofy, select the same bullet character throughout the lists in your presentation for the sake of consistency. You don't want to turn your slide presentation into a showcase for bullets, do you?

To use pictures or unusual symbols for bullets, start by selecting your bulleted list, going the Home tab, and opening the drop-down list on the Bullets button. Do any of the bullets on the drop-down list tickle your fancy? If one does, select it; otherwise, click the Bullets and Numbering option at the bottom of the drop-down list. You see the Bulleted tab of the Bullets and Numbering dialog box. Starting there, you can customize your bullets:

- **Using a picture for bullets:** Click the Picture button and search for a bullet in the Insert Pictures dialog box.
- **Using a symbol for bullets:** Click the Customize button and select a symbol in the Symbol dialog box.
- **Changing bullets' size:** Enter a percentage figure in the Size % of Text box. For example, if you enter **200**, the bullets are twice as large as the font size you choose for the items in your bulleted list.
- **Changing bullets' color:** Click the Color button in the Bullets and Numbering dialog box and choose an option on the drop-down list. Theme colors are considered most compatible with the theme design you chose for your presentation.

Choosing a different list-numbering style, size, and color

PowerPoint offers seven different ways of numbering lists. As well as choosing a different numbering style, you can change the size of numbers relative to the text and change the color of numbers. To select a different list-numbering style, size, or color, begin by selecting your list, going to the Home tab, and opening the drop-down list on the Numbering button. If you like one of the numbering-scheme choices, select it; otherwise choose Bullets and Numbering to open the Numbered tab of the Bullets and Numbering dialog box. In this dialog box, you can customize list numbers:

- **Choosing a numbering scheme:** Select a numbering scheme and click OK.
- **Changing the numbers' size:** Enter a percentage figure in the Size % of Text box. For example, if you enter 50, the numbers are half as big as the font size you choose for the items in your numbered list.
- **Changing the numbers' color:** Click the Color button and choose a color on the drop-down list. Theme colors are more compatible with the theme design you chose than the other colors are.

Putting Footers (and Headers) on Slides

A *footer* is a line of text that appears at the foot, or bottom, of a slide. Figure 3-7 shows a footer. Typically, a footer includes the date, a company name, and/or a slide number, and footers appear on every slide in a presentation if they appear at all. That doesn't mean you can't exclude a footer from a slide or put footers on some slides, as I explain shortly. For that matter, you can move slide numbers, company names, and dates to the top of slides, in which case they become *headers.* When I was a kid, "header" meant crashing your bike and falling headfirst over the handlebars. How times change.

These pages explain everything a body needs to know about footers and headers — how to enter them, make them appear on all or some slides, and exclude them from slides.

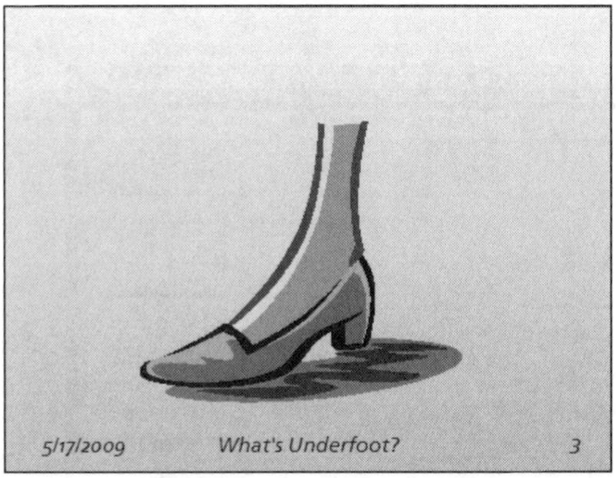

Figure 3-7: An example of a footer.

Some background on footers and headers

PowerPoint provides the Header & Footer command to enter the date, a word or two, and a slide number on the bottom of all slides in your presentation. This command is really just a convenient way to enter a footer on the Slide Master without having to switch to Slide Master view. As Chapter 2 of this mini-book explains, the Slide Master governs the formatting and layout of all slides in your presentation. The Slide Master includes text placeholder frames for a date, some text, and a slide number. Anything you enter on the Slide Master, including a footer, appears on all your slides.

If a date, some text, and a slide number along the bottom of all the slides in your presentation is precisely what you want, you've got it made. You can enter a footer on every slide in your presentation with no trouble at all by using the Header & Footer command. However, if you're a maverick and you want your footers and headers to be a little different from the next person's — if you want the date, for example, to be in the upper-right corner of slides or you want footers to appear on some slides but not others — you have some tweaking to do. You may have to create a nonstandard footer or remove the footer from some of the slides.

Putting a standard footer on all your slides

A standard footer includes the date, some text, and the page number. To put a standard footer on all the slides in your presentation, go to the Insert tab and click the Header & Footer button. You see the Header and Footer dialog box, as shown in Figure 3-8. Choose some or all of these options and click the Apply to All button:

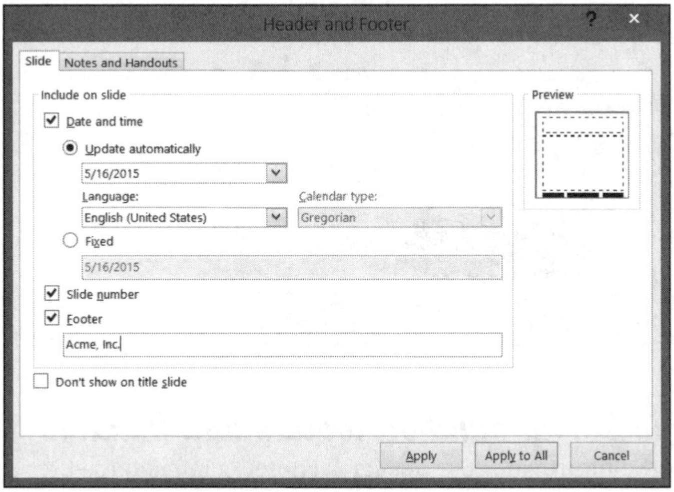

Figure 3-8: Entering a standard footer.

- **Date and Time:** Select this check box to make the date appear in the lower-left corner of all your slides. Then tell PowerPoint whether you want a current or fixed date:
  - *Update Automatically:* Select this option button to make the day's date (or date and time) appear in the footer, and then open the drop-down list to choose a date (or date and time) format. With this option, the date you give your presentation always appears on slides.

- *Fixed:* Select this option button and enter a date in the text box. For example, enter the date you created the presentation. With this option, the date remains fixed no matter when or where you give the presentation.

✦ **Slide Number:** Select this check box to make slide numbers appear in the lower-right corner of all slides.

✦ **Footer:** Select this check box, and in the text box, enter the words that you want to appear in the bottom, middle of all the slides.

Creating a nonstandard footer

As "Some background on footers and headers" explains earlier in this chapter, you have to look elsewhere than the Header and Footer dialog box if you want to create something besides the standard footer. Suppose you want to move the slide number from the lower-right corner of slides to another position? Or you want to fool with the fonts in headers and footers?

Follow these steps to create a nonstandard footer:

1. **Create a standard footer if you want your nonstandard footer to include today's date and/or a slide number.**

   If you want to move the slide number into the upper-right corner of slides, for example, create a standard footer first (see the preceding topic in this chapter). Later, you can move the slide number text frame into the upper-right corner of slides.

2. **On the View tab, click the Slide Master button.**

   You switch to Slide Master view. Chapter 2 of this mini-book explains this view and how to format many slides at once with master slides.

3. **Select the Slide Master, the topmost slide in the Slides pane.**

4. **Adjust and format the footer text boxes to taste (as they say in cookbooks).**

   For example, move the slide number text frame into the upper-right corner to put slide numbers there. Or change the font in the footer text boxes. Or place a company logo on the Slide Master to make the logo appear on all your slides.

5. **Click the Close Master View button to leave Slide Master view.**

   You can always return to Slide Master view and adjust your footer.

Removing a footer from a single slide

On a crowded slide, the date, footer text, page number, and other items in the footer can get in the way or be a distraction. Fortunately, removing one or all of the footer text frames from a slide is easy:

1. **Switch to Normal view and display the slide with the footer that needs removing.**
2. **On the Insert tab, click the Header & Footer button.**

   The Header and Footer dialog box appears.
3. **Deselect check boxes — Date and Time, Slide Number, and Footer — to tell PowerPoint which parts of the footer you want to remove.**
4. **Click the Apply button.**

   Be careful not to click the Apply to All button. Clicking this button removes footers throughout your slide presentation.

Chapter 4: Making Your Presentations Livelier

In This Chapter

- Looking at ways to make a presentation livelier
- Slapping a transition or animation on a slide
- Making sound a part of your presentation
- Playing video during a presentation
- Recording your own voice narration for a presentation

The purpose of this chapter is to make your presentation stand out in a crowd. It suggests ways to enliven your presentation with pictures, charts, slides, and tables. It shows how transitions and animations can make a presentation livelier. Finally, you discover how to play sound and video during a presentation.

Suggestions for Enlivening Your Presentation

Starting on the Insert tab, you can do a lot to make a presentation livelier. The Insert tab offers buttons for putting pictures, tables, charts, diagrams, and shapes on slides:

- **Pictures:** Everyone likes a good graphic or photo, but more than that, audiences understand more from words and pictures than they do from words alone. A well-chosen photo or image reinforces the ideas that you're trying to put across in your presentation. (See Book VIII, Chapter 3.)
- **Tables:** A table is a great way to plead your case or defend your position. Raw table data is irrefutable — well, most of the time, anyway. Create a table when you want to demonstrate how the numbers back you up. (See "Presenting Information in a Table," later in this chapter.)
- **Charts:** Nothing is more persuasive than a chart. The bars, pie slices, or columns show the audience instantaneously that production is up or down, or that sector A is outperforming sector B. The audience can compare the data and see what's what. (See Book VIII, Chapter 1.)

- **Diagrams:** A diagram is an excellent marriage of images and words. Diagrams allow an audience to literally visualize a concept, idea, or relationship. You can present an abstract idea such that the audience understands it better. (See Book VIII, Chapter 2.)
- **Shapes:** Lines and shapes can also illustrate ideas and concepts. You can also use them as slide decorations. (See Book VIII, Chapter 4.)

Presenting Information in a Table

The purpose of a table is to present information for comparison purposes — to see which car gets the best gas mileage, which company made the most money, or who shucked the most corn. Tables on slides can't be used for reference purposes because they appear briefly on screen; viewers can't refer to them later on. Nevertheless, a table is a great way to present a quick summary of the bare facts.

PowerPoint offers no fewer than four ways to create a table. The best slide layout for creating tables is Title and Content because it offers space for a title and provides the Table icon, which you can click to create a table. Create your table with one of these techniques:

- **Dragging on the Table menu:** On the Insert tab, click the Table button, point on the drop-down list to the number of columns and rows you want, as shown in Figure 4-1, and let go of the mouse button.
- **Clicking the Table icon:** Click the Table icon in a content placeholder frame. You see the Insert Table dialog box, shown in Figure 4-1. Enter the number of columns and rows you want for your table and click OK.
- **Using the Insert Table dialog box:** On the Insert tab, click the Table button and choose Insert Table on the drop-down list. The Insert Table dialog box shown in Figure 4-1 appears. Enter the number of columns and rows you want and click OK.
- **Drawing a table:** On the Insert tab, click the Table button and choose Draw Table on the drop-down list. The pointer changes into a pencil. Use the pencil to draw the table borders. On the (Table Tools) Design tab, you can click the Draw Table button and draw the columns and rows for the table.

REMEMBER

After you create a table, PowerPoint places two Table Tools tabs on the Ribbon, one called Design and one called Layout. The (Table Tools) Design tab offers commands for changing the look of the table; the (Table Tools) Layout tab is for changing around the rows and columns.

The techniques for working with tables in Word and PowerPoint are terribly similar. I suggest going to Book II, Chapter 4 if your aim is to create a really, really nice table.

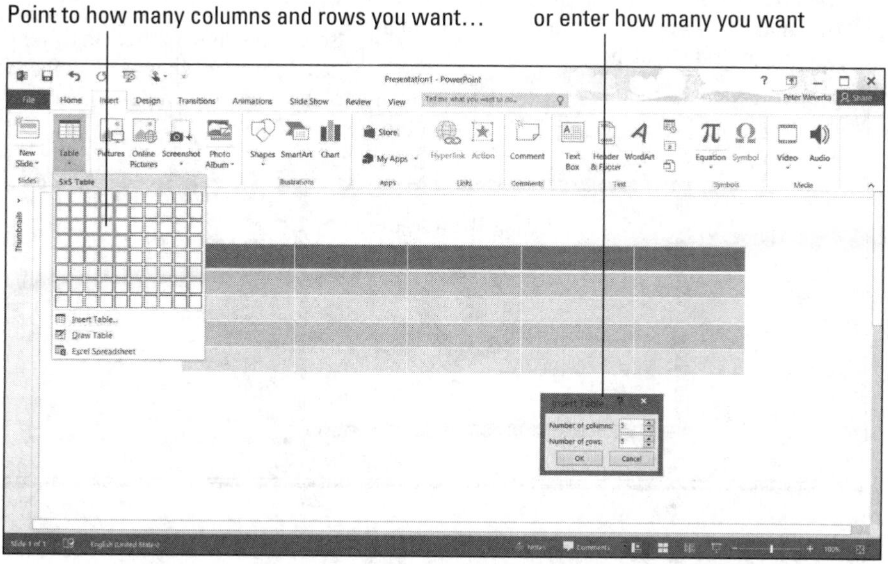

Figure 4-1: Declare how many columns and rows you want for your table.

The grid and drawing guides

The *grid* is an invisible set of horizontal and vertical lines to which objects — images, pictures, and shapes — cling when you move them on a slide. The grid is meant to help you line up objects squarely with one another. When you drag an object, it sticks to the nearest point on the grid.

PowerPoint also offers the *drawing guides* for aligning objects. You can drag these vertical and horizontal lines onscreen and use them to align objects with precision.

To display the grid and the drawing guides:

- **Displaying (and hiding) the grid:** Press Shift+F9 or go to the View tab and select the Gridlines check box.
- **Displaying (and hiding) the drawing guides:** Press Alt+F9 or go to the View tab and select the Guides check box.

By default, objects when you move them "snap to the grid." That means they objects stick to the nearest grid line when you move them

(continued)

(continued)

across a slide. To control whether objects snap to the grid, right-click (but not on an object or frame), choose Grid and Guides, and in the Grid and Guides dialog box, deselect the Snap Objects to Grid check box.

Even if the Snap Objects to Grid check box in the Grid and Guides dialog box is selected, you can move objects without them snapping to a gridline by holding down the Alt key while you drag.

Select the Snap Objects to Other Objects check box if you want shapes to abut each other or fall along a common axis.

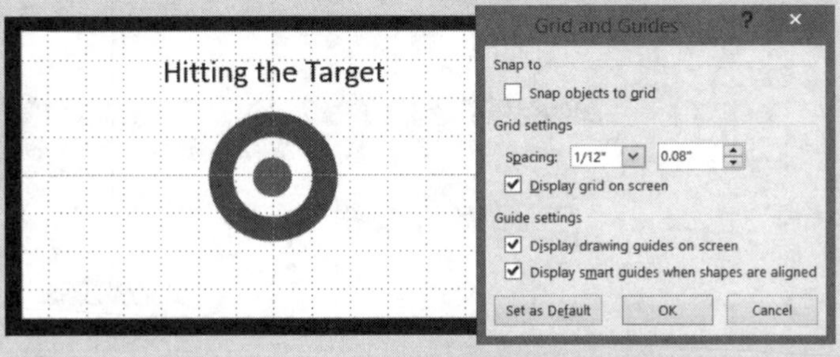

Exploring Transitions and Animations

In PowerPoint-speak, a *transition* is a little bit of excitement that occurs as one slide leaves the screen and the next slide climbs aboard. An *animation* is movement on the slide. For example, you can animate bulleted lists such that the bullet points appear on a slide one at a time when you click the mouse rather than all at one time.

WARNING!

Before you know anything about transitions and animations, you should know that they can be distracting. The purpose of a presentation is to communicate with the audience, not display the latest, busiest, most dazzling presentation technology. For user-run, kiosk-style presentations, however, eye-catching transitions and animations can be useful because they draw an audience. (A user-run presentation plays on its own, as I explain in Chapter 5 of this mini-book.) For audiences that enjoy high-tech wizardry, transitions and animations can be a lot of fun and add to a presentation.

Showing transitions between slides

Transitions include the Switch, Fade, and Push. Figure 4-2 shows how a transition works. For the figure, I chose the Clock transition. This slide doesn't so much arrive onscreen as it does sweep onto the screen in a clockwise fashion. You get a chance to test-drive these transitions before you attach them to slides.

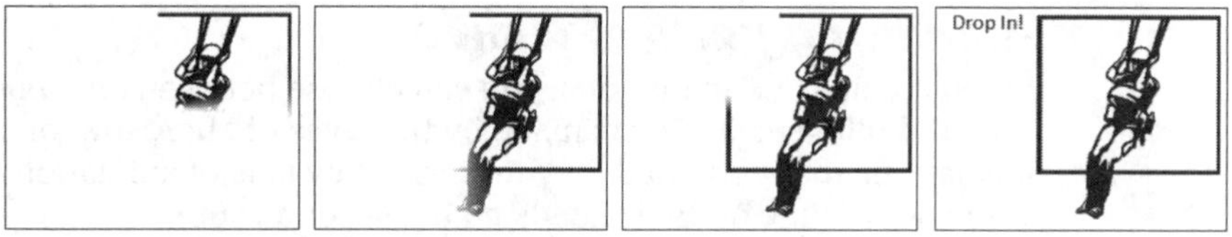

Figure 4-2: The Clock transition in action.

Assigning transitions to slides

To show transitions between slides, select the slide or slides that need transitions, go to the Transitions tab, and select a transition in the Transition to This Slide gallery. (To apply the same transition to all the slides in a presentation, click the Apply To All button after you select a transition.) The names and images in the gallery give you an idea of what the transitions are, and you can click the Preview button on the Transitions tab at any time to watch a transition you chose.

The Transitions tab offers these tools for tweaking a transition:

- ✦ **Effect Options:** Click the Effect Options button and choose an effect on the drop-down list. For example, choose From Top or From Bottom to make a transition arrive from the top or bottom of the screen. Not all transitions offer effect options.
- ✦ **Sound:** Open the Sound drop-down list and choose a sound to accompany the transition. The Loop Until Next Sound option at the bottom of the drop-down list plays a sound continuously until the next slide in the presentation appears.
- ✦ **Duration:** Enter a time period in the Duration box to declare how quickly or slowly you want the transition to occur.

REMEMBER

As I mention earlier, you can click the Apply To All button to assign the same transition to all the slides in your presentation.

Altering and removing slide transitions

In Slide Sorter view and in the Slides pane in Normal view, the transition symbol, a flying star, appears next to slides that have been assigned a transition. Select the slides that need a transition change, go to the Transitions tab, and follow these instructions to alter or remove transitions:

- ✦ **Altering a transition:** Choose a different transition in the Transition to This Slide gallery. You can also choose different effect options and sounds, and change the duration of the transition.
- ✦ **Removing a transition:** Choose None in the Transition to This Slide gallery.

Animating parts of a slide

When it comes to animations, you can choose between *animation schemes,* the pre-built special effects made by the elves of Microsoft, or customized animations that you build on your own. Only fans of animation and people with a lot of time on their hands go the second route.

Choosing a ready-made animation scheme

Follow these steps to preview and choose an animation scheme for slides:

1. **Go to the Animations tab.**
2. **Click to select the element on the slide that you want to animate.**

   For example, select a text frame with a bulleted list. You can tell when you've selected an element because a selection box appears around it.
3. **In the Animation Styles gallery, choose an animation effect, as shown in Figure 4-3.**

   You can choose Entrance, Emphasis, Motion Paths, and Exit animation effects. As soon as you make your choice, the animation springs to life, and you can click the Preview button at any time to see your animation in all its glory.
4. **Click the Effect Options button and experiment with choices on the drop-down list to tweak your animation.**

   Which options are available depends on the animation you chose.

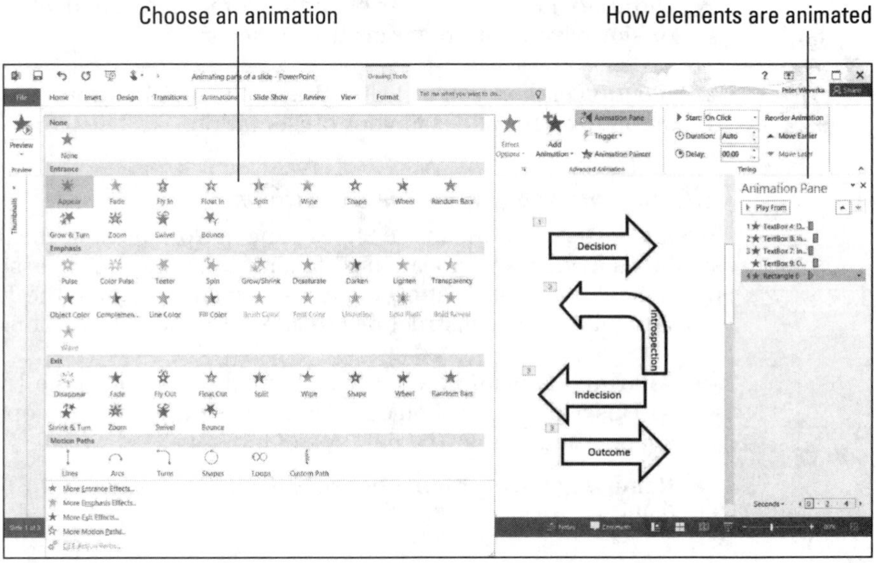

Figure 4-3: Apply effects in the Animation gallery.

5. **If you choose a text-box or text-frame element with more than one paragraph in Step 2, click the Effect Options button and tell PowerPoint whether to animate all the text or animate each paragraph separately from the others.**

   - **As Once Object or All at Once**: All the text is animated at the same time.
   - **By Paragraph:** Each paragraph is treated separately and is animated on its own. For example, each item in a bulleted list is treated as a separate element — each item fades, wipes, or flies in after the one before it, not at the same time as the one before it.

   Very briefly, you see a preview of the animation choice you made. To get a good look at the animation you just chose for your slide, click the Preview button on the Animations tab.

To remove an animation, return to the Animation Styles gallery and choose None.

Fashioning your own animation schemes

To fashion your own animation scheme, go to the Animations tab and click the Animation Pane button. You see the Animation pane, as shown in Figure 4-3. It lists, in order, each animation that occurs on your slide (if animations occur). Select an element on the slide and follow these general instructions to animate it:

✦ Click the Add Animation button and choose an animation.

✦ On the Start drop-down list, declare whether the animation begins when you click your slide (Start On Click), at the same time as the previous animation (Start With Previous), or after the previous animation (Start After Previous).

✦ In the Duration box, enter how long you want the animation to last.

✦ In the Delay box, enter a time period to declare how soon after the previous animation in the Animation pane you want your animation to occur.

✦ Select an animation in the task pane and click a Re-Order button to change the order in which animations occur, if more than one element is animated on your slide.

Making Audio Part of Your Presentation

Especially in user-run, kiosk-style presentations, audio can be a welcome addition. Audio gives presentations an extra dimension. It attracts an audience. PowerPoint offers two ways to make audio part of a presentation:

- **As part of slide transitions:** A sound is heard as a new slide arrives onscreen. On the Transitions tab, open the Sound drop-down list and choose a sound. (See "Showing transitions between slides" earlier in this chapter.)
- **On the slide itself:** The means of playing audio appears on the slide in the form of an Audio icon, as shown in Figure 4-4. By moving the mouse over this icon, you can display audio controls, and you can use these controls to play audio. You can also make audio play as soon as the slide arrives onscreen.

Figure 4-4: Making audio part of a presentation.

Table 4-1 describes the audio files you can use in PowerPoint presentations and whether each file type is a wave or MIDI sound. To find out what kind of audio file you're dealing with, note the file's three-letter extension; or open File Explorer, find the sound file, right-click it, and choose Properties.

Table 4-1 Sound File Formats

File Type	*Extension*	*Wave/MIDI*
MIDI Sequence	`.midi`, `.mid`	MIDI
MP3 audio file	`.mp3`	Wave
Wave audio	`.wav`	Wave
Windows Media Audio File	`.wma`	Wave

Inserting an audio file on a slide

Follow these steps to insert an audio file in a slide:

1. **Go to the Insert tab.**
2. **Click the Audio button.**
3. **Choose Audio on My PC.**

   The Insert Audio dialog box appears.
4. **Locate and select a sound file.**
5. **Click Insert.**

REMEMBER

An Audio icon appears on the slide to remind you that audio is supposed to play when your slide is onscreen. You can change the size of this icon by selecting it and dragging a corner handle or going to the (Audio Tools) Format tab and entering new Height and Width measurements. You can also drag the icon into an out-of-the-way corner of your slide.

To quit playing a sound file on a slide, select its Audio icon and then press the Delete key.

Telling PowerPoint when and how to play an audio file

To tell PowerPoint when and how to play an audio file, start by selecting the Audio icon and going to the (Audio Tools) Playback tab, as shown in Figure 4-5. From there, you can control when and how audio files play:

- **Controlling the volume:** Click the Volume button and choose an option on the drop-down list to control how loud the audio plays.
- **Playing the audio file automatically in the background**: Click the Play in Background button. Clicking this button tells PowerPoint to play the audio automatically, across slides, until you or another presenter clicks the Pause button to stop the audio from playing.

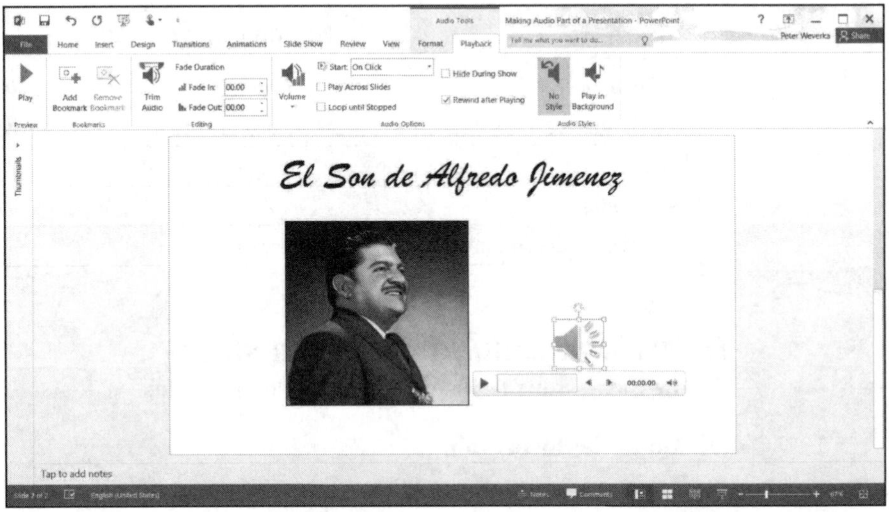

Figure 4-5: Visit the (Audio Tools) Playback tab to control when and how sounds play.

- **Deciding when and how to play audio:** Click the No Style button. Then select these options:
  - *Start:* Choose Automatically to make the audio play as soon as the slide appears; choose On Click to play the audio when you click the Audio icon on your slide.
  - *Play Across Slides:* Play the audio file throughout a presentation, not just when the slide with the audio file appears.
  - *Loop Until Stopped:* Play the audio file continuously until you or another presenter clicks the Pause button.
- **Hiding and unhiding the Audio icon:** Select the Hide During Show check box. If you hide the Audio icon, the file must play automatically; otherwise, you won't see the icon and be able to click it and view the audio controls.
- **Rewind After Playing:** Starts replaying the audio file from the beginning after it is finished playing.

Click the Play button on the (Audio Tools) Playback tab to play an audio file.

Playing audio during a presentation

While an audio file is playing during a presentation, controls for starting, pausing, and controlling the volume appear onscreen (refer to Figure 4-4). They appear onscreen, I should say, if the Audio icon appears on your slide. (If you've hidden the Audio icon, you're out of luck because you can't see the Audio icon or use its audio controls.)

Follow these instructions to start, pause, and control the volume of an audio recording during a presentation:

- **Starting an audio file:** Move the pointer over the Audio icon, and when you see the Audio controls, click the Play/Pause button (or press Alt+P).
- **Pausing an audio file:** Click the Play/Pause button (or press Alt+P). Click the button again to resume playing the audio file.
- **Muting the volume:** Click the Mute/Unmute icon (or press Alt+U).
- **Controlling the volume:** Move the pointer over the Mute/Unmute icon to display the volume slider and then drag the volume control on the slider.

Playing Video on Slides

If a picture is worth a thousand words, what is a moving picture worth? Ten thousand? To give your presentation more cachet, you can play video on slides and in so doing, turn your presentation into a mini-movie theater.

To play video, PowerPoint relies on *Windows Media Player,* the media player that comes with Windows. Therefore, to play video on a slide, stick to formats that Windows Media Player can handle: ASF (Advanced Systems Format), AVI (Audio Visual Interleaved), MPEG (Motion Picture Experts Group), MPG (Media Planning Group), WMV (Windows Media Video), MOV (QuickTime Video), and SWF (Adobe Flash). You can download versions of Windows Media Player at this web page:

`http://windows.microsoft.com/en-US/windows/downloads/windows-media-player`

Inserting a video on a slide

Follow these steps to insert a video on a slide:

1. **On the Insert tab, click the Video button.**
2. **Choose an option on the drop-down list.**

   You can play a video file on your computer or get a video from Office.com.

   - *Online Video:* The Insert Video dialog box appears (you can also open this dialog box by clicking the Insert Video icon on some slide layouts). Obtain a video from a folder on your computer or a OneDrive folder, select a video from YouTube, or embed a video by pasting its URL into the dialog box.
   - *Video on My PC:* You see the Insert Video dialog box. Select a video and click Insert.

The video appears on your slide. If I were you, I would find out how (or whether) the video plays. To do that, click the Play/Pause button (or press Alt+P) or click the Play button on the (Video Tools) Playback or (Video Tools) Format tab.

Fine-tuning a video presentation

As shown in Figure 4-6, select the video and go to the (Video Tools) Playback tab to fine-tune a video presentation. The Playback tab offers all kinds of commands for making a video play the way you want it to play. Here are different ways to fine-tune a video presentation:

- **Adding a bookmark:** Add a bookmark to be able to skip ahead or backward to a place in the video when you play it. To add a bookmark, play the video to the place where you want the book mark to be and then stop playing the video. Next, click the Add Bookmark button. The bookmark appears in the form of a circle. You can click this circle to go to the bookmark while you play the video. To remove a bookmark, select it on the timeline and click the Remove Bookmark button.
- **Trimming the video:** To trim from the start and or end of a video, click the Trim Video button. Then, in the Trim Video dialog box, drag the green slider to trim from the start of the video; drag the red slider to trim from the end.
- **Fading in and out:** Enter time measurements in the Fade In and Fade Out text boxes to make the video fade in or out.

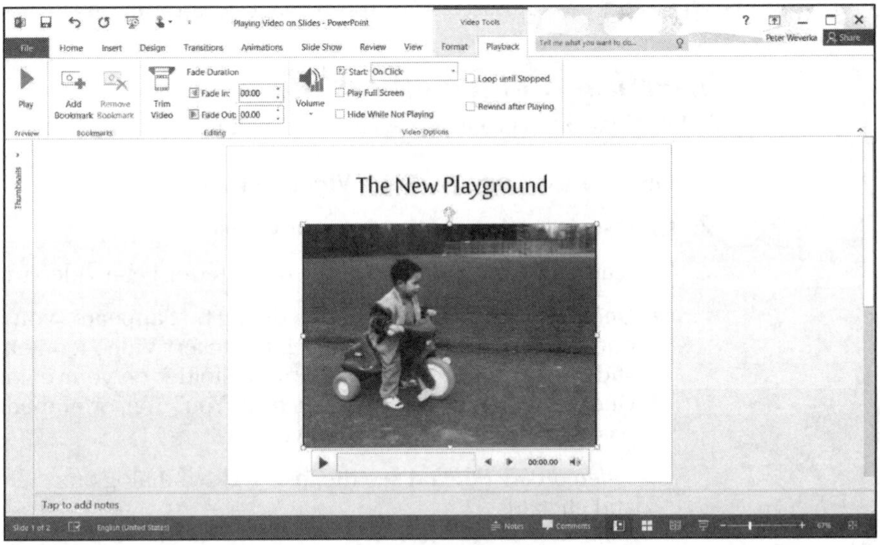

Figure 4-6: Visit the (Video Tools) Playback tab to fine-tune a video presentation.

✦ **Controlling the volume:** Click the Volume button and choose Low, Medium, High, or Mute to control how loud the video sound is.

✦ **Playing the video automatically or when you click the Play/Pause button:** Open the Start drop-down list and choose Automatically or On Click to tell PowerPoint when to start playing the video.

✦ **Playing the video at full-screen:** Make a video fill the entire screen by selecting the Play Full Screen check box. Be careful of this one. Videos can look terribly grainy when they appear on the big screen.

✦ **Hiding the video when it isn't playing:** You can hide the video until you start playing it by selecting the Hide While Not Playing check box. Be sure to choose Automatically on the Start drop-down list if you select this check box.

✦ **Continuously playing, or looping, the video:** Play a video continuously or until you go to the next slide by selecting the Loop Until Stopped check box.

✦ **Rewinding the video when it's finished playing:** Rewind a video if you want to see the first frame, not the last, when the video finishes playing. Select the Rewind After Playing check box to make the start of the video appear after the video plays; deselect this option to freeze-frame on the end of the video when it finishes playing.

Experimenting with the look of the video

Want to make your video look a little sharper? If so, you are hereby invited to experiment with the commands on the (Video Tools) Format tab and Format Video pane shown in Figure 4-7.

To open the Format Video pane, go to (Video Tools) Format tab and do one of the following:

✦ Click the Corrections button and choose Video Corrections Options on the drop-down list.

✦ Click the Video Styles group button.

When you're in an experimental mood, select your video and try these techniques for changing its appearance:

✦ **Recolor the video:** Click the Color button (on the Format tab) or the Recolor button (in the Format Video pane) and select a color or black-and-white option.

✦ **Change the brightness and contrast:** Click the Corrections button and choose a setting in the gallery, or change the Brightness and Contrast settings in the Format Video pane.

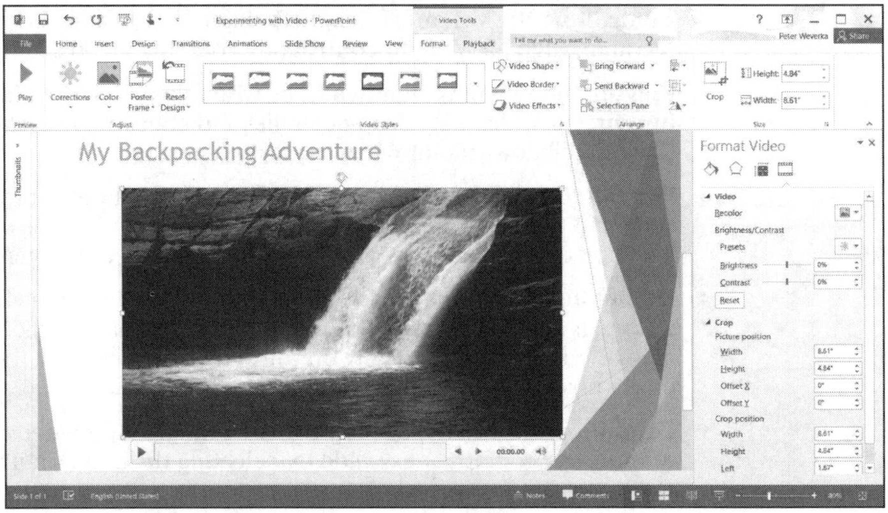

Figure 4-7: You can change the look of a video.

Recording a Voice Narration for Slides

A voice narration in a PowerPoint presentation is sophisticated indeed. A self-playing, kiosk-style presentation can be accompanied by a human voice such that the narrator gives the presentation without actually being there. To narrate a presentation, a working microphone must be attached or built in to your computer. You record the narration for slides one slide at a time or all at one time, and the recording is stored in the PowerPoint file, not in a separate audio file.

The best way to record voice narrations is to do it on a slide-by-slide basis. You can record across several slides, but getting your voice narration and slides to be in sync with one another can be a lot of trouble.

Place your script on your desk and follow these steps to record a voice narration for a slide:

1. **Select the slide that needs a voice narration.**
2. **Go to the Insert tab.**
3. **Open the drop-down list on the Audio button and choose Record Audio.**

   You see the Record Sound dialog box shown in Figure 4-8.

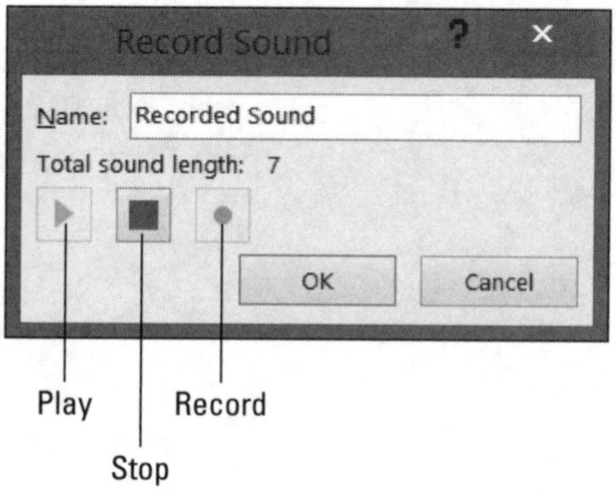

Figure 4-8: Recording in PowerPoint.

4. **Click the Record button and start reading your script.**

   Click the Stop button when you want to pause recording; click the Record button to resume recording.

   You can click the Play button at any time to play back what you have recorded so far. Notice that the dialog box notes how many seconds your recording lasts.

5. **Click the OK button in the Record Sound dialog box when you have finished recording the narration for your slide.**

   The Audio icon appears on your slide to show that your slide is accompanied by an audio file.

Your next task is to select the Audio icon, go to the (Audio Tools) Playback tab, and tell PowerPoint when to play the audio recording, at what volume to play it, and whether you want it to loop. See "Telling PowerPoint when and how to play an audio file," earlier in this chapter.

To play voice narrations during a presentation, make sure that the Play Narrations check box is selected on the Slide Show tab.

Chapter 5: Delivering a Presentation

In This Chapter

- Writing, editing, and printing speaker notes
- Rehearsing a presentation to see how long it is
- Going from slide to slide in a live presentation
- Drawing on slides during a presentation
- Delivering a presentation when you can't be there in person

At last, the big day has arrived. It's time to give the presentation. "Break a leg," as actors say before they go on stage. This chapter explains how to rehearse your presentation to find out how long it is and how to show your presentation. You discover some techniques to make your presentation livelier, including how to draw on slides with a pen or highlighter and blank out the screen to get the audience's full attention. The chapter describes how to handle the speaker notes and print handouts for your audience. In case you can't be there in person to deliver your presentation, this chapter shows you how to create a user-run presentation, a self-running presentation, a presentation designed to be viewed from a CD, and video of a presentation.

All about Notes

Notes are strictly for the speaker. The unwashed masses can't see them. Don't hesitate to write notes to yourself when you put together your presentation. The notes will come in handy when you're rehearsing and giving your presentation. They give you ideas for what to say and help you communicate better. Here are instructions for entering, editing, and printing notes:

- **Entering a note:** To enter a note, start in Normal or Outline view and enter the note in the Notes pane. If the Notes pane isn't displayed, click the Notes button on the Status bar or View tab. Treat the Notes pane like a page in a word processor. For example, press Enter to start a new paragraph and press the Tab key to indent text. You can drag the border above the Notes pane up or down to make the pane larger or smaller.

- **Editing notes in Notes Page view:** After you've jotted down a bunch of notes, switch to Notes Page view and edit them. To switch to Notes Page view, visit the View tab and click the Notes Page button. Notes appear in a text frame below a picture of the slide to which they refer. You may have to zoom in to read them.
- **Printing your notes:** On the File tab, choose Print (or press Ctrl+P). You see the Print window. Under Settings, open the second drop-down list and choose Note Pages on the pop-up menu. Then click the Print button.

Rehearsing and Timing Your Presentation

Slide presentations and theatrical presentations have this in common: They are as good as the number of times you rehearse them. Be sure to rehearse your presentation many times over. The more you rehearse, the more comfortable you are giving a presentation. Follow these steps to rehearse a presentation, record its length, and record how long each slide is displayed:

1. **Select the first slide in your presentation.**
2. **Go to the Slide Show tab.**
3. **Click the Rehearse Timings button.**

   The Recording toolbar appears, as shown in Figure 5-1, and you switch to Slide Show view.

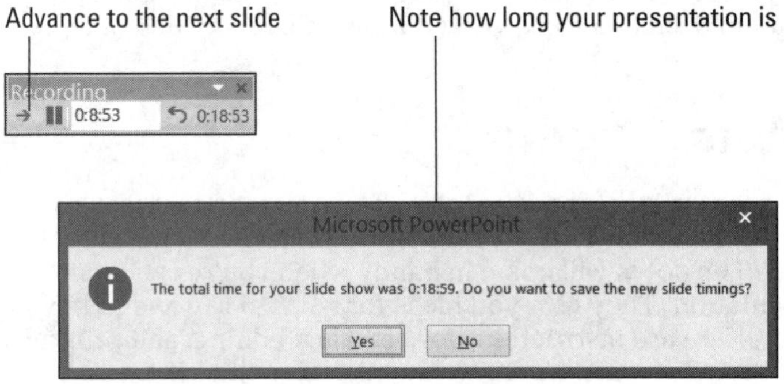

Figure 5-1: Timing a rehearsal.

4. **Give your presentation one slide at a time and click the Next button on the Recording toolbar to go from slide to slide.**

   When each slide appears, imagine that you're presenting it to an audience. Say what you intend to say during the real presentation. If you anticipate audience members asking questions, allot time for questions.

The Recording toolbar tells you how long each slide has been displayed and how long your presentation is so far. You can do these tasks from the Recording toolbar:

- *Go to the next slide:* Click the Next button.
- *Pause recording:* Click the Pause Recording button to temporarily stop the recording so that you can feed the dog or take a phone call. Click the Resume Recording button to resume recording.
- *Repeat a slide:* Click the Repeat button if you get befuddled and want to start over with a slide. The slide timing returns to 0:00:00.

5. **In the dialog box that asks whether you want to keep the slide timings, note how long your presentation is (see Figure 5-1).**

   Is your presentation too long or too short? I hope, like baby bear's porridge, your presentation is "just right." But if it's too long or short, you have some work to do. You have to figure out how to shorten or lengthen it.

6. **In the dialog box that asks whether you want to keep the new slide timings, click Yes if you want to see how long each slide stayed onscreen during the rehearsal.**

   By clicking Yes, you can go to Slide Sorter view and see how long each slide remained onscreen.

WARNING! If you save the slide timings, PowerPoint assumes that, during a presentation, you want to advance to the next slide manually or after the recorded time, whichever comes first. For example, suppose the first slide in your presentation remained onscreen for a minute during the rehearsal. During your presentation, the first slide will remain onscreen for a minute and automatically yield to the second slide unless you click to advance to the second slide before the minute has elapsed. If you recorded slide timings strictly to find out how long your presentation is, you need to tell PowerPoint not to advance automatically to the next slide during a presentation after the recorded time period elapses. On the Slide Show tab, deselect the Use Timings check box.

Showing Your Presentation

Compared to the preliminary work, giving a presentation can seem kind of anticlimactic. All you have to do is go from slide to slide and woo your audience with your smooth-as-silk voice and powerful oratory skills. Well, at least the move-from-slide-to-slide part is pretty easy. These pages explain how to start and end a presentation, all the different ways to advance or retreat from slide to slide, and how to jump to different slides.

Starting and ending a presentation

Here are the different ways to start a presentation from the beginning:

- On the Quick Access toolbar or Slide Show tab, click the From Beginning button (or press F5).
- Select the first slide and then click the Slide Show view button on the Status bar.

You can start a presentation in the middle by selecting a slide in the middle and then clicking the Slide Show view button or going to the Slide Show tab and clicking the From Current Slide button.

Here are the different ways to end a presentation prematurely:

- Press Esc or – (the Hyphen key).
- Click the Slide Control button and choose End Show on the pop-up menu. The Slide Control button is located in the lower-left corner of the screen, as shown in Figure 5-2.
- Right-click and choose End Show in the shortcut menu.

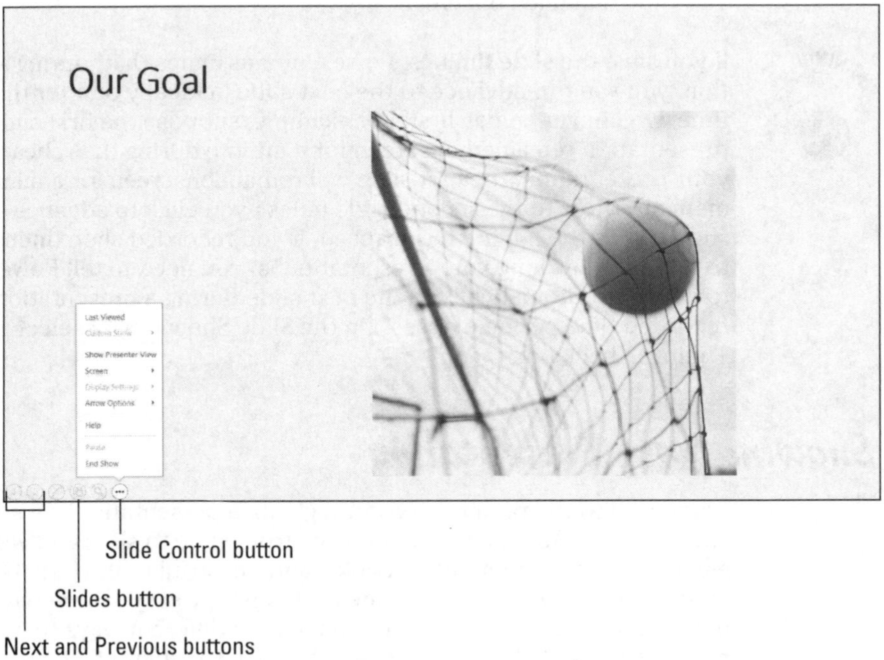

Figure 5-2: Besides using keyboard shortcuts, you can move from slide to slide by clicking onscreen.

Going from slide to slide

In a nutshell, PowerPoint offers four ways to move from slide to slide in a presentation. Table 5-1 describes techniques for navigating a presentation using the four different ways:

- **Click the Next or Previous button:** These buttons are located in the lower-left corner of the screen, as shown in Figure 5-2. If you don't see them, jiggle the mouse.
- **Click the Slides button and choose a slide:** Clicking the Slides button displays thumbnail versions of all the slides in the presentation. Click a thumbnail to go to a specific slide. (To return to the slide you saw previously, right-click and choose Last Viewed on the shortcut menu.)
- **Right-click onscreen:** Right-click and choose a navigation option at the top of the shortcut menu.
- **Press a keyboard shortcut:** Press one of the numerous keyboard shortcuts that PowerPoint offers for going from slide to slide (see Table 5-1).

Table 5-1 Techniques for Getting from Slide to Slide

To Go Here	*Button*	*Right-Click and Choose. . .*	*Keyboard Shortcut*
Next slide*	Next	Next	Enter, spacebar, N, PgDn, ↓, or →
Previous slide	Previous	Previous	Backspace, P, PgUp, ↑, or ←
Specific slide	Slides	See All Slides	*Slide number*+Enter; Ctrl+S and then select *Slide number and title*
Last viewed slide	Slide Control	Last Viewed	
First slide			Home
Last slide			End

**If animations are on a slide, commands for going to the next slide instead make animations play in sequence. To bypass animations and go to the next slide, use a command for going forward across several slides. (See "Jumping forward or backward to a specific slide.")*

Going forward (or backward) from slide to slide

To go forward from one slide to the following slide in a presentation, click onscreen. After you click, the next slide appears. If all goes well, clicking is the only technique you need to know when giving a presentation to go from slide to slide, but Table 5-1 lists other ways to go to the next slide in a presentation as well as techniques for going backward to the previous slide.

TIP

To go to the first slide in a presentation, press Home; to go to the last slide, press End.

Jumping forward or backward to a specific slide

If you find it necessary to jump forward or backward across several slides in your presentation to get to the slide you want to show, it can be done with these techniques:

- ✦ Click the Slides button (in the lower-left corner of the screen, as shown in Figure 5-2). Thumbnail versions of the slides in the presentation appear. Click a thumbnail to view a slide.

Presenter View for Dual Monitors

If two monitors are connected to your computer, you have the option of using Presenter view to give presentations. In Presenter view, the full-screen slide appears on one monitor and a special screen for showing your presentation appears in the other. In this screen, speaker notes are easier to read and the buttons and other controls for getting from slide to slide are larger. Moreover, a timer shows you how long each slide has been onscreen.

Regardless of whether two monitors are connected to your computer, you can test-drive Presenter view by pressing Alt+F5.

To give presentations in Presenter view, go to the Slide Show tab and select Use Presenter View. On the Monitor drop-down list, choose Automatic to allow PowerPoint to choose which monitor the audience sees, or choose a monitor name to select the monitor yourself.

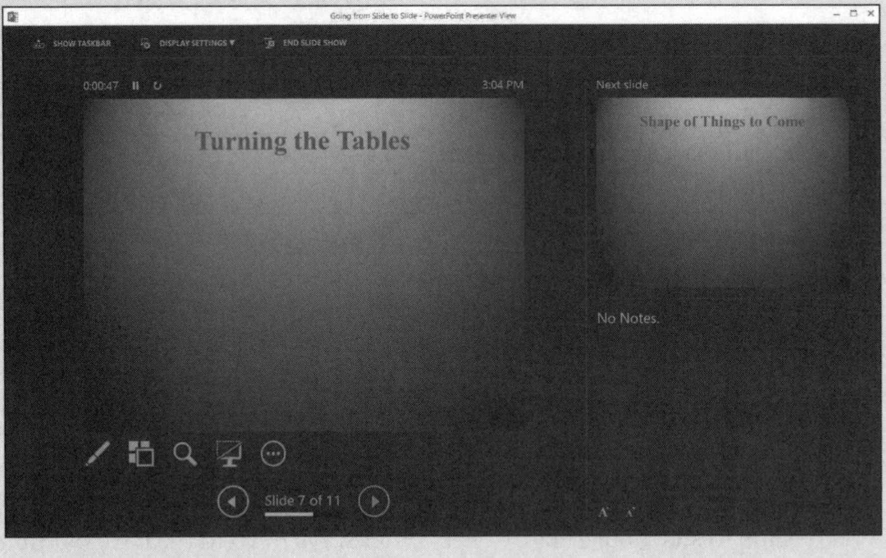

- Press Ctrl+S. You see the All Slides dialog box. It lists all slides in your presentation. Select the slide you want to show and click the Go To button.
- Press the slide number you want on your keyboard (if you can remember the slide's number) and then press the Enter key. For example, to show the third slide in your presentation, press 3 and then press Enter.

Tricks for Making Presentations a Little Livelier

Herewith are a few tricks to make your presentations a little livelier. I explain how to draw on slides, highlight parts of slides, blank the screen, and zoom in. Take this bag of tricks to your next PowerPoint presentation to make your presentation stand out.

Wielding a pen or highlighter in a presentation

Drawing on slides is an excellent way to add a little something to a presentation. Whip out a pen and draw on a slide to get the audience's attention. Draw to underline words or draw check marks as you hit the key points, as shown in Figure 5-3.

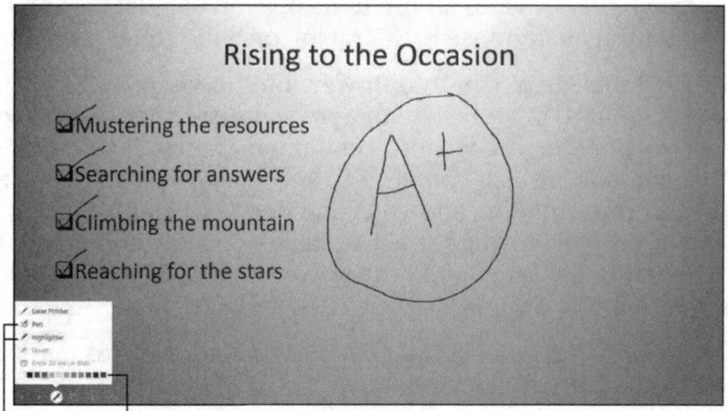

Select a color

Choose a pen or highlighter

Figure 5-3: Choose a pen and ink color on the Pen pop-up list.

Drawing or highlighting on a slide

Follow these steps to draw or highlight on a slide:

1. **Click the Pen button and choose a color on the pop-up menu.**

   The Pen button is located in the lower-left corner of the screen (refer to Figure 5-3).

2. **Click the Pen button again and choose Pen (to draw on slides) or Highlighter (to highlight parts of a slide).**
3. **Drag the mouse to draw or highlight on the slide.**
4. **Press Esc when you're finished using the pen or highlighter.**

   Be careful not to press Esc twice because the second press tells PowerPoint to end the presentation.

You can also right-click, choose Pointer Options, and make selections on the submenu to draw or highlight (choose Ink Color to choose a color).

Hiding and erasing pen and highlighter markings

Follow these instructions to hide and erase pen and highlighter markings:

- **Temporarily showing or hiding markings:** Right-click and choose Screen ⇨ Show/Hide Ink Markup.
- **Permanently erasing markings one at a time:** Click the Pen button and choose Eraser (or right-click and choose Pointer Options ⇨ Eraser). The Eraser appears. Click a line to erase it. Press Esc after you're finished using the Eraser.
- **Permanently erasing all the markings on a slide:** Press E or click the Pen button and choose Erase All Ink on Slide (refer to Figure 5-3).
- **Erasing markings you told PowerPoint to keep:** As I explain shortly, PowerPoint asks at the end of a presentation that you drew on or highlighted whether you want to keep the markings (PowerPoint calls them "ink annotations"). If you elect to keep them, the markings become part of your presentation, and you can't delete them by clicking with the Eraser or by choosing the Erase All Ink on Slide command. To discard these markings later, go to the Review tab, open the drop-down list on the Delete button, and choose one of these options:
  - *Delete All Comments and Ink on this Slide:* Deletes markings you made on a slide you selected
  - *Delete All Comments and Ink in This Presentation:* Deletes markings you made on all the slides in your presentation

Markings aren't permanent, although you can keep them. At the end of a presentation in which you have marked on slides, a dialog box asks whether you want to keep or discard your markings. Click the Keep or Discard button. (If you prefer not to see this dialog box because you intend never to keep your markings, go to the File tab and choose Options. In the PowerPoint Options dialog box, select the Advanced category and deselect the Prompt to Keep Ink Annotations When Exiting check box.)

Blanking the screen

Here's a technique for adding a little drama to a presentation: When you want the audience to focus on you, not the PowerPoint screen, blank the screen. Make an all-black or all-white screen appear where a PowerPoint slide used to be. Every head in the audience will turn your way and listen keenly to what you have to say next. I sure hope you have something important to say.

Follow these instructions to blank out the screen during a presentation:

- **Black screen:** Press B, the period key, or right-click and choose Screen ⇨ Black Screen.
- **White screen:** Press W, the comma key, or right-click and choose Screen ⇨ White Screen.

To see a PowerPoint slide again, click onscreen or press any key on the keyboard.

Zooming In

Yet another way to add pizazz to a presentation is to zoom in on slides. To draw the audience's attention to part of a slide, you can magnify it by following these steps:

1. **Click the Zoom button in the lower-left corner of the screen.**

   You can also right-click and choose Zoom In. The pointer changes to a magnifying glass.

2. **Move to and click the part of a slide you want the audience to focus on.**
3. **Press Esc.**

Delivering a Presentation When You Can't Be There in Person

Let me count the ways that you can deliver a presentation without being there in person:

- Deliver your presentation in the form of a *handout,* a printed version of the presentation with thumbnail slides.
- Create a self-running presentation.
- Create a user-run presentation with action buttons that others can click to get from slide to slide.

- ✦ Show your presentation over the Internet.
- ✦ Make a video of your presentation.
- ✦ Package your presentation so that people who don't have PowerPoint can view it.

The rest of this chapter explains these techniques for delivering a presentation when you can't be there in the flesh.

Providing handouts for your audience

Handouts are thumbnail versions of slides that you print and distribute to the audience. Figure 5-4 shows examples of handouts. Handouts come in one, two, three, four, six, or nine slides per page. If you select three slides per page, the handout includes lines that your audience can take notes on (see Figure 5-4); the other sizes don't offer these lines.

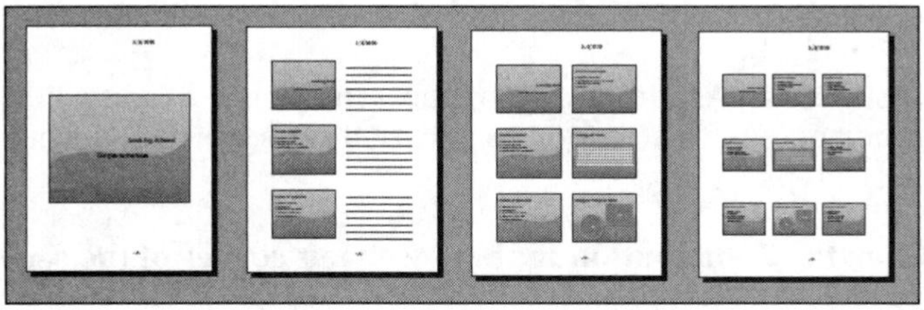

Figure 5-4: Examples of handouts (from left to right) at one, three, six, and nine slides per page.

To tell PowerPoint how to construct handouts, go to the View tab and click the Handout Master button. In Handout Master view, on the Handout Master tab, you can do a number of things to make your handouts more useful and attractive. As you make your choices, keep your eye on the sample handout page; it shows what your choices mean in real terms.

- ✦ **Handout Orientation:** Select Portrait or Landscape. In landscape mode, the page is turned on its side and is longer than it is tall.
- ✦ **Slide Size:** Select Standard or Widescreen.
- ✦ **Slides-Per-Page:** Open the drop-down list and choose how many slides appear on each page. Figure 5-4 shows what some of the choices are.
- ✦ **Header:** Select the Header check box and enter a header in the text frame to make a header appear in the upper-left corner of all handout pages. Candidates for headers include your name, your company name, and the location of a conference or seminar. The point is to help your audience identify the handout.

- **Footer:** Select the Footer check box and enter a footer in the text frame in the lower-left corner of handout pages. Candidates for footers are the same as candidates for headers.
- **Date:** Select this check box if you want the date you print the handout to appear on the handout pages.
- **Page Number:** Select this check box if you want page numbers to appear on the handout pages.
- **Background Styles:** Open the Background Styles drop-down list and select a gradient or color, if you're so inclined. Chapter 2 of this mini-book explains background styles. Make sure that the background doesn't obscure the slide thumbnails or put too much of a burden on your printer.

To print handouts, go to the File tab and choose Print (or press Ctrl+P). You see the Print window. Under Settings, open the second drop-down list, and under Handouts, choose how many slides to print on each page. Then click the Print button.

Creating a self-running, kiosk-style presentation

A self-running, kiosk-style presentation is one that plays on its own. You can make it play from a kiosk or simply send it to co-workers so that they can play it. In a self-running presentation, slides appear onscreen one after the other without you or anyone else having to advance the presentation from slide to slide. When the presentation finishes, it starts all over again from Slide 1.

Telling PowerPoint how long to keep slides onscreen

PowerPoint offers two ways to indicate how long you want each slide to stay onscreen:

- **Entering the time periods yourself:** Switch to Slide Sorter view and go to the Transitions tab. Then deselect the On Mouse Click check box and select the After check box, as shown in Figure 5-5. Next, tell PowerPoint to keep all slides onscreen the same amount of time or choose a different time period for each slide:
  - *All slides the same time:* Enter a time period in the After text box and click the Apply to All button.
  - *Each slide a different time:* One by one, select each slide and enter a time period in the After text box.
- **Rehearsing the presentation:** Rehearse the presentation and save the timings. (See "Rehearsing and Timing Your Presentation" earlier in this chapter.) Be sure to save the slide timings after you're finished rehearsing. In Slide Sorter view, you can see how long each slide will stay onscreen (see Figure 5-5).

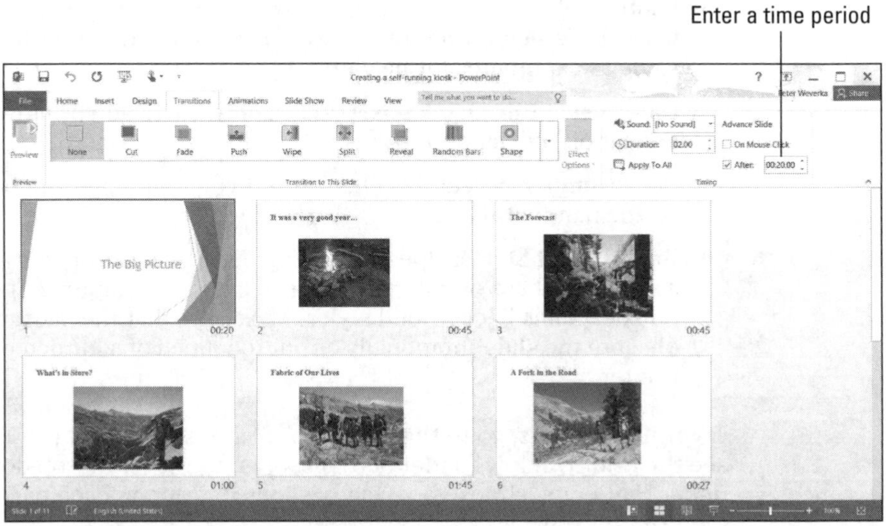

Figure 5-5: Enter how long you want each slide or all the slides to remain onscreen.

Telling PowerPoint that your presentation is self-running

Before you can "self-run" a presentation, you have to tell PowerPoint that you want it to do that. Self-running presentations don't have the control buttons in the lower-left corner. You can't click the screen or press a key to move forward or backward to the next or previous slide. The only control you have over a self-running presentation is pressing the Esc key (pressing Esc ends the presentation).

Follow these steps to make yours a kiosk-style, self-running presentation:

1. **Go to the Slide Show tab.**
2. **Click the Set Up Slide Show button.**

   You see the Set Up Slide Show dialog box.
3. **Under Show Type, choose the Browsed at a Kiosk (Full Screen) option.**

   When you select this option, PowerPoint automatically selects the Loop Continuously Until 'Esc' check box.
4. **Click OK.**

   That's all there is to it.

Creating a user-run presentation

A *user-run,* or *interactive,* presentation is one that the viewer gets to control. The viewer decides which slide appears next and how long each slide remains onscreen. User-run presentations are similar to websites. Users can browse from slide to slide at their own speed. They can pick and choose what they want to investigate. They can backtrack and view slides they saw previously or return to the first slide and start anew.

Self-run presentations are shown in Reading view (click the Reading View button on the status bar to see what self-run presentations look like). A task bar appears along the bottom of the screen. On the right side of the task bar, viewers can click the Previous button or Next button to go from slide to slide. They can also click the Menu button to open a pop-up menu with commands for navigating slides.

Another way to help readers get from slide to slide is to create action buttons. An *action button* is a button that you can click to go to another slide in your presentation or the previous slide you viewed, whatever that slide was. PowerPoint provides 12 action buttons in the Shapes gallery. Figure 5-6 shows some action buttons and the dialog box you use to create them.

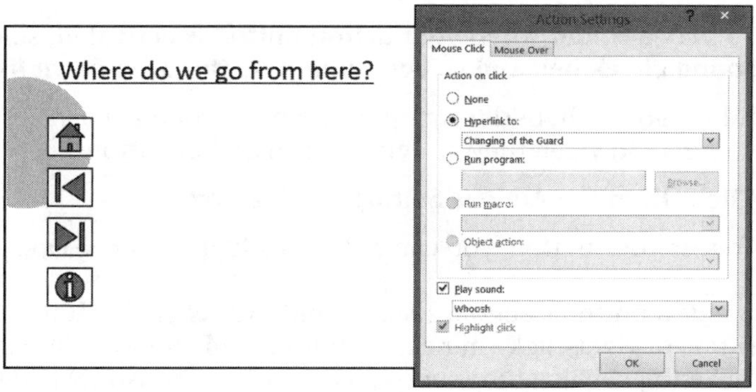

Figure 5-6: Action buttons.

Drawing an action button

After you draw an action button from the Shapes gallery, the Action Settings dialog box shown in Figure 5-6 appears so you can tell PowerPoint which slide to go to when the button is clicked. Select the slide (or master slide) that needs action and follow these steps to adorn it with an action button:

1. **On the Home or Insert tab, open the Shapes gallery and scroll to the Action Buttons category at the bottom.**
2. **Click an action button to select it.**

   Choose the button that best illustrates which slide will appear when the button is clicked.

3. **Draw the button on the slide.**

   To do so, drag the pointer in a diagonal fashion. (As far as drawing them is concerned, action buttons work the same as all other shapes and other objects. Book VIII, Chapter 4 explains how to manipulate objects.) The Action Settings dialog box shown in Figure 5-6 appears after you finish drawing your button.

4. **Go to the Mouse Over tab if you want users to activate the button by moving the mouse pointer over it, not clicking it.**
5. **Select the Hyperlink To option button.**
6. **On the Hyperlink To drop-down list, choose an action for the button.**

   You can go to the next slide, the previous slide, the first or last slide in a presentation, the last slide you viewed, or a specific slide.

   To make clicking the action button take users to a specific slide, choose Slide on the list. You see the Hyperlink to Slide dialog box, which lists each slide in your presentation. Select a slide and click OK.

7. **To play a sound when your action button is activated, select the Play Sound check box and select a sound on the drop-down list.**

   "Mouse-over" hyperlinks require sound accompaniment so that users understand when they've activated an action button.

8. **Click OK in the Actions Settings dialog box.**

   To test your button, you can right-click it and choose Open Hyperlink.

To change a button's action, select it and then click the Action button on the Insert tab, or right-click your action button and choose Edit Hyperlink. In the Action Settings dialog box, choose a new action (or None) and click OK.

Making yours a user-run presentation

Follow these steps to declare yours a user-run presentation:

1. **Go to the Slide Show tab.**
2. **Click the Set Up Slide Show button.**

   You see the Set Up Show dialog box.

3. **Select the Browsed by an Individual (Window) option button.**
4. **Click OK.**

   Your presentation is no longer quite yours. It also belongs to all the people who view it in your absence.

Presenting a Presentation Online

Presenting online means to play a presentation on your computer for others who watch it over the Internet. As you go from slide to slide, audience members see the slides on their web browsers. Presenting online is an excellent way to show a presentation to others during a conference call or to others who don't have PowerPoint.

Presenting online is made possible by the Office Presentation Service, a free service for everyone who has Office software and a Microsoft Account. (What a Microsoft Account is and how to obtain one — it's free — is explained in detail in Book X, Chapter 1.) The first time you attempt to show a presentation online, you are asked to provide your Microsoft Account username and password.

The Office Presentation service creates a temporary web address for you to show your presentation. Before showing it, you send audience members a link to this web address. Audience members, in turn, click the link to open and watch your presentation in their web browsers.

WARNING!

Before presenting online, make sure you know the e-mail addresses of the people who will view your presentation. Make sure as well that they are available to view it. Online presentations are shown in real time. After you close a presentation, its link is broken and the audience can no longer watch it in their web browsers.

Follow these steps to show a presentation online:

1. **On the Slide Show tab, click the Present Online button.**

   The Present Online dialog box appears. You can also open this dialog box on the File tab by choosing Share ➪ Present Online and clicking the Present Online button.

2. Select Enable Remote Viewers to Download the Presentation if you want audience members to have a copy of the presentation as well as view it.

3. **Click the Connect button.**

   The Office Presentation Service generates a URL link for you to send to the people who will view your presentation, as shown in Figure 5-7.

4. **Send the link to your audience.**

   You can send the link with Outlook or another e-mail software.

   - *Copy and send the link by e-mail:* Click Copy Link to copy the link to the Clipboard. Then, in your e-mail software, paste the link into invitations you send to audience members.
   - *Send the link with Outlook:* Click the Send in Email link. An Outlook message window appears. Address and send the message.

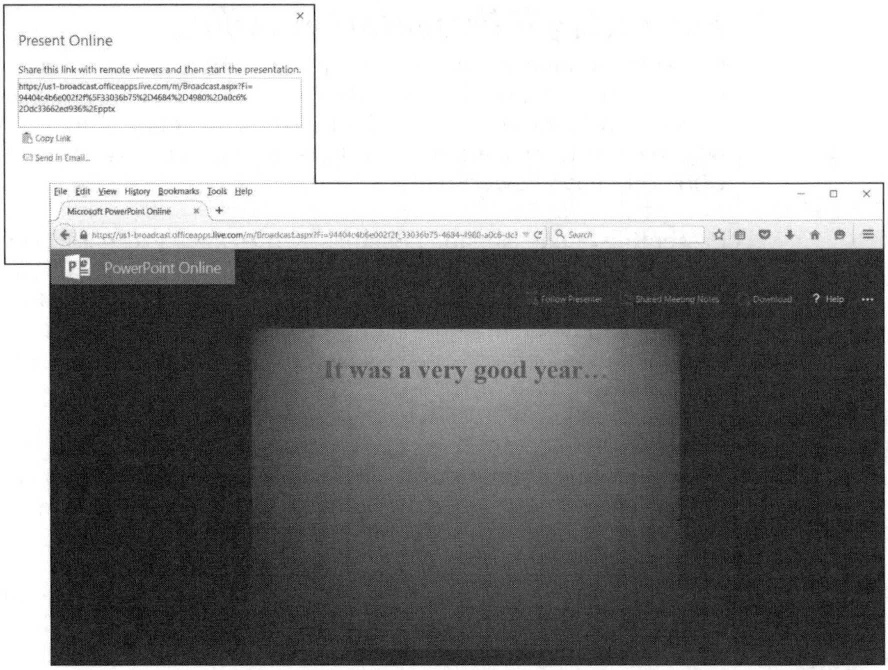

Figure 5-7: Others can click the URL link (top) to view an online presentation in a browser window (bottom).

5. **Make sure that audience members have received the e-mail invitation and are ready to watch your presentation.**

6. **Click the Start Presentation button.**

   Audience members see the presentation in their browsers, as shown in Figure 5-7.

7. **Give the presentation.**

   Use the same techniques to advance or retreat from slide to slide as you use in any presentation.

   When the presentation ends, you land in the Present Online tab.

8. **On the Present Online tab, click the End Online Presentation button; click End Online Presentation in the confirmation dialog box.**

   Your audience sees this notice: "The presentation has ended."

Packaging your presentation on a CD

The Package for CD command copies a presentation to a CD so that you can take a presentation on the road or distribute it to others on CDs. By using the Package for CD command, you can even distribute a presentation to people who don't have PowerPoint. Someone who doesn't have PowerPoint can download the *PowerPoint Viewer,* an abridged version of PowerPoint with all the PowerPoint slide-show commands (but none of the slide-creation commands). With the Package for CD command, you don't have to be concerned whether someone to whom you give your presentation has PowerPoint or whether PowerPoint is installed on the computer where you will give your presentation.

These pages explain the ins and outs of the Package for CD command. You find out how to copy a presentation to a CD or folder and play a presentation in PowerPoint Viewer.

Packaging a presentation on a CD

Follow these steps to copy your presentation and the PowerPoint Viewer to a CD or a folder:

1. **Open the presentation you want to package.**
2. **On the File tab, choose Export.**
3. **Choose Package Presentation for CD, and click the Package for CD button.**

   You see the Package for CD dialog box shown in Figure 5-8.

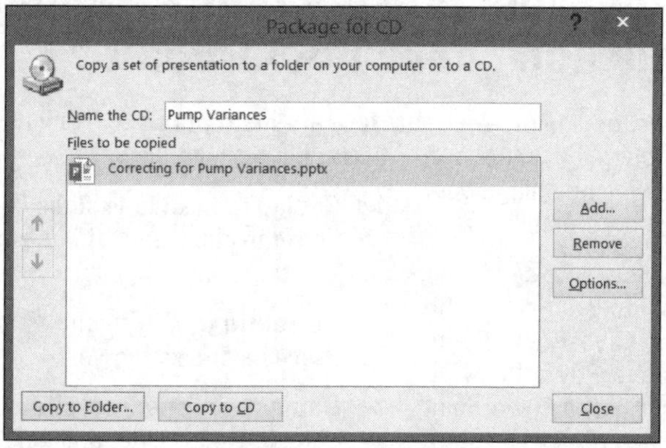

Figure 5-8: Packaging a CD to distribute to others.

4. **Enter a name for the CD or folder in the Name the CD text box.**

   The name you enter will appear as the name of the CD if you view the CD in File Explorer or Windows Explorer; if you're copying your presentation to a folder, the name you enter will be given to the folder PowerPoint creates when it creates the packaged presentation file.

5. **Create the packaged presentation and copy it to a CD or to a folder on your computer.**

   Copy the presentation to a folder if you want to send the presentation by e-mail rather than distribute it by CD.

   - *Copying to a CD:* Click the Copy to CD button.
   - *Copying to a folder:* Click the Copy to Folder button. In the Copy to Folder dialog box, click the Browse button, and in the Choose Location dialog box, select a folder for storing the folder where you will keep your packaged presentation. Then click the Select button and click OK in the Copy to Folder dialog box.

6. **Click Yes in the message box that asks if you want to include linked content in the presentation.**

   It can take PowerPoint several minutes to assemble the files and copy them to the CD or folder.

   If you're copying your presentation to a CD, PowerPoint asks whether you want to copy the same presentation to another CD. Either insert a fresh CD and click Yes, or click the No button.

Distributing your presentation to people who don't have PowerPoint

Not everyone has PowerPoint. Not everyone is so blessed. Some people live along in ignorant bliss without knowing anything about PowerPoint and its slide-show capabilities.

Don't be discouraged if you want to send your PowerPoint presentation to someone who doesn't have or may not have PowerPoint. Someone who doesn't have PowerPoint on his or her computer can still play a PowerPoint presentation by way of *PowerPoint Viewer,* a software program you can download for free from Microsoft starting at this web page (enter **PowerPoint Viewer** in the Search text box and click the Go button):

`www.microsoft.com/downloads`

Here are instructions for running a presentation in PowerPoint Viewer:

- **Getting from slide to slide:** Click onscreen or right-click and choose Next on the shortcut menu.
- **Retreating:** Right-click and choose Previous or Last Viewed.
- **Going to a specific slide:** Right-click, choose Go to Slide, and select a slide on the submenu.
- **Ending the show:** Press Esc or right-click and choose End Show.

Playing a packaged presentation

As shown in Figure 5-9, an AutoPlay window appears when you put a CD-packaged PowerPoint presentation in the computer's CD drive. Tell the people to whom you distribute your CD that they can play the presentation starting in this window whether or not PowerPoint is installed on their computers:

- ✦ **PowerPoint (or PowerPoint Viewer) is installed:** Click Open Folder to View Files in the AutoPlay window. The Computer application opens to show the files on the CD. Double-click the PowerPoint presentation to play it.
- ✦ **PowerPoint isn't installed:** Click Run Presentation Package in the AutoPlay window. A web browser opens. Click the Download Viewer button to go to a web page at Microsoft.com and download the PowerPoint Viewer. After downloading and installing PowerPoint Viewer, you can use it to play the PowerPoint presentation.

Figure 5-9: Playing a CD-packaged presentation.

Creating a presentation video

Yet another way to distribute a video is to record it in an MPEG-4 file and distribute the file on a CD, distribute it by e-mail, or post it on the Internet. PowerPoint offers a command for creating an MPEG-4 version of a presentation. Every aspect of a PowerPoint presentation, including transitions, animations, sound, video itself, and voice narrations, is recorded in the presentation video.

Figure 5-10 shows an MPEG-4 version of a PowerPoint presentation being played in Windows Media Player.

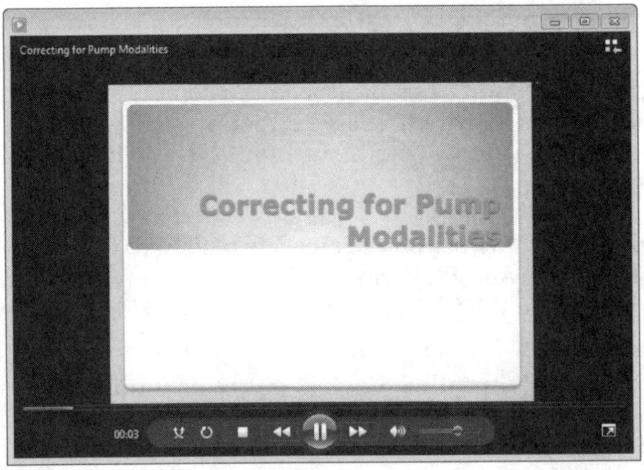

Figure 5-10: Viewing an MPEG-4 version of a PowerPoint presentation in Windows Media Player.

TIP: Before creating your presentation video, consider how long you want each slide to appear onscreen. You can make each slide appear for a specific length of time or make all slides appear for the same length of time. To decide for yourself how long each slide appears, switch to Slide Sorter view, go to the Transitions tab, and for each slide, select the After check box and enter a measurement in the After text box. (Earlier in this chapter, "Creating a self-running, kiosk-style presentation" explains in detail how to establish how long each slide stays onscreen.)

Follow these steps to create an MPEG-4 version of a PowerPoint presentation:

1. **On the File tab, choose Export.**
2. **Choose Create a Video.**

   You see the Create a Video window.
3. **Open the first drop-down list and choose a display resolution for your video.**
4. **Open the second drop-down list and choose whether to use recorded timings and narrations.**

   Your choices are twofold. If you recorded a voice narration for your PowerPoint presentation, choose the second option if you want to preserve the voice narration in the video.

- *Don't Use Recorded Timings and Narrations:* Each slide stays onscreen for the same amount of time. Enter a time period in the Seconds to Spend on Each Slide box to declare how long each slide stays onscreen.
- *Use Recorded Timings and Narrations:* Each slide stays onscreen for the time period listed on the Transition tab (see the Tip at the start of this section to find out how to list slide times on the Transition tab).

5. **Open the second drop-down list and choose Preview Timings and Narrations.**

   Your presentation video plays. How do you like it? This is what your video will look and sound like after you save it in a WMV file.

6. **Click the Create Video button.**

   The Save As dialog box opens.

7. **Choose a folder for storing the MPEG-4 file, enter a name for the file, and click the Save button.**

   The status bar along the bottom of the PowerPoint screen shows the progress of the video as it is being created. Creating a video can take several minutes, depending on how large your PowerPoint presentation is and how many fancy gizmos, such as sound and animation, it contains.

Book V

OneNote 2016

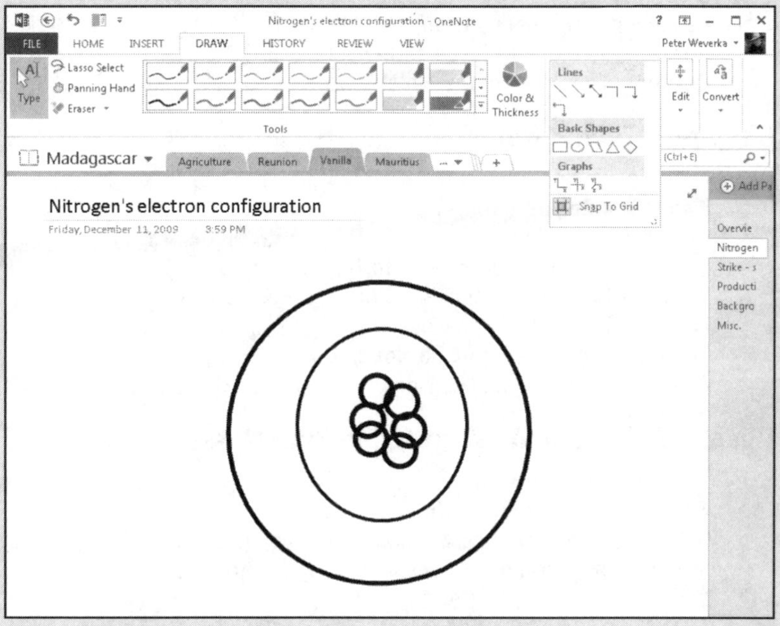

Go to www.dummies.com/extras/office2016aio to see how to quickly copy all the text in an Office 2016 file into a OneNote note.

Contents at a Glance

Chapter 1: Up and Running with OneNote

In This Chapter

- **Getting acquainted with OneNote**
- **Understanding the OneNote screen**
- **Creating notebooks, sections, section groups, and pages**
- **Getting a better view of your notes**
- **Navigating in OneNote**

Microsoft OneNote 2016 is designed for taking notes — at meetings, when talking on the telephone, or in the classroom. Rather than scribble notes indiscriminately in a Word 2016 document, you can enter them in OneNote and be able to retrieve them later. You can use your notes to construct reports and white papers. You can copy them to Excel, PowerPoint, or Word. OneNote comes with all sorts of amenities for finding and filing notes. OneNote can help you brainstorm and organize your ideas.

This chapter explains what OneNote is and how you can use it to store and organize notes. It explains what sections, section groups, and pages are and why to use these items for organizing notes. You also find out how to get from place to place in OneNote and change views so that you can see your notes better.

Introducing OneNote

Everybody who has been in a classroom or participated in a business meeting knows what note taking is. What makes taking notes with OneNote special is that you can store, organize, and retrieve your notes in various ways. OneNote adds another dimension to note taking. Because notes can be copied, moved, and combined with other notes, you can use notes as building blocks for different projects.

A OneNote file is called a *notebook.* Within a notebook, you can write notes and organize your notes into sections, section groups, pages, and subpages. You can use OneNote to refine your thinking about the work you want to do and the subjects you want to tackle. OneNote helps you brainstorm, and when you finish brainstorming, it helps you organize your ideas into something coherent and useful.

OneNote is unusual among Office programs in that it doesn't have a Save button or Save command. Every 30 seconds, OneNote saves all the notes for you. You needn't concern yourself with whether notes are being saved.

Finding Your Way Around the OneNote Screen

OneNote wants you to be able to enter notes and find notes quickly, and to that purpose, the screen is divided into four main areas: the Notebook pane, Section tabs, the Page window, and the Page pane. Figure 1-1 shows where these main areas are located, and the following pages explain each area in detail.

Notebook pane

Located on the left side of the screen, the Notebook pane lists the names of notebooks you created, and within each notebook, it lists sections and section groups. To go to a different notebook, section, or section group, click its name in the Notebook pane.

Click the Unpin Notebook Pane from Side button to pin the Notebook pane to the left side of the screen. This pin-shaped button is located above the Notebook pane. To see the Notebook pane again, double-click the name of your notebook.

Section (and section group) tabs

Section and section group names appear in tabs above the page (refer to Figure 1-1). Click the name of a section to see its pages. (You can also click a section name in the Notebook pane.) Click the name of a section group to make its sections appear on the tabs. Later in this chapter, "Units for Organizing Notes" explains what sections and section groups are.

Page window

After you select a page in the Page pane, it appears in the Page window, and you can read notes you wrote on the page (refer to Figure 1-1). The title of the page appears at the top of the page window in the Title text box. Underneath the Title text box, you can see the date and time that the page was created.

To write a note, click in the Page window and start typing.

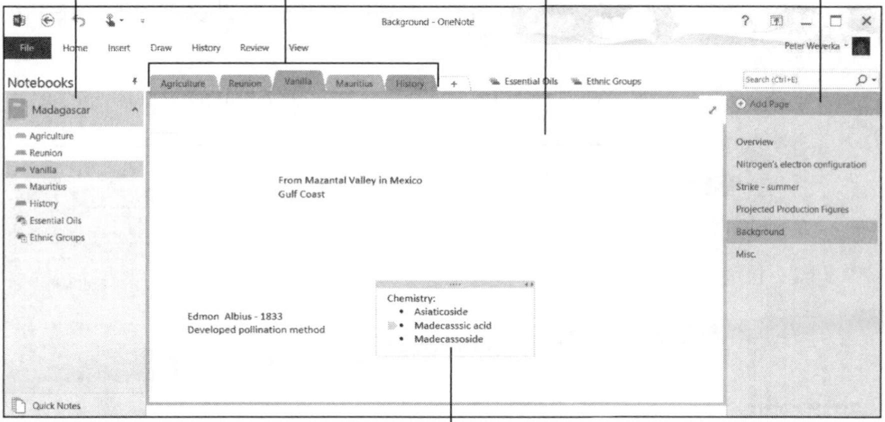

Figure 1-1: The OneNote screen.

Page pane

The names of pages and subpages in the section you selected appear on tabs in the Page pane on the right side of the screen (refer to Figure 1-1).

To go from page to page, click a page's name. The top of the Page pane offers the Add Page button for creating new pages.

Units for Organizing Notes

From largest to smallest, OneNote offers these units for organizing notes:

- **Notebook:** Create a notebook for each important project you're involved in. OneNote places one button on the Notebook pane for each open notebook. By clicking these buttons, you can go from notebook to notebook. The Notebook pane is located on the left side of the window (see Figure 1-1).
- **Sections:** A *section* is a subcategory of a notebook; it is used to store pages. Each notebook can have many different sections, and each section, in turn, can have many pages. In Figure 1-1, there are five sections in the Madagascar notebook: Agriculture, Reunion, Vanilla, Mauritius, and History.
- **Section groups:** A *section group* is a means of organizing and quickly finding sections. In a notebook with many sections, you can store sections

in a group to make finding sections easier. The names of section groups appear below the names of sections on the Notebook pane and to the right of sections in the section tabs, as shown in Figure 1-2.

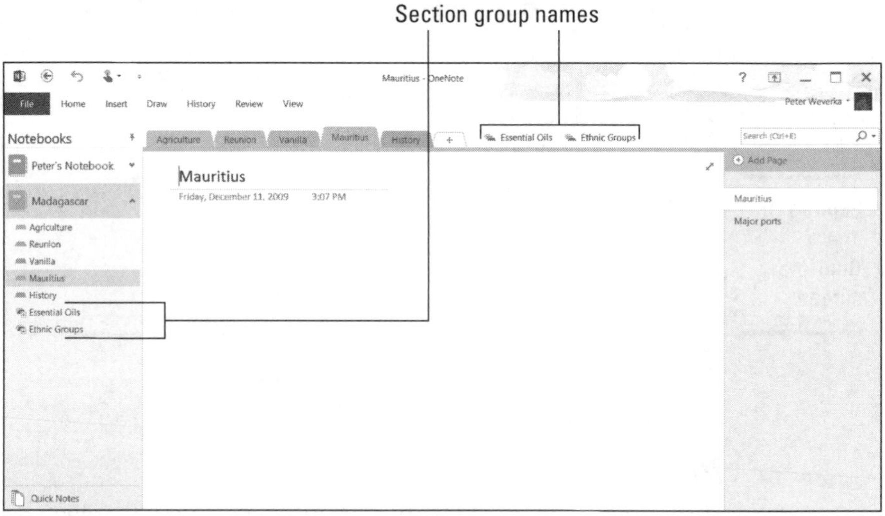

Figure 1-2: Use section groups to organize sections.

✦ **Pages and subpages:** A *page* is for writing and storing notes. Pages are stored in sections. As shown in Figure 1-1, the names of pages appear on the Page pane (on the right side of the screen) on *page tabs.* Within a page, you can also create a *subpage*.

✦ **Notes:** Write your notes on pages and subpages. To write a note, all you have to do is click a page and start typing.

TIP

Before you write your first note, give a moment's thought to organizing notes in the notebook-section-pages hierarchy. Think of descriptive names for your notebook, sections, section groups, and pages. By giving a thought to how to organize notes, you will be able to find them more easily later on.

Creating a Notebook

OneNote creates a new notebook for you the first time you start the program, but you are invited to create a notebook of your own. OneNote is kind of unusual among Office programs in that you name a notebook when you create it, not when you save it for the first time.

Follow these steps to create a new notebook:

1. **On to the File tab, choose New.**

   The New Notebook window opens, as shown in Figure 1-3. You can also right-click the Notebook pane and choose New Notebook to open this window.

2. **Choose This PC to store the notebook on your computer.**

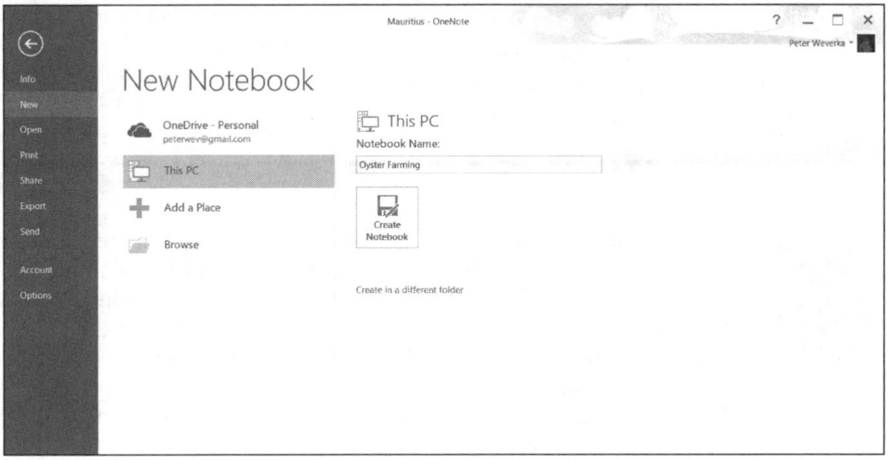

Figure 1-3: Name your notebook when you create it.

   The other options for storing files you create with Office 2016 software are described in Book I, Chapter 1.

3. **Enter a name for the notebook.**
4. **Click the Create Notebook button.**

   The new notebook opens on-screen. OneNote creates a section (called New Section 1) and a page (called Untitled Page) in your notebook.

5. **Change the name of the section and page.**

   Follow these instructions to change section and page names:

   - *Changing the section name:* Right-click the section name, choose Rename on the shortcut menu, and enter a descriptive name. You can also double-click a name and enter a new one.
   - *Changing the page name:* Enter a name in the Title text box at the top of the page (click above the day and date to get to this text box). After you enter the name, the new name appears as well on the Page pane on the right side of the screen.

Removing a notebook from the Notebook pane

Consider removing a notebook's name from the Notebook pane if the Notebook pane gets too crowded with notebooks. Follow these instructions to remove and display a notebook's name on the Notebook pane:

- **Closing a notebook:** Right-click the notebook's name and choose Close This Notebook on the shortcut menu.
- **Re-opening a notebook:** Go to the File tab and choose Open. You see the Open Notebook window. Select a notebook name under Recent Notebooks. If the notebook's name doesn't appear, choose This PC, click the Browse button, and select the notebook's name in the Open Notebook dialog box.

TIP

To delete a notebook, close OneNote, open File Explorer, go to the folder where the notebook is stored, and delete the folder. To find out where a notebook is stored on your computer, hover the pointer over the notebook's name in the Notebook pane; the name and file path to the notebook appear in a pop-up message. To find out where notebooks are stored by default on your computer, go to the File tab, choose Options, go to the Save & Backup category of the OneNote Options dialog box, and look for the Default Notebook Location.

Creating Sections and Section Groups

After the notebook, the next units in the file storage hierarchy are the section and the section group. If a notebook is a book, a section is a chapter in a book. Create a section for each subtopic in the item you're keeping notes on. A section group is a convenient way to organize groups. A group can belong to more than one section.

Creating a new section

Follow these steps to create a new section:

1. **Click the Create a New Section button.**

   This button (indicated by a plus sign) is located to the right of the section tabs, as shown in Figure 1-4. Rather than click the New Section button, you can right-click the Notebook pane or a section tab and choose New Section.

   A new section tab aptly named "New Section 1" appears.

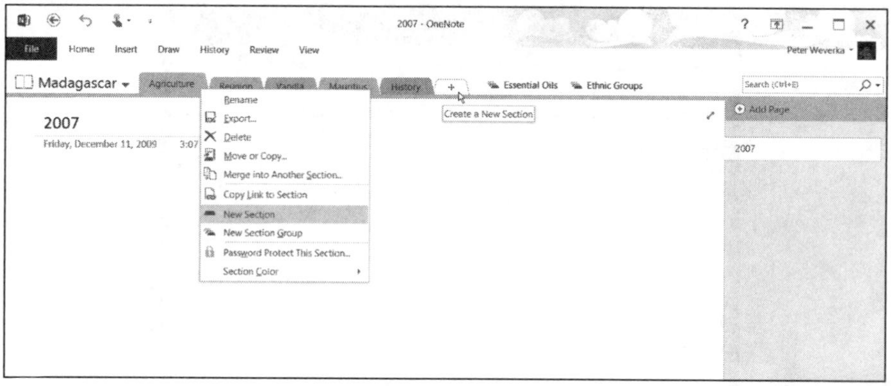

Figure 1-4: Two ways to create a section.

2. **Enter a section name on the tab.**
3. **Press Enter.**

   To rename a section, right-click its name, choose Rename, and enter a new name.

After you create a new section, OneNote automatically creates a new page to go with it. This page is called "Untitled Page." To rename this page, enter a name in the Title text box at the top of the page.

Creating a section group

Follow these steps to create a section group:

1. **Right-click the Notebook pane or a section tab and choose New Section Group.**

   A section group tab appears.
2. **Enter a name for the section group.**
3. **Press the Enter key.**

   Your new section appears on the right side of the section tabs (refer to Figure 1-2). Your next task is to move or copy a section that you already created into the section group.
4. **Right-click a section you want to move or copy into the group and choose Move or Copy on the drop-down list.**

   The Move or Copy Section dialog box appears, as shown in Figure 1-5.
5. **Select the name of the section group you created.**
6. **Click the Move or Copy button.**

   The fastest (but clumsiest) way to move a section name into a group is to drag the section name in the Notebook pane to the section group name.

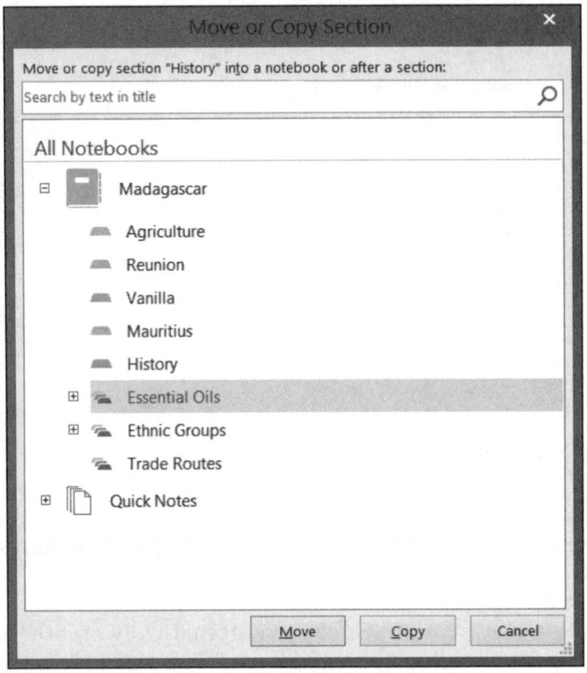

Figure 1-5: Choose a section to move or copy it to a section group.

Creating Pages and Subpages

When you create a section, OneNote automatically creates a new page for you, but that doesn't mean that you can't create more pages for a section. Create a page for each subtopic you want to take notes on. Within each page, you can create subpages to help you organize your notes better.

Creating a new page

Follow these steps to create a page:

1. **Click the Add Page button.**

   This button is located at the top of the Page pane. A new page appears. You can also make a new page appear by pressing Ctrl+N or right-clicking the Page pane and choosing New Page.

2. **Enter a page name in the Title text box.**

   The name you enter appears on a page tab in the Page pane.

TIP

You can rearrange pages (and subpages) in the Page pane by dragging their names higher or lower in the list of pages.

Creating a new subpage

Use these techniques to create a subpage:

- ✦ Right-click a page and choose Make Subpage.
- ✦ In the Page pane, drag the name of the page to the right.

To turn a subpage into a page, right-click the subpage and choose Promote Subpage or drag the page's name to the left.

Renaming and Deleting Groups and Pages

If you're like me, you do a lot of deleting and renaming of groups, section groups, pages, and subpages in OneNote. Making sure that these items have descriptive names is essential for locating notes and entering notes in the right places.

Luckily for all of us, OneNote makes it easy to rename and delete groups and pages. Think the words "right-click" when you want to rename or delete a group, section group, or page. To rename or delete one of these items, right-click it and choose Rename or Delete on the shortcut menu. After you choose Rename, enter a new name for your group, section group, or page.

Getting from Place to Place in OneNote

As you fill up a notebook with sections, section groups, pages, subpages, and notes, finding the place you need to be to enter or read a note gets more complicated. Here are ways to get from section to section or page to page in the OneNote window:

- ✦ **Go to a different notebook:** Click a notebook button on the Notebook pane. Use one of these techniques to find out where clicking a notebook button takes you:
  - *Move the pointer over a button.* You see a notebook's name and the folder where it is stored in a ScreenTip box.
  - *If the Notebook pane is pinned to the side of the screen, double-click its name.* Now you can see the names of open notebooks as well as the names of notebook sections on the Notebook pane.

- **Go to a different section or section group:** Click the name of a section or section group in the Notebook pane or along the top of the page. Section group names are listed at the bottom of the Notebook pane and to the right of section names. You can expand and collapse section groups in the Notebook pane by clicking the plus or minus sign on a section group symbol.
- **Go to a different page:** Click a page or subpage tab on the Page pane on the right side of the window.

To return to the page you last visited, click the Back button on the Quick Access toolbar. This button works like the Back button in a browser. It takes you to where you were previously.

Changing Your View of OneNote

As shown in Figure 1-6, OneNote offers three ways to view the screen:

- **Normal view:** For writing, editing, and organizing notes. In this view, you can see the ribbon, the Notebook pane, the tabs, and the Page pane.
- **Full Page view:** For comfortably reading your notes. In Full Page view, the OneNote buttons and tools aren't there to distract you.
- **Dock to Desktop:** For taking notes on what is in the middle of the screen — a Word document or web page, for example. While looking at a document or website, you can also see the OneNote screen and take notes there.

Use these techniques to change views:

- **View tab:** Click the Normal View, Full Page View, or Dock to Desktop button.
- **Keyboard:** Press F11 to switch between Normal view and Full Page view; press Ctrl+Alt+D to dock OneNote to the desktop or "undock" OneNote.

While the OneNote screen is docked, you can adjust its size by dragging its left side toward or away from the center of your screen. To "undock" the OneNote screen, click the Normal View button or press Ctrl+Alt+D.

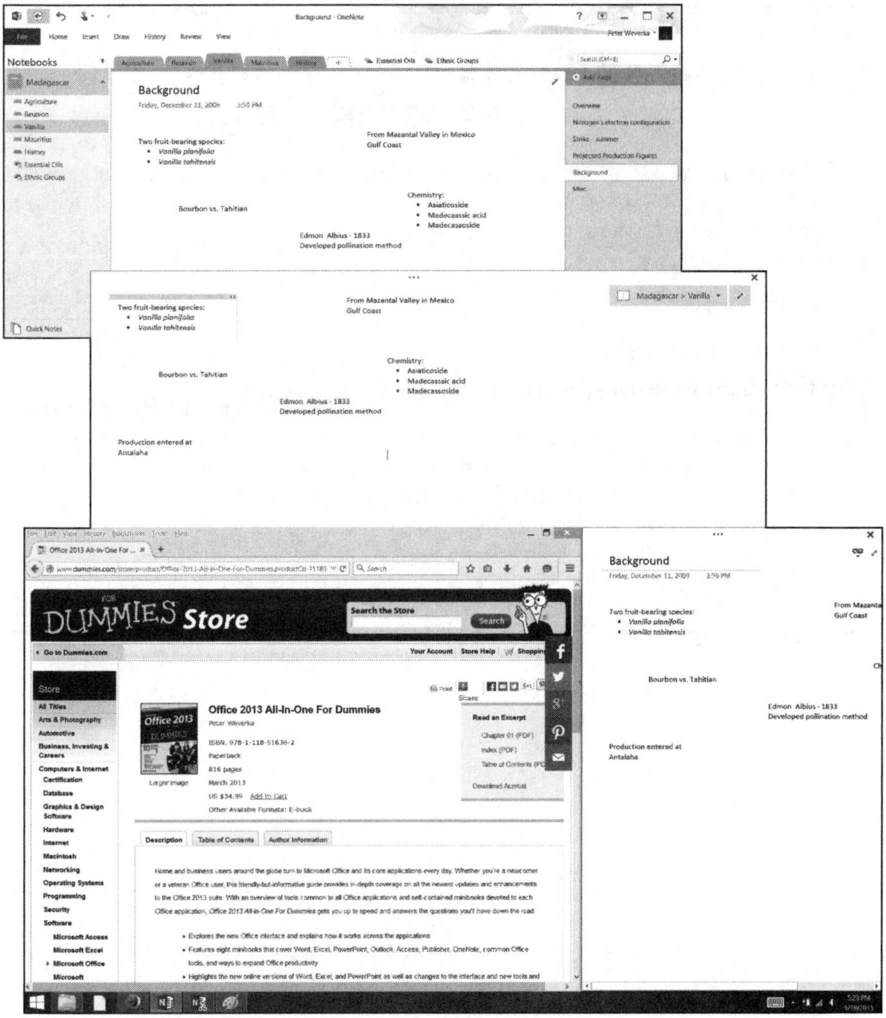

Figure 1-6: OneNote in Normal view (top), in Full Page view (middle), and docked to the desktop (bottom).

Revisiting (and restoring) an earlier version of a page

For each day you work on a page, OneNote saves a copy of the page in case you want to revisit or restore it. To read an earlier version of a page, follow these steps:

1. **Open the page.**
2. **Go to the History tab.**
3. **Click the Page Versions button.**

   The names of page versions appear on the Pages pane. These page versions are dated with an author's name. (You can also see page versions by right-clicking a page's name and choosing Show Page Versions on the shortcut menu.)

4. **Click a page version's name to open and read an earlier version of a page.**

To make an earlier version of a page the one you want for your notes, click the top of the page to open a drop-down list with options for rehiding, deleting, and restoring the page. Then choose Restore on the drop-down list.

To hide page versions, click the Page Versions button a second time or right-click a page's name and choose Hide Page Versions on the shortcut menu that appears.

To delete a page version, choose Delete Version on the drop-down list.

Chapter 2: Taking Notes

In This Chapter

- **Entering notes with the keyboard**
- **Working with note containers**
- **Moving, selecting, and deleting notes**
- **Drawing in OneNote**
- **Turning handwritten notes into text notes**
- **Taking screen-clipping and audio notes**
- **Attaching and linking notes to files**

To OneNote, a "note" is much more than something you scribble on a page. OneNote offers you the chance to create a variety of different notes — drawn notes, audio notes, screen clippings, and linked notes, for example.

This chapter delves into all the kinds of notes you can make with OneNote. It also shows you how to draw on a page, turn handwritten notes into text notes, write mathematical expressions, and attach and link files to notes.

Entering a Typewritten Note

The simplest kind of note is the typewritten note. To type a note, simply click the page where you want the note to be and start typing. Press the Enter key to begin a new paragraph in a note. You can draw upon the commands on the Home tab to format the text or change a note's color. (Later in this chapter, "Formatting the Text in Notes," looks at ways to format text.)

If recording when you made a note is important to you, visit the Insert tab and click the Date, Time, or Date & Time button while writing your note.

Notes: The Basics

Although the program is called OneNote, you can enter many kinds of notes. You can enter typed notes, drawings, and screen clippings, for example. Moreover, if you're using a Tablet PC to scribble your notes, OneNote can (most of the time, anyway) recognize whether you're writing by hand or drawing.

Whatever kind of note you're dealing with, the basics of handling notes are the same. This section's pages look at note containers, how to select and delete notes, and how to get more room onscreen for notes.

Moving and resizing note containers

Notes appear in *containers,* as shown in Figure 2-1. Move the pointer over a note to see its container. Containers make it easier to move notes, resize notes, and arrange notes on the page so that you can read them more easily. Follow these instructions to move and resize notes:

- ✦ **Changing a note's position:** Move the pointer over the top of the note container, and when the pointer changes into a four-headed arrow, click and start dragging.
- ✦ **Changing a note's size:** Move the pointer over the right side of the note container, and when the pointer changes into a double arrow, click and drag to the left or right.

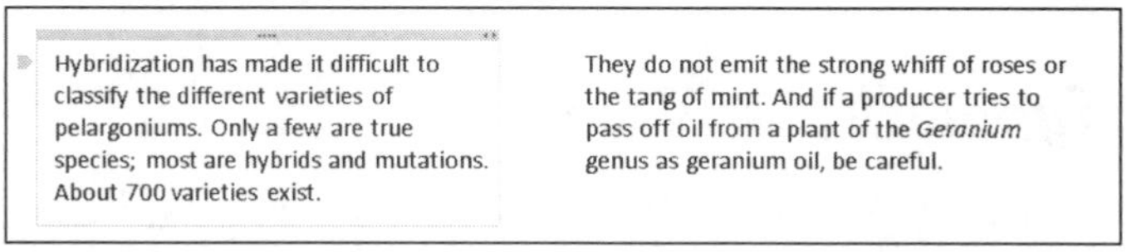

Hybridization has made it difficult to classify the different varieties of pelargoniums. Only a few are true species; most are hybrids and mutations. About 700 varieties exist.
They do not emit the strong whiff of roses or the tang of mint. And if a producer tries to pass off oil from a plant of the Geranium genus as geranium oil, be careful.

Figure 2-1: Notes appear in note containers.

Formatting the Text in Notes

On the Home and Insert tabs, OneNote offers commands for formatting the text in notes. If formatting a note's text makes reading and understanding it easier, by all means format the text. You can do so with these techniques:

- **Basic text formatting:** On the Home tab, you can choose a font for text, change the size and color of text, and create bulleted and numbered lists. Book I, Chapter 2 explains commands for formatting text in OneNote and the other Office applications.
- **Styles:** On the Home tab, styles present an easy way to format text. Click in the text you want to format, open the Styles gallery, and choose an option, as shown in Figure 2-2. Choose Heading 1, for example, to make a heading on a note stand out.

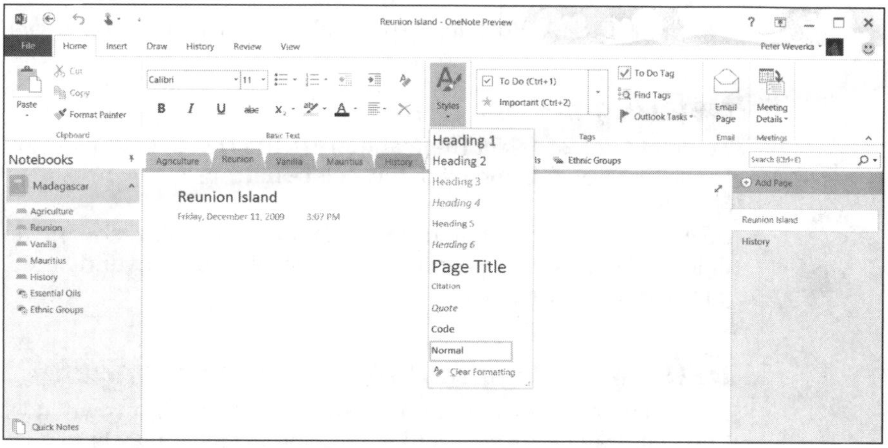

Figure 2-2: Choose a style in the Styles gallery.

- **Tables:** On the Insert tab, click the Table button and choose how many columns and rows you want for your table on the drop-down list. Then enter the table data. The (Table Tools) Layout tab offers commands for laying out the table.

Choosing your default font

By default, notes appear in Calibri font and are 11 points high. (Book I, Chapter 2 explains what fonts and font size are.) Does this font and font size do the job for you?

If it doesn't, you can change the default font and font size by following these steps:

1. **On the File tab, choose Options.**

   The OneNote Options dialog box opens.

2. **In the General category, open the Font drop-down list and choose a font.**
3. **Open the Size drop-down list and choose a font size.**
4. **Click OK.**

Selecting notes

Before you can do anything to a note — move it, delete it — you have to select it. The simplest way to select a note is to click it. After you click, you see the note's container (refer to Figure 2-1). You can also use these techniques to select notes:

- ✦ **Ctrl+click:** Hold down the Ctrl key and click notes to select more than one.
- ✦ **Drag:** Click and drag across a portion of a page to select several notes.
- ✦ **Press Ctrl+A:** Pressing Ctrl+A selects all the notes on a page.

Deleting notes

To delete notes, select them and press the Delete key. You can also go to the Home or Draw tab and click the Delete button.

WARNING!

Be careful about deleting notes, because you can't recover a note you deleted. OneNote gives you the opportunity to recover deleted sections and pages, but not notes you deleted.

Getting more space for notes on a page

How do you make room for a note on a page that is crowded with notes? You can drag notes here and there, but an easier way is to go to the Insert or Draw tab and click the Insert Space button. After you click it, drag downward on the screen where you want to make more space for notes, as shown in Figure 2-3. Notes below where you drag are pushed further down the page.

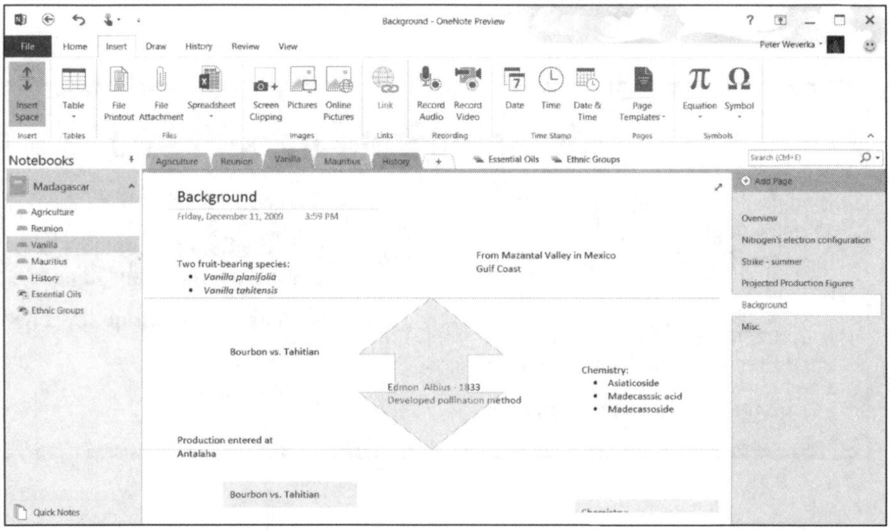

Figure 2-3: Click the Insert Space button to make more room for notes.

Drawing on the Page

Sometimes you can't say it in words, and for those occasions, consider drawing on the page instead of writing a note. OneNote offers the Draw tab precisely for that purpose. On this tab are tools for drawing lines of different colors and widths, drawing shapes, and editing your drawings.

Drawing with a pen or highlighter

Follow these steps to draw on the page with a pen or highlighter:

1. **Go to the Draw tab.**
2. **Choose a pen or highlighter.**

   Use one of these techniques to choose a pen or highlighter:

   - **Tools gallery:** Open the Tools gallery and choose a pen or highlighter, as shown in Figure 2-4.
   - **Color & Thickness dialog box:** Click the Color & Thickness button to open the Color & Thickness dialog box, shown in Figure 2-4. Then select the Pen or Highlighter option button, choose a line thickness, and choose a line color.

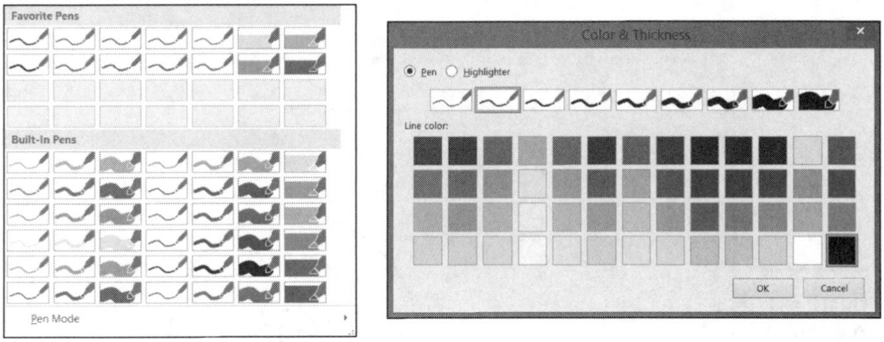

Figure 2-4: On the Draw tab, choose a pen or highlighter from the Tools gallery (left) or Color & Thickness dialog box (right).

3. **Start drawing.**

   As you make your drawing, you can return to the Tools gallery or Color & Thickness dialog box and choose a different color or line type. You can also make shapes and straight lines part of your drawing. (The next topic in this chapter, "Drawing a shape," explains how.)

4. **Press Esc when you finish drawing or highlighting.**

   Later in this chapter, "Changing the size and appearance of drawings and shapes" explains how to change a drawing's size and appearance.

Drawing a shape

As well as drawing freehand (the previous subject of this chapter), you can draw shapes and straight lines on the page. Making shapes and straight lines part of your drawings makes a drawing easier to understand, as shown in Figure 2-5. Follow these steps to draw a shape or straight line:

1. **On the Draw tab, choose a pen or highlighter.**

   Your first step is to choose the color and line style you want for the shape or straight line:

   - **Tools gallery:** Open the Tools gallery and choose a pen or highlighter (refer to Figure 2-4).
   - **Color & Thickness dialog box:** Click the Color & Thickness button to open the Color & Thickness dialog box (refer to Figure 2-4). In the dialog box, select the Pen or Highlighter option button, choose a line thickness, and choose a line color.

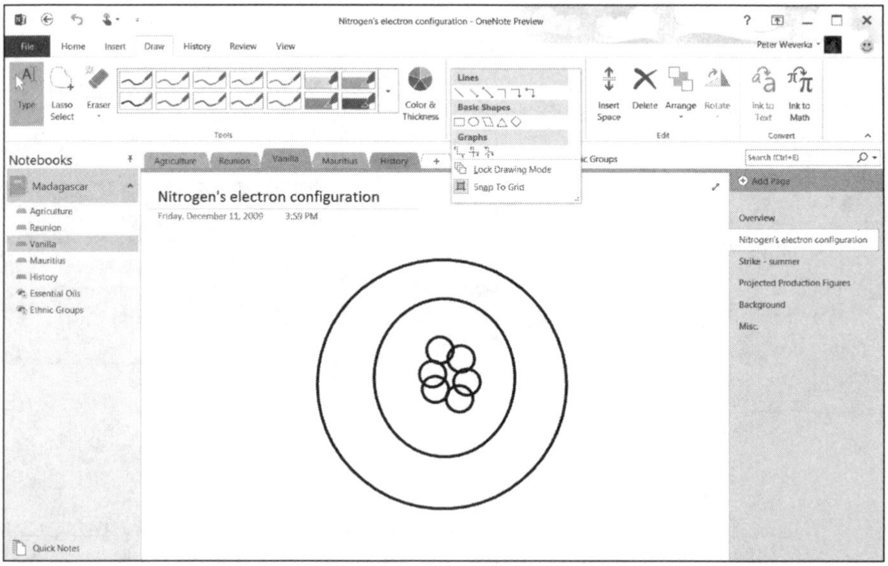

Figure 2-5: You can draw shapes as well as draw freehand.

2. **On the Draw tab, open the Shapes gallery and choose line or shape.**
3. **Drag onscreen to draw the line or shape.**
4. **Press Esc when you finish drawing the line or shape.**

   The next topic in this chapter explains how to change a shape's size and appearance.

Changing the size and appearance of drawings and shapes

Not that you necessarily want to open this can of worms, but you can edit drawings. Starting on the Draw tab, here are instructions for changing the look and appearance of drawings:

- **Selecting a single line or shape:** Click the Type button and then click the line or shape. Dotted lines and selection handles appear around the line or shape to show it is selected.
- **Selecting more than one shape and line:** Click the Lasso Select button and drag slantwise across the drawing.
- **Erasing:** Use the Eraser button to erase all or part of a line or shape. You can open the drop-down list on the Eraser button to choose erasers of different sizes.
  - *To erase part of a line or shape:* Click the Eraser button and drag over the part of the line or shape you want to erase.
  - *To erase entire lines and shapes:* Click the bottom half of the Eraser button to open its drop-down list, choose Stroke Eraser, and drag over or click on lines and shapes.
- **Changing line colors:** After you select a line, shape, or drawing, click Pen Properties in the pop-up menu and select a color.
- **Resizing:** After you select a line, shape, or drawing, use one of these techniques to resize it:
  - Drag a corner handle to change a shape's size and retain its symmetry.
  - Drag a side, top, or bottom handle to stretch or scrunch a shape.
- **Moving:** After you select a line, shape, or drawing, move the pointer on top of it. When you see the four-headed arrow, click and start dragging.
- **Rotating:** After you select a line, shape, or drawing, click the Rotate button and choose a Rotate or Flip option on the drop-down list.

- **Arranging overlapping lines and shapes:** When lines and shapes overlap, choose an Arrange option to determine which is highest and lowest in the stack. Select a line or shape, click the Arrange button, and choose an option on the drop-down list:
  - **Bring Forward:** Moves the line or shape higher in the stack.
  - **Bring to Front:** Moves the line or shape in front of all other lines and shapes in the stack.
  - **Send Backward:** Moves the line or shape lower in the stack.
  - **Send to Back:** Moves the lines or shape behind all other lines and shapes.
- **Deleting:** After you select a line, shape, or drawing, press Delete or click the Delete button.

Converting a Handwritten Note to Text

Want proof that computers are getting smarter? In OneNote, you can write a note by hand using a stylus pen, your finger if your computer is equipped with a touchscreen, or your mouse and tell OneNote to convert it to text. In my experiments, the conversion works most of the time. OneNote is able to recognize my handwriting and render it in text, as shown in Figure 2-6.

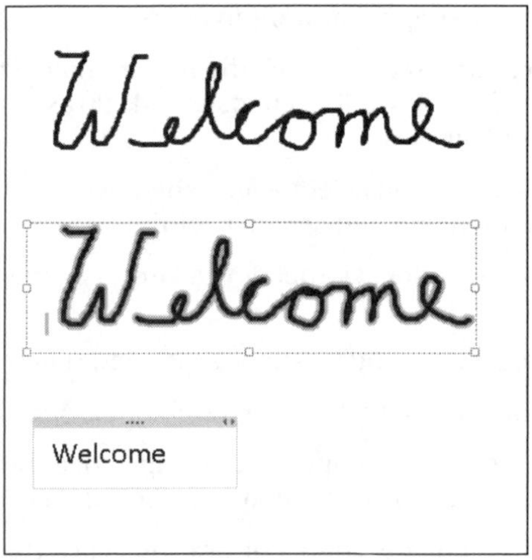

Figure 2-6: A handwritten note converted to text.

Follow these steps to convert a handwritten note to text:

1. **Select the handwritten note.**

   To do that, go to the Draw tab, click the Lasso Select button, and drag slantwise across the note.

2. **On the Draw tab, click the Ink to Text button.**

   Your handwritten note, with a little luck and depending on the quality of your handwriting, is converted to text.

Writing a Math Expression in a Note

The Insert tab offers the Equation Editor (click the Equation button) for writing mathematical equations, and you're welcome to give it a spin, but much more useful than the Equation Editor is another tool called the Ink Equation Editor. As shown in Figure 2-7, you can use it to construct mathematical expressions for notes.

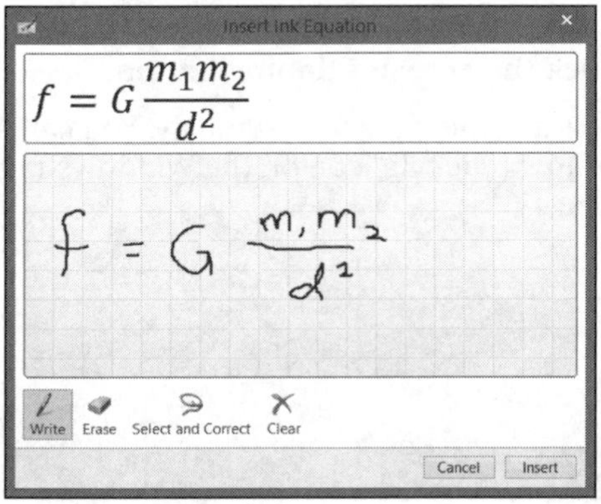

Figure 2-7: Writing a math expression in the Ink Equation Editor.

To open the Ink Equation Editor, go to the Draw tab and click the Ink to Math button. The Ink Equation Editor opens. Keep your eye on the Preview area while you follow these instructions to construct your equation:

- **Writing:** Click the Write button and drag the mouse to write your expression.
- **Erasing numbers and symbols:** Click the Erase button and drag to erase a number or symbol.

- **Correcting errors:** If the Ink Equation Editor enters the wrong number or symbol, click the Select and Correct button and then click on the part of the expression that is incorrect. A drop-down menu appears. If the correct number or symbol is on the menu, select it.
- **Erasing the expression:** Click the Clear button to wipe the slate clean and start anew.

Click the Insert button to turn the equation into a note.

Taking a Screen-Clipping Note

In OneNote lingo, a *screen clipping* is a note with a screen shot inside it, as shown in Figure 2-8. OneNote makes it remarkably easy to take screen clippings. Take them when you want to preserve part of a screen in a note. Follow these steps to make a screen-clipping note:

1. **Go to the web page, Word document, or other item that you need a picture of.**
2. **Switch to OneNote.**
3. **On the Insert tab, click the Screen Clipping button.**

   You return to the program you were in previously. You can also open the Send to OneNote window (click its icon on the Windows taskbar) and choose Screen Clipping.

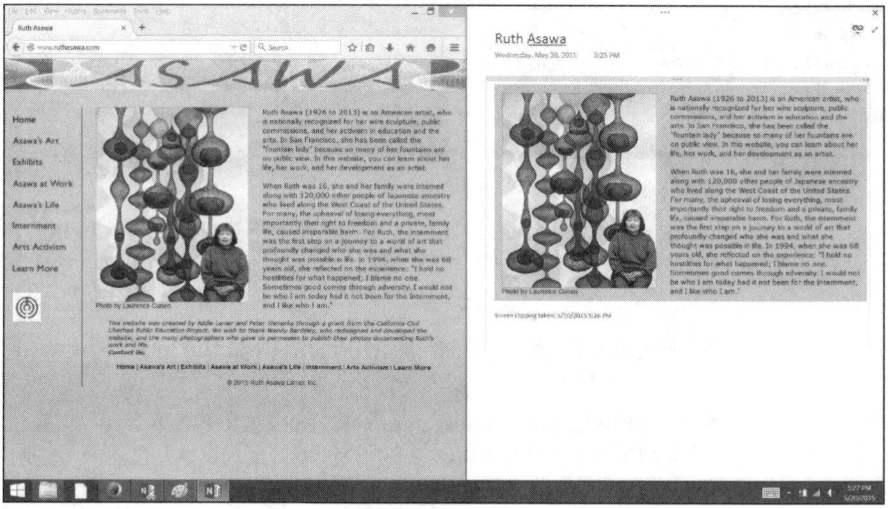

Figure 2-8: A screen clipping taken from a web page.

4. **Drag the pointer to capture the portion of the screen you want for the clipping.**

   When you finish dragging, you return to OneNote, and the screen clipping you took appears in a note.

TIP

You can also take a screen clipping when OneNote isn't running. To do so, start in the Notification tray (located in the lower-right corner of the screen), click the Send to OneNote Tool icon, and choose Screen Clipping in the pop-up window (or press Windows key+S). Then drag the pointer on your screen to capture the part of the screen you want for the clipping. The Select Location in OneNote dialog box appears. Do one of the following:

- **Select a section in the dialog box and click the Send to Selected Location button.** OneNote creates a new page in the section you chose for the clipping and places the clipping on the page.
- **Click the Copy to Clipboard button.** Back in OneNote, right-click a page and choose Paste to paste the clipping into OneNote.

Recording and Playing Audio Notes

If you start to get sleepy in class or a meeting and you can no longer type detailed notes, consider taking an *audio note.* An audio note is a recording stored in a note container. You can take these notes as long as your computer is equipped to record sound. What OneNote calls an *audio note* is really a `.wma` (Windows media audio) file stored in a note container.

After you record an audio note, you can click the note's Playback button or click the Play button on the (Audio & Video) Playback tab to play the recording you made, as shown in Figure 2-9.

TIP

Notes you type while recording an audio note are attached to the audio note. You can click the playback links in these typewritten notes to revisit parts of a recording. For example, to play back a part of your professor's biology lecture, you can go to the note you wrote while your professor spoke, click the playback link inside the note, and hear the part of the lecture that interests you. In this way, you can use audio and typewritten notes to go to and hear specific parts of a lecture or meeting.

Recording an audio note

Make sure your microphone is ready to go because OneNote begins recording audio notes as soon as you click the Record Audio button. Open the page where you want to store the note and follow these steps to record an audio note:

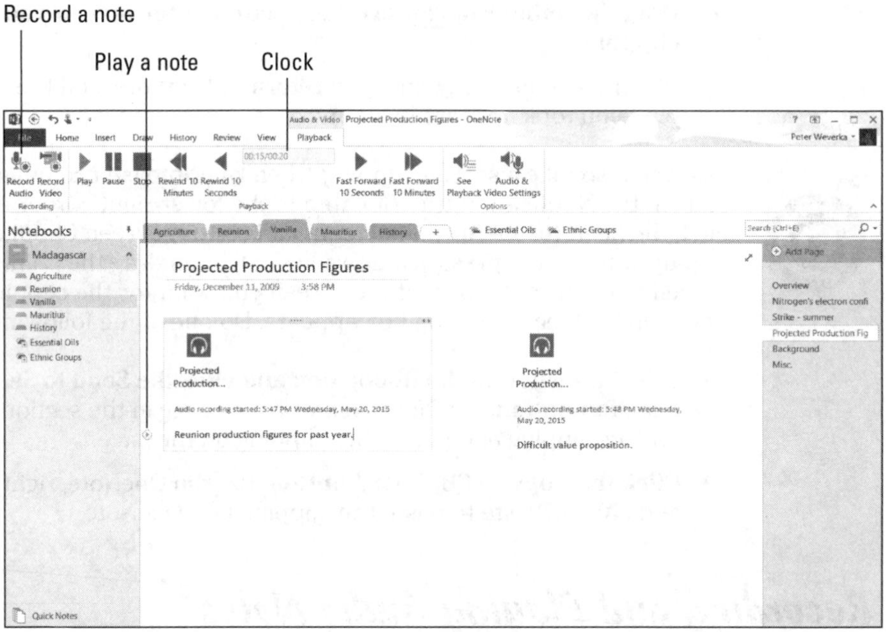

Figure 2-9: Play and record audio notes on the (Audio & Video) Playback tab.

1. **On the Insert tab or (Audio & Video) Playback tab, click the Record Audio button.**

   As shown in Figure 2-9, you go immediately to the (Audio & Video) Playback tab (if you weren't there already), and OneNote begins recording.

2. **Direct your microphone to whatever you're recording — your own voice or someone else's.**

   The clock at the top of the tab tells you how long the recording is. You can click the Pause button to suspend the recording; click Pause a second time to resume recording.

   As you record, type notes to describe what you're hearing. You can use these typewritten notes as references when you play back the recording.

3. **Click the Stop button when you want to finish recording the audio note.**

   Notes are named for the page where they are stored. The WMA icon on the note tells you that the note is a `.wma` (Windows media audio) file recording.

Playing an audio note

To play an audio note, select it and do one of the following:

- ✦ Click the Play icon on the note (refer to Figure 2-9).
- ✦ Right-click the note and choose Play on the shortcut menu that appears.
- ✦ Go to the (Audio & Video) Playback tab and click the Play button.

The Playback group on the (Audio & Video) Playback tab offers buttons for pausing, stopping, rewinding, and fast-forwarding an audio note as it plays (refer to Figure 2-9). Glance at the clock to see how long the note is and how many seconds and minutes have played so far.

While a note is playing, you can type other notes on the page. In other words, you can take notes on the audio recording and capture the information you missed during your catnap.

TIP

On a page with more than one audio note, click the See Playback button on the (Audio & Video) Playback tab to find out which note is currently playing. The note that is playing is highlighted and selected.

Attaching, Copying, and Linking Files to Notes

OneNote endeavors to make it easier for you to take notes on files on your computer. You can attach a note to a file and be able to open the file quickly from inside OneNote, copy a file into a note, and link a Word or PowerPoint file to a OneNote section or page so that you can refer to notes you keep in OneNote while you're working in Word or PowerPoint. These tasks are described forthwith.

Attaching an Office file to a note

Attach a Word, PowerPoint, or Excel file to a note so that you can quickly open the file from inside OneNote. When you attach a file, what you really do is create a shortcut from your note to the Office file. You can click the shortcut and open the attached file right away. Follow these steps to attach an Office file to a note:

1. **Select the note.**
2. **On the Insert tab, click the File Attachment button.**

   You see the Choose a File or Set of Files to Insert dialog box.
3. **Select the file or files.**

   To select more than one file, Ctrl+click their names.

4. Click the Insert button.

The Insert File dialog box appears.

5. Choose Attach File.

As shown in Figure 2-10, filenames and icons appear on notes. The icons indicate what kind of file is attached to the note. To open one of these files, simply click its icon.

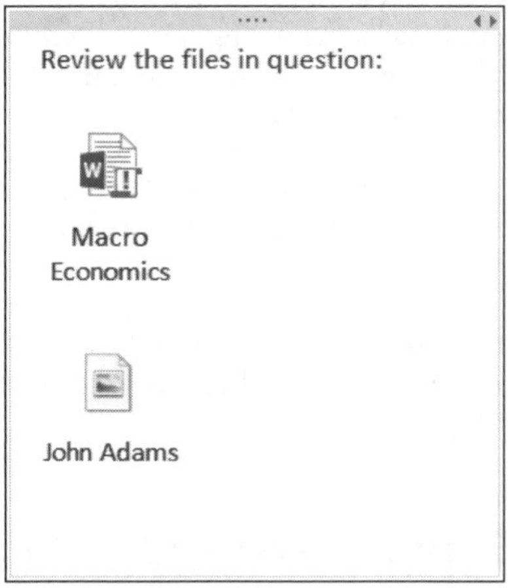

Figure 2-10: Files attached to a note.

Copying an Office file into OneNote

Follow these steps to copy a file from Word, PowerPoint, or Excel onto a OneNote page:

1. On the Insert tab, click the File Printout button.

The Choose Document to Insert dialog box opens.

2. Select a file and click the Insert button.

TIP

Starting in Word, Excel, or PowerPoint, you can copy a file to OneNote by going to the File tab and choosing Print. In the Print window, open the Printer drop-down list, choose Send to OneNote 16, and click the Print button. Then switch to OneNote, and in the Select Location in OneNote dialog box, choose a section or page and click OK. If you select a section, OneNote creates a new page in the section for the material from Word, Excel, or PowerPoint; if you select a page, the material lands on the page you selected.

Linking a Word or PowerPoint file to OneNote

By linking a Word or PowerPoint file to a OneNote section or page, you can open OneNote from inside Word or PowerPoint and refer right away to notes you took. Link a file to OneNote so that you can refer to notes you keep in OneNote while you're working on a Word or PowerPoint file.

Follow these steps to link a Word or PowerPoint file to a section or page in OneNote:

1. **Open the Word or PowerPoint file you want to link to notes you keep in OneNote.**
2. **On the Review tab, click the Linked Notes button.**

   OneNote opens (if it wasn't already open) in Dock to Desktop view, and you see the Select Location in OneNote dialog box, as shown in Figure 2-11.

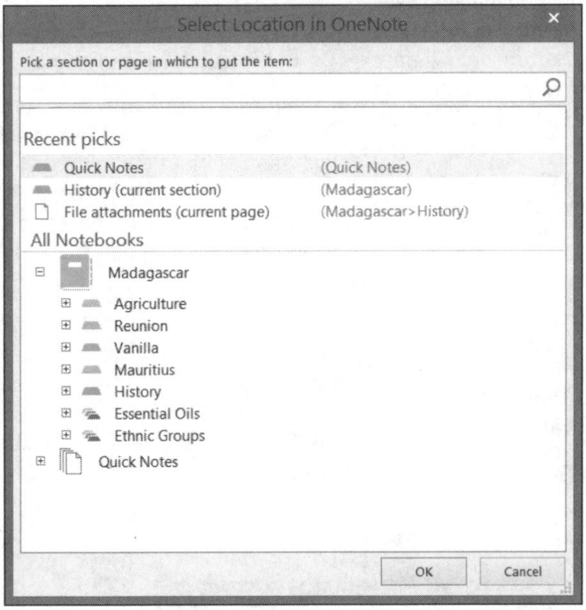

Figure 2-11: Choosing the section or page to link to.

3. **In the dialog box, select the section or page with the notes that refer to your Word or PowerPoint file, and click OK.**

   The Linked Note icon appears in OneNote. This icon tells you that the section or page is linked to a Word or PowerPoint file.

To refer to the OneNote notes while you're working on your Word or PowerPoint file, go to the Review tab and click the Linked Notes button. OneNote opens in Dock to Desktop view. In this view, Word or PowerPoint appears on the left side of your screen, and OneNote appears on the right side. This arrangement makes it easy to work from your notes. (Chapter 1 explains docking to the desktop.)

Copying a note into another Office program

To copy a note into another program, use the copy-and-paste command. Select the note, right-click, and choose Copy. Then go to the other program, right-click, and choose Paste. Typed notes land in the other program in the form of text. Drawings land as Portable Network Graphics (`.png`) files.

Jotting down a quick note

Suppose you're brainstorming and come up with an idea that cries out to be preserved in a note. To quickly jot down your note, write a "quick note" in the small but convenient Quick Note window. This window works in cahoots with OneNote to help you record ideas before you forget them. After you enter a note in the window, it's entered as well in OneNote in the Quick Notes folder. The next time you open OneNote, you can go to the Quick Notes folder, locate your note, and copy or move it to another folder.

Follow these steps to open the Quick Note window and enter a note:

1. **Open the Send to OneNote window:**
   - Click the Send to OneNote button on the Windows taskbar.
   - Press Windows key+N.
   - Click the Send to OneNote Tool icon in the Notification area.
2. **Choose New Quick Note.**
3. **Enter your note and click the Close button in the Quick Note window.**

To find your note the next time you open OneNote, click the Quick Notes button. You can find this button at the bottom of the Notebook pane. Your note is filed away on a page named after the note you entered. From here, you can move your note to a different section.

If the OneNote icon isn't in the Notification area and you want it there, go to the File tab in OneNote and choose Options. In the Options dialog box, go to the Display category and select the Place OneNote Icon in the Notification Area of the Taskbar check box.

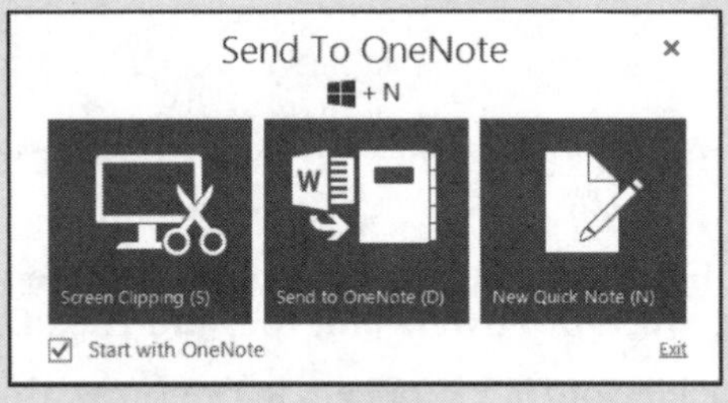

Chapter 3: Finding and Organizing Your Notes

In This Chapter

- Finding lost notes
- Tagging notes so that you can organize them better
- Using colors to identify notebooks, sections, and pages
- Moving and copying sections, pages, and notes

If you're an habitual note taker, you may find yourself drowning in notes. You won't be able to find the note you're looking for. The great idea you had may be lost forever. How do you find the notes you want to review? More important, how can you organize your notes to make finding and recognizing them easier?

This chapter looks at how to organize your notes so that you can find them in a hurry. It tells you how to search for notes, tag notes to make finding them easier, color-code notebooks and sections, and merge and move sections, pages, and notes. You also discover OneNote's Recycle Bin, where sections and pages go to die unless you revive them.

Finding a Stray Note

Notes have a tendency to stray. I'm not saying they move from page to page or section by section on their own in the dead of night, but it sometimes seems that way. To track down and find a stray note, you can search by word or phrase or search by author name. Better keep reading.

Searching by word or phrase

As long as you can remember a word or two in a note, you can find it. Follow these steps to chase down a lost note:

1. **Click in the Search box (or press Ctrl+E).**

   The Search box is located to the right of the Section tabs, above the Page pane, as shown in Figure 3-1. As soon as you click in the Search box, the Search Results pane opens. Terms you searched for since you started OneNote appear on the Search Results pane under "Recent Picks." You can click one of these terms to rerun a search.

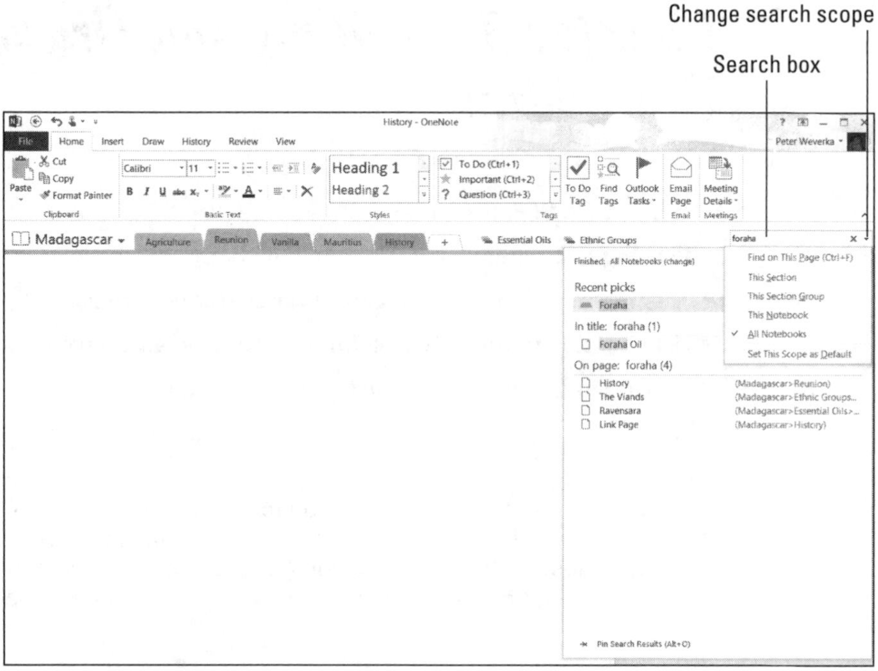

Figure 3-1: Choosing where to conduct a search.

2. **Enter a word or phrase in the Search box.**

   Pages with the word or phrase you entered appear in the Search Results pane (refer to Figure 3-1).

3. **Click a page title or page to open a page with your search term.**

   The Search Results pane remains open so that you can click a different page and open it.

   To close the Search Results pane, click a page or click the Close button (the X in the Search box).

To narrow your search, click the Change Search Scope button (it's on the right side of the Search box) and choose This Section, This Notebook, or another option on the drop-down list (refer to Figure 3-1).

Searching by author

Another way to search is by author name. If you share your OneNote files with others, you can search for notes written by different authors by following these steps:

1. **On the History tab, click the Find by Author button.**

   The Search Results pane opens. It lists notes by author name, as shown in Figure 3-2. If you see the note you're looking for, click it now.

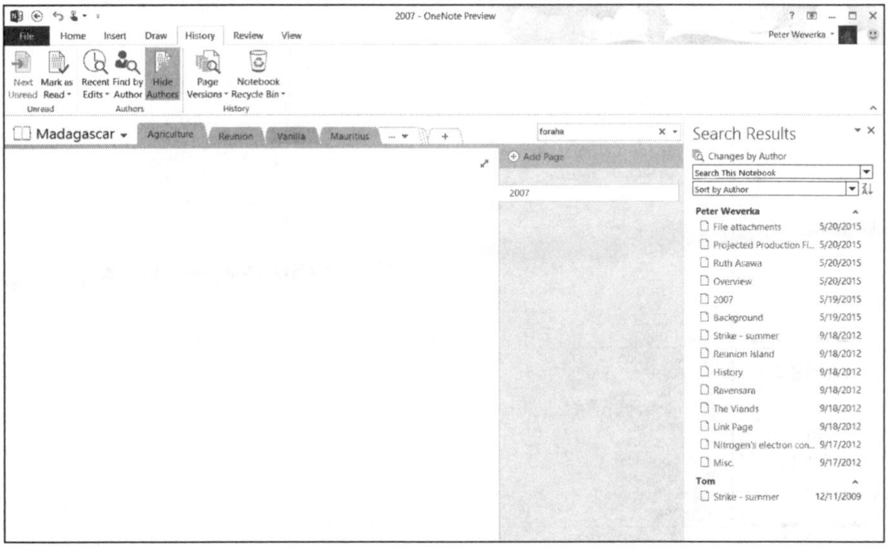

Figure 3-2: Searching for notes by author.

2. **Open the first drop-down list and declare where to search.**
3. **Open the Sort drop-down list and choose an option to sort by author name or the date notes were last modified; you can click the Sort Descending or Sort Descending button to choose how you want to sort notes.**
4. **Click a note in the Search Results pane.**

   OneNote opens the page with the note you clicked so that you can read the note.

5. **Click the Close button (the X) in the Search Results pane to close the pane.**

Tagging Notes for Follow Up

The best way to keep notes from getting lost is to carefully place them in notebooks, sections, and pages. Short of that, you can tag notes to make it easier to follow up on them. OneNote offers numerous ways to tag notes. After you tag a note, you can search for it by opening the Tags Summary task pane, arranging notes according to how they were tagged, and pinpointing the note you want, as shown in Figure 3-3.

Choose how to arrange the tagged notes

Tags Summary ▾ ✕

Search completed

Group tags by:

| Section ▾ |

☐ Show only unchecked items

Vanilla ▲

☐ Check for updates.

? My dinner with Andre.

★ Reunion airplane tix

Search:

| This notebook ▾ |

This page group
This section
This section group
This notebook
All notebooks
Today's notes
Yesterday's notes
This week's notes
Last week's notes
Older notes

Figure 3-3:
Tag notes
so that you
can track
them better.

Choose where to look for notes

Tagging a note

You can tag the same note with more than one tag. Follow these steps to tag a note:

1. **Select the note.**

2. **On the Home tab, open the Tags gallery and choose a tag (or click the To Do Tag button).**

 All options except Remember for Later and Definition place an icon on the note. The aforementioned options highlight the note text, respectively, in yellow or green. Later in this chapter, "Creating and modifying tags" shows you how to add a tag of your own to the Tags gallery.

To remove tags from notes, select the notes and press Ctrl+0 (zero), or open the drop-down list on the Tags gallery and choose Remove Tag.

Arranging tagged notes in the task pane

Follow these steps to arrange notes that you tagged in the Tags Summary task pane:

1. **On the Home tab, click the Find Tags button.**

   You see the Tags Summary task pane (refer to Figure 3-3).

2. **Open the Group Tags By drop-down list and choose an option.**

   These options determine the order in which tagged notes appear in the task pane. Tag Name, for example, arranges notes according to which icon they're tagged with; Section arranges notes under section names; Note Text arranges notes in alphabetical order.

3. **Open the Search drop-down list and choose an option.**

   These options determine which notes appear in the task pane. This Section, for example, assembles only flagged notes from the section that appears onscreen; This Notebook gathers flagged notes from all sections in the notebook you're viewing.

   A list of notes appears in the task pane.

4. **Click the name of a note you want to visit.**

   OneNote opens the page with the note whose name you clicked and selects the note.

Creating and modifying tags

If the tags in the Tags gallery don't do the trick, you can create a tag of your own. Do so either by modifying a tag that is already there or creating a new tag from scratch. Follow these steps to create a tag:

1. **On the Home tab, open the Tags gallery and choose Customize Tags.**

   You see the Customize Tags dialog box, shown in Figure 3-4.

2. **Choose to modify a tag or create a new tag.**

   You've come to a fork in the road:

   - *Creating a new tag:* Click the New Tag button. The New Tag dialog box appears, as shown in Figure 3-4.
   - *Modifying a tag:* Select a tag you don't need in the dialog box and then click the Modify Tag button. The Modify Tag dialog box appears (it looks and works just like the New Tag dialog box shown in Figure 3-4).

Figure 3-4: Giving a name and icon to a tag.

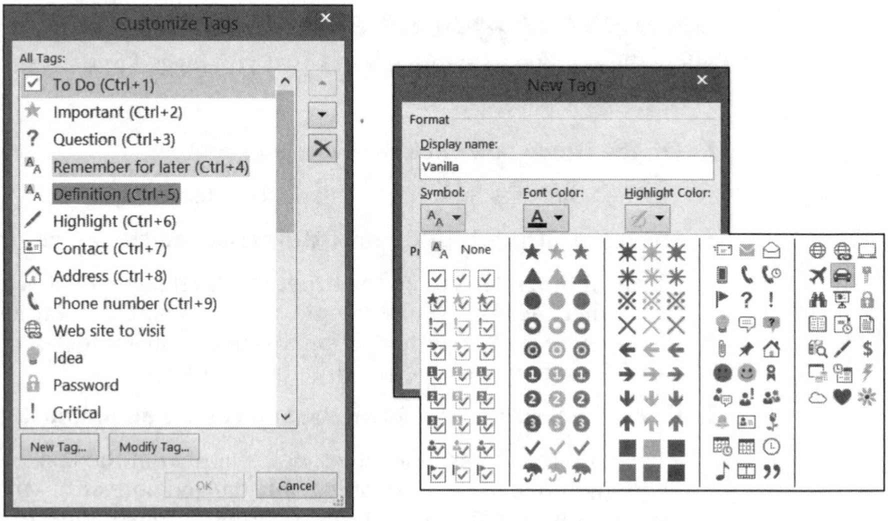

3. **Enter a name for your tag in the Display Name text box.**
4. **Choose a symbol for the tag.**
5. **If you want, choose a font and highlight color.**
6. **Click OK.**

To remove a tag you created, select it in the Customize Tags dialog box and click the Remove button. To change the order of tags in the Tags gallery, open the Customize Tags dialog box, select a tag, and click the Move Tag Up or Move Tag Down button until the tag is where you want it to be.

Color-Coding Notebooks, Sections, and Pages

If color-coding notebooks, sections, and pages helps you understand what is in your notebooks, sections, and pages, by all means start color-coding. Devise a color scheme for assigning colors to different topics and then follow these instructions to color-code your notebooks, sections, and pages:

✦ **Notebook:** Right-click the notebook's name in the Notebook pane and choose Properties. The Notebook Properties dialog box appears, as shown in Figure 3-5. Choose a color on the Color drop-down list and click OK.

- **Section:** Right-click a section's name in the Notebook pane or a section tab and choose Section Color on the drop-down list. Then, on the submenu, choose a color.
- **Page:** On the View tab, click the Page Color button and choose a color on the drop-down list.

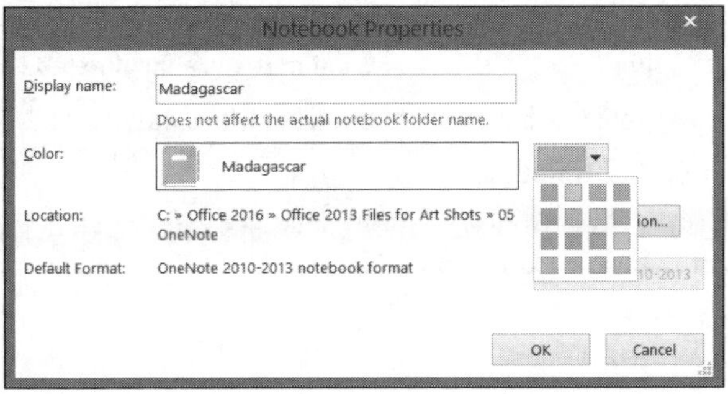

Figure 3-5: Color-coding a notebook.

Merging and Moving Sections, Pages, and Notes

I hope that as you take notes, you find opportunities to combine sections and pages. Combining sections and pages means you're synthesizing your ideas. What used to be a sprawling mass of assorted notes is turning into a handful of rock-solid concepts. Here are instructions for merging sections, moving pages to other sections, and moving notes to different pages:

- **Merging one section into another:** On the Notebook pane or on a section tab, right-click the name of the section you want to merge with another section. On the shortcut menu, choose Merge into Another Section. You see the Merge Section dialog box. Choose a section and click the Merge button.
- **Moving (or copying) a page to another section:** Right-click the page's tab and choose Move or Copy (or press Ctrl+Alt+M). You see the Move or Copy Pages dialog box. Select a section name and click the Move or Copy button.
- **Moving notes to another page:** Use the tried-and-true cut-and-paste method. Select the note, right-click, choose Cut, right-click the page where you want to move the note, and choose Paste.

Visiting the Recycle Bin

OneNote maintains a Recycle Bin of its own. If you mistakenly delete a section or page, you can recover it by going to the History tab and clicking the Notebook Recycle Bin button. Sections and pages you deleted appear (deleted pages appear on the Deleted Pages tab).

Follow these steps to restore a section or page:

- **On the History tab, click the Notebook Recycle Bin button.**
- **Right-click the section or page you want to restore and choose Move or Copy.**

  You see the Move or Copy dialog box.
- **Select the notebook or section where you want to restore the deleted item.**
- **Click the Move button.**

Book VI

Outlook 2016

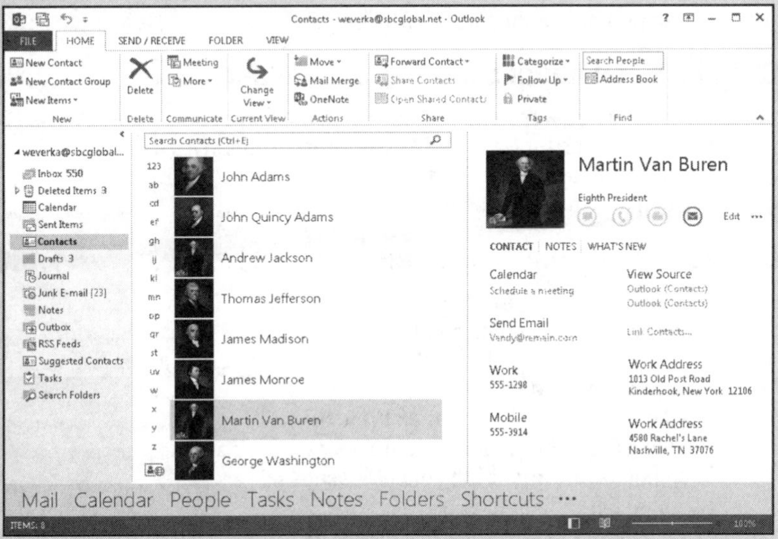

Visit www.dummies.com/extras/office2016aio to discover how to have Outlook alert you whenever email arrives from a specific person.

Contents at a Glance

Chapter 1: Outlook Basics

In This Chapter

- Getting around in Outlook
- Categorizing items so that you can locate them easily
- Searching in folders
- Deleting items
- Backing up your Outlook file
- Archiving old-and-in-the-way items

This chapter pulls back the curtain and gives you a first glimpse of *Outlook*, the emailer, calendar, and personal organizer in the Office 2016 suit of applications. Read on to find out once and for all what Outlook does, how to get from folder to folder, and the different ways to view the stuff in folders. You can find advice about keeping folders well organized, deleting stuff, backing up an Outlook file, and cleaning out items in folders that you no longer need.

What Is Outlook, Anyway?

Outlook isn't in character with the rest of the Office programs. It's a little different in that what you see onscreen changes when you click a Navigation button on the bottom of the window. Click a Navigation button — Mail, Calendar, People, Tasks, Notes, Folders, or Shortcuts — and you go to a different Outlook window altogether.

Outlook serves many different purposes. To wit, Outlook is all this:

- **An email program:** You can use it to send and receive email messages and files, as well as organize email messages in different folders so that you can keep track of them. (See Chapter 3 of this mini-book.)
- **An appointment scheduler:** Outlook is a calendar for scheduling appointments and meetings. You can tell at a glance when and where you're expected, be alerted to upcoming appointments and meetings, and invite coworkers to meetings. (See Chapter 4 of this mini-book.)

Do you need Outlook?

Before you penetrate the mysteries of Outlook, ask yourself whether you need the application. If you don't receive volumes of email, your calendar isn't crowded, and the office where you work doesn't require you to use Outlook, consider using an email program that isn't as cumbersome as Outlook, or better yet, consider using a web-based email program.

Outlook is good at organizing email so that you can find and reply to messages quickly. It is good at handling volumes of email. Outlook can help you manage schedules and coordinate meetings with co-workers. It can help you keep track of where you're supposed to be and when you're supposed to be there.

On the minus side, however, Outlook has many more features than most people need, and all these features clutter Outlook and make it hard to use. What's more, email messages are kept on your computer. Unless you carry around a laptop, you have to be at your home or office computer to collect your email. With a web-based email program, messages are stored on a server on the Internet, and all email activity — composing, sending, and receiving messages — is accomplished through a Web browser. You can be in Timbuktu and still collect your email if you can find a computer with an Internet connection. You don't have to be at home or at the office to read your email.

If web-based emailing appeals to you, ask your Internet service provider whether it offers a web-based email service. Or check out Google Mail (`www.gmail.com`), which is free and easy to use. Google Mail offers a calendar and other amenities as well as emailing. If you want to keep it simple and you can manage to do that, steer clear of Outlook.

- **An address book:** The application can store the addresses, phone numbers, and email addresses of friends, foes, clients, and family members. Looking up this information in the Contacts folder is easy. (See Chapter 2 of this mini-book.)
- **A task reminder:** Outlook is a means of planning projects. You can tell when deadlines fall and plan your workload accordingly. (See Chapter 5 of this mini-book.)
- **A notes receptacle:** This part of the program is a place to jot down notes and reminders. (See Chapter 5 of this mini-book.)

Navigating the Outlook Folders

The first thing you should know about Outlook is this: All items are kept in folders, as shown in Figure 1-1. Recently arrived email messages are kept in the Inbox folder. Calendar items are kept in the Calendar folder. Contact information is kept in the Contacts folder.

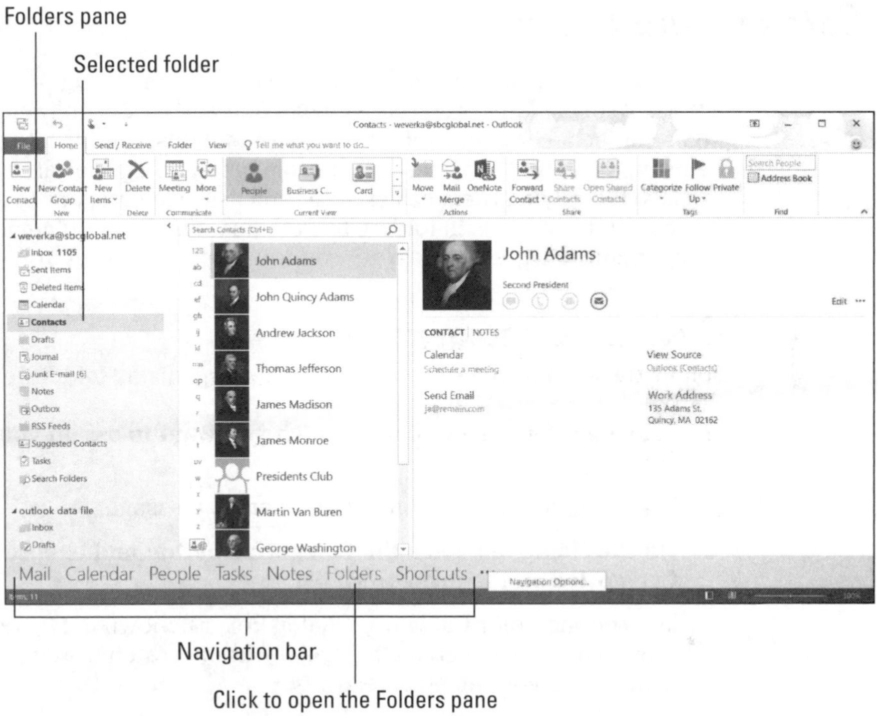

Figure 1-1: Outlook with the Contacts folder selected.

When you want to undertake a new task, you go to a different folder:

- **Folders pane:** Select a folder in the Folders pane (see Figure 1-1). For example, click the Inbox folder to read incoming mail.

  If you don't see the Folders pane, click the Folders button on the Navigation bar (or press Ctrl+6), as shown in Figure 1-1.

- **Navigation bar:** Click a button on the Navigation bar — Mail, Calendar, People, and so on (see Figure 1-1). Clicking one of these buttons displays folders that have to do, respectively, with the Mail, the Calendar, Contacts, and so on.

You can open a folder in a new window. To do so, right-click a Navigation button or folder name and choose Open in New Window.

If an abridged version of the Navigation bar appears along the bottom of the Outlook window and you want it to see a Navigation bar like the one in Figure 1-1, click the Navigation Options button (the three dots on the Navigation bar). The Navigation Options dialog box opens. Deselect the Compact Navigation check box and click OK.

Categorizing Items

One of your biggest tasks in Outlook, if you choose to accept it, is to categorize items in folders so that you can find and deal with them. Finding items can be a chore in a folder with a lot of items, but by categorizing items, you can find the ones you're looking for. Categories are color-coded to make identifying them easier. After you assign a category to an item, you can arrange items in folders by category, and in so doing, find items. Categorizing is a great way to stay on top of all the chores you have to do.

Creating a category

Follow these steps to create a category for organizing folder items:

1. **Select an item in a folder to which you want to assign your new category.**

   For example, select a contact or an email message.

2. **On the Home tab, click the Categorize button and choose All Categories on the drop-down list.**

   You see the Color Categories dialog box, as shown in Figure 1-2. At this point, you can create a category from scratch or revamp one of Outlook's color-named categories:

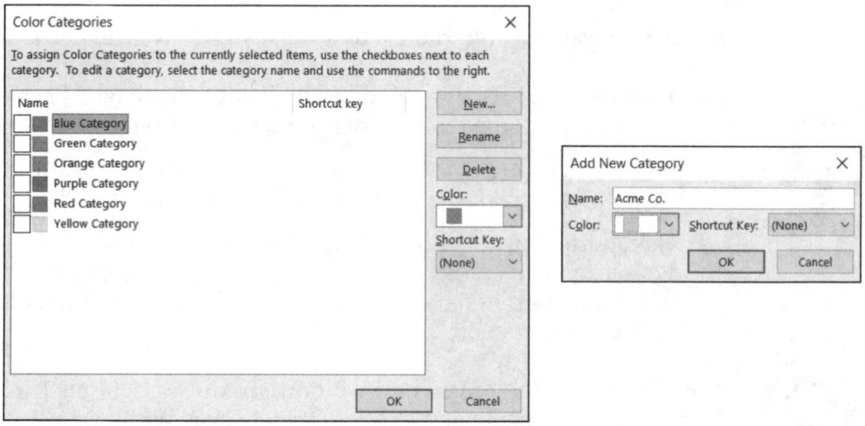

Figure 1-2: Click the New button or Rename button to create a new category.

   - *Creating your own category:* Click the New button to open the Add New Category dialog box, as shown in Figure 1-2. Then enter a name for your category and choose a color on the drop-down list. While you're at it, you can open the Shortcut Key drop-down list and choose a shortcut key combination for assigning your new category to items. Click the OK button in the Color Categories dialog box.

- *Renaming a category:* In the Color Categories dialog box (see Figure 1-2), select a color category, and click the Rename button. Then enter a new name where in place of the old one. You can choose a different color for your category by choosing a color in the Color drop-down list. To assign it a shortcut key, open the Shortcut Key drop-down list and choose a shortcut key combination.

To delete a category, return to the Color Categories dialog box, select the category's name, and click the Delete button. Although the category is deceased, items to which you assigned the category keep their category assignments.

Assigning items to categories

Follow these steps to assign a category to a folder item:

1. **Select the item.**
2. **On the Home tab, click the Categorize button and choose a category on the drop-down list.**

   You can also right-click, choose Categorize, and select a category on the shortcut menu, or press a Ctrl+key combination if you assigned one to the category. An item can be assigned more than one category.

To remove a category assignment, select the item, click the Categorize button, and choose Clear All Categories.

Arranging items by category in folders

To arrange items by category in a folder, select the folder in the Folder pane and use one of these techniques:

- On the View tab, choose Categories in the Arrangement gallery.
- In a list, click the Categories column heading to sort items by category.

You can also click the Categorized button on the (Search Tools) Search tab to organize the results of a search by category.

Searching for Stray Folder Items

If you can't locate an item in a folder by scrolling, changing views, or any other means, run a search. To start a search, go to the folder you want to search and click in the Search box (or press Ctrl+E). You can find the Search box below the Ribbon. As soon as you click in the Search box, Outlook opens the (Search Tools) Search tab so that you can describe what you're seeking, as shown in Figure 1-3.

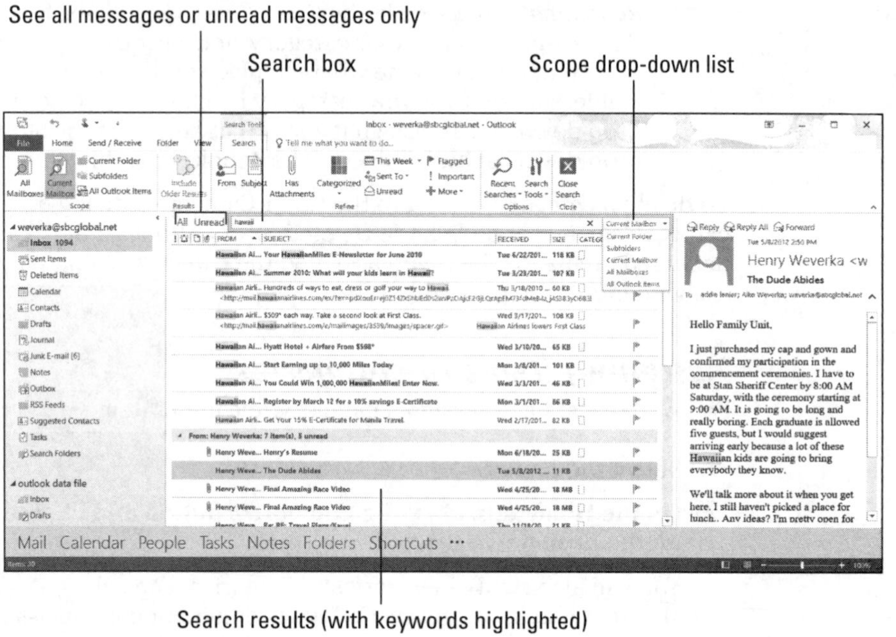

Figure 1-3: Describe what you're searching for on the (Search Tools) Search tab.

As the following pages explain, you can conduct an instant search, narrow your search by choosing Refine options, or conduct an advanced search starting from the (Search Tools) Search tab. Search results appear in the window below the Search box. To close the search and go back to seeing the contents of your folder, click the Close Search button (the *X* on the right side of the Search box).

TIP: Here's a fast way to run a search: Click the Recent Searches button on the (Search Tools) Search tab and choose a search on the drop-down list to rerun one of the last six searches you conducted.

Conducting an instant search

What Microsoft calls an "instant search" is a keyword search of the folder you're viewing. If a keyword you enter in the Search box is found in an email message, calendar appointment, contact, or other item, the item appears in the search results and the keyword is highlighted (refer to Figure 1-3). Search results begin appearing as soon as you start to type. You don't have to press the Enter key to begin the search.

TIP: When searching an email folder, you can click the All or Unread link next to the Search box to see all messages or only those you haven't read yet.

TIP

To change how instant searches are conducted, click the Search Tools button on the (Search Tools) Search tab and choose Search Options on the drop-down list. You go to the Search category in the Outlook Options dialog box. From there, you can choose which folders are searched and how search results are displayed when you conduct an instant search.

Refining a search

Refine a search when an instant search brings up too many or too few search results. Starting on the (Search Tools) Search tab, refine your search by changing its scope and choosing Refine options.

Changing the scope of a search

How wide the scope of a search is determines how many results are found in the search. Use these techniques to narrow or widen searches:

- Click a button in the Scope group on the (Search Tools) Search tab.
- Open the Scope drop-down list to the right of the Search box and choose an option (see Figure 1-3).

The options for changing the scope for searches are the following:

- **Current Mailbox (for email searching only):** Expands a search for email to include all folders that contain email, including the Drafts and Sent Items folders. You can also press Ctrl+Alt+A.
- **All (Calendar, Contact, Task, or Note) Items:** Expands a search to the folder that you selected on the Folder pane as well as folders where calendar items, contacts, tasks, or notes are stored. This button changes names, depending on which folder you selected. You can also press Ctrl+Alt+A.
- **Current Folder:** Searches the folder you selected on the Folder pane. You can also press Ctrl+Alt+K.
- **Subfolders:** Expands the search to include the folder you selected on the Folders pane as well as its subfolders. You can also press Ctrl+Alt+Z.
- **All Outlook Items:** Expands the search to all Outlook folders. Move the pointer over the search results to see a pop-up box that lists which folder an item is stored in.

Choosing Refine options

To narrow a search, click buttons in the Refine group on the (Search Tools) Search tab. After you click a button, Outlook provides a place in the Search box for you to enter a keyword. Which buttons appear in the Refine group depends on which folder you search.

In a folder that contains email, for example, you can click the From button and enter a sender name in the Search box to search for emails you received from a particular person. You can click the Subject button and enter a keyword to search the subject descriptions in email you received.

Conducting an advanced search

If, woe is me, you can't find what you're looking for with an instant search or a refined search, you can try your luck with an advanced search.

On the (Search Tools) Search tab, click the Search Tools button and choose Advanced Find on the drop-down list. You see the Advanced Find dialog box, as shown in Figure 1-4. In the Look drop-down list, choose what you want to search for. Click the Browse button to open the Select Folder(s) dialog box, where you can select more than one folder to search in. Then choose options in the three tabs to formulate your search. Which options are available depends on which folder you're searching.

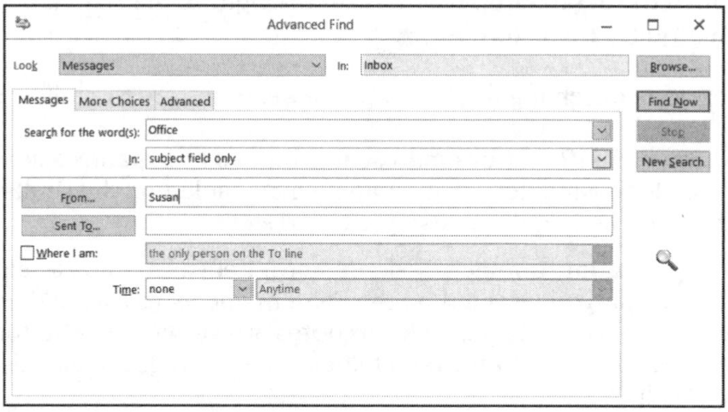

Figure 1-4: Pinpoint what you're searching for in the Advanced Find dialog box.

Deleting Email Messages, Contacts, Tasks, and Other Items

Outlook folders are notorious for filling quickly. Email messages, contacts, and tasks soon clog the folders if you spend any time in Outlook. From time to time, go through the email folders, Contacts window, Task window, and Calendar to delete items you no longer need. To delete items, select them and do one of the following:

- ✦ Click the Delete button.
- ✦ Press the Delete key.
- ✦ Right-click and choose Delete.

Deleted items — email messages, calendar appointments, contacts, and tasks — land in the Deleted Items folder in case you want to recover them. To delete items once and for all, open the Deleted Items folder and start deleting like a madman.

To empty the Delete Items folder altogether, right-click the folder and choose Empty Folder. You can also visit the File tab, choose Info, click the Cleanup Tools button, and choose Empty Deleted Items Folder on the drop-down list.

Be sure to check out "Running the Mailbox Cleanup command" at the end of this chapter. It explains a quick way to delete unwanted Inbox messages.

Finding and Backing Up Your Outlook File

All the data you keep in Outlook — email messages, names and addresses, calendar appointments and meetings — is kept in a `.pst` (Personal Storage Table) file on your computer. Locating this file on your computer sometimes requires the services of Sherlock Holmes. The file isn't kept in a standard location. It can be any number of places, depending on the operating system on your computer and whether you upgraded from an earlier version of Office.

The all-important `.pst` file is hiding deep in your computer, but you need to find it. You need to know where this file is located so that you can back it up to a CD, flash drive, or other backup medium. It holds clients' names and the names of relatives and loved ones. It holds the email messages you think are worth keeping. It would be a shame to lose this stuff if your computer failed.

Here's a quick way to find the `.pst` file on your computer and back it up:

1. **On the File tab, choose Info.**

   The Account Information window opens.

2. **Click the Account Settings button and choose Account Settings on the drop-down list.**

   You see the Account Settings dialog box.

3. **Go to the Data Files tab.**

   This tab is shown in Figure 1-5. It lists the location of your `.pst` file (or files).

4. **Select your `.pst` file and click the Open File Location button.**

   File Explorer opens, and you see the folder where your `.pst` file is kept.

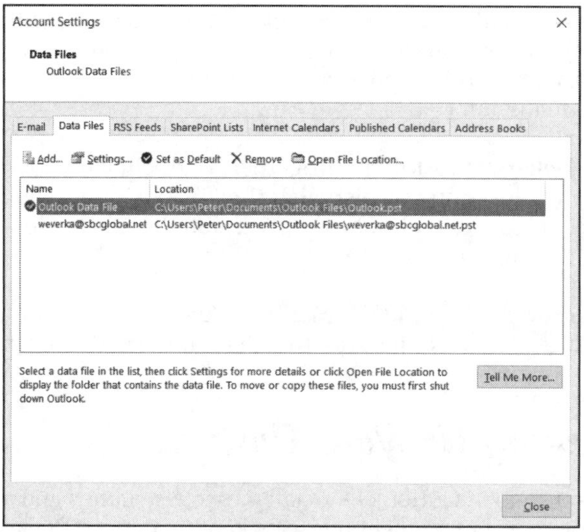

Figure 1-5: Click the Open File Location button to find out where your Outlook file is located.

5. **Close Outlook.**

   Sorry, but you can't back up a `.pst` file if Outlook is running.

6. **To back up the file, right-click it in File Explorer, choose Send To on the shortcut menu, and choose the option on the submenu that represents where you back up files.**

   If an accident befalls your computer, copy the backup `.pst` file that you made into the folder where the `.pst` file is stored on your computer.

Cleaning Out Your Folders

Getting rid of unneeded items in folders is essential for good mental health. All that clutter can be distressing. Earlier in this chapter, "Deleting Email Messages, Contacts, Tasks, and Other Items," explains how to muck out folders by emptying them. These pages explain two more techniques for removing detritus from folders — archiving and the Mailbox Cleanup command.

Archiving the old stuff

In some cases, Outlook puts email messages, tasks, and appointments older than six months in the *Archive folder,* a special folder for items that Outlook thinks are stale and not worth keeping anymore. Outlook calls sending these items to the Archive folder "autoarchiving." Items that have been archived aren't lost forever. You can visit them by opening the Archive Folders folder and its subfolders on the Folder pane. These folders and subfolders are created automatically the first time you archive items.

Archiving is a way of stripping your mail folders, tasks lists, and calendar of items that don't matter anymore. How and when items are archived is up to you. To archive items, you can archive them on your own, establish a default set of archiving rules that apply to all folders, or, if a folder needs individual attention and shouldn't be subject to the default archiving rules, establish special rules for that folder. Each folder can have its own set of archiving rules or be subject to the default rules.

To tell Outlook how to archive old stuff:

- **Establishing default archiving rules:** On the File tab, choose Options to open the Outlook Options dialog box. Then, on the Advanced tab, click the AutoArchive Settings button. You see the AutoArchive dialog box shown in Figure 1-6. See "Default archiving rules."
- **Establishing rules for a specific folder:** Select the folder, go to the Folder tab, and click the AutoArchive Settings button. You see the AutoArchive tab of the Properties dialog box, as shown in Figure 1-6. See "Archiving rules for a folder."
- **Archiving a folder on your own:** On the File tab, choose Info, and in the Account Information window, click the Cleanup Tools button and choose Archive on the drop-down list. You see the Archive dialog box. Select the folder with the items you want to archive and click OK.

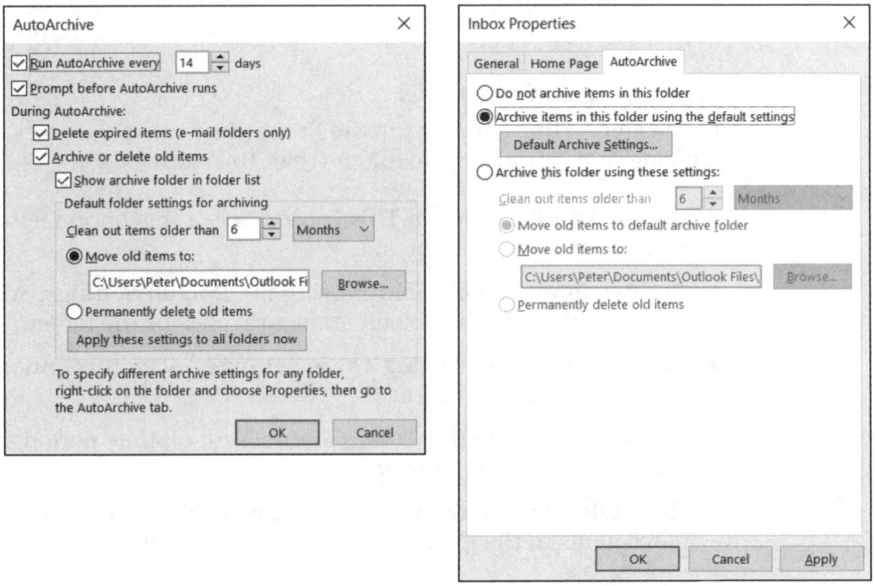

Figure 1-6: Making the default archiving rules (left) and rules for a folder (right).

Default archiving rules

Negotiate these options in the AutoArchive dialog box to establish default archiving rules (see Figure 1-6):

- **Run AutoArchive Every:** Enter a number to tell Outlook how often to archive items.
- **Prompt Before Archive Runs:** If this check box is selected, you see a message box before archiving begins, and you can decline to archive if you want by selecting No in the message box.
- **Delete Expired Items (Email Folders Only):** Select this check box to delete all email messages when the time period has expired.
- **Archive or Delete Old Items:** Deselect this option if you *don't* want to archive items.
- **Show Archive Folder in Folder List:** Select this option if you want to keep the archived version of the folder in the Folder pane. Archived items are kept in this folder so you can review them.
- **Clean Out Items Older Than:** Choose a cut-off time period after which to archive items.
- **Move Old Items To:** Click the Browse button and select a folder if you want to store the Archive file in a certain location.
- **Permanently Delete Old Items:** Select this option if you want to delete, not archive, old items.

Archiving rules for a folder

Choose among these options in the Properties dialog box to establish archiving rules for a specific folder (refer to Figure 1-6):

- **Do Not Archive Items in This Folder:** Select this option if items in the folder aren't worth archiving.
- **Archive Items in This Folder Using the Default Settings:** Select this option to defer to the default archiving rules for the folder.
- **Archive This Folder Using These Settings:** Select this option to establish archiving rules for the folder.
- **Clean Out Items Older Than:** Choose a cut-off time period after which to archive the items in the folder.
- **Move Old Items to the Default Archive Folder:** Select this option to move items to the folder you selected as the default.

- **Move Old Items To:** Click the Browse button and select a folder if you want to store the archived items in a specific location.
- **Permanently Delete Old Items:** Select this option if you want to delete, not archive, items in this folder.

TIP: Besides archiving, another way to remove bric-a-brac automatically is to take advantage of the Rules Wizard to delete certain kinds of email messages when they arrive. See Chapter 3 of this mini-book for more information.

Running the Mailbox Cleanup command

The Mailbox Cleanup command is an all-purpose command for finding email messages, archiving items, deleting items, and deleting alternate versions of items. To use the command, go to the File tab, choose Info, click the Cleanup Tools button, and choose Mailbox Cleanup. You see the Mailbox Cleanup dialog box shown in Figure 1-7. The dialog box offers a speedy entrée into these different Outlook tasks:

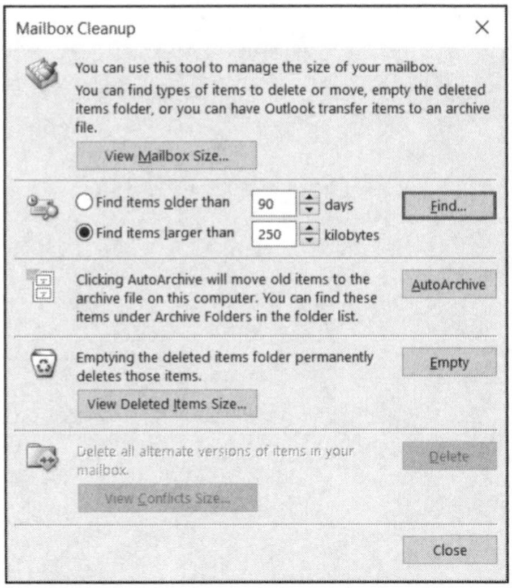

Figure 1-7: Mucking out the mail boxes.

- **Seeing how much disk space folders occupy:** Click the View Mailbox Size button and then take note of folder sizes in the Folder Size dialog box.
- **Finding items:** Select an option button to find items older than a certain number of days or larger than a certain number of kilobytes, enter a days or kilobytes number, and click the Find button. You land in the Advanced Find dialog box. Earlier in this chapter, "Conducting an advanced search" explains this dialog box. Use it to select items and delete them.

- **Archiving items:** Click the AutoArchive button to archive items in your folders. See "Archiving the old stuff" in this chapter for details.
- **Emptying the deleted items folder:** Click the Empty button to empty the Deleted Items folder. See "Deleting Email Messages, Contacts, Tasks, and Other Items," earlier in this chapter.
- **Delete all alternative versions of items:** Click Delete if you conduct emailing through a Exchange Server account and you want to delete alternative versions of items that were created during synchronization.

Chapter 2: Maintaining the Contacts Folder

In This Chapter

- Recording information about a new contact
- Creating a contact group
- Locating a contact in the Contacts folder
- Printing contact information in the Contacts folder

In *pathology* (the study of diseases and how they're transmitted) a *contact* is a person who passes on a communicable disease, but in Outlook, a *contact* is someone about whom you keep information. Information about contacts is kept in the Contacts folder. This folder is a super-powered address book. It has places for storing people's names, addresses, phone numbers, email addresses, web pages, birthdays, anniversaries, nicknames, and other stuff besides. When you address an email, you can get it straight from the Contacts folder to be sure that the address is entered correctly.

This short but happy chapter explains how to maintain a tried-and-true Contacts folder, enter information about people in the folder, create contact groups to make sending the same message to many people easier, find a missing contact, and print the information in the Contacts folder.

To open the Contacts folder, click the People navigation button or click the Contacts folder in the Folders pane.

Maintaining a Happy and Healthy Contacts Folder

A Contacts folder is only as good and as thorough as the information about contacts that you put into it. These pages explain how to enter information about a contact and update the information if it happens to change.

Entering a new contact in the Contacts folder

To place someone in the Contacts List, open the Contacts folder and start by doing one of the following:

- ✦ On the Home tab, click the New Contact button (or click the New Items button and choose Contact on the drop-down list).
- ✦ Press Ctrl+N (in the Contacts window) or Ctrl+Shift+C (in another window).

You see the Contact form, as shown in Figure 2-1. In this form are places for entering just about everything there is to know about a person except his or her favorite ice cream flavor. Enter all the information you care to record, keeping in mind these rules of the road as you go along:

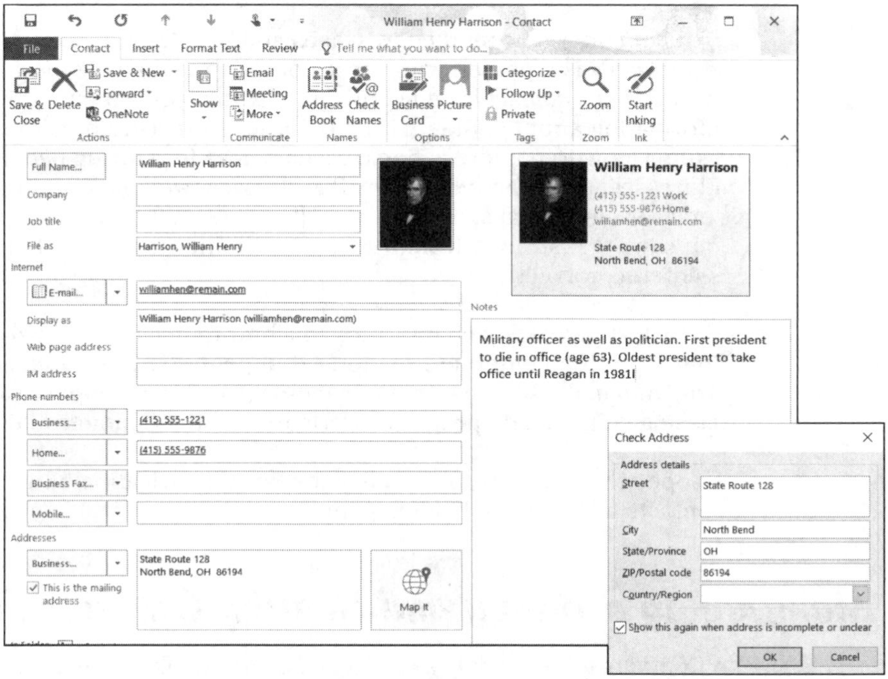

Figure 2-1: A Contact form.

- ✦ **Full names, addresses, and so on:** Although you may be tempted to simply enter addresses, phone numbers, names, and so on in the text boxes, don't do it! Click the Full Name button, for example, to enter a name (see Figure 2-1). Click the Business or Home button to enter an address in the Check Address dialog box (see Figure 2-1). By clicking these buttons and entering data in dialog boxes, you permit Outlook to separate the component parts of names, addresses, and phone numbers. As such, Outlook can use names and addresses as a source for mass mailings and mass emailings.

When entering information about a company, not a person, leave the Full Name field blank and enter the company's name in the Company field.

- **Information that matters to you:** If the form doesn't appear to have a place for entering a certain kind of information, try clicking a triangle button and choosing a new information category from the pop-up menu. Click the triangle button next to the Business button and choose Home, for example, if you want to enter a home address rather than a business address.
- **File As:** Open the File As drop-down list and choose an option for filing the contact in the Contacts folder. Contacts are filed alphabetically by last name, first name, company name, or combinations of the three. Choose the option that best describes how you expect to find the contact in the Contacts folder.
- **Mailing addresses:** If you keep more than one address for a contact, display the address to which you want to send mail and select the This Is the Mailing Address check box. This way, in a mass mailing, letters are sent to the correct address.
- **Email addresses:** You can enter up to three email addresses for each contact. (Click the triangle button next to the Email button and choose Email 2 or Email 3 to enter a second or third address.) In the Display As text box, Outlook shows you what the To: line of email messages looks like when you send email to a contact. By default, the To: line shows the contact's name followed by his or her email address in parentheses. However, you can enter whatever you wish in the Display As text box, and if entering something different helps you distinguish between email addresses, enter something different. For example, enter Lydia – Personal so that you can tell when you send email to Lydia's personal address as opposed to her business address.
- **Photos:** To put a digital photo in a Contact form, click the Add Contact Picture placeholder, and in the Add Contact Picture dialog box, select a picture and click OK.
- **Details:** To keep a detailed dossier on a contact, click the Details button (you may have to click the Show button first, depending on the size of your Contact form) and enter information in the Details window. This window offers places for recording birthdays and other minutia.

Be sure to write a few words in the Notes box to describe how and where you met the contact. When the time comes to weed out contacts in the Contacts folder list, reading these descriptions helps you decide who gets weeded and who doesn't.

When you finish entering information, click the Save & Close button. If you're in a hurry to enter contacts, click the Save & New button. Doing so opens an empty form so that you can record information about another contact.

Want to add the name of someone who sent you an email message to the Contacts folder? Right-click the sender's name in the message window and choose Add to Outlook Contacts on the shortcut menu.

Changing a contact's information

Outlook offers a simple and comprehensive way to change a contact's information. No matter which path you take, start by going to the Home tab. From there, choose People as the Current View to make simple changes or one of the other views to make comprehensive changes to a contact:

- In People view, double-click a contact name to open the Edit window, as shown in Figure 2-2. Make your changes in the Edit window and click the Save button.
- In Business Card, Card, Phone, or List view, double-click the contact's name to open the Contact window. Click the Save & Close button after making your changes. While you're in the Contact window, try clicking the All Fields button and entering information in the All Fields window, as shown in Figure 2-2. The All Fields window lists fields in a line-by-line fashion. Choose an option on the Select From drop-down list, scroll in the form, and update fields as necessary.

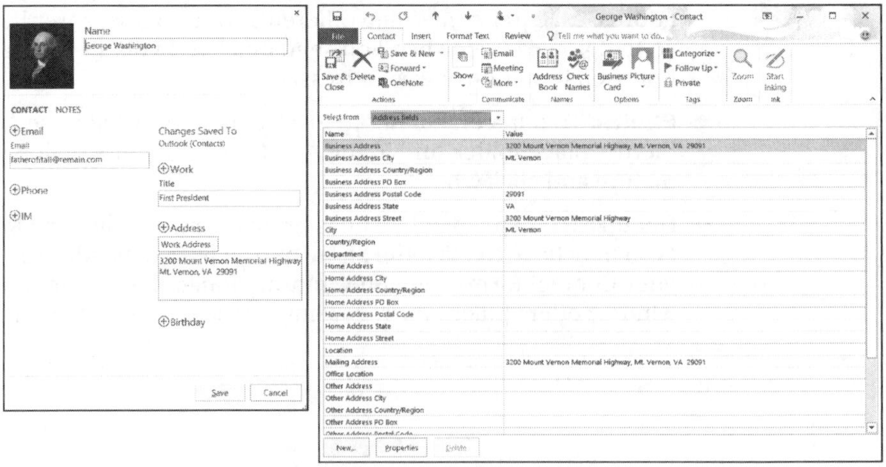

Figure 2-2: Editing contact data in the Edit window (left) and the All Fields window (right).

Mapping out an address

To find your way to a contact's home or place of business, click the Map It button in the Contact window. As long as your computer is connected to the Internet and an address is on file for the contact, your web browser opens to the Bing.com website, where you find a map with the address at its center. You can get driving directions from this map. Good luck getting there!

Contact Groups for Sending Messages to Groups

The captain of the volleyball team and the secretary of the PTA are examples of people who have to send email messages to the same group of people on a regular basis. You might be in the same boat. You might have to send email messages to the same 10 or 12 people from time to time. Entering email addresses for that many people each time you want to send email is a drag. To keep from having to enter so many email addresses, you can create a *contact group*, a list with multiple email addresses. To address your email message, you simply enter the name of the contact group, not the individual names, as shown in Figure 2-3.

Creating a contact group

Follow these steps to bundle email addresses into a contact group:

1. **On the Home tab, click the New Contact Group button (or press Ctrl+Shift+L).**

   You see the Contact Group window, as shown in Figure 2-4.

2. **Enter a descriptive name in the Name text box.**
3. **Click the Add Members button and choose an option on the drop-down list to tell Outlook where you store the addresses of friends and colleagues.**

   If you're a loyal user of Outlook, you likely choose From Outlook Contacts. You see the Select Members dialog box.

4. **Hold down the Ctrl key and select the name of each person you want to include in the contact group.**
5. **Click the Members button and click OK.**

   You can find the Members button in the lower-left corner of the dialog box. The names you chose appear in the Contact Group window.

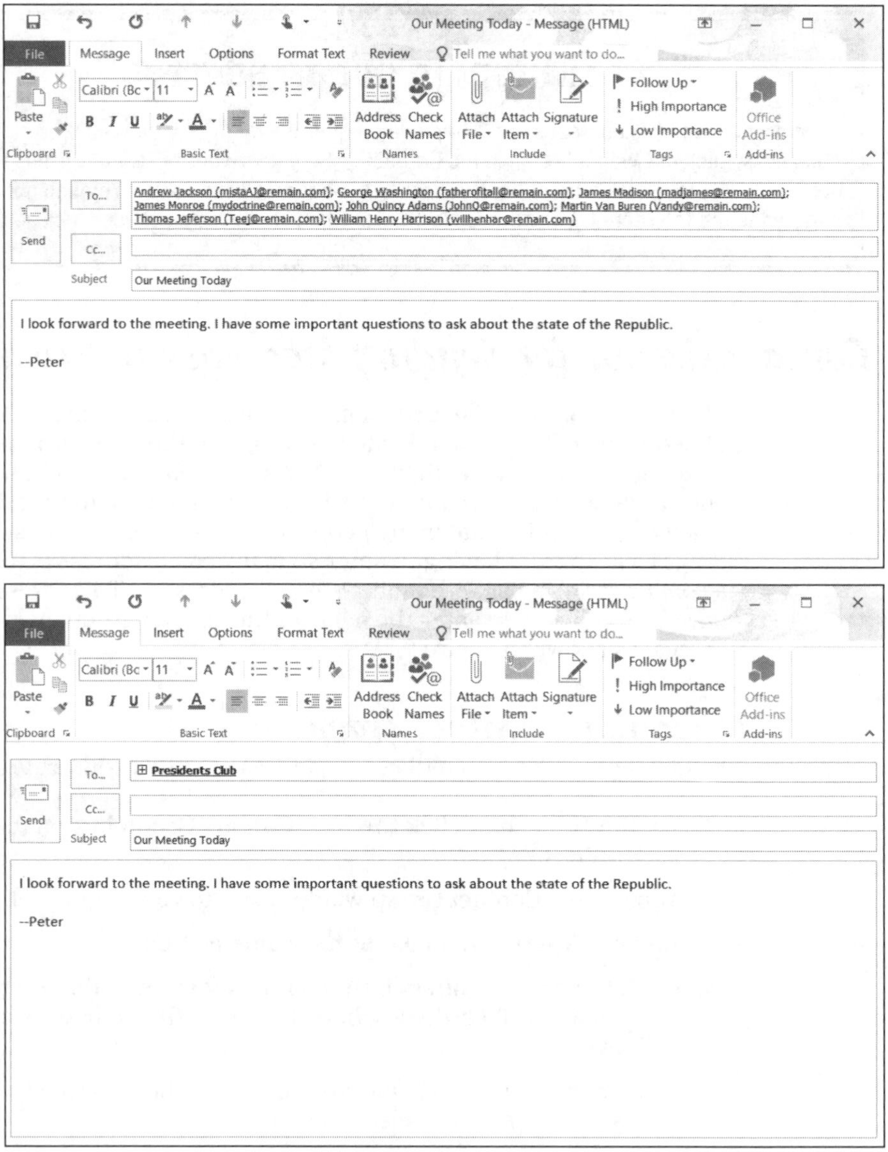

Figure 2-3: Instead of entering many addresses (top), enter a contact group name (bottom).

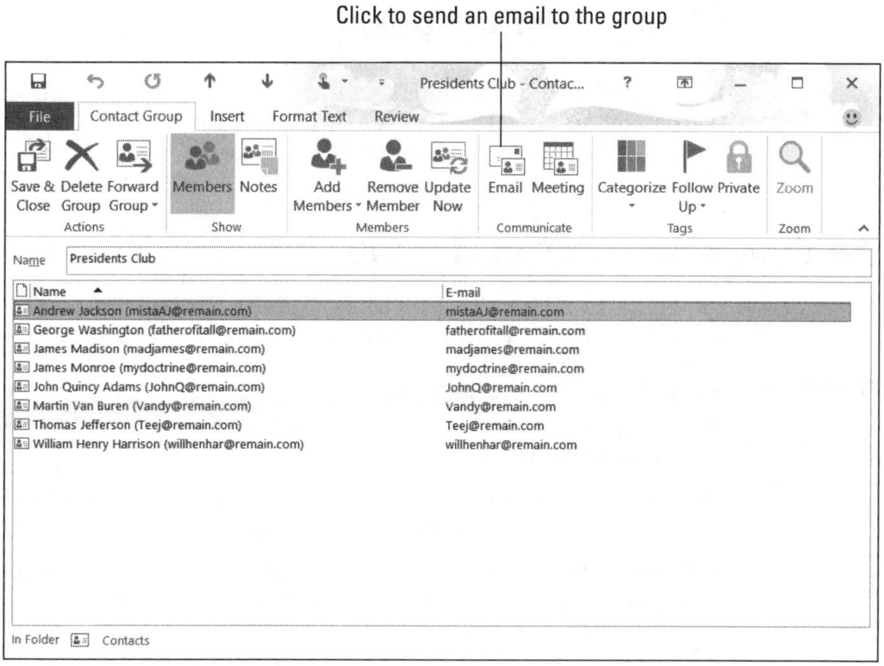

Figure 2-4: Entering addresses for a contact group.

You can add the names of people who aren't in your Contacts folder by clicking the Add Members button, choosing New Email Contact on the drop-down list, and filling out the Add New Member dialog box.

6. **Click the Save & Close button in the Contact Group window.**

   In the Contacts folder, contact group names and are marked with the Contact group icon.

Addressing email to a contact group

To address an email message to a contact group, start in the Inbox folder and click the New Email button. A Message window opens. Click the To button to open the Select Names dialog box and then select a contact group name. Contact group names appear in boldface and are marked with a Contact Group icon.

TIP

The fastest way to address email to a contact group is to start in the Contacts folder, double-click the group's name to open Group window (refer to Figure 2-4), and then click the Email button.

Editing a contact group

The names of contact groups appear in the Contacts folder, You can treat the groups like other contacts. In the Contacts folder, double-click a contact group name to open the Contact Group window (refer to Figure 2-4). From there, you can add names to and remove names from the group.

Finding a Contact in the Contacts Folder

The Contacts folder can grow very large, so Outlook offers a number of ways to locate contacts. Here are some techniques for locating a contact in the Contacts folder:

- **Use the scrollbar:** Click the arrows or drag the scroll box to move through the list.
- **Click a letter button:** Click a letter button on the left side of the window to move in the list to names beginning with a specific letter.
- **Change views:** On the Home tab, go to the Current View gallery and choose a view option: People, Business Card, Card, Phone, or List. Changing views often helps in a search.
- **Search Contacts text box:** Enter a keyword in the Search Contacts text box (see Chapter 1 of this mini-book for instructions about searching for items in folders).

Printing the Contacts Folder

The paperless office hasn't arrived yet in spite of numerous predictions to the contrary, and sometimes it's necessary to print the Contacts folder on old-fashioned paper. For times like these, I hereby explain the different ways to print the Contacts folder and how to fiddle with the look of the printed pages.

To print information about a single contact, double-click his or her name to open the Contact window. Then press Ctrl+P, and in the Print window, click the Print button.

Different ways to print contact information

Follow these steps to print information about contacts in the Contacts folder:

1. **On the Home tab, open the Current View gallery and choose a view.**

   Which printing options you get when you print information from the Contacts folder depends on which view of the Contacts folder is showing when you give the command to print:

- If you start in People, Business Card, or Card view, you can print Contacts information in these styles: card style, booklet style, memo style, or phone directory style (you find out what these styles are shortly).
- If you start in Phone or List view, you can print only in table style.

2. **Press Ctrl+P.**

   You see the Print window, as shown in Figure 2-5.

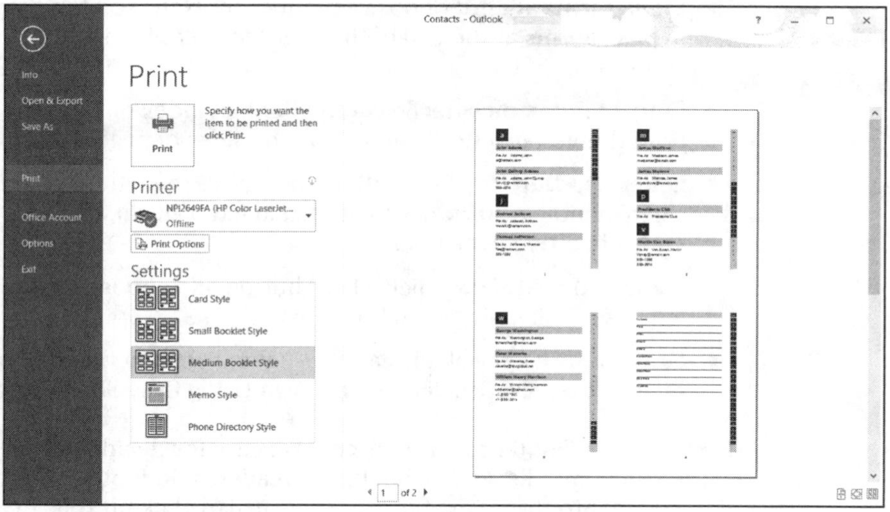

Figure 2-5: Printing contact information.

3. **Under Settings, choose an option.**

   Glance at the right side of the window to see what the option choices are and choose the option that suits you best.

4. **Click the Print Options button if you want to change the number of columns that are printed, change fonts, change headers and footers, or otherwise fiddle with the printed pages.**

   The next section in this chapter explains these options.

5. **Click the Print button to start printing.**

Changing the look of printed pages

To determine what Contact folder information looks like when you print it, click the Print Options button in the Print window (refer to Figure 2-5). You see the Print dialog box. In this dialog box, click the Page Setup button and choose options on the Format tab of the Page Setup dialog box to change the look of the printed pages:

- **Where contact information is printed:** Contact information is printed alphabetically with a letter heading to mark where the As, Bs, Cs, and so on begin. To place contacts that begin with each letter on separate pages, select the Start on a New Page option button.
- **Number of columns:** Choose a number in the Number of Columns drop-down list to tell Outlook how many columns you want.
- **Blank forms at end:** Choose a number (or None) on the drop-down menu to place forms at the end of the pages for people to write down more addresses.
- **Contact index on side:** Select the Contact Index on Side check box to print thumbnail letter headings on the sides of pages.
- **Letter headings for each letter:** To remove the letter headings that mark where contacts starting with a certain letter begin, deselect the Headings for Each letter check box.
- **Fonts and font sizes:** Click a Font button and choose a different font or font size for headings and body text.
- **Gray shades:** Gray shades appear behind contact names, but you can remove them by deselecting the Print Using Gray Shading check box.

In the Header/Footer tab, the three boxes are for deciding what appears on the left side, middle, and right side of headers and footers. Type whatever you please into these text boxes. You can also click buttons in the dialog box to enter fields — a page number, total page number, printing date, printing time, or your name — in headers and footers.

Chapter 3: Handling Your Email

In This Chapter

- Configuring an email account for Outlook
- Addressing, sending, replying to, and forwarding email messages
- Sending files and pictures with email
- Receiving email and files over the Internet
- Organizing and managing your email
- Creating and using different folders to store email
- Preventing junk email

"Neither snow nor rain nor heat nor gloom of night stays these couriers from the swift completion of their appointed rounds," reads the inscription on the Eighth Avenue New York Post Office Building. Emailers face a different set of difficulties. Instead of snow, rain, or gloomy nights, they face the task of having to manage volumes of email.

This chapter explains the basics of sending and receiving email, but it also goes a step further to help you organize and manage your email messages. It shows you how to send files and pictures with email messages. You also find out how to reorganize email in the Inbox window and be alerted to incoming messages from certain people or from people writing about certain subjects. This chapter shows you how to create folders for storing email and explains how to prevent junk email from arriving on your digital doorstep.

Setting Up an Email Account

Before you can send and receive email, you must provide Outlook with connection information about your email service. Outlook needs your name, your email address, and the password with which you log on to the email service.

Follow these steps to configure an email account with Outlook:

1. **On the File tab, choose Info.**

   The Account Information window opens.

2. **Click the Add Account button.**

   You see the Add Account dialog box.

3. **Provide your name, address, and password; and click Next.**

4. **Click the Finish button when Outlook finishes configuring your email account.**

If Outlook can't configure your account, you are asked to configure the account manually. To do so, you likely need the following, which you can obtain by seeking help online from your email service provider:

- *POP (post office protocol),* the protocol for retrieving messages from your email provider's incoming mail server. Outlook needs an IP address or domain name system (DNS) name, something like *inbound.att.net.*
- *SMPT (simple mail transfer protocol),* the protocol for sending messages through your provider's outgoing mail server. Outlook needs an IP address or DNS name, something like *outbound.attn.net.*

You can configure Outlook to send and retrieve email from more than one account. For each email account you configure, Outlook places a new folder profile in the Folder pane.

To delete an email account, go to the File tab and choose Info. Then click the Account Settings button and choose Account Settings on the drop-down list. In the Account Settings dialog box, select the account and click the Remove button.

Addressing and Sending Email Messages

Sadly, you can't send chocolates or locks of hair by email, but you can send digital pictures and computer files. These pages explain how to do it. You also discover how to send copies and blind copies of email messages, reply to and forward email, send email from different accounts, and postpone sending a message. Better keep reading.

The basics: Sending an email message

The first half of this chapter addresses everything you need to know about sending email messages. Here are the basics:

1. **In any mail folder, click the New Email button on the Home tab (or press Ctrl+N).**

A Message window like the one in Figure 3-1 appears. You can open this window in a folder apart from mail folders by clicking the New Items button and choosing Email Message on the drop-down list (or by pressing Ctrl+Shift+M). The New Items button is located on the Home tab.

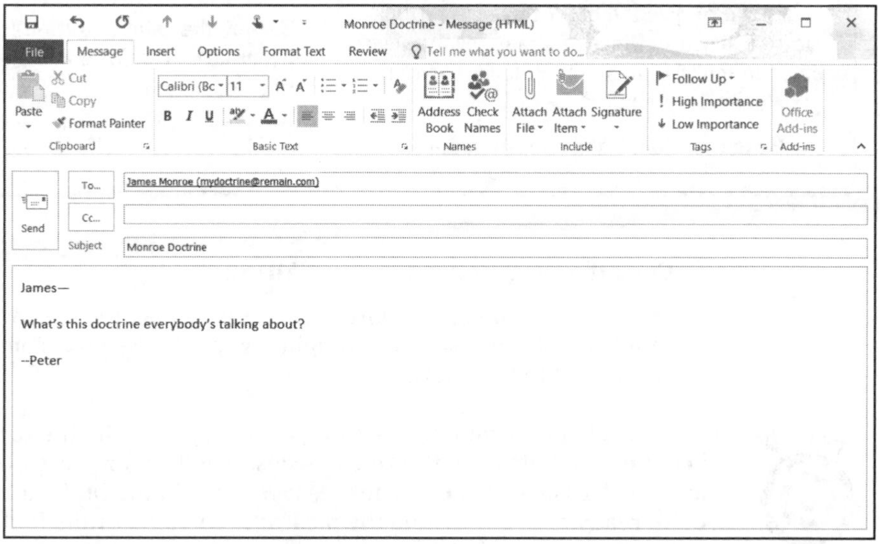

Figure 3-1: Addressing and composing an email message.

2. **Enter the recipient's email address in the To text box.**

   The next topic in this chapter, "Addressing an email message," explains the numerous ways to address an email message. You can address the same message to more than one person by entering more than one address in the To text box. For that matter, you can send copies of the message and blind copies of the message to others (see "Sending copies and blind copies of messages," later in this chapter).

3. **In the Subject text box, enter a descriptive title for the message.**

   When your message arrives on the other end, the recipient sees the subject first. Enter a descriptive subject that helps the recipient prioritize the message. After you enter the subject, it appears in the title bar of the Message window.

4. **Type the message.**

   Whatever you do, don't forget to enter the message itself! You can spell check your message by pressing F7 or clicking the Spelling & Grammar button on the Review tab.

Making Outlook your default email program

The default email program is the one that opens when you click an email hyperlink on a web page or give the order to send an Office file from inside an Office program. Follow these steps to make Outlook the default email program on your computer:

1. **Go to the File tab and choose Options.**
2. **In the Outlook Options dialog box, visit the General category.**
3. **Select the Make Outlook the Default Program for Email, Contacts, and Calendar check box.**
4. **Click OK.**

5. **Click the Send button (or press Alt+S).**

   Messages remain in the Outbox folder if you postpone sending them or if Outlook can't send them right away because your computer isn't connected to the Internet.

TIP: If you decide in the middle of writing a message to write the rest of it later, click the Save button on the Quick Access Toolbar (or press Ctrl+S) and close the Message window. The message lands in the Drafts folder. When you're ready to finish writing the message, open the Drafts folder and double-click your unfinished message to resume writing it.

Copies of the email messages you send are kept in the Sent Items folder, where you can review messages you sent.

Addressing an email message

How do you address an email message in the To text box of the Message window (refer to Figure 3-1)? Let me count the ways:

- **Type a person's name from the Contacts folder:** Simply type a person's name, as shown in Figure 3-2. If the name is on file in the Contacts folder, a drop-down menu with the name appears, and you can select the name on the drop-down menu.
- **Get the address (or addresses) from the Contacts folder:** Click the To (or Cc) button to send a message to someone whose name is on file in your Contacts folder. You see the Select Names dialog box, as shown in Figure 3-2. Click or Ctrl+click to select the names of people to whom you want to send the message. Then click the To-> button (or the Cc-> or Bcc-> button) to enter addresses in the To text box (or the Cc or Bcc text box) of the Message window. Click OK to return to the Message window. This is the easiest way to address an email message to several different people.

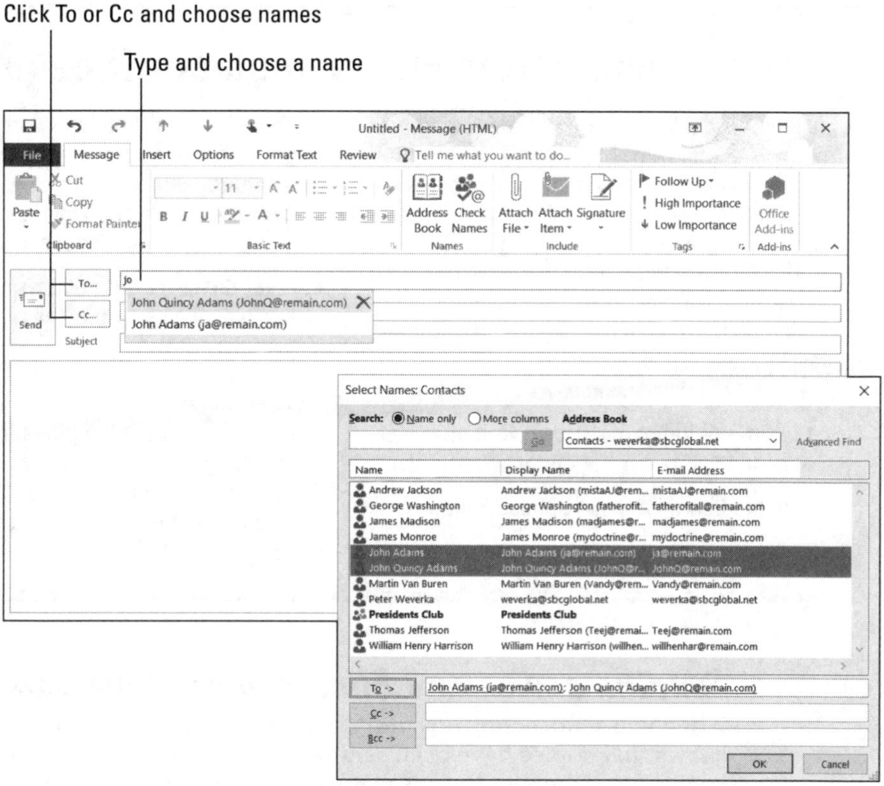

Figure 3-2: Getting addresses from the Contacts folder.

- **Type the address:** Type the address if you know it offhand. You can paste an address into the Message window by right-clicking and choosing the Paste command.
- **Reply to a message sent to you:** Select the message in the Inbox folder and click the Reply button. The Message window opens with the address of the person to whom you're replying already entered in the To text box. You can also click the Reply All button to reply to enter the email addresses of all the people to whom the original message was sent.

TIP

You can create contact groups for sending the same email message to a group of people without having to enter an address for each recipient. For information about contact groups, see Chapter 2 of this mini-book.

Sending email from inside another Office program

As long as Outlook is your default email program (I explain how to make it the default program earlier in this chapter), you can send email messages or file attachments from other Office programs without opening Outlook. If the Word document, Excel worksheet, PowerPoint presentation, or Publisher publication needs sending right away, save it and follow these steps to send it as a file attachment to an email message:

1. **With the file you want to send onscreen, go to the File tab and choose Share.**
2. **In the Share window, choose Email.**
3. **Choose a Send option.**

   These options differ from program to program. For example, you can send the file as an attachment to an email message or send it as a PDF file. The Message window appears after you choose a Send option.

4. **Enter the recipient's address in the To box and type a message in the Message box.**
5. **Click the Send button.**

   That was fast! It was faster than opening Outlook and attaching the file to the email message on your own. The message is sent right away if Outlook is running. Otherwise, the message is sent next time you open Outlook.

Sending copies and blind copies of messages

When you send a copy of a message, the person who receives the message knows that copies have been sent because the names of people to whom copies were sent appear at the top of the email message. But when you send blind copies, the person who receives the message doesn't know that others received it.

Follow these instructions to send copies and blind copies of messages:

- **Send a copy of a message:** Enter email addresses in the Cc text box of the Message window, or in the Select Names dialog box (refer to Figure 3-2), select names and then click the Cc->button.
- **Send a blind copy of a message:** Use one of these techniques:
  - On the Options tab of the Message window, click the Bcc button and then enter addresses in the Bcc text box.
  - Click the To or Cc button in the Message window to open the Select Names dialog box (refer to Figure 3-2), select names, and click the Bcc-> button or else enter addresses in the Bcc-> text box.

Why are these buttons called Cc and Bcc? The Cc stands for "carbon copy" and the Bcc stands for "blind carbon copy." These terms originated in the Mesozoic era when letters were composed on the typewriter, and to make a copy of a letter, you inserted carbon paper between two paper sheets and typed away.

Replying to and forwarding email messages

Replying to and forwarding messages is as easy as pie. For one thing, you don't need to know the recipient's email address to reply to a message. In the Inbox, select or open the message you want to reply to or forward and do the following on the Home tab, Message tab, or Reading pane:

- **Reply to author:** Click the Reply button (or press Ctrl+R). The Message window or Reading pane opens with the sender's name already entered in the To box and the original message in the text box below. Write a reply and click the Send button.
- **Reply to all parties who received the message:** Click the Reply All button (or press Ctrl+Shift+R). The Message window or Reading pane opens with the names of all parties who received the message in the To and Cc boxes and the original message in the text box. Type your reply and click the Send button.
- **Forward a message:** Click the Forward button (or press Ctrl+F). The Message window or Reading pane opens with the text of the original message. Either enter an email address in the To text box or click the To button to open the Select Names dialog box and then select the names of the parties to whom the message will be forwarded. Add a word or two to the original message if you like; then click the Send button.

  Forwarding a message to a third party without the permission of the original author is a breach of etiquette and very bad manners. I could tell you a story about an email message of mine that an unwitting editor forwarded to a cantankerous publisher, but I'm saving that story for the soap opera edition of this book.

To add a sender's name to the Contacts folder, right-click the name in the Message window and choose Add to Outlook Contacts.

Auto-replying to messages

An *auto-reply* (automatic reply) is a message sent automatically to everyone who sends you a message. An auto-reply goes something like this: "I'm on vacation till Tuesday and can't reply to your message. But as soon as I return, I'll reply to you." Use auto-replies to inform people that you aren't neglecting them, you just can't reply because you're in meetings, on vacation, or otherwise occupied.

Only people who run Outlook through a Microsoft Exchange server can send auto-replies. What this means in real terms is that only people whose computers are connected to a network can auto-reply to messages. Follow these steps to find out whether your Outlook account is run through a Microsoft Exchange server:

1. **On the File tab, choose Info to open the Account Information window.**
2. **Click the Account Settings button and choose Account Settings to open the Account Settings dialog box.**
3. **In the Type column, look for the words "Microsoft Exchange." If you see these words, you can send auto-replies to messages.**

Follow these steps to write an auto-reply and instruct Outlook to send it to all who send you messages:

1. **On the File tab, choose Info.**
2. **Choose Automatic Replies (Out of Office) to open the Automatic Replies dialog box.**
3. **Click the Send Automatic Replies check box.**
4. **Choose a start time and end time for sending auto-replies.**
5. **On the Inside My Organization tab, enter the auto-reply that you want to send to your co-workers.**
6. **On the Outside My Organization tab, enter the auto-reply you want to send people outside your network.**
7. **Click OK.**

Sending Files and Photos

Yes, it can be done. You can send files and photos along with your email messages. As long as you know where the file or photo is stored on your computer or OneDrive, you can send it lickety-split (Book X, Chapter 1 explains OneDrive).

Sending a file along with a message

Sending a file along with an email message is called *attaching* a file in Outlook lingo. You can send a file or several files along with an email message by following these steps:

1. **In the Message window, go to the Message or Insert tab and click the Attach File button.**

   A drop-down list appears with the names of files you sent recently. If the file you want to send is on the list, select its name and be done with it; if the file's name isn't on the list, keep reading.

2. **Choose Browse This PC (or if you keep files on OneDrive, choose Browse Web Locations and select OneDrive on the submenu).**

   You see the Insert File dialog box.

3. **Locate and select the file that you want to send along with your email message.**

   Ctrl+click filenames to select more than one file.

4. **Click the Insert button.**

   The name of the file (or files) appears in the Attached text box in the Message window. Address the message and type a note to send along with the file. You can open the drop-down menu on a filename in the Attach text box and choose Open to open a file you're about to send. Or, if you change your mind about sending the file, you can choose Remove Attachment.

TIP

Here's a fast way to attach a file to a message: Find the file in File Explorer and drag it into the Message window. The file's name appears in the Attach box as though you placed it there by clicking the Attach File button.

Including a photo in an email message

As shown in Figure 3-3, you can include a photo in the body of an email message. Follow these steps:

1. **In the Message window, go to the Insert tab.**

2. **Click in the body of the email message where you want the picture to go.**

3. **Click the Pictures button.**

   You see the Insert Picture dialog box. If the Pictures button is grayed out and you can't click it, go to the Format Text tab and click the Aa HTML button. Choosing Aa HTML as the format for email messages enables you to send photos in the body of email messages.

4. **Locate and select the digital picture you want to send; then click the Insert button.**

   The picture lands in the Message window. Book VIII, Chapter 3 explains how to manipulate graphic images in Outlook and the other Office applications.

Want to remove a picture from an email message? Select it and press the Delete key.

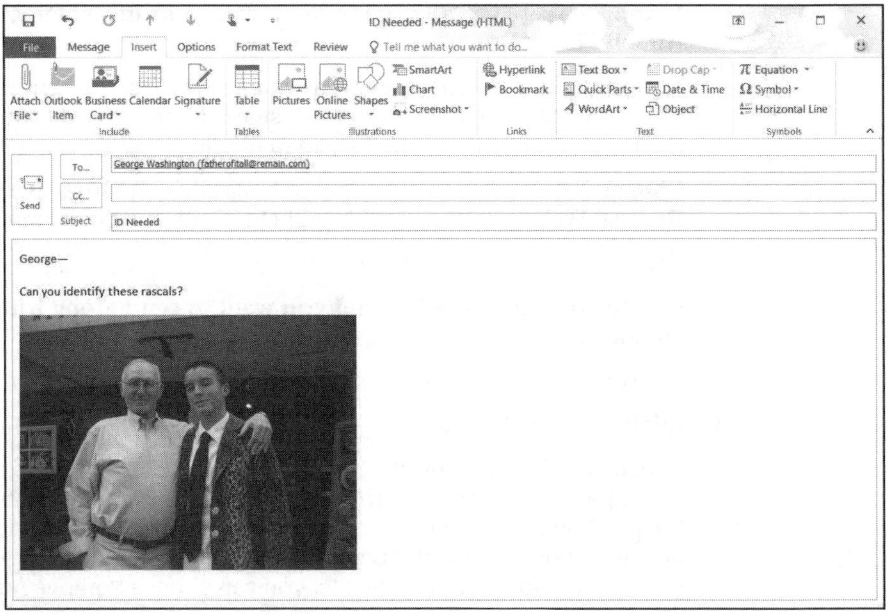

Figure 3-3: Inserting a photo in an email message.

Receiving Email Messages

Let's hope that all the email messages you receive carry good news. These pages explain how to collect your email and all the different ways that Outlook notifies you when email has arrived. You can find several tried-and-true techniques for reading email messages in the Inbox window. Outlook offers a bunch of different ways to rearrange the window as well as the messages inside it.

Getting your email

Starting in the Inbox folder on the Send/Receive tab, here are all the different ways to collect email messages that were sent to you:

- **Collect all email:** Click the Send/Receive All Folders button (or press F9). Mail is sent from and delivered to all your email accounts.
- **Collect mail for the Inbox folder only:** Click the Update Folder button (or press Shift+F9).
- **Send all unsent mail:** Click the Send All button.

✦ **Collect email from a single account (if you have more than one):** Click the Send/Receive Groups button, and on the drop-down list, choose the name of a group or an email account.

Being notified that email has arrived

Take the email arrival quiz. Winners get the displeasure of knowing that they understand far more than is healthy about Outlook. You can tell when email has arrived in the Inbox folder because

A) You hear this sound: *ding*.

B) The mouse cursor briefly changes to a little envelope.

C) A little envelope appears in the notification area to the left of the Windows clock. (You can double-click the envelope to open the Inbox folder.)

D) A pop-up *desktop alert* with the sender's name, the message's subject, and the text of the message appears briefly on your desktop.

E) All of the above.

The answer is E, "All of the above," but if four arrival notices strike you as excessive, you can eliminate one or two. On the File tab, choose Options, and in the Mail category of the Options dialog box, go the Message Arrival area and change the settings.

Reading Your Email in the Inbox Window

Messages arrive in the Inbox window, as shown in Figure 3-4. You can tell a thing or two about messages by glancing in the window:

✦ Unread messages are shown in boldface type.

✦ Messages that you've read (or at least opened to view) are shown in Roman type.

✦ In the Folder pane, a number beside a folder tells you how many unread messages are in those folders. (The number in square brackets beside the Drafts and Junk Email folders tells you how many items, read and unread, are in those folders.)

To read a message, select it and look in the Reading pane, or to focus more closely on a message, double-click it to open it in a Message window, as shown in Figure 3-4.

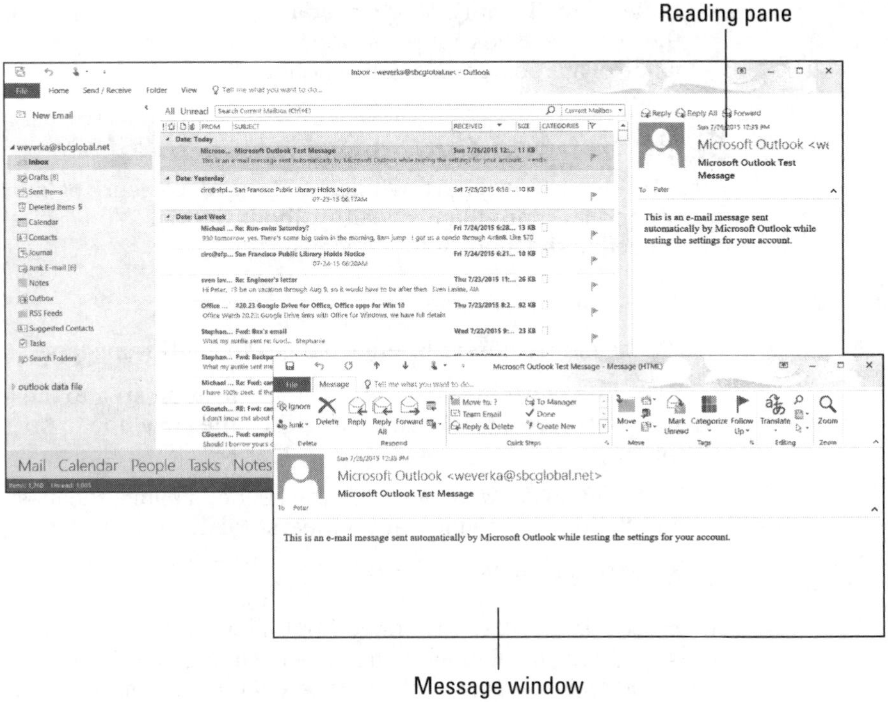

Figure 3-4: Reading a message in the Reading pane and Message window.

Later in this chapter, "Techniques for Organizing Email Messages," explains how to organize messages in the Inbox folder. Meanwhile, here are some simple techniques you can use on the View tab to unclutter the Inbox folder and make messages easier to read:

- **Changing your view of messages:** Click the Change View button and choose Compact, Single, or Preview on the drop-down list. Compact and Single display more messages onscreen. In Preview view, the first two lines of unread messages appear so that you can read them.
- **Rearranging messages:** In the Arrangement gallery, choose an option. For example, choose Date to arrange messages according to the date and time they were received. Choose From to arrange messages by sender name in alphabetical order. Click the Reverse Sort button to reverse the way the messages are arranged.
- **Hiding and displaying the Reading pane:** Click the Reading Pane button and choose Off, Right, or Bottom on the drop-down list to make the Reading pane appear or disappear. The Reading pane gives you an opportunity to read messages without opening them in a Message window.

  The Reading pane offers a Reply, Reply All, and Forward button for quickly replying to and forwarding email messages.

+ **Hiding and displaying the Folder pane:** Click the Folder Pane button and choose Normal or Minimized (or press Alt+F1 or click the Minimize the Folder Pane button on the Folder pane itself). By hiding the Folder pane, you get even more room to display messages.

Suppose you open an email message but you regret doing so because you want the unopened envelope icon to appear beside the message's name. In other words, you want to handle the message later on. To make a message in the Inbox window appear as if it has never been opened, right-click it and choose Mark As Unread.

Handling Files That Were Sent to You

You can tell when someone sends you files along with an email message because the paper clip icon appears in the Attachment column of the Inbox window (if column headings are displayed). Moreover, the name of the file or files appears in the Reading pane (if the Reading pane is open). When you double-click to open the message in a window, the names of files sent to you appear across the top of the message window, as shown in Figure 3-5.

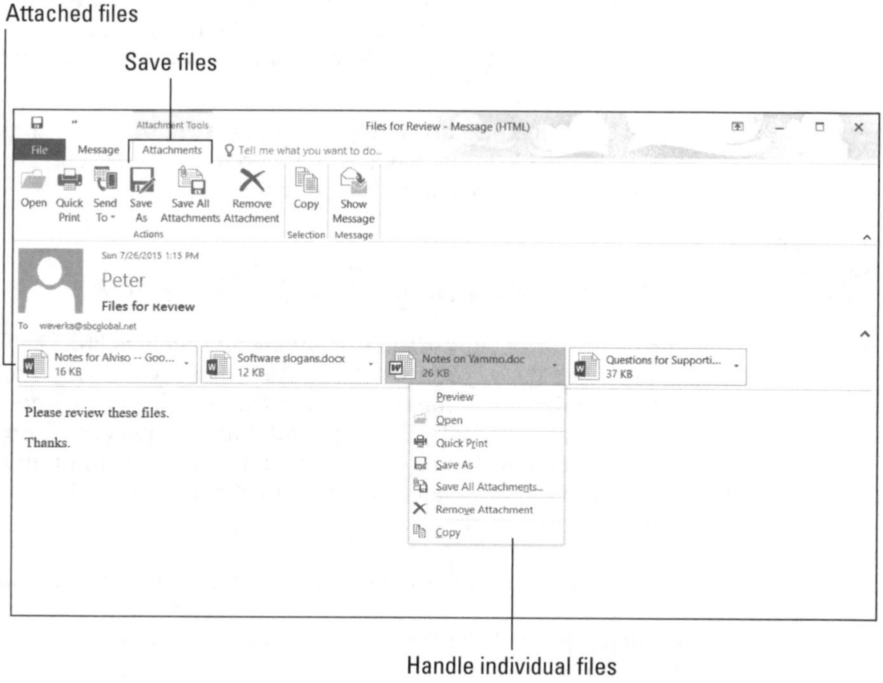

Figure 3-5: Receiving a file.

Opening a file you received

Follow these instructions to open a file that was sent to you:

- ✦ Double-click the filename.
- ✦ Click to select the filename, and on the (Attachment Tools) Attachments tab, click the Open button.
- ✦ Open the drop-down menu on the filename and choose Open on the shortcut menu (see Figure 3-5).

As long as the file being sent to you is a Word, PowerPoint, Excel, or Publisher file, you can preview it inside the Message window or Reading pane. To do so, click the filename (or choose Preview on the file's drop-down menu). Click Back to Message to see the message again, not the file preview.

Saving a file you received

Follow these instructions to save a file that was sent to you in a folder of your choice:

- ✦ Click to select the filename, and on the (Attachment Tools) Attachments tab, click the Save As button and save the file using the Save Attachment dialog box. Click the Save All Attachments button to save more than one file.
- ✦ Open the filename's drop-down menu (see Figure 3-5), choose Save As, and save the file in the Save Attachment dialog box. Choose Save All Attachments to save more than one file.

Techniques for Organizing Email Messages

If you're one of those unfortunate souls who receives 20, 30, 40 or more email messages daily, you owe it to yourself and your sanity to figure out a way to organize email messages such that you keep the ones you want, you can find email messages easily, and you can quickly eradicate the email messages that don't matter to you. Outlook offers numerous ways to manage and organize email messages. Pick and choose the techniques that work for you.

In a nutshell, here are all the techniques for organizing email messages:

- ✦ **Change views in the Inbox window:** On the View tab, click the Change View button and choose a view. Earlier in this chapter, "Reading Your Email in the Inbox Window" explains all the ways to change views.

- **Delete the messages that you don't need:** Before they clutter the Inbox, delete messages that you're sure you don't need as soon as you get them. To delete a message, select it and click the Delete button on the Home tab, press the Delete key, or right-click and choose Delete.
- **Move messages to different folders:** Create a folder for each project you're involved with, and when an email message about a project arrives, move it to a folder. See "All about Email Folders," later in this chapter.
- **Move messages automatically to different folders as they arrive:** Instead of moving messages yourself after they arrive, you can tell Outlook to move messages automatically to different folders. See "Rules for earmarking messages as they arrive," later in this chapter.
- **Destroy junk mail as it arrives:** You can delete junk mail automatically. See "Yes, You Can Prevent Junk Mail (Sort Of)," later in this chapter.
- **Ignore messages from pesky senders:** On the Home tab, select a message and click the Ignore button to prevent messages from a sender from appearing in the Inbox. Ignored messages go straight to the Deleted Items folder.
- **Flag messages:** Flag a message with a color-coded flag to let you know to follow up on it. See "Flagging email messages," the next section in this chapter.
- **Categorize messages:** Assign email messages to categories; then, arrange email messages by category in the Inbox window. See Chapter 1 of this mini-book for info about categorizing items in a folder.
- **Have Outlook remind you to reply to a message:** Instruct Outlook to make the Reminder message box appear at a date and time in the future so that you know to reply to a message. See "Being reminded to take care of email messages," later in this chapter.
- **Make liberal use of the Search commands:** You can always find a stray message with the Search commands. (See Chapter 1 of this mini-book to know more about searching for items in folders.)
- **Archive messages you no longer need:** Archiving is a good way to strip the Inbox folder of items that you don't need. See Chapter 1 of this mini-book for more about archiving.
- **Use the Mailbox Cleanup command:** This handy command archives messages, deletes them, and deletes alternative versions of messages. See Chapter 1 of this mini-book for more about the Mailbox Cleanup command.

Flagging email messages

One way to call attention to email messages is to flag them with a color-coded flag. You can use red flags, for example, to mark urgent messages and green flags to mark not-so-important ones. After you flag a message, you can arrange messages by their flag status in the Inbox folder. Follow these instructions to flag an email message:

- **Starting in the Message window:** Click the Follow Up button and choose a flag on the drop-down list, as shown in Figure 3-6.
- **Starting in the Inbox folder:** Select the message, and on the Home tab, click the Follow Up button and choose a flag. You can also right-click, choose Follow Up, and choose a flag.

To "unflag" a message, click the Follow Up button and choose Clear Flag, or right-click and choose Clear Flag. You can also choose Mark Complete to put a checkmark where the flag used to be and remind yourself that you're done with the message. Later in this chapter, "Rules for earmarking messages as they arrive" explains how you can flag messages automatically as they arrive.

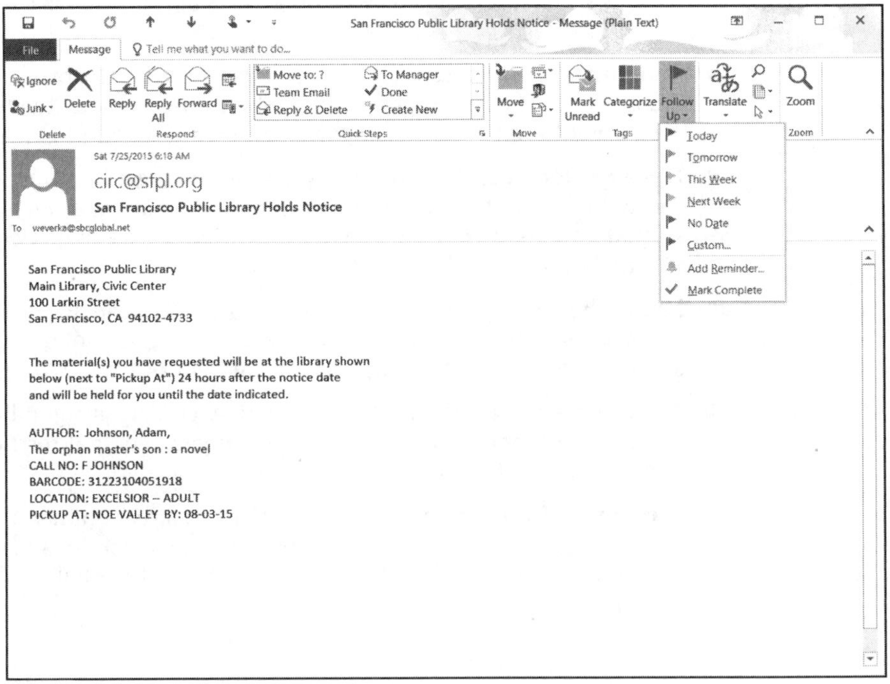

Figure 3-6: Flagging a message in the Message window.

Being reminded to take care of email messages

If you know your way around the Calendar and Tasks windows, you know that the Reminder message box appears when an appointment or meeting is about to take place or a task deadline is about to arrive. What you probably don't know, however, is that you can put the Reminders dialog box to work in regard to email messages by following these steps:

1. **Select the message.**
2. **Click the Follow Up button and choose Add Reminder.**

   You see the Custom dialog box, as shown in Figure 3-7. You can also right-click a message and choose Follow Up ➪ Add Reminder to see the dialog box.

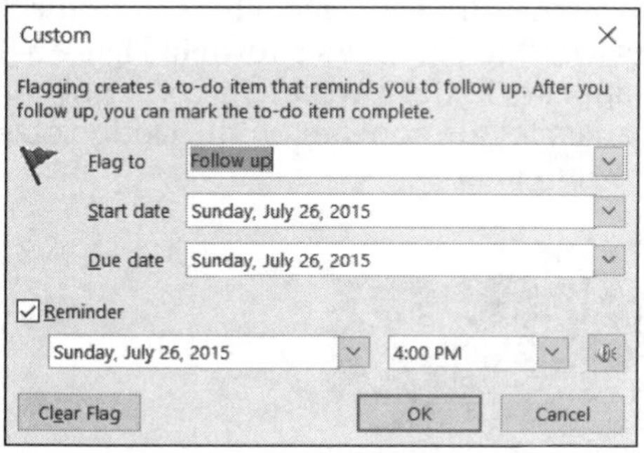

Figure 3-7: Reminding yourself to take care of an email message.

3. **On the Flag To drop-down list, choose an option that describes why the email message needs your attention later, or if none of the options suits you, enter a description in the Flag To text box.**

   The description you choose or enter will appear above the message in the Reading pane and message window, as well in the Reminder message box.
4. **In the Due Date drop-down list, choose when you want the Reminder message box to appear.**

   As Chapter 5 explains in detail, the Reminder message box appears 15 minutes before the default due date time.
5. **Click OK.**

   When the reminder falls due, you see the Reminder message box, where you can double-click the name of the email message to open it. See Chapter 5 of this mini-book if you need to find out how the Reminder message box works.

Rules for earmarking messages as they arrive

To help you organize messages better, Outlook gives you the opportunity to earmark messages in various ways and even move messages as they arrive automatically to folders apart from the Inbox folder. Being able to move messages immediately to a folder is a great way to keep email concerning different projects separate. If you belong to a newsgroup that sends many messages per day, being able to move those messages instantly into their own folder is a real blessing because newsgroup messages have a habit of cluttering the Inbox folder.

To earmark messages for special treatment, Outlook has you create so-called rules. You can create a rule to:

✦ Move email from a particular person automatically to a folder.

✦ Be alerted when email arrives from a certain person or the Subject line of a message includes a certain word. As shown in Figure 3-8, a New Item Alerts message appears in the lower-right corner of your screen to alert you. Moreover, an envelope appears on the Outlook taskbar icon to remind you to check your email.

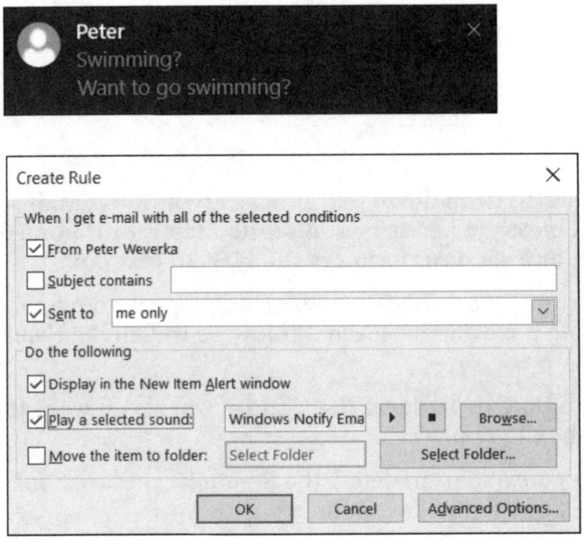

Figure 3-8: A New Item Alerts message (top) and the Create Rule dialog box (bottom).

Follow these instructions to create a rule so that incoming email messages are given special treatment:

1. **Select an email message from a person whose messages require a rule.**

   You can skip this step if your goal is to create a rule for messages that contain a certain word in the Subject line.

2. **On the Home tab, click the Rules button.**

3. **Choose an option on the drop-down list.**

   Choose an option to move messages to a folder or be alerted about messages.

   - *Automatically move messages from this person to a folder:* Choose Always Move Messages From, and in the Rules and Alerts dialog box, select a folder. (Later in this chapter, "Creating a new folder for storing email" explains how to create a folder of your own.")
   - *Be alerted about messages:* Choose Create Rule. You see the Create Rule dialog box shown in Figure 3-8. Fill in the dialog box and click OK.

TIP

To change or delete a rule, click the Rules button and choose Manage Rules & Alerts. On the Email Rules tab of the Rules and Alerts dialog box, select a rule and change, copy, or delete it.

All about Email Folders

Where Outlook email is concerned, everything has its place and everything has its folder. Email messages land in the Inbox folder when they arrive. Messages you write go to the Outbox folder until you send them. Copies of email messages you send are kept in the Sent Items folder. And you can create folders of your own for storing email.

If you're one of those unlucky people who receive numerous email messages each day, you owe it to yourself to create folders in which to organize email messages. Create one folder for each project you're working on. That way, you know where to find email messages when you want to reply to or delete them. These pages explain how to move email messages between folders and create folders of your own for storing email.

Moving email messages to different folders

Open or select the message you want to move and use one of these techniques to move an email message to a different folder:

✦ On the Home tab or a Message window, click the Move button and choose a folder name on the drop-down list. If the folder's name isn't on the list, choose Other Folder and select a folder in the Move Item To dialog box.

- ✦ Right-click, choose Move, and select a folder name or choose Other Folder and select a folder in the Move Item To dialog box.
- ✦ Display the folder you want to receive the message in the Folder pane. Then drag the message from the Inbox to the folder in the Folder pane.

Earlier in this chapter, "Rules for earmarking messages as they arrive" explains how to move email messages automatically to folders as email is sent to you.

Creating a new folder for storing email

Follow these steps to create a new folder:

1. **On the Folder tab, click the New Folder button.**

   You see the Create New Folder dialog box, as shown in Figure 3-9. You can also open this dialog box by pressing Ctrl+Shift+E or right-clicking a folder in the Folder list and choosing New Folder.

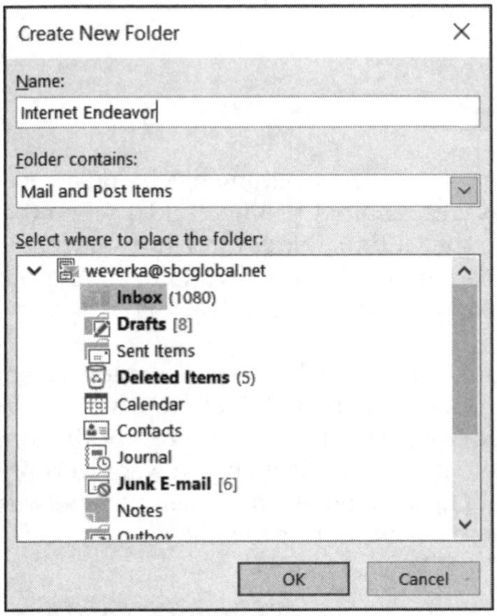

Figure 3-9: Creating a new folder.

2. **Select the folder that the new folder will go inside.**

   To create a first-level folder, select Personal Folders (or the name of the topmost folder in the hierarchy).

3. **Enter a name for the folder.**
4. **Click OK.**

To delete a folder you created, open it, go to the Folder tab, and click the Delete Folder button. Items in the folder are deleted along with the folder itself. To rename a folder, open it, go to the Folder tab, click the Rename Folder button, and enter a new name.

Yes, You Can Prevent Junk Mail (Sort of)

Outlook maintains a folder called Junk E-mail especially for storing junk email, or *spam* as the digital variety is sometimes called. Email messages with certain words or phrases in the Subject line — *for free!*, *money-back guarantee*, *order now* — are routed automatically to the Junk E-mail folder, where they needn't bother you. What's more, you can add senders' names to the Blocked Senders list and route mail from those senders straight into the Junk Email folder.

WARNING!

As nice as it is, the Junk E-mail folder has one fatal flaw — sometimes a legitimate email message finds its way into the folder. From time to time, you have to look in the Junk E-mail folder to see whether something of value is in there — and that sort of defeats the purpose of routing messages automatically to the Junk E-mail folder. You still have to look through all that junk email!

Realistically, the only way to prevent getting junk email is to safeguard your email address. These pages explain how to help stamp out junk mail in your lifetime by using features inside Outlook and taking preventative measures.

Defining what constitutes junk email

Outlook maintains a *Safe Senders* and *Blocked Senders list* to help distinguish email from junk email. To help Outlook recognize junk email and route it to the Junk Email folder, you can take these measures to add addresses to the lists:

- **Add a sender to the Safe Senders list:** Senders on this list are deemed legitimate, and their email messages are always routed to the Inbox folder. In the Message window or Home tab of a mail folder, click the Junk button and choose Never Block Sender. Choose this option if you find a legitimate email message in the Junk E-mail folder.
- **Add an address to the Blocked Senders list:** Email from senders on the Blocked Senders list goes straight to the Junk E-mail folder. In the Message window or Home tab of a mail folder, click the Junk button and choose Block Sender.

- **Editing the Safe Senders and Blocked Senders lists:** Click the Junk button and choose Junk E-mail Options. The Junk E-mail Options dialog box opens. On the Safe Senders and Blocked Senders tab, select email addresses as necessary, and click the Remove button.

To quickly move an email message from the Junk E-mail folder to the Inbox folder, click the Junk button and choose Not Junk on the drop-down list. The Mark As Not Junk dialog box appears. Click the Always Trust E-mail From check box and click OK.

Preventative medicine for junk email

TIP

As zealous as Outlook is about preventing junk email, the program can't really do the job. Junk emailers change addresses frequently. They are clever about putting words in the subject lines of their messages so that the messages aren't recognized as spam. The only foolproof way to keep your email address free of junk email is to follow these suggestions:

- **Use a secondary email address:** Create a secondary email account and give its email address to businesses and merchants on the Internet who might sell your address to spammers or might themselves be spammers. The Internet offers many places to create free web-based email accounts. For example, check out Gmail (`http://gmail.google.com`) and Yahoo! Mail (`http://mail.yahoo.com`). Never give your primary email address to strangers.
- **Don't reply to spam:** Don't reply to junk email messages under any circumstances. By replying, all you do is alert the spammer to the fact that your email address is legitimate, and that makes you a target of even more spam.
- **Don't unsubscribe to junk email messages:** Some spam messages contain an Unsubscribe link that you can click to prevent more messages from coming. The links are a ruse. All you do by clicking them is make spammers aware that your email address is live and therefore, worth targeting with more spam.
- **Don't buy anything advertised by spam:** Even if the message is selling what looks to be a terrific bargain, resist the temptation. By buying, you expose yourself to all the risks of replying to junk email.
- **Be careful where (and how) you post your email address:** Spammers gather email addresses from the Internet. They get the addresses from web pages, newsgroups, chat rooms, and message boards. Harvestware, a variety of spamware, can scour the Internet for the tell-tale at symbol (@) found in email addresses and copy those addresses back to a spammer's computer. If you have to post your email address on the Internet, get around the problem by putting blank spaces between the letters in your address, or spell out the address like so:

  ```
  johndoe at earthlink dot net
  ```

Chapter 4: Managing Your Time and Schedule

In This Chapter

- **Understanding how the Calendar works**
- **Going to different dates in the Calendar**
- **Scheduling appointments and events**
- **Rescheduling an activity**
- **Getting different views of your schedule**

The purpose of the Outlook Calendar is to keep you from arriving a day late and a dollar short. Use the Calendar to schedule meetings and appointments. Use it to make the most of your time. This chapter explains how to go from day to day, week to week, and month to month in the Calendar window. It shows you how to schedule and reschedule appointments and meetings and look at your schedule in different ways.

Introducing the Calendar

Use the Calendar to juggle appointments and meetings, remind yourself where you're supposed to be, and get there on time. Surveying your schedule in the Calendar window is easy. Merely by clicking a button, you can tell where you're supposed to be today, any given day, this week, this work week, this month, or any month.

Figure 4-1 shows, for example, someone's schedule during the work week of June 29 – July 3 (a work week comprises Monday through Friday, not Monday through Sunday). All you have to do to find out how busy you are on a particular day, week, or month is gaze at the Calendar window. When someone invites you to a meeting or wants to schedule an appointment, you can open the Calendar and see right away if your schedule permits you to attend the meeting or make the appointment.

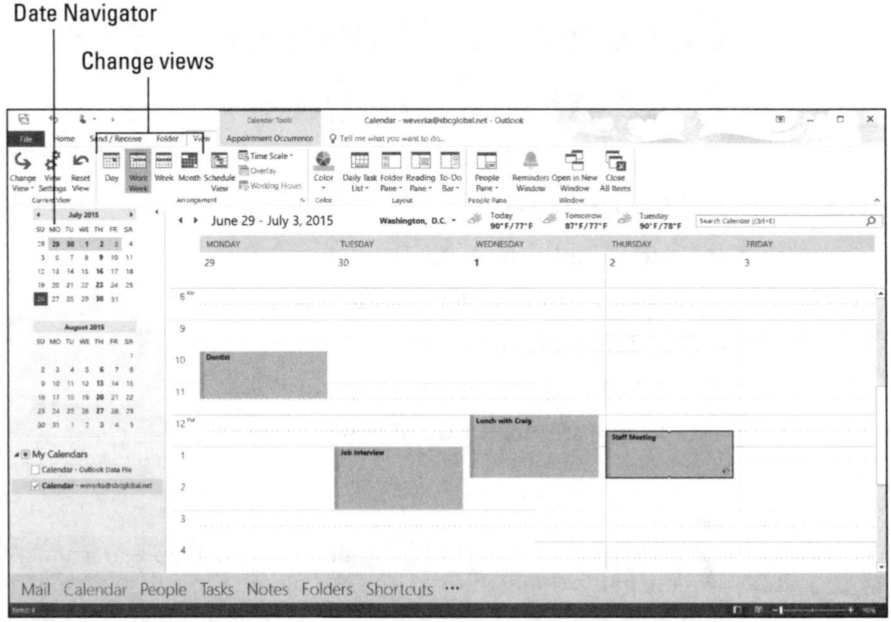

Figure 4-1: The Calendar in Work Week view.

Outlook gives you opportunities to categorize meetings and appointments so that you can tell at a glance what they're all about. Moving a meeting or appointment is simply a matter of dragging it elsewhere in the Calendar window. By double-clicking a meeting or appointment in the Calendar window, you can open a window to find out where the meeting takes place or read notes you jotted down about the meeting. You can even make a bell ring and the Reminder message box appear when a meeting or appointment is forthcoming.

The Different Kinds of Activities

REMEMBER

For scheduling purposes, Outlook makes a distinction between appointments, events, and meetings. Meetings, however, aren't everybody's concern. If your computer is connected to a network and the network uses the Microsoft Exchange Server, you can use Outlook to invite colleagues on the network to come to meetings. But if your computer isn't on a network, don't bother with meetings. Schedule appointments and events instead. You can schedule the following activities:

- **Appointment:** An activity that occupies a certain time period on a certain day. For example, a meeting that takes place between 11 a.m. and 12 p.m. is an appointment.

✦ **Recurring appointment:** An appointment that takes place daily, weekly, or monthly on the same day and same time each day, week, or month. A weekly staff meeting is a recurring appointment. The beauty of recurring appointments is that Outlook enters them weeks and months in advance in the Calendar window. You don't have to re-enter these appointments over and over.

✦ **Event:** An activity that lasts all day. A trade show, for example, is an event. A birthday is an event. A day spent on vacation is also an event (is it ever!). On the Calendar, events and recurring events appear first.

✦ **Recurring event:** An all-day activity that takes place each week, month, or year. Unromantic (or forgetful) users of Outlook are hereby advised to schedule these recurring events in the Calendar: Valentine's Day, their significant other's birthday, and first-date and wedding anniversaries. Thanks to Outlook, no one will ever accuse you again of being cold-hearted or unromantic.

✦ **Meeting:** Same as an appointment except that you can invite others to attend. Scheduling meetings isn't covered in this book. See your network administrator for details.

Seeing Your Schedule

Days on which meetings or appointments are scheduled appear in boldface in the Date Navigator, the calendar located in the Folder pane (refer to Figure 4-1). Following are techniques for getting around in the Calendar window and viewing your schedule in different ways.

Going to a different day, week, or month

Use these techniques to go to different days, weeks, or months in the Calendar window:

✦ **To today:** On the Home tab, click the Today button. Clicking this button selects today's date on your calendar in whatever view you happen to be in.

✦ **To the next seven days:** On the Home tab, click the Next 7 Days button to see the next seven days starting with today's date.

✦ **To a specific day:** Click a day in the Date Navigator (located on the Folder pane). You can also press Ctrl+G and select a day in the Go To Date dialog box. If you don't see the Date Navigator, go to the View tab, click the Folder Pane button, and choose Normal on the drop-down list.

- **To the previous or next day, work week, week, or month:** Click a Back or Forward arrow. These arrows are in the upper-left corner of the Calendar window and on either side of the month name in the Date Navigator.

  Here's a quick way to go from month to month in the Date Navigator: Click the month name in the Date Navigator and hold down the mouse button. You see a list of month names. Drag the pointer to the name of the month you want to go to.

Use the scroll bar on the right side of the window to travel from hour to hour in Day, Work Week, and Week view. In Month view, manipulating the scroll bar takes you from month to month.

Rearranging the Calendar window

To get a sense of what is expected of you and where you're supposed to be, go to the Home or View tab and click one of these buttons to rearrange your view of the Calendar window:

- **Day:** Shows today's date only (press Ctrl+Alt+1).
- **Work Week:** Shows Monday through Friday of this week (press Ctrl+Alt+2).
- **Week:** Shows the entire week, Sunday through Saturday (press Ctrl+Alt+3).
- **Month:** Shows the entire month (press Ctrl+Alt+4).

Scheduling Appointments and Events

Now that you know how the Calendar window works, the next step is to fill the pages of the Calendar with all kinds of busywork. These pages explain how to schedule activities, schedule recurring activities, and magically transform an email message into a Calendar item. You can find many intriguing shortcuts on these pages.

Scheduling an activity: The basics

Follow these basic steps to schedule an appointment, recurring appointment, event, or recurring event:

1. **Select the day in which you want to schedule the activity.**

   If the activity occupies a certain time period, you can select the time period in Day, Work Week, or Week view and save yourself the trouble of entering a time period in the Appointment window. To select a time period, drag downward in the Calendar window. To create a half-hour appointment, simply double-click a half-hour slot in Day, Work Week, or Week view. The Appointment dialog box opens with the Start and End time entered already.

2. **On the Home tab, click the New Appointment button (or press Ctrl+N).**

   As shown in Figure 4-2, you see the Appointment window for naming the activity, stating its starting and ending time, and choosing whether you want to be alerted to its occurrence. In a folder apart from the Calendar, you can display this window by going to the Home tab, clicking the New Items button, and choosing Appointment on the drop-down list.

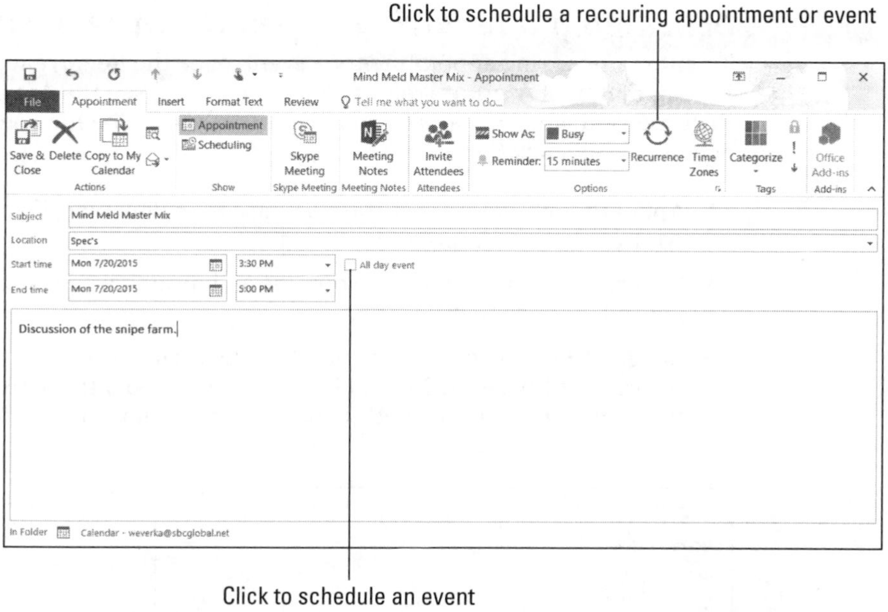

Figure 4-2: The window for scheduling activities.

3. **Enter information in the Appointment tab.**

   Enter a subject, location (you can open the drop-down list and choose one you've entered before), start date and time, and end date and time. To enter a recurring event or appointment, click the Recurrence button. To enter an event instead of an appointment, click the All Day Event check box.

   If the appointment time you enter conflicts with an appointment you've already scheduled, the Appointment window tells you as much. You can click the Calendar button to view the calendar and look for open timeslots.

4. **Open the Reminder drop-down list (located in the Options group) and choose an option if you want to be reminded when the activity is imminent (or choose None if you don't care to be reminded).**

   Choose an option from the drop-down list to make the Reminder message box appear before the activity begins. Chapter 5 of this mini-book explains how reminders work.

5. **Click the Save & Close button when you finish describing the appointment or event.**

   The appointment or event is entered in the Calendar window.

Scheduling a recurring appointment or event

To enter a recurring appointment or event, click the Recurrence button in the Appointment window (refer to Figure 4-2). You see the Appointment Recurrence dialog box, as shown in Figure 4-3. Describe how persistent the activity is and click OK:

- **Appointment Time:** Enter the starting and ending time, if you didn't do so already in the Appointment form.
- **Recurrence Pattern:** Use the options and drop-down lists to describe how often the activity recurs.
- **Range of Recurrence:** Describe when the recurring events will cease recurring. Choose the No End Date option button if the activity occurs *ad infinitum, ad nauseum* (that's Latin for "unto infinity, most nauseously").

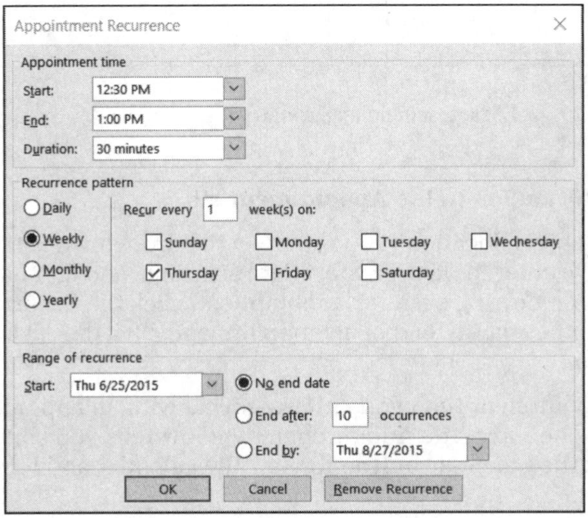

Figure 4-3: My, this appointment is persistent!

Using an email message to schedule an appointment

Here's a neat little trick that can save you time when email correspondence has to do with scheduling an appointment. To get a head start on scheduling, drag the email message from the Inbox folder to the Calendar folder in the Folder pane. On the theory that you want to schedule an appointment around the information in the email message, the Appointment window appears onscreen. For the subject of the appointment, Outlook enters the subject of the email message. The text of the email message appears in the window as well. Fiddle with the particulars of the appointment and click the Save & Close button.

In the Calendar window, recurring activities are marked by the arrow chasing its tail icon.

Scheduling an event

Select the All Day Event check box in the Appointment window (refer to Figure 4-2) to schedule an event, not an appointment. As I explain earlier, an event is an activity that lasts all day. In the Calendar, events are listed at the start of the day before appointments and meetings.

Canceling, Rescheduling, and Altering Activities

Canceling, rescheduling, and altering appointments and events is pretty easy. You can always double-click an activity to open an Appointment or Event window and change the particulars there. And you can take advantage of these shortcuts:

- **Canceling:** Select an activity, go the (Calendar Tools) Appointment tab, and click the Delete button. When you click the Delete button to cancel a recurring activity, a drop-down list appears on the Delete button so that you can delete one occurrence of the activity or the entire series.
- **Rescheduling:** Drag the activity to a new location in the schedule. Release the mouse button when the activity is in the new timeslot.
- **Changing start and end times:** In Day, Work Week, or Week view, move the pointer over the top or bottom of the activity and start dragging when you see the double arrow.
- **Changing the description:** Click in the activity's box and start typing or editing.

Chapter 5: Tasks, Reminders, and Notes

In This Chapter

- **Creating, handling, and managing tasks**
- **Being reminded when deadlines and activities are forthcoming**
- **Jotting down digital notes**

This short chapter describes some Outlook goodies that were neglected in the other chapters of this mini-book. It explains how the Tasks window can help you meet your deadlines and how to be alerted when an activity is looming, a task deadline is arriving, an email message needs a reply, or someone in your Contacts folder needs love and attention. Finally, it explains Outlook's digital stick 'em notes.

Tasks: Seeing What Needs to Get Done

As shown in Figure 5-1, use the Tasks window to see what needs to be done, when it's due, and whether it's overdue. On this list, due dates clearly show how smartly the whip is being cracked and how close you are to meeting or missing deadlines. A gray line appears across tasks that are done. Tasks that are overdue appear in red. Read on if you want to find out how to enter a task, attach a file to a task, and manage tasks in the Tasks window.

TIP

The best way to examine tasks is to display the Reading pane. This way, you can select a task and read notes you've made about it, as shown in Figure 5-1. To display the Reading pane, go to the View tab, click the Reading Pane button, and choose Right or Bottom on the drop-down list.

Entering a task in the Tasks window

Outlook offers two ways to enter a task in the Tasks window:

- **The fast way:** Click at the top of the window where it says "Click here to add a new Task," type a few words to describe the task, press the Tab key to enter the start date and due date. To enter the date, type it or open the drop-down calendar and choose a date there.

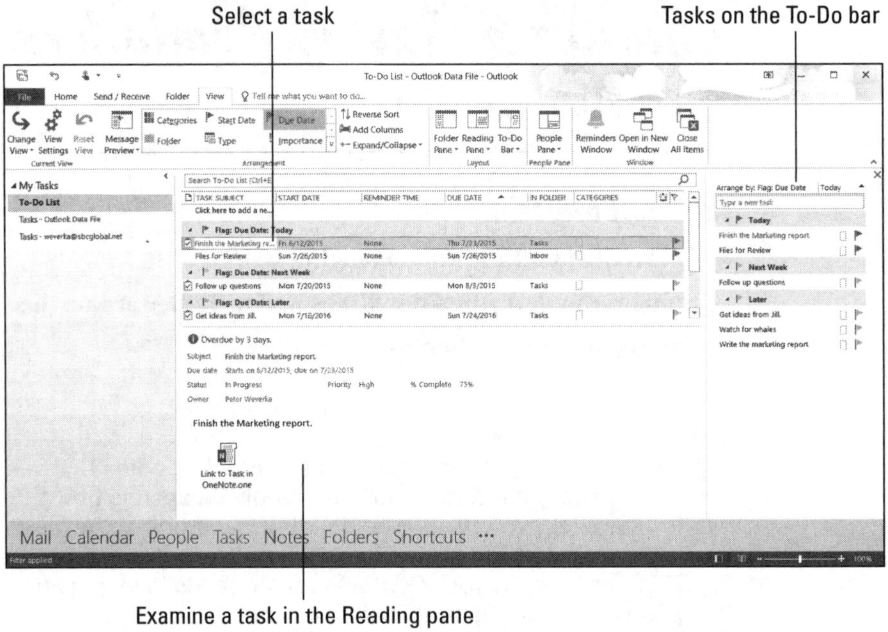

Figure 5-1: The Tasks window shows what has been done and what needs doing.

- **The slow but thorough way:** On the Home tab, click the New Task button (or press Ctrl+N). You see the Task window, as shown in Figure 5-2. In this window are places for describing the task, entering start and due dates, describing the task's status, prioritizing the task, and jotting down notes about it. Click the Save & Close button when you finish describing the task.

Figure 5-2: Describing a task.

Attaching a file to a task

Attaching a file to a task is a neat way to get down to work quickly. Instead of fumbling in your computer for a Word document, Excel worksheet, or other type of file to work on, you can open it merely by double-clicking its name in the Tasks window or Reading pane of the Tasks window. To attach a file to a task:

- Go to the Insert tab in the Task window and click the Attach File button. Then, either select a file on the drop-down list or choose Browse This PC and select a file in the Insert File dialog box.
- Drag and drop a file to the Task window.

By clicking the Recurrence button in the Task window, you can enter a Sisyphean task that gets repeated over and over again. In the Task Recurrence dialog box, describe how often the task recurs. Recurring tasks are marked in the Tasks window with a special recurring icon.

Click the Details button in the Task window to track the hours you worked on a project, the companies you worked for, and how many miles you logged going to and fro in your work.

Examining tasks in the Tasks window

Juggling many different tasks is a high art, and to help you get better at it, the Tasks window offers these techniques for examining tasks that need doing:

- **Choose To-Do List or Tasks in the Folder pane:** Under My Tasks at the top of the Folder pane, choose To-Do List to examine all tasks, including those you fashioned from email messages and Calendar appointments; choose Tasks to see only the tasks you set for yourself in the Tasks folder.
- **Arrange tasks:** On the View tab, open the Arrangement gallery and choose an option to arrange tasks on the Tasks list by Due Date, Category, Importance, or one of the other options.
- **Change views:** On the View tab, click the Change View button and choose a View option. For example, choose Overdue or Next 7 Days to focus on the tasks that *really* need doing.

TIP

To display tasks on the To-Do bar (refer to Figure 5-1), go to the View tab, click the To-Do Bar button, and choose Tasks. No matter which folder you're viewing in Outlook, you can double-click a task on the To-Do bar and see it in a Task window.

Handling and managing tasks

When the time comes to manage the tasks in the Tasks window, I hope you are a stern taskmaster. Here's advice for handling and managing tasks:

- **Marking a task as complete:** Click the check box beside the task name in the Tasks window. Outlook draws a line through completed tasks.
- **Deleting a task:** Select the task and click the Delete button (it's on the Home tab) or press the Delete key.
- **Editing a task:** Double-click a task in the Tasks window to open the Task window and change the particulars there.

Reminders for Being Alerted to Activities and Tasks

Outlook offers the Reminder message box to alert you when an appointment or event from the Calendar is about to take place (see Chapter 4 of this mini-book), when a task deadline is looming (see the preceding topic in this chapter), when an email message needs a reply (see Chapter 3 of this mini-book), or when someone whose name is in your Contacts folder needs attention (see Chapter 2 of this mini-book).

Figure 5-3 shows the Reminder message box. When Outlook is running and you least expect it, a Reminder message box similar to the one in the figure may appear to keep you on your toes. These pages explain how to handle reminder messages, schedule messages, and make the messages appear when you want them to appear.

Figure 5-3: The Reminder message box.

Handling reminder messages

Select a reminder in the Reminder message box and do the following to handle a reminder:

- **Dismiss it:** Click the Dismiss button to shelve the reminder notice. If more than one notice appears in the Reminder message box and you want to erase them all, click the Dismiss All button.
- **Be reminded later:** Click the Snooze button. At the bottom of the dialog box, the Click Snooze to Be Reminded Again In text box tells you when the next reminder message will arrive. To change this setting, open the drop-down list and choose a different time period.
- **Open the item:** Double-click the reminder to examine the appointment, task, email message, or contact to which the reminder pertains.
- **Procrastinate:** Click the Close button (the *X*) in the Reminder message box to make it disappear. To open the message box later, go to the View tab and click the Reminders Window button.

REMEMBER

Reminders work only for items that are stored in these folders: Tasks, Calendar, Inbox, and Contacts. Store an item in another folder or a subfolder of one of the folders I just named, and you won't see the Reminder message box when the reminder is due. To make sure you get reminded, store items in these folders: Tasks, Calendar, Inbox, or Contacts.

Scheduling a reminder message

Follow these instructions to schedule a reminder message:

- **Calendar appointment or event:** In the Appointment window, open the Reminder drop-down list and choose how many minutes, hours, or weeks in advance of the appointment or event to make the reminder appear.
- **Task deadline:** In the Task window (refer to Figure 5-2), select the Reminder check box and choose a day and time to be reminded in the drop-down menus.
- **Email message:** In the Message window or Inbox window, click the Follow Up button and choose Add Reminder on the drop-down list. You see the Custom dialog box. Select the Reminder check box and choose a date and time in the drop-down lists. If you enter a date but not a time, the Reminder message box appears at 5:00 p.m.
- **Contacts name:** In a Contact window or the Contacts window, click the Follow Up button and choose Add Reminder on the drop-down list. The Custom dialog box opens. Treat this dialog box the same way you treat the one for email messages (see the preceding item in this list).

Making reminders work your way

You can do two or three things to make reminders work your way. On the File tab, choose Options to open the Options dialog box. Then follow these instructions to have your way with reminder notices:

- **Changing the reminder time for appointments and events:** By default, the Reminder message box appears 15 minutes before appointments and events start. To change this setting, go to the Calendar category, and enter a new setting in the Default Reminders drop-down list (look under "Calendar Options").
- **Changing the default time for task reminders:** When a task's deadline arrives, the Reminders dialog box lets you know at 8:00 a.m. (or when you start Outlook, if you start the program after 8:00 a.m.). To change this default setting, go to the Tasks category and choose a new time from the Default Reminder Time drop-down list.
- **Playing a different sound (or no sound):** By default, you hear a little chime when the Reminder message box appears onscreen. To hear a different sound or no sound at all, go to the Advanced category of the Options dialog box. To play no sound, deselect the Play Reminder Sound check box. To play a different sound, click the Browse button and then select a .wav sound file in the Reminder Sound File dialog box.

Making Notes to Yourself

As shown in Figure 5-4, notes resemble the yellow stick 'em notes that you often see affixed to manuscripts and refrigerator doors. Click the Notes button in the Navigation pane to go to the Notes window. Write a note to mark down a deadline, for example, or remind yourself to take out the cat. Here are instructions for doing all and sundry with notes:

- **Creating a note:** Click the New Note button (or press Ctrl+N) and type the note in the Note window. Then click outside the window. You can create a note when you're not in the Notes window by pressing Ctrl+Shift+N.
- **Opening a note:** Double-click a note to read it in its Note window.
- **Forwarding a note:** To forward a note to someone in an email message, right-click the note and choose Forward. A Message window opens so that you can address the message. The note arrives in the form of a file attachment, and the recipient must have Outlook in order to read it.
- **Deleting a note:** Select the note and click the Delete button, press the Delete key, or right-click and choose Delete.

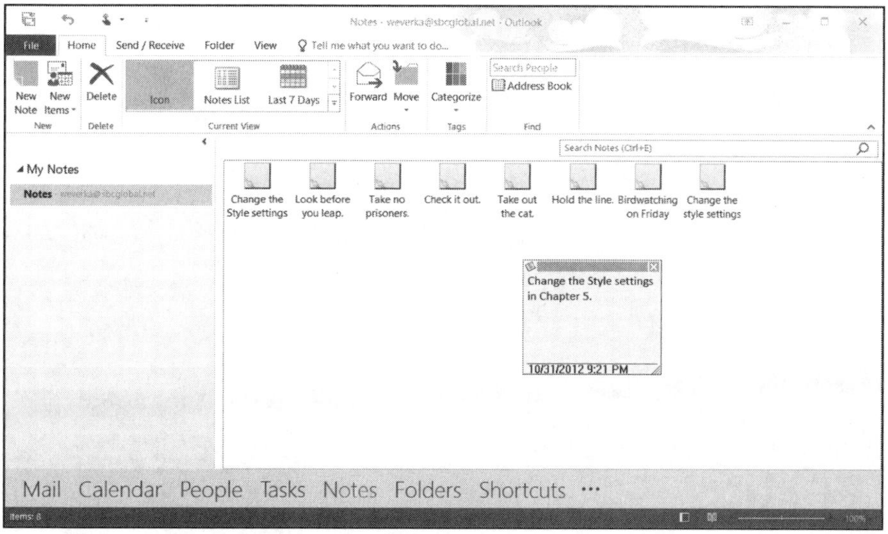

Figure 5-4: Notes, notes, and more notes.

Book VII

Access 2016

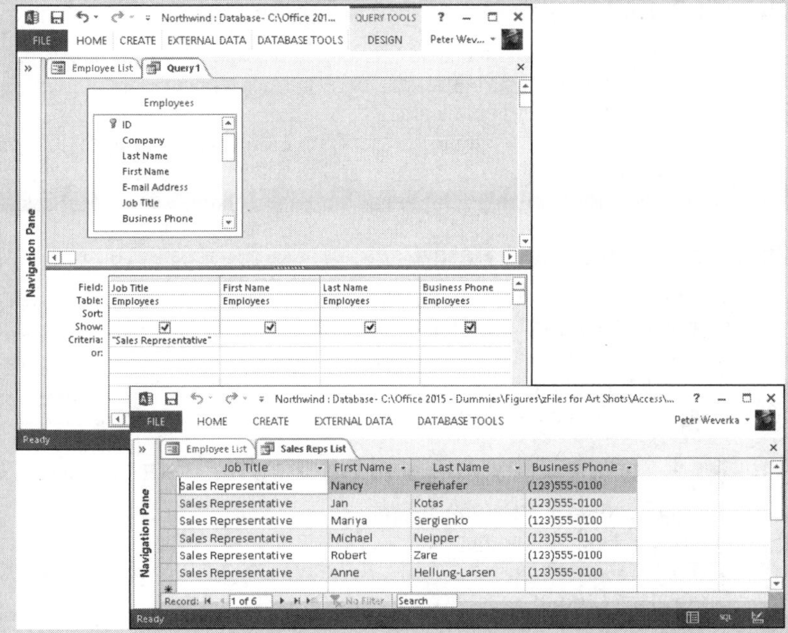

Check out www.dummies.com/extras/office2016aio to see how you can copy an Access report into Word so that you can edit and lay it out there.

Contents at a Glance

Chapter 1: Introducing Access

In This Chapter

- **Understanding how databases work**
- **Looking at tables, queries, forms, and other database objects**
- **Creating a database**
- **Opening and closing tables**
- **Designing the tables, queries, forms, and the other parts of a database**

The word *database* is prone to making most people feel kind of queasy. Can you blame them? Database terminology — record, field, and filter — is the worst of the worst. It even puts other computer terminology to shame. Databases intimidate most people. Even brave souls with a considerable amount of experience in Word and Excel shy away from *Access,* the Office 2016 database program. However, Access can be invaluable for storing and organizing customer lists, inventories, addresses, payment histories, donor lists, and volunteer lists. What's more, Access is easy to use, after you get the hang of it. No kidding!

This chapter introduces databases and the concepts behind databases. It shows you how to create a database and database tables for storing information. The second half of this chapter explains how to design databases. Sorry, but you have to know about database design before you can start fooling with databases. You can't jump right in as you can with the other Office programs.

TIP

Access offers a practice database called Northwind that you can experiment with as you get to know your way around databases. To open this database, click the File tab and choose New. Then, in the New window, enter **Northwind** in the Search box and click the Start Searching button.

What Is a Database, Anyway?

Whether you know it, you're no stranger to databases. The address book on your computer is a database. The telephone directory in the desk drawer is, too. A recipe book is also a database in that recipes are categorized under different headings. If you ever arranged a CD collection in a certain way — in alphabetical order or by musical genre, for example — you created a database of CDs, one that makes finding a particular CD easier. Any place where information is stored in a systematic way can be considered a *database*. The only difference between a computerized database and a conventional database, such as a telephone directory, is that storing, finding, and manipulating data is much easier in a computerized database.

Imagine how long it would take to find all the New York addresses in an address list with 10,000 entries. In Access, you can query a 10,000-entry database and find all New York addresses in a matter of seconds. For that matter, you can query to find all the addresses in a certain ZIP code. You can put the list in alphabetical order by last name or in numerical order by ZIP code. Doing these chores without a computer requires many hours of dreary, monotonous labor.

Tables, Queries, Forms, and Other Objects

One problem with getting to know a database program — and the primary reason that people are intimidated by databases — is that you can't jump right in. You have to know how data is stored in a database and how it is extracted, to use database terminology. You have to know about *objects,* Access's bland word for database tables, queries, forms, and all else that makes a database a database. To help you get going, these pages offer a crash course in databases. They explain the different *objects* — tables, queries, forms, and reports — that make up a database. Fasten your seatbelt. If you complete the crash course without crashing, you're ready to create your first database.

Database tables for storing information

Information in databases is stored in *database tables* like the one in Figure 1-1. In a database table, you include one field for each category of information you want to keep on hand. *Fields* are the equivalent of columns in a table. Your first duty when you create a database table is to name the fields and tell Access what kind of information you propose to store in each field. The database table in Figure 1-1 is for storing employee information. It has eight fields: ID, First Name, Last Name, E-mail Address, Business Phone, Company, Job Title, and Home Phone.

A database can comprise one database table or many different tables that are linked together. If you're dealing with a lot of information, storing data in more than one table is to your advantage. Later in this chapter, "Separating information into different database tables" explains why storing data across several database tables is advantageous.

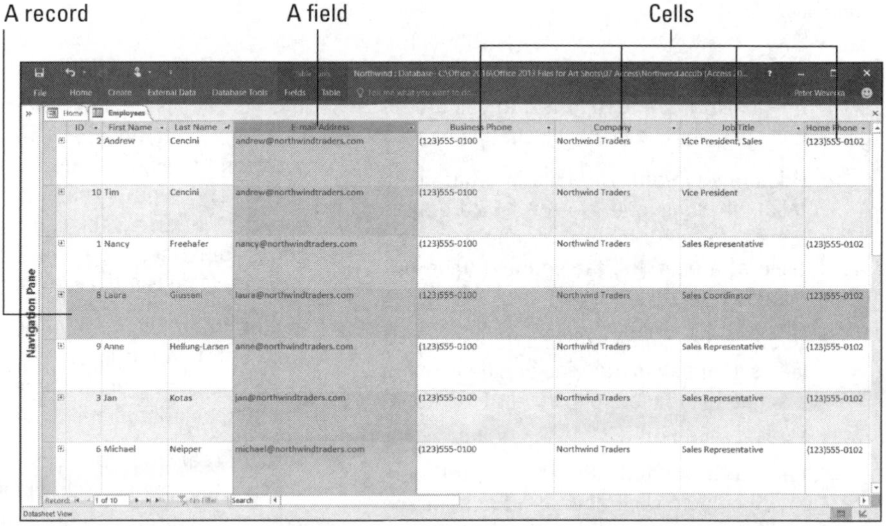

Figure 1-1: A database table.

Access database terminology

Stumbling over database terminology is easy. To keep yourself from stumbling, fold back the corner of this page and return here if one of these database terms puzzles you:

- **Cell:** In a database table, a place for entering one piece of data. Cells appear in a database table where a field and record intersect.
- **Database:** A systematic way of organizing information so that it can be retrieved and manipulated easily.
- **Database table:** A collection of data records arranged into well-defined categories, or fields. Most relational databases have more than one table.
- **Dynaset:** The results of a search for data in a database. (This term is short for dynamic set.) A dynaset is not to be confused with a dinosaur.
- **Field:** One category of information in a database table. Fields are the equivalent of columns in a conventional table.
- **Filtering:** Finding the records in a database table that have the same or nearly the same field value. Filtering is a more convenient but not as sophisticated means of querying a database.
- **Foreign field:** In a relationship between two database tables, the field that is on the "many" side of a one-to-many relationship. The primary key field is on the "one" side.
- **Form:** Similar to a dialog box, a place with text boxes and drop-down lists for entering records in a database table.
- **Module:** A Visual Basic procedure whose job is to perform a certain task in Access.

(continued)

(continued)

- **Object:** The catch-all term for the tables, queries, forms, and reports that you create and open starting in the Navigation pane.
- **Primary key field:** The field in a database table where unique, one-of-a-kind data is stored. To query more than one database table at a time, the tables must have primary key fields.
- **Query:** A question asked of a database that yields information. Queries can be made of a single database table, several tables, or even other queries.
- **Record:** In a database table, all the data that has been recorded about one person or thing. A record is the equivalent of a row in a conventional table.
- **Relational database:** A database program in which data is kept in more than one database table, relationships are established between tables, and queries can be conducted and reports made by assembling data from different tables. Access is a relational database. A database that permits only one table is a *flat-file database.*
- **Report:** Information gathered from a database and laid out in such a way that it's easy to read and understand. Reports are meant to be printed and distributed.
- **Sort:** To rearrange records in a database table so that the records appear in alphabetical, numerical, or date order in one field.

Forms for entering data

After you create the fields in the database table, you can start entering the records. A *record* describes all the data concerning one person or thing. Although you can enter records straight into a database table, the easiest way to enter a record is with a *form*. Similar to a dialog box, a form has convenient text boxes and drop-down lists for entering information, as shown in Figure 1-2. On a form, you can see clearly what kind of information needs entering in each field.

Queries for getting the data out

Figure 1-3 shows a simple query for finding out which employees in the database table shown in Figure 1-1 are Sales Representatives. A *query* is a question you ask of a database. The question here is, "Who is a Sales Representative?" Notice the criterion "Sales Representative" in the Job Title field on the Query grid.

In an address database, you can use a query to find all the people in a particular ZIP code or state. If information about contributions is stored in the database, you can find out who contributed more than $500 last year. Queries can get very complex. For example, you can find all the people in a particular city who contributed between $50 and $500 and volunteered more than eight hours in the past year. You can construct the query so that it produces each person's name and telephone number, or you can construct it so that all the information you have concerning each person appears in the query results.

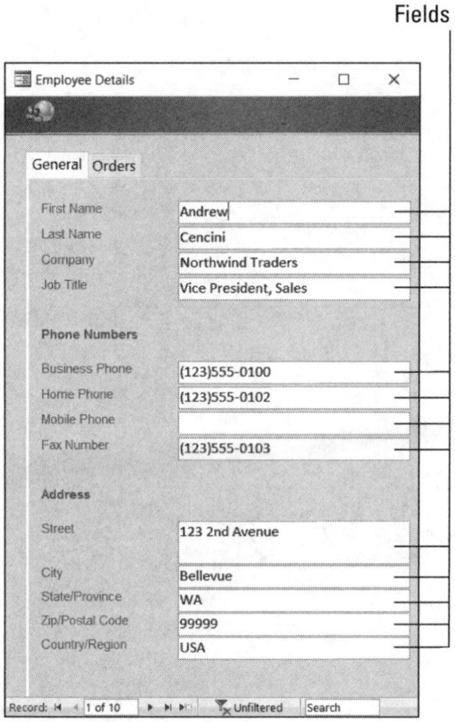

Figure 1-2: A form for entering data.

When you get junk mail, it likely comes to your mailbox as the result of a database query. Companies routinely buy and sell customer databases. They query these databases to gather the names of people who they believe are well-disposed to purchasing the products they sell. Next time you get junk mail solicitation, study the letter and ask yourself, "How did I get in this database, and which database query produced my name?" The junk mailer is probably targeting extraordinarily beautiful, intelligent people.

After you create a query, you can save it and run it again. You can use it as the basis for constructing new queries. The information in database tables usually changes over time. Customers change addresses. New products come online, and others are discontinued. But no matter how much the data changes, you can find out exactly what you want to know from a database by running a well-crafted query.

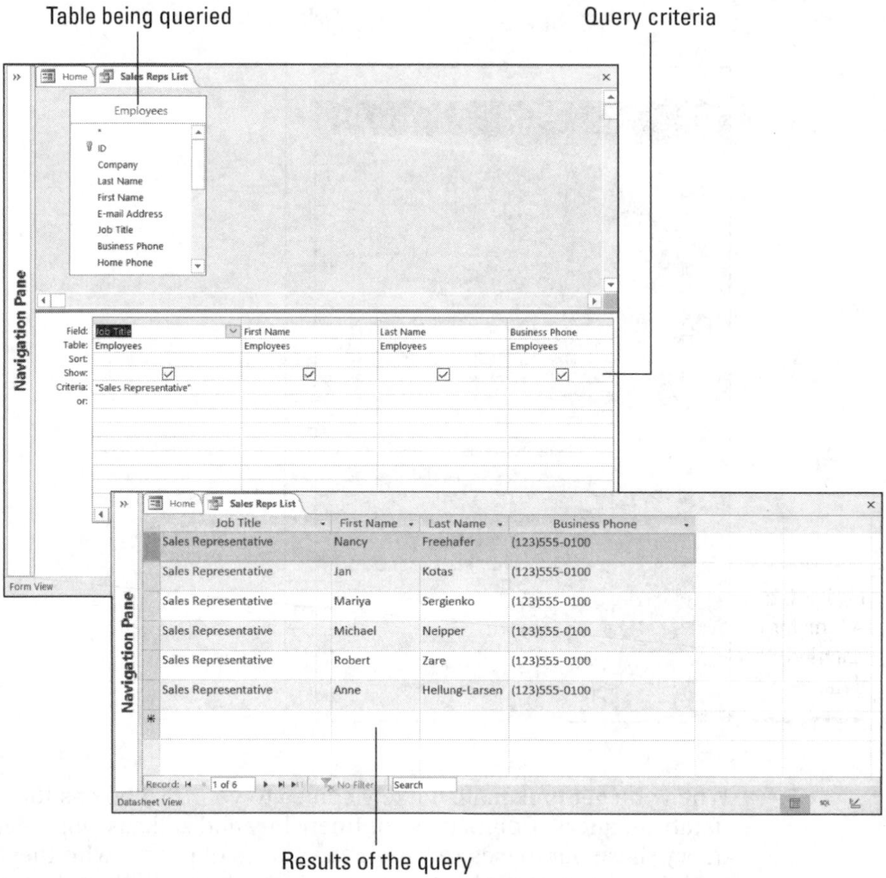

Figure 1-3: Querying a database.

Reports for presenting and examining data

Figure 1-4 shows a *report.* Reports can be made from database tables or from the results of queries. Reports are usually read by managers and others who don't get their hands dirty in databases. They're meant to be printed and distributed so that the information can be scrutinized and analyzed. Access offers many attractive reports. Don't worry — the program does most of the layout work for you, and exporting reports to a Word file is easy.

Macros and modules

Macros and modules aren't covered in this mini-book, but they are also database objects. A *macro* is a series of commands. You can store macros for running queries and doing other Access tasks. A *module* is a collection of Visual Basic procedures and declarations for performing tasks in Access.

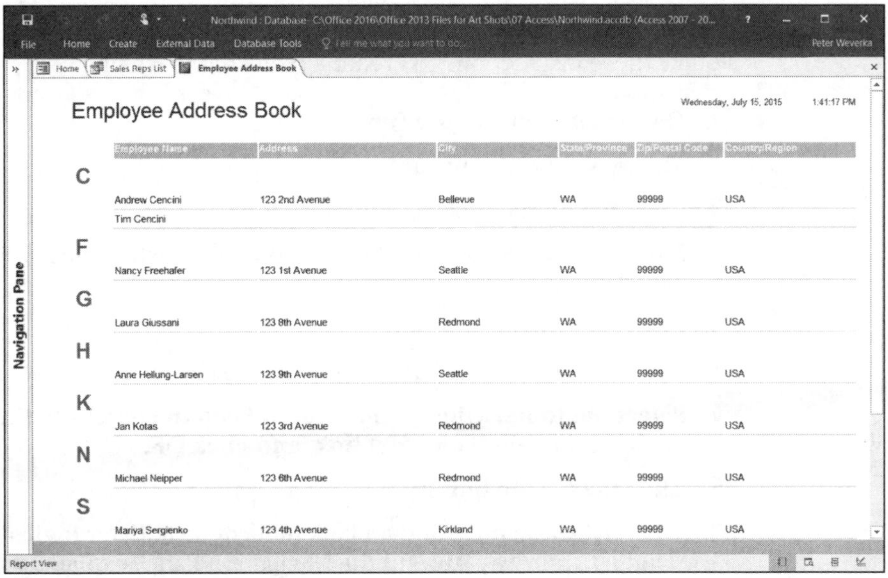

Figure 1-4: A report gathers data for scrutiny and analysis.

Creating a Database File

Creating a database is a lot of work, at least in the beginning. You have to design the database (a subject that I explain shortly). You have to enter the raw information into the tables. You have to construct queries that allow yourself and others to read meaning into the data (see Chapter 4 of this mini-book). By contrast, creating a database file for storing the information is the easy part.

Access offers two ways to create a new database file. You can do it from scratch or get the help of a template. With a template, some of the work is done for you. The template comes with prefabricated queries, forms, and reports. However, templates are for people who already know their way around Access databases. To make use of a template, you have to know how to modify a pre-existing database.

REMEMBER

Before you create a database file, start by deciding where in your computer to store it. Unlike other Office programs, Access requires you to save and name a new database file as soon as you create it.

Creating a blank database file

Follow these instructions to create a blank database file:

1. **On the File tab, choose New.**

   The New window appears.

2. **Click the Blank Desktop Database icon.**

   A dialog box appears for choosing the folder where you will store your new database.

3. **Click the Browse button.**

   You see the File New Database dialog box.

4. **Select the folder where you want to keep the database file, enter a name in the File Name text box, and click OK.**

5. **Click the Create button.**

   The Navigation pane and a blank table appear. Later in this chapter, "Finding Your Way Around the Navigation Pane" explains what this pane is all about. I suggest you go there without delay or deferral.

Getting the help of a template

As I explain earlier, templates are wonderful if you have the wherewithal to modify them. Access offers prefabricated databases for tracking assets, keeping inventory, scheduling resources, and doing other things. Unfortunately, the only way to find out whether one of the templates is worthwhile is to go to the trouble to create a database from a template, open up the database file, and look around.

Follow these steps to create a database file from a template:

1. **On the File tab, choose New.**

   The New window opens.

2. **Select a template or use the Search box to obtain a template online from Microsoft.**

   Templates showing the globe icon are applications, not databases. Access applications are designed for use with web browsers.

3. **Click the Browse button.**

   The File New Database dialog box opens.

4. **Select the folder where you want to keep the database file, enter a name in the File Name text box, and click OK.**

5. **Click the Create button.**

   The Navigation pane and a blank table appear. Read on to find out how to find your way around the Navigation pane.

Finding Your Way Around the Navigation Pane

The first thing you see when you open most database files is a Navigation pane like the one in Figure 1-5. This is the starting point for doing all your work in Access. From here, you can select an object — that horrible word again! — and begin working. Tables, queries, and other objects you create are added to the Navigation pane when you create them.

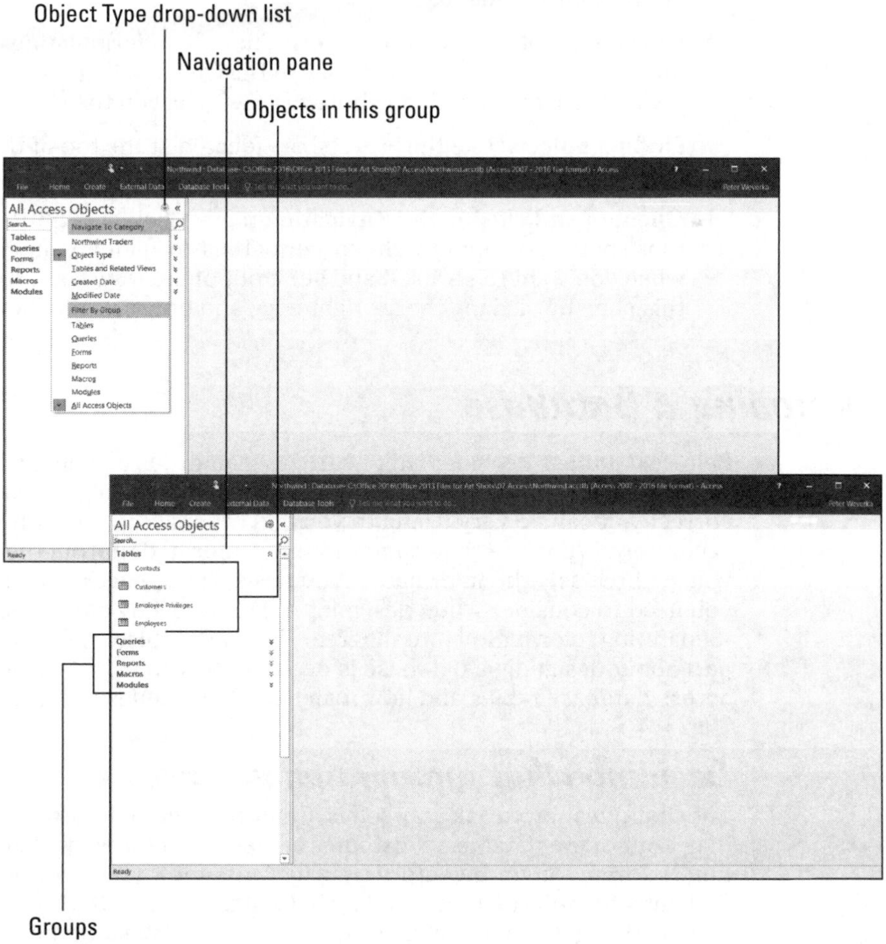

Figure 1-5: Finding and selecting objects with the Navigation pane.

Here are shorthand instructions for doing this, that, and the other thing in the Navigation pane:

- **Choosing an object type:** Select a group (Tables, Queries, Forms, Reports, and so on) from the Object Type drop-down list at the top of the Navigation pane, or select All Access Objects to see all the groups, as shown in Figure 1-5.
- **Creating a new object:** Go to the Create tab and choose what type of object you want to create. When creating new forms and reports, click a table or query in the Navigation pane to base the new form or report on a table or query.
- **Opening an object:** To open a database table, query, form, or report, double-click it; select it and press Enter; or right-click it and choose Open on the shortcut menu.
- **Opening an object in Design view:** The task of formulating database tables, forms, and queries is done in Design view. If an object needs reformulating, right-click it and choose Design View on the shortcut menu.
- **Finding objects:** Use the Search bar (located at the top of the Navigation pane) to search for objects.
- **Opening and closing the Navigation pane:** Click the Shutter Bar Open/Close button on upper-right corner of the Navigation pane (or press F11) when you want to shrink it and get it out of the way. You can also resize this pane by clicking the far right edge and dragging it left or right.

Designing a Database

Being a database designer isn't nearly as glamorous as being a fashion designer, but it has its rewards. If you design your database carefully and correctly, it can be very useful to you and others. You can enter information accurately. When the time comes to draw information from the database, you get precisely the information you need. These pages explain everything you need to consider when designing a database. Pay close attention to "Separating information into different database tables" because the hardest part about designing a database is deciding how to distribute information across database tables and how many database tables to have.

Deciding what information you need

The first question to ask yourself is about the kind of information you want to get out of the database. Customer names and addresses? Sales information? Information for inventory tracking? Interview your co-workers to find out what information could be helpful to them. Give this matter some serious thought. Your goal is to set up the database so that every tidbit of information your organization needs can be recorded.

TIP

A good way to find out what kind of information matters to an organization is to examine the forms that the organization uses to solicit or record information. These forms show precisely what the organization deems worthy of tracking in a database. Figure 1-6, for example, shows the paper form that players fill out to sign up for a baseball league whose database tables appear in Figure 1-7. Compare Figure 1-6 with Figure 1-7, and you can see that the Players, Teams, and Divisions database tables all have fields for entering information from this form.

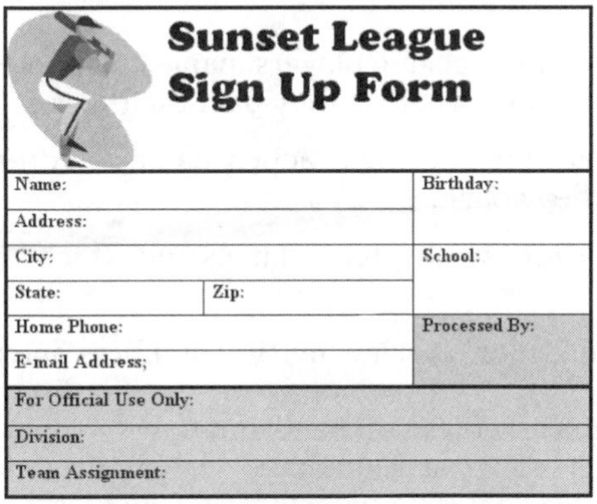

Sunset League Sign Up Form

Name:		Birthday:
Address:		
City:		School:
State:	Zip:	
Home Phone:		Processed By:
E-mail Address;		
For Official Use Only:		
Division:		
Team Assignment:		

Figure 1-6: Paper forms also have fields.

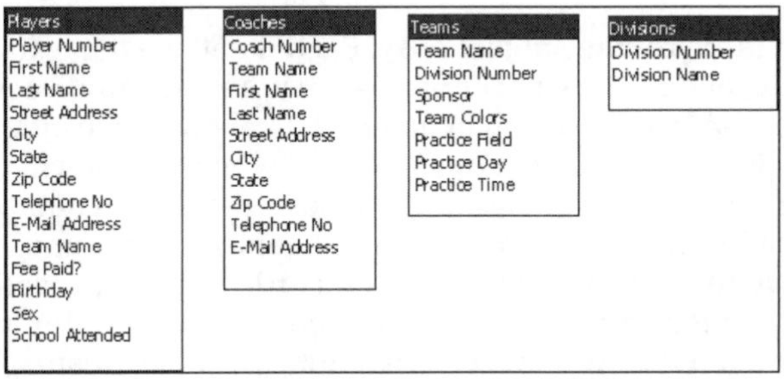

Figure 1-7: Plans for database tables and field names.

Separating information into different database tables

After you know the information you want to record in the database, think about how to separate the information into database tables. Many are tempted to put all the information into a single database table, but because Access is a *relational database,* you can query more than one table at a time, and in so doing, assemble information from different tables.

To see how it works, consider the simple database, as shown in Figure 1-7. The purpose of this little database and its four tables is to store information about the players, coaches, and teams in a baseball league. The Team Name field appears in three tables. It serves as the link between the tables and permits more than one to be queried. By querying individual tables or combinations of tables in this database, I can assemble team rosters, make a list of coaches and their contact information, list teams by division, put together a mailing list of all players, find out which players have paid their fee, and list players by age group, among other things. This database comprises four tables:

- **Players:** Includes fields for tracking players' names, addresses, birthdays, which teams they're on, and whether they paid their fees.
- **Coaches:** Includes fields for tracking coaches' names, addresses, and the names of the teams they coach.
- **Teams:** Includes fields for tracking team names and which division each team is in.
- **Divisions:** Includes fields for tracking division numbers and names.

Deciding how many database tables you need and how to separate data across the different tables is the hardest part of designing a database. To make the task a little easier, do it the old-fashioned way with a pencil and eraser. Here are the basic rules for separating data into different tables:

- **Restrict a table to one subject only:** Each database table should hold information about one subject only — customers, employees, products, and so on. This way, you can maintain data in one table independently from data in another table. Consider what would happen in the little league database (refer to Figure 1-7) if coach and team data were kept in a single table, and one team's coach was replaced by someone new. You would have to delete the old coach's record, delete information about the team, enter information about the new coach, and re-enter information about the team that you just deleted. But by keeping team information separate from coach information, you can update coach information and still maintain the team information.
- **Avoid duplicate information:** Try not to keep duplicate information in the same database table or duplicate information across different tables. By keeping the information in one place, you have to enter it only once, and if you have to update it, you can do so in one database table, not several.

Entire books have been written about database design, and this book can't do the subject justice. You can, however, store all your data in a single table if the data you want to store isn't very complex. The time you lose entering all the data in a single table is made up by the time you save not having to design a complex database with more than one table.

Choosing fields for database tables

As I explain earlier, *fields* are categories of information. Each database table needs at least one field. If the table itself is a subject, you could say that its fields are facts about the subject. An Address database table needs fields for recording street addresses, cities, states, and ZIP Codes. A Products database table needs fields for product ID numbers, product names, and unit prices. Just the facts, ma'am. Within the confines of the subject, the database table needs one field for each piece of information that is useful to your organization.

When you're planning which fields to include in a database table, follow these guidelines:

- Break up the information into small elements. For example, instead of a Name field, create a First Name field and a Last Name field. This way, you can sort database tables by last name more easily.
- Give descriptive names to fields so that you know what they are later. A more descriptive name, such as *Serial Number,* is clearer than *SN.*
- Think ahead and include a field for each piece of information your organization needs. Adding a field to a database table late in the game is a chore. You have to return to each record, look up the information, and enter it.
- Don't include information that can be derived from a calculation. As I explain in Chapter 4 of this mini-book, calculations can be performed as part of a query or be made part of a table. For example, you can total the numbers in two fields in the same record or perform mathematical calculations on values in fields.

Deciding on a primary key field for each database table

REMEMBER

Each database table must have a *primary key field.* This field, also known as the *primary key,* is the field in the database table where unique, one-of-a-kind data is stored. Data entered in this field — an employee ID number, a part number, a bid number — must be different in each record. If you try to enter the same data in the primary key field of two different records, a dialog box warns you not to do that. Primary key fields prevent you from entering duplicate records. They also make queries more efficient. In a query, you tell Access what to look for in database tables, Access searches through the tables, and the program assembles information that meets the criteria. Primary key fields help Access recognize records and not collect the same information more than once in a query.

Social security numbers make good primary key fields because no two people have the same social security number. Invoice numbers and serial numbers also make excellent primary key fields. Returning to the sample baseball league database (refer to Figure 1-7), which fields in the little league database tables are primary key fields? In the Teams table, Team Name can be the primary key field because no two teams have the same name. Division Number can also be a primary key field because divisions in the league are numbered and no two divisions have the same number.

The Players and Coaches database tables, however, present a problem when it comes to choosing a primary key field. Two players might have the same last name, which rules out Last Name as a primary key field. A brother and sister might have the same telephone number, which rules out a Telephone No. field. Because no field holds values that are certain to be different from record to record, I introduce fields called Player Number and Coach Number. For the purpose of this database, players and coaches are assigned numbers. (Chapter 2 in this mini-book explains how Access can assign sequential numbers for you in a database table.)

Mapping the relationships between tables

If your database includes more than one table, you have to map how the tables relate to one another. Usually, relationships are formed between the primary key field in one table and the corresponding field in another, called the *foreign key.* Figure 1-8 shows the relationships between the tables in the little league database. Because these tables are linked by common fields, I can gather information from more than one table in a query or report. Chapter 2 in this mini-book takes up the subject of linking tables in more detail. For now, when you design your database, consider how to connect the various tables with common fields.

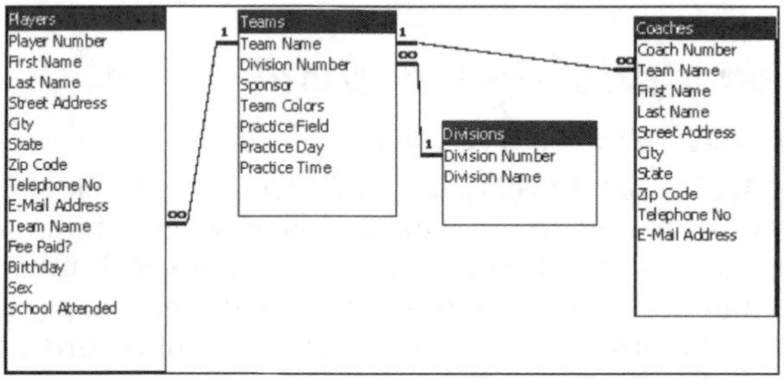

Figure 1-8: Table relationships.

Chapter 2: Building Your Database Tables

In This Chapter

- **Creating database tables**
- **Creating fields for a database table**
- **Choosing a primary key field**
- **Using field properties to make data entries more accurate**
- **Indexing fields in a table**
- **Forming relationships between tables**

Database tables are the building blocks of a database. They hold the raw data. Relationships between the tables permit you to query and generate reports from several different tables. How well your database tables are put together and how accurately data is entered in the tables determine whether your database is a thing of beauty or a wilted flower.

This chapter explains how to create database tables and fields for the tables. It explains what primary key fields are and how primary key fields and indexed fields make it easier for Access to sort, search, and query a database. This chapter describes how to forge relationships between tables. Fasten your seatbelts. In this chapter, you find numerous tips and tricks for making sure that data is entered accurately in your database tables.

Creating a Database Table

Raw data is stored in database tables (or in a single table if you decide to keep all the data in one place). The first and most important part of setting up a database is creating the tables and entering the data. After you enter the data, you can harass your database for information about the things and people your database keeps track of. If you haven't done so already, read the sections in Chapter 1 of this mini-book that pertain to storing information and designing a database before you create a database table. Chapter 1 of this mini-book explains what database tables are and how to fashion a splendid one.

The business of creating a database table starts on the Create tab. As I explain in detail in the next few pages, Access offers three ways to create a database table:

- **Create the database table from scratch:** Enter and format the fields one at a time on your own.
- **Get the help of a template:** Get prefabricated fields assembled in a table. This is the way to go if you know Access well, and you can modify database tables and table fields.
- **Import the database table from another database:** This technique can be an enormous timesaver if you can recycle data that has already been entered in a database table in another Access database.

Creating a database table from scratch

Creating a table from scratch entails creating the table and then entering the fields one by one. After you open a database file, follow these steps to create a database table from scratch:

1. **Go to the Create tab.**
2. **Click the Table Design button.**

   The Design window appears. From here, you enter fields for your database table. I hate to be like a City Hall bureaucrat who gives everybody the runaround, but I can't help myself. Turn to "Entering and Altering Table Fields" later in this chapter to find out how to enter fields in a database table.
3. **Click the Save button on the Quick Access toolbar.**

   The Save As dialog box appears.
4. **Enter a descriptive name for your table and click OK.**

   Return to the Navigation pane and you see the name of the table you created. If you don't believe me, click the Tables group to see the names of tables in your database.

Creating a database table from a template

If you know your way around Access and know how to modify database tables, you can do worse than create a database table with a template. Access offers four template types: Contacts (for storing contact addresses and phone numbers), Issues (for prioritizing issues), Tasks (for tracking projects, their status, and when they are due), and Users (for storing e-mail addresses). As well as creating a table, Access creates ready-made queries, forms, and reports to go along with the table. After you create a table with a template, you can remove fields that you don't want. It's always easier to delete fields than add new ones.

Follow these steps to use a template to create a table (and accompanying queries, forms, and reports):

1. **Close all objects if any objects are open.**

   To close an object, click its Close button or right-click its tab and choose Close on the shortcut menu.

2. **On the Create tab, click the Application Parts button.**

   A drop-down list with options for creating forms and tables appears. (The tables are listed under "Quick Start.")

3. **Choose Contacts, Issues, Tasks, or Users.**

   If there are other tables in your database, a dialog box asks whether you want to create a relationship between the table you're creating and another table.

4. **Select the There Is No Relationship option button and click Create.**

   Later in this chapter, "Establishing Relationships between Database Tables" explains how to create relationships on your own. If you want to create these relationships now and you have the wherewithal to do it, select an option besides There Is No Relationship, choose a table on the drop-down list, and click the Next button to choose which field to forge the relationship with.

5. **On the Navigation pane, right-click the name of the table you created and choose Design View (or click the Design View button in the lower-right corner of the screen).**

   In Design view, you can see the names of the fields in the table. If the table contains fields you don't want or you want to change the names of the fields, turn to "Entering and Altering Table Fields," later in this chapter.

Importing a table from another database

Few things are more tedious than entering records in a database table. If the records you need were already entered elsewhere, more power to you. Follow these steps to get a database table from another Access database:

1. **Go to the External Data tab.**

2. **Click the Access button in the Import & Link group.**

   WARNING!

   This button's full name is Import Access Database. There is a second Access button in the Export group; don't click it. The Get External Data – Access Database dialog box opens.

3. **Click the Browse button, and in the File Open dialog box, select the Access database with the table you need and click Open.**

   You return to the Get External Data – Access Database dialog box.

4. **Select the first option button (Import Tables, Queries, Forms, Reports, Macros, and Modules into the Current Database) and click OK.**

   You see the Import Objects dialog box, as shown in Figure 2-1.

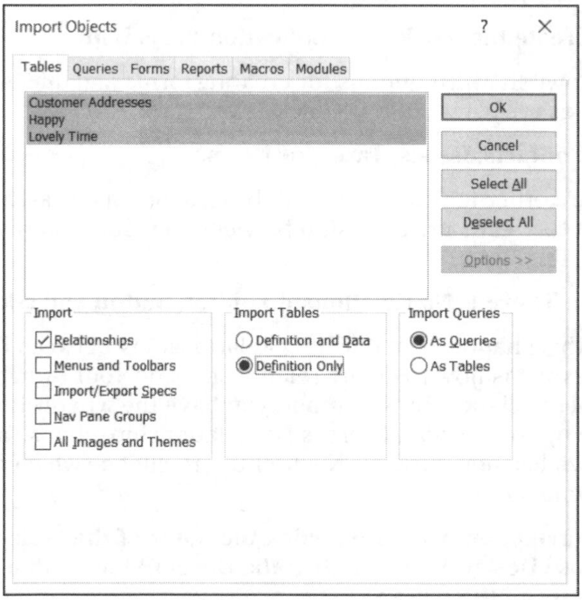

Figure 2-1: Fetching a table from another database.

5. **On the Tables tab, select the database table you want.**

   You can import more than one database table by clicking several table names or clicking the Select All button.

   TIP: You can import a table structure — its field names and formats — without importing the data in the table. To do so, click the Options button in the Import Objects dialog box, and under Import Tables, select the Definition Only option button (refer to Figure 2-1).

6. **Click OK.**

WARNING! If the table you want to import includes lookup fields, import the tables or queries that the lookup fields refer to as well as the table itself. Without those tables or queries, the lookup fields won't be able to obtain any values. Later in this chapter, "Creating a lookup data-entry list" explains what lookup fields are.

Opening and Viewing Tables

To open a table, start in the Navigation pane and select the Tables group to view the names of database tables you created. How you open a table depends on whether you want to open it in Datasheet view or Design view. Figure 2-2 illustrates the difference between these views.

- ✦ Datasheet view is for entering and examining data in a table.
- ✦ Design view is for creating fields and describing their parameters.

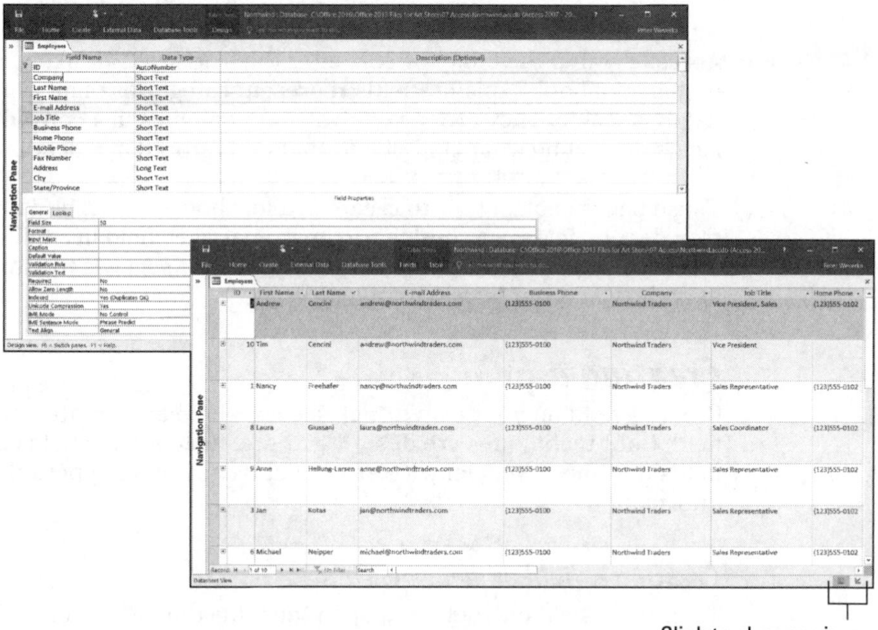

Figure 2-2: A table in Design view (top) and Datasheet view (bottom).

Select a table on the Navigation pane and use one of these techniques to open and view it:

- ✦ **Opening in Design view:** Right-click the table's name in the Navigation pane and choose Design View on the shortcut menu.
- ✦ **Opening in Datasheet view:** On the Navigation pane, double-click the table's name or right-click its name and choose Open on the shortcut menu.

- **Switching between views with the View button:** On the Home tab, click the View button. This button changes appearance, depending on whether you're in Design view or Datasheet view.
- **Switching between views on the status bar:** Click the Datasheet View or Design View button on the right side of the status bar (refer to Figure 2-2).
- **Switching between views by right-clicking:** Right-click the table's tab and choose Datasheet View or Design View.

Entering and Altering Table Fields

After you create a database table, the next task is to enter the fields, or if Access created the table for you, alter the fields to your liking. As Chapter 1 of this mini-book explains, fields represent categories of information in a database table. They are the equivalent of columns in a conventional table. Fields determine what kind of information is stored in a database table.

These pages explain how to create a field, choose the right data type, display data in fields, and designate the primary key field in a table. While I'm on the subject of fields, W.C. Fields said, "Horse sense is the thing a horse has which keeps it from betting on people."

Creating a field

Create a field on your own or get Access's help and create a ready-made field. Both techniques are described here. Ready-made fields include fields designed especially for storing currency data, hyperlinks, and date information.

Creating a field on your own

To create a field on your own, open the table that needs a new field and follow these steps on the (Table Tools) Design tab:

1. **Switch to Design view if you aren't already there.**

   To switch to Design view, click the View button on the Home tab and choose Design View on the drop-down list.

2. **If necessary, insert a new row for the field.**

   To do so, click in the field that is to go after the new field, and then click the Insert Rows button on the (Table Tools) Design tab.

3. **Enter a name in the Field Name column.**

   Names can't include periods or be longer than 64 letters, but you don't want to enter a long name anyway because it won't fit very well along the top of the table.

WARNING! Some database programs don't permit spaces in field names. If you intend to export Access data to other database programs, don't include spaces in field names. Instead, run the words together or separate words with an underscore character, like this: underscore_character.

4. **Press the Tab key or click in the Data Type column, and choose a data type from the drop-down list, as shown in Figure 2-3.**

   Data types classify what kind of information is kept in the field. The next topic in this chapter, "All about data types," explains data types.

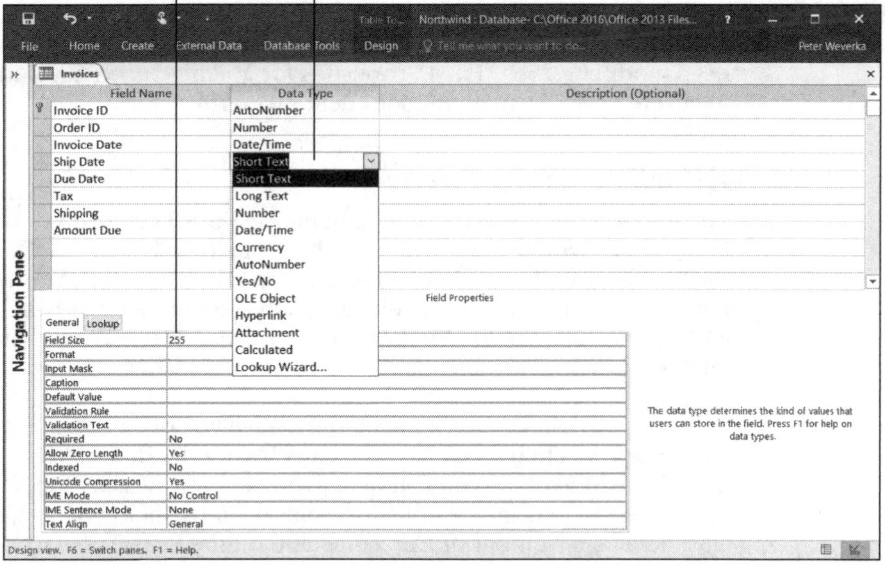

Figure 2-3: Choosing a data type.

5. **If you want, enter a description in the Description column.**

   These descriptions can be very helpful when you need to reacquaint yourself with a field and find out what it's meant to do.

TIP In case the name you choose for your field isn't descriptive enough, you can give the field a second name. The name appears in Datasheet view, on forms, and on reports. To enter a second, descriptive field name, enter the name in the Caption field on the General tab of the Design view window.

Later in this chapter, "Field Properties for Making Sure That Data Entries Are Accurate" demonstrates how to define field properties in the Design view window to make it easier for data-entry clerks to enter the data.

Taking advantage of ready-made fields

You can get a head start creating a field by using a ready-made field and then modifying it, if necessary. To create a ready-made field, switch to Datasheet view and select the field that you want your new field to go after. Then, on the (Table Tools) Fields tab, click a field button or click the More Fields button and choose the name of a field on the drop-down list.

Look for field buttons in the Add & Delete group. Field buttons include Short Text, Number, and Currency. After you create your new field, switch to Design view and examine its field properties. Some of these properties may need modifying. See "Field Properties for Making Sure That Data Entries Are Accurate" for information about field properties.

All about data types

To choose a data type for a field, open the Data Type drop-down list in the Design view window and choose a data type (see Figure 2-3). Data types are the first line of defense in making sure that data is entered correctly in a table. Try to enter text in a field assigned the Currency or Number data type, and Access tells you that your entry is invalid. You get the chance to fix your mistake as soon as you make it.

Table 2-1 explains the options on the Data Type drop-down list. Choose data types carefully because how you classify the data that is entered in a field determines how you can query the field for information. Querying for a number range is impossible, for example, if the field you're querying isn't classified as a Number or Currency field on the Data Type drop-down list.

Table 2-1 Data Types for Fields

Data Type	*What It's For*
Short Text	For storing text (city names, for example), combinations of text and numbers (street addresses, for example), and numbers that won't be calculated or used in expressions (telephone numbers, ZIP codes, and social security numbers, for example). A Short Text field can be no longer than 255 characters.

Data Type	*What It's For*
Long Text	For storing long descriptions. Fields assigned this data type can hold 65,535 characters, not that anyone needs that many.
Number	For storing numbers to be used in calculations or sorting. (If you're dealing with monetary figures, choose the Currency data type.)
Date/Time	For storing dates and times and being able to sort data chronologically or use dates and times in calculations.
Currency	For storing monetary figures for use in calculations and sorting.
AutoNumber	For entering numbers in sequence that will be different from record to record. Use the AutoNumber data type for the primary key field if no other field stores unique, one-of-a-kind data. (See "Designating the primary key field," later in this chapter.)
Yes/No	For storing True/False, Yes/No, On/Off type data. Choose this data type to enter data with a check box in the field. When the box is selected, the data in the field is True, Yes, or On, for example.
OLE Object	For embedding an OLE link in your Access table to another object — an Excel worksheet or Word document. (Consider the using the Attachment data type as well.)
Hyperlink	For storing hyperlinks to other locations on the Internet or on the company intranet.
Attachment	For storing an image, spreadsheet, document, chart, or other file. Attaching a file to a database table is similar to attaching a file to an e-mail message. Attachments do not require as much disk space as OLE objects because they don't require Access to store a bitmap image of the original file.
Calculated	For entering a mathematical expression that uses data from other fields in the database table.
Lookup Wizard	For creating a drop-down list with choices that a data-entry clerk can choose from when entering data. See "Creating a lookup data-entry list," later in this chapter.

Deciding how the data in fields is displayed

To decide how numbers, times, dates, currency values, and Yes/No data are displayed in fields, go to the General tab in the Field Properties part of the Design view and choose an option on the Format drop-down list. The display options are useful indeed. Choose the Currency format, for example, and you don't have to enter the dollar signs or commas when you enter a dollar figure in the field because the dollar sign and commas are entered for you.

Moreover, you can create a format of your own by entering these placeholder symbols in the Format text box:

- @ (at symbol): A character or space is required. For example, @@@@-@@ inserts a hyphen between the first set of numbers and the second. You don't have to enter the hyphen, only the text or numbers.
- & (ampersand): A character or space is optional. For example, @@@@@-&&&& in a ZIP Code field tells Access that either entry is correct, a five-character ZIP code or a five-character plus the four extra characters ZIP code.
- > (right bracket): Displays all characters in the field as uppercase. Merely by entering this symbol in the Format text box, you can display all entries in the field as uppercase without the data-entry clerk having to hold down the Shift or Caps Lock key.
- < (left bracket): Displays all characters in the field as lowercase.

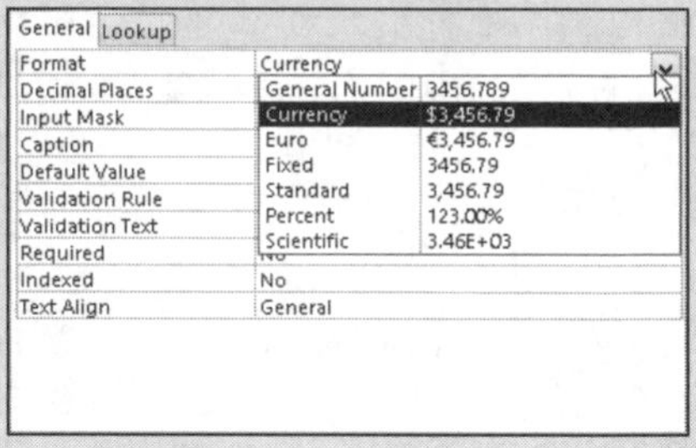

Designating the primary key field

As I explain in Chapter 1 of this mini-book, no database table is complete without a primary key field. The *primary key field* identifies which field in the table is unique and contains data that differs from record to record. Duplicate values and null values can't be entered in the primary key field. (A *null value* indicates a missing or unknown value.) Choosing a primary key field is so important that Access doesn't let you close a table unless you choose one.

TIP

If no field in your table holds one-of-a-kind data that is different from record to record, get around the problem with one of these techniques:

- **The AutoNumber data type:** Create a new field, give it a name, choose AutoNumber from the Data Type drop-down list (refer to Figure 2-3), and make your new field the primary key field. This way, when you enter data, Access enters a unique number to identify each record in the field. (To generate random numbers instead of sequential numbers in an AutoNumber field, go the General tab of the Design view window, open the New Values drop-down list, and choose Random instead of Increment.)

- **A multiple-field primary key:** Combine two or more fields and designate them as the primary key. For example, if you're absolutely certain that no two people whose names will be entered in your database table have the same name, you can make the First Name and Last Name fields the primary key. The problem with multiple-field primary keys, however, is that it takes Access longer to process them, and you run the risk of entering duplicate records.

Follow these steps on the (Table Tools) Design tab to designate a field in a database table as the primary key field:

1. **In Design view, select the field or fields you want to be the primary key.**

   To select a field, click its *row selector,* the small box to its left; Ctrl+click row selectors to select more than one field.

2. **Click the Primary Key button.**

   A small key symbol appears on the row selector to let you know which field or fields is the primary key field.

To remove a primary key, click its row selector and then click the Primary Key button all over again.

Moving, renaming, and deleting fields

Suppose that you need to move, rename, or delete a field. To do so, switch to Design view and follow these instructions:

- **Moving a field:** Select the field's row selector (the box to its left) and release the mouse button. Then click again and drag the selector up or down to a new location.
- **Renaming a field:** Click in the Field Name box where the name is, delete the name that's there, and type a new name.
- **Deleting a field:** Click in the Field Name box, go to the (Table Tools) Design tab, and click the Delete Rows button. You can also right-click the field and choose Delete Rows on the shortcut menu.

Field Properties for Making Sure That Data Entries Are Accurate

Unfortunately, entering the data in a database table is one of the most tedious activities known to humankind. And because the activity is so dull, people are prone to make mistakes when they enter data in a database table. One way to cut down on mistakes is to take advantage of the Field Properties settings on the General tab in the Design view window. Figure 2-4 shows the General tab.

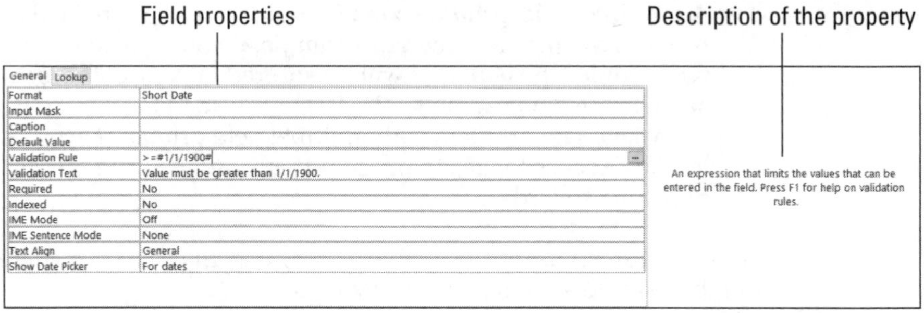

Figure 2-4: Establishing field properties.

These properties determine what can and can't be entered in the different fields of a database table. Some of the settings are invaluable. The Field Size property, for example, determines how many characters can be entered in a field. In a State field where two-letter state abbreviations are to be entered, make the Field Size property 2 to be certain that no one enters more than two characters. If the majority of people you're tracking in an address database live in New York, enter NY in the Default Value property. That way, you spare data-entry clerks from having to enter NY the majority of the time. They won't have to enter it because NY is already there.

The Lookup tab in the Field Properties part of the Design view window is for creating a data-entry drop-down list. It, too, is invaluable. If you happen to know that only four items can be entered in a field, create a drop-down list with the four items. That way, data-entry clerks can choose from a list of four valid items instead of having to enter the data themselves and perhaps enter it incorrectly. (See "Creating a lookup data-entry list," later in this chapter.)

A look at the Field Properties settings

Especially if yours is a large database, you're encouraged to study the field properties carefully and make liberal use of them. The Field Properties settings safeguard data from being entered incorrectly. Following is a description of the different properties (listed here in the order in which they appear in the Design view window) and instructions for using them wisely. Which properties you can assign to a field depends on which data type the field was assigned.

Field Size

In the Field Size box for Text fields, enter the maximum number of characters that can be entered in the field. Suppose that the field you're dealing with is ZIP code, and you want to enter five-number ZIP codes. By entering **5** in the Field Size text box, only five characters can be entered in the field. A sleepy data-entry clerk couldn't enter a six-character ZIP code by accident.

For Number fields, select a value for the field size from the drop-down list. Table 2-2 describes these field sizes.

Table 2-2 Numeric Field Sizes

Field Size	*Description*
Byte	An integer that holds values from 0–255.
Integer	An integer that holds values from -32,768– +32,767.
Long Integer	An integer that holds values from -2,147,483,648– +2,147,483,647.
Single	A floating point number that holds large values up to 7 significant digits.
Double	A floating point number that holds large values up to 15 significant digits.
Replication ID*	A globally unique identifier (GUID) required for replication; this number is generated randomly.
Decimal	A number with defined decimal precision. The default precision is 0, but you can set the scale up to 28.

**Not supported by the .accdb file format.*

TECHNICAL STUFF

The Single, Double, and Decimal field size options hold different ranges of numbers. For now, if you need to store numbers after the decimal point, choose the Double field size so that you cover most situations.

Format

Earlier in this chapter, "Deciding how the data in fields is displayed" (a sidebar) explains the Format property. Click the drop-down list and choose the format in which text, numbers, and dates and times are displayed.

Decimal Places

For a field that holds numbers, open the Decimal Places drop-down list and choose how many numbers can appear to the right of the decimal point. This property affects how numbers and currency values are displayed, not their real value. Numbers are rounded to the nearest decimal point. The Auto option displays the number of decimal places that the format you choose on the Format drop-down list permits.

Input Mask

For Text and Date field types, this feature provides a template with punctuation marks to make entering the data easier. Telephone numbers, social security numbers, and other numbers that typically are entered along with dashes and parentheses are ideal candidates for an input mask (another ridiculous database term!). On the datasheet, blank spaces appear where the numbers go, and the punctuation marks stand at the ready to receive numbers, as shown in Figure 2-5.

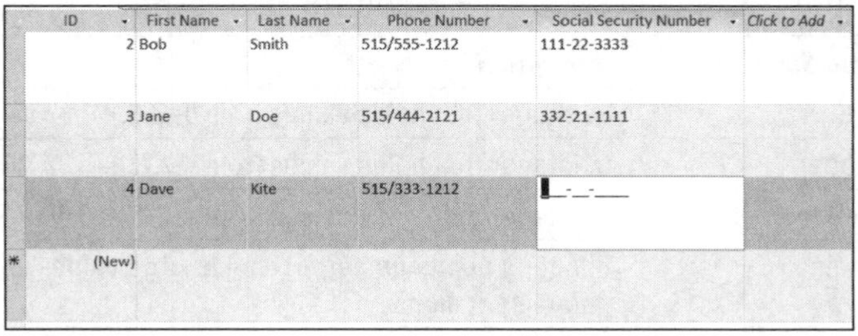

ID
First Name
Last Name
Phone Number
Social Security Number
Click to Add
2 Bob
Smith
515/555-1212
111-22-3333
3 Jane
Doe
515/444-2121
332-21-1111
4 Dave
Kite
515/333-1212
(New)

Figure 2-5: Input masks.

In the Input Mask text box, enter a **0** where numbers go, and enter the punctuation marks where they go. For example, enter (000) 000-0000 or 000/000-0000 to enter an input mask for a telephone number like the one shown in Figure 2-5. You can also create input masks by clicking the three dots beside the Input Mask text box. Doing so opens the Input Mask Wizard dialog box, where you can fashion a very sophisticated input mask.

Caption

If the field you're working on has a cryptic or hard-to-understand name, enter a more descriptive name in the Caption text box. The value in the Caption property appears as the column heading in Datasheet view, as a label on forms, and on reports in place of the field name. People entering data understand what to enter after reading the descriptive caption.

Default Value

When you know that the majority of records require a certain value, number, or abbreviation, enter it in the Default Value text box. That way, you save yourself the trouble of entering the value, number, or abbreviation most of the time because the default value appears already in each record when you enter it. You can always override the default value by entering something different.

Validation Rule

As long as you know your way around operators and Boolean expressions, you can establish a rule for entering data in a field. For example, you can enter an expression that requires dates to be entered in a certain time frame. Or you can require currency figures to be above or below a certain value. To establish a validation rule, enter an expression in the Validation Rule text box. To use dates in an expression, the dates must be enclosed by number signs (#). Here are some examples of validation rules:

>1000	The value you enter must be over 1000.
<1000	The value you enter must be less than 1000.
>=10	The value you enter must be greater than or equal to ten.
<>0	The value you enter cannot be zero.
>=#1/1/2016#	The date you enter must be January 1, 2016, or later.
>=#1/1/2016# And <#1/1/2017#	The date you enter must be in the year 2016.

To get help forming expressions, click the three dots beside the Validation Rule text box to open the Expression Builder, as shown in Figure 2-6, and build an expression there. Try clicking the Help button in the Expression Builder dialog box. Doing so opens the Access Help program, where you can get advice about building expressions.

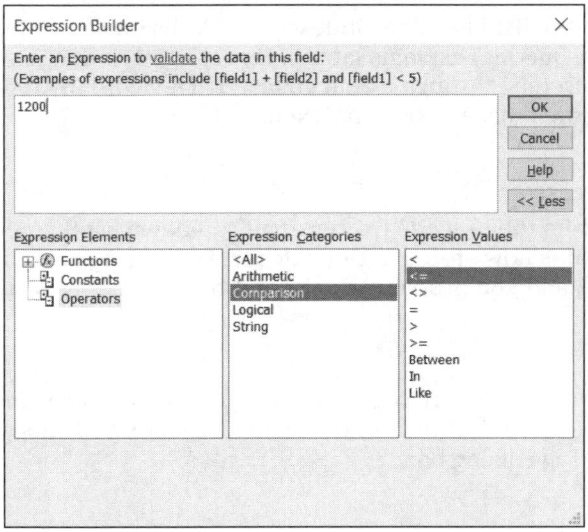

Figure 2-6: Creating a validation rule.

Validation Text

If someone enters data that violates a validation rule that you enter in the Validation Rule text box, Access displays a standard error message. The message reads, "One or more values are prohibited by the validation rule set for [this field]. Enter a value that the expression for this field can accept." If this message is too cold and impersonal for you, you can create a message of your own for the error message dialog box. Enter your friendly message in the Validation Text text box.

Required

By default, no entry has to be made in a field, but if you choose Yes instead of No in the Required box and you fail to make an entry in the field, a message box tells you to be sure to make an entry.

Allow Zero Length

This property allows you to enter zero-length strings in a field. A *zero-length string* — two quotation marks with no text or spaces between them ("") — indicates that no value exists for a field. To see how zero-length strings work, suppose that your database table calls for entering e-mail addresses. If you didn't know whether one person has an e-mail address, you would leave the E-Mail Address field blank. If, however, you knew that the person didn't have an e-mail address, you could indicate as much by entering a zero-length string. Choose Yes on the drop-down list to permit zero-length strings to be entered in the field.

Indexed

Indicates that the field has been indexed. As "Indexing for Faster Sorts, Searches, and Queries" explains later in this chapter, indexes make sorting a field and searching through a field go faster. The word *No* appears in this text box if the field has not been indexed.

Unicode Expression

Choose Yes from the Unicode Expression drop-down list if you want to compress data that is now stored in Unicode format. Storing data this way saves on disk space, and you probably don't want to change this property.

Smart Tags

If you intend to enter Smart Tags in the field, indicate which kind you enter by clicking the three dots next to the Smart Tags box and choosing an option in the Action Tags dialog box.

Text Align

This property determines how the text is aligned in a column or on a form or report. Select General to let Access determine the alignment, or select Left, Right, Center, or Distribute.

Text Format

Available on Long Text fields, this drop-down list lets you choose to allow rich text in the field. With this property set to Rich Text, you can make different words bold, italic, underline, and change font sizes and colors. Set it to Plain Text for plain, boring text with no formatting. I wonder why that isn't the setting's name.

Append Only

Available on Long Text fields, this lets you add data only to a Long Text field to collect a history of comments.

Show Date Picker

Available on Date/Time fields, choosing For Dates places a button next to the column that data-entry clerks can click to open a calendar and select a date instead of typing numbers.

IME Mode/IME Sentence mode

These options are for converting characters and sentences from East Asian versions of Access.

Creating a lookup data-entry list

Perhaps the best way to make sure that data is entered correctly is to create a data-entry drop-down list. Whoever enters the data in your database table has to only choose an item from the list, as shown in Figure 2-7. This saves time and prevents invalid data from being entered. Access offers two ways to create the drop-down list:

✦ **Create the list by entering the items yourself:** Go this route when you're dealing with a finite list of items that never change.

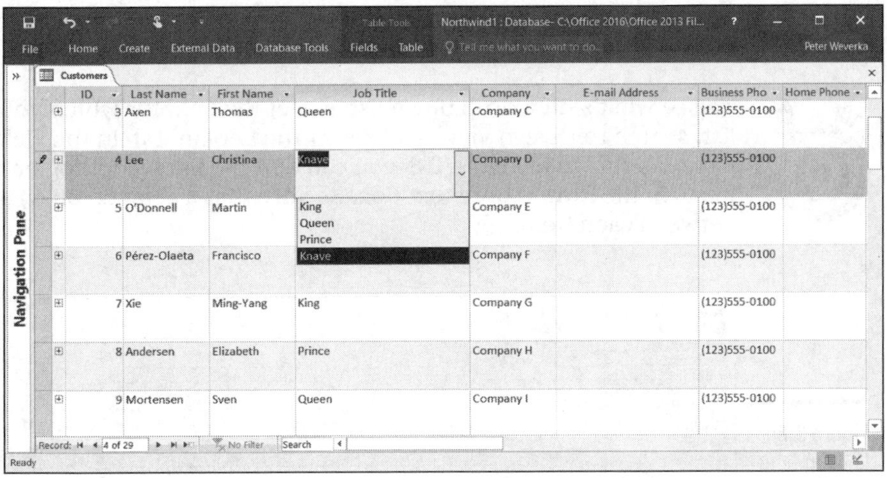

Figure 2-7: A so-called lookup list.

- **Get the items from another database table:** Go this route to get items from a column in another database table. This way, you can choose from an ever-expanding list of items. When the number of items in the other database table changes, so does the number of items in the drop-down list because the items come from the other database table. This is a great way to get items from a primary key field in another table.

Creating a drop-down list on your own

Follow these steps to create a drop-down, or *lookup,* list with entries you type:

1. **In Design view, click the field that needs a drop-down list.**
2. **Open the Data Type drop-down list and choose Lookup Wizard, the last option in the list.**

   The Lookup Wizard dialog box appears.
3. **Select the second option, I Will Type in the Values That I Want, and click the Next button.**
4. **Under Col1 in the next dialog box, enter each item you want to appear in the drop-down list; then click the Next button.**

   You can create a multicolumn list by entering a number in the Number of Columns text box and then entering items for the list.
5. **Enter a name for the field, if necessary, and click the Finish button.**

   Switch to Datasheet view and open the drop-down list in the field to make sure that it displays properly.

To remove a lookup list from a field, select the field, go to the Lookup tab in the Design view window, and choose Text Box on the Display Control drop-down list.

TIP: To see what's on a drop-down list, select the field for which you created the list, switch to Design view, and select the Lookup tab in the Field Properties pane. As shown in Figure 2-8, you can edit the list by editing or removing items in the Row Source text box. Be sure that a semi-colon (;) appears between each item.

General
Lookup
Display Control
Combo Box
Row Source Type
Value List
Row Source
"King";"Queen";"Prince";"Knave"
Bound Column
1
Column Count
1
Column Heads
No
Column Widths
1"
List Rows
16
List Width
1"
Limit To List
No
Allow Multiple Values
No
Allow Value List Edits
No
List Items Edit Form
Show Only Row Source Values
No
The type of control to use to display this field on forms.

Figure 2-8: Lookup field properties.

Getting list items from a database table

Before you can get list items from another database table, you might want to define a relationship between the tables; it's not required, but it's recommended. Later in this chapter, "Establishing Relationships between Database Tables" explains how to do that. Follow these steps to get items in a drop-down list from another database table:

1. **In Design view, click the field that needs a list, open the Data Type drop-down list, and choose Lookup Wizard.**

   The Lookup Wizard dialog box appears.

2. **Select the first option, I Want the Lookup Field to Get the Values from Another Table or Query, and click Next.**

   You see a list of tables in your database.

3. **Select the table with the data you need and click the Next button.**

   The dialog box shows you a list of available fields in the table.

4. **Select the field where the data for your list is stored.**
5. **Click the > button.**

   The name of the list appears on the right side of the dialog box, under Selected Fields.

6. **Click the Next button.**

   Normally, lists are displayed in ascending order, but you can select a field and click the Ascending button to reverse the order of the list. (Note that the button turns into the Descending button.)

7. **Click the Finish button.**

   If you're so inclined, you can change the width of the list before clicking Finish, but you can always do that on the datasheet, as Chapter 3 of this mini-book explains.

TIP

Suppose that you obtain the items from the wrong field or wrong database table? To fix that problem, select the field for which you created the list, and in Design view, select the Lookup tab (refer to Figure 2-8). Choose Text Box instead of Combo Box on the Display Control drop-down list and start all over.

Indexing for Faster Sorts, Searches, and Queries

Indexing means to instruct Access to keep information about the data in a field or combination of fields. Because Access keeps this information on hand, it doesn't have to actually search through every record in a database table to sort data, search for data, or run a query. In a large database table, indexes make sorting, searching, and querying go considerably faster because Access looks through its own data rather than the data in tables. The performance difference between querying a database table that has and has not been indexed is astonishing. That's the good news. The bad news is that indexes inflate the size of Access files.

By default, the field you choose as the primary key field is indexed. I recommend choosing other fields for indexing if you often conduct queries and searches. When you choose a field to index, choose one with data that varies from record to record and is likely to be the subject of searches, sorts, and queries. That way, the index means something. However, a field with data that is mostly the same from record to record is a waste of a good index, not to mention disk space. By the way, Access automatically indexes fields whose names include the words *ID, Code, Num,* and *Key*, the idea being that these fields are likely to store essential information worthy of indexing.

Indexing a field

To index a field, switch to Design view, select the field you want to index, and on the General tab of the Field Properties part of the Design window, open the Indexed drop-down list and choose one of these options:

- **Yes (Duplicates OK):** Indexes the field and allows duplicate values to be entered in the field.
- **Yes (No Duplicates):** Indexes the field and disallows duplicate values. If you choose this option, the field works something like a primary key field in that Access does not permit you to enter the same value in two different records.

Indexing based on more than one field

An index created on more than one field is called a *multifield index.* Multifield indexes make sorting, querying, and searching the database table go faster. They are especially valuable in sorting operations where records in one field are usually the same but records in a companion field are different. In a large database table that stores names and addresses, for example, many names in the Last Name field are the same, so indexing on the Last Name field isn't worthwhile, but indexing the First Name and Last Name fields helps Access distinguish records from one another.

Follow these steps to generate a multifield index:

1. **Switch to Design view, and on the (Table Tools) Design tab, click the Indexes button.**

   You see the Indexes dialog box, as shown in Figure 2-9. The dialog box lists the primary key field already because it's indexed by default. You also see any fields to which you set the Indexed property to Yes.

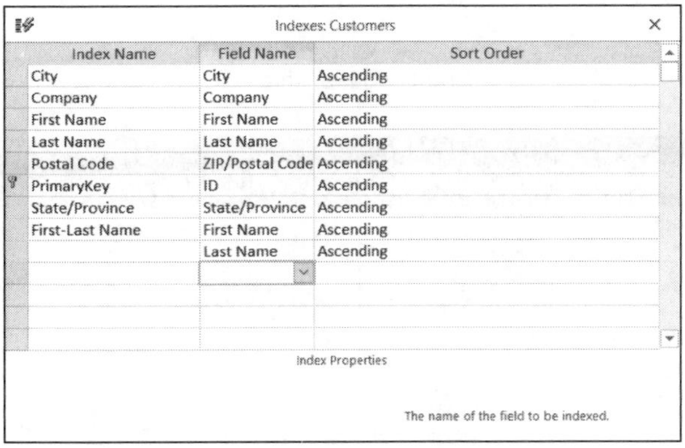

Figure 2-9: The Indexes dialog box.

2. **On a blank line in the dialog box, enter a name for the index in the Index Name column.**
3. **In the Field Name column, open the drop-down list and choose the first field you want for the multifield index.**

   Access sorts the records first on this field and then on the second field you choose.
4. **In the next row, leave the Index Name blank and choose another field name from the drop-down list.**

   This field is the second field in the index. You can use as many as ten different fields in a multifield index. In Figure 2-9, two fields are in a multifield index: First Name and Last Name.
5. **Choose Descending in the Sort Order column if you want the field sorted in descending order.**

   Most of the time, you want leave the Sort Order set to Ascending because most people read from A to Z.
6. **Click the Close button.**

   Click the Indexes button in Design view if you need to return to the Indexes dialog box and change how fields are indexed.

Establishing Relationships Between Database Tables

As Chapter 1 of this mini-book explains, you have to establish relationships between tables if you want to query or generate reports with data from more than one database table. Relationships define the field that two different tables have in common. To understand why relationships between tables are necessary, consider the query shown in Figure 2-10. The purpose of this query is to list all companies that ordered items in 2016, list the companies by name, and list the city where each company is located.

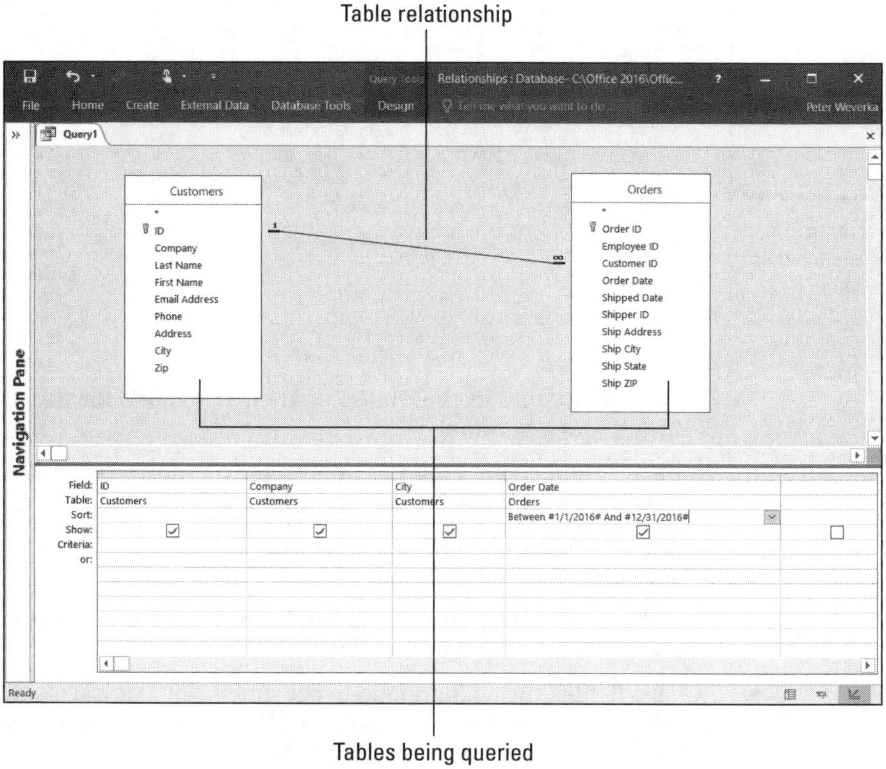

Figure 2-10: To conduct a query with more than one table, the tables must have a relationship.

Consider what Access does to run this query:

- Access deals with two database tables, Customers and Orders.
- In the Orders table, Access looks in the Order Date field to isolate all records that describe orders made in the year 2016. The expression for finding these records is shown on the Criteria line in Figure 2-10: `Between #1/1/2016# And #12/31/2016#`.

- Because there is a relationship between the ID field in the Customers table and the Customer ID field in the Orders table — because the two fields hold the same type of information — Access can match the 2016 records it finds in the Orders table with corresponding records in the Customers table. Where the Customer ID of a 2016 record in the Orders table and an ID in the Customers table match, Access assembles a new record and places it in the query results.
- Data for determining which records appear in the query results is found in the Order Date field in the Orders table. But the information compiled in the query results — customer IDs, company names, and cities — comes from fields in the Customers table. Thanks to the relationship between the ID and Customer ID fields in these tables, Access can draw upon information from both tables.

Types of relationships

The vast majority of relationships between tables are *one-to-many relationships* between the primary key field in one database table and a field in another. Table relationships fall in these categories:

- **One-to-many relationship:** Each record in one table is linked to many records in another table. The relationship in Figure 2-10 is a one-to-many relationship. Each ID number appears only once in the ID field of the Customers table, but in the Orders table, the same Customer ID number can appear in many records because the same customer can order many different products. When you link tables, Access creates a one-to-many relationship when one of the fields being linked is either a primary key field or an indexed field assigned the No (No Duplicates) setting. (See "Indexing for Faster Sorts, Searches, and Queries" earlier in this chapter.)
- **One-to-one relationship:** Two fields are linked. This relationship is rare and is sometimes used for security purposes.
- **Many-to-many relationship:** This complex relationship actually describes crisscrossing relationships in which the linking field is not the primary key field in either table. To create a many-to-many relationship, an intermediary table called a *junction table* is needed. This relationship is rare.

REMEMBER

Sometimes, fields in separate tables that hold the same data also have the same name, but that isn't necessary. For example, a field called ZIP Code in one table might be called Postal Code in another. What matters is that fields that are linked have the same data type. For example, you can't create a relationship between a text field and a number field.

Placing tables in the Relationships window

The first time you open the Relationships window, you see the Show Table dialog box. Use this dialog box to tell Access which tables to put in the Relationships window. Ctrl+click to select tables and then click the Add button.

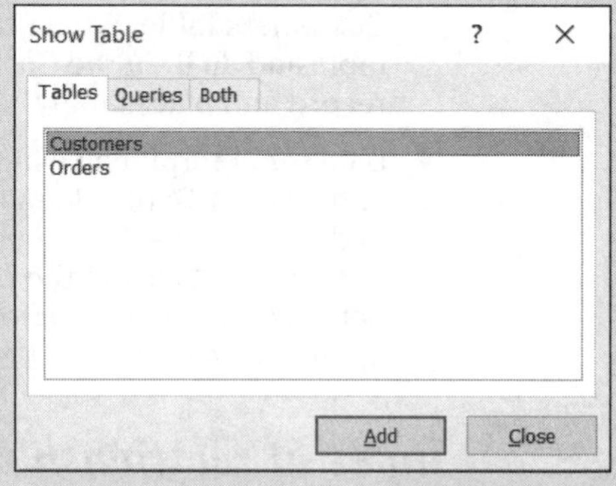

If you create a new database table and want to place it in the Relationships window, click the Relationships button to display the Relationships window; then click the Show Table button on the (Relationship Tools) Design tab. The Show Table dialog box appears. Select your new table and click the Add button.

Handling tables in the Relationships window

To display the tables in a database and link tables to one another or see how they're related to each other, go to the Database Tools tab and click the Relationships button. You see the Relationships window, as shown in Figure 2-11. Notice the field names in each table. The primary key field is shown with a picture of a key next to it. Lines in the window show how relationships have been established between tables.

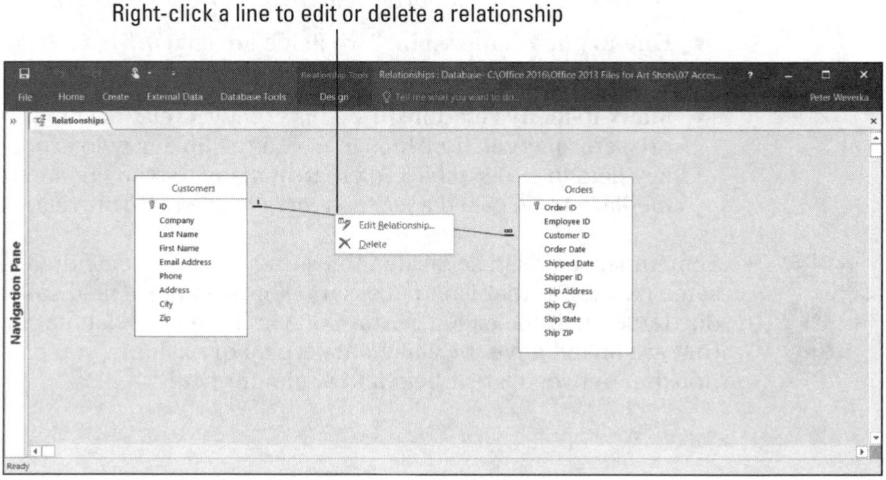

Figure 2-11: The Relationships window.

Apart from linking tables in the Relationships window (a subject I explain shortly), use these techniques on the (Relationship Tools) Design tab to handle tables:

- **Repositioning and resizing the tables:** Each table appears in its own window. Drag tables from place to place, drag a border to change a window's size, and scroll to see field names.
- **Removing a table from the window:** Select the table and click the Hide Table button.
- **Removing all tables from the window:** Click the Clear Layout button and choose Yes in the confirmation box.
- **Placing tables back on the window:** Click the Show Table button, and in the Show Table dialog box, select the tables and click the Add button.
- **Placing all tables back in the window:** To put all the tables with relationships back in the window, click the All Relationships button.
- **Studying a table's relationships:** Click the Clear Layout button to remove all tables from the window; then place the table back in the window, select it, and click the Direct Relationships button. All tables that are related to the selected table are added to the layout.

TIP

To generate and print an Access report that shows how tables in your database are linked, go to the (Relationship Tools) Design tab and click the Relationship Report button. Then save the report and print it. Chapter 5 of this mini-book explains reports.

Forging relationships between tables

On the (Relationship Tools) Design tab (refer to Figure 2-11), make sure that both tables are on display and then follow these steps to forge a relationship between them:

1. **Click to select the field in one table; then hold down the mouse button, drag the pointer to the field in the other table where you want to forge the link, and release the mouse button.**

   You see the Edit Relationships dialog box, as shown in Figure 2-12. This dragging between table fields is probably the most awkward thing you undertake in Office 2016! If you do it right, a bar appears where the pointer is while you move it over the second table, and the names of the two fields appear in the Edit Relationships dialog box.

   Notice the Relationship Type at the bottom of the dialog box. If you accidentally create a link to the wrong field, choose the correct field from the drop-down list in the dialog box.

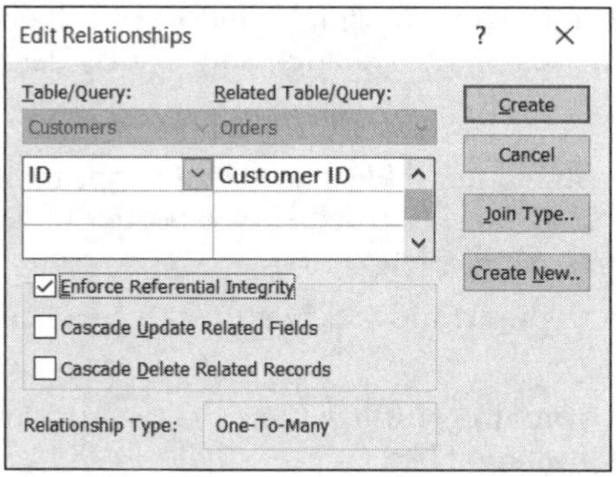

Figure 2-12: Creating a table relationship.

2. **Select the Enforce Referential Integrity check box.**

   If you don't select this box, the relationship between the tables is indeterminate, instead of being a one-to-many relationship. *Referential integrity* (another hideous database term!) has to do with whether values in the two different fields corroborate each other.

3. **Select Cascade options if you so choose.**

   One of these options is excellent, and the other is dangerous:

   - **Cascade Update Related Fields:** If you change a value on the "one" side of the relationship, a matching value on the "many" side changes as well to preserve referential integrity. For example, if you create a multifield primary key of First Name and Last Name and then change the name of someone, the related fields in the other table change automatically to preserve referential integrity. This is a great way to make sure that information is up to date.
   - **Cascade Delete Related Records:** If you delete a record in the "one" table, all records in the "many" table to which the deleted record is linked are also deleted. For example, if you delete an employee from the "one" table, all records in the "many" table that include that employee are deleted! Access warns you before making the deletion, but still! This option is dangerous, and I don't recommend selecting it.

4. **Click the Create button to forge the relationship.**

   In the Relationships window (refer to Figure 2-11), a line is drawn between the table fields. The number 1 appears on the "one" side of the relationship and the infinity symbol (∞) appears on the "many" side.

After you create a one-to-many relationship between tables with the Enforce Referential Integrity check box selected, you can't enter a value in the "many" table unless it's already in the "one" table. For example, suppose that the "one" table includes a primary key field called Employee Number, and this field is linked to a field in the "many" table that is also called Employee Number. If you enter an Employee Number in the "many" table that isn't in the "one" table, Access warns you that it can't be done without violating referential integrity. The best way to solve this problem is to create a lookup data-entry list in the "many" table with values from the primary key field in the "one" table. See "Creating a lookup data-entry list," earlier in this chapter.

Editing table relationships

In the Relationships window (refer to Figure 2-11), select the line that represents the relationship between two database tables and follow these instructions to edit or remove the relationship:

- **Editing the relationship:** Click the Edit Relationships button or right-click and choose Edit Relationship. You see the Edit Relationships dialog box, where you can overhaul the relationship (the previous topic in this chapter explains how).
- **Deleting the relationship:** Press the Delete key or right-click and choose Delete. Then select Yes in the confirmation box.

Chapter 3: Entering the Data

In This Chapter

- Entering data on a datasheet
- Changing the look of a datasheet
- Creating a form for entering data
- Finding records in a field or database table
- Finding and replacing your data

At last — you can start entering the data. If you set up your database tables, named the fields, and established relationships between the tables, you're ready to go. This short chapter explains how to enter the data in a database table. It shows you how to enter data on a datasheet or enter data by way of a form. This chapter also describes how to find missing records in case one goes astray.

There's no getting around it: Entering data is truly a tedious activity. But if you set up the fields well and take advantage of input masks and other field properties, it isn't so bad. It's better than stepping on a shovel blade, anyway.

The Two Ways to Enter Data

When it comes to entering data in a database table, you can take your pick between Datasheet view and a form. Figure 3-1 compares and contrasts the two. Here are the advantages of entering data in Datasheet view:

- Many records appear simultaneously.
- You can compare data easily between records.
- You can sort by column with the commands in the Sort and Filter group on the Home tab (as discussed in Chapter 4 of this mini-book).
- You can scroll up or down to locate records.

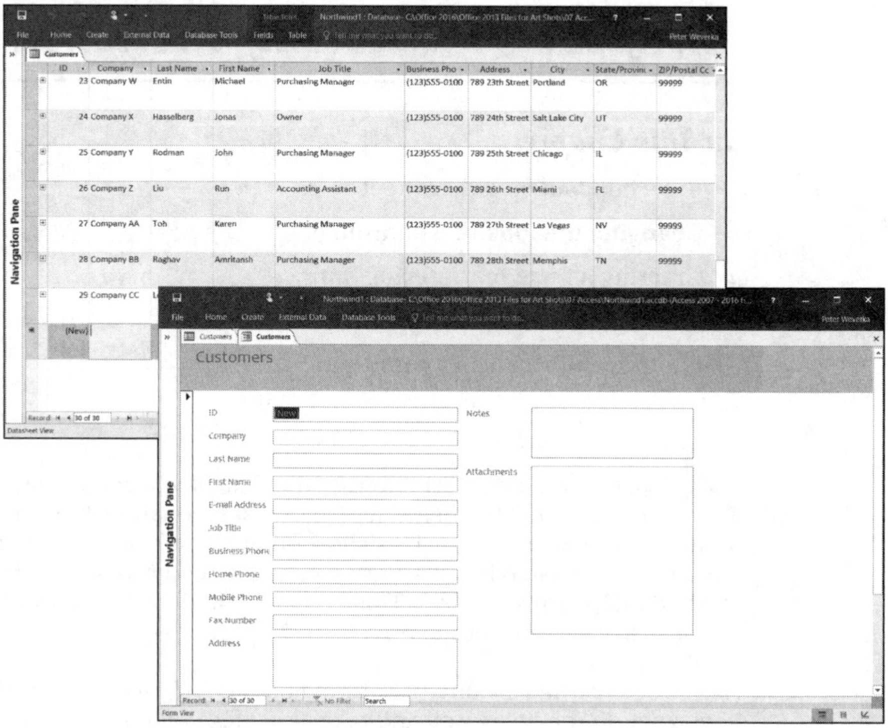

Figure 3-1: Entering records in Datasheet view (left) and in a form (right).

Here are the advantages of entering the data in a form:

- ✦ You don't have to scroll left or right to see all the fields.
- ✦ Getting from field to field is easier.
- ✦ Fields are clearly labeled so that you always know what to enter.

Entering the Data in Datasheet View

Entering data in Datasheet view is like entering data in a conventional table. As with a table, a datasheet has columns and rows. Records are entered in rows, and each column represents a field. Fans of Datasheet view like being able to look at a dozen records simultaneously. For fans of Datasheet view, these pages explain how to enter data in a datasheet and change a datasheet's appearance.

Database tables open in Datasheet view when you double-click their names in the Navigation pane. But if you happen to be gazing at a table in Design view, click the View command on the Home tab or the Datasheet View button on the status bar.

Entering data

In Datasheet view, the bottom of the window tells you how many records are entered in the database table and which record the cursor is in. To enter a new record, move to a new, empty row and start entering the data. To create a new row, do one of the following:

- ✦ On the Home tab, click the New button.
- ✦ Click the New (Blank) Record button in the Datasheet navigation buttons. These buttons are located at the bottom of the Datasheet view window.
- ✦ Scroll to the bottom of the Datasheet view window and begin typing in the row with an asterisk (*) next to it.
- ✦ Press Ctrl++ (the plus key).

A pencil icon appears on the row selector to let you know which record you're dealing with. To get from field to field, click in a field, press the Tab key, or press Enter. Table 3-1 lists keyboard shortcuts for getting around in a datasheet.

Table 3-1 Datasheet Shortcuts

Press. . .	*To Move. . .*
↑	To the previous record. You can also press the Previous button on the Navigation buttons.
↓	To the next record. You can also press the Next button.
Tab or Enter	To the next field in the record.
Shift+Tab	To the previous field in the record.
Home	To the first field in the record.
End	To the last field in the record.
Ctrl+Home	To the first field in the first record. You can also press the First button.
Ctrl+End	To the last field in the last record. You can also press the Last button.
Page Up	Up one screen.
Page Down	Down one screen.

To delete a record, click its row selector and press the Delete key or the Delete button (located on the Home tab). You can also click in a record, go to the (Table Tools) Fields tab, and click the Delete button there.

Two tricks for entering data quicker

In a database table with many fields, it's sometimes hard to tell what data to enter. When the pointer is in the sixth or seventh field, for example, you can lose sight of the first field, the one on the left side of the datasheet that usually identifies the person or item whose record you're entering.

TIP

To freeze a field so that it appears onscreen no matter how far you travel toward the right side of the datasheet, right-click the column's heading and choose Freeze Fields on the shortcut menu. To unfreeze the fields, right-click the column heading and choose Unfreeze All Fields on the shortcut menu. You can freeze more than one field by dragging across field names at the top of the datasheet before choosing to freeze the columns. Is it getting cold in here?

Another way to handle the problem of not being able to identify where data is supposed to be entered is to hide columns in the datasheet. To perform this trick, select the columns you want to hide by dragging the pointer across their names; then right-click the column heading and choose Hide Fields on the shortcut menu. To see the columns again, right-click any column heading and choose Unhide Fields on the shortcut menu. You see the Unhide Columns dialog box. Select the fields that you want to see on the datasheet.

TIP

The fastest way to hide a column is to drag the border between it and the next column to the left until the column disappears.

Entering data in the Zoom box

To make putting a long entry in a field a little easier, Access offers the Zoom box. Instead of having to stay within the narrow confines of a datasheet field, you can press Shift+F2 to open the Zoom box and enter the data there. After you click OK, the data is entered in the field. The Zoom box is especially convenient for entering data in a Memo field. As Chapter 2 in this mini-book explains, Memo fields can hold a whopping 65,535 characters. Move the cursor into a field and press Shift+F2 to open the Zoom box and read all the text in the field.

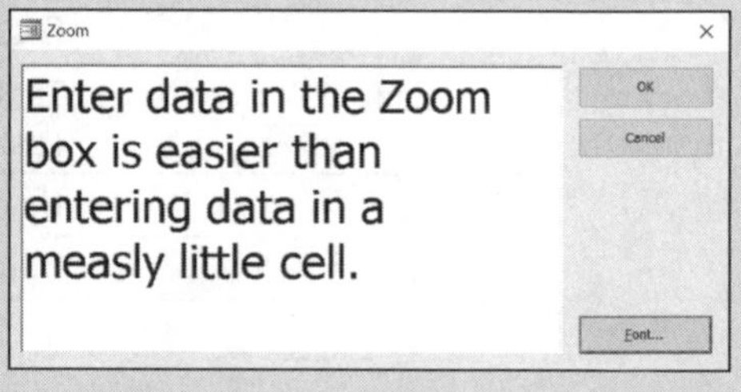

Changing the appearance of the datasheet

To make the datasheet a little less cluttered and unwieldy, try experimenting with its appearance. Access offers a few handy shortcuts for doing just that:

- **Rearranging columns:** To move a column to a different location, click its name at the top of the datasheet and drag it to the left or right.
- **Resizing columns:** Move the pointer between column names at the top of the datasheet, and when you see the double-headed arrow, click and start dragging. To make a column just large enough to fit its widest entry, move the pointer between column names and double-click when you see the double-headed arrow.
- **Changing fonts:** The default font for a datasheet is Calibri 11-point, but the Home tab offers commands for changing fonts and font sizes. Look for these commands in the Text Formatting group.
- **Changing the look of gridlines:** On the Home tab, open the drop-down list on the Gridlines button and choose options to change the number and thickness of gridlines.
- **Alternate row colors:** On the Home tab, open the drop-down list on the Alternate Row Color button and choose a color for alternating rows on the datasheet.

TIP

To experiment all at one time with the many options for changing a datasheet's appearance, go to the Home tab and click the Text Formatting group button. You see the Datasheet Formatting dialog box, as shown in Figure 3-2. If you want a customized look for all the datasheets you work on, visit the File tab and select Options. Then go to the Datasheet category in the Options dialog box and go to town.

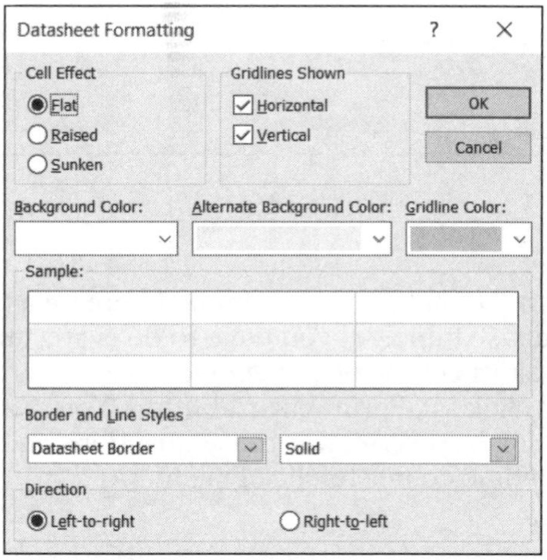

Figure 3-2: The Datasheet Formatting dialog box.

Entering the Data in a Form

Forms like the one shown in Figure 3-3 are very convenient for entering data. The labels tell you exactly what to enter. Personally, I prefer entering data in a form to entering data on a datasheet. On a form, you take it one step — make that one record — at a time. Not looking at a dozen records makes the task of entering data a little easier. These pages explain how to create a form for entering information in a database table. You also get tried-and-true advice for moving around with the Navigation buttons.

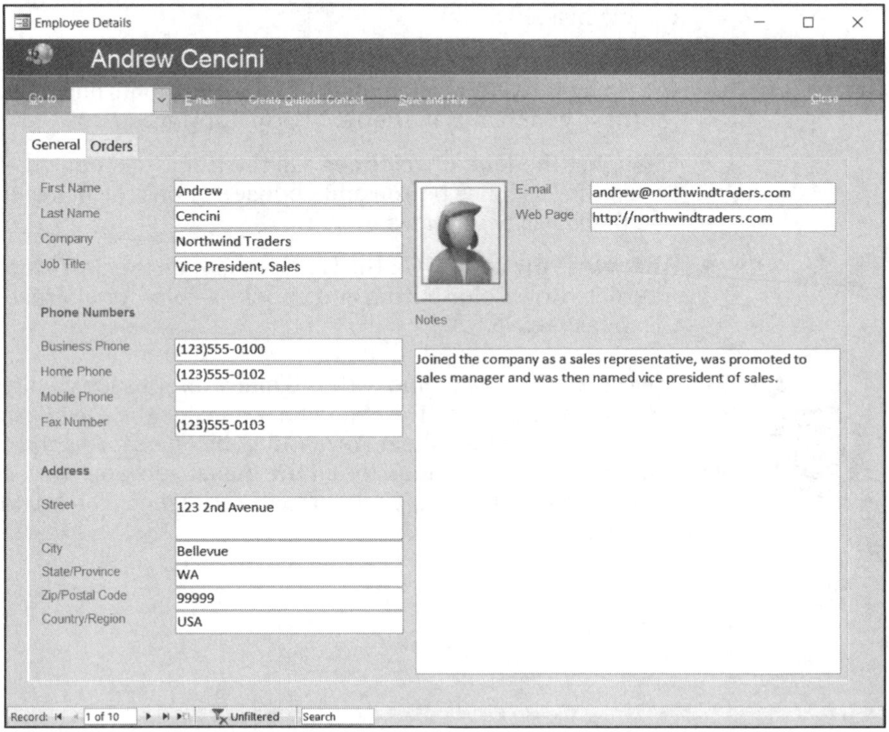

Figure 3-3: A form.

Creating a form

Fortunately, the Form Wizard makes it very simple to create a form for entering information in a database table. All you have to do is start the wizard, choose the table, and make a couple of design decisions. To create a form, go to the Create tab and click the Form Wizard button. You see the first of several Form Wizard dialog boxes. Answer these questions and keep clicking the Next button until the time comes to click Finish:

- **Tables/Queries:** From the drop-down list, choose the name of the database table you need to enter data in.
- **Selected Fields:** Click the >> button to enter all the field names in the Select Fields box.
- **Layout:** Select the Columnar option button. The other layouts aren't much good for entering data in a table. If you choose Tabular or Datasheet, you may as well enter data straight into the datasheet rather than rely on a form.
- **Title:** Name your form after the table you created it for so you can identify the form easily in the Navigation pane.

To delete a form, right-click its name in the Navigation pane and choose Delete on the shortcut menu.

Entering the data

To open a form and begin entering data in its database table, display the form's name in the Navigation pane and then double-click the form's name. You can also right-click the name of the form and choose Open.

To enter data in a form, click the New (Blank) Record button. This button is located with the Navigation buttons at the bottom of the form window. A new, empty form appears. Start typing. Press the Tab key, press the Enter key, or click to move from field to field. You can move backward through the fields by pressing Shift+Tab. If you enter half a record and want to start over, press the Esc key to empty the current field. Press Esc again to empty all the fields.

The Navigation buttons at the bottom of the form window tell you how many records are in the database table and which record you're looking at. From left to right, the Navigation buttons take you to the first record, previous record, next record, and last record.

Finding a Missing Record

Sometimes data goes astray. You scroll through a datasheet but simply can't find the item or record you need so badly. For times like those, Access offers the Find command. Use the command to scour a database for errant information.

Open the database table with the data that needs finding. If you know in which field the data is located, click in the field. You can save a little time that way. Then, on the Home tab, click the Find button (or press Ctrl+F). You see the Find and Replace dialog box, as shown in Figure 3-4. Fill in the dialog box as follows:

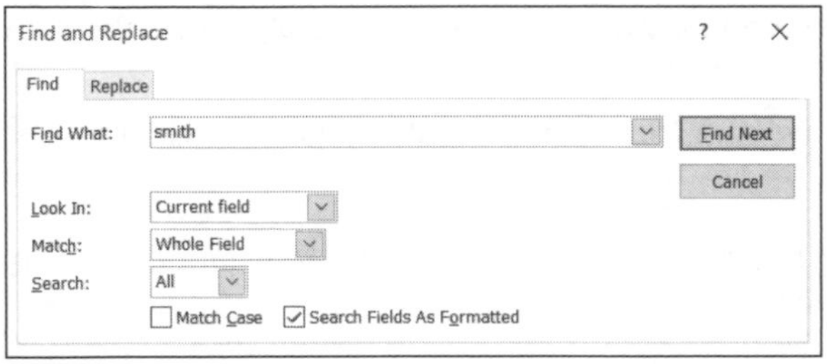

Figure 3-4: Finding data.

- **Find What:** Enter the item you're looking for. If you're looking for a null value, enter **null** in this text box. Enter "" (two double-quotation marks) to find zero-length strings. Table 3-2 describes the wildcard characters you can use in searches.
- **Look In:** If you clicked in a field before choosing the Find command, Current Field is selected in this box. To search the entire database table, choose Current Document on the drop-down list.
- **Match:** Choose the option that describes what you know about the item. Choosing the Any Part of Field option can make for a long search. For example, a search for the letters *chin* finds, among others, China, Ching, and itching — any word with the consecutive letters *chin.*
- **Search:** Choose an option — All, Up, or Down — that describes which direction to start searching.
- **Match Case:** If you know the combination of upper- and lowercase letters you're after and you enter the combination in the Find What text box, select this check box.
- **Search Fields As Formatted:** If you're searching for a field that has been formatted a certain way, select this check box and make sure that the text or numbers you enter in the Find What text box are formatted correctly. For example, if you're searching for a record with the date July 31, 1958, and you choose the *mm/dd/yyyy* format, enter the date as 07/31/1958.

Click the Find Next button to conduct the search. The item might be found in more than one location. Keep clicking Find Next (or pressing Alt+F) until you find the item or you die of thirst on the hot sands of the digital desert.

Table 3-2	Wildcard Characters for Searches	
Character	*Description*	*Example*
?	A single character	**b?t** finds *bat, bet, bit,* and *but.*
#	A single numeric digit	**9411#** finds *94111, 94112, 94113,* and so on.
*	Any group of consecutive characters	**t*o** finds *to, two,* and *tattoo.*
[xyz]	Any character in the brackets	**t[aio]pper** finds *tapper, tipper,* and *topper,* but not *tupper.*
[!xy]	Any character not in the brackets	**p[!io]t** finds *pat* and *pet,* but not *pit* and *pot.*
x–z	Any character in a range of characters	**[1–4]000** finds *1000, 2000, 3000,* and *4000,* but not *5000.* The range must be in ascending order.

TIP

To quickly find the first value of a search term, start typing in the Search box in the form window or in Datasheet view. As soon as you start typing, the cursor moves to the first instance of the data you enter. The search box is located at the bottom of the screen.

Finding and Replacing Data

Finding and replacing data is remarkably similar to finding data. The difference is that you enter data in the Replace With text box as well as the familiar Find What text box and other option boxes. Figure 3-5 shows the Replace tab of the Find and Replace dialog box. Does it look familiar? If it doesn't, read the preceding topic in this chapter.

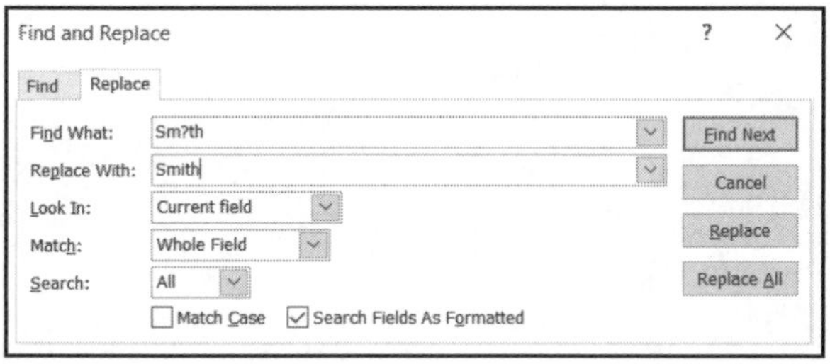

Figure 3-5: Replacing data.

To find and replace data, go to the Home tab and click the Replace button (or press Ctrl+H). You see the Replace tab of the Find and Replace dialog box. After you enter the replacement data in the Replace With text box, make sure that Whole Field is selected in the Match drop-down list. Conducting a find-and-replace operation with Any Part of Field or Start of Field selected in the Match drop-down list can have unintended consequences. For example, a search for *Brook* also finds *Brooklyn, Middlebrook,* and other words that include *brook.* Blindly replacing the *brook* text string with *stream* produces, for example, *Streamlyn* and *Middlestream.*

Unless you're as confident as a gambler with four aces, don't click the Replace All button to replace all instances of the text or numbers in the database table or field you're searching in. Instead, click the Replace button to find and replace text or numbers one instance at a time.

By the way, you can also find and replace data with an update query. Chapter 4 of this mini-book covers update queries.

Chapter 4: Sorting, Querying, and Filtering for Data

In This Chapter

- **Sorting, or rearranging, records in a database table**
- **Filtering records in a table to see only the records you need**
- **Querying to collect and examine information stored in a database**
- **Looking at different kinds of queries**

Now that you've laid the groundwork, you can put your database through its paces and make it do what databases are meant to do — provide information of one kind or another. This chapter explains how to pester a database for names, addresses, dates, statistical averages, and what not. It shows how to sort records and filter a database table to see records of a certain kind. You also find out how to query a database to get it to yield its dark secrets and invaluable information.

Sorting Records in a Database Table

Sorting rearranges records in a database table so that the records appear in alphabetical, numerical, or date order in one field. By sorting the records in a database, you can locate records faster. What's more, being able to sort data means that you don't have to bother about the order in which you enter records because you can always sort them later to put them in a particular order.

Ascending vs. descending sorts

Records can be sorted in ascending or descending order:

- **Ascending order:** Arranges records in alphabetical order from A to Z, numbers from smallest to largest, and dates chronologically from earliest to latest.
- **Descending order:** Arranges text from Z to A, numbers from largest to smallest, and dates chronologically from latest to earliest.

Sorting records

Follow these steps to sort the records in a database table:

1. **In Datasheet view, click anywhere in the field by which you want to sort the records.**
2. **On the Home tab, click the Ascending or Descending button.**

   You can also right-click a field name at the top of a column and choose Sort A to Z or Sort Z to A on the shortcut menu. The menu choices change based on the type of data. For Number fields, you can sort smallest to largest and vice versa; for Date fields, choose to sort oldest to newest, or vice versa.

TIP

You can sort on more than one field by clicking a field and sorting it, and then clicking a second field and sorting it. Just make sure you sort the fields in reverse order. For example, to sort the database by the Employee, Customer, and Order ID fields, click in Order ID and sort it in ascending order; click in Customer and sort it in ascending order; click in Employee and sort it in ascending order. If you mess up and forget how the table is sorted, click the Remove Sort button. This button is located on the Home tab underneath the Ascending and Descending buttons.

Filtering to Find Information

Filtering isolates all the records in a database table that have the same field values or nearly the same field values. Instead of all the records in the table appearing on the datasheet, only records that meet the filtering criteria appear, as shown in Figure 4-1.

The basic idea behind filtering is to choose a field value in the database table and use it as the standard for finding or excluding records. For example, you can find all the orders for a particular customer, all orders taken in the month of April, or all the orders that a particular customer placed in April. For that matter, you can filter by exclusion and see the records of all the orders in a database table *not* taken in April and *not* for a particular customer. Filtering is useful when you need to find records with specific information in a single database table.

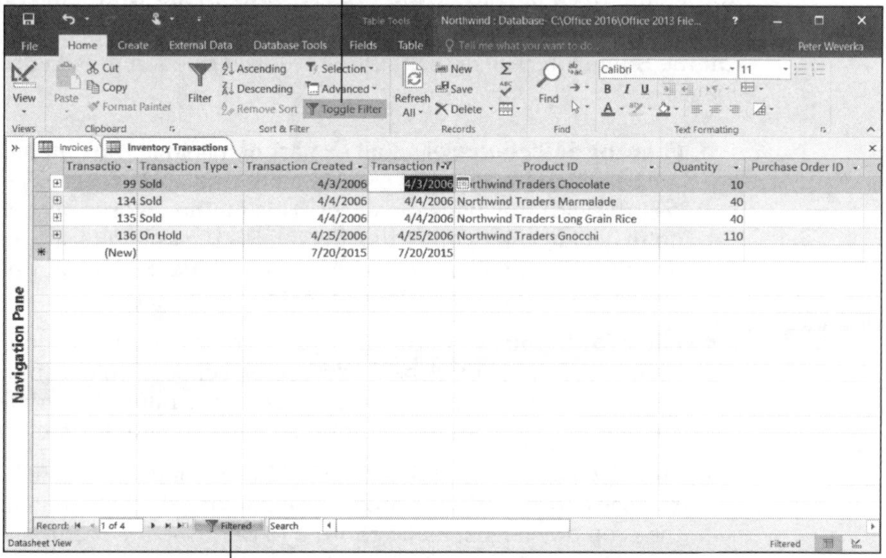

Figure 4-1: Results of a filtering operation.

The difference between a filter and a query

The biggest difference between filtering and querying is that you can save a query and call upon it more than once. Queries are kept at the ready in the Navigation pane. A filter, on the other hand, is as good as the first time you use it, although you can save and run it as a query. Filters apply to a single database table, whereas you can query to assemble information from more than one table. In the results of a query, you can include as many fields as you want, but the results of a filtering operation show all the fields in the database table, regardless of whether you want them.

When it comes to examining data, a query is more sophisticated than a filter. Although you can use standard comparison operators to find records by filtering, querying gives you the opportunity to use complex expressions as well as comparison operators. You can filter, for example, to find people whose income is greater than or less than a certain amount. However, because you can write expressions in queries, you can query to find people whose income falls within a certain range.

Different ways to filter a database table

For comparison purposes, here are shorthand descriptions of the four ways to filter a database table. All filtering operations begin in Datasheet view on the Home tab. These techniques are described in detail in the upcoming pages.

- **Filter by Selection:** Select all or part of a field in the database table, click the Selection button, and choose a filtering option. Access isolates all records with the data you select. This method works best when you can't quite decide what you're looking for. It's the only filtering method that permits you to look for data found in a whole field or part of a field. You can also filter data that doesn't match the selection.
- **Filter for Input:** Select the field you want to filter with and click the Filter button. A dialog box appears so you can choose values in the field or enter comparison operators to describe the numeric or date values you are filtering for. With this technique, you can filter for data ranges.
- **Filter by Form:** Click the Advanced button and choose Filter by Form. You see a form with one drop-down list for each field in your table. From the drop-down lists, make choices to describe the records you're looking for and then click the Toggle Filter button. This method is more flexible than the others because you can conduct OR as well as AND filtering operations. For example, you can isolate the records of people named Smith who also live in California, or the people who live in California or New York.
- **Advanced Filter/Sort:** Click the Advanced button and choose Advanced Filter/Sort. The Filter window opens. Drag the name of the field you want to filter onto the grid. Then choose a Sort option and enter a search criterion. This filtering technique has more in common with queries than filters. Truth be told, the Advanced Filter/Sort command is merely a way to query a single table.

TIP

After you filter a database table, you can run a second (or third or fourth) filter operation to filter the data even more and further isolate the data you are looking for.

"Unfiltering" a database table

REMEMBER

You can tell when you're looking at a database table that has been filtered rather than a database table with all its records because the word *Filtered* appears at the bottom of the window next to the Navigation buttons (refer to Figure 4-1). Moreover, the filter icon appears in the field names of columns used in the filter operation and the Toggle Filter button on the Ribbon is highlighted.

When you have finished filtering a database table, use one of these techniques to "unfilter" it and see all the records in the table again:

- Click the word *Filtered* at the bottom of the window. You can click this word again or click the Toggle Filter button to repeat the filter operation.
- On the Home tab, click the Toggle Filter button. You can click this button again to repeat the filter operation.
- On the Home tab, click the Advanced button and choose Clear All Filters on the drop-down list. Choosing this option kills the filter operation; you can't repeat it except by reconstructing it in the Datasheet window.

Filtering by selection

Filtering by selection is the fastest way to filter a database table. It's also the best way when you're not sure what you're looking for because you can search for partial words and phrases. Follow these steps to filter by selection:

1. **Display the database table that needs filtering in Datasheet view.**
2. **Tell Access how to filter the records.**

   To find all records with the same value or text in a particular field, simply click in a field with the value or text. If you aren't quite sure what to look for, select part of a field. For example, to find all names that start with the letters *St,* select St in one of the name fields.
3. **On the Home tab, click the Selection button and choose a filtering option.**

   The options you see are specific to the cell you clicked or the data you selected in Step 2. For example, if you click a Last Name field that contains the name *Smith*, your options include Equals "Smith" and Does Not Contain "Smith." Select an option to include or exclude records in the filter operation.

Filtering for input

Filtering for input gives you the advantage of being able to filter for data ranges. Use this technique to isolate records that fall within a numerical or date range. Follow these steps to filter for input:

1. **Display the database table that you want to filter in Datasheet view.**
2. **Select the field with the data you want to use for the filter operation.**
3. **On the Home tab, click the Filter button.**

   As shown in Figure 4-2, a dialog box appears so that you can describe records that you want to filter for. You can also open this dialog box by clicking the button to the right of a field name.

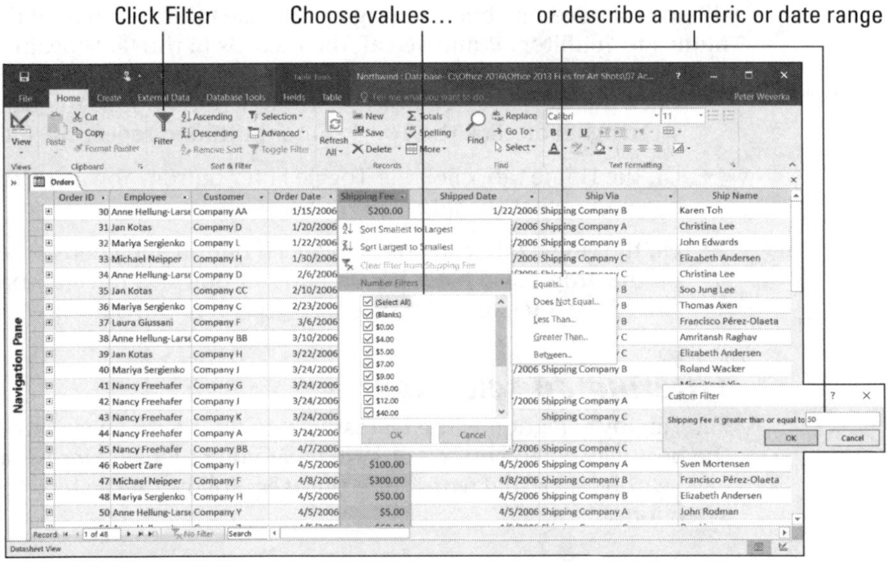

Figure 4-2: Filtering by input for numeric data values.

4. **Tell Access how to filter the database table.**

   You can choose values or describe a data range:

   - *Choose values in the field:* The dialog box lists all values in the field. Deselect the Select All check box and then click to select the values you want to filter with.
   - *Describe a numeric or date range:* Choose Number Filters or Date Filters and select a comparison operator on the submenu (refer to Figure 4-2). The Custom Filter dialog box appears. Enter a comparison value and click OK.

You can repeat Steps 2 through 4 to filter the database table even further.

Filtering by form

Filtering by form is a sophisticated filtering method. It permits you to filter in more than one field using an *OR search.* For example, you can tell Access to look in the Last Name field for people named *Martinez,* as well as look in the City field for *Martinez*es who live in Los Angeles *or* San Francisco. Moreover, you can use comparison operators in the filter operation. Follow these steps to filter by form:

1. **In Datasheet view, go to the Home tab, click the Advanced button, and choose Filter by Form on the drop-down list.**

   Only field names appear on the datasheet, as shown in Figure 4-3.

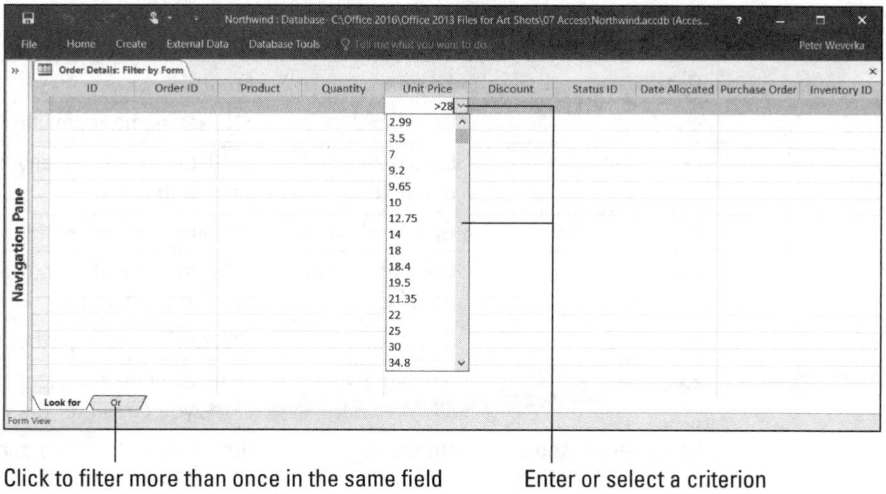

Figure 4-3: Filtering by form.

2. **Click in a field, open its drop-down list, and enter a comparison value or select a value on the drop-down list.**

   You can choose a value on the drop-down list or, in Number and Currency fields, enter a comparison operator and a value. Table 4-1 explains the comparison operators.

3. **If you want, enter more criteria for the filtering operation.**

   You can enter values in other fields as well as filter more than once in the same field.

   - *Enter values in other fields:* Open the drop-down list in a field and enter a comparison value or select a value on the drop-down list.
   - *Filter more than once in the same field:* Select a field in which you already entered a search criterion. Then click the Or tab and either enter a comparison value or choose a value from the drop-down list.

   When you click the Or tab, the search choices you made previously disappear from the screen. Don't worry — Access remembers them on the Look For tab. You can click the Or tab again if you want to enter more criteria for Or searching.

4. **Click the Toggle Filter button.**

   The results of the filtering operation appear in the datasheet.

Table 4-1 Comparison Operators for Filtering and Querying

Operator	*Name*	*Example*
<	Less than	<10, any number smaller than ten
<=	Less than or equal to	<=10, ten as well as any number smaller than ten
>	Greater than	>10, any number larger than ten
>=	Greater than or equal to	>=10, ten as well as any number equal to or larger than ten
=	Equal to	=10, ten — not any other number
<>	Not equal to	<>10; all numbers except ten (instead of <>, you can enter the word *not*)
Between . . . And . . .	Between	Between 10 And 15, a number between 10 and 15 or equal to 10 or 15

Querying: The Basics

Querying means to ask a question of a database and get an answer in the form of records that meet the query criteria. Query when you want to ask a detailed question of a database. "Who lives in Los Angeles and donated more than $500 last year?" is an example of a query. So is, "Which orders were purchased by people who live in California and therefore, have to pay sales tax, and how much sales tax was charged with these orders?" A query can search for information in more than one database table. For that matter, you can query other queries for information. A query can be as sophisticated or as simple as you need it to be. In the results of the query, you can show all the fields in a database table or only a few necessary fields.

Access offers several different ways to query a database (the different techniques are described later in this chapter in "Six Kinds of Queries"). Still, no matter which kind of query you're dealing with, the basics of creating and running a query are the same. You start on the Create tab to build new queries. To open a query you already created, double-click its name on the Navigation pane. The following pages introduce you to queries, how to create them, and how to modify them.

Creating a new query

To create a new query, start on the Create tab and click the Query Design or Query Wizard button.

✦ **Create the query in Design view:** Click the Query Design button to see the Query Design window, as shown in Figure 4-4, as well as the Show Table dialog box for telling Access which database tables to query. Construct your query in the Design window (the following pages explain how).

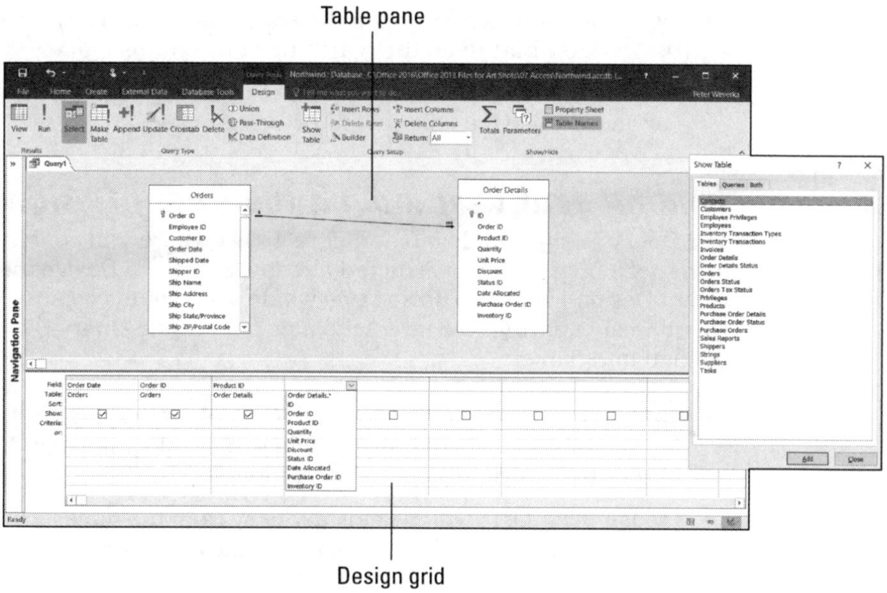

Figure 4-4: The Query Design window.

✦ **Create the query with a wizard:** Click the Query Wizard button to display the New Query dialog box and then choose a wizard option (four possible Query Wizards are available) and answer the questions that the Query Wizard asks. You're asked which table or tables to query, which fields to include in the query, and which fields to include in the query results (the following pages explain these issues).

To run a query, open the query in the Query window, go to the (Query Tools) Design tab, and click the Run button. The results of the query appear in Datasheet view.

Viewing queries in Datasheet and Design view

Select a query on the Navigation pane and use these techniques to view it in Datasheet or Design view. Datasheet view shows the results of running a query. Create and modify queries in Design view.

✦ **Opening in Design view:** Right-click the query's name in the Navigation pane and choose Design View on the shortcut menu.

- **Opening in Datasheet view:** On the Navigation pane, double-click the query's name or right-click its name and choose Open on the shortcut menu.
- **Switching between views with the View button:** On the Home tab, click the View button. This button changes appearance, depending on whether you're in Design view or Datasheet view.
- **Switching between views on the status bar:** Click the Datasheet View or Design View button on the right side of the status bar.
- **Switching between views by right-clicking:** Right-click the query's title bar and choose Datasheet View or Design View.

Finding your way around the Query Design window

The Query Design window (see Figure 4-4) is where you construct a query or retool a query you constructed already. Switch to Design view to see the Query Design window. You see this window straightaway after you click the Query Design button to construct a new query. The Query Design window is divided into halves:

- **Table pane:** Lists the database tables you're querying as well as the fields in each table. You can drag the tables to new locations or drag a table border to change its size and view more fields.
- **Design grid:** Lists which fields to query from the tables, how to sort the query results, which fields to show in the query results, and criteria for locating records in fields.

Choosing which database tables to query

To choose which database tables (and queries as well) to get information from, go to the (Query Tools) Design tab and click the Show Table button. You see the Show Table dialog box (refer to Figure 4-4). The Tables tab lists all the database tables you created for your database. Ctrl+click to select the tables you want to query and then click the Add button. To query a query, go to the Queries tab and select the query.

The tables and queries you choose appear in the Table pane of the Query Design window (refer to Figure 4-4). To remove a table from a query, right-click it in the Table pane and choose Remove Table on the shortcut menu.

REMEMBER

In order to query more than one table, you need to establish relationships between tables. (Chapter 2 of this mini-book has information about establishing relationships between database tables.) So-called *join lines* in the Query Design window show how the tables are related to one another.

If you haven't defined relationships between the tables, you can still join them together by dragging a field from one table onto a field in another table. This is the same method used to create relationships between tables. Joining tables in a query doesn't create an actual relationship; it's just a temporary join for the sake of the query.

Choosing which fields to query

After you choose which tables to query, the next step is to choose which fields to query from the tables you selected. The object is to list fields from the Table pane in the first row of the Design grid. Fields whose names you enter in the first row of the Design grid are the fields that produce query results, as demonstrated by Figure 4-5.

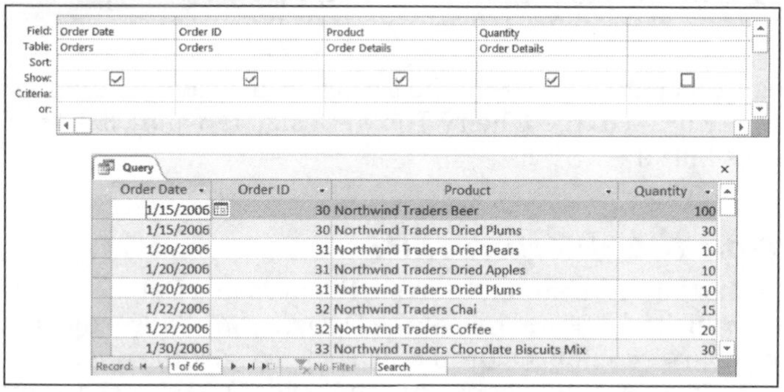

Figure 4-5: How query fields translate into query results.

Access offers these techniques for listing field names in the first row of the Design grid:

- **Dragging a field name:** Drag a field name into a column on the Design grid. The field name appears on the grid, as does the name of the table that you drag the field name from.
- **Double-clicking a field name:** Double-click a field name to place it in the next available column in the Design grid.
- **Choosing a table and field name:** Click in the Table row, open the drop-down list, and choose the name of a table. Then, in the Field box directly above, open the drop-down list and choose a field name.
- **Selecting all the fields in a table:** In the unlikely event that you want all the fields from a table to appear in the query results, either double-click the asterisk (*) at the top of the list of field names or drag the asterisk into the Design grid. Access places the name of the table followed by an asterisk in the Field text box. The asterisk signifies that all the fields from the table are included in the query.

Moving field columns on the Query grid

The order in which field names appear in the Query grid is also the order in which they appear in the query results (refer to Figure 4-5). Follow these steps to put field columns in the right order in the Query grid:

1. **Click a column's selector button to select a column.**

   This button is the narrow gray box directly above the field name. The pointer turns into a downward-pointing arrow when you move it over the selector button.

2. **Click the selector button again and drag the column to the left or right.**

To remove a field name from the Design grid, select it and press the Delete key or go to the (Query Tools) Design tab and click the Delete Columns button.

Sorting the query results

At the start of this chapter, "Sorting Records in a Database Table" explains what sorting is. The Sort row of the Design grid — directly underneath the Table name — contains a drop-down list. To sort the query, click the drop-down list in a field and choose Ascending or Descending to sort the results of a query on a particular field. To sort the results on more than one field, make sure that the first field to be sorted appears to the left of the other fields. Access reads the sort order from left to right.

Choosing which fields appear in query results

Although a field is part of a query and is listed in the Query grid, it isn't always necessary to display information from the field in the query results. Consider the Query grid shown in Figure 4-6. The object of this query is to get a list of customers by ZIP Code that ordered products in the year 2016. To that end, the query criteria cell in the Order Date field is `Between #1/1/2016# And #12/31/2016#`. However, when the query results are generated, listing the precise dates when the orders shipped isn't necessary because the object of the query is to get a list of customers by ZIP Code who ordered products in 2016.

REMEMBER

Whether a field's Show check box is selected in the Query grid determines whether its results are part of the query results. Deselect the Show box if a field is necessary for producing records in a query but not necessary in the query results. By the way, after you save and reopen a query, Access moves deselected Show fields to the right side of the Query grid, where you usually have to scroll to see them.

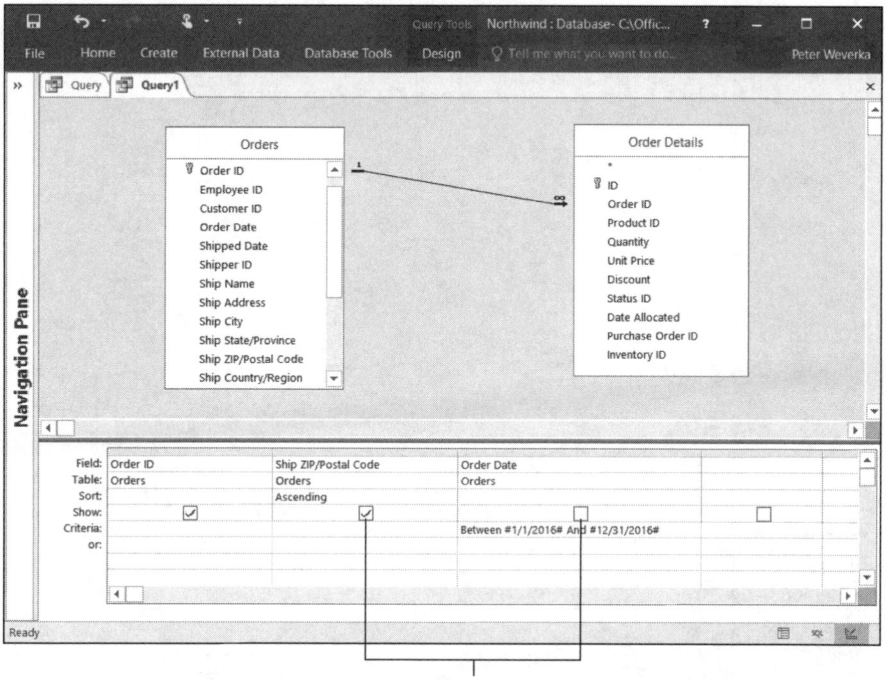

Select or deselect to show a field's data in query results

Figure 4-6: Choosing what appears in the query results.

Entering criteria for a query

What separates a run-of-the-mill query from a supercharged query is a *criterion,* an expression or value you enter on the Criteria line under a field. Enter criteria on the Criteria line of the Query grid. By entering criteria, you can pinpoint records in the database with great accuracy. In Figure 4-7, the Query grid instructs Access to retrieve orders with invoices due before January 1, 2016 that charged more than $2000 and were shipped to Massachusetts (MA), Connecticut (CT), or New York (NY).

REMEMBER: As Figure 4-7 shows, Access places double quotation marks ("") around text criteria and number signs (#) around date criteria. When you enter text or date criteria, don't enter the double quotation marks or number signs. Access enters them for you.

TIP: When you need help writing an expression for a query, try clicking the Builder button to construct your query in the Expression Builder dialog box. This button is located on the (Query Tools) Design tab.

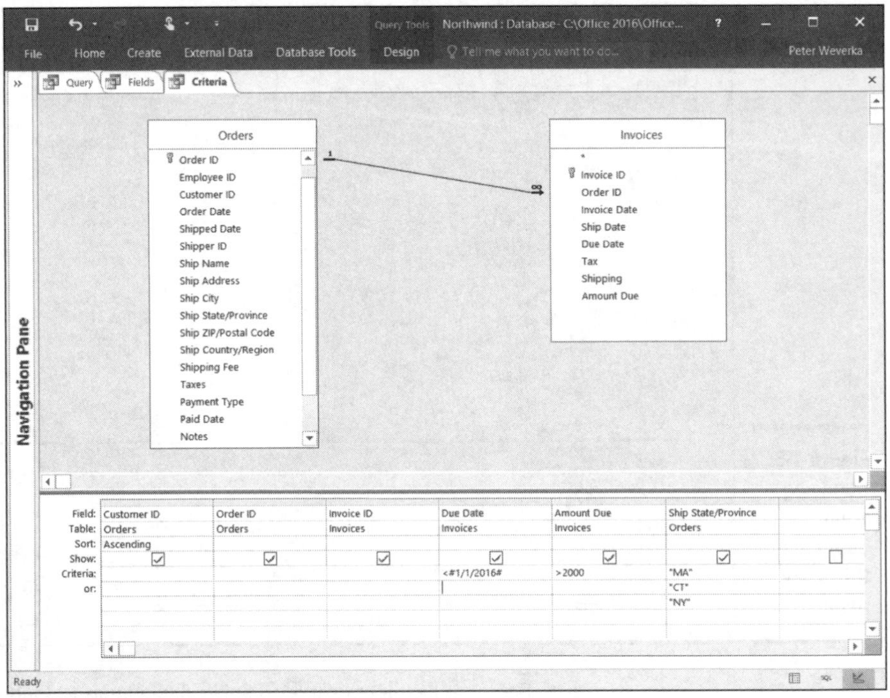

Figure 4-7: Including criteria in a query.

Entering numeric criteria

Enter numeric criteria in Number and Currency fields when you want to isolate records with specific values. Earlier in this chapter, Table 4-1 describes comparison operators you can use for querying and filtering. These operators are invaluable when it comes to mining a database for information. Use the greater than (>) and less than (<) operators to find values higher or lower than a target value. Use the Between operator to find values between two numbers. For example, *Between 62 And 55* in a Currency field isolates records with all items that sell for between $62.00 and $55.00.

Do not include commas in numbers when you enter them as criteria. For example, enter 3200, not 3,200. Enter a comma and you get a "The expression you entered contains invalid syntax. . ." error message.

Entering text criteria

To enter a text criterion, type it in the Criteria text box. For example, to find students who attended Ohio State University, enter Ohio State in the Criteria text box of the University field. Access places double quotation marks ("") around the text you enter as soon when you move the pointer out of the Criteria text box.

Wildcards and the Not operator can come in very handy when entering text criteria:

- **Wildcards:** Wildcards make it possible to query for data whose spelling you aren't quite sure of. (In Chapter 3 of this mini-book, Table 3-2 explains what the wildcard characters are and how to use them.) For example, entering Sm?th in the Criteria box of the Last Name field finds all Smiths and Smyths. Entering E* in the Company field finds all company names that begin with the letter *E*.
- **Not operator:** Use the Not operator to exclude records from query results. For example, to exclude records with Belgium in the Shipped To field, enter Not Belgium in the Criteria text box. This is a great way to strip unneeded records from a query.

Entering date criteria

All the operators that work for numeric data (see Table 4-1 earlier in this chapter) also work for data entered in a Date field. For example, you would enter **>7/31/1958** in a Birth Date field to find all people born after (greater than) July 31, 1958. You would enter **Between 1/1/1920 And 12/31/1929** to retrieve data about people born in the Roaring Twenties.

Access places number signs (#) around date criteria after you enter it. You can enter dates in these formats:

- 11/22/13
- 11/22/2013
- 22-Nov-13
- November 22, 2013

For the purpose of entering two-digit years in dates, the digits 30 through 99 belong to the 20th Century (1930–1999), but the digits 00 through 29 belong to the 21st Century (2000–2029). For example, *>4/1/24* refers to April 1, 2024, not April 1, 1924. To enter a date in 1929 or earlier, enter four digits instead of two to describe the year: **>4/1/1929**. To enter a date in 2030, or later, enter four digits instead of two: **>4/1/2038**. To avoid any confusion, enter four-digit years all the time.

The Date() function can come in very handy when you want to retrieve data relative to today's date, whatever it happens to be. For example, to retrieve purchase orders made between January 1, 2009, and today's date, enter this expression: **Between 1/1/2009 And Date()**.

At last — saving and running a query

To save a query and inscribe its name forever in the Navigation pane, click the Save button on the Quick Access toolbar and enter a descriptive name in the Save As dialog box. The name you enter appears in the Queries group in the Navigation pane.

After you laboriously construct your query, take it for a test drive. To run a query:

- **Starting from the Query Design window:** Click the Run button on the (Query Tools) Design tab.
- **Starting from the Navigation pane:** Double-click an existing query's name, or right-click its name and choose Open on the shortcut menu.

Six Kinds of Queries

For your pleasure and entertainment, the rest of this chapter describes six useful types of queries. Access offers a handful of other queries, but I won't go there. Those queries are pretty complicated. If you become adept at querying, however, you're invited to look into the Help system for advice about running the query types that aren't explained here.

Select query

A *select query* is the standard kind of query, which I explain earlier in this chapter. A select query gathers information from one or more database tables and displays the information in a datasheet. A select query is the most common query, the primal query, the starting point for most other queries.

Top-value query

A *top-value query* is an easy way to find out, in a Number or Currency field, the highest or lowest values. On the Query grid, enter the name of the Number or Currency field you want to know more about; then choose Ascending in the Sort drop-down list to rank values from lowest to highest or Descending in the Sort drop-down list to rank values from highest to lowest. Finally, on the (Query Tools) Design tab, enter a value in the Return text box or choose a value on the Return drop-down list:

- **Highest or lowest by percentage:** Enter or choose a percentage to find, for example, the highest or lowest 25 percent of the values. To enter a percentage, type a percent sign (%) after your entry and press the Enter key.
- **Highest or lowest by ranking number:** Enter or choose a number to find, for example, the top-ten or lowest-ten values. Press the Enter key after you enter a number.

This may seem counterintuitive, but to see the top values, you have to sort the field you're ranking in descending order. For example, if you sort employees by number of sales in descending order, the employees with the top sales appear at the top. To see the bottom values, sort in ascending order.

Summary query

Similar to a top-value query, a *summary query* is a way of getting cumulative information about all the data in a field. In a field that stores data about sales in Kentucky, for example, you can find the average amount of each sale, the total amount of all the sales, the total number of all the sales, and other data.

To run a summary query, go to the (Query Tools) Design tab and click the Totals button. A new row called Total appears on the Query grid. Open the Total drop-down list in the field whose contents you want to summarize and choose a function. Table 4-2 describes the functions.

Table 4-2 Summary Query Functions

Function	*Returns*
Sum	The total of all values in the field
Avg	The average of all values
Min	The lowest value
Max	The highest value
Count	The number of values
StDev	The standard deviation of the values
Var	The variance of the values
First	The first value
Last	The last value

The Group By, Expression, and Where choices in the Totals drop-down list are for including fields you're not performing a function on:

- **Group By:** For choosing which fields to show totals for.
- **Expression:** For creating a calculated field.
- **Where:** For setting criteria (you can't include the field in the query).

Calculation query

A *calculation query* is one in which calculations are performed as part of the query. For example, you can calculate the sales tax on items sold or total the numbers in two fields in the same record. The beauty of a calculation query is that the data is recomputed each time you run the query. If the data used to make a calculation changes, so does the result of the calculation. If you were to include the calculation in a database table, you would have to recalculate the data yourself each time one of the values changed. With a calculation query, Access does the math for you.

To construct a calculation query, you create a new field in the Query grid for storing the results of the calculation; then enter a name for the field and a formula for the calculation. Follow these steps to create a calculation query:

1. **Create a query as you normally would, and be sure to include the fields you want to use for calculation purposes in the Query grid.**
2. **In the Field box of a blank field, enter a name for the Calculation field and follow it with a colon.**

   In Figure 4-8, I entered **Subtotal:**. The purpose of the new Subtotal field is to calculate the Unit Price × the Quantity.

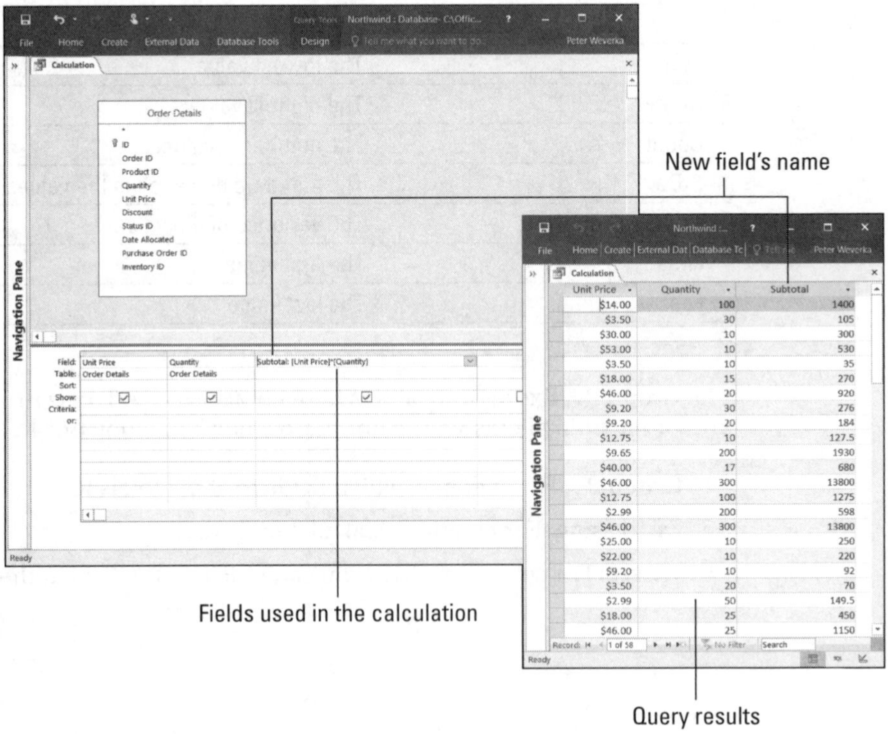

Figure 4-8: A calculation query.

3. **After the colon, in square brackets ([]), enter the name of a field whose data you use for the calculation.**

   In Figure 4-8, data from the Unit Price and Quantity fields are used in the calculation, so their names appear in square brackets: [Unit Price] and [Quantity]. Be sure to spell field names correctly so that Access can recognize them.

4. **Complete the calculation.**

   How you do this depends on what kind of calculation you're making. In Figure 4-8, I entered an asterisk (*) to multiply two fields together. The equation multiplies the values in the Unit Price and Quantity fields. You can add the data from two different fields — including calculated fields — by putting their names in brackets and joining them with a plus sign, like so: [SubTotal]+[Shipping Cost].

Sometimes the results of the query aren't formatted correctly on the datasheet. To assign a new format to a field you create for the purposes of making a calculation query, right-click the field on the Query grid and choose Properties. The Property Sheet appears. On the General tab, click the Format drop-down list and choose the correct format for your new, hand-crafted field.

Delete query

Be careful about running delete queries. A *delete query* deletes records and doesn't give you the opportunity to get the records back if you change your mind about deleting them. If used skillfully, however, a delete query is a great way to purge records from more than one database table at once. Back up your database file before running a delete query. Edith Piaf didn't regret her delete query, but you might regret yours.

To run a delete query, start a new query, and in on the (Query Tools) Design tab, click the Delete button. Then make as though you were running a select query but target the records you want to delete. Finally, click the Run button to run the query.

You can delete records from more than one table as long as the tables are related and you chose the Cascade Delete Related Records option in the Edit Relationships dialog box when you linked the tables. (See Chapter 2 of this mini-book for advice about forging relationships between tables.)

To preview the records that will be deleted before you run the delete query, switch to Datasheet view (click the View button). Those records you see? The delete query will delete them if you click the Run button.

Update query

An *update query* is a way to reach into a database and update records in several different tables all at one time. Update queries can be invaluable, but as with delete queries, they can have untoward consequences. Back up your database before you run an update query; then follow these steps to run it:

1. **Starting in Design view, go to the (Query Tools) Design tab and click the Update button.**
2. **In the field with the data that needs updating, enter text or a value in the Update To line. You can even enter another field name in square brackets ([ ]).**

   What you enter in the Update To line replaces what's in the field of the records you collect.
3. **Click the Run button.**

To update records in more than one table, you must have chosen the Cascade Update Related Fields option in the Edit Relationships dialog box when you linked the tables. (See the section in Chapter 2 of this mini-book about forging relationships between tables.)

Chapter 5: Presenting Data in a Report

In This Chapter

- Creating a new report
- Opening a report
- Changing the look of a report

The prettiest way to present data in a database table or query is to present it in a report. Even people who are allergic to databases can put up with database material in a report. Reports are easy to read and understand. They succinctly present the data so that you and others can interpret it. This brief chapter explains how to create reports, open them, and edit them.

Creating a Report

Access comes with all kinds of complicated tools for fashioning your own report — for laying out the pages in different ways and making data fields show up in different parts of the page. If ever a task called for relying on a wizard, creating a report is it. You can save yourself a lot of trouble, and fashion sophisticated-looking reports as well, by dispensing with the fancy report-making tools and letting the wizard do the job.

What's more, the easiest and best way to make a report is to base your report on a query. As part of fashioning a report with a wizard, you can tell Access which database tables and which fields to get the data from — in other words, you can query your database from inside the Report Wizard. However, doing that requires turning somersaults and cartwheels. It's far easier to run a query to produce the results you want in your report, save your query, and then fashion a report from the query results. Chapter 4 in this mini-book explains how to create a query.

Figure 5-1 shows a report created with the Report Wizard. To create a report with the Report Wizard, go to the Create tab and click the Report Wizard button. You see the first of several Report Wizard dialog boxes. Negotiate the dialog boxes as follows, clicking the Next button as you go along:

- **Tables/Queries:** Open this drop-down list and choose the query where the information in the report will come from. A list of fields in the query appears in the Available Fields box.
- **Available Fields and Selected Fields:** Select the fields whose data you want in the report by selecting the fields one at a time and clicking the > button. Doing so moves field names from the Available Fields box to the Selected Fields box. Add all the fields by clicking the >> button.
- **Do You Want to Add Any Grouping Levels?:** Include subheadings in your report by selecting a field name and clicking the > button to make it a subheading. If you're building your report on a query that includes related tables, the Report Wizard automatically adds subheadings.
- **What Sort Order Do You Want?:** Select up to four fields to sort the data in your report. Even if you sort the fields in a query, the report handles sorting on its own. If you include grouping levels, the report already sorts on these fields.
- **How Would You Like to Lay Out Your Report?:** Experiment with the options, and watch the Preview box, to choose a layout for your report. If your report has a lot of fields, you may want to print it in Landscape view.
- **What Title Do You Want for Your Report?:** Enter a descriptive title. The name you choose appears in the Reports group in the Navigation pane. From there, you double-click the name when you want to see the report.
- **Preview the Report:** Select this option button and click Finish.

The report appears in the Preview window. How do you like it? Later in this chapter, "Tweaking a Report" offers some tips for making a report look spiffier.

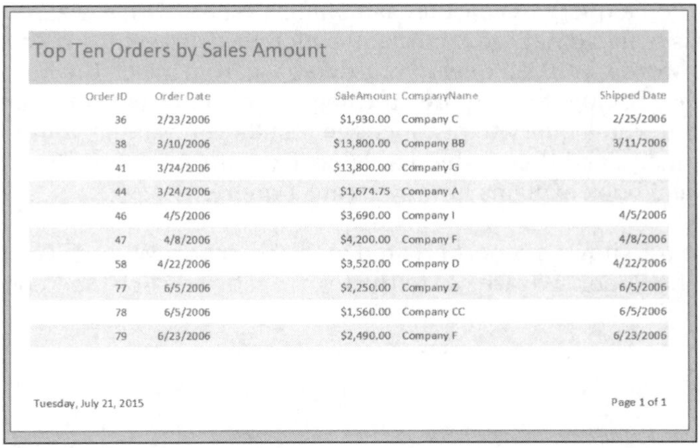

Top Ten Orders by Sales Amount

Order ID	Order Date	SaleAmount	CompanyName	Shipped Date
36	2/23/2006	$1,930.00	Company C	2/25/2006
38	3/10/2006	$13,800.00	Company BB	3/11/2006
41	3/24/2006	$13,800.00	Company G	
44	3/24/2006	$1,674.75	Company A	
46	4/5/2006	$3,690.00	Company I	4/5/2006
47	4/8/2006	$4,200.00	Company F	4/8/2006
58	4/22/2006	$3,520.00	Company D	4/22/2006
77	6/5/2006	$2,250.00	Company Z	6/5/2006
78	6/5/2006	$1,560.00	Company CC	6/5/2006
79	6/23/2006	$2,490.00	Company F	6/23/2006

Tuesday, July 21, 2015 Page 1 of 1

Figure 5-1: An example of a report.

Opening and Viewing Reports

If you've spent any time whatsoever in Access, you know the drill for opening a so-called object. Follow these steps to open a report:

1. **In the Navigation pane, select the Reports group.**

   You see the names of reports you created.

2. **Double-click a report name or right-click a name and choose Open from the shortcut menu.**

   The report appears in Report view.

TIP

To update a report so it includes recently added data, go to the Home tab and click the Refresh All button.

Tweaking a Report

As I mention at the start of this chapter, Access offers a bunch of complex tools for changing the layout and appearance of a report. If you're courageous and have lots of time on your hands, you're invited to take these tools in hand and go to it. In the Reports group of the Navigation pane, right-click a report and choose Layout View on the shortcut menu. Your report appears in Layout view, as shown in Figure 5-2. In this view, using tools on the Report Layout Tools tabs, you can tweak your report's appearance.

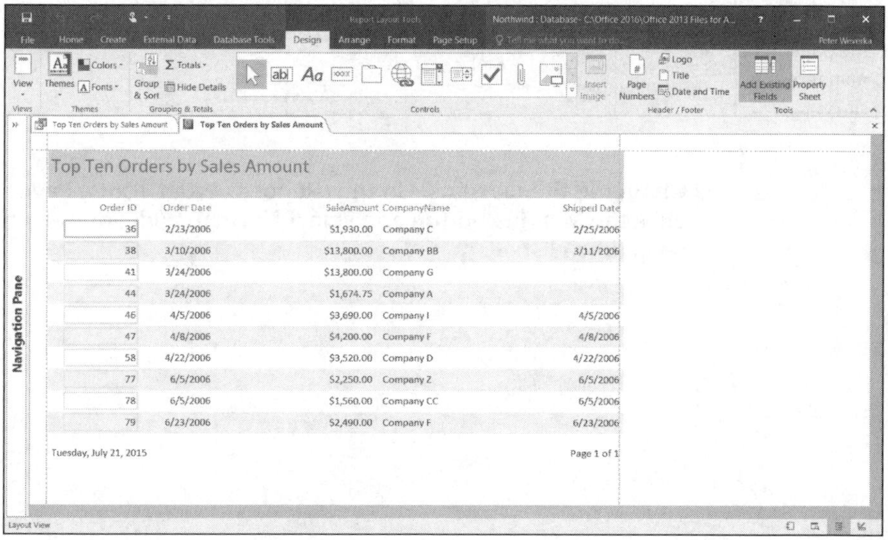

Figure 5-2: The report in Figure 5-1 in Layout view.

I tell you how to create a report with the Report Wizard in order to avoid your having to visit this imposing window. However, you can change a report's appearance in Layout view without going to very much trouble if you follow these instructions:

- **Choosing a new layout:** On the (Report Layout Tools) Arrange tab, click the Stacked or Tabular button, or click the Gridlines button and choose an option on the drop-down list, to change your report's layout.
- **Including page numbers:** To include page numbers on the report, go the (Report Layout Tools) Design tab and click the Page Numbers button. You see the Page Numbers dialog box shown in Figure 5-3. Choose the Page N option button to display a page number only, or select the Page N of M option button to display a page number as well as the total number of pages in the report (as in "Page 2 of 4"). Choose Position and Alignment options to describe where on the page to put the page number.

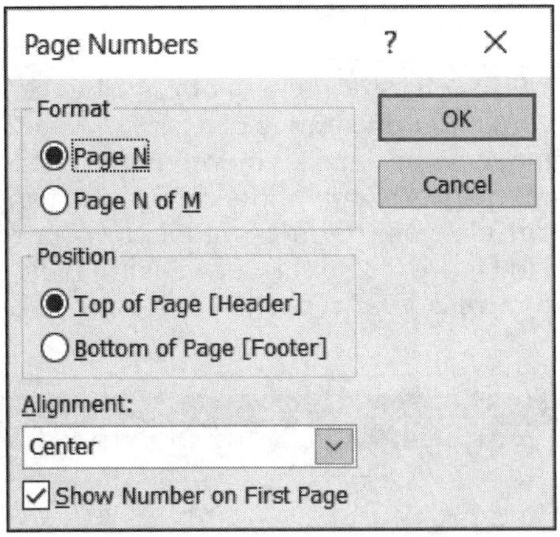

Figure 5-3: Putting on the page numbers.

- **Changing the margins:** On the (Report Layout Tools) Page Setup tab, click the Margins button and select Normal, Wide, or Narrow on the drop-down list.

An easier way to tweak a report — in Word

An easier way to tweak a report is to transfer your report to Microsoft Word and edit it there. Follow these steps to turn an Access report into a Word document:

1. **On the External Data tab, click the More button in the Export group and choose Word on the drop-down list.**

   You see the Export - RTF File dialog box.

2. **Click the Browse button, and in the File Save dialog box, choose a folder for storing the Word document, and click the Save button.**
3. **In the Export - RTF File dialog box, choose Open the Destination File After the Export Operation Is Complete.**
4. **Click the OK button.**

In a moment, your Access report appears in Word. The file is an RTF (rich text format) file. To save it as a Word file, go to the File tab, choose Save As, click the Browse button, and in the Save As dialog box, open the Save As Type drop-down list and choose Word Document. Books I and II describe how to work with files in Word.

Book VIII

Working with Charts and Graphics

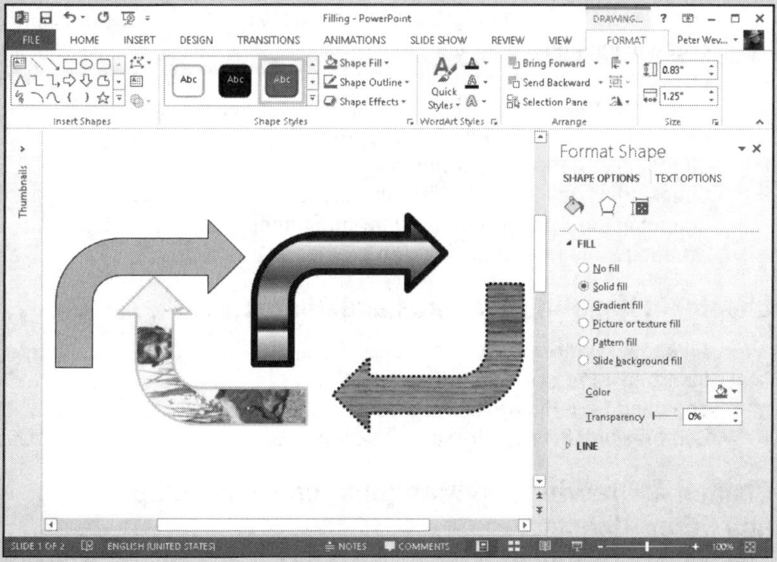

web extras

Check out www.dummies.com/extras/office2016aio to see how you can use descriptive images in place of bars in a bar chart.

Contents at a Glance

Chapter 1: Creating a Chart

In This Chapter

- Creating a chart
- Examining the different types of charts
- Entering chart data in an Excel worksheet
- Positioning a chart in Excel, Word, and PowerPoint
- Changing the appearance of a chart
- Saving a customized chart as a template so that you can use it again
- Exploring some fancy-schmancy chart tricks
- Fixing common problems with charts

Nothing is more persuasive than a chart. The bars, pie slices, lines, or columns show immediately whether production is up or down, cats are better than dogs or dogs better than cats, or catsup tastes better than ketchup. Fans of charts and graphs will be glad to know that putting a chart in a Word document, Excel worksheet, or PowerPoint slide is fairly easy.

This chapter explains how to create a chart. It looks at which charts are best for presenting different kinds of data, how to change a chart's appearance, and how to save charts in a template that you can use again. You discover some nice chart tricks, including how to make a picture the backdrop for a chart and how to annotate a chart. This chapter also addresses common chart problems.

The Basics: Creating a Chart

Throughout this chapter, I explain the whys, wherefores, and whatnots of creating a chart. Before going into details, here are the basic steps that everyone needs to know to create a chart in Word, Excel, and PowerPoint:

1. **Go to the Insert tab.**
2. **If you're working in Excel, select the data you'll use to generate the chart (in Word and PowerPoint, skip to Step 3).**

   In Excel, you select the data on a worksheet before creating the chart, but in Word and PowerPoint, you enter the data for the chart after you create the chart.

3. **Select the kind of chart you want.**

   How you select a chart type depends on which program you're working in:

   - *Excel:* On the Insert tab, open the drop-down list on one of buttons in the Charts group (Column, Bar, and so on) and select a chart type; or click the Recommended Charts button or Charts group button to open the Insert Chart dialog box and select a chart there. As shown in Figure 1-1, the Insert Chart dialog box shows all the kinds of charts you can create. Go to the Recommended Charts tab to see which charts Excel recommends.

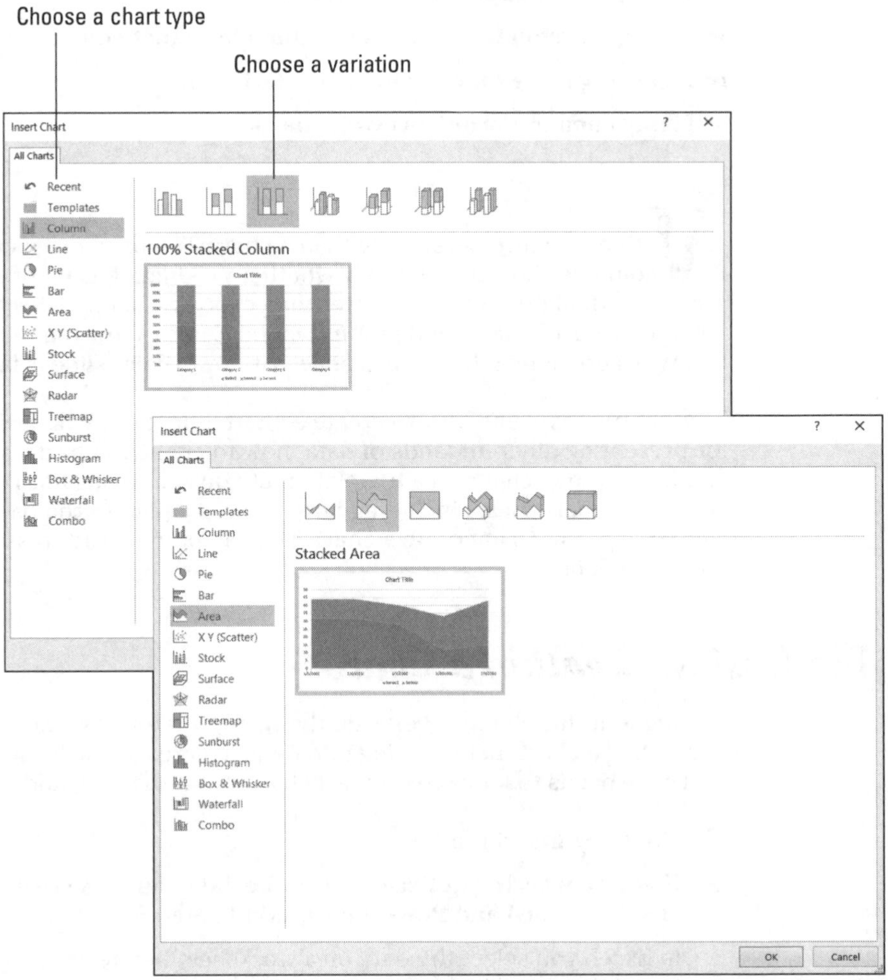

Figure 1-1: Which chart do you want?

   - *Word and PowerPoint:* Click the Chart button. You see the Insert Chart dialog box shown in Figure 1-1. Select a chart type, select a variation, and click OK. A data grid opens on your screen. (In PowerPoint, you can also click the Chart icon on a placeholder frame to open the Insert Chart dialog box.)

   The next topic in this chapter, "Choosing the Right Chart," describes all the charts types and advises you which to choose.

4. **In Word and PowerPoint, replace the sample data in the data grid with the data you need for generating your chart.**

   Later in this chapter, "Providing the Raw Data for Your Chart" explains how to enter data in the data grid, and the sidebar "Getting chart data from a table (Word and PowerPoint)" explains how to copy the data from a table.

   After you finish entering the data, click the Close button in the data grid.

5. **Modify your chart, if you desire.**

   The Chart Tools tabs and buttons to the right of the chart offer commands for making a chart look just-so (see "Changing a Chart's Appearance," later in this chapter).

TIP

Click the Recent button in the Insert Chart dialog box to see all the charts you examined in your search for the right chart.

And if you decide to delete the chart you created? Click its perimeter to select it and then press the Delete key.

Choosing the Right Chart

If you're a fan of charts, the huge selection of charts can make you feel like a kid in a candy store, but if charts aren't your *forté,* the wealth of charts you can choose from can be daunting. You can choose among 58 charts in 15 categories (refer to Figure 1-1). Which chart is best? The golden rule for choosing a chart type is to choose the one that presents information in the brightest possible light. The purpose of a chart is to compare information across different categories. Select a chart that draws out the comparison so that others can clearly make comparisons. Table 1-1 describes the 15 chart types and explains in brief when to use each type of chart.

Table 1-1 Chart Types

Chart Type	*Best Use/Description*
Area	Examine how values in different categories fluctuate over time, and see the cumulative change in values. (Same as a line chart except that the area between trend lines is colored in.)
Bar	Compare values in different categories against one another, usually over time. Data is displayed in horizontal bars. (Same as a column chart except that the bars are horizontal.)
Box & Whisker	Examine how data is distributed (the whiskers define the range of data and the boxes define the median).
Column	Compare values in different categories against one another, usually over time. Data is displayed in vertical columns. (Same as a bar chart except that the bars are vertical.)
Combo	Contrast two sets of data, with one chart overlying the other to draw out the contrast. Data is displayed in lines, bars, and stacks.
Histogram	Measure the frequency of data. Data is displayed in bars, with the width of each bar representing a data range and the height of each bar representing the frequency of data within the range.
Line	Examine how values fluctuate over time. Data is displayed in a set of points connected by a line.
Pie	See how values compare as percentages of a whole. Data from categories is displayed as a percentage of a whole.
Radar	Examine data as it relates to one central point. Data is plotted on radial points from the central point. This kind of chart is used to make subjective performance analyses.
Stock	See how the value of an item fluctuates as well as its daily, weekly, or yearly high, low, and closing price. This chart is used to track stock prices, but it can also be used to track air temperature and other variable quantities.
Surface	Examine color-coded data on a 3D surface to explore relationships between data values.
Sunburst	Compare values at different levels of a hierarchy. This chart is a stacked, or multilevel, pie chart.
Treemap	Evaluate data in nested rectangles that show the relative size of data and the relationship between data items.
Waterfall	See how positive and negative values contribute to a cumulative value.
XY (Scatter)	Compare different numeric data point sets in space to reveal patterns and trends in data. (Similar to a bubble chart except that the data appears as points instead of bubbles.)

Providing the Raw Data for Your Chart

Every chart is constructed from *raw data* — the numbers and labels you select in an Excel worksheet (in Excel) or enter in the data grid (in Word and PowerPoint). If you're operating in Word or PowerPoint, you see, in the data grid, sample data in a *data range*, as shown in Figure 1-2. The information inside the data range is used to generate the chart. You can tell where the data range begins and ends because it is enclosed in a blue border. Your job is to replace the sample data in the data range with data of your own. As you enter your data, the chart on your slide or page takes shape.

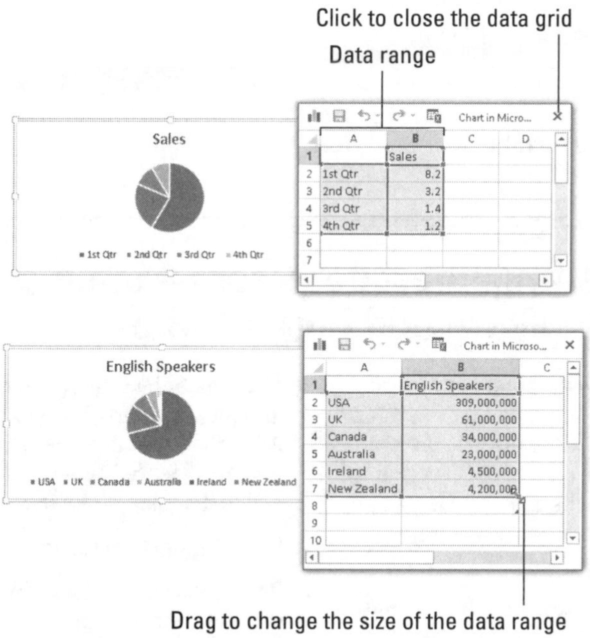

Figure 1-2: To create a chart in Word or PowerPoint, enter data in the data grid.

As you enter numbers and labels in the data grid, watch your chart take shape. Here are the basics of entering data in the data grid:

- **Entering the data in a cell:** A cell is the box in a data grid where a column and row intersect; each cell can contain one data item. To enter data in a cell, click the cell and start typing. When you're finished, press Enter, press Tab, or click a different cell.
- **Deleting the data in a cell:** To delete the data in a cell, including the sample data, click the cell and press Delete.

REMEMBER

- **Displaying the numbers:** When a number is too large to fit in a cell, the number is displayed in scientific notation (you can double-click the number to enlarge the cell in which it is located). Don't worry — the number is still recorded and is used to generate your chart. You can display large numbers by widening the columns in which the numbers are found. Move the pointer between column letters (A, B, and so on at the top of the worksheet) and when you see the double-headed arrow, click and drag to the right.
- **Changing the size of the data range:** To enclose more or fewer cells in the data range, move the pointer to the lower-right corner of the data range, and when the pointer changes into a two-headed arrow, click and drag so that the blue box encloses only the data you want for your chart (refer to Figure 8-2).

TIP

The data grid offers the Edit Data in Microsoft Excel button in case you want to enter data for your chart in Excel. Click this button and enter data in Excel if you're comfortable working there.

Getting chart data from a table (Word and PowerPoint)

Rather than painstakingly enter data in the data grid, you can get the data you need for a chart from a Word or PowerPoint table. In fact, entering the data in a Word or PowerPoint table and copying it to the data grid is easier than entering data in the narrow confines of the data grid.

Follow these steps to generate a chart from data in a table you created in Word or PowerPoint:

1. **Click the table to select it.**
2. **On the (Table Tools) Layout tab, click the Select button and choose Select Table on the drop-down list.**
3. **Press Ctrl+C to copy the table data to the Clipboard.**
4. **Click your chart to select it.**
5. **On the (Chart Tools) Design tab, click the Edit Data button to open the data grid.**
6. **Click the Select All button in the data grid (or press Ctrl+A). Clicking the Select All button selects all cells in the grid. The button is located above 1 in the first row and to the left of the A in the first column.**
7. **Press Delete to erase the data in the grid.**
8. **Press Ctrl+V to copy the data from the table into the data grid.**

If the table you copied into the data grid is larger than the sample data that was there before, you're done. You can breathe easy. But if the table is smaller than the sample data, you have to make the data range smaller so that it encompasses only the data you copied from your table. Move the pointer to the lower-right corner of the data range and then drag in a northwesterly direction until the blue box encloses the data from your Word or PowerPoint table.

In Word and PowerPoint, click the Edit Data button on the (Chart Tools) Design tab at any time to open the data grid and fiddle with the numbers and data from which your chart is generated.

Positioning Your Chart in a Workbook, Page, or Slide

To change the position of a chart, click to select it, click its perimeter, and when you see the four-headed arrow, start dragging. Otherwise, follow these instructions to land your chart where you want it to be:

- **Excel:** To move your chart to a different worksheet or create a new worksheet to hold your chart, go to the (Chart Tools) Design tab and click the Move Chart button. You see the Move Chart dialog box.
  - To move your chart to a different worksheet, click the Object In option button, choose the worksheet in the drop-down list, and click OK.
  - To create a new worksheet for a chart, click the New Sheet option button, enter a name for the new worksheet, and click OK.
- **Word:** Starting in Print Layout view, select your chart, and in the Layout or (Chart Tools) Format tab, click the Position button (you may have to click the Arrange button first, depending on the size of your screen). You see a drop-down list with text-wrapping options. Choose the option that describes how you want surrounding text to behave when it crashes into your chart. Book II, Chapter 6 looks in detail at wrapping text around charts and other objects in Word.

  TIP: You can also position a chart by selecting it, clicking the Layout Options button, and choosing an option on the Layout Options drop-down menu. The Layout Options button appears to the right of a chart after you select a chart.
- **PowerPoint:** Select the chart and drag it on the slide to the right position.

Changing a Chart's Appearance

Charts are awfully nice already, but perhaps you want to redesign one. Perhaps you're an interior decorator type and you want to give charts your own personal touch. As shown in Figure 1-3, Office presents many different ways to refine a chart. You can click one of the three buttons — Chart Elements, Chart Styles, or Chart Filters — that appear beside a chart when you select it. You can also go to (Chart Tools) Design tab and the (Chart Tools) Format tab. Your opportunities for tinkering with a chart are many.

These pages explain how to change a chart's appearance and layout, starting with the biggest change you can make — exchanging one type of chart for another.

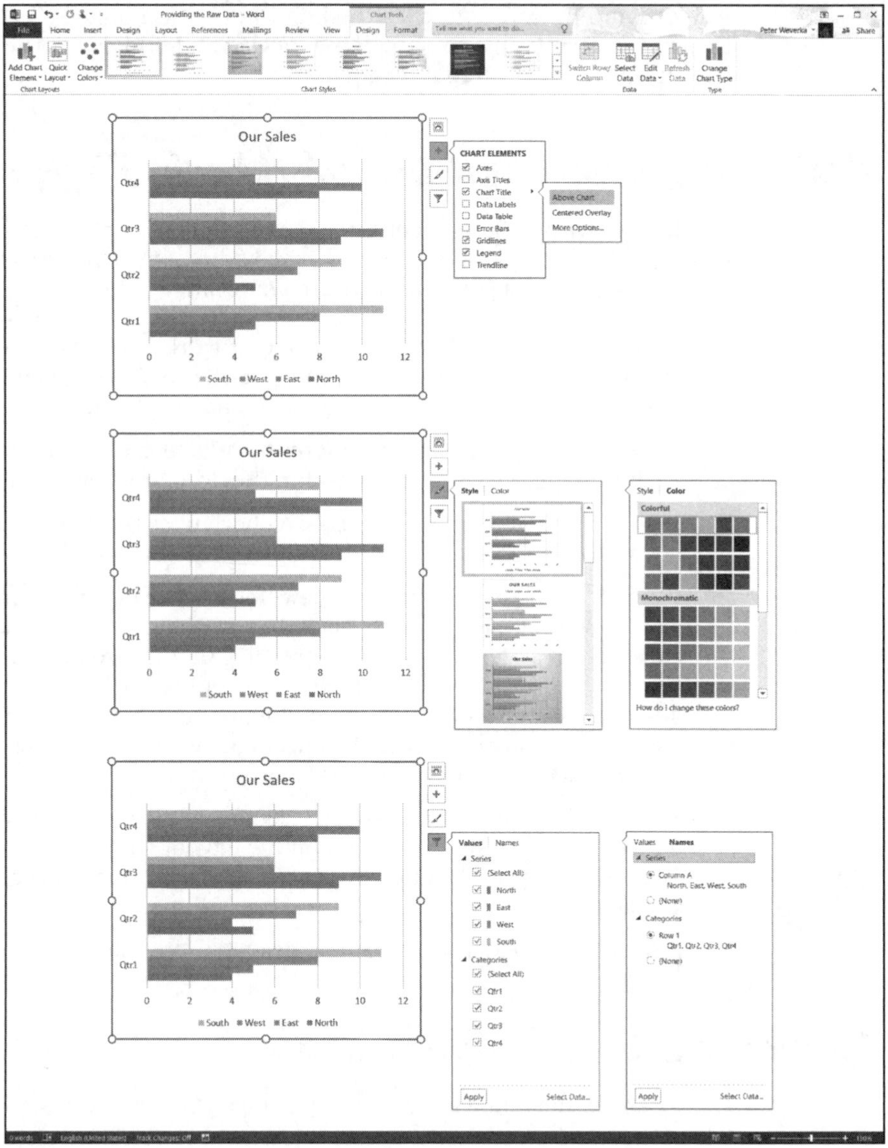

Figure 1-3: Click a button or go to the (Chart Tools) Design or Format tab to change the look of a chart.

Changing the chart type

The biggest way to overhaul a chart is to ditch it in favor of a different chart type. Luckily for you, Office makes this task simple. I wish that changing jobs was this easy. Follow these steps to change a pumpkin into a carriage or an existing chart into a different kind of chart:

1. **Click your chart to select it.**
2. **On the (Chart Tools) Design tab, click the Change Chart Type button, or right-click your chart and choose Change Chart Type on the shortcut menu.**

   The Change Chart Type dialog box appears. Does it look familiar? This is the same dialog box you used to create your chart in the first place.
3. **Select a new chart type and click OK.**

   Not all chart types can be converted successfully to other chart types. You may well have created a monster, in which case go back to Step 1 and start all over or click the Undo button.

Changing the size and shape of a chart

To make a chart taller or wider, follow these instructions:

- Click the perimeter of the chart to select it and then drag a handle on the side to make it wider, or a handle on the top or bottom to make it taller.
- Go to the (Chart Tools) Format tab and enter measurements in the Height and Width boxes. You can find these boxes in the Size group (you may have to click the Size button to see them, depending on the size of your screen).

Choosing a new look for your chart

Select your chart and experiment with these different ways to change its look:

- **Select a chart style:** On the (Chart Tools) Design tab, choose an option in the Chart Styles gallery. Or click the Chart Styles button and select a style on the drop-down menu (refer to Figure 1-3).These gallery options are quite sophisticated. You would have a hard time fashioning these charts on your own.
- **Change the color scheme:** On the (Chart Tools) Design tab, click the Change Colors button and select a color on the drop-down list. Or click the Chart Styles button and select a color on the drop-down menu (refer to Figure 1-3).

Later in this chapter, "Changing a chart element's color, font, or other particular" explains how to dig down deep and change one particular aspect of a chart — its legend, plot area, or vertical axis, for example.

If your file includes more than one chart, make the charts consistent with one another. Give them a similar appearance so that your file doesn't turn into a chart fashion show. You can make charts consistent with one another by choosing similar options for charts in the Chart Styles gallery.

Changing the layout of a chart

Charts are composed of different elements — the legend, the labels, and the titles. Figure 1-4 identifies chart elements. Where these elements appear is up to you. Whether to include them is up to you as well. You can, for example, place the legend on the right side of your chart or go without a legend. By choosing which elements to include and where to put elements, you fashion a layout for your chart.

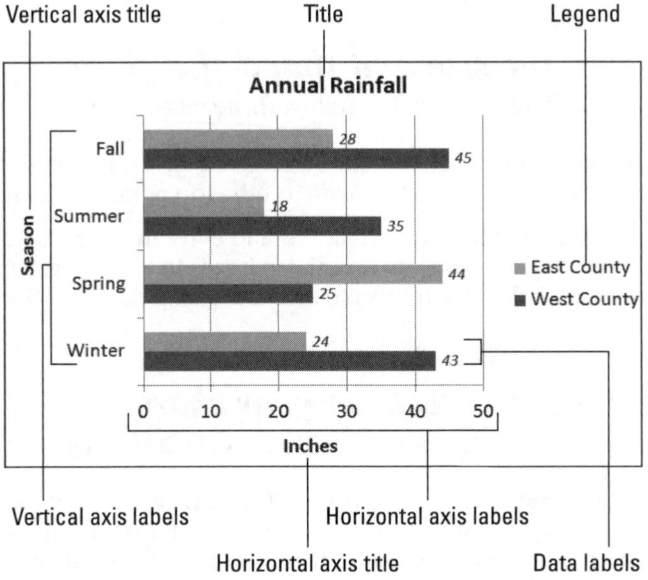

Figure 1-4: The layout elements of a chart.

Select your chart and experiment with these techniques to decide on a layout:

- On the (Chart Tools) Design tab, click the Quick Layout button and select an option in the gallery.
- On the (Chart Tools) Design tab, click the Add Chart Element button. Then choose an element on the drop-down list, and on the submenu, choose whether to place the element (the None option) or where to place it.
- Click the Chart Elements button, choose an element on the drop-down menu, and choose whether to place it (the None option) or where to place it. Figure 1-5, for example, shows how to choose where to place the legend.

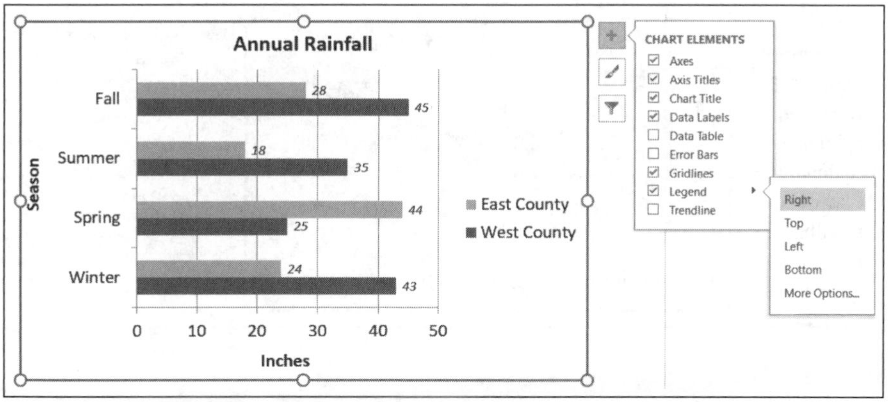

Figure 1-5: Clicking the Chart Elements button is one way to handle chart layouts.

TIP

Hover the pointer over the options on the Chart Elements menus and glance at your chart. You can see right away what each option does to your chart.

TIP

To remove series or category names from a chart, click the Chart Filters button and, on the drop-down menu, deselect a column or row option button (see Figure 1-3).

Handling the gridlines

Gridlines are lines that cross a chart and indicate value measurements. Most charts include major gridlines to show where bars or columns meet or surpass a major unit of measurement, and you can also include fainter, minor gridlines that mark less significant measurements.

Use these techniques to handle gridlines:

- On the (Chart Tools) Design tab, click the Add Chart Element button, choose Gridlines on the drop-down list, and select or deselect an option on the submenu.
- Click the Chart Elements button, choose Gridlines, and select or deselect a check box on the submenu, as shown in Figure 1-6.

Deselecting all the gridline options removes the gridlines from a chart. Choose More Options on the submenu to open the Format Major Gridlines task pane, where you can change the color of gridlines, make gridlines semi-transparent, and make gridlines wider or narrower.

WARNING!

Gridlines are essential for helping read charts, but be very, very careful about displaying minor gridlines on charts. These lines can make your chart unreadable. They can turn a perfectly good chart into a gaudy pinstripe suit.

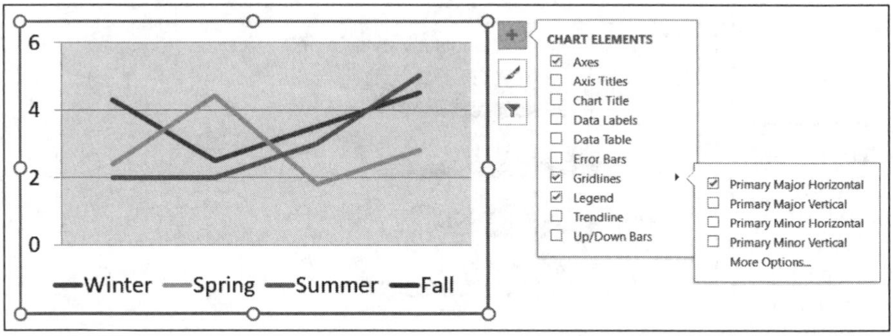

Figure 1-6: Choosing a Gridlines option by way of the Chart Elements button.

Changing a chart element's color, font, or other particular

The (Chart Tools) Format tab is the place to go to change the color, line width, font, or font size of a chart element. Go to the (Chart Tools) Format tab, for example, to change the color of the bars in a bar chart, the color of text, or the chart background color.

Follow these basic steps to change a color, line width, font, or font size in part of a chart:

1. **Go to the (Chart Tools) Format tab.**
2. **In the Chart Elements drop-down list, select the chart element that needs a facelift.**

   You can find this list in the upper-left corner of the screen, as shown in Figure 1-7.
3. **Click the Format Selection button.**

   The Format task pane opens (see Figure 1-7).
4. **Format the chart element you selected.**

   In the Format task pane, you can find all the tools you need to change the color, outline, and size of a chart element. These tools are explained in detail in Chapter 4 of this mini-book.

TIP

If your experiments with retouching a chart go awry and you want to start over, click the Reset to Match Style button on the (Chart Tools) Format tab.

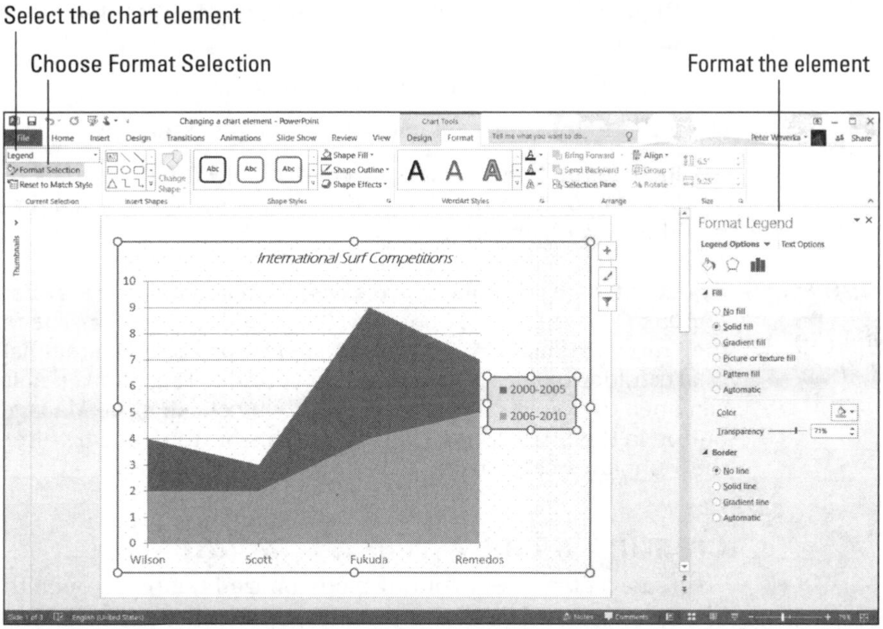

Figure 1-7: Choose what you want to format on the Chart Elements drop-down list.

Saving a Chart as a Template So That You Can Use It Again

If you go to the significant trouble of redecorating a chart and you expect to do it again the same way in the future, save your chart as a template. This way, you can call on the template in the future to create the same chart and not have to decorate it again. Perhaps you've created charts with your company's colors or you've created a chart that you're especially proud of. Save it as a template to spare yourself the work of reconstructing it.

A chart template holds data series colors, gridline settings, plot area colors, font settings, and the like. It doesn't hold data. These pages explain how to save a chart as a template and how to create a chart with a template you created.

Saving a chart as a template

Follow these steps to make a template out of a chart:

1. **Save your file to make sure the chart settings are saved on your computer.**
2. **Select your chart.**

3. **Right-click your chart and choose Save As Template on the shortcut menu.**

   You see the Save Chart Template dialog box.

4. **Enter a descriptive name for the template and click the Save button.**

   Include the type of chart you're dealing with in the name. This will help you understand which template you're selecting when the time comes to choose a chart template.

TECHNICAL STUFF

By default, chart templates are saved in this folder: `C:\Users\`*`Username`*`\AppData\Roaming\Microsoft\Templates\Charts`. The templates have the `.ctrx` extension. If you want to delete or rename a template, open the Charts folder in File Explorer and do your deleting and renaming there. You can open the Charts folder very quickly by clicking the Manage Templates button in the Insert Chart dialog box (this button appears after you choose the Templates category).

Creating a chart from a template

To create a chart from your own customized template, open the Create Chart dialog box (click the Chart button) and go to the Templates category. The dialog box shows a list of templates you created. Move the pointer over a template to read its name in a pop-up box. Select a template and click OK.

Chart Tricks for the Daring and Heroic

This chapter wouldn't be complete without a handful of chart tricks to impress your friends and intimidate your enemies. In the pages that follow, you discover how to make charts roll over and play dead. You also find out how to decorate a chart with a picture, annotate a chart, display worksheet data alongside a chart, and create a combo chart.

Decorating a chart with a picture

As shown in Figure 1-8, a picture looks mighty nice on the plot area of a chart — especially a column chart. If you have a picture in your computer that would serve well to decorate a chart, you are hereby encouraged to start decorating. Follow these steps to place a picture in the plot area of a chart:

1. **Select your chart.**
2. **On the (Chart Tools) Format tab, open the Chart Elements drop-down list and choose Plot Area.**

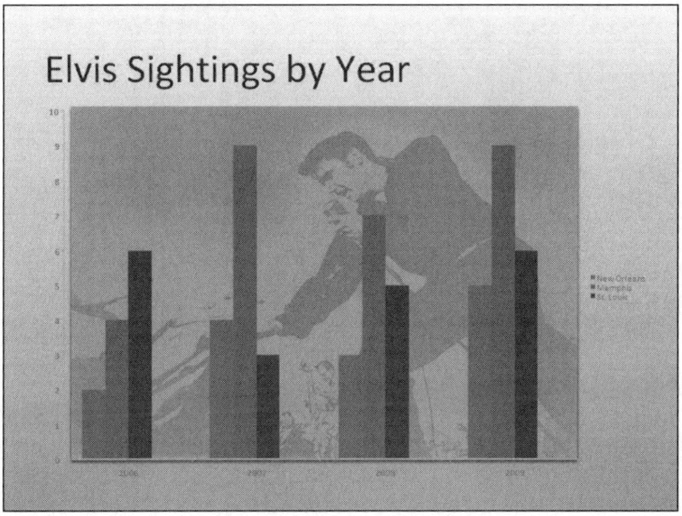

Figure 1-8: Using a picture as the back-drop of a chart.

3. **Click the Format Selection button.**
4. **In the Format Plot Area task pane, click the Picture or Texture Fill option button.**
5. **Click the File button.**

   You see the Insert Picture dialog box.

6. **Locate the picture you need and select it.**

   Try to select a light-colored picture that will serve as a background. Chapter 3 of this mini-book explains how you can recolor a picture to make it lighter.

7. **Click the Insert button.**

   The picture lands in your chart.

   You may need to change the color of the *data markers* — the columns, bars, lines, or pie slices — on your chart to make them stand out against the picture. See "Changing a chart element's color, font, or other particular," earlier in this chapter.

Annotating a chart

To highlight part of a chart — an especially large pie slice, a tall column, or a bar showing miniscule sales figures — annotate it with a callout text box and place the text box beside the pie slice, column, or bar. Figure 1-9 shows an example of an annotated chart. The annotation tells you that one sector isn't performing especially well and somebody ought to get on the ball.

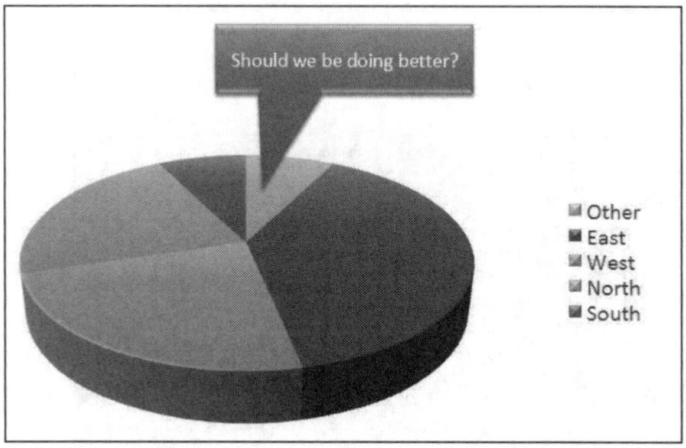

Figure 1-9: Annotations point out a chart's salient features.

To annotate a chart, select a callout shape, enter text in the callout shape, and connect the shape to part of your chart. Follow these steps to annotate a chart:

1. **Select your chart and go to the (Chart Tools) Format tab.**
2. **Open the Shapes gallery, scroll to the Callouts section of the drop-down list, and choose a callout.**

   Depending on the size of your screen, you may have to click the Insert button to get to the Shapes button.
3. **Drag on the page or slide to draw the callout shape.**

   Chapter 4 of this mini-book explains drawing shapes in gory detail.
4. **Type the annotation inside the callout shape.**

   After you type the text, you can select it, go to the Home tab, and choose a font and font size for it.
5. **Resize the callout shape as necessary to make it fit with the chart.**
6. **Drag the yellow square on the callout shape to attach the callout to the chart.**

   You probably have to do some interior decorating to make the callout color fit with the chart. Chapter 4 of this mini-book explains how to change an object's color.

Displaying the raw data alongside the chart

Showing the worksheet data used to produce a chart is sort of like showing the cops your I.D. It proves you're the real thing. It makes your chart more authentic. If yours is a simple pie chart or other chart that wasn't generated with a large amount of raw data, you can display the data alongside your chart in a data table. Anyone who sees the table knows you're not kidding or fudging the numbers.

To place a table with the raw data below your chart, go to the (Chart Tools) Design tab, open the Quick Layout gallery, and select a layout that includes a data table.

To format a data table, go to the (Chart Tools) Format tab, open the Chart Element drop-down list, and choose Data Table. Then click the Format Selection button. You see the Format Data Table task pane, where you can fill the table with color and choose colors for the lines in the table.

Placing a trendline on a chart

Especially on column charts, a *trendline* can help viewers more clearly see changes in data. Viewers can see, for example, that sales are going up or down, income is rising or falling, or annual rainfall is increasing or decreasing. Figure 1-10 shows an example of a trendline on a chart. In this case, the trendline shows that the deer population in Sacramento County is rising.

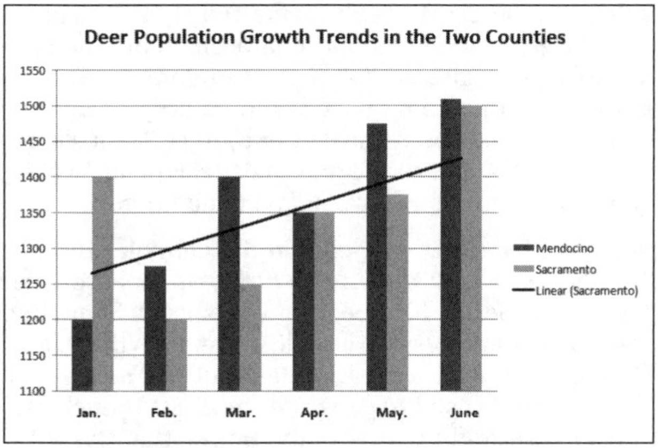

Figure 1-10: A trendline helps viewers recognize changes in data.

Follow these steps to put a trendline on a chart:

1. **On the (Chart Tools) Design tab, click the Add Chart Element button.**
2. **Choose Trendline on the drop-down list and select a trendline option on the submenu.**

   The Add Trendline dialog box appears.
3. **Choose the data series that you want to highlight with a trendline and click OK.**

To remove a trendline from a chart, go to the (Chart Tools) Design tab, click the Add Chart Element button, choose Trendline on the drop-down list, and choose None on the submenu.

Troubleshooting a Chart

Sometimes tinkering with a chart opens a Pandora's Box of problems. You find yourself having to correct little errors that appear in charts. Here are some shorthand instructions for fixing common chart problems:

- **The dates in the chart aren't formatted right.** To change the way in which dates are formatted on a chart, go to the (Chart Tools) Format tab, open the Chart Elements drop-down list, and choose Horizontal (Value) Axis or Vertical (Value) Axis. Then click the Format Selection button, and in the Format Axis task pane, go to the Number category, select Date in the Category menu, and choose a date format.
- **The numbers in the chart aren't formatted right.** To change the number of decimal places, include comma separators in numbers, display currency symbols, or do all else that pertains to numbers, go to the (Chart Tools) Format tab, open the Chart Elements drop-down list, and choose Horizontal (Value) Axis or Vertical (Value) Axis. Then click the Format Selection button. You see the Format Axis task pane. Visit the Number category and select options for displaying numbers.
- **"Category 1" or "Series 1" appears in the chart legend.** To direct you to the right place to enter data in the data grid, phantom names such as "Category 1" and "Series 1" appear in worksheets. Sometimes these phantoms wind up in chart legends as well. To remove them, go to the (Chart Tools) Design tab and click the Edit Data button. You see the data grid, where the data range used to generate the chart is enclosed in a blue box. Drag the lower-right corner of the box so that the box encloses only the data you want for your chart.
- **In 3D charts, small markers are obscured by large markers in the foreground.** For all the data markers to be shown in a 3D chart, the smaller ones have to be in the foreground. To rearrange data markers, go to the (Chart Tools) Design tab and click the Select Data button to open the Select Data Source dialog box. Then select a series and click the Up or Down button to rearrange the series in your chart. Series that are high on the list go to the back of the chart; series that are low on the list go to the front.
- **The chart doesn't gather all data from the worksheet.** On the (Chart Tools) Design tab, click the Edit Data button, and in the data grid that stores data for your chart, enlarge the blue data-range box so that it encloses all your data. You can enlarge the box by dragging its lower-right corner.

Chapter 2: Making a SmartArt Diagram

In This Chapter

- Creating a diagram
- Repositioning and resizing diagrams
- Laying out and changing the look of diagram shapes
- Entering text on a diagram shape
- Changing the appearance of a diagram
- Creating a diagram from shapes

Along with charts and tables, diagrams are the best way to present your ideas. Diagrams clearly show, for example, employees' relationships with one another, product cycles, workflow processes, and spheres of influence. A diagram is an excellent marriage of images and words. Diagrams allow an audience to literally visualize a concept, idea, or relationship.

This chapter explains how to construct diagrams from SmartArt graphics and how to create a diagram. It shows how to customize diagrams by changing the size of diagrams and diagram shapes, adding and removing shapes, and changing shapes' colors. You also discover how to change the direction of a diagram and enter the text. Finally, this chapter demonstrates how to create a diagram from scratch with shapes and connectors.

The Basics: Creating SmartArt Diagrams

In Word, PowerPoint, and Excel, diagrams are made from *SmartArt graphics.* These diagram graphics are "interactive" in the sense that you can move, alter, and write text on them. In other words, you can use them to construct diagrams. You can alter these diagrams to your liking. You can make a diagram portray precisely what you want it to portray, although you usually have to wrestle with the diagram a bit.

Choosing a diagram

The first step in creating a diagram is to select a layout in the Choose a SmartArt Graphic dialog box, shown in Figure 2-1. To open this dialog box, go to the Insert tab and click the SmartArt button. After you create the initial diagram, you customize it to create a diagram of your own. About 160 diagrams are in the dialog box. They fall into these nine categories:

Diagram Type	***Use***
List	For describing blocks of related information as well as sequential steps in a task, process, or workflow
Process	For describing how a concept or physical process changes over time or is modified
Cycle	For illustrating a circular progression without a beginning or end, or a relationship in which the components are in balance
Hierarchy	For describing hierarchical relationships between people, departments, and other entities, as well as portraying branchlike relationships in which one decision or action leads to another
Relationship	For describing the relationship between different components (but not hierarchical relationships)
Matrix	For showing the relationship between quadrants
Pyramid	For showing proportional or hierarchical relationships
Picture	For creating diagrams that include photographs and pictures (This catch-all category presents picture diagrams from the other categories.)
Office.com	For presenting data in tabbed arcs, radials, block processes, and other unusual ways

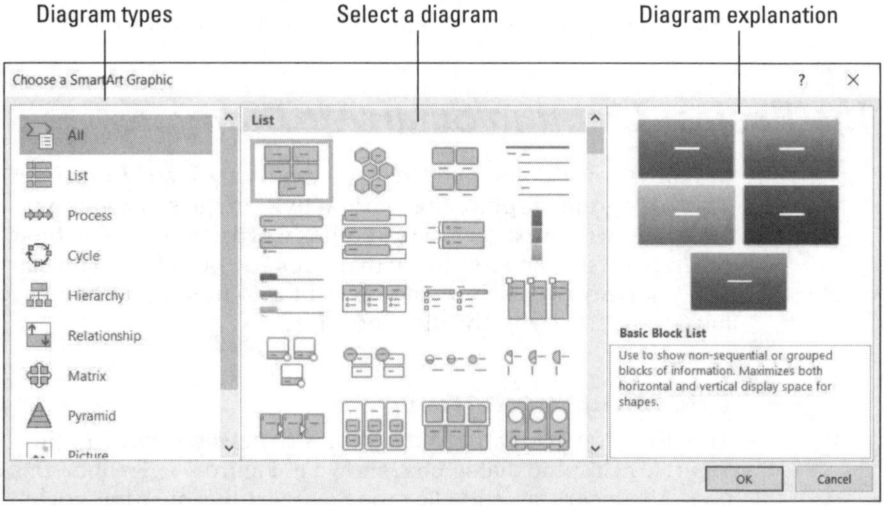

Figure 2-1: To create a diagram, start by selecting a diagram in this dialog box.

If you intend to construct a "flow chart type" diagram with many branches and levels, go to the Hierarchy category and select the Organization Chart or one of the hierarchy diagrams. As "Laying Out the Diagram Shapes" explains later in this chapter, only these choices permit you to make a diagram with many different branches and levels.

Making the diagram your own

After you select a generic diagram in the Choose a SmartArt Graphic dialog box and click OK, the next step is to make the diagram your own by completing these tasks:

- **Change the diagram's size and position:** Change the size and position of a diagram to make it fit squarely on your page or slide. See "Changing the Size and Position of a Diagram," later in this chapter.
- **Add shapes to (or remove shapes from) the diagram:** Adding a shape involves declaring where to add the shape, promoting or demoting the shape with respect to other shapes, and declaring how the new shape connects to another shape. See "Laying Out the Diagram Shapes," later in this chapter.
- **Enter text:** Enter text on each shape, or component, of the diagram. See "Handling the Text on Diagram Shapes," later in this chapter.

If you so desire, you can also customize your diagram by taking on some or all of these tasks:

- **Changing its overall appearance:** Choose a different color scheme or 3D variation for your diagram. See "Choosing a Look for Your Diagram," later in this chapter.
- **Changing shapes:** Select a new shape for part of your diagram, change the size of a shape, or assign different colors to shapes to make shapes stand out. See "Changing the Appearance of Diagram Shapes," later in this chapter.

If you're comfortable creating a diagram of your own by drawing shapes and lines, no law says you have to begin in the Choose a SmartArt Graphic dialog box. Later in this chapter, "Creating a Diagram from Scratch" looks into creating a diagram by making use of text boxes, lines, and shapes.

Creating the Initial Diagram

The first step in fashioning a diagram is to choose a SmartArt graphic in the Choose a SmartArt Graphic dialog box. After that, you roll up your sleeves, change the diagram's size and shape, and enter the text. If you select the wrong diagram to start with, all is not lost. You can choose another diagram in its place, although how successful swapping one diagram for another is depends on how lucky you are and how far along you are in creating your diagram. These pages explain how to create an initial diagram and swap one diagram for another.

Creating a diagram

Follow these steps to create a diagram:

1. **On the Insert tab, click the SmartArt button.**

   You see the Choose a SmartArt Graphic dialog box (refer to Figure 2-1). In PowerPoint, you can also open the dialog box by clicking the SmartArt icon in a content placeholder frame.

2. **Select a diagram in the Choose a SmartArt Graphic dialog box.**

   Diagrams are divided into nine categories, as I explain earlier in this chapter. The dialog box offers a description of each diagram. Either select a type on the left side of the dialog box or scroll the entire list to find the graphic that most resembles the diagram you want.

   TIP: If you want to create a graph with many levels and branches, go to the Hierarchy category and select one of these charts: Organization Chart or Name and Title Organization Chart. These two diagrams are much more complex than the others and allow for branching. See "Laying Out the Diagram Shapes" later in this chapter for details.

3. **Click OK.**

   The next topic in this chapter explains how to swap one diagram for another, in case you chose wrongly in the Choose a SmartArt Graphic dialog box.

Starting from a sketch

You can spare yourself a lot of trouble by starting from a sketch when you create a diagram. Find a pencil with a good eraser, grab a blank piece of paper, and start drawing. Imagine what your ideal diagram looks like. Draw the arrows or lines connecting the different parts of the diagram. Write the text. Draw the diagram that best illustrates what you want to communicate.

Later, in the Choose a SmartArt Graphic dialog box (refer to Figure 2-1), you can select the diagram that most resembles the one you sketched. The dialog box offers more than 200 types of diagrams. Unless you start from a sketch and have a solid idea of the diagram you want, you can get lost in the dialog box. Also, if you don't start from a sketch, adding shapes to the diagram and landing shapes in the right places can be a chore.

Swapping one diagram for another

If the diagram you chose initially doesn't do the job, you can swap it for a different diagram. How successful the swap is depends on how far along you are in creating your diagram and whether your diagram is simple or complex. Follow these steps to swap one diagram for another:

1. **Click your diagram to select it.**
2. **Go to the (SmartArt Tools) Design tab.**
3. **Open the Layouts gallery (you may have to click the Change Layout button first).**

   You see a gallery with diagrams of the same type as the diagram you're working with.
4. **Select a new diagram or choose More Layouts to open the Choose a SmartArt Graphic dialog box and select a diagram there.**

You may have to click the trusty Undo button and start all over if the diagram you selected for the swap didn't do the job.

Changing the Size and Position of a Diagram

To make a diagram fit squarely on a page or slide, you have to change its size and position. Resizing and positioning diagrams and other objects is the subject of Chapter 4 of this mini-book, but in case you don't care to travel that far to get instructions, here are shorthand instructions for resizing and positioning diagrams:

- ✦ **Resizing a diagram:** Select the diagram, move the pointer over a selection handle on the corner or side, and start dragging after the pointer changes into a two-headed arrow. You can also go to the (SmartArt Tools) Format tab and enter new measurements in the Width and Height boxes. (You may have to click the Size button to see these text boxes, depending on the size of your screen.)
- ✦ **Repositioning a diagram:** Select the diagram, move the pointer over its perimeter, and when you see the four-headed arrow, click and start dragging.

REMEMBER

Notice when you resize a diagram that the shapes in the diagram change size proportionally. Most diagrams are designed so that shapes fill out the diagram. When you change the size of a diagram, remove a shape from a diagram, or add a shape, shapes change size within the diagram.

Laying Out the Diagram Shapes

At the heart of every diagram are the rectangles, circles, arrows, and whatnots that make the diagram what it is. These shapes illustrate the concept or idea you want to express. Your biggest challenge when creating a diagram is laying out the diagram shapes.

The following pages explain how to select diagram shapes, add shapes, reposition shapes, and remove shapes from diagrams. They also offer instructions specific to working with hierarchy diagrams.

Selecting a diagram shape

Before you can remove a shape from a diagram or indicate where you want to add a new shape, you have to select a diagram shape. To select a diagram shape, move the pointer over its perimeter and click when you see the four-headed arrow appear on your pointer.

REMEMBER

You can tell when a diagram shape is selected because a solid line, not a dotted line, appears around the shape, as shown in Figure 2-2. When you see dotted lines around a shape, you're expected to enter text.

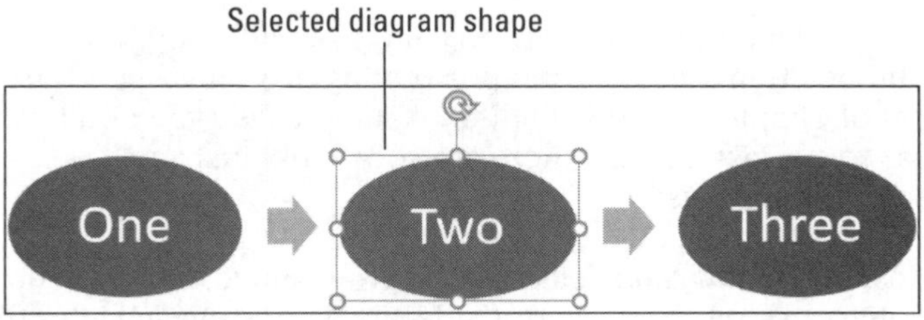

Figure 2-2: A selected diagram shape is surrounded by solid lines.

Removing a shape from a diagram

Removing a shape from a diagram is as easy as falling off a turnip truck as long as you correctly select the shape before you remove it. To remove a shape, select it and press Delete. Other shapes grow larger when you remove a shape, in keeping with the "fill out the diagram by any means necessary" philosophy.

Moving diagram shapes to different positions

If a shape in a diagram isn't in the right position, don't fret because you can change the order of shapes very easily by going to the (SmartArt Tools) Design tab and clicking the Move Up or Move Down button.

Select the diagram shape that needs repositioning and click the Move Up or Move Down button as many times as necessary to land the shape in the right place.

Adding shapes to diagrams apart from hierarchy diagrams

Unlike hierarchy diagrams, list, process, cycle, relationship, and matrix diagrams don't have branches. They always travel in one direction only. This makes adding shapes to these diagrams fairly straightforward. To add a shape, you select a shape in the diagram and then add the new shape so that it appears before or after the shape you selected, as shown in Figure 2-3.

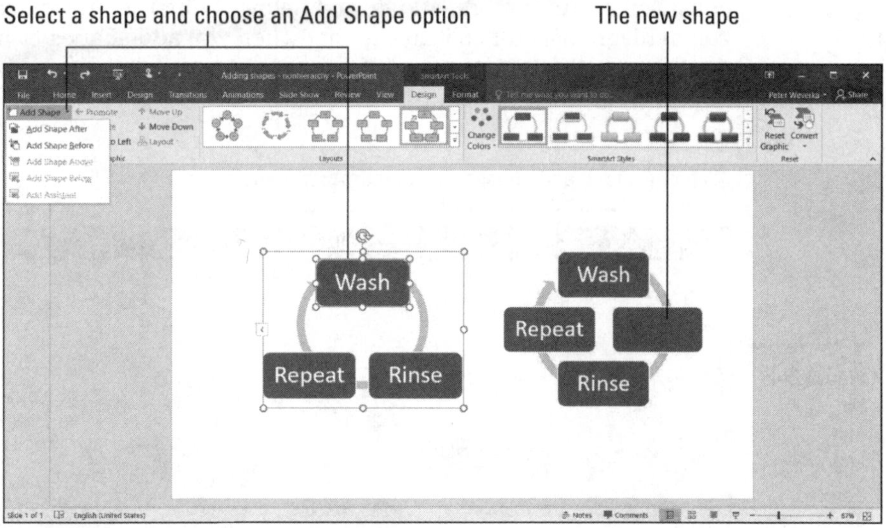

Figure 2-3: To add a shape, start by selecting the shape that your new shape will go before or after.

Follow these steps to add a shape to a list, process, cycle, relationship, matrix, or pyramid diagram:

1. **In your diagram, select the shape that your new shape will appear before or after.**

   Earlier in this chapter, "Selecting a diagram shape" explains how to select diagram shapes.

2. **Choose the Add Shape After or Add Shape Before command.**

   To get to these commands, use one of these techniques:

   - On the (SmartArt Tools) Design tab, open the drop-down list on the Add Shape button and choose Add Shape After or Add Shape Before, as shown in Figure 2-3.

- Right-click the shape you selected, choose Add Shape on the shortcut menu, and then choose Add Shape After or Add Shape Before on the submenu.

Adding shapes to hierarchy diagrams

Hierarchy diagrams are more complex than other diagrams because they branch out such that shapes are found on different levels. This branching out makes adding shapes to hierarchy diagrams problematic.

As shown in Figure 2-4, Office offers four Add Shape commands for adding shapes to hierarchy diagrams: Add Shape After, Add Shape Before, Add Shape Above, and Add Shape Below. What these commands do depends on whether the diagram is horizontally or vertically oriented, because what constitutes after, before, above, and below is different in vertical and horizontal diagrams. Suffice it to say that when you add shapes to hierarchy diagrams, you often have to try different commands, clicking the Undo button and starting all over until you get it right.

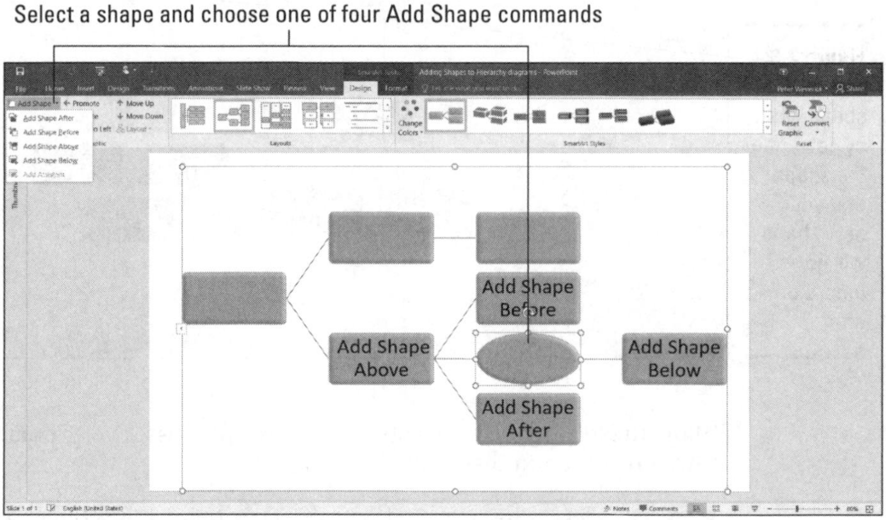

Figure 2-4: You can add a shape after, before, above, or below a shape in a hierarchy diagram.

Follow these steps to add a shape to a hierarchy diagram:

1. **In your diagram, select the shape to which your new shape will be connected.**

   Earlier in this chapter, "Selecting a diagram shape" describes how to select a shape.

2. **Choose an Add Shape command.**

   Figure 2-4 shows what Add Shape commands do. You can choose Add Shape commands with one of these techniques:

   - On the (SmartArt Tools) Design tab, open the drop-down list on the Add Shape button and choose an Add Shape command (refer to Figure 2-4).
   - Right-click the shape you selected, choose Add Shape on the shortcut menu, and choose an Add Shape command on the submenu.

Adding shapes to Organization charts

An Organization chart diagram offers many opportunities for connecting shapes. The shapes can branch out from one another in four directions as well as appear to the side in the "assistant" position. When you place one shape below another shape, you can make the new shape *hang* so that it is joined to a line that drops, or hangs, from another shape. These pages explain how to add shapes and create hanging relationships between one shape and the shapes subordinate to it.

Adding an Organization Chart shape

Besides adding a shape after, before, above, or below a shape, you can add an assistant shape to an Organization Chart diagram, as shown in Figure 2-5. An assistant shape is an intermediary shape between two levels. Follow these steps to add a shape to an Organization Chart diagram:

1. **Select the shape to which you will add a new shape.**

   Earlier in this chapter, "Selecting a diagram shape" explains how to select shapes. As shown in Figure 2-5, shapes are surrounded by solid lines, not dotted lines, when you select them properly.

2. **Choose an Add Shape command.**

   You can choose Add Shape commands in two ways:

   - On the (SmartArt Tools) Design tab, open the drop-down list on the Add Shape button and choose an Add Shape (or Add Assistant) command (see Figure 2-5).
   - Right-click the shape you selected, choose Add Shape on the shortcut menu, and then choose an Add Shape (or Add Assistant) command on the submenu.

Figure 2-5 demonstrates what the Add Shape commands do to a vertically oriented diagram. Notice that Add Shape Before places a new shape to the left of the shape you selected; Add Shape After places a new shape to the right.

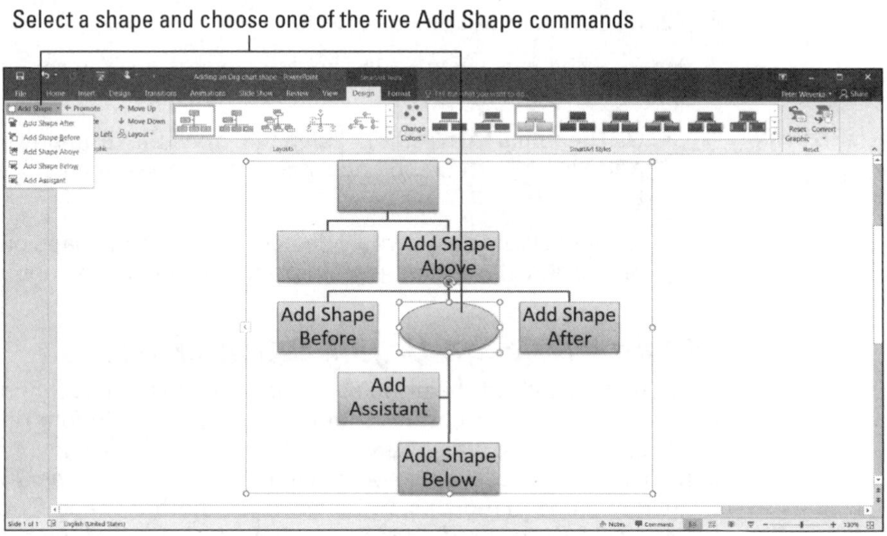

Figure 2-5: Adding a shape to an Organization Chart diagram.

WARNING! Be careful about choosing the Add Shape Above command. This command effectively bumps the shape you selected to a lower level in order to make room for the new shape. In effect, you demote one shape when you place a new shape above it.

TIP Shapes created with the Add Assistant command land on the left side of the line to which they're attached, but if you prefer the assistant shape to be on the right side of the line, you can drag it to the right.

Hanging a shape below another shape in an Organization Chart

Besides the standard relationship between shapes above and below one another, you can create a *hanging relationship* in an Organization Chart diagram. Figure 2-6 shows the four kinds of hanging relationships — Standard, Both, Left Hanging, and Right Hanging. In a hanging relationship, the line hangs from a shape, and subordinate shapes are connected to the line.

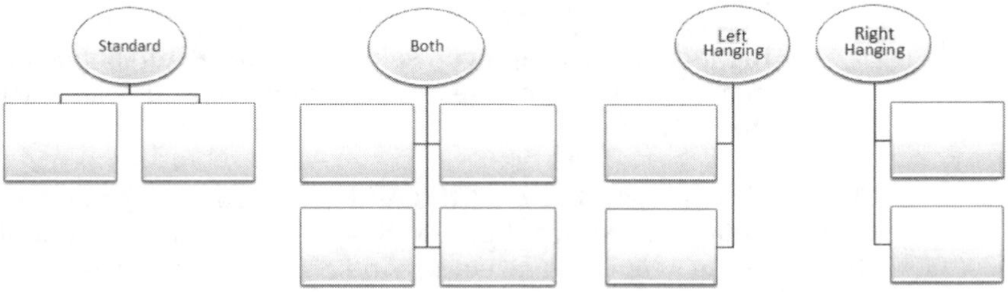

Figure 2-6: Ways that shapes can hang in Organization Chart diagrams.

You can create a hanging relationship between shapes before or after you create the subordinate shapes. Follow these steps to create a hanging relationship:

1. **Select the shape to which other shapes will hang or are hanging.**
2. **On the (SmartArt Tools) Design tab, click the Layout button.**
3. **On the drop-down list, choose Standard, Both, Left Hanging, or Right Hanging.**

Promoting and demoting shapes in hierarchy diagrams

Shapes in hierarchy diagrams are ranked by level. If a shape is on the wrong level, you can move it higher or lower in the diagram by clicking the Promote or Demote button on the (SmartArt Tools) Design tab. Promoting and demoting shapes can turn into a donnybrook if you aren't careful. If the shapes being promoted or demoted are attached to subordinate shapes, the subordinate shapes are promoted or demoted as well. This can have unforeseen and sometimes horrendous consequences.

Follow these steps to promote or demote a shape (and its subordinates) in a hierarchy diagram:

1. **Select the shape that needs a change of rank.**

   You can select more than one shape by Ctrl+clicking.
2. **Go to the (SmartArt Tools) Design tab.**
3. **Click the Promote or Demote button.**

   Do you like what you see? If not, you may have to click the Undo button and start all over.

Handling the Text on Diagram Shapes

When you create a new diagram, "[Text]" (the word *Text* enclosed in brackets) appears on shapes. Your job is to replace this generic placeholder with something more meaningful and less bland. These sections explain how to enter text and bulleted lists on shapes.

Entering text on a diagram shape

Use one of these techniques to enter text on a diagram shape:

- **Click in the shape and start typing:** The words you type appear in the shape, as shown in Figure 2-7.

✦ **Enter text in the Text pane:** Enter the text by typing it in the Text pane, as shown in Figure 2-7. The text pane opens to the left of the diagram. To open the text pane, go to the (SmartArt Tools) Design tab and click the Text Pane button.

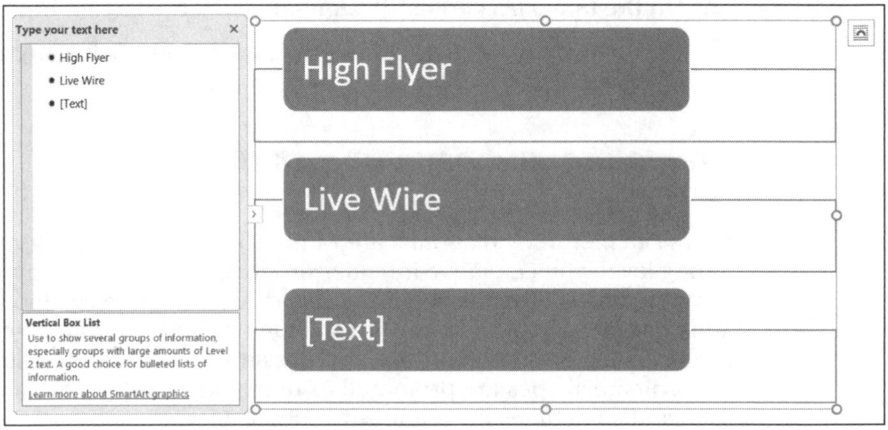

Figure 2-7: Type directly on diagram shapes or enter text on the Text pane.

The text in diagrams shrinks as you enter more text so that all text is the same size. If you want to make the text larger or smaller in one shape, see "Changing fonts and font sizes on shapes" later in this chapter.

Entering bulleted lists on diagram shapes

Some diagram shapes have built-in bulleted lists, but no matter. Whether or not a shape is prepared to be bulleted, you can enter bullets in a diagram shape. Here are instructions for entering and removing bullets:

✦ **Entering a bulleted list:** Select the shape that needs bullets, and on the (SmartArt Tools) Design tab, click the Add Bullet button. Either enter the bulleted items directly into the shape (pressing Enter as you type each entry) or click the Text Pane button to open the Text pane (refer to Figure 2-7) and enter bullets there.

✦ **Removing bulleted items:** Click before the first bulleted entry and keep pressing the Delete key until you have removed all the bulleted items. You can also start in the Text pane (refer to Figure 2-7) and press the Delete key there until you've removed the bulleted items, or drag to select several bulleted items and then press Delete.

Turning a bulleted list into a diagram (PowerPoint)

Suppose you're working along in PowerPoint when suddenly the realization strikes you that a bulleted list in a text frame or text box would work much better as a diagram. For those occasions, you can click the Convert to SmartArt button. By clicking this button, you can turn the text in a text frame or text box into a diagram. If the text frame or box contains a bulleted list, each bulleted item becomes a diagram shape.

Follow these steps to turn a text frame or text box into a diagram:

1. **Select the text frame or text box.**
2. **On the Home tab, click the Convert to SmartArt Graphic button.**

   You see a drop-down list with basic diagram choices.
3. **Either select a diagram on the list or choose More SmartArt Graphics to open the Choose a SmartArt Graphic dialog box and select a diagram there.**

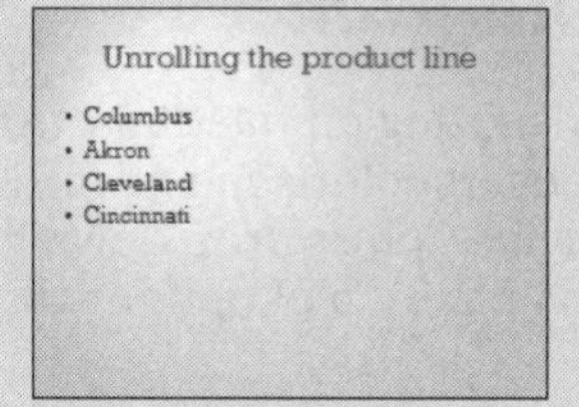

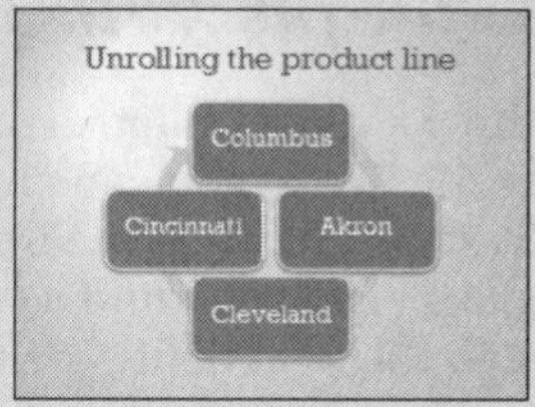

Changing a Diagram's Direction

As long as your diagram is horizontally oriented, you can change its direction. As shown in Figure 2-8, you can flip it over such that the rightmost shape in your diagram becomes the leftmost shape, and what was the leftmost shape becomes the rightmost shape. If arrows are in your diagram, the arrows point the opposite direction after you flip the diagram. You can't flip vertically oriented diagrams this way. Sorry, but diagrams that run north to south, not west to east, can't be rolled over.

Follow these steps to flip a horizontally oriented diagram:

1. **Select the diagram.**
2. **On the (SmartArt Tools) Design tab, click the Right to Left button.**

   If you don't like what you see, click the button again or click the Undo button.

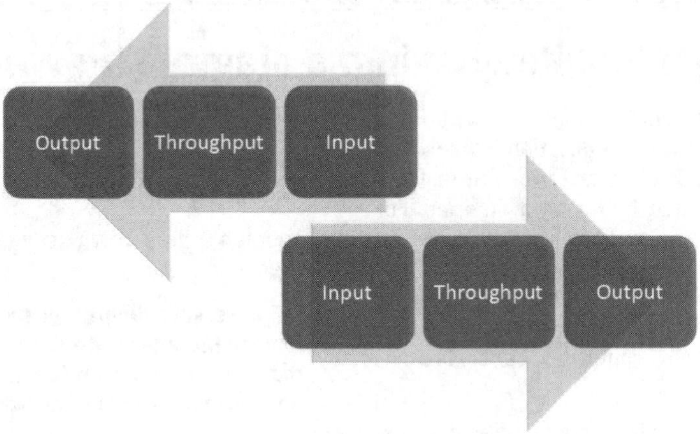

Figure 2-8: You can flip horizontal diagrams so that they run the opposite direction.

Choosing a Look for Your Diagram

Decide how a diagram looks by starting on the (SmartArt Tools) Design tab. Starting there, you can choose a color scheme for your diagram and a different style. Between the Change Colors drop-down list and the SmartArt Styles gallery, you can find a combination of options that presents your diagram in the best light:

- **Change Colors button:** Click the Change Colors button to see color schemes for your diagram on the drop-down list, as shown in Figure 2-9. Point at a few options to live-preview them.
- **SmartArt Styles gallery:** Open the SmartArt Styles gallery to choose simple and 3-D variations on the diagram.

TIP

If you experiment too freely and wish to backpedal, click the Reset Graphic button on the (SmartArt Tools) Design tab. Clicking this button reverses all the formatting changes you made to your diagram.

TIP

If your Word document, Excel worksheet, or PowerPoint presentation includes many diagrams, make sure your diagrams are consistent in appearance. Choose similar colors for diagrams. If you like 3-D diagrams, make the majority of your diagrams 3-D. Don't let the diagrams overwhelm the ideas they are meant to express. The point is to present ideas in diagrams, not turn your work into a SmartArt diagram showcase.

Select a color scheme

Select a diagram style

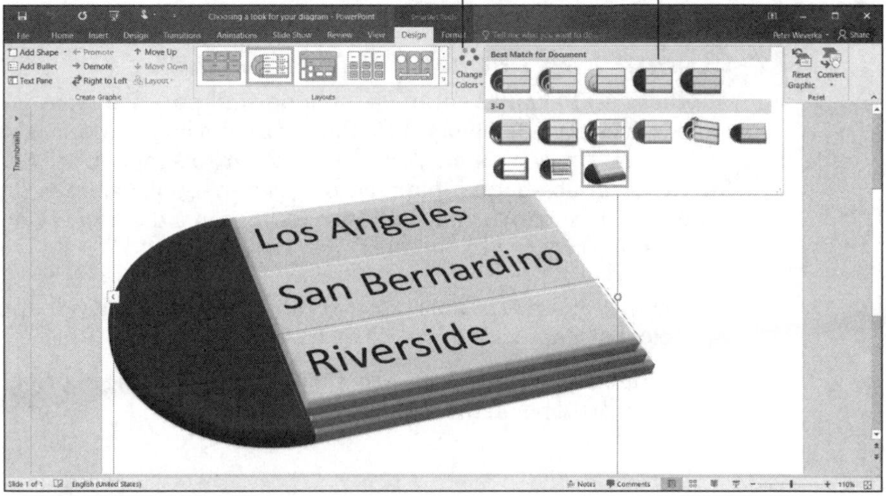

Figure 2-9: Experiment freely with the Change Colors and SmartArt Styles gallery options.

Changing the Appearance of Diagram Shapes

To call attention to one part of a diagram, you can change the appearance of a shape and make it stand out. Any part of a diagram that is different from the other parts naturally gets more attention. To change the appearance of a shape, consider changing its size or color, exchanging one shape for another, or changing the font and font size of the text. These topics are covered in the following pages.

Changing the size of a diagram shape

A shape that is larger than other shapes in a diagram gets the attention of the audience. Select your shape and use one of these techniques to enlarge or shrink it:

- ✦ On the (SmartArt Tools) Format tab, click the Larger or Smaller button as many times as necessary to make the shape the right size.
- ✦ Move the pointer over a corner selection handle, and when the pointer changes to a two-headed arrow, click and start dragging.

Notice that the text inside the shape remains the same size although the shape is larger. To change the size of the text in a shape, see "Changing fonts and font sizes on shapes," later in this chapter.

TIP

To return a diagram shape to its original size after you've fooled with it, right-click the shape and choose Reset Shape.

Exchanging one shape for another

Another way to call attention to an important part of a diagram is to change shapes, as shown in Figure 2-10. Rather than a conventional shape, use an oval, block arrow, or star. You can substitute a shape in the Shapes gallery for any diagram shape (Chapter 4 of this mini-book explores the Shapes gallery). To exchange one shape for another in a diagram, select the shape and use one of these techniques:

- On the (SmartArt Tools) Format tab, click the Change Shape button and select a shape in the Shapes gallery.
- Right-click the shape, choose Change Shape on the shortcut menu, and select a shape on the submenu.

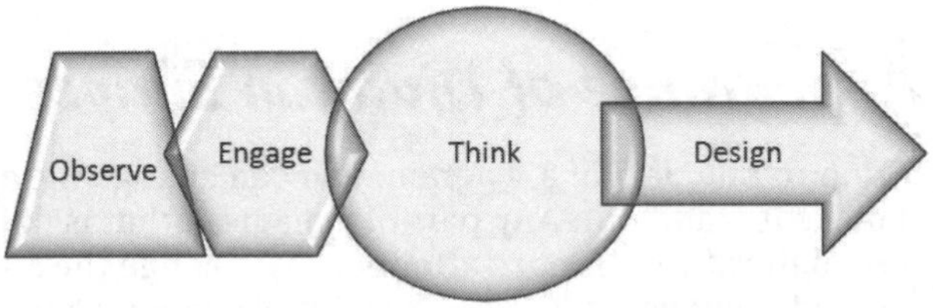

Figure 2-10: Using different shapes and different-sized shapes in a diagram.

Changing a shape's color, fill, or outline

Yet another way to call attention to a shape is to change its color, fill, or outline border, as shown in Figure 2-11. Select a shape and go to the (SmartArt Tools) Format tab to change a shape's color, fill, or outline.

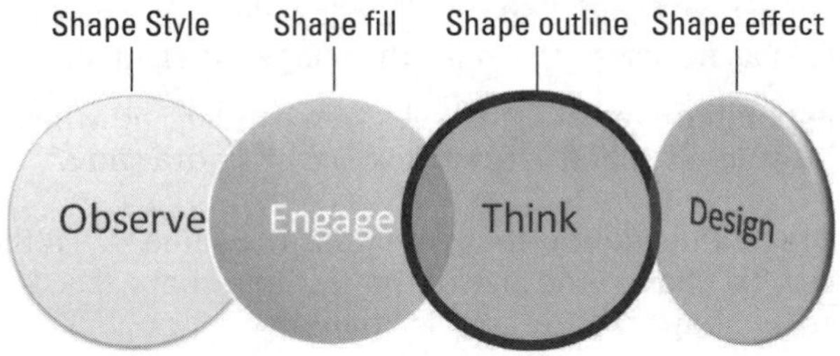

Figure 2-11: Ways to make a diagram shape stand out.

Editing 3-D diagrams in 2-D

Three-dimensional diagrams are wonderful. You can impress your friends with a 3-D diagram. All you have to do to turn a mundane two-dimensional diagram into a three-dimensional showpiece is go to the (SmartArt Tools) Design tab, open the SmartArt Styles gallery, and select a 3-D option.

Unfortunately, editing a 3-D diagram can be difficult. The shapes and text are all aslant. It's hard to tell where to click or what to drag when you're editing a 3-D diagram.

Fortunately, you can get around the problem of editing a 3-D diagram by temporarily displaying it in two dimensions. On the (SmartArt Tools) Format tab, click the Edit in 2-D button to temporarily render a 3-D graphic in two dimensions. Click the button a second time to return to the third dimension.

- **Restyling a shape:** Select an option in the Shape Styles gallery to give a shape a makeover.
- **Filling a shape with a new color:** Click the Shape Fill button and make a choice from the drop-down list to select a color, picture, two-color gradient, or texture for the shape.
- **Changing the outline:** Click the Shape Outline button and choose a color and weight for the shape's border on the drop-down list.
- **Applying a shape effect:** Click the Shape Effects button to select a shape effect for your shape.

Changing fonts and font sizes on shapes

To make a diagram shape stand out, try changing the font and font size of the text on the shape. Before you change fonts and font sizes, however, you should know that changing fonts in a shape effectively disconnects the shape from the other shapes in the diagram. Normally text changes size throughout a diagram when you add or remove shapes, but when you change the font or font size in one shape, it is no longer associated with the other shapes; its letters don't change their size or appearance when shapes are added or removed from the diagram of which it is a part.

To alter the text on a diagram shape, select the text, go to the Home tab, and choose a different font, font size, and font color, too, if you want.

Creating a Diagram from Scratch

If you have the skill and the wherewithal, you can create a diagram from scratch by piecing together shapes, arrows, and connectors. The diagram in Figure 2-12, for example, was made not from SmartArt graphics but from shapes, arrows, and connectors. Chapter 4 of this mini-book explains how to draw shapes and lines between shapes. You can enter text on any shape merely by clicking inside it and wiggling your fingers over the keyboard.

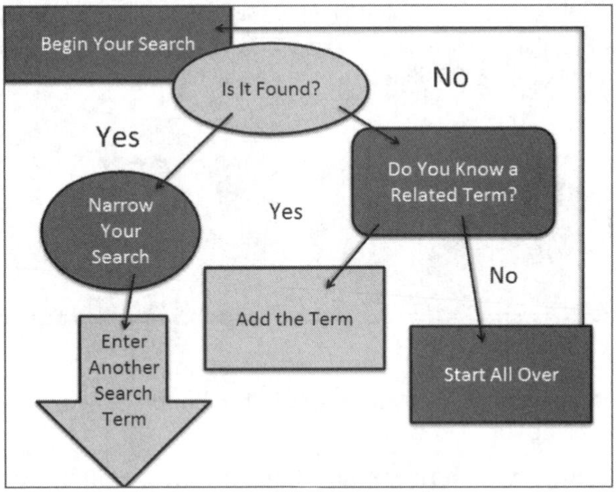

Figure 2-12: A home-grown diagram made without SmartArt graphics.

Making a diagram from scratch has some advantages. You can draw the connectors any which way. Lines can cross the diagram chaotically. You can include text boxes as well as shapes (the diagram in Figure 2-12 has four text boxes). Don't hesitate to fashion your own diagrams when a presentation or document calls for it.

Chapter 3: Handling Graphics and Photos

In This Chapter

- Understanding the different graphic file formats
- Placing a graphic in a Word document, PowerPoint slide, or Excel worksheet
- Recoloring, cropping, and otherwise altering a picture
- Compressing graphics

A picture, so they say, is worth a thousand words. Whether it's worth a thousand words or merely 950 is debatable. What is certain is that visuals help people remember things. A carefully chosen image in a PowerPoint presentation, Word document, or Excel worksheet helps others understand you better. The image reinforces the ideas or information that you're trying to put across.

This chapter explains how you can make pictures — photographs and graphics — part of your Word documents, PowerPoint presentations, and Excel worksheets. It looks into graphic file formats and other issues pertaining to graphics as well as how to touch up graphics in an Office application.

All about Picture File Formats

Graphics and photographs come in many different file formats, and as far as Office 2016 is concerned, some are better than others. These pages explain what you need to know about graphic files to use them wisely in Office files. Here, you find out what bitmap and vector graphics are, what resolution and color depth are, and how graphic files are compressed.

Bitmap and vector graphics

All graphic images fall into either the bitmap or vector category:

- A *bitmap graphic* is composed of thousands upon thousands of tiny dots called *pixels* that, taken together, form an image (the term "pixel" comes from "picture element"). A photograph is a bitmap graphic.

- A *vector graphic* is drawn with the aid of computer instructions that describe the shape and dimension of each line, curve, circle, and so on.

The difference between the two formats is that vector graphics do not distort when you enlarge or shrink them, whereas bitmap graphics lose resolution when their size is changed. Furthermore, vector images do not require nearly as much disk space as bitmap graphics. Drop a few bitmap graphics in a file and soon you're dealing with a file that is close to 750K in size.

Table 3-1 describes popular bitmap graphic formats; Table 3-2 lists popular vector graphic formats.

Table 3-1 Bitmap (Photograph) File Formats

Extension	*File Type*	*Color Depth*	*Compression*
BMP, BMZ, DIB	Microsoft Windows Bitmap	To 24-bit	None
GFA, GIF	Graphics Interchange Format	To 8-bit	Lossy
JPEG, JPG, JFIF, JPE	JPEG File Interchange Format	To 24-bit	Lossy
PICT	Macintosh PICT	To 32-bit	None
PNG	Portable Network Graphics	To 48-bit	Lossless
RLE	Bitmap File in RLE Compression Scheme	To 24-bit	None
TIF, TIFF	Tagged Image File Format	To 24-bit	Lossless

Table 3-2 Vector File Formats

Extension	*File Type*
CDR	CorelDRAW
CGM	Computer Graphics Metafile
EMF	Enhanced Windows Metafile
EMZ	Windows Enhanced Metafile
EPS	Encapsulated PostScript
PCT	Macintosh PICT
WMF	Windows Metafile
WPG	WordPerfect Graphics

Resolution

Resolution refers to how many pixels comprise a bitmap image. The higher the resolution, the clearer the image. Resolution is measured in *dots per inch* (dpi), sometimes called *pixels per inch* (ppi). Images with more dots — or pixels — per inch are clearer and display more fineness of detail. When you scan an image, the scanner permits you to choose a dots-per-inch setting.

High-resolution images look better but require more disk space than low-resolution images. Figure 3-1 illustrates the difference between a high-resolution and low-resolution photograph.

Figure 3-1: A high-resolution photo (left) and the same photo at low resolution (right).

Compression

TECHNICAL STUFF

Compression refers to a mathematical algorithm by which bitmap graphic files can be made smaller. In effect, compression enables your computer to store a bitmap graphic with less disk space. Some bitmap graphic types can't be compressed; other bitmap graphic types are compressed using either lossless or lossy compression:

- **Lossless compression:** To maintain the picture's integrity, the same number of pixels are stored in the compressed file as in the original. Because the pixels remain intact, you can change the size of a file that has undergone lossless compression without losing picture quality.
- **Lossy compression:** Without regard for the picture's integrity, pixel data in the original picture is lost during compression. Therefore, if you try to enlarge a picture that has undergone lossy compression, the picture loses quality.

Color depth

Color depth refers to the number of colors that can be displayed in a graphics file. The larger the color depth, the larger the number of colors that can be displayed, the richer the graphic looks, and the larger its file size is. Color depth is measured in bits. To get technical on you, color depth is measured in the number of bits that are needed to describe each pixel's color in the image. A bit, or "binary digit," is the smallest unit of data measurement in computing. These are the color-depth measurements:

Bit Size	***Color Depth***
1-bit	Black and white only
8-bit	256 colors
16-bit	65,536 colors
24-bit	16,777,216 colors
32-bit	4,294,967,296 colors

To look like photographs and not cartoons, photographs require a color depth of at least 16-bits. Sometimes color depth is described in terms of a color palette. For example, a graphic format with an 8-bit color depth is said to have a 256-color palette.

Choosing file formats for graphics

One of the challenges of using photographs and graphics in Office files is keeping file sizes to a minimum. A file that is loaded down with many photographs can take a long time to load and send over the Internet.

The trick is to find a balance between high-quality, high-resolution graphics and the need to keep file sizes low. Here are some tips for choosing graphic file formats:

- ✦ Consider sticking with vector graphics if you're including graphics in your file strictly for decoration purposes. Vector images are easy to come by, don't require very much disk space, and can be edited in Office.
- ✦ For photographs, make JPEG your first choice for graphics. JPEG images have a fairly high resolution. JPEG is the de facto photograph standard on the Internet.
- ✦ If you're dealing with black-and-white photos or resolution doesn't matter, use GIF files. These files eat up the least amount of disk space.

Inserting a Picture in an Office File

After you've weighed the merits of different kinds of graphics and decided which one is best for you, you can insert it. To insert a picture, either use one stored on your computer or get one from the Internet.

After a picture lands in a file, it becomes an object. Chapter 4 of this minibook explains how to manipulate objects — how to move them, change their size, and change their borders. Later in this chapter, "Touching Up a Picture" looks into various ways to change the appearance of graphics.

Inserting a picture of your own

Inserting a picture stored on your computer (or computer network) is as simple as choosing it in the Insert Picture dialog box. Follow these steps to insert a picture on a PowerPoint slide, Word document, or Excel worksheet:

1. **Go to the Insert tab.**
2. **Click the Pictures button.**

   You see the Insert Picture dialog box, as shown in Figure 3-2. In PowerPoint, you can also open this dialog box by clicking the Pictures icon in a content placeholder frame.

3. **Select a file in the Insert Picture dialog box.**

   As Figure 3-2 shows, you can choose a View option to see what a graphic looks like.

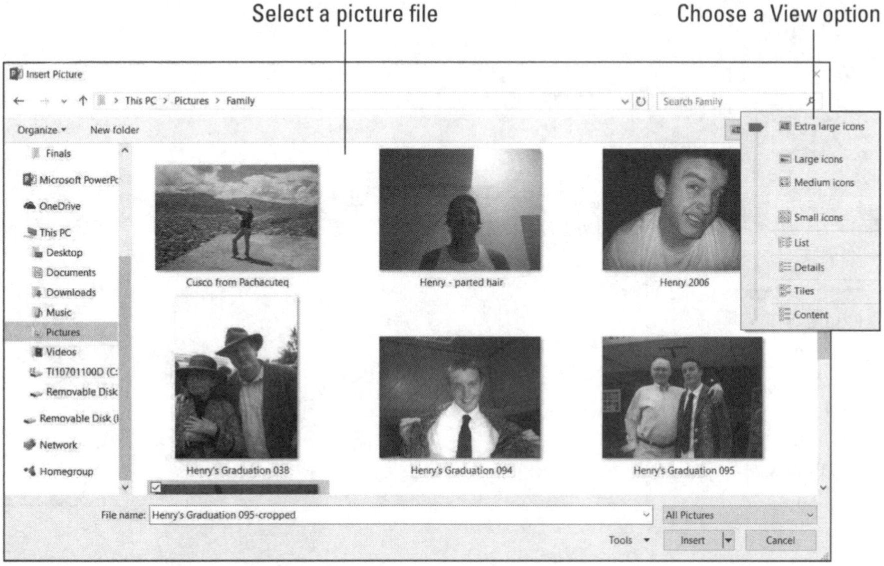

Figure 3-2: You can preview a picture file before you insert it.

You can click the File Types button to open a drop-down list and choose a file type to locate files of a certain type in the dialog box. This button is located above the Insert and Cancel buttons.

4. **Click the Insert button.**

   Go to the (Picture Tools) Format tab to see all the different ways you can manipulate a picture after you insert it.

If you chose the wrong picture, don't fret because you can exchange one picture for another. On the (Picture Tools) Format tab, click the Change Picture button and select a different picture in the Insert Picture dialog box.

Obtaining a picture online

Don't have a suitable picture on your computer? You can obtain a picture online. As shown in Figure 3-3, the Insert Pictures dialog box gives you the opportunity to obtain a picture from these places:

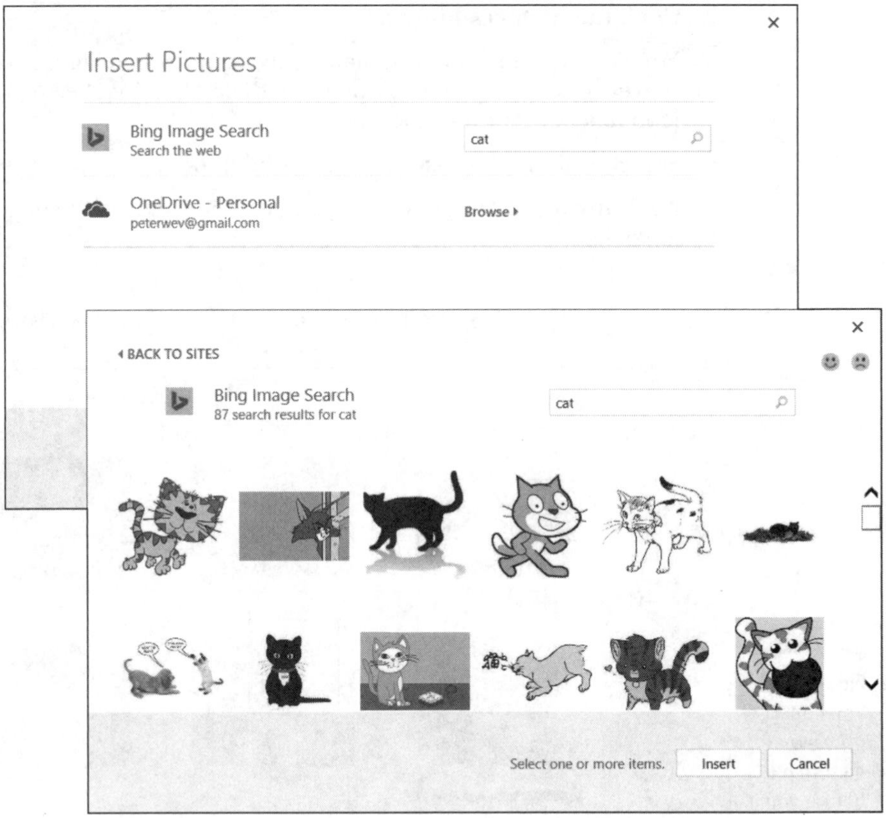

Figure 3-3: A picture search in the Insert Pictures dialog box.

- **The Internet:** Search the Internet for pictures using the Bing search engine.
- **A OneDrive folder:** Obtain a picture from a folder you maintain or share at OneDrive (Book X explains OneDrive).

Follow these steps to obtain a picture from the Internet:

1. **Go to the Insert tab.**
2. **Click the Online Pictures button.**

   The Insert Pictures dialog box opens (see Figure 3-3).
3. **Direct your search to the Internet or a OneDrive folder.**

   You have come to a junction in the road:

   - **The Internet:** Enter a search term in the Bing Image Search box and click the Search button (or press Enter). Then scroll through the search results, select a picture, and click Insert.
   - **A OneDrive folder:** Click the Browse button to open your OneDrive folder and its subfolders. Then locate the picture you want and click Insert.

   Your next task is to move the image into position and perhaps change its size. Chapter 4 of this mini-book explains how to manipulate pictures and other objects.

Shooting a screenshot

Word, PowerPoint, Excel, and Outlook make it easier than ever to take a picture of a screen on your computer and insert it in a document, slide, worksheet, or e-mail message. Follow these steps to take a picture of a screen:

1. **If you want to capture a portion of one screen, open the screen.**
2. **On the Insert tab, click the Screenshot button.**

   A drop-down list shows you thumbnail images of each screen that is open on your computer.
3. **Choose a thumbnail image to shoot an entire screen, or choose Screen Clipping and drag onscreen to shoot a portion of a screen.**

A picture of the screen or a portion of the screen lands in your document, slide, worksheet, or e-mail message.

Here are a couple of other tried-and-true techniques for capturing screens:

- Press PrtScn (the key to the right of F12) to capture an entire screen to the Clipboard.
- Press Alt+PrtScn to capture the active part of the screen to the Clipboard. For example, to capture a dialog box, select the dialog box and press Alt+PrtScn.

After the screen capture is on the Clipboard, you can paste it where you will.

Touching Up a Picture

Every picture can be a collaboration. You can do the following to make a picture your own as well as the work of the original artist:

- **Softening and sharpening:** Mute or polish a picture. See "Softening and sharpening pictures," later in this chapter.
- **Changing the brightness and contrast**: Adjust a picture's tone. See "Correcting a picture's brightness and contrast."
- **Recoloring:** Give your picture a brand-new set of colors or gray shades. See "Recoloring a picture."
- **Choosing an artistic effect:** Take your picture for a walk on the wild side. See "Choosing an artistic effect."
- **Choosing a picture style:** Present your picture in an oval fame, soft-edged frame, or other type of frame. See "Selecting a picture style."
- **Cropping:** Cut out the parts of a picture that you don't want. See "Cropping off part of a picture."
- **Removing picture areas:** Keep the essentials of a picture and remove the rest. See "Removing the background."

If you regret experimenting with your picture and you want to start all over, go to the (Picture Tools) Format tab and click the Reset Picture button. Clicking this button restores a picture to its original condition.

Softening and sharpening pictures

Figure 3-4 shows the effects of the softening/sharpening settings. These settings mute a picture or make it look more succinct. To soften or sharpen a picture, select it and use one of these techniques:

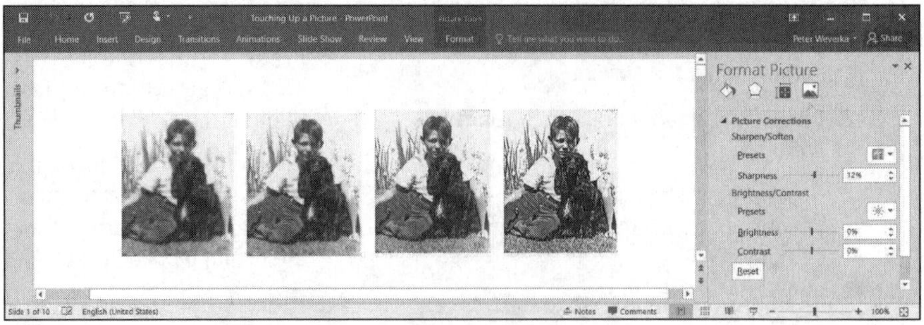

Figure 3-4: Effects of the Soften/Sharpen settings.

- On the (Picture Tools) Format tab, click the Corrections button and choose a Sharpen and Soften option on the drop-down list.
- Open the Format Picture task pane and drag the Sharpness slider or enter a negative or positive number in the text box. Negative numbers soften the picture; positive numbers sharpen it. To open the Format Picture task pane, click the Corrections button and choose Picture Corrections Options on the drop-down list.

Correcting a picture's brightness and contrast

Figure 3-5 shows a picture that has been made over several times with the Brightness and Contrast settings. Brightness settings govern the overall brightness of a picture; contrast settings determine how distinguishable the different parts of the picture are from one another. Change a picture's brightness and contrast to make it fit better on a page or slide. Select your picture and use one of these techniques:

- On the (Picture Tools) Format tab, click the Corrections button and choose a Brightness and Contrast option on the drop-down list.
- Open the Format Picture task pane and change the Brightness and Contrast settings. Negative Brightness settings make a picture darker; positive settings make it brighter. Negative Contrast settings mute the differences between the parts of a picture; positive settings heighten the differences. To open the Format Picture task pane, click the Corrections button and choose Picture Corrections Options on the drop-down list.

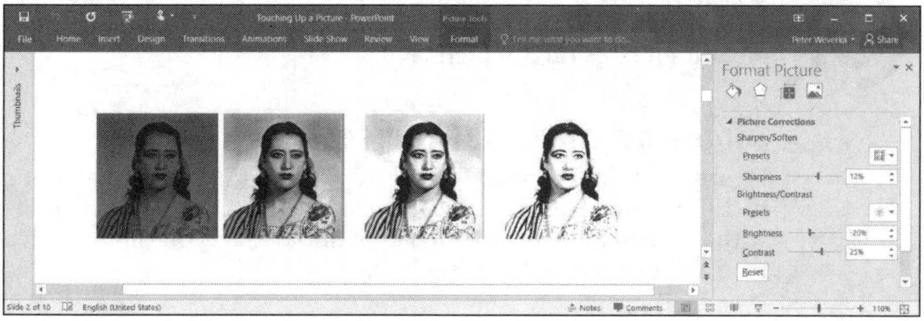

Figure 3-5: Effects of the Brightness and Contrast settings.

Recoloring a picture

Recolor a picture to give it a makeover. Figure 3-6 shows examples of Recolor options. As well as recoloring a picture, you can change its color saturation and color tone settings. *Color saturation* refers to the purity and intensity of the colors; *color tone* determines the degree of lightness and darkness.

Recoloring is useful for giving a picture a uniform appearance. Select your picture and use these techniques to recolor it:

- On the (Picture Tools) Format tab, click the Color button and choose a Color Saturation, Color Tone, or Recolor option on the drop-down list. You can choose More Variations at the bottom of the list and choose a color on the sublist.
- Open the Format Picture task pane and change the Color Saturation and Color Tone settings. Change the Saturation setting to mute or bring out the colors; change the Temperature setting to make the color tones darker or lighter. To open the Format Picture task pane, click the Color button and choose Picture Color Options.

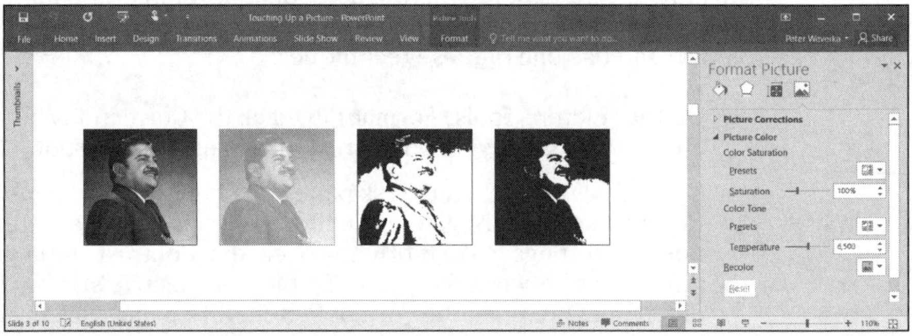

Figure 3-6: Examples of Recolor options.

Live-previewing really comes in handy when you're recoloring a graphic. As you change Color Saturation and Color Tone settings, you can see the effect of your choices on the picture.

Choosing an artistic effect

Figure 3-7 demonstrates four of the 23 artistic effects that you can apply to a picture: Pencil Sketch, Glow Diffused, Glass, and Glow Edges. To experiment with the artistic effects and maybe find one to your liking, select your picture and use one of these techniques:

- Go to the (Picture Tools) Format tab, click the Artistic Effects button, and choose an effect on the drop-down list.
- Open the Format Picture task pane and choose an artistic effect. To open the Format Picture dialog box, click the Effects button and choose Artistic Effects Options.

Making a color transparent

The (Picture Tools) Format tab offers the Set Transparent Color command for making one color in a picture transparent and thereby allowing the background to show through in certain parts of a picture. The Set Transparent Color command works by making all the pixels in a picture that are the same color transparent. In a picture in which one color predominates, you can make this color transparent and get some interesting effects.

To experiment with the Set Transparent Color command:

- **Select the picture.**
- **On the (Picture Tools) Format tab, click the Color button and choose Set Transparent Color on the drop-down list.**
- **Click in your picture on the color that you want to be transparent.**

You can choose the Set Transparent Color command again and make another color in your picture transparent.

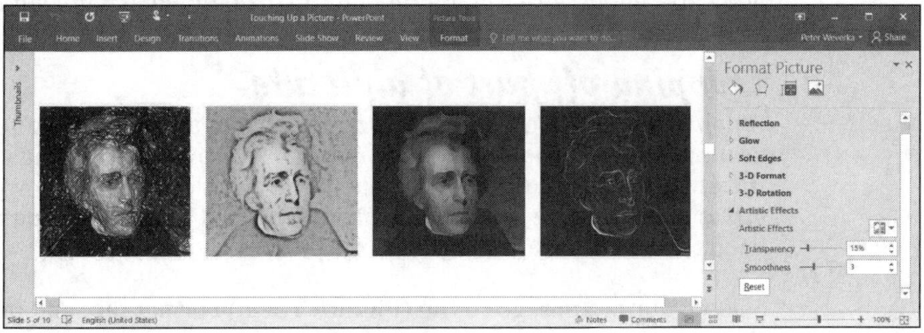

Figure 3-7: Examples of artistic effects.

Selecting a picture style

A *picture style* is way of presenting or framing a picture. Figure 3-8 shows examples of picture styles. Picture styles include Simple Frame, Soft Edge Rectangle, Perspective Shadow, and Reflected Bevel. To choose a picture style for a picture, select it, go to the (Picture Tools) Format tab, open the Picture Styles gallery, and choose a style.

Figure 3-8: Examples of picture styles.

If you don't like the picture style you chose (or you don't care for any change you made to a picture), click the Reset Picture button to reverse all your format changes and start over.

If you like the picture styles, you may be enamored as well with the picture effects. On the (Picture Tools) Format tab, click the Picture Effects button and experiment with the options on the drop-down list and sublists.

Cropping off part of a picture

Cropping means to cut off part of a picture. I'm afraid you can't use the Office cropping tool like a pair of scissors or an Xacto knife to zigzag cut around the edges of a picture or cut a hole in the middle. You can, however, cut strips from the side, top, or bottom. In Figure 3-9, the cropping tool is being used to cut off extraneous parts of a picture.

Select your picture, go to the (Picture Tools) Format tab, and use one of these techniques to crop it:

- ✦ **Crop manually:** Crop the picture by dragging its cropping handles. Click the Crop button. Cropping handles appear around the picture, as in Figure 3-9. Drag cropping handles to lop off a part or parts of the picture. Click the Crop button again or press Esc after you finish cropping.

Figure 3-9: Cropping off parts of a picture.

✦ **Crop to a shape:** Crop the picture to a rectangle, circle, or other shape. Open the drop-down list on the Crop button, choose Crop to Shape, and select a shape in the Shapes gallery.

✦ **Crop to proportions:** Crop the picture to a proportional size setting. Open the drop-down list on the Crop button, choose Aspect Ratio, and choose a ratio. For example, choose 1:1 to crop to a perfect square with the width and height the same size.

✦ **Crop by filling:** For placing an image in a picture placeholder, crop the image to make it fit in the placeholder box.

✦ **Crop by fitting:** For placing an image in a picture placeholder, shrink the picture to make it fit.

TIP

With the cropping handles showing, you can drag the picture left, right, up, or down to determine where it is cropped.

WARNING!

When you crop a picture, you don't cut off a part of it — not as far as your computer is concerned. All you do is tell Office not to display part of a graphic. The graphic is still whole. You can, however, compress a graphic after you crop it, and in so doing truly shave off a part of the graphic and thereby decrease the size of the file you're working with, as "Compressing Pictures to Save Disk Space" explains later in this chapter.

Removing the background

Yet another way to diddle with pictures is to use the Remove Background command. This command endeavors to locate the unessential parts of a picture so that you can remove them. In Figure 3-10, I removed the sky and then placed a rainbow image behind the skyline.

Select a picture and follow these steps to test-drive the Remove Background command:

1. **On the (Picture Tools) Format tab, click the Remove Background button.**

   The Background Removal tab opens and the parts of your picture that Office wants to remove turn a lurid shade of magenta, which you could see in Figure 3-10 if this book were in color.

Figure 3-10: Removing parts of a picture (in this case the sky).

2. **On the Background Removal tab, indicate what you want to keep and remove.**

   Keep your eye on what's magenta and what's not as you use these techniques, and consider zooming to 200 percent or more so that you can get a good look at your picture:

   - *Changing the size of the box:* Drag the side and corner handles of the box to capture what you want to keep or remove.
   - *Marking what you want to keep:* Click the Mark Areas to Keep button. The pointer changes into a pencil. Click your picture to indicate what you want to keep. Each time you click, a keep mark (a plus sign icon) appears on your picture.
   - *Marking what you want to remove:* Click the Mark Areas to Remove button. The pointer changes to a pencil. Click your picture to indicate what you want to remove. When you click, a remove mark (a minus sign) appears.
   - *Deleting keep and remove marks:* Click the Delete Mark button and then click a keep or remove mark to remove a mark and change what is and isn't removed from the picture.

   Of course, you can click the Undo button to backtrack as you work. If you get thoroughly lost on the Background Removal tab, click the Discard All Changes button and start all over.

3. **Click the Keep Changes button when you finish marking what you want to keep and remove.**

   How do you like your picture now? If it needs more work, click the Remove Background button again and diddle some more on the Background Removal tab. Click the Discard All Changes button if you want your original picture without the background removed.

Compressing Pictures to Save Disk Space

By compressing pictures, you reduce their file size and consequently the size of the file you're working on. Not all pictures can be compressed, as "Compression" explains earlier in this chapter, and some types of graphics lose their integrity when they're compressed. You can't resize lossy-compressed graphics without their looking odd.

Compress pictures to make files load faster and make e-mail messages with file attachments travel faster over the Internet. Compressing a picture file reduces its pixels per inch (ppi) setting. Follow these steps to compress pictures:

1. **Optionally, select the picture or pictures you want to compress if you want to compress only one or two.**

   The Compress Pictures command compresses all the graphics in a file unless you select graphics first.

2. **Go to the (Picture Tools) Format tab.**
3. **Click the Compress Pictures button.**

   You see the Compress Pictures dialog box, as shown in Figure 3-11.

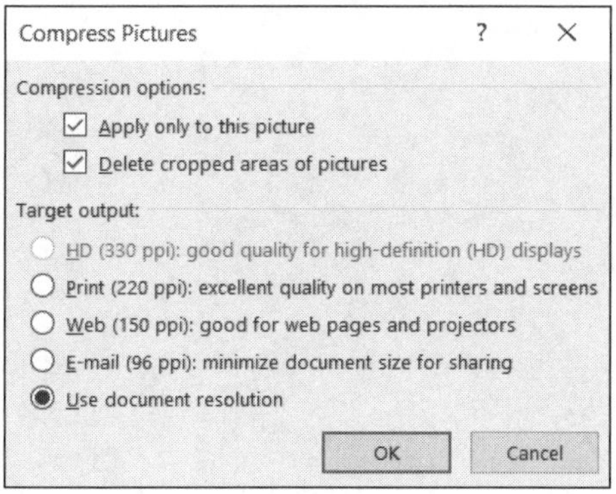

Figure 3-11: Compress pictures to reduce file sizes.

4. **Select the Apply Only to This Picture check box if you selected graphics in Step 1 and you want to compress only a couple of graphics.**

5. **Click the Delete Cropped Areas of Pictures check box if you want to delete the unused portions of pictures you cropped.**

   As "Cropping off part of a picture" explains earlier in this chapter, Office crops graphics in name only. It retains the cropped part of the graphic in case you want it back, but you can remove the cropped part as well by selecting this check box.

6. **Choose a target output for the pictures.**

   These options tell Office which pixels per inch (ppi) setting to use when compressing graphics. Which setting you choose depends on where you intend to show your graphics.

7. **Click OK.**

Chapter 4: Drawing and Manipulating Lines, Shapes, and Other Objects

In This Chapter

- **Drawing and manipulating lines, arrows, and connectors**
- **Creating and modifying shapes**
- **Creating WordArt images**
- **Changing the color and border around an object**
- **Selecting, resizing, moving, aligning, overlapping, rotating, and grouping objects**

Office 2016 comes with drawing commands for drawing lines, arrows, shapes, block arrows, stars, banners, and callout shapes. And Office provides numerous ways to manipulate these objects after you draw them. The drawing commands are meant to bring out the artist in you. Use them to make diagrams, fashion your own ideagrams, and illustrate difficult concepts and ideas. Lines and shapes give you a wonderful opportunity to exercise your creativity. A picture is worth a thousand words, so they say, and the drawing commands give you a chance to express yourself without having to write a thousand words.

In this chapter, you discover the many ways to manipulate lines, shapes, text boxes, WordArt images, and graphics. You discover how to lay out these objects on a page or slide, flip them, change their colors, resize them, move them, and otherwise torture them until they look just right. You discover how to draw lines and arrows, draw connections between shapes, and draw ovals, squares, other shapes, and WordArt images.

Use the techniques I describe in this chapter to bring something more to your Word documents, PowerPoint presentations, and Excel worksheets: originality. With the techniques I describe in this chapter, you can bring the visual element into your work. You can communicate with images as well as words and numbers.

The Basics: Drawing Lines, Arrows, and Shapes

Figure 4-1 demonstrates how you can use lines, arrows, and shapes (not to mention text boxes) to illustrate ideas and concepts. Sometimes, saying it with lines and shapes is easier and more informative than saying it with words. Even in Excel worksheets, you can find opportunities to use lines, arrows, and shapes. For example, draw arrows and lines on worksheets to illustrate which cells are used to compute formulas.

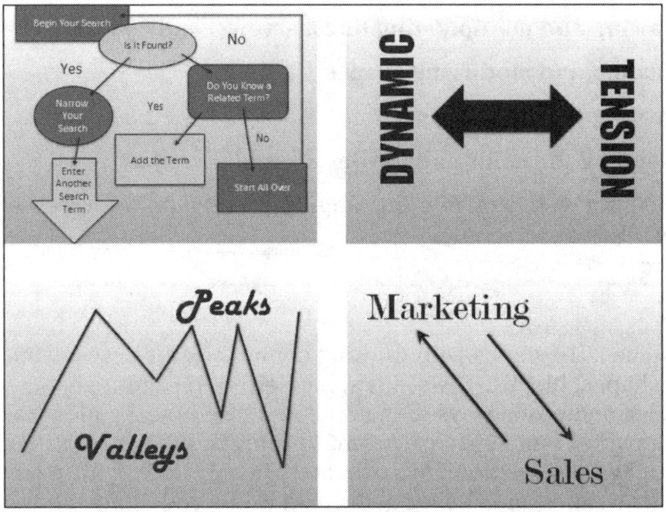

Figure 4-1: Exercise your creativity by including lines, arrows, and shapes in your work.

Follow these basic steps to draw a line, arrow, or shape:

1. **Go to the Insert tab.**

   In Word, you must be in Print Layout view to draw and see lines and shapes.

2. **Click the Shapes button to open the Insert Shapes gallery.**

   As shown in Figure 4-2, the Shapes gallery appears. The shapes are divided into several categories, including Lines, Basic Shapes, and Block Arrows, as well as a category at the top of the gallery where shapes you chose recently are shown. (PowerPoint also offers the Shapes button on the Home tab.)

3. **Select a line, arrow, or shape in the Shapes gallery.**

4. **Drag on your page, slide, or worksheet.**

   As you drag, the line, arrow, or shape appears before your eyes.

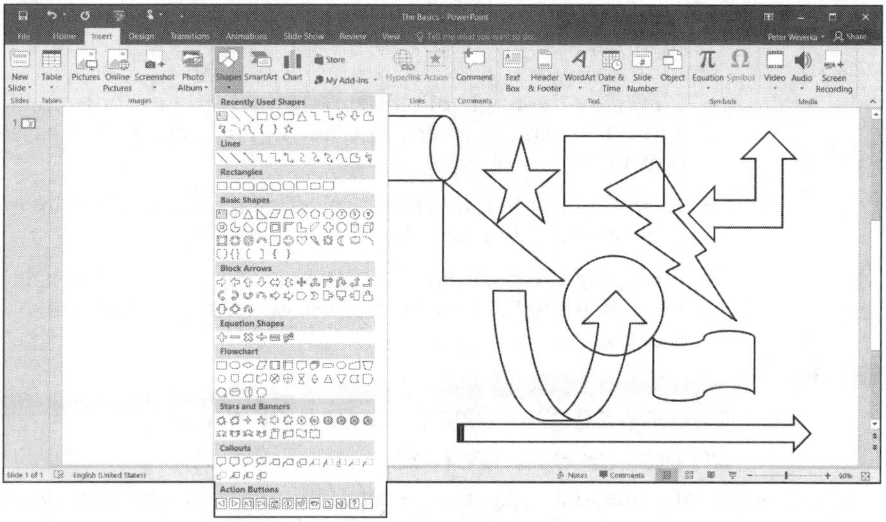

Figure 4-2: To draw a line, arrow, or shape, choose it in the Shapes gallery.

5. **To alter your line, arrow, or shape — that is, to change its size, color, or outline — go to the (Drawing Tools) Format tab.**

   This tab offers many commands for manipulating lines and shapes. (Those commands are explained throughout this chapter.) You must select a line or shape to make the (Drawing Tools) Format tab appear.

   In the upper-left corner of the (Drawing Tools) Format tab is another Shapes gallery for creating new shapes to go along with the one you created.

Handling Lines, Arrows, and Connectors

Earlier in this chapter, Figure 4-1 shows examples of how you can use lines and arrows to present ideas. As well as lines and arrows, the Insert Shapes gallery offers *connectors,* the special lines that link shapes and can bend and stretch as you move shapes around. Use connectors along with lines and arrows to describe the relationships between the people or things in a diagram. These pages explain how to handle lines, arrows, and connectors.

Changing the length and position of a line or arrow

To change anything about a line or arrow, start by clicking to select it. You can tell when a line has been selected because square selection handles appear at either end. Follow these instructions to move a line or adjust its length or angle:

- **Changing the angle of a line:** Drag a selection handle up, down, or sideways. You can see where your line will be when you release the mouse button.
- **Changing the length:** Drag a selection handle away from or toward the opposite selection handle.
- **Changing the position:** Move the pointer over the line itself and click when you see the four-headed arrow. Then drag the line to a new location.

Changing the appearance of a line, arrow, or connector

What a line looks like is a matter of its color, its *weight* (how wide it is), its *dash status* (it can be filled out or dashed), and its *cap* (its ends can be rounded, square, or flat). To change the appearance of a line, start by selecting it, going to the (Drawing Tools) Format tab, and opening the drop-down list on the Shape Outline button (this button is in the Shape Styles group). As shown in Figure 4-3, you see a drop-down list with commands for handling the appearance of lines, arrows, and connectors:

- **Color:** Select a color on the drop-down list (refer to Figure 4-3).
- **Width:** Choose Weight on the drop-down list (refer to Figure 4-3) and then choose a line width on the submenu. You can also choose More Lines on the submenu to open the Format Shape task pane and change the width there. Enter a Width setting in points to make the line heavier or thinner.

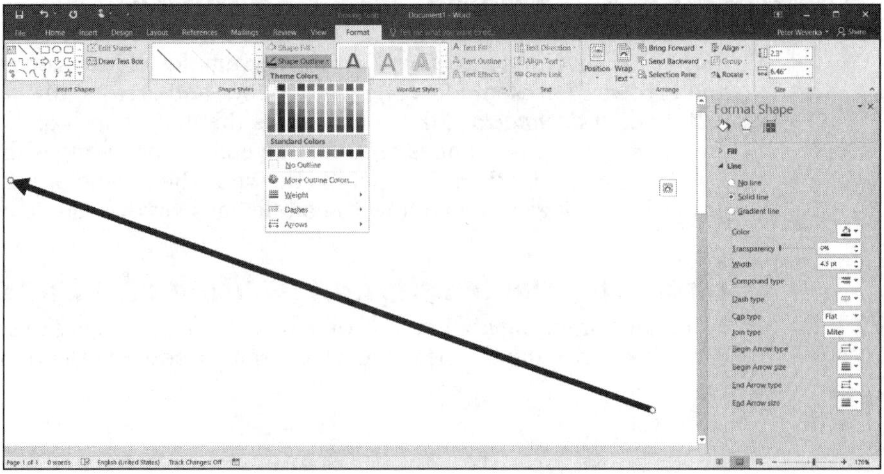

Figure 4-3: Change the appearance of lines on the Shape Outline drop-down list and Format Shape task pane.

Choosing a default line style for consistency's sake

One of the secrets to making an attractive drawing is to make the lines consistent with one another. Lines should be the same width and color. They should be the same style. Unless you observe this rule, your drawings will be infested with lines of varying width and different colors. They will look like a confetti parade in a windstorm.

You can get around the problem of making lines consistent with one another by creating a model line and making it the default line style. After you declare a default style, all new lines you create are assigned the style. You don't have to spend as much time making the lines look alike.

Give a line the style, weight, and color that you want for all (or most) lines and then follow these steps to make that line the default style:

1. **Select and right-click the line.**
2. **Choose Set As Default Line on the shortcut menu.**

- **Dotted or dashed lines:** Choose Dashes on the drop-down list and then choose an option on the submenu. Again, you can choose More Lines to open the Format Shape task pane and choose from many dash types and compound lines (refer to Figure 4-3).
- **Line caps:** Click the Shape Styles group button to open the Format Shape task pane (refer to Figure 4-3). Then select a cap type (Square, Round, or Flat).

TIP

You can also change the appearance of a line on the (Drawing Tools) Format tab by opening the Shape Styles gallery and selecting a style.

Attaching and handling arrowheads on lines and connectors

Arrows, of course, have arrowheads, and arrowheads on lines and connectors can go on either side or both sides of a line. What's more, arrowheads come in different sizes and shapes. To handle arrowheads on lines and connectors, select your line or connector and go to the (Drawing Tools) Format tab. Then use one of these techniques to handle the arrowheads:

- Open the drop-down list on the Shape Outline button, choose Arrows (refer to Figure 4-3), and select an arrow on the submenu.
- Click the Shape Styles group button to open the Format Shape task pane. Then choose Arrow settings to describe where you want the arrowheads to be, what you want them to look like, and what size you want them to be.

To attach an arrowhead or arrowheads to a line or connector you've already drawn, select the line and proceed as though you were attaching arrowheads to a line that already has an arrow.

Connecting shapes by using connectors

Under Lines, the Shapes gallery offers six different connectors. Use *connectors* to link shapes and text boxes to form a diagram. Connectors differ from conventional lines in an important way: After you attach one to a shape, it stays with the shape when you move the shape. You don't have to worry about remaking all the connections after you move a shape. You can move shapes at will and let the connectors between shapes take care of themselves.

Figure 4-4 shows three types of connectors in action. (By the way, if you came here to explore how to make a diagram, be sure to check out Chapter 2 of this mini-book as well. It explains Office SmartArt diagramming.)

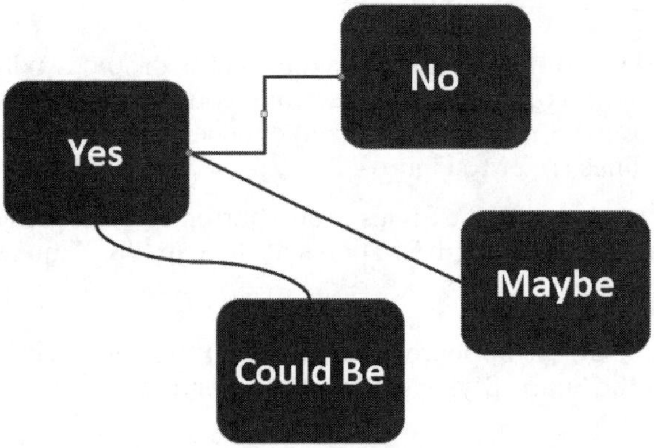

Figure 4-4: The three types of connectors (from top to bottom): elbow, straight, and curved.

To connect shapes in Word, the shapes must be on the drawing canvas. Book II, Chapter 6 describes the Word drawing canvas. (Click the Shapes button and choose New Drawing Canvas to create one.)

Making the connection

Before you draw the connections, draw the shapes and arrange them on the slide where you want them to be in your diagram. Then follow these steps to connect two shapes with a connector:

1. **Select the two shapes that you want to connect.**

   To select the shapes, hold down the Ctrl key and click each one.

2. **On the (Drawing Tools) Format tab, open the Shapes gallery.**
3. **Under Lines, select the connector that will best fit between the two shapes you want to link together.**

   The three connectors are located on the right side of the Lines choices: Curved Connector, Curved Arrow Connector, and Curved Double-Arrow Connector,
4. **Move the pointer over a side selection handle on one of the shapes you want to connect.**
5. **Click and drag the pointer over a selection handle on the other shape, and when you see green selection handles on that shape, release the mouse button.**

   When you click a connector, you see round, green selection handles on the shapes that are joined by the connector. These green handles tell you that the two shapes are connected and will remain connected when you move them.

If your connector is attached to the wrong shape, don't despair. Select the connector, and on the (Drawing Tools) Format tab, click the Edit Shape button and choose Reroute Connectors. Then move the pointer over the green handle on the side of the connector that needs to be attached elsewhere, click, drag the connector elsewhere on the other shape, and release the mouse button when you see the green selection handles.

Adjusting a connector

Chances are, your connector needs adjusting to make it fit correctly between the two shapes. Click to select your connector and follow these techniques to adjust it:

- **Changing the shape of a connector:** Drag the yellow circle (or circles) on the connector. As you drag, the connector assumes different shapes.
- **Changing the connector type:** Right-click the connector, choose Connector Types, and choose Straight Connector, Elbow Connector, or Curved Connector on the submenu.
- **Handling arrows on connectors:** If the arrows on the connector aren't there, are pointing in the wrong direction, or shouldn't be there, change the arrowheads around using the same techniques you use with standard arrows. See "Attaching and handling arrowheads on lines and connectors" earlier in this chapter.

Make sure that the connector lines in your diagram are consistent with one another. Give them the same style and appearance, or else it will be hard to make sense of your diagram.

Handling Rectangles, Ovals, Stars, and Other Shapes

Figure 4-5 illustrates how shapes can come in very handy for illustrating concepts and ideas. You can combine shapes to make your own illustrations. Apart from the standard rectangle and oval, you can draw octagons and various other "-agons," arrows, stars, and banners. You are hereby encouraged to make shapes a part of your work, and you'll be glad to know that drawing shapes is not difficult. These pages explain how to draw a shape, exchange one shape for another, change a shape's symmetry, and enter words on a shape.

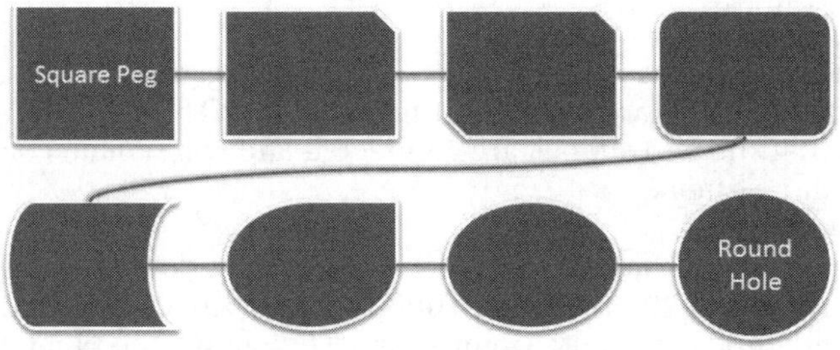

Figure 4-5: An example of using shapes (and connectors) to convey an idea.

WARNING! In Word, you must be in Print Layout view to draw and handle shapes. If you intend to draw more than one shape in Word, create a drawing canvas to hold the shapes (click the Shapes button and choose New Drawing Canvas). Book II, Chapter 6 describes the drawing canvas in Word.

Drawing a shape

Follow these steps to draw a shape:

1. **On the Insert tab, click the Shapes button to open the Shapes gallery.**

   You can also insert shapes from the Shapes gallery on the (Drawing Tools) Format tab.

2. **Select a shape in the gallery.**

   If you've drawn the shape recently, you may be able to find it at the top of the gallery under Recently Used Shapes.

3. **Click and drag slantwise to draw the shape, as shown at the top of Figure 4-6.**

   TIP: Hold down the Shift key as you drag if you want the shape to retain its proportions. For example, to draw a circle, select the Oval shape and hold down the Shift key as you draw.

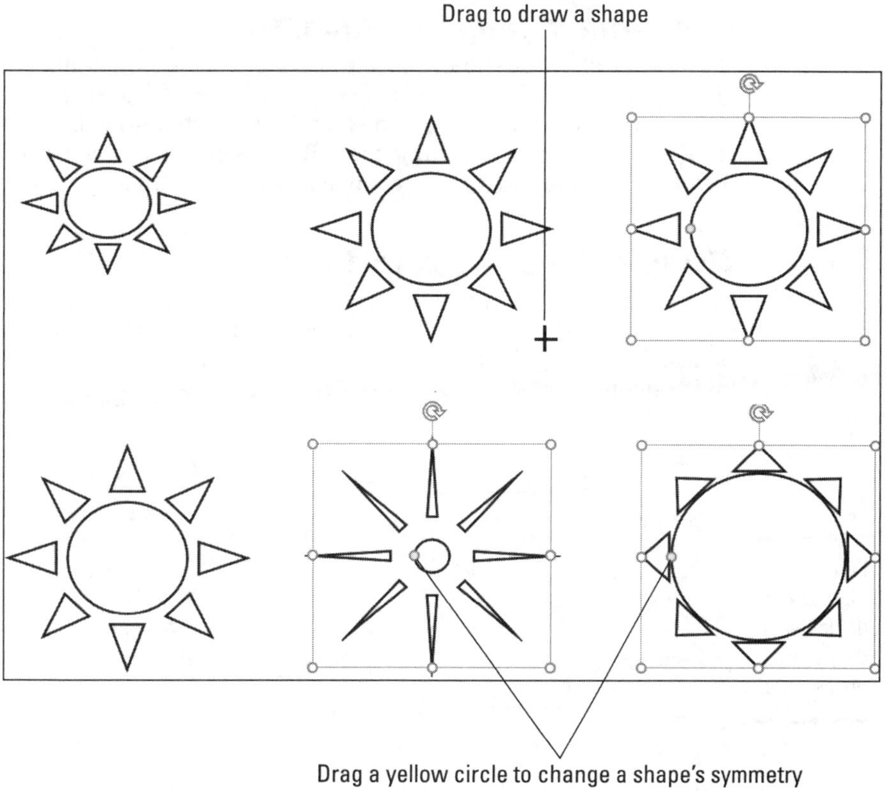
Drag to draw a shape
Drag a yellow circle to change a shape's symmetry

Figure 4-6: Drag to draw a shape (top); drag a yellow circle to change a shape's symmetry (bottom).

Changing a shape's size and shape

Selection handles appear on the corners and sides of a shape after you select it. With the selection handles showing, you can change a shape's size and shape:

- Hold down the Shift key and drag a corner handle to change a shape's size and retain its symmetry.
- Drag a side, top, or bottom handle to stretch or scrunch a shape.

Choosing a different shape

To exchange one shape for another, select the shape and follow these steps:

1. **On the (Drawing Tools) Format tab, click the Edit Shape button.**

   You can find this button in the Insert Shapes group.
2. **Choose Change Shape on the drop-down list.**
3. **Select a new shape in the Shapes gallery.**

Changing a shape's symmetry

A yellow circle, sometimes more than one, appears on some shapes. By dragging a circle, you can change a shape's symmetry. Figure 4-6, for example, shows the same shape (the Sun shape) altered to show different symmetries. Notice where the yellow circles are. By dragging a yellow circle even a short distance, you can do a lot to change a shape's symmetry.

Using a shape as a text box

Here's a neat trick: Rather than use the conventional rectangle as a text box, you can use a shape. Figure 4-7 shows examples of shapes being used as text boxes. By placing words on shapes, you can make the shapes illustrate ideas and concepts.

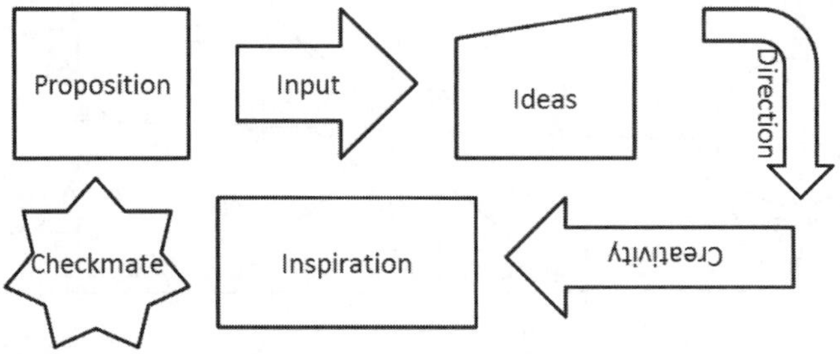

Figure 4-7: Shapes can do double duty as text boxes.

Follow these instructions to handle text box shapes:

- **Entering the text:** Click in the shape and start typing. In Word, you can right-click and choose Add Text if you have trouble typing in the shape.
- **Editing the text:** Click in the text and start editing. That's all there is to it. If you have trouble getting inside the shape to edit the text, select the shape, right-click it, and choose Edit Text on the shortcut menu.
- **Changing the font, color, and size of text:** Select the text, right-click the text, and choose Font. Then, in the Font dialog box, choose a font, font color, and a font size for the text.
- **Allowing the shape to enlarge for text:** You can allow the shape to enlarge and receive more text. On the (Drawing Tools) Format tab, click the Shape Styles group button, and in the Text Options/Text Box category of the Format Shape task pane, select the Resize Shape to Fit Text option button.

Turning a text box into a text box shape

To turn a conventional text box into a text box shape, follow these instructions:

1. **Select the text box by clicking its perimeter.**
2. **On the (Drawing Tools) Format tab, click the Edit Shape button, choose Change Shape, and then select a shape in the Shapes gallery.**

After the conversion, you usually have to enlarge the shape to accommodate the text.

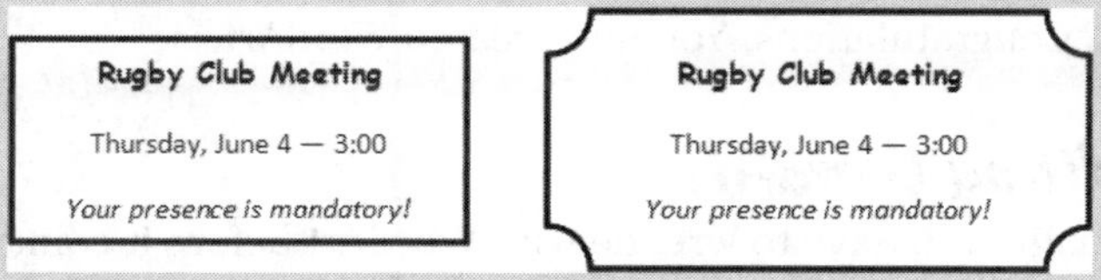
Rugby Club Meeting
Thursday, June 4 — 3:00
Your presence is mandatory!
Rugby Club Meeting
Thursday, June 4 — 3:00
Your presence is mandatory!

WordArt for Embellishing Letters and Words

WordArt gives you the opportunity to decorate letters and words like letters and words on a birthday cake. Figure 4-8 shows the WordArt gallery, where WordArt is made, and an example of WordArt in action. After you insert WordArt, you can fool with the WordArt Styles buttons on the (Drawing Tools) Format tab and embellish the word or phrase even further.

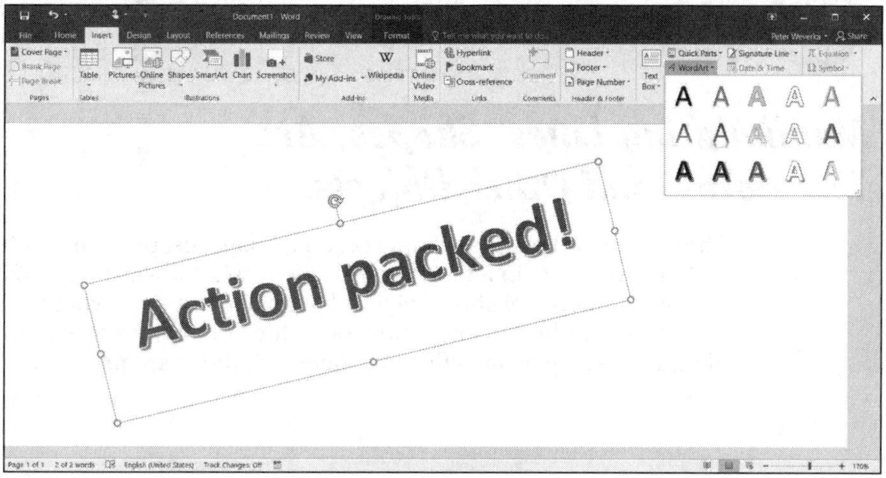
Action packed!

Figure 4-8: Creating a WordArt image.

Creating WordArt

Follow these steps to create WordArt:

1. **On the Insert tab, click the WordArt button.**

   A drop-down list with WordArt styles appears.

2. **Select a WordArt style.**

   Don't worry about selecting the right style; you can choose a different one later on.

3. **Enter text in the WordArt text box.**

   Congratulations. You just created WordArt.

Editing WordArt

Usually, you have to wrestle with WordArt before it comes out right. Select the words, go to the (Drawing Tools) Format tab, and use these techniques to win the wrestling match:

- **Editing the words:** Click in the WordArt text box and edit the text there.
- **Choosing a new WordArt style:** Open the WordArt Styles gallery and choose a style.
- **Changing the letters' color:** Click the Text Fill button and choose a color on the drop-down list.
- **Changing the letters' outline:** Click the Text Outline button and make choices to change the letters' outline.

TIP

To apply color or an outline to some of the letters or words, select the letters or words before choosing options on the (Drawing Tools) Format tab.

Manipulating Lines, Shapes, Art, Text Boxes, and Other Objects

After you insert a shape, line, text box, image, graphic, diagram, chart, or embedded object in a file, it ceases being what it was before and becomes an *object*. Figure 4-9 shows eight objects. I'm not sure whether these eight objects resent being objectified, but Office objectifies them. As far as manipulating these items in Office is concerned, these are just objects.

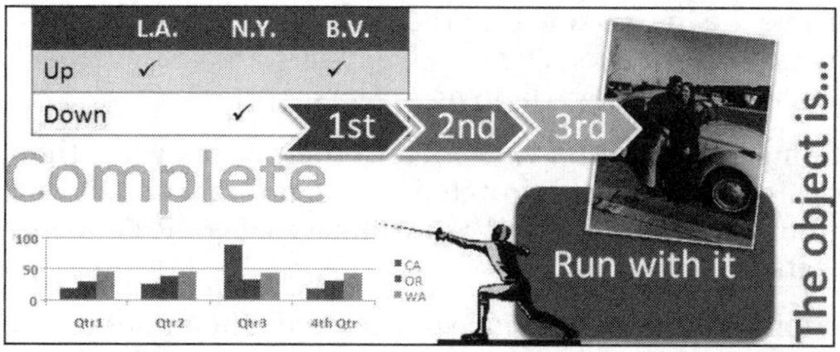

Figure 4-9: Examples of objects.

The techniques for manipulating objects are the same whether you're dealing with a line, shape, graphic, diagram, or text box. The good news from your end is that you have to master only one set of techniques for handling these objects. Whether you want to move, change the size of, change the color of, or change the outline of a text box, graphic, or shape, the techniques are the same.

In the remainder of this chapter are instructions for doing these tasks with objects:

- **Selecting:** Before you can do anything to objects, you have to select them. See "Selecting objects so that you can manipulate them."
- **Making use of the rulers and grid:** Rulers (in Word, PowerPoint, Excel, and Publisher) and the grid (in Word and PowerPoint) can be very helpful for aligning and placing objects. See "Hiding and displaying the rulers and grid."
- **Changing an object's size and shape:** You can enlarge, shrink, stretch, and scrunch objects to make them wider or taller. See "Changing an object's size and shape."
- **Applying color:** Changing an object's color makes it stand out. You can apply patterns to some objects. See "Changing an Object's Color, Outline Color, and Transparency."
- **Moving and positioning:** You can land objects with precision in a Word document, PowerPoint slide, or Excel worksheet. See "Moving and Positioning Objects."
- **Aligning and distributing:** Another way to move and position objects is to realign or redistribute them across a page, slide, or worksheet. See "Tricks for aligning and distributing objects."
- **Overlapping:** When you're dealing with several objects, they're bound to overlap — and sometimes overlapping objects make for an interesting effect. On the right side of Figure 4-9, for example, several objects overlap

and give the impression that they were "dropped there." See "When objects overlap: Choosing which appears above the other," later in this chapter, to handle overlapping objects.

- **Rotating and flipping:** Viewers turn their heads when they see an object that has been flipped or rotated. You can rotate and flip shapes, lines, text boxes, graphics, and WordArt images. See "Rotating and flipping Objects."
- **Grouping:** To make working with several different objects easier, you can *group* them so that they become a single object. After objects have been grouped, manipulating them — manipulating it, I should say — is easier. See "Grouping objects to make working with them easier," later in this chapter.

If you sighed after you finished reading this long list, I don't blame you. But be of good cheer: Most of these commands are easy to pick up, and including lines, shapes, text boxes, WordArt images, and graphics in your work is a good way to impress your friends and intimidate your enemies.

Selecting objects so that you can manipulate them

Before you can move or change the border of a graphic, text box, or other object, you have to select it. To select an object, simply click it. Sometimes, to align or decorate several objects simultaneously, you have to select more than one object at the same time. To select more than one object:

- Ctrl+click them. In other words, hold down the Ctrl key as you click the objects.
- On the Home tab, click the Select button and choose Select Objects on the drop-down list. Then click on one side of the objects you want to select and drag the pointer across the other objects.
- Display the Selection pane. It lists objects on the drawing canvas (Word), slide (PowerPoint), or worksheet (Excel). You can click or Ctrl+click object names in the pane to select objects. Figure 4-10 shows the Selection pane. Use these techniques to open it:
  - On the (Drawing Tools) Format tab, click the Selection Pane button.
  - On the Home tab, click the Select button and choose Selection Pane on the drop-down list. (You may have to click the Editing button first, depending on the size of your screen.)

Figure 4-10: Click an object in the Selection pane to select it.

After you select an object, its selection handles appear. Objects have eight selection handles, one at each corner and one at each side. To tell whether an object is selected, look for its selection handles.

Hiding and displaying the rulers and grid

Word, PowerPoint, and Excel offer two rulers, one along the top of the window and one along the left side. Use the rulers to help place and align objects. To display or hide these rulers, use one of these techniques:

- ✦ On the View tab, click the Ruler check box. (You may have to click the Show button first, depending on the size of your screen.) To see the rulers, you must be in Print Layout view In Word and Page Layout view in Excel.
- ✦ In PowerPoint, you can also hide or display rulers by right-clicking a slide (but not an object or frame) and choosing Ruler on the shortcut menu.

In Word and PowerPoint, the grid can come in very handy for aligning objects. On the View tab, click the Gridlines check box to see the grid. (You may have to click the Show button first.) The grid settings in PowerPoint are quite sophisticated (see Book IV, Chapter 4 for details).

By the way, fans of the metric system will be pleased to know that you can display centimeters (or millimeters, points, or picas) on the ruler instead of inches. On the File tab, choose Options. In the Options dialog box, go to the Advanced category, open the Show Measurements in Units Of drop-down list, and choose a unit of measurement.

Changing an Object's Size and Shape

Usually when an object arrives onscreen, you have to wrestle with it. You have to change its size (and sometimes its shape as well). Figure 4-11 demonstrates how to resize an object. Select your object and use one of these methods to change its size and shape:

- **"Eyeball it":** Hold down the Shift key and drag a *corner* selection handle to make the object larger or smaller but maintain its proportions. Drag a selection handle on the *side* to stretch or crimp an object and change its shape as well as its size.

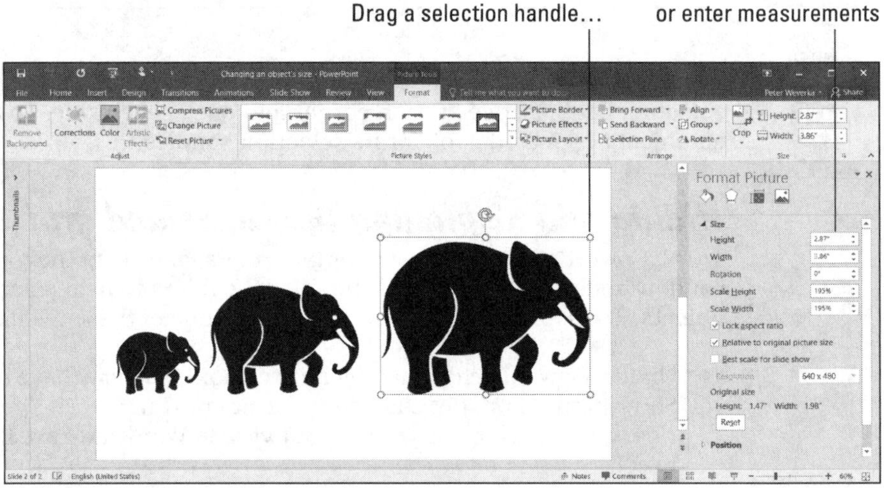
Drag a selection handle...
or enter measurements
Format Picture

Figure 4-11: Ways to resize an object.

- **Enter height and width measurements:** On the Format tab, enter measurements in the Height and Width boxes (see Figure 4-11). Depending on the size of your screen, you may have to click the Size button before you can see these boxes.
- **Open the Format task pane or Layout dialog box:** Click the Size group button on the Format tab to open the Format task pane (in PowerPoint and Excel) or the Layout dialog box (in Word). Then change the Height and Width settings (see Figure 4-11).

TIP

Whether you can change an object's shape as well as its size depends on whether the object's aspect ratio is *locked.* If you're wrestling with an object and it won't do your bidding — if it refuses to change shape or it changes shape, and you don't want it to do that — unlock its aspect ratio setting. Click the Size group button, and in the task pane or dialog box that appears, select or deselect the Lock Aspect Ratio check box. When an object's aspect ratio is *locked*, it maintains its shape as you change its size, but when it's *unlocked,* you can change its shape as well as its size.

TIP

You can change the size and shape of several objects at one time by selecting all the objects before giving a command to change sizes. Being able to change objects' size this way is convenient when you want to change the size of many objects but maintain their relationships to one another.

Changing an Object's Color, Outline Color, and Transparency

If an object's color doesn't suit you, you have the right to change colors. For that matter, you can opt for a "blank" object with no color or make the object semitransparent. As the saying goes, "It's a free country."

Office has its own lingo when it comes to an object's color. Remember these terms when you make like Picasso with your shapes, text boxes, and graphics:

- ✦ **Fill colors:** The color that fills in an object is called the *fill.* You can apply fill color to shapes, text boxes, and WordArt, but not pictures. Besides colors, you can use a picture, gradient, or texture as the fill. (See the next topic in this chapter, "Filling an object with color, a picture, or a texture.")
- ✦ **Outline colors:** The line that goes around the perimeter of an object is called the *outline.* You can choose a color, style, and line width for outlines. (See "Putting the outline around an object," later in this chapter.)

REMEMBER

The easiest way to decorate a shape, text box, or WordArt image is to visit the Format tab and make a selection in the Styles gallery. These ready-made gallery selections can spare you the work of dealing with fill color and, outlines. Just remember not to mix and match different Style options; use them with consistency.

Filling an object with color, a picture, or a texture

Shapes, text boxes, and WordArt images are empty when you first create them, but you can fill them with a color, picture, gradient, or texture by following these basic steps:

1. **Select the object that needs a facelift.**
2. **Apply a color, picture, gradient, or texture to the object.**

Use one of these application techniques:

- On the Format tab, click the Shape Fill button. Then, on the drop-down list, choose a color, picture, gradient, or texture.
- Click the Shape Styles group button to open the Format task pane, as shown in Figure 4-12. Then choose a color, picture, gradient, or texture.

Click the Shape Fill button and choose No Fill to remove the color, picture, gradient, or texture from an object.

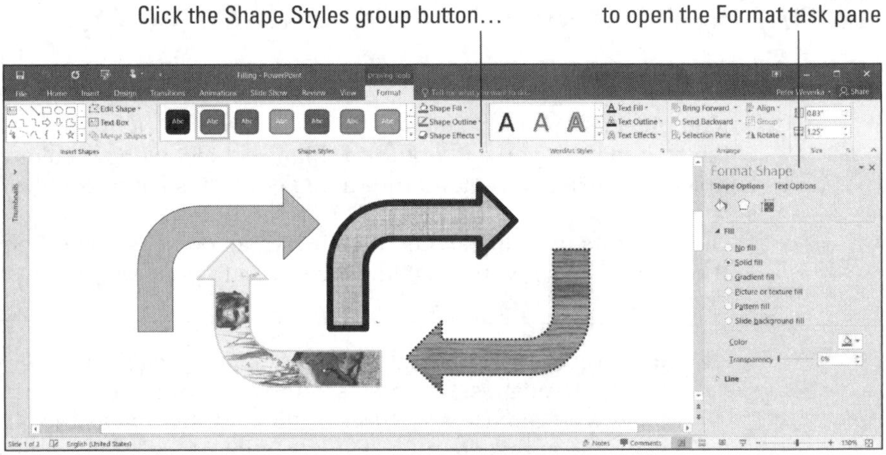
Click the Shape Styles group button...
to open the Format task pane

Figure 4-12: Shape fills (from left to right): color, picture, gradient, and texture.

Figure 4-12 shows the same object filled with a color, picture, gradient, and texture. Which do you prefer? Your choices are as follows:

✦ **Color:** Applies a single color to the object.

✦ **Picture:** Places a picture in the object. You see the Insert Picture dialog box. Choose a picture and click the Insert button.

✦ **Gradient (Word and PowerPoint only):** Applies gradient color shading to the object. You can choose between various shading styles.

✦ **Texture:** Offers 24 patterns meant to simulate various surfaces. The choices include Granite, Paper Bag, and Pink Tissue Paper. Be sure to use the scroll bar to see all the choices.

✦ **Pattern:** Applies a pattern to the object. Select Pattern Fill in the Format task pane and then choose a pattern.

Using the eyedropper to select an onscreen color (PowerPoint only)

Suppose you become enamored of a color that you see on your screen and you want to apply this color to an object. For example, suppose you want to apply the particular shade of yellow in your company logo to a shape. Using the eyedropper, you can select the color you like so well and apply it to an object on a page or slide. Follow these steps:

1. **Select the text box, shape, slide, WordArt image, or other object that needs recoloring.**
2. **On the Format tab, click the Shape Fill button and choose Eyedropper on the drop-down list.**

   The pointer changes to an eyedropper.
3. **Move the eyedropper over the onscreen color that you want for the object you selected in Step 1.**

   How you move the eyedropper depends on where the color you want is located on the screen.

   If the onscreen color is on a PowerPoint slide, simply move the eyedropper over the color.

   If the onscreen color is outside your PowerPoint application — if it's on a web page, for example — hold down the left mouse button as you drag the eyedropper outside the PowerPoint window. Drag the eyedropper until it is over the color you want.

   A pop-up color box shows the color that the eyedropper is on, the name of the color, and the color's RGB (red green blue) settings.
4. **Click when the pop-up color box shows you the color you want for the object you selected in Step 1.**

   The object you selected in Step 1 gets the new color.

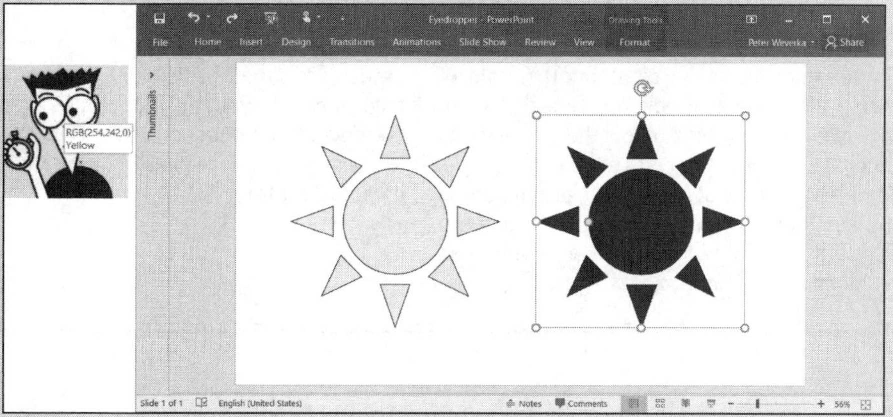

Making a color transparent

A transparent color is like gauze because instead of being solid, it shows what's behind it. Transparent colors are especially useful in text boxes because the text shows through and can be read easily. Follow these steps to make the fill color in a text box, shape, or WordArt image transparent or semi-transparent:

1. **Right-click the object and choose Format.**

   The Format task pane opens (see Figure 4-12).

2. **In the Fill category, drag the Transparency slider to choose how transparent a color you want.**

   At 100%, the color is completely transparent and, in fact, not there; at 1%, the color is hardly transparent at all.

You can also make a graphic transparent by recoloring it. See Chapter 3 of this mini-book.

Putting the outline around an object

The *outline* is the line that runs around the perimeter of an object. Put an outline color around an object to give it more definition or make it stand out. Figure 4-13 shows examples of outlines. What a shape outline looks like has to do with the color, width, and dash style you choose for it.

Designating a fill and outline color for all your objects

Rather than go to the significant trouble of giving all or most of your objects the same look, you can make one object the model for all others to follow and declare it the default style. After that, all new objects you insert appear in the same style, your objects have a uniform appearance, and you don't have to spend as much time formatting objects.

Select an object with a fill and an outline color that you want as your model, right-click the object, and choose Set As Default Shape to make your object the default that all other objects start from.

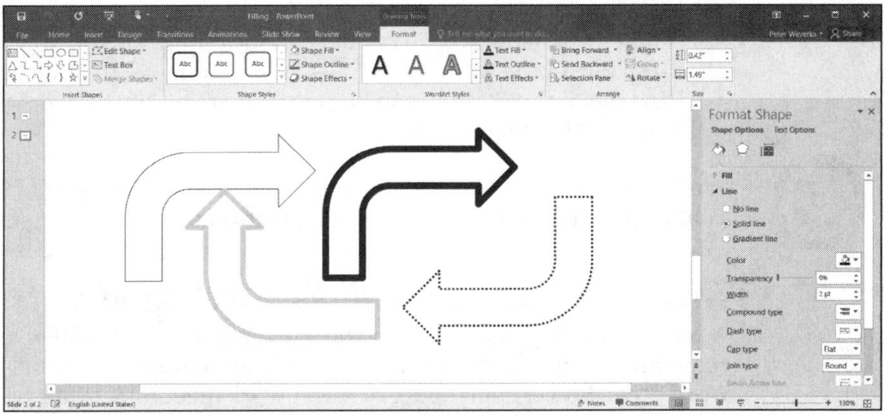

Figure 4-13: An object's outline has to do with its color, width, and dash type.

Follow these steps to change an object's outline:

1. **Select the object.**
2. **Change the outline.**

   Use one of these techniques to change the outline:

   - On the Format tab, click the Shape Outline button. Then, on the drop-down list, choose a color, weight, and dash type.
   - Click the Shape Styles group button to open the Format task pane (see Figure 4-13). Then, under Line, choose a color, width, and dash type.

   To remove the outline from an object, click the Shape Outline button and choose No Outline or choose No Line in the Format task pane.

Moving and Positioning Objects

Moving objects is considerably easier than moving furniture. Select the object you want to reposition and use one of these techniques to land it in the right place:

- **Dragging:** Move the pointer over the perimeter of the object, click when you see the four-headed arrow, and drag the object to a new location. Hold down the Shift key as you drag to move an object either horizontally or vertically in a straight line.
- **Using a task pane or dialog box (in PowerPoint and Word):** On the Format tab, click the Size group button. (Depending on the size of your screen, you may have to click the Size button first.) You see the Format task pane or Layout dialog box. On the Position category or tab, enter Horizontal and Vertical position measurements to place the object on the slide or page.

- **Nudging:** If you can't quite fit an object in the right place, try using a Nudge command. Nudge commands move objects up, down, left, or right. Press one of the arrow keys (↑, ↓, ←, →) to move the object a little bit. Hold down the Ctrl key as you press an arrow key to make the object move by tiny increments.

TIP

Use the task pane or dialog box method of positioning objects when you want objects to be in the exact same position on different pages or slides.

Tricks for aligning and distributing objects

When several objects appear in the same place, use the Align and Distribute commands to give the objects an orderly appearance. You can make your Word page, PowerPoint slide, or Excel worksheet look tidier by aligning the objects or by distributing them so that they are an equal distance from one another. Office offers special commands for doing these tasks.

Aligning objects

The Align commands come in handy when you want objects to line up with one another. Suppose you need to align several shapes. As shown in Figure 4-14, you can use an Align command to line up the shapes with precision. You don't have to tug and pull, tug and pull until the shapes are aligned with one another. In the figure, I used the Align Top command to line up the shapes along the top. In Word and PowerPoint, besides aligning objects with respect to one another, you can align objects or with respect to the page (in Word) or the slide (in PowerPoint). For example, you can line up objects along the top of a slide.

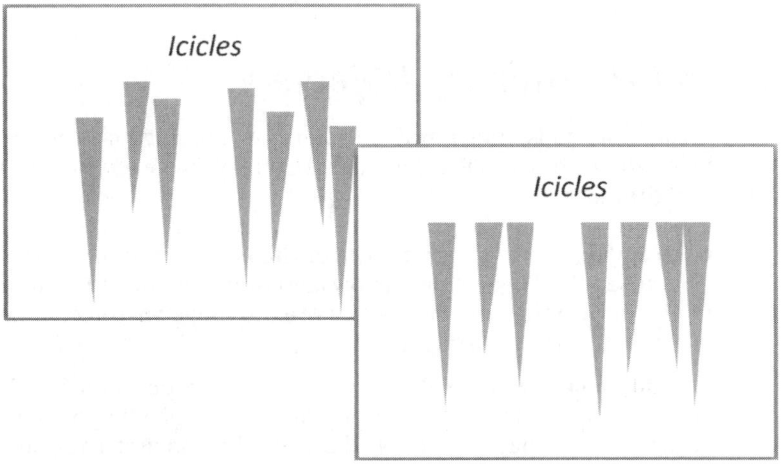

Figure 4-14: Use the Align commands to align objects. These objects are aligned along the top.

Follow these steps to line up objects:

1. **Move the objects where you roughly want them to be, and if you want to align objects with respect to one another, move one object to a point that the others will align to.**

   When Office aligns objects with respect to one another, it aligns them to the object in the leftmost, centermost, rightmost, topmost, middle-most, or bottommost position, depending on which Align command you choose.

2. **Select the objects you want to align.**

   Earlier in this chapter, "Selecting objects so that you can manipulate them" looks at selection techniques.

3. **Go to the Format tab.**

   You can also go to the Layout tab in Word.

4. **Click the Align button, and on the drop-down list, choose whether to align the objects with respect to one another or with respect to the page or page margin (in Word) or a slide (in PowerPoint).**

   Depending on the size of your screen, you may have to click the Arrange button to get to the Align button.

5. **Click the Align button again and choose an Align command — Left, Center, Right, Top, Middle, or Bottom.**

6. **If necessary, drag the objects on the page.**

   That's right — drag them. After you give an Align command, the objects are still selected, and you can drag to adjust their positions.

Distributing objects so that they are equidistant

The Distribute commands — Distribute Horizontally and Distribute Vertically — come in handy for laying out objects on a page or slide. These commands arrange objects so that the same amount of space appears between each one. Rather than go to the trouble of pushing and pulling objects until they are distributed evenly, you can simply select the objects and choose a Distribute command.

Figure 4-15 demonstrates how the Distribute commands work. In the figure, I chose the Distribute Horizontally command so that the same amount of horizontal (side-by-side) space appears between the objects. Distributing objects such as these on your own is a waste of time when you can use a Distribute command.

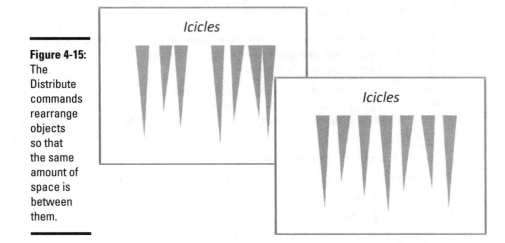

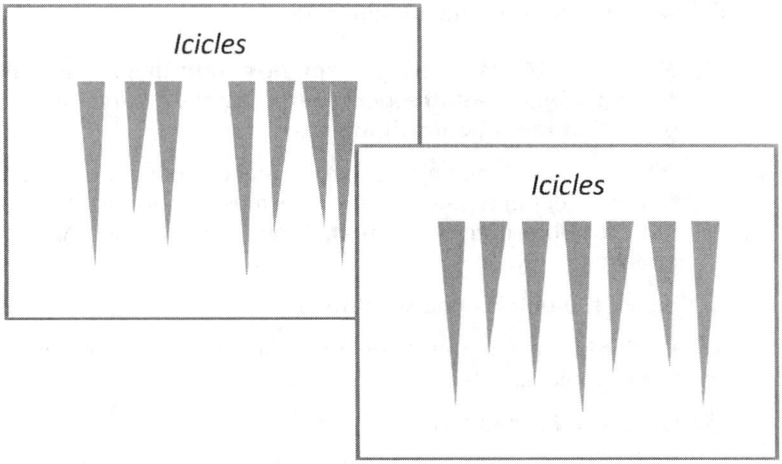

Figure 4-15: The Distribute commands rearrange objects so that the same amount of space is between them.

Follow these steps to distribute objects horizontally or vertically on a page or slide:

1. **Arrange the objects so that the outermost objects — the ones that will go on the top and bottom or left side and right side — are where you want them to be.**

   In other words, if you want to distribute objects horizontally across a page, place the leftmost object and rightmost object where you want them to be. Office will distribute the other objects equally between the leftmost and rightmost object.

2. **Select the objects.**
3. **Go to the Format tab.**

   You can also go to the Layout tab in Word.

4. **Click the Align button and choose a Distribute option on the drop-down list.**

   To find the Align button, you may have to click the Arrange button first, depending on the size of your screen.

When objects overlap: Choosing which appears above the other

On a page or slide that is crowded with text boxes, shapes, and graphics, objects inevitably overlap, and you have to decide which object goes on top of the stack and which on the bottom. In a Word document, you have to decide as well whether text appears above or below objects.

Objects that deliberately overlap can be interesting and attractive to look at. On the right side of Figure 4-16, for example, a graphic image and text box appear in front of a shape. Makes for a nice effect, no? These pages explain controlling how objects overlap with the Bring and Send commands and the Selection pane.

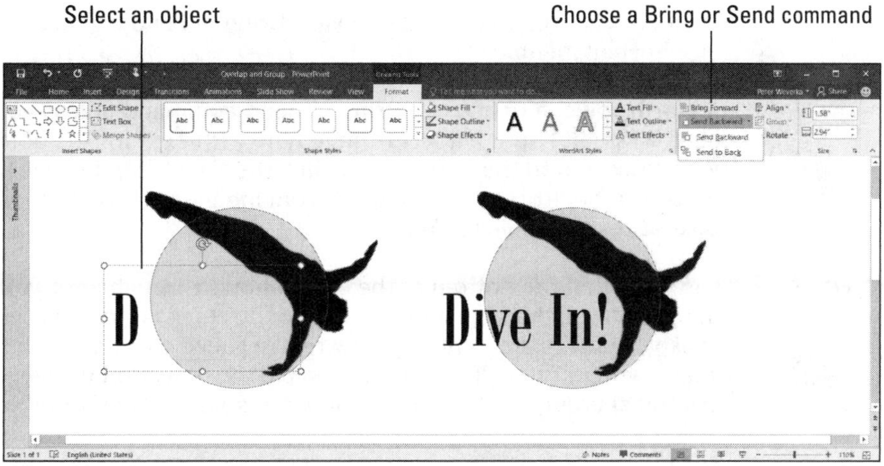
Select an object
Choose a Bring or Send command
D
Dive In!

Figure 4-16: An example of objects overlapping.

Controlling overlaps with the Bring and Send commands

Word, PowerPoint, and Excel offer these commands for handling objects in a stack:

- **Bring Forward:** Moves the object higher in the stack
- **Bring to Front:** Moves the object in front of all other objects in the stack
- **Send Backward:** Moves the object lower in the stack
- **Send to Back:** Moves the object behind all other objects

Word offers these additional commands:

- **Bring in Front of Text:** Moves the object in front of text on the page
- **Send Behind Text:** Moves the object behind text on the page so that the text appears over the object

Select an object and use one of these techniques to give a Bring or Send command:

- On the Format tab, click the Bring Forward or Send Backward button, or open the drop-down list on one of these buttons and choose a Bring or Send command (refer to Figure 4-16). Depending on the size of your screen, you may have to click the Arrange button before you can get to a Bring or Send command.

In Word, the Bring and Send commands are also available on the Layout tab; in Excel, they are available on the Page Layout tab; in PowerPoint, they are also available on the Home tab, although you may have to click the Arrange button first, depending on the size of your screen.

- Right-click an object and choose a Bring or Send command on the shortcut menu.

In Word, you can't choose a Bring or Send command unless you've chosen a text-wrapping option apart from In Line with Text for the object. Select your object, go to the Format tab, click the Text Wrap button, and choose an option on the drop-down list apart from In Line with Text. Book II, Chapter 6 looks at text wrapping in Word.

If an object on the bottom of the stack shows through after you place it on the bottom, the object on the top of the stack is transparent or semi-transparent. Transparent objects are like gauze curtains — they reveal what's behind them. If you want to make the object on the top of the stack less transparent, see "Making a color transparent," earlier in this chapter.

Controlling overlaps with the Selection pane

Another way to control how objects overlap is to open the Selection pane, select an object, and click the Bring Forward or Send Backward button as necessary to move the object up or down in the stack. Earlier in this chapter, "Selecting objects so that you can manipulate them" explains the Selection pane. (On the Format tab, click the Selection Pane button to open it.)

Rotating and flipping objects

Rotating and flipping objects — that is, changing their orientation — is a neat way to spruce up a page or slide, as Figure 4-17 demonstrates. You can rotate and flip these kinds of objects: lines, shapes, text boxes, graphics, and WordArt images. To flip or rotate an object, select it and do one of the following:

- **Roll your own:** Drag the object's *rotation handle,* the semicircle that appears after you select it. Hold down the Shift key as you drag to rotate the shape by 15-degree increments.
- **Choose a Rotate or Flip command:** On the Format tab, click the Rotate button and choose an option on the drop-down list (refer to Figure 4-17). The Rotate commands rotate objects by 90 degrees; the Flip commands flip objects over. The Rotate button is also found on the Page Layout tab (in Word and Excel) and the Home tab (in PowerPoint). You may have to click the Arrange button to see the Rotate button, depending on the size of your screen.

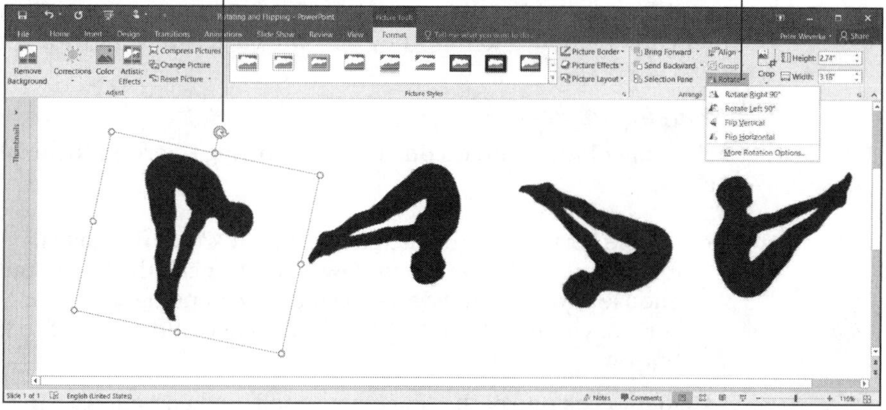
Drag the rotation handle...
or choose a Rotate or Flip command

Figure 4-17: Members of an audience turn their heads when objects are rotated or flipped.

✦ **Open the Format task pane or Layout dialog box:** On the Rotate drop-down list, choose More Rotation Options to open the Format task pane or Layout dialog box. Enter a degree measurement in the Rotation text box.

TIP

To rotate several objects simultaneously, Ctrl+click to select each object and then give a rotation command.

Grouping objects to make working with them easier

Consider the graphic image, shape, and text box in Figure 4-18. To move, resize, or reshape these objects, I would have to laboriously move them one at a time — that is, I would have to do that if it weren't for the Group command.

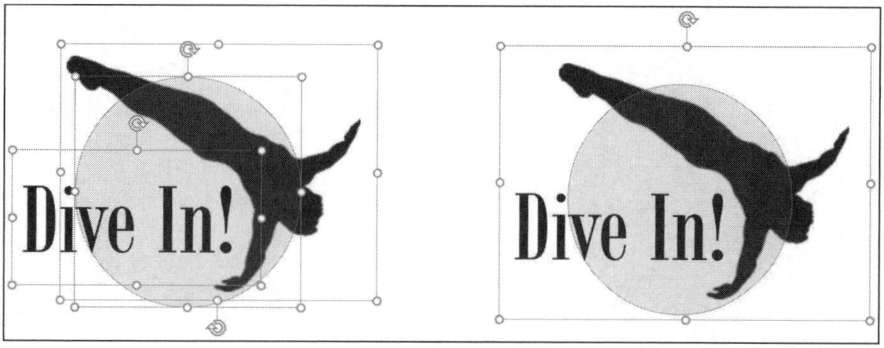
Dive In!
Dive In!

Figure 4-18: You can move, resize, and reshape grouped objects as though they were a single object.

The Group command assembles different objects into a single object to make moving, resizing, and reshaping objects easier. With the Group command, you select the objects that you want to "group" and then you wrap them into a bundle so that they become easier to work with.

Grouping objects

Select the objects and do one of the following to group them into one happy family:

- ✦ On the Format tab (or the Layout tab in Word, the Page Layout tab and Excel, and the Home tab in PowerPoint), click the Group button and choose Group on the drop-down list. Depending on the size of your screen, you may have to click the Arrange button to get to the Group button.
- ✦ Right-click one of the objects you selected and choose Group ➪ Group.

After objects are grouped, they form a single object with the eight selection handles.

TIP

To add an object to a group, select the object and the grouped objects by Ctrl+clicking and then choose the Group command.

Ungrouping objects

To ungroup an object and break it into its components parts, perhaps to fiddle with one of the objects in the group, select the object, go to the Format tab, click the Group button, and choose Ungroup.

Book IX

Office 2016 — One Step Beyond

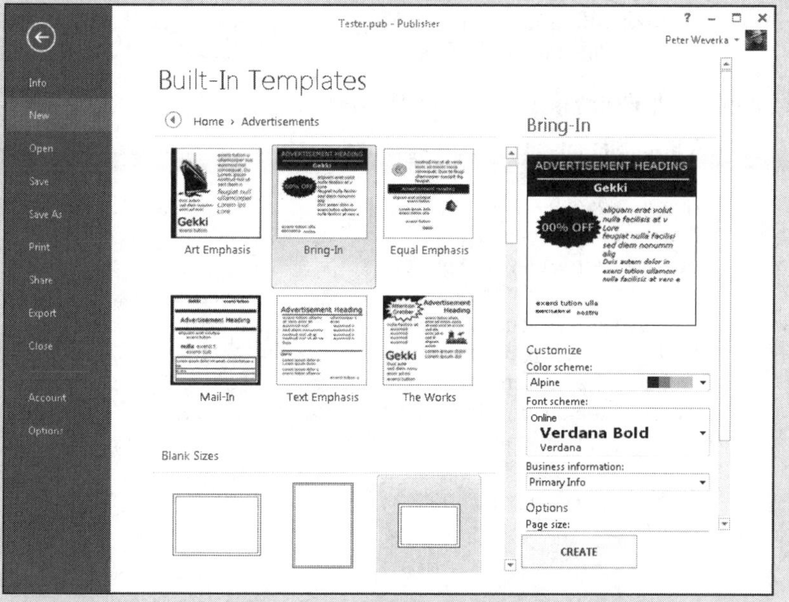

Visit www.dummies.com/extras/office2016aio to see how you can very quickly place your favorite buttons on the Quick Access toolbar.

Contents at a Glance

Chapter 1: Customizing an Office Program

In This Chapter

- **Personalizing the Ribbon**
- **Changing around the Quick Access toolbar**
- **Choosing what appears on the status bar**
- **Choosing a new screen background and Office theme**
- **Devising keyboard shortcuts in Word**

This short chapter describes a handful of things you can do to customize Office 2016 programs. Don't be afraid to make like a software developer and change a program to your liking. Many people are wary of retooling Office programs, but you can always reverse the changes you make if you don't like them, as I explain throughout this chapter.

This chapter shows how to put your favorite button commands on the Ribbon and Quick Access toolbar. Instead of fishing around for your favorite commands, you can assemble them on the Ribbon or Quick Access toolbar and locate them right away. You also discover how to change around the status bar, dress up an Office program in a new set of clothes, and designate your own keyboard shortcuts in Word.

Customizing the Ribbon

As you surely know by now, the Ribbon is the stretch of ground across the top of all Office programs. The Ribbon is composed of tabs. On each tab, commands are arranged by group. To undertake a task, you visit a tab on the Ribbon, find the group with the command you want, and choose the command. If you are so inclined, you can customize the Ribbon. You can place the tabs and commands you know and love where you want to find them on the Ribbon. And you can remove tabs and commands that aren't useful to you.

To customize the Ribbon, open the Customize Ribbon tab of the Options dialog box with one of these techniques:

- ✦ On the File tab, choose Options, and select the Customize Ribbon category in the Options dialog box.
- ✦ Right-click a tab or button and choose Customize the Ribbon.

You see commands for customizing the Ribbon, as shown in Figure 1-1. The right side of the dialog box ("Customize the Ribbon") lists the names of tabs, groups within tabs, and commands within groups that are currently on the Ribbon. To customize the Ribbon, you arrange the right side of the dialog box to your liking. You list the tabs, groups, and commands that you want for the Ribbon on the right side of the dialog box.

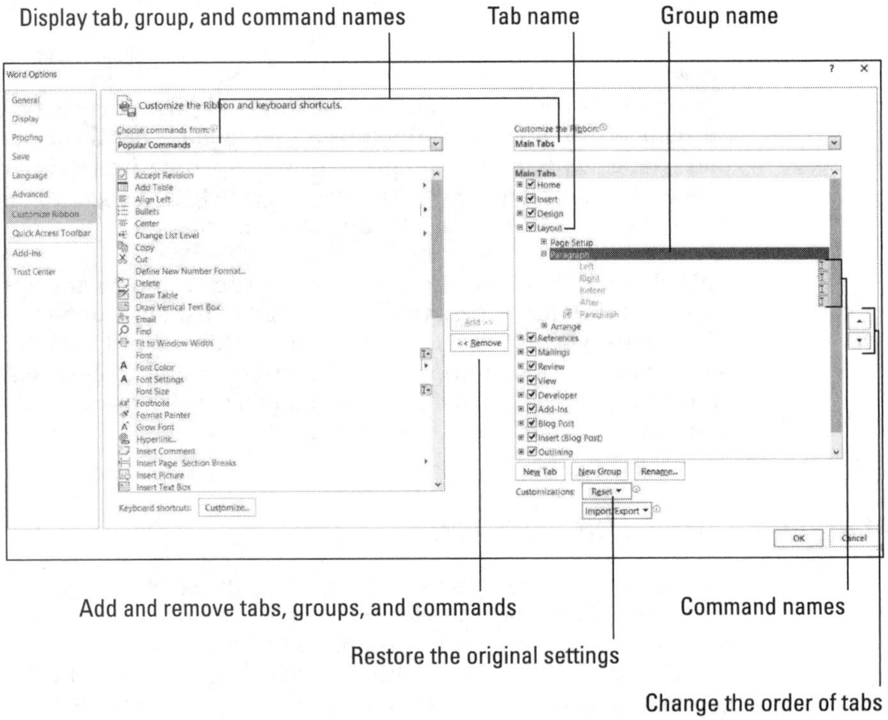

Figure 1-1: Starting in the Customize Ribbon category of the Options dialog box, you can customize the Ribbon.

The left side of the dialog box ("Choose Commands From") presents every tab, group, and command in your Office program. To customize the Ribbon, you select a tab, group, or command on the left side of the dialog box and move it to the right side by clicking the Add button.

Keep reading to find out how to display tabs, groups, and commands in the Options dialog box and how to do all else that pertains to customizing the Ribbon. In case you make a hash of the Ribbon, you also find instructions for restoring the Ribbon to its original state.

Displaying and selecting tab, group, and command names

To customize the Ribbon, you need to display and select tab names, group names, and command names in the Options dialog box (refer to Figure 1-1). Start by opening the drop-down lists and choosing a display option:

- **Choose Commands From:** Choose an option to locate the tab, group, or command you want to add to the Ribbon. For example, choose All Commands to see an alphabetical list of all the commands in the Office program you're working in; choose Main Tabs to see a list of tabs.
- **Customize the Ribbon:** Choose an option to display the names of all tabs, main tabs, or tool tabs. Tool tabs are the context-sensitive tabs that appear after you insert or click something. For example, the Table Tools tabs appear when you construct tables in Word.

After you choose display options on the drop-down lists, you can display the names of groups and commands (refer to Figure 1-1):

- **Displaying group names:** Click a plus sign icon next to a tab name to see the names of its groups. You can click the minus sign icon to fold group names back into a tab name.
- **Displaying command names in groups**: Click the plus sign icon next to a group name to see the names of its commands. You can click the minus sign icon to collapse command names.

After you display the tab, group, or command name, click to select it.

Moving tabs and groups on the Ribbon

To change the order of tabs on the Ribbon or groups on a tab, go to the Customize Ribbon category of the Options dialog box (refer to Figure 1-1) and select the name of a tab or group on the right side of the dialog box. Then click the Move Up or Move Down button (the arrow buttons located on the right side of the dialog box). Click these buttons as necessary until tabs or groups are in the order that you see fit.

WARNING!

Be careful about moving groups by clicking the Move Up or Move Down button. Clicking these buttons too many times can move a group to a different tab on the Ribbon.

Adding, removing, and renaming tabs, groups, and commands

In the Options dialog box (refer to Figure 1-1), display and select the tab, group, or command you want to add, remove, or rename. Then proceed to add, remove, or rename it. (Earlier in this chapter, "Displaying and selecting tab, group, and command names" explains how to display items in the Options dialog box.)

Adding items to the Ribbon

Follow these steps to add a tab, group, or command to the Ribbon:

1. **On the left side of the Customize Ribbon category of the Options dialog box, select the tab, group, or command you want to add.**

   For example, to add the Tables group to the Home tab, select the Tables group.

   WARNING! Commands can be added only to custom groups. To add a command to the Ribbon, create a new group for the command (see "Creating new tabs and groups," later in this chapter).

2. **On the right side of the dialog box, select the tab or custom group where you want to place the item.**

   If you're adding a tab to the Ribbon, select a tab. The tab you add will go after the tab you select.

3. **Click the Add button.**

Removing items from the Ribbon

Follow these steps to remove a tab, group, or command from the Ribbon:

1. **On the right side of the Customize Ribbon category of the Options dialog box, select the tab, group, or command you want to remove.**
2. **Click the Remove button.**

   WARNING! Except for tabs you create yourself, you can't remove tabs from the Ribbon. And you can't remove a command unless you remove it from a group you created yourself.

Renaming tabs and groups

Sorry, you can't rename a command. Follow these steps to rename a tab or group:

1. **On the right side of the Customize Ribbon category of the Options dialog box, select the tab or group you want to rename.**

2. **Click the Rename button.**

   You see the Rename dialog box, as shown in Figure 1-2.

3. **Enter a new name and click OK.**

   When renaming a group that you created yourself, you can choose a symbol for the group in the Rename dialog box (see Figure 1-2).

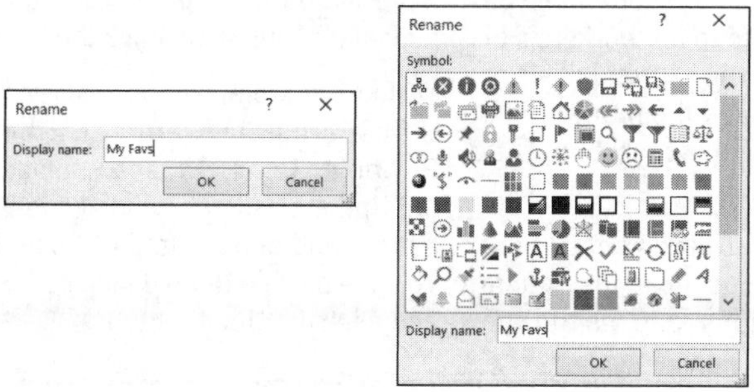

Figure 1-2: Renaming a tab (left) and a group (right).

Creating new tabs and groups

Create new tabs and groups on the Ribbon for commands that are especially useful to you. Follow these steps on the Customize Ribbon category of the Options dialog box (refer to Figure 1-1) to create a new tab or group:

1. **On the right side of the dialog box, display and select the name of a tab or group.**

   Earlier in this chapter, "Displaying and selecting tab, group, and command names" explains how to select items in the Options dialog box.

   - *Tab:* If you're creating a tab, select a tab name. The tab you create will appear after the tab you select.
   - *Group:* If you're creating a group, select a group name. The group you create will appear after the group you select.

2. **Click the New Tab or New Group button.**

   Your Office program creates a new tab or group called "New Tab (Custom)" or "New Group (Custom)." If you created a tab, Office also creates a new group inside your new tab.

3. **Click the Rename button to give the tab, group, or both a name.**

   In the Rename dialog box, enter a descriptive name and click OK. If you're naming a group, the Rename dialog box gives you the opportunity to select an icon to help identify the group (see Figure 1-2).

4. **Add groups, commands, or both to your newly made tab or group.**

   For instructions, see "Adding items to the Ribbon," earlier in this chapter.

Exporting and importing program customizations

You can preserve your Ribbon and Quick Access toolbar customizations for posterity in a special file called an Import Customization file; these files have the `.exportedUI` file extension. Keep the file on hand for when you need it, or distribute the file to co-workers. For that matter, a co-worker who is proud of his or her customizations can send them to you in a file and you can load the customizations into your Office program.

To save your Ribbon and Quick Access toolbar customization settings in a file, go to the File tab, choose Options, and visit to the Customize Ribbon or Quick Access Toolbar category of the Options dialog box. Then click the Import/Export button and choose Export All Customizations on the drop-down list. The File Save dialog box opens. Give the customizations file a name and click the Save button.

To load customizations from a file into your Office program, return to the Customize Ribbon or Quick Access Toolbar category of the Options dialog box, click the Import/Export button, and choose Import Customization File. You see the File Open dialog box. Select the file and click the Open button.

Resetting your Ribbon customizations

If you make a hash of the Ribbon, all is not lost because you can restore the original settings. In the Options dialog box, click the Reset button (refer to Figure 1-1) and choose one of these commands on the drop-down list:

- **Reset Only Selected Ribbon Tab:** Select a tab name on the right side of the Options dialog box and choose this command to restore a tab to its original state.
- **Reset All Customizations:** Choose this command to restore the Ribbon in its entirety. All changes you made are reversed.

You can also remove tabs and groups you created if you discover you don't need them. See "Removing items from the Ribbon," earlier in this chapter.

Customizing the Quick Access Toolbar

No matter where you go in Office, you see the Quick Access toolbar in the upper-left corner of the screen. This toolbar offers the Save, Undo, and Redo buttons, as well as the Touch/Mouse Mode button if your computer has a touchscreen. However, which buttons appear on the Quick Access toolbar is entirely up to you. You can put your favorite buttons on the toolbar to keep them within reach. And if the Quick Access toolbar gets too big, you can move it below the Ribbon, as shown in Figure 1-3. Adding buttons to and removing buttons from the Quick Access toolbar is, I'm happy to report, a piece of cake. And moving the toolbar below the Ribbon is as easy as pie.

Right-click a button to add it to the Quick Access toolbar

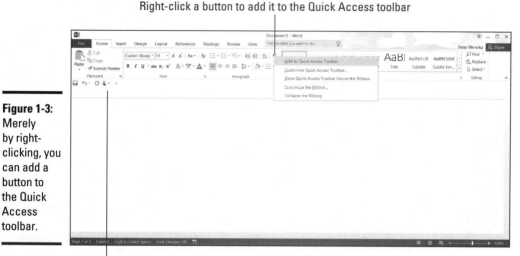

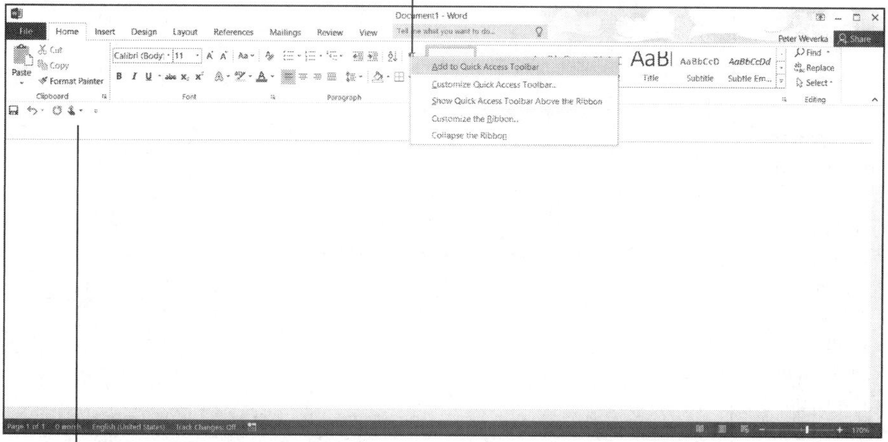

The Quick Access toolbar below the Ribbon

Figure 1-3: Merely by right-clicking, you can add a button to the Quick Access toolbar.

Adding buttons to the Quick Access toolbar

Use one of these techniques to add buttons to the Quick Access toolbar:

- Right-click a button you want to see on the toolbar and choose Add to Quick Access Toolbar on the shortcut menu (refer to Figure 1-3). You can add all the commands in a group to the Quick Access toolbar by right-clicking the group name and choosing Add to Quick Access Toolbar.
- Click the Customize Quick Access Toolbar button (this button is located to the right of the Quick Access toolbar) and choose a button on the drop-down list. The list offers buttons deemed most likely to be placed on the Quick Access toolbar by the makers of Office.
- On the File tab, choose Options, and go to the Quick Access Toolbar category in the Options dialog box (or right-click any button or tab and choose Customize Quick Access Toolbar on the shortcut menu). You see the Quick Access Toolbar category of the Options dialog box, as shown in Figure 1-4. On the Choose Commands From drop-down list, select the name of the button you want to add to the Quick Access toolbar. Then click the Add button.

TIP

To restore the Quick Access toolbar to its original buttons, click the Reset button in the Options dialog box (see Figure 1-4) and choose Reset Only Quick Access Toolbar on the drop-down list. Choosing Reset All Customizations resets Ribbon customizations as well as Quick Access toolbar customizations.

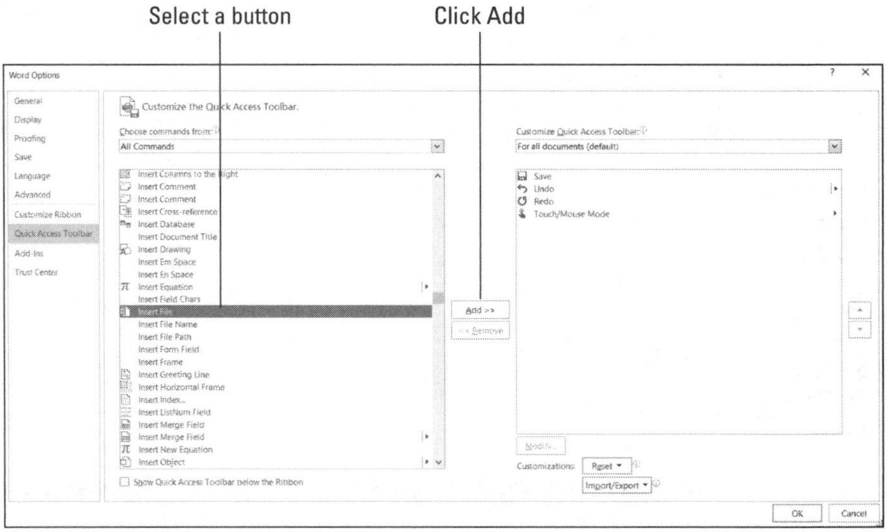

Figure 1-4: Add, remove, and reorder Quick Access toolbar buttons in the Options dialog box.

Changing the order of buttons on the Quick Access toolbar

Follow these steps to change the order of buttons on the Quick Access toolbar:

1. **Click the Customize Quick Access Toolbar button and choose More Commands on the drop-down list.**

   The Quick Access Toolbar category of the Options dialog box appears (see Figure 1-4). You can also open this dialog box by right-clicking any button or tab and choosing Customize Quick Access Toolbar.

2. **Select the name of a button on the right side of the dialog box and click the Move Up or Move Down button.**

   These arrow buttons are located on the right side of the dialog box.

3. **Repeat Step 2 until the buttons are in the right order.**
4. **Click OK.**

Removing buttons from the Quick Access toolbar

Use one of these techniques to remove buttons from the Quick Access toolbar:

- Right-click a button and choose Remove from Quick Access Toolbar on the shortcut menu.

- Right-click any button or tab and choose Customize Quick Access Toolbar. You see the Quick Access Toolbar category of the Options dialog box (refer to Figure 1-4). Select the button you want to remove on the right side of the dialog box and click the Remove button.

You can click the Reset button in the Options dialog box (refer to Figure 1-4) to remove all the buttons you placed on the Quick Access toolbar.

Placing the Quick Access toolbar above or below the Ribbon

The Ribbon is the stretch of ground along the top of the screen where the tabs and buttons are found. If your Quick Access toolbar contains many buttons, consider placing it below the Ribbon, not above it (refer to Figure 1-3). Follow these instructions to place the Quick Access toolbar above or below the Ribbon:

- **Quick Access toolbar below the Ribbon:** Right-click the toolbar, and on the shortcut menu, choose Show Quick Access Toolbar Below the Ribbon.
- **Quick Access toolbar above the Ribbon:** Right-click the toolbar, and on the shortcut menu, choose Show Quick Access Toolbar Above the Ribbon.

The Options dialog box offers a check box called Show Quick Access Toolbar Below the Ribbon (refer to Figure 1-4). You can select this check box as well to move the toolbar below the Ribbon.

Customizing the Status Bar

The status bar along the bottom of the window gives you information about the file you're working on. The Word status bar, for example, tells you which page you're on, how many pages are in your document, and several other things. In PowerPoint, the status bar tells you which slide you're looking at. It also presents the view buttons and Zoom controls.

To choose what appears on the status bar, right-click the status bar. You see a drop-down list similar to the one in Figure 1-5. By selecting and deselecting items in this list, you can decide what appears on the status bar.

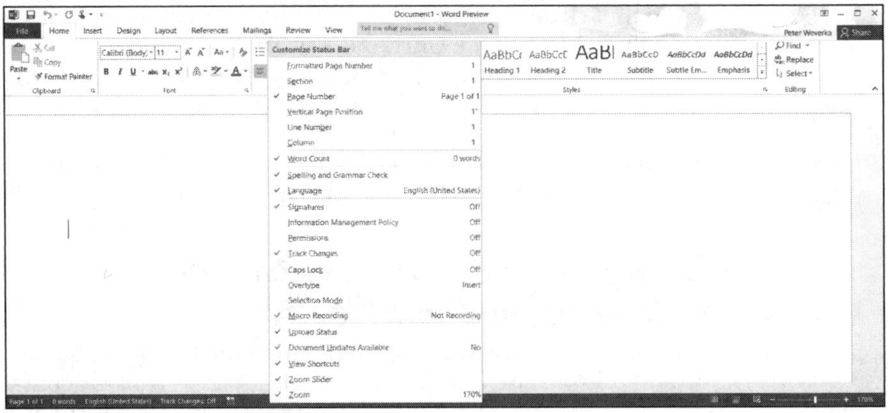

Figure 1-5: Right-click the status bar to customize it.

Changing the Screen Background and Office Theme

Starting on the Accounts screen, you can change the screen background and Office theme. The *screen background* is the fluff that appears along the top of Office application windows. The *Office theme* is the color (or lack thereof) that appears around the perimeter of Office application windows. You are encouraged to experiment with screen backgrounds and Office themes until you find a combination that works for you.

Follow these steps to choose a screen background and Office theme:

1. **On the File tab, choose Account.**

   You see the Account screen, as shown in Figure 1-6.

2. **Open the Office Background drop-down list and choose an option.**
3. **Open the Office Theme drop-down menu and choose an option.**
4. **Click the Back button.**

   How do you like your new get-up? If you don't like it, repeat these steps until you get it right.

WARNING!

A screen background and Office theme you apply in one Office program applies to all the other programs as well.

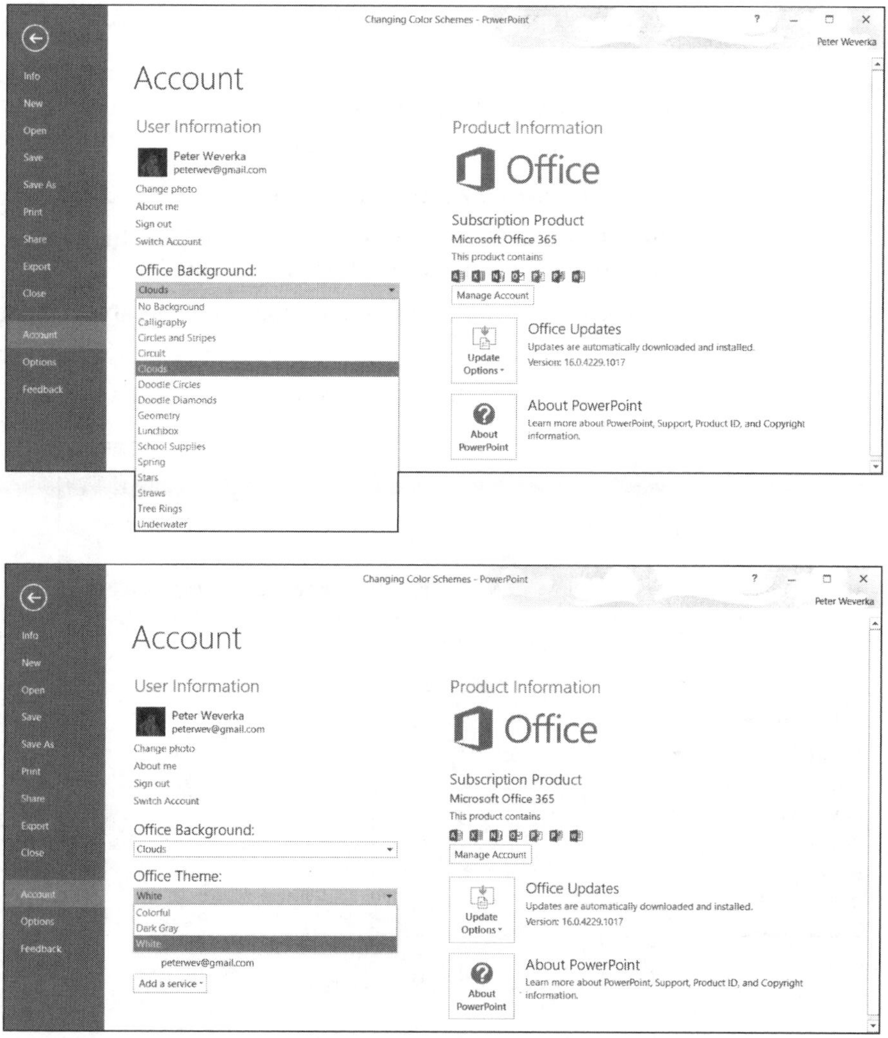

Figure 1-6: Changing the screen background (top) and Office theme (bottom).

Customizing Keyboard Shortcuts in Word

In Microsoft Word, you can change the keyboard shortcuts. A *keyboard shortcut* is a combination of keys that you press to give a command. For example, pressing Ctrl+P opens the Print window; pressing Ctrl+S gives the Save command. If you don't like a keyboard shortcut in Word, you can change it and invent a keyboard shortcut of your own. You can also assign keyboard shortcuts to symbols, macros, fonts, building blocks, and styles.

Follow these steps to choose keyboard shortcuts of your own in Microsoft Word:

1. **On the File tab, choose Options.**

   You see the Word Options dialog box.

2. **Go to the Customize Ribbon category.**

3. **Click the Customize button (you can find it at the bottom of the dialog box next to the words "Keyboard Shortcuts").**

   You see the Customize Keyboard dialog box, as shown in Figure 1-7.

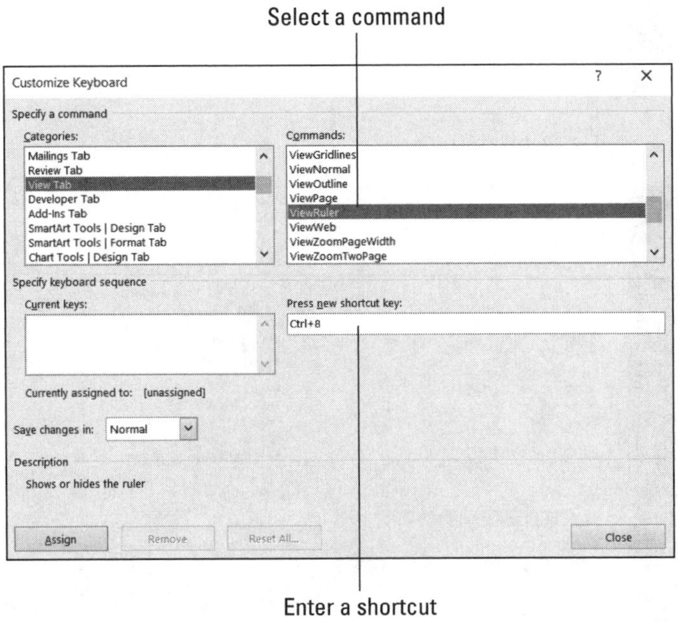

Figure 1-7: Assigning keyboard shortcuts to Word commands.

4. **In the Categories list, choose the category with the command to which you want to assign the keyboard shortcut.**

   At the bottom of the list are the Macros, Fonts, Building Blocks, Styles, and Common Symbols categories.

5. **Choose the command name, macro, font, building block, style, or symbol name in the Commands list.**

6. **In the Press New Shortcut Key box, type the keyboard shortcut.**

   Press the actual keys. For example, if the shortcut is Ctrl+8, press the Ctrl key and the 8 key — don't type out C-t-r-l-+8.

   If you try to assign a shortcut that has already been assigned, the words "Currently assigned to" and a command name appear below the Current Keys box. You can override the preassigned keyboard assignment by entering a keyboard assignment of your own.

7. **If you want the keyboard shortcut changes you make to apply to the document you're working on, not to all documents created with the template you're working with, open the Save Changes In drop-down list and choose your document's name.**

8. **Click the Assign button.**

9. **When you finish assigning keyboard shortcuts, close the Customize Keyboard dialog box.**

To delete a keyboard shortcut, display it in the Current Keys box, select it, and click the Remove button.

REMEMBER

You can always get the old keyboard shortcuts back by clicking the Reset All button in the Customize Keyboard dialog box.

Chapter 2: Ways of Distributing Your Work

In This Chapter

- Printing files
- Saving files so that others can read them in Adobe Acrobat Reader
- Sending a file by email
- Saving a file so that it can be viewed in a web browser
- Writing and keeping a blog from inside Word

This chapter explains how to distribute your work to co-workers and friends. You'll be glad to know that people who don't have Office 2016 can still read and review an Office 2016 file you created. You can print it for them, save it so it can be read in Adobe Acrobat Reader, or save it as a web page. This chapter explains all that as well as how to send a file right away by email and write and post blog entries from inside Word. By the way, Book IV, Chapter 5 describes other ways to distribute PowerPoint presentations. You can provide audience handouts, ship presentations on CDs, and save presentations as video files.

Printing — the Old Standby

In spite of predictions to the contrary, the paperless office is still a pipe dream. The day has yet to materialize when Johnny at his computer is completely digitized and communicating with his colleagues without having to print anything on paper. As for Jane, she can hardly go a day without printing reports, spreadsheets, and brochures. The office is still awash in paper, and all Jane and Johnny can do for consolation is try their best to recycle.

To print a file, preview a file before you print it, and do all else that pertains to printing, go to the File tab and choose Print (or press Ctrl+P). You land in the Print window, as shown in Figure 2-1. From here, you can choose how many copies to print, choose a part of a file to print, and get a look at your file before you print it. Notice that the Print window offers Zoom controls buttons and buttons for going from page to page (or slide to slide).

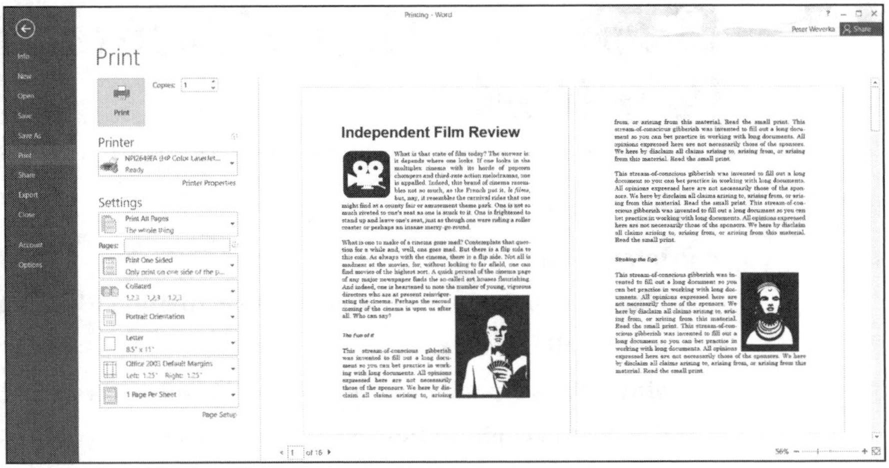

Figure 2-1: Starting in the Print window, you can preview and print files.

Distributing a File in PDF Format

As shown in Figure 2-2, you can save and distribute a file in the PDF (Portable Document File) format if the person to whom you want to give the file doesn't have the program with which it was created. For example, someone who doesn't have Excel can still view your Excel file in PDF format. Moreover, you can post PDF files on the Internet so others can view them there.

Figure 2-2: A Word document as seen through the eyes of Adobe Acrobat Reader.

About PDF files

PDF files are designed to be viewed and printed in a program called Adobe Acrobat Reader. This program is very good at acquiring data from other programs and presenting it so it can be read and printed easily. Nearly every computer has Adobe Acrobat Reader. If someone to whom you sent a PDF file doesn't have the program, they can download it for free at this web page:

```
http://get.adobe.com/reader/
```

Windows 10 (and the Microsoft Store) offers a program called Reader that is also capable of handling PDF files.

Book II, Chapter 2 explains how you can open and edit PDF files in Word 2016.

Saving an Office file as a PDF

Follow these steps to save an Office file as a PDF file:

1. **Go to the File tab and choose Export to open the Export window.**
2. **Choose Create PDF/XPS Document.**
3. **Click the Create a PDF/XPS button.**

   The Publish as PDF or XPS dialog box appears. If your goal is to create an XPS file, not a PDF file, open the Save As Type drop-down list and choose XPS Document (*.xps). Microsoft created the XPS format to compete with the PDF format. As are PDF files, XPS files are meant to present data from different programs, in this case in Internet Explorer. However, the XPS format is not nearly as well known or frequently used as the PDF format.
4. **Select a folder for storing your PDF (or XPS) file, give it a name, and click the Publish button.**

   The Adobe Acrobat Reader program opens and you see your file. (If you created an XPS file, Internet Explorer opens.)

Later in this chapter, "Saving an Office File as a Web Page" explains another way to distribute Office files to people who don't have Office — by saving the files as web pages.

Sending Your File in an Email Message

As long as you handle your email with Outlook 2016, you can send the file you're working on to a friend or co-worker without having to open Outlook 2016. Moreover, you can send a PDF or XPS version of the file. You simply choose a command and send the thing over the Internet. Follow these steps to send an open file you're working on to a friend or co-worker:

1. **Go to the File tab and choose Share.**

   The Share window opens.

2. **Choose Email.**
3. **Choose an Email option on the right side of the window.**

   How do you want to send your file? Click one of these buttons:

   - *Send as Attachment:* Send the file as an attachment to an email message.
   - *Send a Link:* Send an email link with a hyperlink to the file on a shared workspace.
   - *Send as PDF:* Send a PDF version of the file as an attachment to an email message.
   - *Send as XPS:* Send an XPS version of the file as an attachment to an email message.
   - *Send as Internet Fax:* Send the file as an Internet fax (you must have signed up with an Internet fax service provider).

   An Outlook 2016 message window appears with the name of your file on the subject line and the file itself in the Attached box. Your presentation is ready to send along with the email message.

4. **Enter the recipient's address in the To box and a message in the Message box.**

   Book VI, Chapter 3 explains how to address, compose, and send email messages with Outlook.

5. **Click the Send button.**

   That was fast! It was faster than opening Outlook and attaching the file to the email message on your own.

Saving an Office File as a Web Page

Figure 2-3 shows what a Word document looks like after it is saved as a web page and displayed in a web browser. Looks like a normal Word document, doesn't it? Anyone with a web browser can view a Word document or other Office file after it's saved as a web page. Save an Office file as a web page and post it on the Internet so that people who don't have Office can view it.

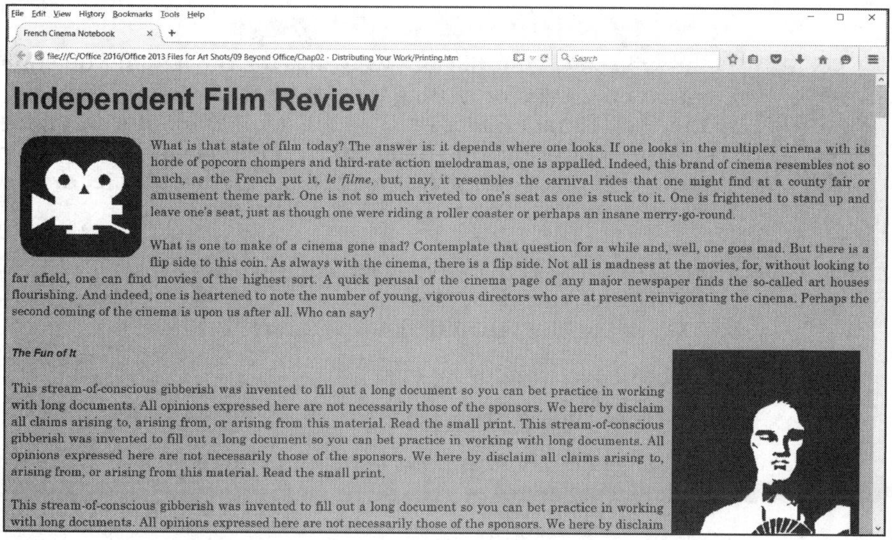

Figure 2-3: A Word document saved as a web page, as seen through the eyes of a web browser.

These pages explain the different ways to save an Office file as a web page, as well as how to open a web page you created in a web browser.

Choosing how to save the component parts

When you save an Office file as a web page, you have the choice of saving it as a Single File Web Page (`.mht`, `.mhtml`) or Web Page (`.htm`, `.html`).

WARNING!

- **Single File Web Page (`.mht`, `.mhtml`):** All component parts of the file — graphics, separate pages, and sounds, for example — are bundled into a single file. Keeping all the component parts in one file makes moving, copying, and sending the file easier. However, only the Internet Explorer browser can open and read `.mht` and `.mhtml` files. The popular Mozilla Firefox, Safari, and Opera browsers can't handle them.
- **Web Page (`.htm`, `.html`):** All the component parts of the file are kept in separate files and are saved in the same folder. Keeping the component parts in separate files is the standard way to present pages on the Internet. Handling the half-dozen or more files that are needed to display the web page can be troublesome, but you can be certain that the web page displays properly in all browsers.

Turning a file into a web page

TIP

Before you save your file as a web page, create a folder on your computer or computer network for storing the page if you intend to save it in several files in the `.htm` format. Unless you create a folder for storing all the files, you'll have a hard time locating them later, and you must be able to locate them to transfer them to a web server for display on the Internet or to send them to someone else.

Follow these steps to save an Office file as a web page:

1. **Go to the File tab and choose Export.**

   The Export window opens.

2. **Choose Change File Type.**

   Change File Type options appear on the right side of the window, as shown in Figure 2-4.

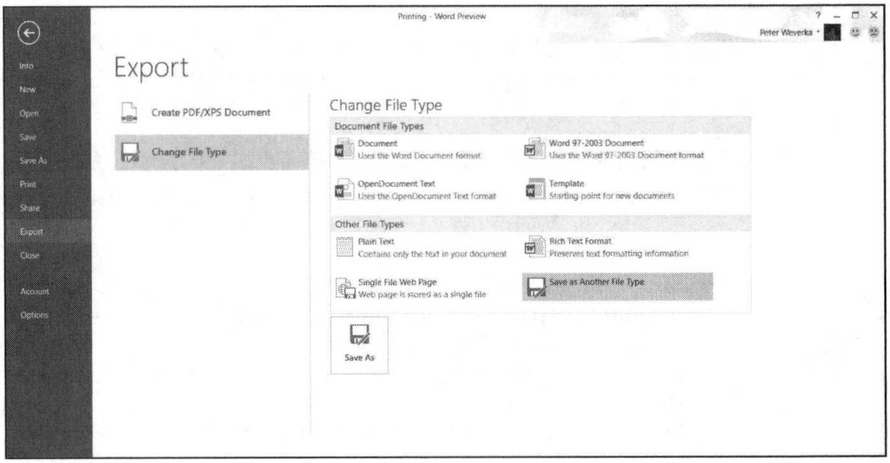

Figure 2-4: Change the file type to turn an Office file into a web page.

3. **Save your file as a single file web page or web page.**

   The previous topic in this chapter, "Choosing how to save the component parts," explains the difference between the two.

   - *Single File Web Page:* Choose the Single File Web Page option and click the Save As button. The Save As dialog box opens.
   - *Web Page:* Choose the Save as Another File Type option, click the Save As button, and in the Save As dialog box, open the Save as Type drop-down list and choose Web Page.

4. **In the Save As dialog box, click the Change Title button, enter a descriptive title in the Enter Text dialog box, and click OK.**

   The title you enter will appear in the title bar along the top of the web browser window.

5. **Choose a folder for storing your new web page.**

   If you followed my advice about creating a web page, choose the folder you recently created for storing the page and its attendant files.

6. **Click the Save button.**

   If your file includes features that can't be displayed in a web browser, the Compatibility Checker dialog box tells you what those features are. Click the Continue button to create your web page.

Opening a web page in your browser

To open a web page you fashioned from an Office file, open the folder where you stored the web page in File Explorer and double-click the `.htm` or `.mht` file. For example, if your file is called Sales Projections, double-click the `Sales Projections.htm` or `Sales Projections.mht` file to open the web page.

Blogging from inside Word

The word *blog* is shorthand for *web log*. A typical blog is a hodgepodge of commentary and links to online news sources and often other blogs where topics of concern to the blogger are discussed. Many blogs are online diaries. You get a daily picture of what the blogger is interested in — dating, technology, politics, and just about anything else under the sun.

To make it easier to keep a blog, Word offers special commands for writing blog entries and posting them immediately with a blogging service. Figure 2-5 shows the blogging feature in action. The title and the blog entry in the Word document are transported *in toto* to the blog without your having to enter a password or even visit a blogging service. What's more, Word offers a special Blog Post tab for posting blog entries and managing accounts with your blogging service. To take advantage of Word's blogging feature, you must already have an account with a blogging service.

Describing a blog account to Word

Word can't post entries to a blog unless you tell it where the blog is located, what your password is, and some other juicy tidbits. As of this writing, Word is compatible with these blogging services: Blogger, SharePoint Blog, Telligent Community, TypePad, and WordPress.

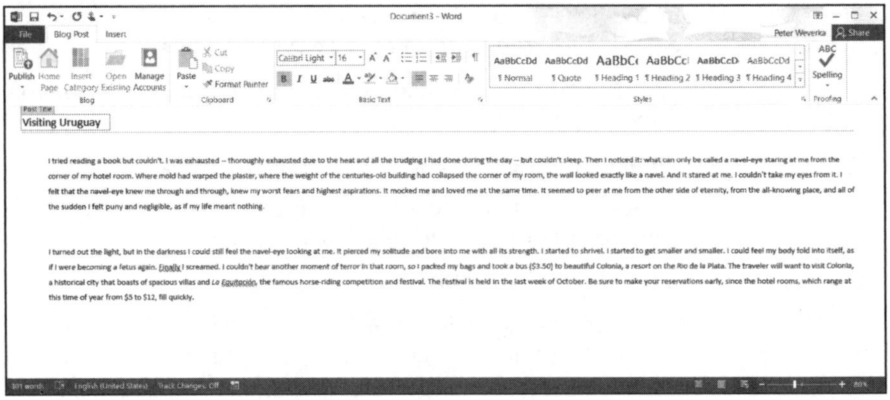

Figure 2-5: Word offers the Blog Post tab for composing and submitting blog entries.

Follow these steps to register your blogging account with Word so Word can upload blog entries:

1. **Go to the File tab and choose Share.**

   The Share window opens.

2. **Choose Post to Blog.**
3. **Click the Post to Blog button.**

   You see the Register a Blog Account dialog box.

4. **Click the Register Now button and answer questions in the dialog box to describe the blogging service you use.**

   Which questions you are asked depends on which blogging service you use. You're asked for a username and password, and also perhaps an http or ftp address for publishing pictures on your blog.

After you finish describing your blogging service, you will be pleased to discover a new tab in Word — the Blog Post tab (refer to Figure 2-5). You can use this tab to post blog entries and manage your blog accounts.

Posting an entry to your blog

When you're ready to share your thoughts with the world, follow these steps to write and post an entry to your blog from inside Word:

1. **In Word, write the entry from scratch or open a document you've already written.**

   You can start from a new document, or if you've written the entry, open the Word document with the entry.

2. **Go to the File tab, choose Share, choose Publish as Blog Post, and click the Publish as Blog Post button.**

   You land in the Blog Post tab (refer to Figure 2-5). It offers all the character styles and proofing tools that you find in Word. Go to the Insert tab to enter a hyperlink. (Book I, Chapter 2 explains hyperlinks.)

3. **Enter a title for your blog entry in the space provided.**
4. **When you're finished writing and preparing your blog entry, click the Publish button on the Blog Post tab.**

   If all goes well, Word informs you that your post has been published on your blogging service, and it lists the time and date it was published. This information appears in the Word document itself.

TIP

Instead of publishing your blog entry right away, you can open the drop-down list on the Publish button and choose Publish as Draft. Doing so uploads the blog entry to your blogging service without posting it. The entry lands on the Editing page, where you can select it, click the Editing button, and edit it online before publishing it.

Taking advantage of the Blog Post tab

By clicking buttons on the Blog Post tab, you can manage blog entries:

- **Go to your blog page:** Click the Home Page button to open your browser and display the home page of your blog.
- **Edit a blog entry:** Click the Open Existing button, and in the Open Existing Post dialog box, select a blog entry and click OK. The entry appears in Word. Edit it and click the Publish button to post it on your blog.
- **Manage accounts:** Click the Manage Accounts button to describe a new account to Word, change a blog account, or remove a blog account. Word provides the Blog Accounts dialog box for doing these activities.

Chapter 3: Working with Publisher

In This Chapter

- **Understanding frames**
- **Creating a new publication**
- **Designing your publication**
- **Changing your view of the Publisher window**
- **Entering the text and handling text frames**
- **Inserting pictures**
- **Finalizing and printing your publication**

Welcome to Publisher 2016. Not long ago, creating professional publications like the kind you can create with Publisher required sophisticated printing equipment and a background in graphic design. However, even a novice can now create professional-looking publications with Publisher. As long as you rely on a publication design — a template that comes with Publisher — most of the layout work is done for you. All you have to do is enter the text and the other particulars.

"A Print Shop in a Can"

Publisher has been called "a print shop in a can" because the program is great for creating prefabricated brochures, business cards, calendars, newsletters, resumes, posters, and the like. To make these publications without going to a great deal of trouble, however, you have to stick to the template. Each *template* provides you with a readymade brochure, calendar, and so on.

Chances are you can find a suitable template for whatever kind of publication you want to create. Figure 3-1 shows examples of informational templates. Templates include placeholders for graphics and text. To create a publication, you choose a template, choose a design, enter graphics and text in the publication where the placeholders are, and tweak the publication to your liking.

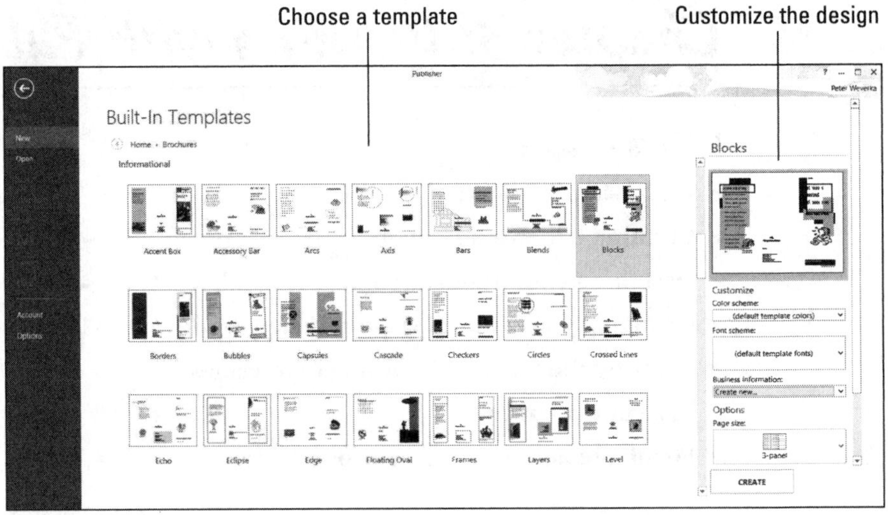

Figure 3-1: Creating a publication in the New window.

Introducing Frames

The publications that you make with Publisher are composed of frames. A *frame* is a placeholder for text, a graphic, or a table. Complex publications have dozens of frames; simple publications have only a few. Frames keep text and graphics from overlapping. They make sure that everything stays on the page where it should be. As you create a publication, you enter text or graphics in frames.

The publication in Figure 3-2 is made up of several frames that were stitched together to form a poster. On the left side of the figure, I selected the frames, and you can see the frame boundaries; the right side of the figure shows what the poster looks like after it is printed. Frames make laying out publications easier. When you want to move text, a picture, a table, or an image, you simply drag its frame to a new location. After you select a frame, the commands you give apply to the text or graphic in the frame. Frames do not appear in the finished product — they are meant strictly to help with the laying out of text and graphics.

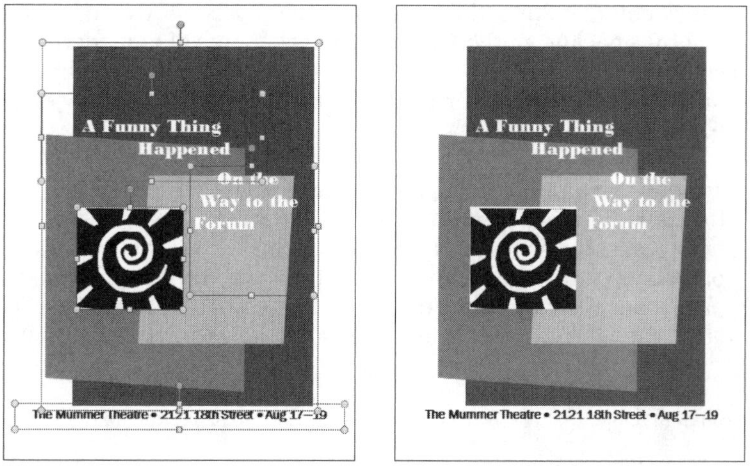

Figure 3-2: A poster with frames showing (left); the poster as it looks when printed (right).

Creating a Publication

To create a new publication, go to the File tab and choose New (or press Ctrl+N). You see the New window, where you create a publication with any of these techniques:

- **Search online for a template:** In the Search for Online Templates text box, enter the name of a publication type and click the Start Searching button (or press Enter). Select a category and click a template to examine it in a preview screen. Click the Create button to create a publication.
- **Choose a featured template:** On the Featured tab, select a template. A preview screen opens so that you can examine the template. Click Create to create a publication.
- **Choose a built-in template:** On the Built-In tab (see Figure 3-1), select the icon representing a category (Brochures, Business Cards, and so on). You see a dozen or more templates. Scroll through the list, select a template, and click Create.

REMEMBER

As you search for a template, you can click the Back or Home button to retrace your search in the New window.

Redesigning a Publication

WARNING!

Make your design choices carefully. In theory, you can change publication designs, color schemes, and design options when you are well along in a project, but in practice, changing these designs can have unforeseen consequences. If you change the color of a headline, for example, and then choose a new color scheme, the headline might be swallowed or rendered invisible by a background color in the new scheme. If you enter a bunch of text, change the size of a few frames, and then choose a new template for your publication, you may turn your publication into corned-beef hash and have to start over.

To redesign a publication, go to the Page Design tab. As shown in Figure 3-3, this tab offers opportunities for changing templates, the orientation and size of pages, color schemes, and font schemes. If your publication has more than one page, click page thumbnails in the Page Navigation pane to visit different pages and see what they look like. (If you don't see the Page Navigation pane, go to the View tab and select the Page Navigation check box.)

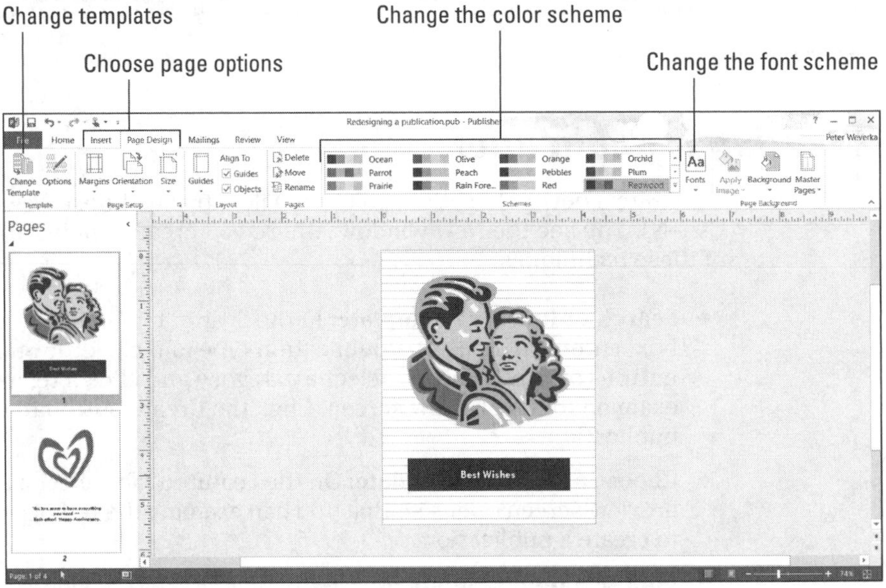

Figure 3-3: Go to the Page Design tab to change templates, color schemes, font schemes, color schemes, and page options.

Choosing a different template

Not happy with the template you chose when you created your publication? To exchange it for a new one, go to the Page Design tab, click the Change Template button, and choose Change Template. You go to the Change Template window, where you can select a different template (refer to Figure 3-1).

Choosing a color scheme

To choose a different color scheme for your publication, go to the Page Design tab and select a scheme in the Schemes gallery (refer to Figure 3-3). If you're daring, choose Create New Color Scheme at the bottom of the gallery and fashion your own color scheme in the Create New Color Scheme dialog box.

Setting up your pages

On the Page Design tab, visit the Page Setup group to determine the margin size, orientation, and page size of your publication:

- ✦ **Margins:** Click the Margins button and choose an option on the drop-down list or click Custom Margins to enter margin measurements in the Layout Guides dialog box.
- ✦ **Orientation:** Click the Orientation button and choose Portrait or Landscape on the drop-down list to stand your publication upright or turn it on its side.
- ✦ **Size:** Click the Size button and select a page size on the drop-down list. You can choose Create New Page Size on the menu to declare a page size of your own for your publication in the Create New Page Size dialog box. Decide right away which page size to use for your publication. How large or small the page is determines how the headings, graphics, and text fit on the pages.

Getting a Better View of Your Work

Because seeing the little details as well as the big picture matters so much in a publication, Publisher offers many tools for changing views of your work. Figure 3-4 shows what these tools are. They are described in the following pages.

Zooming in and out

Apart from the standard Zoom controls found in most Office programs (Book I, Chapter 3 describes the Zoom controls in the lower-right corner of the screen), Publisher offers a handful of other commands for zooming in or out. Go to the View tab and take advantage of these techniques as you refine your publication:

- ✦ **Make the page fit squarely in the window:** Click the Whole Page button (or press Ctrl+Shift+L) to make the entire page fit in the window. The lower-right corner of the window also offers a Whole Page button; you can click it when you're not working in the View tab.

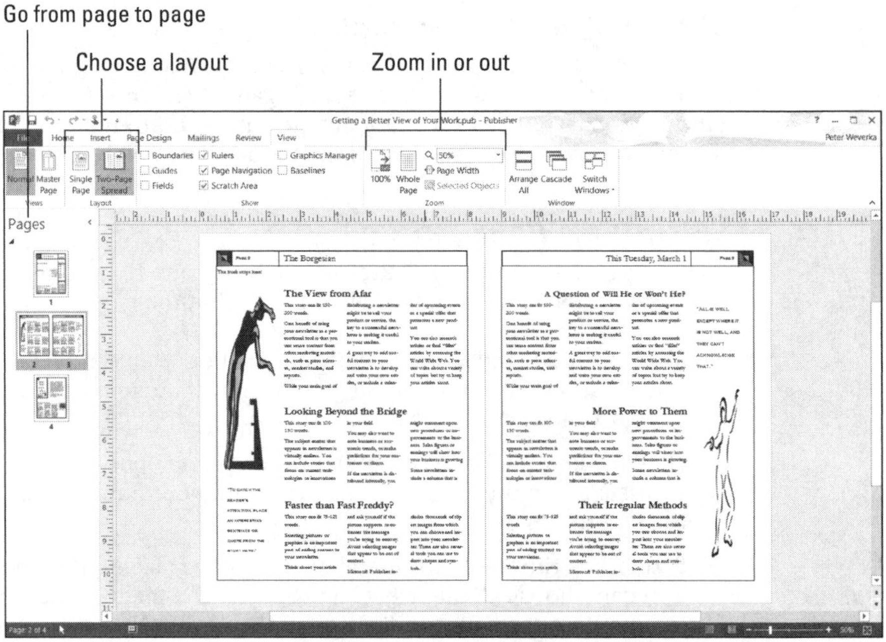

Figure 3-4: Go to the View tab to change views of your work.

- **Make the width of the page fit in the window:** Click the Page Width button.
- **Focus on objects:** Select an object (a text frame or graphic, for example) or a handful of objects and click the Selected Objects button to zoom in on what you selected. Being able to focus this way is very helpful when you're working on a publication that is crowded with words and images.
- **View your publication at its actual size:** Click the 100% button.

Viewing single pages and two-page spreads

On the View tab, click the Two-Page Spread button to see facing pages in newsletters, brochures, and other publications with more than one page (refer to Figure 3-4). Choose this command early and often. It permits you to see what readers of your publication will see when they view facing pages. Click the Single Page button to see a single page in the window.

Going from page to page

Use these techniques to get from page to page in a publication:

- **Page Navigation pane:** In a publication with more than one page, go from page to page by clicking thumbnail pages in the Page Navigation pane (refer to Figure 3-4). To display this pane, visit the View tab and click the Page Navigation check box.

✦ **The Go To Page dialog box:** On the Home tab, open the drop-down list on the Find button and choose Go To Page (or press Ctrl+G). Then enter a page number in the Go To Page dialog box.

TIP

To help you identify pages, you can name them. When you move the pointer over a page thumbnail in the Page Navigation pane, the name appears in a pop-up box. To name a page, right-click its thumbnail in the Page Navigation pane and choose Rename on the shortcut menu. In the Rename Page dialog box, enter a descriptive name.

Entering Text on the Pages

The placeholder text that appears in publication designs has to go, of course. One of your first tasks is to replace the placeholder text with your own words. If you're putting together a sign or greeting card, you have only a handful of words to write, and you can write them in Publisher. But if you're working on a story (*story* is Publisher's term for an article that reaches across several text frames), the easiest way to handle the text is to write it in Word and import it.

If you have to replace more than two dozen words, follow these steps to replace the placeholder text in a text frame with text from a Word document:

1. **In Word, write the text and save the text in a file.**

   You can call on all of the Word commands to edit the text. Book II covers Word.

2. **In Publisher, click in the placeholder text, go to the Home tab, click the Styles button, and note on the Styles drop-down list which style has been assigned to the placeholder text.**

   You can tell which style has been assigned to the text because it is selected on the Styles drop-down list. In Step 6, you will assign the style that is currently applied to the text to the replacement text you insert into the text frame.

3. **If necessary, press Ctrl+A to select the text in the story.**
4. **On the Insert tab, click the Insert File button.**

   You see the Insert Text dialog box. You can also open this dialog box by right-clicking and choosing Change Text ➪ Text File.

5. **Select the Word file with the replacement text and click the OK button.**

   Replacement text from the Word file "flows" into the text frame or frames. If the replacement text doesn't fit in the text frames allotted to the story, you see the Autoflow dialog box. You can click the Yes button to tell Publisher to flow the text into different text frames in the publication, but I recommend clicking No in the Autoflow dialog box. Later in this chapter, "Making text flow from frame to frame" explains how to decide on your own where to put overflow text from a story.

The replacement text maintains the styles assigned to it in the Word document. In the next step, you reassign a style to the text.

6. **Press Ctrl+A to select the text in the story, go to the Home tab, click the Styles button, and choose the style that was assigned to the placeholder text.**

   In Step 2, you noted which style this was.

Making Text Fit in Text Frames

When text doesn't fit in a text frame, red selection handles appear around the frame, and if the text frame holds a story, the Text In Overflow icon appears in the lower-right corner of the text frame, as shown in Figure 3-5. When you see this icon and the red selection handles, it means that you must make decisions about how to fit stray text into text frames. You can either fit the text into an existing frame, or, if you're dealing with a story, flow the text to other frames. These pages explain strategies for handling text that doesn't fit in text frames.

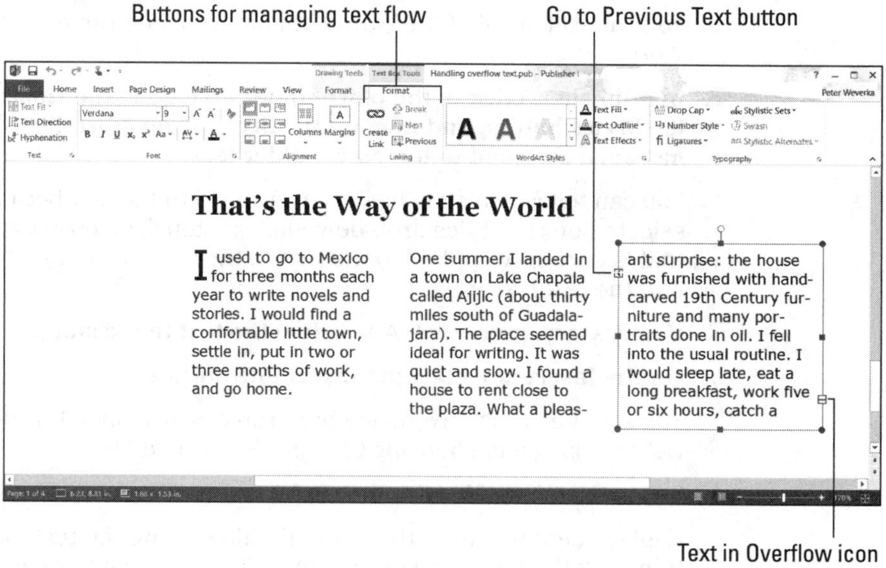

Figure 3-5: "Flowing" text from frame to frame.

Fitting overflow text in a single frame

To fit a heading or paragraph into a single text frame, try one of these techniques:

- **Shrink the text automatically:** On the (Text Box Tools) Format tab, click the Text Fit button and choose Shrink Text On Overflow on the drop-down list. This command shrinks the point size of text so that all text fits in the frame. Sometimes, however, shrinking the text this way makes the heading or paragraph hard to read.
- **Edit the text:** Snip out a word or sentence here and there to make the text fit. Have you ever wondered why magazine articles always fill the page and never end in the middle? That's because skillful editors and typesetters remove and add words here and there to make the story fit the page.
- **Make the text frame larger:** Click the frame to display the selection handles; then, drag a handle.
- **Make the text frame margins smaller:** Like a page, text frames have internal margins to keep text from getting too close to the frame border. To shrink these margins and make more room for text, go to the (Text Box Tools) Format tab, click the Margins button, and choose Narrow on the drop-down list. You can also choose Custom Margins, and on the Text Box tab of the Format Text Box dialog box, enter smaller measurements for the text box margins.

Making text flow from frame to frame

As shown in Figure 3-5, the Text In Overflow icon and red selection handles appear when story text overflows a text frame. How do you flow story text from frame to frame and handle a story that is spread across several frames? Better keep reading.

Flowing text to another frame

If necessary, create a new text box for the overflow text and follow these steps to direct text from one frame to another in your publication:

1. **Select the text frame with overflowing text.**

   You can tell when text is overflowing because the Text in Overflow icon appears in the lower-right corner of the frame (refer to Figure 3-5).

2. **On the (Text Box) Format tab, click the Create Link button.**

   The pointer turns into an overflowing pitcher (or is that a beer stein?) after you click the button.

3. **Move the pointer over the box that you want the text to flow into.**

   You may have to click a page navigation button to go to another page.

4. **Click in the target text box to make the text flow there.**

Handling text frames in a story

As I mention earlier, text frames that are linked are known as a story in Publisher-speak. Here are techniques for handling text frames that are linked in a story:

- **Going from text frame to text frame:** On the (Text Box Tools) Format tab, click the Next or Previous button to go from frame to frame. You can also select a text frame and click its Go to Next Text Box or Go to Previous Text Box icon.
- **Selecting the text in all the text frames:** Press Ctrl+A; or go to the Home tab, click the Select button, and choose Select All Text in Text Box on the drop-down list.
- **Breaking the link between frames:** Select the frame that you want to be the last one in the chain, and on the (Text Box Tools) Format tab, click the Break button.

TIP

In a crowded publication, it's easy to overlook a text frame with overflowing text. To find these text frames, go to the File tab, and on the Info page, click the Run Design Checker button. Then, in the Design Checker task pane, look for "Story with Text in Overflow Area."

Making Text Wrap around a Frame or Graphic

Wrap text around a frame, an image, a picture, or a WordArt image and you get a very elegant layout. Figure 3-6 shows text that has been wrapped around an image. Looks nice, doesn't it? Wrapping text may be the easiest way to impress innocent bystanders with your layout prowess. As Figure 3-6 shows, text wrapped tightly follows the contours of the picture, whereas text wrapped squarely runs flush with the picture's frame.

Figure 3-6: Text wrapped tightly (left) and squarely (right).

TIP

Here are shorthand instructions for wrapping text:

1. **Select the item that text is to wrap around.**

   In Figure 3-6, you would select the image.

2. **On the Format tab, click the Wrap Text button and choose a wrapping option on the drop-down list.**

   For Figure 3-6, I chose Tight for the picture on the left and Square for the picture on the right.

The Wrap Text commands are identical in Word and Publisher. Book II, Chapter 6 (about wrapping objects in Word) explains the wrapping commands in detail.

Replacing the Placeholder Pictures

As you must have noticed by now, publication designs are littered with generic pictures and graphics. Besides writing your own words where the placeholder ones are, replace the generic pictures with pictures of your own. Well, do it if you please. You are welcome to pass off the generic pictures as your own. I won't tell anybody.

Follow these steps to put a picture of your own where a placeholder picture is now:

1. **Click the placeholder picture to select it.**

   TIP

   You can also select a picture by clicking its name in the Graphics Manager. To use the Graphics Manager, go to the View tab and click the Graphics Manager check box. The Graphics Manager opens on the right side of the screen.

2. **On the (Picture Tools) Format tab, click the Change Picture button and choose Change Picture on the drop-down list.**

   The Insert Pictures dialog box appears.

3. **Select a picture and click the Insert button.**

   Book VIII, Chapter 3 describes the Insert Pictures dialog box and how to handle graphics in all the Office programs. You'll be delighted to discover that graphics are handled the same way, no matter which program you're toiling in.

TIP

You can postpone choosing a picture to replace a placeholder picture. Right-click the picture in question and choose Change Picture ➪ Remove Picture on the drop-down list. Publisher places a picture icon in the frame to remind you to insert a picture later on. You can click this picture icon to open the Insert Pictures dialog box.

Taking advantage of the scratch area

To make experimenting with pictures a little easier, Publisher offers the *scratch area.* You can keep pictures on hand in the scratch area as you decide which pictures to use in a publication. On the Insert tab, click the Online Pictures button and select pictures from the Internet in the Insert Pictures dialog box. The pictures you select land in the scratch area on the right side of the screen.

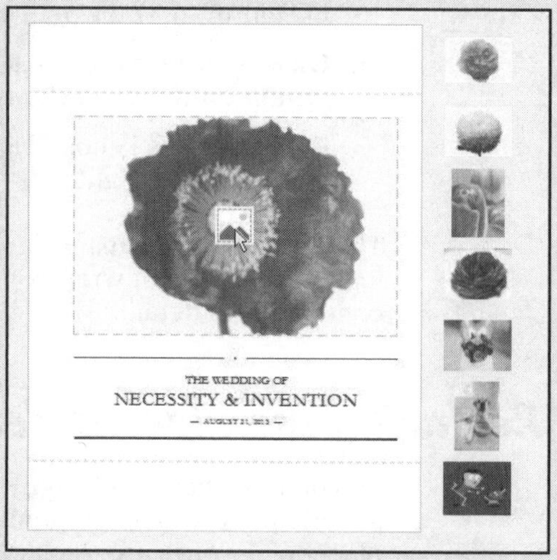

You can compare and contrast pictures in the scratch area. To swap a picture in your publication with one in the scratch area, move the pointer over the middle of the picture you want to swap out. When you see the picture icon, drag it into the scratch area over the picture you'd like to see in your publication. In this way, you can quickly swap pictures in and out of publications to find the picture that does the job best.

Inserting, Removing, and Moving Pages

Suppose that you have too many pages or you need to add a page or two. On the Page Navigation pane (select the Page Navigation check box on the View tab), click a thumbnail to select the page where you want to insert, remove, or move pages. Then follow these instructions:

- **Inserting a new page:** On the Insert tab, click the Page button and choose an option on the drop-down list:
  - *Insert Blank Page:* Inserts an empty page.
  - *Insert Duplicate Page:* Inserts a page identical to the thumbnail page you selected.
  - *Insert Page:* Opens the Insert Pages dialog box, shown in Figure 3-7, where you can enter the number of pages you want to insert and click the More button to put the new pages before or after the page you selected. You can also tell Publisher what to put on the new page or pages.

- **Removing a page:** On the Page Design tab, click the Delete button. You can also right-click a page thumbnail and choose Delete.
- **Moving a page:** On the Page Design tab, click the Move button. Give instructions for moving the page in the Move Page dialog box and click OK.

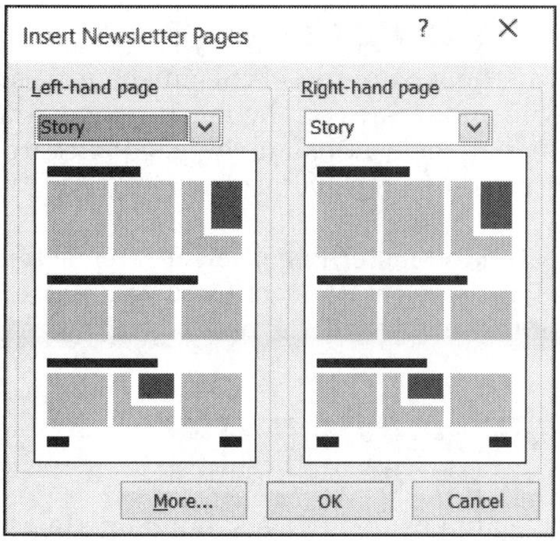

Figure 3-7: Inserting a new page.

Master Pages for Handling Page Backgrounds

In a publication with many pages, the same object sometimes goes on every page. A company logo on the corner of each page looks mighty elegant. Page numbers and copyright information are also found on all the pages of some publications. The good news is that you don't have to place the objects on each page individually. Instead, you can place the objects on the *master page*. Whatever is on the master page appears on all pages in a publication (unless you decide that the master page shouldn't apply to a particular page). Forthwith are instructions for handling master pages.

Switching to Master Page view

To change the appearance of the master page, place an object on the master page, or see precisely what is on the master page, start by switching to Master Page view:

- On the View tab, click the Master Page button.
- On the Page Design tab, click the Master Pages button and choose Edit Master Pages on the drop-down list.

You can tell when you're looking at a master page because you see the Master Page tab on the ribbon and the page thumbnails in the Page Navigation pane show letters instead of numbers.

To leave Master Page view, go to the Master Page tab and click the Close Master Page button.

Changing the look of a master page

All commands for changing the look of run-of-the-mill pages also apply to master pages. Place objects and frames on the master page as if you were putting them on run-of-the-mill pages. Change the page background as if you were changing the background of a normal page.

To edit a master page, switch to Master Page, select the master page you want to work with in the Page Navigation tab (if you've created more than one master page), and get to work.

Applying (or unapplying) a master page to publication pages

By default, the master page applies to all pages, but sometimes unapplying a master page is necessary because objects on the master page get in the way. And if you created more than one master page, you have to tell Publisher which master page to apply to which publication page.

Follow these instructions to unapply or apply master pages to pages in a publication:

- **Unapplying a master page:** In Normal view, go to the Page Design tab, display the page you want to unattach from the master page, click the Master Pages button, and choose None on the drop-down list.
- **Applying a different master page:** Use one of these techniques to apply a different master page to pages in your publication:
  - In Normal view, display a page, go to the Page Design tab, click the Master Pages button, and choose a different master page on the drop-down list.
  - In Master Page view, go to the Master Page tab, select a master page in the Navigation pane, and click the Apply To button. On the Apply To drop-down list, choose Apply to All Pages to apply a different master page to all the pages in your publication. Choose Apply Master Page on the drop-down list and enter page-range numbers in the Apply Master Page dialog box to apply the master page to a select group of pages.

Running the Design Checker

When at last your publication is ready for printing, be sure to run the Design Checker. This helpful tool can alert you to frames that fall on nonprinting parts of the page, stories that "overflow" without finding a text frame to go to, invisible objects, and a host of other problems.

On the File tab, choose Info, and click the Run Design Checker button to run the Design Checker. As shown in Figure 3-8, the Design Checker task pane opens and lists items that need your attention. Open an item's drop-down list and choose Go to This Item to locate it in your publication. Sometimes the drop-down list offers a quick fix as well.

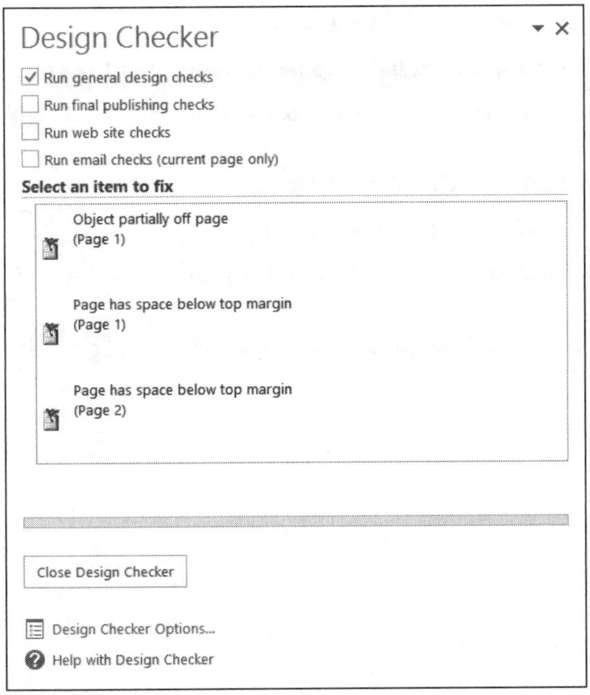

Figure 3-8: Running the Design Checker.

TIP: To see which design flaws the Design Checker looks for, click the Design Checker Options hyperlink in the Design Checker task pane. Then, in the Design Checker Options dialog box, select the Checks tab and read the list.

Commercially Printing a Publication

You know the routine for printing a publication on your computer: Go to the File tab, choose Print, negotiate the Print window, and click the Print button. To print a publication with a commercial printer, Publisher offers the Save for a Commercial Printer command. This command creates a PDF file for use by print shops. PDF is now the standard file format for print shops.

Follow these steps to save your publication as a PDF that you can hand off to a printer:

1. **On the File tab, choose Export.**

   The Export window opens.

2. **Choose Save for a Commercial Printer.**
3. **On the first drop-down list, choose Commercial Press.**
4. **On the second drop-down list, choose Both PDF and Publisher .pub Files.**
5. **Click the Pack and Go Wizard button.**

   The Pack and Go Wizard dialog box opens.

6. **Choose a location for your publication file or choose to burn it to a CD.**
7. **Click Next and follow the instructions for creating the PDF and `.pub` file.**

Book X

File Sharing and Collaborating

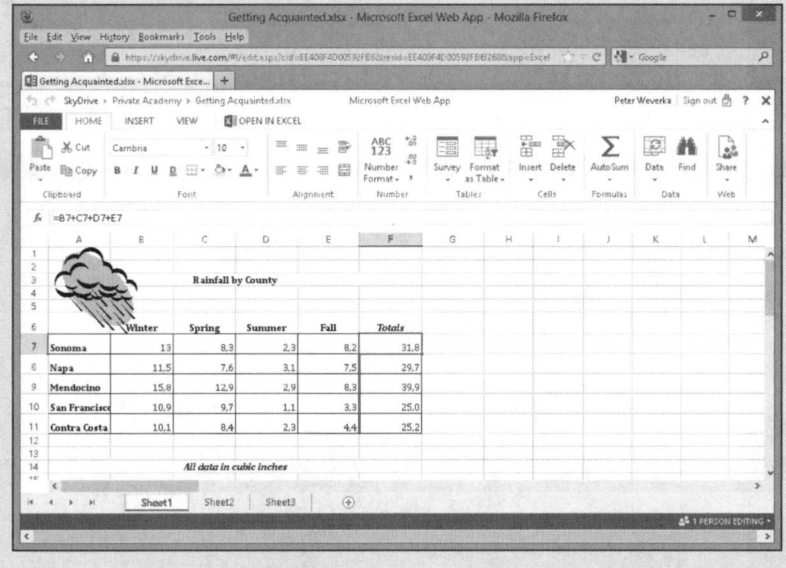

Visit `www.dummies.com/extras/office2016aio` to find out how to share a file with others online and generate a hyperlink so that others can find the file in their browsers.

Contents at a Glance

Chapter 1: Up and Running on OneDrive

In This Chapter

- **Getting into OneDrive**
- **Understanding how the OneDrive window works**
- **Creating, navigating, renaming, and deleting folders**
- **Uploading and downloading files to and from OneDrive**
- **Opening a file stored at OneDrive**
- **Managing files at OneDrive**

This chapter introduces you to OneDrive, Microsoft's online facility for storing files, sharing files, and co-editing files with other people. It describes how to sign in and out of OneDrive so that you can get to your OneDrive folders. You also discover how to navigate in OneDrive, manage folders, and upload and download files from your computer to OneDrive. Finally, this chapter shows how to open, delete, and move a file you store at OneDrive.

To use OneDrive, you must be an Office 365 subscriber. Book 1, Chapter 1 explains what Office 365 is and how to subscribe to it.

Signing In to OneDrive

OneDrive is a component of Office 365, Microsoft's online suite of services. Before you can store, share, or co-edit files in OneDrive, you have to sign in to OneDrive. Open a web browser and follow these steps to sign in to Office 365:

1. **Go to this web address:** `onedrive.live.com`
2. **Click the Sign In button.**

   The Sign In window opens.
3. **Enter the email address of your Office 365 account and click Next.**

   The OneDrive window opens.
4. **Enter your password and click Sign In.**

   The OneDrive window opens in your browser, as shown in Figure 1-1.

To sign out of Office 365 in a web browser, click your username or picture in the upper-right corner of the screen and choose Sign Out on the drop-down menu.

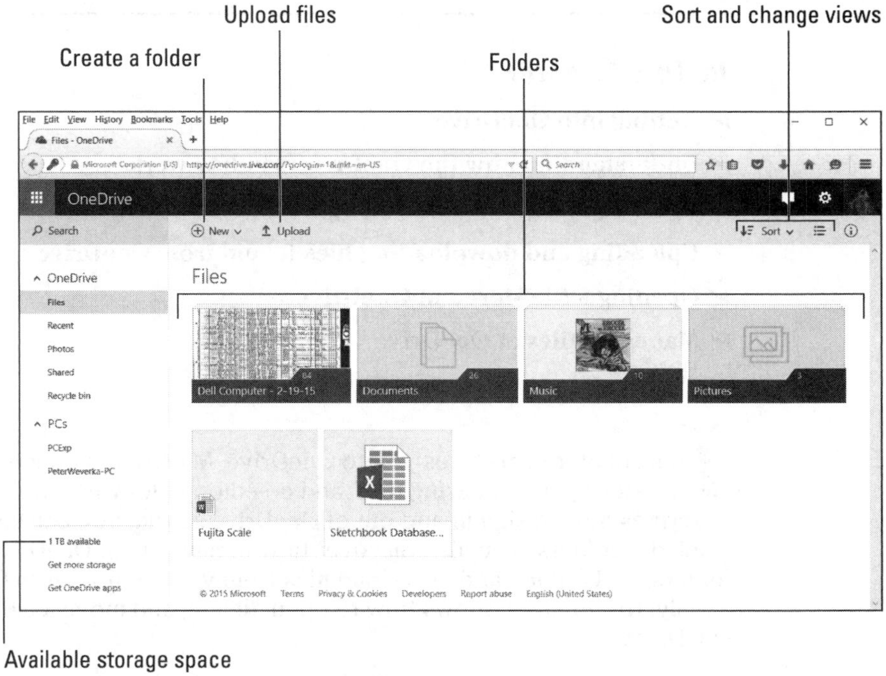

Figure 1-1: OneDrive in a web browser.

SharePoint: The other way to store and share files

In this book, I describe how to store and share files with OneDrive, a Microsoft website, but you can also store and share files using a software product called SharePoint. With SharePoint, files are maintained on a local network. They are kept on a server that is owned and operated by a company.

Keeping files on a network server close to home helps solve the privacy problem. Meddlers and spies who want to steal files have a harder time getting them from a server on a closed network than they do from a OneDrive folder on the Internet. To run SharePoint, however, you need a fair amount of technical expertise. If SharePoint interests you, see *SharePoint 2013 For Dummies,* by Ken Withee (Wiley).

Exploring the OneDrive Window

To start with, OneDrive gives you two folders — Documents and Pictures — for storing files, and you can create additional folders as well. OneDrive can store up to from 15GB to 1TB (that's 1000 GB) of files, depending on the type of subscription you have. The lower-left corner of the browser window tells you how much storage space you have for storing files.

You can tell how many files are stored in each folder because folders list how many files they hold. To open a folder and view its contents, click a folder name.

Glance back at Figure 1-1 and take note of these tools in the OneDrive window for managing files:

- **Create folders:** Click the New button and choose Folder to create a folder for storing files. See "Creating a folder," later in this chapter, for details.
- **Upload files:** Click the Upload button to upload files from your desktop or laptop computer to OneDrive. See "Uploading Files to a Folder on OneDrive," later in this chapter.
- **Arranging folders and files in the window:** Use the tools in the upper-right corner of the screen to arrange and locate folders and files. See "Viewing and locating folders in the OneDrive window," later in this chapter.

REMEMBER

To return to the main OneDrive window, click OneDrive in the upper-left corner, or click Files, the first link on the left side of the screen.

Managing Your OneDrive Folders

All folders you create for storing files are kept in OneDrive. OneDrive gives you two folders — Documents and Pictures — for storing files, and you can create folders of your own, as well as subfolders. These pages explain how to create folders, get from folder to folder in OneDrive, and do folder-management tasks such as renaming, deleting, and moving folders.

Creating a folder

Create folders to store and organize your files on OneDrive. Sign in to OneDrive with your web browser and follow these steps to create a folder:

1. **If you want to create a subfolder (a folder inside another folder), open the folder that your new folder will go into.**

   To open a folder, click its name.

2. **Click the New button and choose Folder on the drop-down list.**

   A dialog box appears.

3. **Enter a name for the folder.**
4. **Click Create.**

   Later in this chapter, "Uploading Files to a Folder on OneDrive" explains how to upload files from your computer to a folder in OneDrive.

Viewing and locating folders in the OneDrive window

Use the OneDrive window to store and locate folders, subfolders, and files in OneDrive. The OneDrive window offers these tools for managing folders:

- **Searching:** Enter a search term in the Search box to search for a folder or file. The Search box is located in the upper-left corner of the window.
- **Sorting:** Click the Sort button and choose an option to rearrange folders and files in the OneDrive window. Sorting is helpful for finding a folder or file in a long list.
- **Viewing:** Click the Details button to switch between Details view and Thumbnails view, as shown in Figure 1-2:
  - *Details view* presents detailed information about folders and files — when they were last modified, whether they are shared, and file sizes.
  - *Thumbnails view* presents folders and files in thumbnail form.
- **Displaying the Information pane:** Select a folder or file and click the Information button to open the Information pane (see Figure 1-2). You can also display the Information pane by right-clicking a folder or file and choosing Details.

REMEMBER

Click the check box (looks like a circle, actually) on a folder or file to select it. Before you can rename, delete, or move a folder or file, you have to select it.

Going from folder to folder in OneDrive

After you accumulate a few folders on OneDrive, getting to the folder you want to open can be an arduous, interminable journey. To help you on your way, OneDrive offers different techniques for going to a folder:

- **The drill-down method:** Starting in the OneDrive window, click a top-level folder to display its subfolders. If necessary, keep drilling down this way until you reach the folder you want to open.

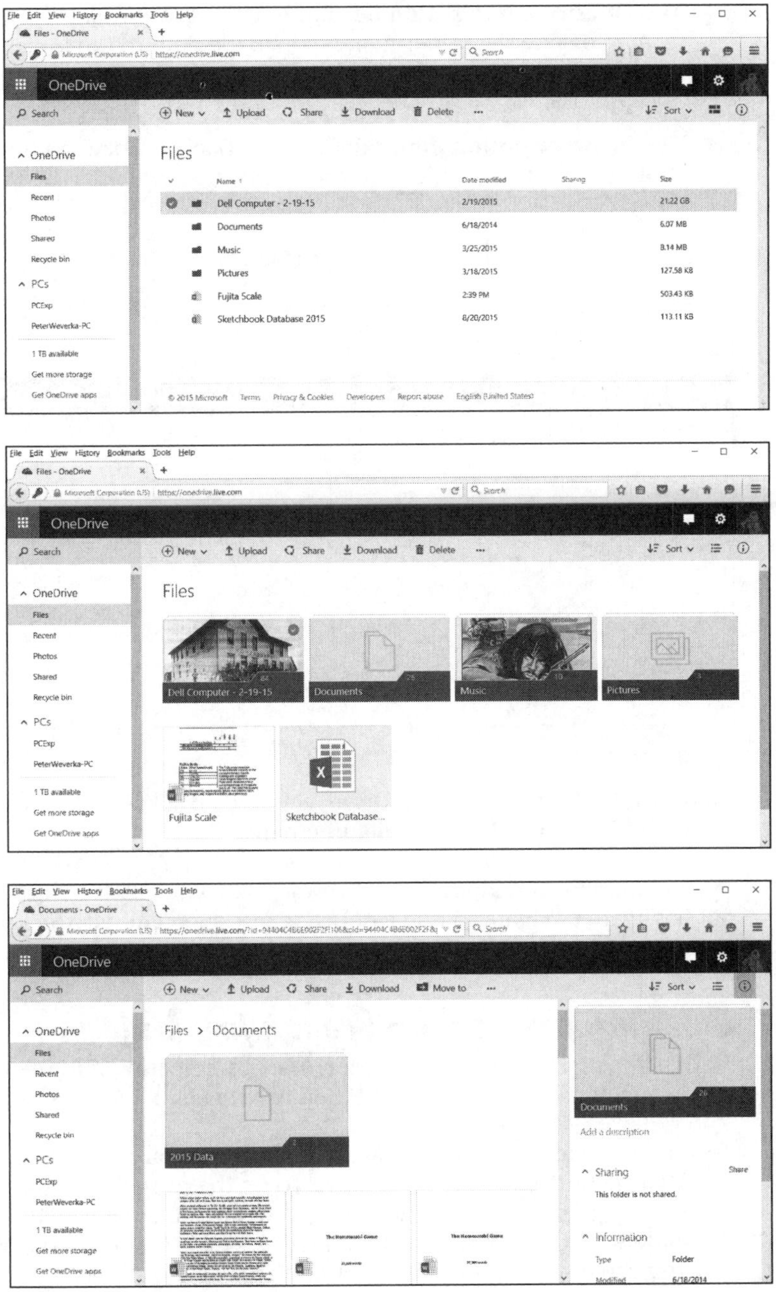

Figure 1-2: The OneDrive window in Details view (top), Thumbnails view (middle), and Thumbnails view with the Information pane showing (bottom).

- **The OneDrive Navigation bar method:** The *OneDrive Navigation bar* — located beside the folder name — lists the path to the folder that is currently open. To backtrack, click the name of a folder on the path, as shown in Figure 1-3.
- **The browser button method:** Click the Back or Forward button in your browser to open a folder you previously opened.

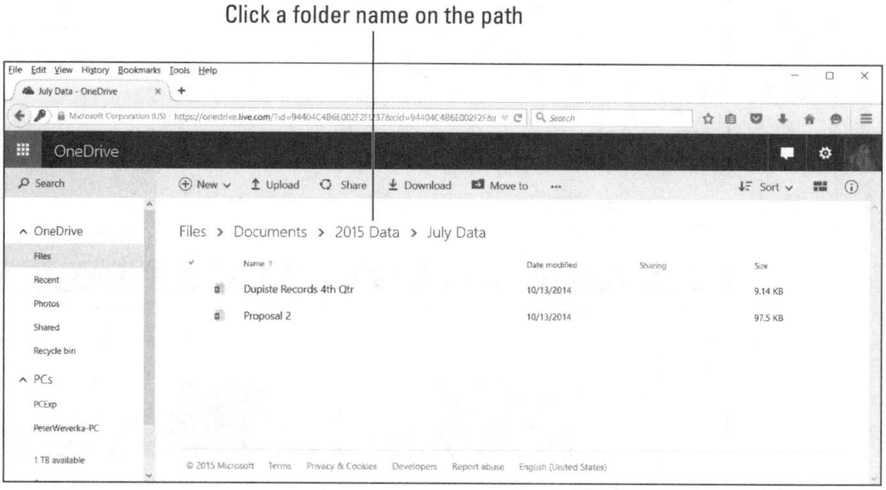

Figure 1-3: Click a folder name on the Navigation bar to open a folder.

To return to the top-level OneDrive window, click the OneDrive button or click Files in the OneDrive Navigation pane.

TIP

By bookmarking a folder in your browser, you can go straight to a folder without having to navigate to it in OneDrive. After you choose the bookmark (and enter your ID and password if you haven't yet signed in yet), the folder opens.

Deleting, moving, and renaming folders

To delete, move, or rename a folder, start by selecting it in the OneDrive window (select its check circle). Then use these techniques:

- **Moving a folder:** Click the Move To button (you may have to click the Manage button and choose Move To on the drop-down list, depending on the size of your browser window). A dialog box opens with a list of your folders on OneDrive. Select a folder in the list and click the Move button. You can also right-click a folder and choose Move To.
- **Deleting a folder:** Click the Delete button. You can also right-click and choose Delete.
- **Renaming a folder:** Click the Rename button and enter a name. You can also right-click and choose Rename.

The Office Online applications

As an Office 365 subscriber, you are entitled to use the Office Online applications — Word, Excel, PowerPoint, and OneNote. These applications are available from the Office 365 toolbar. Click the Navigation button (the button to the left of the OneDrive button) to open this toolbar. Then choose Word Online, Excel Online, PowerPoint Online, or OneNote Online to test-drive an Office Online application.

To open a file in an online application, select it in the OneDrive window, click the Open button, and choose an option for opening the file in an online application.

Anyone can use these applications. You don't have to pay a fee of any kind or install Office. All you need is an Internet connection and an Office 365 subscription. Moreover, users of Office Online apps can collaborate online with one another to create Word documents, Excel worksheets, PowerPoint presentations, and OneNote notebooks.

The Office Online applications are lightweight versions of Office software. You store the files you create with Office Online applications on OneDrive.

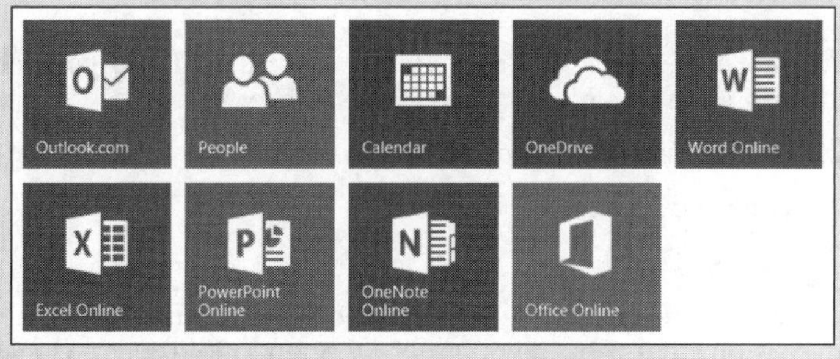

Uploading Files to a Folder on OneDrive

Upload a file from your computer to OneDrive so that you can share the file with others or be able to access it when you are not at the computer you normally use. Sign in to OneDrive with your web browser and follow these steps to upload files from your computer to a folder you keep on OneDrive:

1. **On OneDrive, open the folder where you want to store the files.**
2. **Click the Upload button.**

   The File Upload dialog box opens.
3. **Select the files.**
4. **Click the Open button.**

   The file or files are uploaded to the folder you selected in OneDrive.

TIP

Another way to upload files is to drag them from File Explorer (Windows 10, 8.1, and 8) or Windows Explorer (Windows 7). Open File Explorer or Windows Explorer, locate the files you want to upload, and select them. Then drag them into the OneDrive window.

You can also upload an Excel, Word, or PowerPoint by opening it in an Office 2016 program and saving it to a OneDrive folder. See "Saving a File from Office 2016 to OneDrive," the next topic in this chapter.

Saving a File from Office 2016 to OneDrive

Starting in Word, Excel, or PowerPoint, you can save a file to a folder on OneDrive. In effect, saving a file this way is the same as uploading it to OneDrive.

Follow these steps to save an Office 2016 file on your computer to a OneDrive folder:

1. **In Word, Excel, or PowerPoint, open the file on your computer that you want to save to a OneDrive folder.**
2. **On the File tab, choose Save As.**

   The Save As window opens.
3. **Choose OneDrive.**

   As shown in Figure 1-4, the Recent Folders list shows the names of folders on OneDrive (if you recently opened folders on OneDrive).
4. **Select the OneDrive folder where you want to save the file.**

   Select the folder from the Recent Folders list or browse for the folder.

   - **Recent folder:** Click the name of the folder on the Recent Folders list. The Save As dialog box opens to the folder you selected.
   - **Click the Browse button.** The Save As dialog box appears. On the left side of the dialog box, scroll to and select OneDrive. Then go to the OneDrive folder where you want to save the file.

   In the Save As dialog box, notice the path to the OneDrive folder where the file will be saved. You are about to save the file to a OneDrive folder on the Internet.

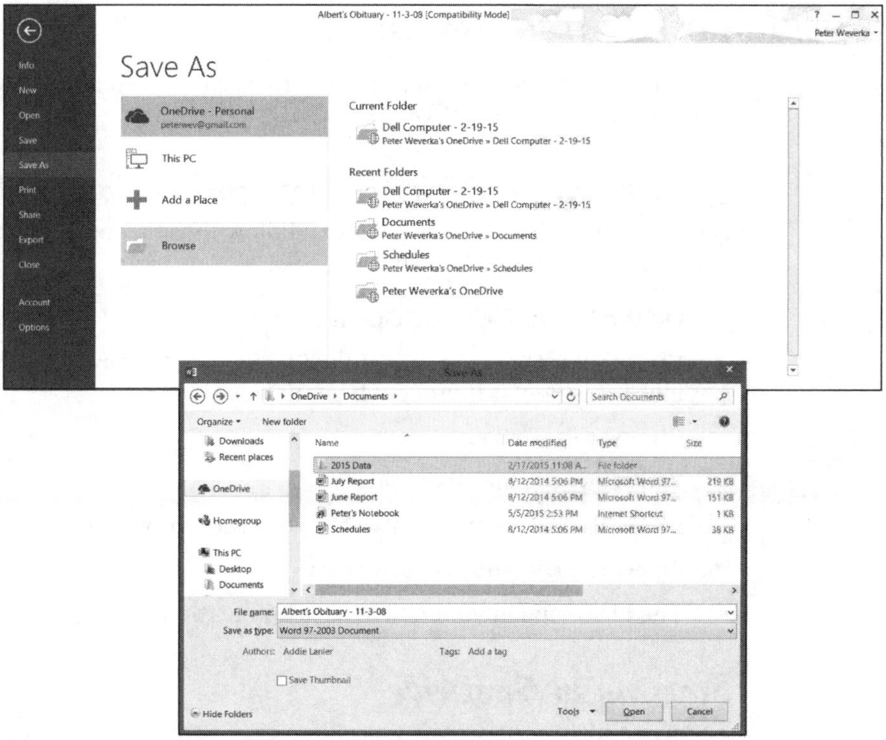

Figure 1-4: Choose OneDrive in the Save As window to save a file from your computer to a OneDrive folder.

5. **Click the Save button in the Save As dialog box.**

   TIP: Take a look at the Save button on the Quick Access toolbar after you save your file. It looks a little different from the conventional Save button. Those circular lines on the Save button tell you that the file is stored at OneDrive. When you click the Save button, you save your work and also refresh the file with work done by people who share the file with you.

WARNING! When you save an Excel, Word, or PowerPoint from your computer in a OneDrive folder, you create a second copy of the file. Be careful not to get the two copies mixed up — the one on your computer and the one at OneDrive.

Opening a File from OneDrive

Read on to find out the different ways to open a file that you keep on OneDrive in an Office 2016 application.

Starting in an Office 2016 application

Starting in an Office 2016 application, follow these steps to open an Office 2016 file you keep on OneDrive:

1. **On the File tab, choose Open.**

   You see the Open window. If the file you want to open is on the Recent files list, select it there and be done with it.

2. **Choose OneDrive.**

   You see your OneDrive folders.

3. **Select the folder where the file you want to open is stored.**
4. **Select the file you want to open.**

   The file opens in your Office 2016 application.

Starting in OneDrive

To open a file on OneDrive in an Office 2016 application, start by selecting the file. Then use these techniques to open it:

- Open the drop-down list on the Open button and choose an Open option (Open in Word, Open in Excel, or Open in PowerPoint).
- Right-click the file and choose an Open option.

Downloading Files from OneDrive to Your Computer

Follow these instructions to download files to your computer:

- **Downloading a file:** Select the file you want to download and click the Download button. You see the standard dialog box for downloading files from the Internet. Choose to open or save the file after you download it and click OK.
- **Downloading several files or all the files in a folder:** Select several files or, to download all the files in a folder, select the folder. Then click the Download button. The standard dialog box for downloading files appears. Click the Save File option button and click OK to download the files in a zip file.

Chapter 2: File Sharing and Collaborating

In This Chapter

- Understanding how file sharing works
- Sharing files and folders with your collaborators
- Seeing files you share with others and others share with you
- Changing how you share folders and files

Starting in the OneDrive window, you can collaborate online by sharing Word documents, Excel worksheets, and PowerPoint presentations. This chapter explains how file sharing works. It shows you how, using OneDrive, you can share your folders and files with others, and how to change how files and folders are shared.

Sharing Files: The Big Picture

OneDrive generates a link for each file that is shared. This link is the means by which the people who share the file open it. Someone who has the link can click it and, in their web browser, open the file for viewing or editing in an Office program (or Office Online application).

The owner of a folder or file can share it using these methods:

- **Invite people by email:** Send the link by email on a person-by-person basis to the people with whom you will share the file. Figure 2-1 shows an example of sending links by email to share files. The recipient of this email message can click a link to open an Office file stored at OneDrive. In this case, the sender shared a folder with five files in it.
- **Get a link:** Generate a link and distribute it on your own or post it on a blog or web page.
- **Share with embedded HTML code:** Generate HTML code that you can embed in a blog or web page.

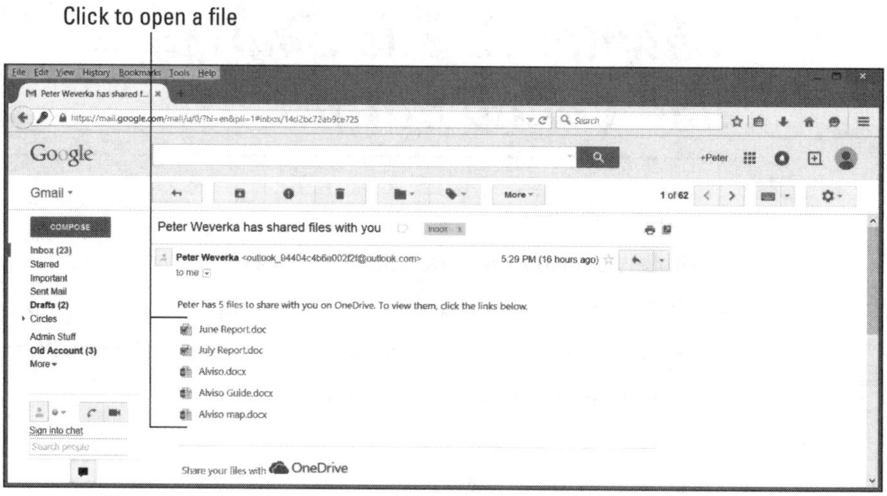

Figure 2-1: An email invitation to share files stored on OneDrive.

Sharing Your Files and Folders with Others

Share files with others so that they can view or edit your work. Sharing is a way to collaborate with others on Office files. Starting in the OneDrive window, you can share a folder (that is, all the files in the folder) or an individual file.

Inviting people by email

Follow these steps to share a file (or all the files in a folder) by sending out an email message with links to the files (see Figure 2-1). All the recipient of your email message has to do to read or view the file is click a link.

1. **In OneDrive, select the file or folder you want to share.**
2. **Click the Share button.**

   You can find the Share button on the OneDrive toolbar along the top of the screen.

   As shown in Figure 2-2, you see the Share window. If you're sharing the file or folder already, the sharers' names appear on the left side of the window.
3. **Choose Invite People.**
4. **Enter the email addresses of the people with whom you will share the file or folder. Enter a message as well, if you want (see Figure 2-2).**

   If you want the recipients of your email invitation to be able to view the files without subscribing to Office 365, click the Share button now; otherwise, keep reading.

Figure 2-2: File sharing by email.

5. **Click the Recipients Can Edit link.**

   As shown in Figure 2-2, drop-down menus appear.

6. **Choose access privileges on the drop-down menus.**

   On the first menu, choose whether recipients can view the file(s) or view and edit the file(s).

   On the second menu, choose whether recipients need an Office 365 subscription to view or view and edits the file(s).

7. **Click the Share button.**

   The Share window opens. It tells you who shares the file or folder with you. You can return to this window at any time to unshare files or folders as well as change how files and folders are shared. See "Investigating and Changing How Files and Folders Are Shared," later in this chapter for details.

Generating a link to shared files

Follow these instructions to share a file (or all the files in a folder) by generating a hyperlink. After OneDrive generates the link, you can post it or send it to others. Anyone who clicks the link can view (or view and edit) the file.

1. **In the OneDrive window, select the file or folder you want to share.**
2. **Click the Share button.**

   As shown in Figure 2-3, you see the Share window for generating a link to your file or folder.

3. **Choose Get a Link.**

Figure 2-3: File sharing by generating a link.

4. **Choose an access option on the drop-down menu.**

   Herewith are your choices:

   - **View Only:** Others can view the file (or all files in the folder if a folder is being shared), but not edit the file(s).
   - **Edit:** Others can view *and* edit the file (or all files in the folder if a folder is being shared).

5. **Click Create Link.**

   OneDrive generates the link. You can click Shorten Link to generate a shorter and more manageable version of the link.

6. **Select the link (double-click it).**

7. **Right-click the link and choose Copy.**

   You can now paste the link where you will — to a blog, web page, or email message. Later in this chapter, "Investigating and Changing How Files and Folders Are Shared" explains how to unshare files and change how they are shared.

Sharing a file directly

Word, Excel, and PowerPoint offer the Share button (it's located in the upper-right corner of the screen) for sharing a file without having to visit the OneDrive window. After you click the Share button, the Share pane opens. From there, you can decide how a file is to be shared and invite others to share the file with you.

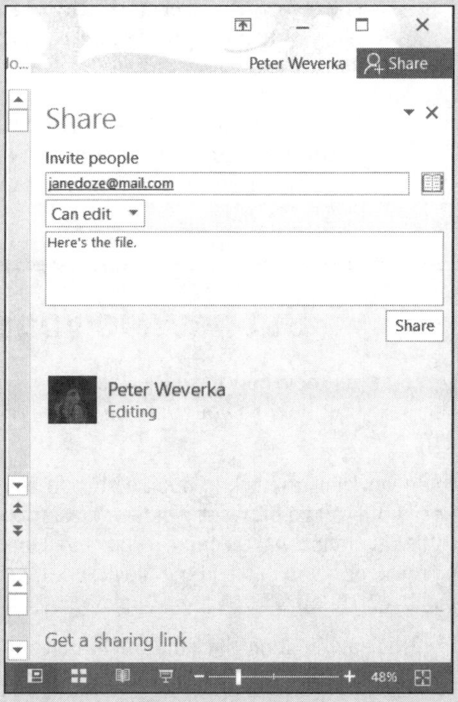

On the Permissions drop-down menu, choose Can Edit or Can View to determine what editing privileges the sharer has. Then decide how to share the file:

- **Sharing the file by email:** Enter the sharer's name in the Invite People text box and click the Share button.
- **Sharing the file by generating a link:** Click Get a Sharing Link. Then click the Copy button to copy the link to the Clipboard. From there you can copy the link to a blog, web page, or email message.

Generating HTML code

Yet another way to share files is to generate HTML code for a link and embed the HTML code in a web page or blog. A visitor to the web page or blog can click the link and open the file you want to share. Follow these steps to generate HTML code for file-sharing purposes:

1. **In the OneDrive window, select the file you want to share.**
2. **Click the Embed button on the OneDrive toolbar.**

   You may have to click the Manage button and choose Embed on the drop-down list, depending on the size of your browser screen. The Embed window opens.
3. **Click the Generate button.**

   OneDrive generates the HTML code.
4. **Right-click the code and choose Copy.**

   Embed this code into a web page to create the link.

Seeing Files and Folders Others Shared with You

Go to the Shared window to see the names of folders and files that you shared with other and others shared with you. To go to the Shared window, click Shared in the OneDrive Navigation pane (located on the left side of the window).

Open files and folders in the Shared Window the same way you open them in the Files or Recent window — by clicking. You can also right-click and choose Open on the shortcut menu.

But how do you work on the files?

Now that you know how to share files, you may well ask, "But how do you work on a shared file?"

When you click the link to open a shared file, the file opens in a browser window, as shown in this illustration. At this point, if you have editing privileges, you can edit the file in an Office application or an Office Online application:

- **Office application:** Click the Edit button and the first option on the drop-down menu.
- **Office Online application:** Click the Edit button and choose the second option on the drop-down menu.

What the Edit button is named depends on the type of file you're dealing with. In the illustration shown here, the file in question is a Word document, so the button is named Edit Document. Meanwhile, the options on the drop-down menu are Edit in Word and Edit in Word Online.

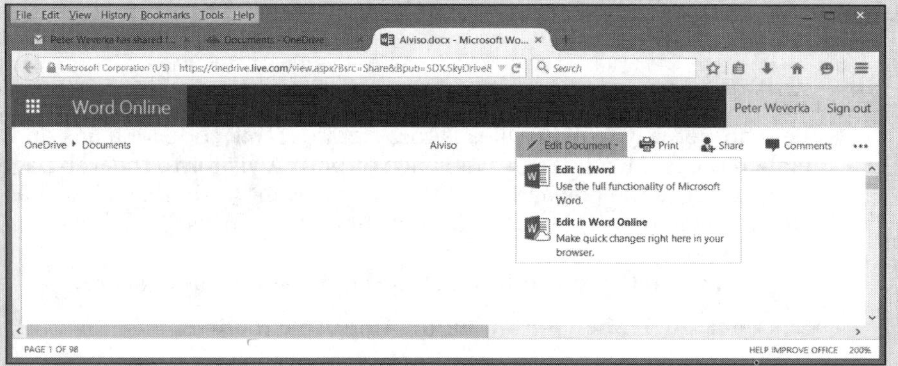

Investigating and Changing How Files and Folders Are Shared

The Information pane tells you everything you need to know about who shares a file or folder. To open the Information pane, select a shared file or folder and click the Information button (located in the upper-right corner of the screen). Then look in the Information pane to investigate how a file is being shared.

Follow these steps to stop sharing a file or change how you share a file with someone:

1. **In the OneDrive window, select the file or folder in question.**
2. **Click the Share button.**

   The Share window opens, as shown in Figure 2-4. This is the same window you use to share folders and files. The left side of the window tells you who shares the file with you.

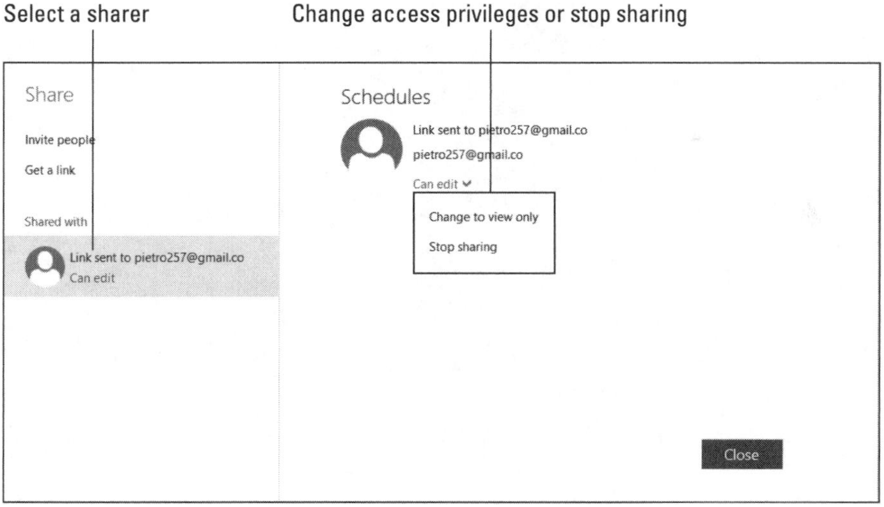

Figure 2-4: Changing how a file is shared.

3. **Select a name on the left side of the window.**

   The person's name appears in the center of the window.

4. **On the drop-down menu, choose Allow Editing, Change to View Only, or Stop Sharing.**

   If you choose Stop Sharing, the person's name is removed from the Share window and the person is no longer permitted to view or edit the file.

   The Share window remains open in case you want to change how you share the file with others whose names are listed.

5. **Close to close the Share window.**

Index

Symbols

A

B

C

D

E

F

G

H

I

J

K

L

M

N

O

P

Q

R

S

T

U

V

W

X

Y

Z

About the Author

Peter Weverka is the bestselling author of many *For Dummies* books, including *Windows 10 For Seniors For Dummies* and *Office For iPad & Mac For Dummies,* as well as three-dozen other computer books about various topics.

Dedication

For Sofia and Henry

Acknowledgments

This book owes a lot to many hard-working people at the offices of Wiley Publishing in Indianapolis, and I want to express my gratitude to all of them. I would especially like to thank Steve Hayes for giving me the opportunity to write it, Susan Christophersen for editing it, BIM Creatives, LLC for indexing it, and Michelle Krasniak for making sure all instructions are correct.

Publisher's Acknowledgments

Acquisitions Editor: Steve Hayes
Project Manager, Development Editor, and Copy Editor: Susan Christophersen
Technical Editor: Michelle Krasniak
Editorial Assistant: Bridget Feeney
Sr. Editorial Assistant: Cherie Case
Production Editor: Antony Sami
Cover Image: © iStock.com/Magnilion; © iStock.com/Robert Churchill